D0906995

DATE DUE

THE OUTLOOK
FOR WATER

THE OUTLOOK FOR WATER

QUALITY, QUANTITY, AND NATIONAL GROWTH

By

Nathaniel Wollman and Gilbert W. Bonem

Published for Resources for the Future, Inc.

by The Johns Hopkins Press,
Baltimore and London

Resources for the Future is a nonprofit corporation for research and education in
the development, conservation, and use of natural resources and the improvement
of the quality of the environment. It was established in 1952 with the cooperation
of the Ford Foundation. Part of the work of Resources for the Future is carried out
by its resident staff; part is supported by grants to universities and other nonprofit
organizations. Unless otherwise stated, interpretations and conclusions in RFF pub-
lications are those of the authors; the organization takes responsibility for the
selection of significant subjects for study, the competence of the researchers, and
their freedom of inquiry.

This book is one of RFF's studies in environmental quality, which are directed by
Allen V. Kneese. The research was supported by a grant to the University of New
Mexico, where Nathaniel Wollman is professor of economics and dean of the Col-
lege of Arts and Sciences. Gilbert W. Bonem, formerly research associate in the
Economics Department, University of New Mexico, is now chief of research and
evaluation, Model Cities Program, Albuquerque. The charts and maps were drawn
by Clare and Frank Ford. The index was prepared by Florence Robinson.

RFF editors: Henry Jarrett, Vera W. Dodds, Nora E. Roots, Tadd Fisher.

The Johns Hopkins Press, Baltimore, Maryland 21218
The Johns Hopkins Press Ltd., London

Library of Congress Catalog Card Number 75-149243

International Standard Book Number 0-8018-1260-7

FOREWORD

The people of the United States are fast coming to realize the role some major resources have played in our growth and development and how disastrously we have come to overuse and misuse them. These are what the economist calls "common property resources" — resources which in a sense are owned by everyone and therefore not owned by anyone. Major examples are the air mantle, most of our watercourses, the electromagnetic spectrum, landscapes, and ecological systems. The private market, which has been our main instrument for developing and allocating natural resources, provides little or no incentive to conserve or enhance these resources, to develop new technology for using them more efficiently, or even to gather information about them.

While our collective responsibility for these resources has been recognized to some extent, we are just becoming aware of the large and pervasive public management task that confronts us in regard to them. Since they are rarely priced, even though in our contemporary world they are scarce and valuable, we find them used promiscuously and their quality degraded. The seriousness of this problem perhaps becomes clearer to us when we recall a recent study of the General Accounting Office[1] which found that in every river basin studied the quality of water has deteriorated in recent years. The period under study was one during which much federal and state legislation was passed and an endless stream of well-meaning rhetoric flowed. The present situation is symptomatic of the fact that we have not achieved a national understanding of the basic causes and dimensions of the problem and therefore have not developed a consis-

tent, coherent, and adequate national strategy for dealing with it. The present book is a contribution toward improving our understanding of the water resources problem and the strategic choices available to us.

The Outlook for Water is one in an RFF series of studies projecting the demand and supply of major natural resource commodities. But it pioneers by being the first to venture into the realm of the commodity property resource, and this presents some really major new problems. There is not the benefit of the immense amount of information which market exchange generates about most natural resource commodities, since hardly any market exchange occurs. Because most common property resources are large natural systems with their pulses and rhythms, we face supplies that are highly variable in time, both systematically and randomly. Water is heavy and must be used in large quantities, so that purposefully transporting it over long distances is usually foreclosed. Accordingly, dealing in national aggregates as the other projection studies have done has very little meaning — intraregional and interregional analyses must be performed.

The full dimensions of the difficulties posed by these characteristics can be apparent only to those who worked closely with the authors during the years they labored on the book. New methodologies had to be developed. In this connection, the studies by Reid and Hardison and Löf should be mentioned. They are amply cited in the text and were sponsored by RFF specifically in support of this study. New data had to be collected and tabulated — as, for example, the data on existing reservoirs and their storage allocation. It was a long, ardous, and often frustrating process, and the senior author is to be complimented not least for his perseverance and the ability to take criticisms which were sometimes fundamental. One or two of these criti-

---

[1] *Examination into the Effectiveness of the Constructions Grant Program for Abating, Controlling, and Preventing Water Pollution*, Report of the Comptroller General of the United States (1969).

cisms literally sent the authors back to the "drawing boards."

Even so, the authors find it necessary to be modest in the claims they make for their study. The range of salient variables included is narrow and the uncertainties inherent in many of the numbers generated are great. The authors go much further than most would have done in pointing to the deficiencies and limitations of their conclusions and in emphasizing that the contribution of the study is perhaps primarily methodological. Still, we can get an impression of the broader significance of the results when we consider some of the conclusions the authors believe they can draw with confidence.

1. Rapid growth projections a half century into the future suggest that high-quality water on a wide scale will be possible only if we can find quite new technologies for using the resource.

2. Even in the nearer term, high growth combined with high water quality targets mean vastly expanded capital and operating costs for facilities – primarily waste treatment.

3. The Southwest will remain a hard-core area of quantitative water shortage with the upper Arkansas-White-Red and perhaps several other regions sharing its fate within fifty years, even with medium growth.

4. On a national scale, quality is a much more difficult and costly problem than quantity, and large-scale investment in water facilities will shift from its traditional home in the irrigated West to the East.

Nathaniel Wollman and Gilbert Bonem have plowed new ground with thoroughness and persistence. Their work should aid efforts now under way in the federal government to do the job in a continuing, systematic, and detailed manner, which Wollman started more than a decade ago in his work with the Senate Select Committee on Water Resources. In 1960 he was the author of Senate Select Committee Print No. 32, *Water Supply and Demand*, which contained the first presentation of the general methodology underlying his work since then.

ALLEN V. KNEESE
Director, Quality of
the Environment Program

PREFACE

We are appreciative of the patience and kindly tolerance of Resources for the Future in its support of this study. A draft had been completed in 1964; only then, on review by Howard Cook (then of the Office of the Chief, Corps of Engineers, now Deputy Director of the National Water Commission) was it found that certain flow-storage relationships were in error, leading to an understatement of required storage and costs of storage for relatively high sustained flows, especially in western regions.

When the senior author returned to the United States from Chile in December 1965, it was decided that a new attempt would be undertaken. In the meantime, at the instance of RFF, corrected flow-storage relationships were prepared by George Löf and Clayton Hardison and published in *Water Research* (April 1966).

George Reid, Chairman of the Department of Civil Engineering at the University of Oklahoma, agreed to restudy the flow requirements for alternative BOD loadings and costs of treatment for alternative levels of BOD removal and secured the assistance of Wesley Eckenfelder, then of the University of Texas at Austin and now at Vanderbilt University. The resulting study by Reid, Eckenfelder, Streebin, Nelson, and Love is published in this volume as appendix D, and constitutes, of course, a basic element of the revised study. To these people — Löf, Hardison, Reid, and colleagues — the authors' debt is very large, since without their contributions a new go at the study would have been pointless.

The original undertaking owed much of its impetus and structure to the guidance and enthusiasm of Irving Fox, then Vice President of RFF and now Associate Director of the Water Resources Center at the University of Wisconsin. Without the comfort, support, guidance, and research contributions of Allen Kneese and Blair Bower of RFF, the manuscript would never have been revised and completed.

The authors are grateful to Henry Jarrett for his participation in the writing of the first four chapters, and to Tadd Fisher, who edited the manuscript.

The authors express their thanks to the Water Resources Research Institute, New Mexico State University; to Ralph Stucky, its Director; and to the Office of Water Resources Research, U.S. Department of the Interior, for funds that financed a computer model without which the various sensitivity responses could not have been ascertained. Many others, in addition, have given us help, some of which is footnoted elsewhere within the volume. To all we express our gratitude.

We have searched diligently but in vain for someone we can hold responsible for the next major error that may appear. We hope, at least, that our insistent disavowals of gift of prophesy will put the reader sufficiently on notice to recall the fragile basis of projections and estimates of regionwide coefficients and to weight all conclusions with the properly computed chance of error.

NATHANIEL WOLLMAN
GILBERT W. BONEM

TABLE OF CONTENTS

FOREWORD v

PREFACE vi

PART I – THE STUDY IN BRIEF

1. THE PROBLEM AND THE APPROACH 3
   Ultimate Goals   *4*

2. THE BASIC MODEL AND ITS VARIATIONS 6
   Definitions and Methods   *7*
       Supply   *7.*   Demand   *8.*   Choice among Programs   *10.*   Estimation
       of Costs   *10.*   Technology   *11.*
   How the Model Works   *11*
   Limitations   *14*
   Uses of the Study   *17*

3. A SUMMARY OF THE FINDINGS 18
       Population and Economic Activity   *18.*   Projected Water
       Requirements   *18.*   Dilution Flow   *19.*   Adequacy of Total
       Supply   *20.*   Regional Prospects   *20.*
   Alternative Programs Compared   *21*
       Breakdown by Purpose and Area   *23.*   Costs by Industry   *24.*
       Costs of Meeting Deficits   *24.*   Capital Costs   *25.*   Coupling
       the Basic Model with Short-Term Chemical Treatment   *25.*
       Variations of the Basic Model   *26.*   Dissolved Oxygen   *27.*
       Annual Factor   *28.*   Simultaneous Changes   *28.*
   Impact of Technology   *28*
   Comparison with Committee Print No. 32   *29*
   Comparison with Water Resources Council Assessment   *30*

4. CONCLUSIONS, POLICY ISSUES, AND RESEARCH PRIORITIES 32
   Qualifications and Omissions   *33*
   Some Issues of Policy   *34*
       Is High Growth Always a Good Thing?   *34.*   More Lakes
       versus Undisturbed Flow   *34.*   Who Should Bear the Costs?   *34.*
       How Much Risk of Deficiency?   *35.*   What Standards of Quality?   *35.*
       Weighing Aesthetic Values   *35.*

Some Urgent Research Needs   *35*
Treatment of Dissolved Solids   *36*.   Interbasin Transfers   *36*.
Waste Collection and Thermal Pollution   *36*.   Waste Treatment
versus Water Treatment   *36*.   Inputs per Unit of Output   *36*.
Regional Data and Analysis   *36*.   Price Elasticity of Water   *37*.

PART II – THE STUDY IN DETAIL

5. POPULATION AND ECONOMIC ACTIVITY PROJECTIONS TO THE YEAR 2020 41
Gross National Product   *42*.   Manufacturing   *42*.   Steam-
Electric Power   *43*.   Mining   *43*.   Agriculture   *43*.
Some Comparisons with Other Projections   *44*.

6. COEFFICIENTS OF WATER USE: WITHDRAWAL USES 48
Agriculture   *49*.   Mining   *50*.   Manufacturing   *50*.
Steam-Electric Power   *51*.   Municipal   *51*.   Onsite
and Flow Uses   *52*.

7. WITHDRAWALS AND LOSSES: ALL USES 55
Withdrawals   *55*.   Losses   *56*.   Onsite Uses   *56*.
Swamps and Wetlands   *56*.   Regional Variation in
Total Losses   *56*.

8. WATER QUALITY 66
Amount of Waste Produced   *66*.   Dilution Flows   *68*.   Costs of
Treatment   *70*.   Thermal Pollution and Recirculation Costs   *72*.
Collection Costs   *73*.   Short-Term Tertiary Treatment   *74*.
Short-Term Treatment versus Lower Permanent Treatment   *74*.

9. THE "SUPPLY" OF WATER AND THE COSTS OF FLOW 96
The Cost of Flow   *97*.

10. THE BASIC MODEL: THE RESULTS 105
Minimum Treatment Program   *105*.   Required Storage   *106*.
Level of Treatment   *107*.   Expenditures for Quality
Standards and Flow Regularity   *107*.   Future Costs   *108*.
Regional Shortages and Aggregate Gross Deficits   *109*.
Regional Variation in Costs   *110*.

11. SHORT-TERM TERTIARY TREATMENT AND REDUCED STORAGE 121
Savings Yielded by Short-Term Chemical Treatment   *121*.
Continuous Chemical Treatment   *123*.

12. VARIATIONS IN SELECTED PARAMETERS 131
Change in Certainty of Flow   *131*.   Variation in Annual
Factor   *132*.   Variation in Dissolved Oxygen   *133*.
Combined Variations   *134*.   Reduction in Industrial Waste Output   *136*.
Recirculation in Municipal Coastal Intake   *136*.   Reservation
of Water for Recreation   *137*.   Regional Characteristics   *137*.

APPENDIXES

A. BASIC ECONOMIC PROJECTIONS 155
Population   *155*
Gross National Product   *159*

B. WATER USE COEFFICIENTS AND SELECTED AGGREGATES 174

C. AGGREGATE WITHDRAWALS AND LOSSES BY MAJOR USE 195

D. TREATMENT, DILUTION, AND TREATMENT COSTS OF MUNICIPAL AND
    INDUSTRIAL WASTES 203
        Detailed Model Development   *210*

E. ESTIMATION OF WASTELOADS AND TREATMENT COSTS 221
        BOD Waste Loads   *221*
        Thermal Waste Loads   *222*
        Waste Treatment Costs   *222*

F. FLOW-STORAGE RELATIONSHIPS AND THE COSTS OF FLOW 244

INDEX 281

LIST OF TABLES

Text

1. U.S. Flows and Costs at Various Marginal Costs per 1,000 Gallons 31
2. Effect of Parametric Changes on U.S. Total Costs of New Storage and Treatment, Minimum Cost Programs: 2000 Medium 31
3. Total Population of the Conterminous United States, by Region: 1960 and Projections 45
4. Urban Population of the Conterminous United States, by Region: 1960 and Projections 45
5. Population of Standard Metropolitan Statistical Areas, by Region: 1960 and Projections 46
6. Index of Manufacturing Output for Selected Industries: 1980, 2000, 2020 46
7. Power Generated by Utility Steam-Electric Plants: 1960 and Projections 46
8. Mining Output: 1960 and Projections 47
9. Index of Livestock Production: 1980, 2000, 2020 47
10. Irrigated Acreage, by Region: 1960 and Projections 47
11. Gross and Net Use of Water per Acre for Agriculture: 1960 and Projections 53
12. Mining Withdrawal Coefficients: 1960 and Projections 53
13. Mining Loss Coefficients: 1960 and Projections .. 53
14. Manufacturing Water Use Coefficients: 1954, 1959, 1964 54
15. Steam-Electric Power, Rates of Water Use with Recirculation High Enough to Avoid Thermal Pollution: 1980, 2000, 2020 54
16. Municipal Withdrawals, by Region: 1960 and Projections 54
17. Municipal Losses, by Region: 1960 and Projections 54
18. U.S. Withdrawals for Withdrawal Uses, Original Recirculation Rate: 1960 and Projections 58
19. Gross Use (Withdrawal and Onsite Uses), Original and Revised Recirculation Rates: 1960 and Projections 58

20. Total Withdrawals and Onsite Gross Uses, by Major Use and Region: 1960 59
21. Total Withdrawals and Onsite Gross Uses, by Major Use and Region: 1980 Medium 59
22. Total Withdrawals and Onsite Gross Uses, by Major Use and Region: 2000 Medium 60
23. Total Withdrawals and Onsite Gross Uses, by Major Use and Region: 2020 Medium 60
24. Total Withdrawls for Intake and Onsite Uses at Original Rates of Recirculation, by Region: 1960 and Projections 61
25. U.S. Losses from Withdrawal Uses: 1960 and Projections 61
26. U.S. Losses from Withdrawal and Onsite Uses: 1960 and Projections 61
27. Land Treatment and Structures: Withdrawals and Losses, by Region, Increase over 1960 for 1980, 2000, 2020 62
28. Swamps and Wetlands: Withdrawals and Losses by Region, Increase over 1960 for 1980, 2000, 2020 62
29. Losses, by Region and Type of Use: 1960 63
30. Losses, by Region and Type of Use: 1980 Medium 63
31. Losses, by Region and Type of Use: 2000 Medium 64
32. Losses, by Region and Type of Use: 2020 Medium 64
33. Total Losses from Withdrawals and Onsite Uses, by Region: 1960 and Projections 65
34. Percentage of Total Waste Discharged to Streams, by Region 74
35. BOD Waste Loads in Population Equivalents, by Major Source and Region: 1960 75
36. BOD Waste Loads in Population Equivalents, by Major Source and Region: 1980 Medium 76
37. BOD Waste Loads in Population Equivalents, by Major Source and Region: 2000 Medium 77
38. BOD Waste Loads in Population Equivalents, by Major Source and Region: 2020 Medium 78

39. BOD Waste Loads in Population Equivalents, by Major Source and Region: 2020 High *79*

40. Total Population Equivalents to Fresh Water before Treatment, by Region: 1960 and Projections *80*

41. Mix of Treatment by Percentage of Industrial BOD Reduction *80*

42. Basic and Variant Assumptions for Waste Loads per Unit of Output: 1960 and Projections *80*

43. Percentage of Phosphorus and Nitrogen Removed by Various Levels of Treatment *81*

44. Percentage Distribution of Total BOD Produced, by Major Source: 1960 and Projections *81*

45. Dilution Flow for New England, 4 mg/l D.O.: 2000 Medium *81*

46. Ruling Dilution Flows at Selected Levels of Treatment, by Region, 4 mg/l D.O.: 1960 .... *81*

47. Ruling Dilution Flow at 95% Treatment, by Region, 4 mg/l D.O.: 1980, 2000, 2020 .... *82*

48. Ruling Dilution Flows at Selected Levels of Treatment, by Region, 4 mg/l D.O.: Medium Projections for 1980, 2000, 2020 .... *83*

49. Ruling Dilution Flows at 95% Treatment, by Region: 1960 and Medium Projections *84*

50. Ruling Dilution Flows at 97½% Treatment, by Region, 4 mg/l D.O.: 1980, 2000, 2020 .... *85*

51. Ruling Dilution Flows at 97½% Treatment, by Region: 1960 and Medium Projections *86*

52. Ruling Dilution Flows at 97½% Treatment, Variant 1, by Region: 1960 and Medium Projections *87*

53. Ruling Dilution Flows at 97½% Treatment, Variant 2, by Region: 1960 and Medium Projections *88*

54. Industrial Waste Treatment Costs per p.e., by Level of Treatment and Selected Industries *89*

55. Municipal Waste Treatment Costs per p.e., by Level of Treatment *89*

56. U.S. Annual Costs of Standard Treatment, by Level of Treatment: 1960 and Projections *89*

57. Municipal and Industrial Costs for 95% Treatment, by Region: 1960 and Projections *90*

58. Municipal and Industrial Costs for 95% Treatment, Variants 1 and 2, by Region: 2020 Medium and High *91*

59. Cooling Water Discharge at Original Recirculation Rates, by Region: 1960 and Projections *92*

60. Thermal Dilution Requirements at Original Recirculation Rates, 98% Availability, 0.0425 Annual Factor, 4 mg/l D.O.: 1960 and Projections *93*

61. Steam-Electric Power Intake and Costs of Recirculation at Original and Revised Recirculation Rates: 1960 and Projections *94*

62. Projected U.S. Collection, Treatment, and Recirculation Costs for 95% Treatment *95*

63. Annual Urban Waste Collection Costs at $4.12 per Capita, by Region: 1960 and Projections *95*

64. Estimates of Maximum Physical Development, 98% Availability, by Region *100*

65. Maximum Regulated Flow, Storage, and Costs of Storage, by Region: 98%, 95%, and 90% Availability *101*

66. U.S. Storage Requirements at Full and Constrained Capacity *102*

67. Regional Comparison of Physical Maximum Net Flow with Net Flow Limited by Marginal Cost: 98% Availability, 0.0425 Annual Factor *102*

68. Marginal Cost Constraint: Selected Storage Flows and Costs, by Region, 0.0425 Annual Factor ... *103*

69. U.S. Marginal and Average Costs for Selected Flows *103*

70. Selected Flows and Average Costs of Flow, U.S. Aggregates: 0.0425 Annual Factor *104*

71. Required Flows for the United States, by Program, 98% Availability, 0.0425 Annual Factor, 4 mg/l D.O.: 1960 and Projections *111*

72. Deficits of Flows, by Regions, Minimum Flow Programs, 98% Availability, 4 mg/l D.O.: Selected Projections *112*

73. Required Flows at 70/50% Treatment, 4 mg/l D.O., by Region: 2020 .... *113*

74. U.S. New Storage, 98% Availability, 0.0425 Annual Factor, 4 mg/l D.O.: 1960 and Projections *113*

75. New Storage, East and West, for the Minimum Cost Program, 0.0425 Annual Factor, 4 mg/l D.O.: 1960 and Projections *113*

76. Treatment Levels for Alternative Programs, by Region, 98% Availability, 0.0425 Annual Factor, 4 mg/l D.O.: 1960 and Projections *114*

77. Costs of Alternative Programs, 98% Availability, 0.0425 Annual Factor, 4 mg/l D.O.: 1960 .... *114*

78. Annual Costs of New Storage plus Treatment, 98% Availability, 0.0425 Annual Factor, 4 mg/l D.O.: 1960 and Projections *115*

79. U.S. "Costs of Quality," Minimum Cost Program, 98% Availability, 0.0425 Annual Factor, 4 mg/l D.O.: 1960 and Projections *115*

80. U.S. Annual Total Costs, by Program, 98% Availability, 0.0425 Annual Factor, 4 mg/l D.O.: 1960 and Projections *116*

81. Costs of Water Related to GNP, Minimum Cost Programs: 1960 and Projections *116*

82. Total Required Flows (Losses plus Dilution) for Minimum Flow Programs, by Region, 0.0425 Annual Factor, 4 mg/l D.O.: 1960 and Projections *117*

83. Minimum Flow Requirements Exceeding Constrained Maximum Net Flow, by Region: 1980, 2000, 2020 .... *118*

84. Deficit Regions with a Maximum Marginal Cost of 2 Cents per 1,000 Gallons, 98% Availability: Selected Projections *118*

85. Projected Water-Short Regions: Minimum Flow Program, Maximum Marginal Cost of 2 Cents per 1,000 Gallons, 98% Availability, 4 mg/l D.O. *119*

86. East and West Storage, Treatment, and Collection Costs for Minimum Flow Programs, 98% Availability, 0.0425 Annual Factor, 4 mg/l D.O.: 1960 and Projections *119*

87. East and West Storage, Treatment, and Collection Costs for Minimum Treatment Programs, 98% Availability, 0.0425 Annual Factor, 4 mg/l D.O.: 1960 and Projections *120*

88. East and West Storage, Treatment, and Collection Costs for Minimum Cost Programs, 98% Availability, 0.0425 Annual Factor, 4 mg/l D.O.: 1960 and Projections *120*

89. East and West Costs Variable by Program, 98% Availability, 0.0425 Annual Factor, 4 mg/l D.O.: 1960 and Projections *120*

90. Short-Term Treatment, Minimum Cost Base, 0.0425 Annual Factor, 4 mg/l D.O.: 2000 Medium *126*

91. Dollar Savings with Short-Term Tertiary Treatment, 90% Availability, 0.0425 Annual Factor, 4 mg/l D.O.: 1960 and Projections *127*

92. Continuous Chemical Treatment (Q_p Unresponsive and Responsive), Minimum Cost Base, 98% Availability, 0.0425 Annual Factor, 4 mg/l D.O.: 2000 Medium *128*

93. Two-Layer Treatment with Q_p Responsive, Minimum Cost Base, 90% Availability, 0.0425 Annual Factor, 4 mg/l D.O.: 2000 Medium *129*

94. Summary: Chemical Treatment Alternatives Based on the Standard Minimum Cost Program, 98% Availability, 0.0425 Annual Factor, 4 mg/l D.O.: 2000 Medium *130*

95. Required New Storage, by Program and Availability Variants, 0.0425 Annual Factor, 4 mg/l D.O.: 1960 and Projections *139*

96. Annual Costs for New Storage, by Program and Availability Variants, 0.0425 Annual Factor, 4 mg/l D.O.: 1960 and Projections *139*

97. Annual Costs for Treatment, by Program and Availability Variants, 0.0425 Annual Factor, 4 mg/l D.O.: 1960 and Projections *139*

98. Annual Total Costs for New Storage and Treatment, by Program and Availability Variants, 0.0425 Annual Factor, 4 mg/l D.O.: 1960 and Projections *140*

99. Annual Treatment Costs, by Program and Annual Factor Variants, 98% Availability, 4 mg/l D.O.: 1960 and Projections *140*

100. New Storage, by Program and Annual Factor Variants, 98% Availability, 4 mg/l D.O.: 1960 and Projections *140*

101. Annual Costs for New Storage, by Program and Annual Factor Variants, 98% Availability, 4 mg/l D.O.: 1960 and Projections *141*

102. Annual Total Costs, by Program and Annual Factor Variants, 98% Availability, 4 mg/l D.O.: 1960 and Projections *141*

103. Annual Treatment Costs, by Program and D.O. Variants, 98% Availability, 0.0425 Annual Factor: 1960 and Projections *141*

104. Required Flows, by Program and D.O. Variants, 98% Availability, 0.0425 Annual Factor: 1960 and Projections *142*

105. Annual Storage Costs, by Program and D.O. Variants, 98% Availability, 0.0425 Annual Factor: 1960 and Projections *142*

106. Total Annual Costs, by Program and D.O. Variants, 98% Availability, 0.0425 Annual Factor: 1960 and Projections *142*

107. Total Required New Storage for Minimum Cost Programs, by Selected Variants: 1960 and Projections *143*

108. Total Annual Costs for New Storage, Minimum Cost Programs, by Selected Variants: 1960 and Projections *143*

109. Annual Total Costs for New Storage and Treatment, Alternative Programs, as a Percentage of Minimum Cost Programs for 98% Availability, 0.0425 Annual Factor, 4 mg/l D.O.: 1960 and Projections *144*

110. Annual Total Costs for New Storage and Treatment, Minimum Cost Programs, by Selected Variants: 1960 and Projections *145*

111. Major Characteristics of Alternative Programs, by Industrial Waste Variants, 98% Availability, 0.0425 Annual Factor, 4 mg/l D.O.: Selected Projections *146*

112. Withdrawals and Losses, Municipal Coastal Intake Recirculated, by Region: 2000 Medium *147*

113. Treatment Levels for Minimum Cost Programs, by Region and Selected Variants: 2000 Medium and 2020 High *148*

114. Treatment Levels for Minimum Treatment Programs, by Region and D.O. Variants, 98% Availability: 1960 and Projections *149*

115. Required Flows for Minimum Cost Programs, by Region and Selected Variants: 2000 Medium ... *150*

116. Required Flows for Minimum Cost Programs, by Region and Selected Variants, 98% Availability, 0.0425 Annual Factor: Selected Projections *151*

117. Gross Deficits of Flow under Minimum Cost Programs, by Region and D.O. Variants, 98% Availability, 0.0425 Annual Factor: Selected Projections *152*

Appendixes

A-1. Comparative Projections of the U.S. Population for 1980 .... *165*

A-2. Population of Selected Regions as a Percentage of the Population of the Conterminous United States: 1960 and Projections *165*

A-3. Population of Selected Divisions as a Percentage of the Population of the Conterminous United States: 1960, 1975, 1980 .... *165*

A-4. Comparative Projections of GNP *165*

A-5. Comparative Projections of Irrigated Acreage, East and West *166*

A-6. Comparative Projections of Irrigated Acreage, by Region: 1980 166

A-7. Comparative Projections of Mining Production for 1980 166

A-8. Comparative Projections of Manufacturing Output for 1980 167

A-9. Value Added by Food and Kindred Products, by Region: 1960 and Projections 167

A-10. Value Added by Pulp and Paper Products, by Region: 1960 and Projections 168

A-11. Value Added by Chemicals and Allied Products, by Region: 1960 and Projections 168

A-12. Value Added by Petroleum Refining, by Region: 1960 and Projections 169

A-13. Value Added by Primary Metals, by Region: 1960 and Projections 169

A-14. Comparative Projections of Power Generated by Utility Steam-Electric Plants 170

A-15. Utility Steam-Electric Power Generation, by Region: 1960 and Projections 170

A-16. New England Region: Comparative Projections of Population, Urban Ratio, and Value Added by Selected Industries 171

A-17. Chesapeake Bay Region: Comparative Projections of Population and of Value Added by Selected Industries 171

A-18. Ohio Region: Comparative Projections of Population, Urban Ratio, and Value Added by Selected Industries 171

A-19. Eastern Great Lakes: Comparative Projections of Population and of Value Added by Selected Industries 172

A-20. Cumberland and Tennessee Regions: Comparative Projections of Population and of Value Added by Selected Industries 172

A-21. Upper Missouri Region: Comparative Projections of Population and of Value Added by Selected Industries 172

A-22. Western Gulf Region: Comparative Population Projections 173

A-23. Pacific Northwest Region: Comparative Projections of Population, Irrigated Acreage, and Value Added by Selected Industries 173

B-1. Delivery Efficiencies (Percentage of Diversions Reaching Farms), by Region: 1960 and Projections 185

B-2. Withdrawals (and Losses) for Livestock, by Region: 1960 and Projections 185

B-3. Mining Output by Region as a Percentage of the U.S. Total, Selected Minerals: 1960 and Projections 186

B-4. Mining Output by Region as a Percentage of the U.S. Total, Coal, Oil, and Gas: 1960, 1980-2020 186

B-5. Freshwater Withdrawals from Municipal Systems by Users of 20 MGY and Over as a Percentage of the Users' Total Freshwater Withdrawals 187

B-6. Estimated Industrial Freshwater Withdrawals in Estuarine Areas as a Percentage of Total Regional Freshwater Withdrawals by Industry 187

B-7. Withdrawal Coefficients for Food and Kindred Products, by Region: 1960 and Projections ... 187

B-8. Withdrawal Coefficients for Pulp and Paper, by Region: 1960 and Projections 187

B-9. Withdrawal Coefficients for Chemicals, by Region: 1960 and Projections 188

B-10. Withdrawal Coefficients for Petroleum and Coal Products, by Region: 1960 and Projections ... 188

B-11. Withdrawal Coefficients for Primary Metals, by Region: 1960 and Projections 188

B-12. Withdrawals for Selected Manufacturing Industries, by Region: 1960 189

B-13. Index of Withdrawals and Losses per Dollar of Value Added by Selected Industries: 1960 and Projections 189

B-14. Total Loss Coefficients for Selected Industries for All Years, by Region 190

B-15. Losses from Selected Manufacturing Industries: 1960 190

B-16. Cooling Water as a Percentage of Discharge, Manufacturing Sectors, All Years 191

B-17. Withdrawals for Steam-Electric Power at Original Recirculation Rates, by Region: 1960 and Projections 191

B-18. Original and Revised Recirculation Rates for Steam-Electric Power, by Region: 1960 and Projections 191

B-19. Annual Growth Rates of Municipal per Capita Water Intake, by Division: 1954-80, 1980-2000, 2000-2020 192

B-20. Municipal Losses as a Percentage of Intake, by Region 192

B-21. Major Coastal Cities with an Upland Water Supply (Including Groundwater) and Ocean Discharge 193

B-22. Estimated Percentage of Land under Treatment, by Region: 1960, 1980, 2000 194

B-23. Estimated Losses from Swamps and Wetlands, by Region: 1960 194

C-1. Withdrawals for Agriculture, by Region: 1960 and Projections 195

C-2. Withdrawals for Mining, by Region: 1960 and Projections 196

C-3. Withdrawals for Manufacturing, by Region: 1960 and Projections 196

C-4. Withdrawals for Steam-Electric Power at Original Recirculation Rates, by Region: 1960 and Projections 197

C-5. Withdrawals for Steam-Electric Power at Revised Recirculation Rates, by Region: 1960 and Projections 197

C-6. Withdrawals for Municipal Uses, by Region: 1960 and Projections 198

C-7. Withdrawals for All Uses at Revised Recirculation Rates, by Region: 1960 and Projections . 198

C-8. Losses from Agriculture, by Region: 1960 and Projections 199

C-9. Losses from Mining, by Region: 1960 and Projections 199

C-10. Losses from Manufacturing, by Region: 1960 and Projections 200

C-11. Losses from Steam-Electric Power, by Region: 1960 and Projections *200*

C-12. Losses from Municipal Uses, by Region: 1960 and Projections *201*

C-13. Losses from Land Treatment and Structures, by Region: Increase over 1960 for 1980, 2000, 2020 .... *201*

C-14. Losses from Swamps and Wetlands, by Region: Increase over 1960 for 1980, 2000, 2020 .... *202*

D-1. Values of Selected Parameters, by Region *214*

D-2. F Schedule Used to Modify a Formula Based on Domestic Waste to Accommodate Nutrients from Industrial Wastes *214*

D-3. Values of Selected Parameters, by Region *214*

D-4. Characteristics of Industrial Wastewaters, Selected Industries *215*

D-5. Population Equivalent Constants, Selected Industries *215*

D-6. Treatment Efficiency Schemes *216*

D-7. Average Percentage Removal of Wastes by Municipal Sewage Processes *216*

D-8. Capital Costs and Operation and Maintenance Costs, Municipal Sewage Treatment Processes . *217*

D-9. Industrial Waste Treatment Costs *218*

D-10. Stream Characteristics, by Region *218*

D-11. Temperature and Related Stream Characteristics, by Region *218*

D-12. Discrete Point Analysis, by Region: 1960 .... *219*

D-13. Usable Reservoir Capacity and Capacity when Regulated to Median Flow, by Region *219*

D-14. Selected Parameters Related to Thermal Pollution, by Region *219*

D-15. Definitions of Treatment Processes *220*

E-1. Capital Costs and Operation and Management Costs, Municipal Waste Treatment, by Plant Size and Treatment Level *224*

E-2. Mean Design Capacities of Municipal Waste Treatment Plants in Non-SMSA Areas *225*

E-3. Mean Design Capacity of Municipal Waste Treatment Plants in SMSA Areas *225*

E-4. Cost of Standard Treatment, by Level of Treatment and Region: 1960 .... *225*

E-5. Cost of Standard Treatment, by Level of Treatment and Region: 1980 Low *226*

E-6. Cost of Standard Treatment, by Level of Treatment and Region: 1980 Medium *226*

E-7. Cost of Standard Treatment, by Level of Treatment and Region: 1980 High *227*

E-8. Cost of Standard Treatment, by Level of Treatment and Region: 2000 Low *227*

E-9. Cost of Standard Treatment, by Level of Treatment and Region: 2000 Medium *228*

E-10. Cost of Standard Treatment, by Level of Treatment and Region: 2000 High *228*

E-11. Cost of Standard Treatment, by Level of Treatment and Region: 2020 Low *229*

E-12. Cost of Standard Treatment, by Level of Treatment and Region: 2020 Medium *229*

E-13. Cost of Standard Treatment, by Level of Treatment and Region: 2020 High *230*

E-14. Recirculation Rates Required to Offset Thermal Waste Loads, Selected Regions: 1980, 2000, 2020 .... *230*

E-15. Thermal Waste Loads: Cooling Water Discharge, by Industry and Region, 1960 .... *231*

E-16. Thermal Waste Loads: Cooling Water Discharge at Original Recirculation Rates, by Industry and Region, 1980 Medium *232*

E-17. Thermal Waste Loads: Cooling Water Discharge at Original Recirculation Rates, by Industry and Region, 2000 Medium *233*

E-18. Thermal Waste Loads: Cooling Water Discharge at Original Recirculation Rates, by Industry and Region, 2020 Medium *234*

E-19. Costs of Recirculation, Steam-Electric Power: 1960 .... *235*

E-20. Costs of Recirculation at Original Rates: 1980 Medium *236*

E-21. Steam-Electric Power: Costs of Recirculation at Original Rates, 2000 Medium *237*

E-22. Steam-Electric Power: Costs of Recirculation at Original Rates, 2020 Medium *238*

E-23. Steam-Electric Power: Costs of Recirculation at Original Rates, 2020 High *239*

E-24. Steam-Electric Power: Costs of Recirculation at Revised Rates, 1980 Medium *240*

E-25. Steam-Electric Power: Costs of Recirculation at Revised Rates, 2000 Medium *241*

E-26. Steam-Electric Power: Costs of Recirculation at Revised Rates, 2020 Medium *242*

E-27. Steam-Electric Power: Costs of Recirculation at Revised Rates, 2020 High *243*

F-1. Storage Required to Produce Gross Flows Equal to Indicated Percentages of Mean Annual Flow, with 98% Availability and No Deduction for Reservoir Losses, by Region *254*

F-2. Storage Required to Produce Gross Flows Equal to Indicated Percentages of Mean Annual Flow, with 95% Availability and No Deduction for Reservoir Losses, by Region *255*

F-3. Storage Required to Produce Gross Flows Equal to Indicated Percentages of Mean Annual Flow, with 90% Availability and No Deduction for Reservoir Losses, by Region *256*

F-4. Capital Costs of Storage Capacity per Acre-Foot, by Physiographic Zone and Size Class, 1964 Prices *257*

F-5. Capacity of Reservoirs in Thousands of Acre-Feet, Existing or under Construction: 1964 ... *257*

F-6. Distribution of Existing Reservoirs by Size Class, U.S. Summary: 1960, 1964 .... *257*

F-7. Percentage Distribution of Existing (1964) Reservoirs, by Physiographic Zone and Region *258*

F-8. Synthetic Schedule of Reservoirs: Percentage of Total New Capacity in Each Region Assigned to Various Physiographic Zones *258*

F-9. Synthetic Schedule of Reservoirs: Percentage of Total New Capacity in Each Region Assigned to Various Size Classes *259*

F-10. Inventories of Existing Reservoir Capacity, by Region *260*

F-11. Existing Storage Capacity, by Function and
Region: 1964 .... *261*

F-12. Distribution of Reservoir Capacity, by Divi-
sion: 1964 .... *262*

F-13. Distribution of Reservoir Capacity, by Function
and Region *263*

F-14. Synthetic Storage Schedules, by Region *264*

F-15. Adjusted Mean Annual Flow After Accounting
for Reservoirs Built or under Construc-
tion: 1954–64 .... *268*

F-16. Maximum Physical Development, by Region: 98%, 95%, and 90% Availability *269*

F-17. Synthetic Schedules of Flow, Storage, and
Costs, by Region: 98% Availability, 0.0425
Annual Factor *270*

F-18. Synthetic Schedules of Flow, Storage, and
Costs, by Region: 90% Availability, 0.0425
Annual Factor *275*

LIST OF FIGURES

Text

1. Water resource regions. *7*

2. Alternative programs for the Eastern Great Lakes
region, based on 98% availability, 0.0425 annual factor, and 1, 4, and 6 mg/l D.O. stan-
dards: 2000 Medium. *13*

3. Comparison of flow and storage requirements
with short-term tertiary treatment. *122*

Appendixes

A-1. Comparative population trends. *157*

D-1. Relationship of point loading to continuous load-
ing. *211*

D-2. Efficiency term-ratio of point loading to uniform
loading. *211*

F-1. Physiographic zones of the United States. *245*

PART ONE
THE STUDY IN BRIEF

The Problem and the Approach

The Basic Model and Its Variations

A Summary of the Findings

Conclusions, Policy Issues, and Research Priorities

Chapter 1

THE PROBLEM AND THE APPROACH

Concern over adequate supplies of fresh water, long a pre-occupation in the arid western states, has spread in recent decades to many other parts of the United States. It will become more intense and spread still more rapidly as population — especially urban population — and industrial activity continue to grow.

Many of the installations used in modern water management, like dams or waste treatment plants, are expensive and take time to build. Years pass from authorization, through the planning and construction stages, to operation. Also, the installations are durable. Once built, they can freeze a region's patterns of water management for generations, influencing rates of economic growth, levels of health, and the amenities of living. The fact that most of the major decisions on water policies and programs are public rather than private accentuates the importance of having a systematic and accessible body of information on future projects to serve as a basis for discussion and action.

In view of all this, the need for well-grounded projections of future supplies and requirements is as great for water as for any other of the country's major natural resources or resource commodities. Yet the art of making comprehensive projections remains more primitive for water than for a number of other resource commodities, notably the major metals and mineral fuels. This is not for lack of thought and effort; most of the reasons for the lag are inherent in the unique and elusive characteristics of water as a natural resource.

1. Most water problems are local or regional rather than national. Transporting water for long distances outside its natural lines of flow is expensive — often prohibitively so — in relation to its value in all but a few small, specialized uses. For some purposes, the national data on water

are useful — for instance, to estimate the limit that water availability might set on economic expansion throughout the whole nation, even if water were diverted on a large scale from one basin to another and people and industry could move freely from deficit regions to areas where water is more plentiful. But for the most part, knowledge that some regions of the country have plenty of water means little in an area where supplies are short.

2. There is no true market for water; a national market is ruled out for the reasons stated above and even regional or local markets are absent. Water is unlike most resource commodities for which planning, investment, and operations are carried on largely through the mechanism of the price system. Although many users of water pay something for it, the charges are rarely based on total costs and sometimes do not even relate to the amounts used. Other users pay no direct charges.

3. Water from the same source is used for many different purposes, and the various uses affect the supply in many different ways. Demands on the same water source may include withdrawals for use on irrigated land, in factories, or in steam-generation plants; falling water for hydropower; impoundments for recreational lakes or for flood control; flow of streams for carrying wastes or for navigation; and the maintenance of wetlands for wildfowl. If upstream users discharge inordinate amounts of waste into a river, the supply of usable water available to downstream users is diminished. In some withdrawal uses in which there is no recirculation most of the water is returned to the stream in good condition. In others, notably irrigation, most of the water is lost. Neither the uses of water nor their effects on the supply can always be estimated in monetary terms. Hence, some uses of water are priced, or could be; others could not.

4. Because of the very close relationship between quality and quantity, volume alone — so many acre-feet or cubic feet per second — is often of little value as a measure of water supply. The problem is seldom one of how much water, but of how much water is acceptable for particular uses. Timing is also important. In most areas there is so much variation in flow among and within years that an average gives no assurance that supply can be depended on when needed.

5. There are few absolute requirements for establishing either quality or quantity. Requirements are governed by the many different objectives of water management throughout the country. For example, 4 milligrams per liter is often cited as a desirable level of dissolved oxygen. Yet some authorities prefer 6 mg/l, while others believe that 1 mg/l will do in some circumstances. Similarly, should a reach of a river be clean enough for boating and fishing, or still cleaner to make it fit for swimming? The issue becomes one of how much the public is willing to pay for. The same issue arises with quantities of water. Is the amount of storage that would assure a desired rate of flow 98 percent of the time worth the increases over the cost of storage that would assure the same flow 95 or 90 percent of the time?

6. Once agreement has been reached on the desired level of quality and the amount and dependability of flow, there are widely different ways of achieving these aims. Emphasis can be put on storage to assure a large dependable flow; in this case, waste treatment would be at a minimum and used only as a supplementary means of maintaining the desired standards. Or emphasis can be put on waste treatment, with storage as the supplementary element. Or emphasis can be put on regulating the character of use, in which case economic projections must be adjusted. Within these extremes many variations are possible, including whatever combination would meet the agreed-upon requirements at minimum cost for a particular economic projection.

Even the best-grounded projections are influenced by uncertainties — the rate of technological advance, developments in national and world politics, and the sheer unpredictability of human events. Because of the additional uncertainties that attend the supply-demand outlook for fresh water, not even the conventional kind of projection is yet within reach. The best that can be done under the circumstances — and what is attempted in this study — is to construct an economic "model" in which several important factors are necessarily excluded, either because the basic data are still lacking or because some interrelationships are not well enough understood to be handled with any confidence. On the other hand, we have tried to cover as much ground as we could and to make our assumptions as realistic as possible, so that the findings can be offered as at least provisional projections.

There have been several previous studies of the water situation and its prospects, including the report of the President's Water Resources Policy Commission and portions of the report of the President's Materials Policy Commission and of Resources for the Future's *Resources in America's Future.* Numerous other studies have dealt with particular areas or with particular characteristics of water. More closely akin to the present volume are the group of studies undertaken for the U.S. Senate Select Committee on National Water Resources, 1959 and 1960;[1] and *The Nation's Water Resources* (1968), the first national assessment of the Water Resources Council. Other comprehensive studies can be expected in the future, certainly by the Council, which plans to maintain its assessment on a continuing basis, and by the National Water Commission, a body created by Congress to prepare a report on long-range water resources policies.

The nation has been slow to respond on any broad, systematic basis to the restrictions on people's activities imposed by competition for water in the humid as well as the arid regions. This is not only because of the time required for engineering and ecological modifications to take hold; there has been an intellectual lag. Substantial changes in the institutional framework — legal, economic, political, and social — of water policies and programs seem likely within the next decade or two, although the exact nature of such changes remains vague. But a few major endeavors are under way, largely in response to the activity of the Office of Water Resources Research and to the various river basin studies and programs being developed through the collaboration of national, state, and local governments. In the present study, we have hoped to contribute to the advancement of water management in the United States by marshalling available facts, illustrating several ways in which they can be applied, and indicating the kinds of additional facts that are most needed.

Ultimate Goals

The object of any projection (or in this case something short of a true projection) is to serve as a general guide to planning and investment that ought to be undertaken now in order to deal with the situations most likely to arise in the future. A desire for guides to action has followed the realization that the nation's water resources will increasingly affect decisions regarding where we live and what we do, and will also affect the degree of pleasure we can derive from the environment. Among economists, and sometimes for the political record, these guides are usually demanded in the name of "efficiency," but one must also always ask: "Efficiency for what?"

Ultimately all decisions rest on a complex evaluation of the quality of life for which a common unit of measurement would be helpful but does not now, and may never exist. A partial substitute for such a unit is market price, but the price structure itself is never a completely adequate tool for resource allocation, and water is one of the resources for which the inadequacies are greatest. Water and air have traditionally been used by economists as examples of "free" goods. It is now readily apparent that over most

---

[1] President's Water Resources Policy Commission, *Report* (1950), 3 vols.; President's Materials Policy Commission, *Resources for Freedom*, vol. 5, "Selected Reports to the Commission" (1952); Hans H. Landsberg, Leonard L. Fischman, and Joseph L. Fisher, *Resources in America's Future* (The Johns Hopkins Press for Resources for the Future, 1963); *Water Resources Activities in the United States*, Committee Prints Nos. 1–32, 86th Cong.

of the world water is not free, and that in many urban concentrations air is also no longer free, yet neither is adequately coupled with other prices and costs. This accentuates the problem of externality — the degree to which the costs or gains to an individual, firm, or unit of local government differ from the social costs or gains to a large area or the whole nation. Dumping wastes in the river may be the cheapest means of disposal for a manufacturer or a municipal government, but the costs of water treatment to downstream users may exceed the upstream savings. Because of these externalities and the inapplicability of the price system to water, the economist's technical apparatus at present is insufficient for all except simple models. Therefore, in choosing a particular analytical scheme — for instance, determination of a water resource policy that maximizes net national product — the economist may introduce unintended bias if he selects a method because it is workable rather than because it satisfactorily encompasses all relevant elements.

A complete analysis of the nation's water resources would encompass an inventory of "natural" supplies, changes in supply, uses to which water resources are put, changes in quality as a consequence of use, and restrictions on use imposed by quantity and quality constraints. It would be based on a thorough knowledge (much more than we now have) of the behavior of water throughout the various phases of the hydrologic cycle and of the effects of man's intervention at particular points of the cycle.

Ideally, one would like to look toward a national water resources system within which all manner of adjustments are possible — changes in final product mix, changes in types of inputs, changes in geographic location of production and consumption, changes in aesthetic response to the environment, and changes in the environment. But the models that we know how to construct at present are quite limited and do not respond with equal precision to all adjustments.

Our study seeks to develop a systematic economic model that (1) recognizes the regional aspects of the water problem yet yields a national perspective; (2) permits aggregation of demand and supply into usefully parallel concepts; (3) takes into account the fugitive and probabilistic characteristics of supply as well as the interdependence between supply and demand; and (4) identifies important choices to be made and tensions to expect within and among water resource regions.

It is now understood that "shortage" is a phenomenon of quality as well as quantity and that our adjustments to both constraints will ultimately reflect broad social preferences. Therefore, one purpose of the study is to make explicit how aesthetic judgments can be incorporated into the body of an economic analysis of water resources. This is done, albeit imperfectly, by postulating alternative goals of quality (measured by the single characteristic of dissolved oxygen) and by comparing their impact on water resource policies.

Chapter 2

THE BASIC MODEL AND ITS VARIATIONS

A great many factors — and a far greater number of possible combinations of these factors — are involved in trying to determine how adequate the supplies of fresh water will be in the United States during the next five decades. But the first step in any conscientious effort to look ahead is to reduce the number of factors to be considered. Selectivity is necessary, not only because reliable data are lacking, but also because the field of inquiry must be diminished to manageable proportions.

The present study is an outgrowth of the work done a decade ago by the Senate Select Committee on National water-related activity in each region. In aggregating projected uses, the possibility of an absolute deficiency of dant of the Committee's report *Water Supply and Demand*.[1] Many of the basic data and analyses of the earlier study have been updated and some new data have been incorporated, but the framework and rationale are little changed.

As in the earlier study, attention is confined to the forty-eight contiguous states; the water problems of Alaska and Hawaii are too separate to be included in any useful way. Restricted definitions of "supply" and "demand" have been retained, and this study, like the earlier one, introduces quality into the concept of supply by stipulating required levels of dissolved oxygen content. The additional quality characteristic of heat has been added. But because many other factors are treated sketchily or omitted entirely, our effort to make forward estimates is better described as an economic model than as a set of formal projections.

---

[1] Nathaniel Wollman, *Water Supply and Demand*, Committee Print No. 32, Senate Select Committee on National Water Resources, 86th Cong., 2d sess. (1960). Referred to hereinafter as Committee Print No. 32.

The essential steps are these:

1. The supply of fresh water for each of the twenty-two water resource regions is calculated at three levels — the flow that can be depended on 98 percent, 95 percent, and 90 percent of the time. These are amounts obtainable through maximum regulation — the point at which more storage would result in net losses through evaporation — regardless of cost. Supplementary estimates are made of the supplies that would be available at maximum costs of 10 cents and of 2 cents per 1,000 gallons.

2. Water "requirements" for each of the regions are estimated for the years 1980, 2000, and 2020. (For a definition of "requirements" as used in this study, see the section on demand in this chapter.) The estimates for each year are made at three levels, based on assumptions of high, medium, and low rates of economic growth. Separate calculations are made for three minimum levels of dissolved oxygen content — 1, 4, and 6 milligrams per liter.

3. Estimates of supplies are compared with the requirements of each region to indicate the surplus or deficit to be expected in 1980, 2000, or 2020 under various combinations of the assumptions and constraints noted above.

4. Three alternative types of programs for meeting indicated regional deficits (up to the limits of maximum dependable flow) are developed and their estimated costs compared. The principal reason for presenting these choices is that the quality of water, as measured in this study by dissolved oxygen content, can be maintained through either larger dilution flows or higher levels of waste treatment. The alternative programs are based on:

   a) minimum levels of treatment (implying maximum flows through additional storage),

   b) minimum storage (with maximum reliance on treatment), and

Figure 1. Water resource regions.

c) minimum cost (the least expensive combination of treatment and storage).

Comparison of the alternative programs leads deep into the realm of policy — questions of economic efficiency, of regional versus national advantage, and of aesthetic values.

Even the limited number of factors explored in this study presents a large array of possible combinations. *Consequently, we give most of our attention to a "basic" model which calls for an instream dissolved oxygen standard of 4 milligrams of oxygen per liter of water, and a 98 percent availability of flow (that is, a 2 percent chance of deficiency).* We frequently use the other parameters to test how costs, required flows, and required levels of treatment are affected by changing the constraints of the basic model. Variants similarly tested are the rates of recirculating withdrawn water, the costs of short-term chemical treatment of wastes compared with the higher storage costs for which they would substitute, changes in the assumed amounts of waste discharged per unit of industrial output, and an assumption that all reservoirs would include some water for use exclusively in recreation.

Definitions and Methods

Supply

In this study water supply is always measured by streamflow, with no allowance for importation of water, desalination, weather modification, or exportation to another region or to Canada or Mexico. We assume that aquifers discharge sooner or later into a water course. This assumption contains at least two sources of error: (1) some underground movement never appears as surface flow but is discharged underground outside the land boundaries of the United States; and (2) some groundwater exists as a stock that is more or less fixed or is being replenished much more slowly than the rate of exhaustion. While both of these exceptions are important in the economies of particular regions, it is assumed that their overall magnitude is small relative to average annual runoff.

Failure to account for groundwater as a resource that can be mined until economically exhausted is serious in at least two respects: (1) the level of water-related activity is understated during the active life of the resource; and (2) adjustments to exhaustion may involve large water-related expenditures that might not have been undertaken had the local economy been geared to a rate of water use equal to the rate of natural recharge. An example of such an adjustment is the plan now under consideration by the state of Texas and federal agencies to import water to the high plains.

A high degree of accuracy is presumably attainable regarding estimates of expected precipitation and runoff. All that is needed is an extended series of historical observations, since, to the best of our knowledge, climate and watershed conditions are fairly stable even though weather is variable. If groundwater reservoirs and movements are added to information about precipitation and runoff, we have reasonably accurate knowledge of the availability of water as it can be captured for use. The *costs* of regulating this physical supply in order to reduce diurnal, seasonal, and annual fluctuations are also theoretically ascertainable with a high degree of accuracy but in actuality can only be estimated by crude techniques. Because of limited historical data on precipitation and runoff, as well as limited information regarding groundwater, potential reservoir sites, and alternative devices for regulating water supplies, the confidence with which we can make statements about the costs of future supply may be no greater than that for statements about future demands.

In economic terms "supply" is a functional relationship between costs and output. In most of our analysis we show cost of regulation as the marginal cost (per 1,000 gallons of additional sustained flow) or as the cumulative total cost required to attain a specified flow by use of surface storage, both expressed as annual equivalents. The reader will note that the term "supply" sometimes refers to physical availability and sometimes to cost-output functions, but the context should make clear which meaning is intended. Also, at times costs refer to capital outlays and at other times to annual equivalents.

The "supply" of water in the cost-function sense, is a schedule of successively higher minimum flows (with a designated level of certainty) and the associated costs of regulatory storage for each water resource region. If a region has a single river system, such as the Colorado, supply is defined by the regulated flow at the point of discharge from the United States. If a region has a number of separate basins, such as New England or the Southeast, supply is the aggregate of regulated flows at the mouths of the region's rivers.

The "supply" of water is the minimum flow that is assured with a chance of deficiency equal to 2 percent, 5 percent, and 10 percent of the time. The chance of deficiency should be interpreted as the *percentage of years*, although in connection with a special short-term treatment program we treat the deficiency as the percentage of days within the year. In nineteen of the twenty-two regions the present minimum flow can be raised by constructing regulatory storage. In the other three – Upper Missouri, Rio Grande–Pecos, and Colorado – the amount of storage already constructed or under construction in 1964 was deemed ample to achieve full, or maximum, regulation. By "full regulation" is meant the degree of regulation by use of surface storage beyond which a further increase in reservoir capacity would result in greater loss from evaporation than in addition to regulated flow. Each increment in minimum flow is the result of a specified increment in reservoir capacity. The annual equivalent cost of reservoir capacity is the "cost of storage," or "cost of flow," the two terms being used interchangeably.

It is the conclusion of hydrologists that maximum assurance of certainty does not exceed the likelihood that a designated flow will be available 98 percent of the time.[2]

The validation of this 2 percent uncertainty, however, depends on a reasonable replication of past history. A significant change in watershed conditions could lead to a violation of the specified chance of deficiency.

Demand

Whereas "supply" in this study usually means a cost-output relationship, the term "demand" usually refers simply to a physical target for fresh water. That is, no consideration is given to the effects on demand of any change in the cost of water to its users.

There are three traditional categories of water use: (1) "withdrawal uses" (or "intake") – industry, irrigation, and household water supply systems – which actually remove water from its source; (2) "onsite uses," which consist mainly of water requirements for swamps and wetlands and for land treatment to abate soil erosion; and (3) "flow uses" – navigation, hydroelectric power, sport fish habitat, waste dilution, and freshwater discharges that maintain a proper salinity balance in estuaries.

The principal factors in demand are withdrawal uses and the dilution flow needed to maintain water quality. Under the assumptions of this study, onsite requirements are comparatively small, and, with the exception of dilution flow, we largely ignore the flow uses. Navigation and sport fishery flows are omitted on the assumption that they are sufficient if adequate waste dilution flows are provided. Hydroelectric flows are omitted because (1) projected storage for flow regulation would allow generation of hydroelectric power at many, perhaps most, sites; and (2) local peaking-power requirements could be met by building reregulatory capacity without restricting other uses of water, except, perhaps, as the result of additional surface evaporation and limitation of available reservoir sites. Flows into estuaries are needed for breeding and nursery habitat along the coast, but in view of the uncertain state of knowledge regarding effects of upstream losses on the one hand and regularity of flow on the other, we decided to omit such flows from the models.

Starting from estimates of total U.S. population and of urban population in the years 1980, 2000, and 2020, levels of water-related activity are projected for each of the twenty-two regions on the assumption that regional economic activity will grow or decline relative to the growth of the national economy at rates consistent with recent trends. Population projections are used in estimating municipal water use, municipal waste, waste collection costs, and rural domestic requirements and also to update the projections of food manufacturing and processing presented in 1960 in Committee Print No. 32. Estimates of gross national product are used to update the 1960 projections of other activities if a more direct basis of revision is not available. By modifying particular assumptions, applicable either to the economy as a whole or to a particular sector, we established a range of High, Medium, and Low growth rates for each water-related activity in each region. In aggregating projected uses, the possibility of an absolute deficiency of water did not influence the result; the totals stood. However, to the extent that they are reflected in the historical record of economic activity, the constraints of water short-

[2] George O. G. Löf and Clayton H. Hardison, "Storage Requirements for Water in the United States," *Water Resources Research*, vol. 2, no. 3 (Third Quarter 1966), pp. 323–54.

age or the stimuli of large supplies were implicitly taken into account in the projection of each activity by itself.

Activity projections consisting of national indexes of output or measurements, such as regional irrigated acreage or urban population, were then coupled with unit water requirements that reflected foreseeable technological changes. Water inputs were calculated on both a gross (withdrawals) and a net (losses) basis, depending on how much of the withdrawn water is returned to the stream for later use. Net inputs represent the amount lost from a region by evaporation, transpiration, incorporation into a product, or discharge into salty water or irretrievably into the ground. In manufacturing and steam-electric power plants withdrawal is inversely related to the degree of in-plant recirculation. Water loss by evaporation is, so far as we know, relatively insensitive to changes in recirculation rates, but the facts have yet to be established.

Many projections are updatings of estimates made for the Senate Select Committee on National Water Resources and published in the 1960–61 series of committee prints. If new regional information was available — e.g., for agriculture and mining — it was used to update the material published in the committee prints. If new national, but not regional, projections were available, original projections were adjusted in accordance with the percentage change in projected GNP. No attempt was made to use more sophisticated methods, such as those being developed by the Office of Business Economics, U.S. Department of Commerce; or by the Economic Research Service, U.S. Department of Agriculture, for the Water Resources Council and various river basin or regional planning committees.[3]

The method of estimation takes no account of the price elasticity of water, i.e., the substitutions among products and factors that result from changes in the price (cost) of water relative to other final products or factor inputs. Price elasticity for water varies for each use and for different price-of-water ranges. And, as already noted, most pricing of water is not geared into the free market system. In our model we assume that during the next five decades price elasticity will be unimportant as a predictive element in water use except where the marginal cost of water rises to levels fixed by the upper limits of regulation or costs of transbasin diversions or desalination.

It is also probable that changes in technology or changes in the mix of final products, or both, will occur in a fashion not incorporated in the technical coefficients or projections of economic sectors. It is virtually certain that the future as realized will be different from the future as projected. (Part of the divergence may be attributable to policies established in response to studies such as this.) That is the reason for making projections of High, Low, and Medium growth paths. When the time comes for action, the underlying assumptions can be verified and, if necessary, corrected before an irreversible error is committed.

A complete measure of water requirements includes attention to quality. We partially meet this need in our model by postulating that the streams of each region shall contain no less than 4 milligrams of dissolved oxygen per liter[4] (with some testing of the results of 6 mg/l and 1 mg/l as alternative standards) and undergo no more than a 5.4°F. increase in temperature after industrial and municipal use. One way to avoid violation of the oxygen constraint is to have an adequate flow of well-oxygenated water available when decomposable organic material is introduced into the streams. The other way is to reduce the discharge of decomposable organic material by treatment that induces accelerated decomposition, so that wastes discharged into a stream are composed of a larger fraction of nondecomposable inorganic matter than would be the case in the absence of treatment. Thus, quantity of flow and level of treatment are physical substitutes by means of which a specified in-stream oxygen level can be maintained.[5] The relationship is not wholly linear but may be treated as logarithmically linear for rough estimates.

Violation of the heat constraint is avoided by in-plant recirculation or provision of a dilution flow. The reader will note that even if a dissolved oxygen constraint is not violated the quality of water may deteriorate from other causes, e.g., a build-up of dissolved solids from multiple recycling or drainage of irrigation water.

The absolute quantity of dilution flow is a function of the discharge of waste associated with a given bill of goods after reduction by treatment. Waste dilution curves (waste dilution flow as a function of treatment levels) must be computed for each bill of goods — i.e., for each projection of population and production. In this study nine such curves were computed for each region for a specified level of water quality: Low, Medium, and High projections for 1980, 2000, and 2020.

The total of required waste dilution flow plus losses incurred through use and reservoir evaporation plus the discharge of fresh water into coastal waters is the measure of a region's "requirement," or "demand." "Withdrawal," or "intake," cannot serve as a measure of "requirement." So long as the river's flow is equal to, or more than, the intake requirement at any single point, aggregate intake for the region can exceed the rate of flow by any amount.

An alternative definition of "requirement," or "required flow," is the sum of "upstream" losses plus "downstream" intake. In this study "downstream" implies that a user's discharge is into a brackish or salty receiving body of water so that his entire intake, by definition, is lost.

Bays and estuaries, the aquatic environment that lies between the freshwater river and the salty ocean, pose special problems that we largely ignore, not because they are un-

---

[4] The "natural" level varies according to the physical and biological characteristics of the stream. A range of 4 mg/l to 8 mg/l is common.

[5] There are other techniques as well, but our model deals only with these two, supplemented by short-term chemical treatment. For a discussion of the various techniques, with special reference to an estuary, see Robert K. Davis, *The Range of Choice in Water Management: A Study of Dissolved Oxygen in the Potomac Estuary* (The Johns Hopkins Press for Resources for the Future, 1968).

[3] See, for example, *North Atlantic Regional Water Resources Study*, app. B, "Economic Base," prepared by the Office of Business Economics, Regional Economics Division, U.S. Department of Commerce, for the North Atlantic Regional Water Resources Study Coordinating Committee (May 1968).

important but because knowledge is still insufficient. We cannot, at present, establish a "required" freshwater flow into estuaries, nor can we specify what level of treatment of discharged wastes is necessary to avoid impairment of the waters, nor can we measure the social costs of successively higher levels of impairment.

Recent studies, such as those of the Potomac and Delaware estuaries,[6] conclude that incremental costs of reaching successively higher levels of water quality in an estuary are substantially greater than those implied by our figures. The differences are explainable, at least in part, by our simple assumption that maintenance of quality along the course of a stream above tidewater automatically assures the quality of the estuary, provided that waste discharged into the estuary is given primary treatment. The effect of our assumptions may have been to understate the cost of maintaining water quality in regions in which lakes and estuaries are important, as well as to suppress the increase in costs associated with attaining successively higher levels of quality.

Choice among Programs

Our model specifies various rates of water loss per unit of output and provides for a range of treatment from a minimum of 70 percent biochemical oxygen demand (BOD) removal for municipal wastes and a minimum of 50 percent for industrial wastes[7] to a maximum of 97½ percent for both. The residue of waste discharged after treatment determines the amount of water required as a dilution flow.

Comparison of a region's water requirements – losses from withdrawal and onsite uses, plus dilution flow – with its supply at various levels up to dependable flow at maximum regulation will show the surplus or deficit that can be expected in 1980, 2000, and 2020 at various levels of economic growth. Since deficits can be overcome either by adding storage to increase dependable flow – provided flow is not already at a maximum – or by raising the level of waste treatment in order to reduce required dilution flows, there is a choice among the three types of programs already mentioned: one that holds new storage to a minimum, one that minimizes treatment, and one that aims at a least-cost combination of treatment and storage.

As projected requirements increase, the range of choice among programs narrows. When maximum regulated flow is sufficient only if all waste treatment is carried to 97½ percent, the minimum flow program is the only solution. Beyond that point the model can merely indicate the size of the water deficit that will have to be dealt with by means outside the scope of this study – changes in the assumed national bill of goods in response to changes in the cost of flow or treatment; changes in the assumed distribution of population and economic activity among regions; increases

in regional supply through importation, desalination, weather modification, evaporation control, and other methods. However, in the course of the study, rough side computations seek to indicate an order of magnitude of some of these adjustments.

Sensitivity of costs, required flows, and required levels of treatment of the minimum cost and other programs are tested by changing the chance of deficiency, the annual factor, the level of dissolved oxygen, and the implied rate of recirculation of cooling water in the production of power.

A variant of the basic model compares the costs of special chemical waste treatment for a thirty-day period with the saving in storage costs achieved by providing a reservoir capacity geared to a 10 percent chance of deficiency of flow rather than a 2 percent chance. Further variants are constructed by changing the assumed amount of waste discharge per unit of output, by assuming that municipal water in downstream areas was recirculated, and by providing for a dead pool devoted to recreation in all reservoirs.

Estimation of Costs

In this study, "cost of water" means the annual equivalent costs of dams and waste treatment plants. These are the costs incurred in maintaining a designated quantity of regulated flow, plus the costs of treating wastes at the level consistent with the regulated flow in order to maintain a specified amount of dissolved oxygen in a region's streams. A number of costs are *not* included: (1) municipal and industrial water treatment at point of intake; (2) local distribution – municipal, agricultural; (3) pumping from groundwater aquifers; (4) onsite preparation and onsite maintenance to conserve moisture and soils, e.g., contour furrowing to reduce erosion, river bank and beach erosion controls, reseeding of land, and artificial groundwater recharge; (5) creation of recreational areas (other than the lakes designed to regulate flow) and related engineering and biological activities; (6) dredging of channels and maintenance of navigational facilities; and (7) installation of hydroelectric turbines and related facilities. These items were omitted as parts of the "costs of water" because they are not necessarily related to pressure against a "fixed" water supply – conceiving of the "fixed" supply as the average annual runoff in a region. The exclusion from "costs of water" of antierosion and sedimentation controls is not wholly logical, since the benefits of such controls are enjoyed as much by a region's river as by its land; nor is it logical to exclude the costs of pumping water from aquifers, since surface and ground storage are usually connected.

In estimating storage costs, a 4 percent interest rate is assumed in the basic model. In converting the capital costs of a project, a factor of 0.0425 is used on the assumption of a 50-year life for the installation, and annual operation and maintenance costs of one-quarter of 1 percent of capital cost. Two alternative factors are frequently used for the purposes of comparison: 0.0200 (representing 2 percent interest, a 100-year life, and zero operating and maintenance costs) and 0.0525 (based on 5½ percent interest, a

---

[6] See Davis, *Range of Choice*; and Edwin L. Johnson, "A Study in the Economics of Water Quality Management," *Water Resources Research*, vol. 3 (Second Quarter 1967).

[7] Hereinafter, levels of treatment are sometimes expressed as 70/50 percent, 70/60 percent, and so on. The first number always refers to municipal wastes; the second to industrial wastes.

50-year life, and annual operating and maintenance costs of one-half of 1 percent). Annual equivalent costs of waste treatment plants are calculated uniformly on the basis of a 4 percent interest charge and a 50-year life.

Costs of treatment are the estimated costs of treating a designated aggregate amount of waste to a specified level of BOD reduction. Unit costs of treatment vary by type of waste. Hence, costs of treatment are computed separately for each projection in each region. Marginal costs per unit-reduction in BOD increase as the level of treatment increases, just as marginal costs of flow increase as regulated flow approaches its theoretical maximum. The play between the changes in costs of flow and costs of treatment affords us the opportunity of selecting the combination of treatment and storage that minimizes their combined cost. The minimum cost combination of flow and treatment usually falls somewhere between the minimum treatment program and the minimum flow program, but not always. This leads us to the matter of options, restrictions on choice, and how our model may be put to use.

The treatment cost function employed in our model is held constant over the entire projection period but assumes substantial technological improvement in waste treatment at high levels. Whereas it is generally accepted today that total treatment costs double when the rate of BOD removal is raised from secondary (90–95 percent) to tertiary (97½ percent), our cost functions postulate about a 25 percent increase for various industrial wastes and about 60 percent for municipal wastes. If it turns out that cost reductions in waste treatment are less than those we have assumed in our model, we shall have understated required flows and overstated treatment levels for minimum cost programs and, of course, understated treatment costs.

Aggregate costs for successively higher average levels of treatment within a region ascend less rapidly but begin at a higher level than is indicated by the scale of costs that applies to a single waste treatment system. A rise in the level of treatment does not represent a uniform increase but a difference in the proportion of firms treating at primary (35 percent), secondary (95 percent), and tertiary (97½ percent) levels. The effect of this procedure is to dampen the rise in cost resulting from a uniform increase in treatment level from, say, 95 percent to 97½ percent BOD removal. Moreover, by assuming that wastes discharged into major bodies of water are given primary treatment only, the increase in treatment costs is further dampened in coastal regions, in the Eastern and Western Great Lakes regions, and in the Great Basin.

Technology

The state of technology figures prominently in public discussion of water use, but it is an implicit rather than an explicit element in our study. Technology appears at five points of our analysis, and any change in technological capabilities beyond those implicitly taken into account in our models can upset our conclusions. The five points are: (1) cost of storage; (2) cost of biophysical and biochemical characteristics of waste treatment; (3) intake and loss per unit of product; (4) output of waste (including thermal) per unit of product; and (5) methods of maintaining stream quality other than by treatment and dilution. Technology not only might affect the costs of storage and treatment but also might provide alternatives to either or both. Perhaps the element most likely to respond to technological change is the output of waste per unit of product. An indication of the sensitivity of water use to such technological innovation is provided later in the study by introducing arbitrary changes in the industrial waste produced per unit of product. Technology will affect intake of new water per unit of product by regulating the number of times water may be recirculated. Since our computation of water requirement is dependent on loss rather than intake, changes in the rate of recirculation are assumed to have no effect on our measure of "requirements." One polluting characteristic, heat, is dependent on the level of recirculation, and in order to prevent undue warming of our streams, especially in the East, we assumed higher rates of recirculation than were indicated by extrapolating from past experience. Costs of recirculation to avoid an increase in stream temperature beyond 5.4°F. could be a major component of future costs of water.

How the Model Works

We will use the year 2000 Medium projection for the Eastern Great Lakes region to illustrate how we constructed our model and how we arrived at our findings. Urban and rural population, value added in manufacturing, irrigated acreage, and mining and electric power output are projected for the region as follows (see chapter 5 and appendix A):

Total population	22,360,000
Urban population	19,679,000
Irrigated acres	87,000
Selected minerals *(percentage of U.S. total)*	
Phosphate rock, etc.	16
Metal ores	3
Petroleum & natural gas	2
Manufacturing, value added *($ million, 1960)*	
Food	1,197
Pulp & paper	417
Chemicals, etc.	3,896
Petroleum refining & coal production	289
Primary metals	5,941
Steam electric *(billion kwh)*	290

From these estimates, gross and net water requirements were inferred by use of coefficients described in chapters 4 and 5 and appendix B. Water requirements for land treatment and structures and for swamps and wetlands were negligible for the 2000 Medium projections and were ignored. On the basis of population and output of food, pulp and paper, chemicals, and petroleum and coal products, amounts of waste measured in population equivalents (p.e.'s)[8] were estimated (chapter 8 and appendixes D and

---

[8] "Population equivalent," a measure of industrial waste in millions of units when in capital letters. One unit (p.e.) is equivalent to the domestic waste produced per day by one person, i.e., that amount of waste that exhausts from the stream 0.25 lb. of oxygen per day in the process of decomposition.

E). It was assumed that 75 percent of municipal wastes and 50 percent of industrial wastes were discharged into lakes; the amount of waste discharged into streams was correspondingly reduced. The 2000 Medium projections of Eastern Great Lakes withdrawals, losses, and p.e.'s are given below. (Dashes indicate negligible quantities, and there is some discrepancy due to rounding and the inclusion of omitted quantities in the tables.)

	Withdrawals (bgd)	Losses (bgd)	P.e.'s produced before treatment (1,000's)
Agriculture	0.3	0.2	
Mining	1.8	0.2	
Manufacturing			
Food	–	–	12,385
Textiles	–	–	135
Pulp & paper	0.4	–	4,269
Chemicals	2.4	0.6	41,711
Petroleum & coal prod.	0.2	–	396
Primary metals	4.1	0.3	–
Other	1.1	0.1	–
Total mfg.	8.2	1.1	58,896
Steam-electric power	31.0	0.4	–
Municipal	5.7	1.4	19,679
Totals	47.0	3.3	78,575
Amount of p.e.'s (before treatment) into streams			34,368

It was assumed that wastes discharged into lakes required no dilution provided that primary treatment (35 percent BOD removal) was imposed — an assumption that bears watching because of the growing concern with eutrophication. Given the average characteristics of streams in the Eastern Great Lakes region (see appendix D), the following waste dilution flows for different levels of treatment, plus losses of 3.3 billion gallons per day, represent the required flows to maintain instream dissolved oxygen at 4 mg/l:

Treatment (percent)	Waste dilution (bgd)	Total required flows (bgd)
70/50	87.1	90.4
70/60	72.9	76.2
70	56.7	60.0
80	37.8	41.1
90	18.9	22.2
95	9.5	12.7
97½	4.7	8.0

It was also determined that if stream temperatures were not to rise more than 5.4°F., recirculation rates had to reach maximum level, i.e., a rate of 70 (see appendix E). Costs of recirculation were estimated but did not affect the model's solution, since the rate of recirculation was held constant as the level of treatment was allowed to vary. Costs of waste collection were treated in the same way as costs of recirculation. If large-scale industrial waste treat-

ment plants are developed to collect the wastes of many manufacturing plants, industrial waste collection costs are likely to be a significant part of total costs.

The next step was to ascertain what range of treatment levels and total required flows came within the physical limits of the region. Hydrologic analysis (chapter 9 and appendix F) indicated that while mean annual flow was 40 bgd, maximum attainable regulated flow was 33.3 bgd as a consequence of increased evaporation losses from reservoir surfaces. Thus, the minimum treatment program required 84 percent treatment and 33.3 bgd flow. Since standard treatment was assumed to go no higher than 97½ percent, 8 bgd was the treatment-flow combination for the minimum flow program. Whereas minimum treatment and minimum flow could be ascertained from the physical relationships, the minimum cost program required additional cost data.

Estimated existing storage in the Eastern Great Lakes region was 1.7 million acre-feet (as of 1964), including 0.6 million acre-feet of flood control capacity. On the assumption that 1.1 million acre-feet could be used for flow regulation, minimum flow of 3.5 bgd could be sustained with existing storage. By adding additional storage and gradually absorbing flood control capacity into flow regulation capacity, the following flow-storage-cost table was determined:

Flow (bgd)	Required new storage (billion acre-feet)	Annual equivalent cost ($ million)
19.2	12.3	19.9
26.4	28.7	54.8
30.8	45.2	98.0
32.1	61.6	157.4
32.9	73.9	240.1
33.1	78.0	275.0
33.3	82.1	318.6

For full regulation, storage would be 83.8 million acre-feet, of which 82.1 million acre-feet would be new and 1.7 million acre-feet would be existing. Quantities of flow, storage, and costs that fell between the indicated intervals were estimated by straight-line interpolation in spite of the fact that this introduced a small error.

Costs of the different levels of treatment (appendix E) were as follows:

Treatment (percent)	Annual costs ($ million)
70/50	71
70/60	73
70	75
80	80
90	85
95	90
97½	102

As noted elsewhere, the flatness of the cost curve is partly explained by the fact that treatment of 75 percent of municipal wastes and 50 percent of industrial wastes, assumed to be discharged into lakes, remained fixed at the primary level. Treatment levels were assumed to move by discrete steps, except for the minimum treatment program. The minimum cost combination was ascertained by comparing total costs of treatment and flow for the alternative combinations that are possible between the physical limits given by the minimum treatment and minimum flow programs. It was established that treatment and flow costs were minimized when treatment was 95 percent and flow was 12.7 bgd.

Treatment *(percent)*	Flow *(bgd)*	Cost of flow *($ million)*	Cost of treatment *($ million)*	Total cost *($ million)*
90	22.2	34.4	84.5	118.9
95	12.7	11.7	90.3	102.0
97½	8.0	5.7	102.3	108.0

The three programs are summarized as follows:

	Treat-ment *(percent)*	Flow *(bgd)*	New storage *(mil. af)*	Cost of treat-ment *($ mil.)*	Cost of flow *($ mil.)*	Total cost *($ mil.)*
Minimum flow	97½	8.0	3.5	102.3	5.7	108.0
Minimum treatment	84	33.3	82.1	81.8	318.6	400.4
Minimum cost	95	12.7	7.2	90.3	11.7	102.0

Figure 2 presents the three programs diagrammatically and shows the comparable solutions for instream standards of 1 mg/l and 6 mg/l. The lowest solid line shows the annual cost of storage for successively greater minimum flows

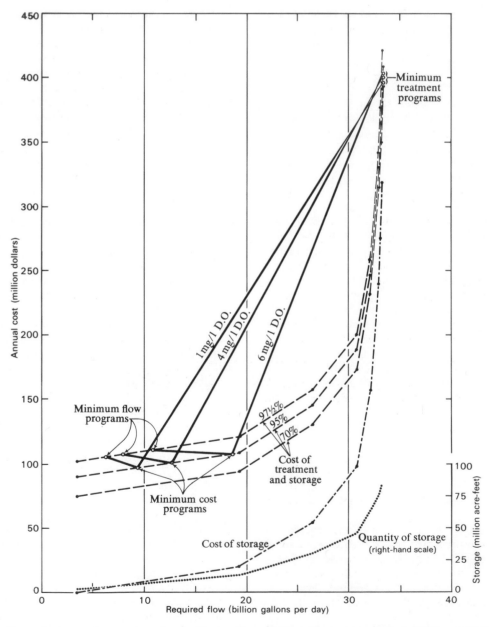

Figure 2. Alternative programs for the Eastern Great Lakes region, based on 98% availability, 0.0425 annual factor, and 1, 4, and 6 mg/l D.O. standards: 2000 Medium.

up to the region's maximum of 33.3 bgd. Parallel to this line are others that show the combined cost of a specified level of treatment and specified flow. The vertical distance between the cost-of-flow curve and any of the other curves parallel to it represents the cost of the designated level of treatment. The family of lines showing combined flow-treatment costs serves as a grid on which is superimposed the flow-cost-treatment points for the alternative programs and alternative levels of dissolved oxygen. For a given level of dissolved oxygen the point farthest to the left is the minimum flow program, the point farthest to the right is the minimum treatment program, and the lowest point is the minimum cost program. The path that connects the points for 1, 4, and 6 mg/l shows what is implied by raising the instream level of dissolved oxygen according to one or another of the programs.

A similar analysis was applied to the variants (chapter 12). In addition, the possibility of a tradeoff between chance of deficiency of flow and short-term chemical treatment was explored (chapter 11).

Limitations

From what has been said already it is clear that the model with which we must work at this stage of knowledge is highly restrictive. So long as (1) the population and final bill of goods are given for each region; (2) no account is taken of the effects of water costs on demand; and (3) other important assumptions are just as rigid, the policy question of how "best" to meet water requirements is relatively simple. For the most part, it can be dealt with through one of the three programs outlined above, or a combination of them. Eventually, when more data have been gathered and interpreted and methods of analysis have been refined, both the field of study and the range of choice in water management will be wider.

By changing the national bill of goods or its regional projection, the present model could be used to explore the implications of other objectives. For example, policies designed to elevate the income of a particular region may imply a greater relative increase in nonagricultural pursuits than is given by our projections. The same effect might be engendered by a policy of converting farm land to recreational land. The extension of navigation deeper into the central part of the country may induce changes in product mix that have not been accurately anticipated. Similarly, the effect of a reduction in the costs of electrical energy and the diffusion of such a reduction throughout a national power grid may also induce departures from our projections. We can only hope that continual surveillance will enable us to anticipate these changes and to alter projections accordingly.

It is not yet feasible to develop a general equilibrium model by which water resource policy is determined simultaneously with all the other variables in the social system. The models used in this study are of such partial nature that internal consistency is taken for granted. Whether or not this faith is misplaced is itself a suitable subject for further investigation.

In a comprehensive "efficiency" model the bill of goods, the geographic distribution, and the specified level of water quality would not be accepted as given. Not even the size of population and labor force would be a given except in the very short run. Instead, we would expect these measurements to fall out as part of the solution.

In a truly comprehensive model, the final bill of goods would include all environmental characteristics that are subject to modification by man and for which preference functions could be elicited. Furthermore, the institutional arrangements (e.g., income distribution and locus of power) whereby preferences, technology, and resources are brought together would color the result, since they introduce various "weights" into the decision process. It is perfectly clear that any economic model now capable of being constructed is restricted by a large number of givens.

The minimum cost program of our model is restricted by a limited definition of environmental quality, namely, a designated oxygen content and a maximum temperature increase in a region's streams and rivers. The only test of sensitivity of costs to a change in environmental quality that we perform on our model is to introduce a hypothetical change in instream dissolved oxygen. Other tests that could be introduced with comparative ease would be a population density restriction; alternative land use patterns (increases or decreases in area devoted to crops, forests, wetlands, and water surface); and water quality requirements other than dissolved oxygen and temperature. In our minimum cost model we have no idea how much, if at all, a dissolved oxygen content of, say, 4 mg/l, conforms to an efficiency model, since we have virtually no information on (1) the technical relationship between water quality and the whole array of goods and services which provide the basis for the preference functions; nor (2) the direct sensitivities of people to alternative levels of water quality (including size of flow) per se, nor (3) well-verified costs of achieving various levels of water quality either by treating waste or by modifying production processes. If, for the purposes of the model, we had defined the "cost of water" to include water treatment instead of confining the term to costs of storage and waste treatment, we might have reached different solutions for minimum cost programs. Under the broader definition, the minimum cost program might have called for a higher level of dissolved oxygen than the 4 mg/l specified in the basic model; the oxygen level would not then have been a given but would have varied with the required quality of treated water and the costs of such treatment.

The minimum flow and minimum treatment programs are indicators of the effects of fairly small changes in social objectives: What is implied by policies that put maximum emphasis (minimum treatment) or minimum emphasis (minimum flow) on maintaining water quality by provision of waste dilution? We can consider the minimum treatment and minimum flow programs as proxies for a preference for more lakes or for maintenance of undisturbed rivers, respectively. Also, depending on the nature of the financial arrangements, the two programs might represent alternative distributions of the cost of water quality between the public and private sectors. This line of thought, however, cannot be pursued very far, since various cost-distributional schemes are possible regardless of the physical form a water resource program assumes. The model does not account systematically for other possible ways of achieving a given level of water quality: lagooning of wastes, collection and discharge of wastes far out to sea, conversion of liquid wastes to solids by use of heat, disposal of wastes into the ground, and so forth. (One side computation is made showing the savings in treatment and flows that would follow a reduction in waste per unit of product.)

Our model also departs from a maximum "efficiency" model in that water uses as projected — e.g., irrigation and municipal — reflect current pricing practices which do not conform to an efficiency model.

The model gives no explicit attention to the "negative" aspects of water management: drainage of swamps and wetlands and flood control. By implication, a component of flood control is automatically incorporated into reservoirs designed for flow regulation and another component is implicit in land treatment and structures to conserve soil and moisture, but all other flood control outlays are ignored: dikes and levees, flood proofing, relocation of activity subject to flood hazard, and flood control reservoirs in excess of those required for flow regulation. The area of swamps and wetlands for fish and wildlife habitat in each region is incorporated into the model as a component of onsite water requirements; otherwise drainage has been ignored.

The aesthetic qualities of land and water use are not covered except for specification of instream dissolved oxygen. We therefore may have failed to account for the aesthetic costs or benefits of both reservoirs and estuaries. Consequently, we may have reached an incorrect solution to a minimum cost program, in part, by having improperly projected recreational demands and some municipal requirements. For the same reason we may have ignored solutions to water resource problems that will, in fact, be prominently relied on in the future. These future solutions may be more costly than traditional ones but may yield aesthetic benefits or avoid aesthetic costs in amounts great enough to justify additional costs. We are just beginning to incorporate into the planning processes differences in taste regarding environmental quality, but we still lack adequate information on psychic response to various environments and a weighting scale by which we aggregate such response.

Our model does not account fully for certain hydrologic elements. One of these is the possibility of artificial groundwater recharge. Another is required reregulation — a requirement that may change the treatment-flow combination of the minimum cost program. A related omission is failure to account for required single-purpose flood control reservoir capacity. In our model we assumed that when regulation of minimum flow approached full regulation, requirements for flood control capacity approached zero.[9] Two errors are contained in this assumption: (1) local protection works may be needed in spite of adequate storage capacity for the region as a whole; and (2) if a marginal cost constraint is imposed, the synthetic cost curve indicates how much storage would be available within the marginal cost constraint (and what the related minimum flow would be)

but does not reveal flood hazards remaining to be countered on a regionwide basis.

Another omission related to hydrology is the adjustment that will have to be made in 2 percent of the years in which regulated flow is deficient. Various compensatory responses are possible, but we have merely assumed they would take place without regard for their nature. It might turn out that this inattention has glossed over serious potential shortages and quality impairments.

Such forms of manipulation of water supply as evaporation suppression, weather modification, or modification of ground cover (including, but not limited to, elimination of "nonbeneficial" evapotranspiration) are not considered, mainly because data are fragmentary. Preliminary investigations indicate that changes in ground cover, upland or valley, may substantially affect "wild" evapotranspiration and therefore affect runoff. In some instances — e.g., phreatophyte eradication in the Rio Grande valley — there is strong opposition to any elimination of wildlife habitat in order to increase water supplies for other uses.[10] At the moment there is no satisfactory method for comparing the contribution to aggregate social welfare of using water to maintain habitat with that of use for alternative purposes.

We have ignored the probable increase in the salinity of freshwater streams resulting from heavy reuse and persisting despite the high levels to which conventional treatment may be carried. This means that the costs of desalination may dominate future treatment costs and change the cost-minimizing combination of treatment and flow. We also have ignored the problems of pollution created by storm drainage from agricultural and urban land and the costs of abating such pollution, except for a brief reference to separation of storm and sanitary sewers. The questions of land subsidence and the intrusion of saline waters resulting from pumping groundwater or from withdrawals from streams have been overlooked as well. These are problems that would have to be taken into account in operating a regionwide system of surface and ground reservoirs.

We have not accounted systematically for the effects of erosion and sedimentation. Suspended solids constitute the largest single source of stream pollution when measured by volume. We have taken into account some of the effects of soil and moisture conservation programs by including water loss associated with land treatment and structures, and have given a passing nod to the social cost of sedimentation by assuming a fifty-year life for reservoirs. But other aspects have gone unnoticed, notably, instream quality as a function of suspended solids, effect on lakes and estuaries of silt deposition, and additional costs of water treatment attrib-

---

[9] Even at less than full regulation, we made no attempt to account separately for flood control storage.

[10] William C. Hughes concluded that in the Pecos Valley of New Mexico eradication of salt cedar would yield benefits in excess of costs and that evaporation suppression measures in the summer would also yield net benefits, but that removal of timber in watershed areas would not, as a result of the loss of recreational values. No recreational or aesthetic values were assigned to stands of salt cedar in the computation of the costs of eradication. See "Economic Feasibility of Increasing Pecos Basin Water Supplies Through Reduction of Evaporation and Evapo-Transpiration" (preliminary draft, Department of Economics, University of New Mexico, 1968, mimeo.).

utable to high sediment loads. We also have not considered costs of land treatment and structures and instream devices designed to reduce channel erosion.

Prospective levels of pollution may be greater than anticipated because of an increase in the production of water-borne domestic waste per capita as a result of new techniques of waste disposal; an increasing scarcity of suitable solid-waste disposal sites; and our assumption that primary treatment of wastes discharged into estuaries, coastal waters, and large lakes will be adequate. Reductions in industrial waste loads per unit of output may offset these adverse possibilities. Still other sources of underestimation of pollution are (1) the failure to account for local problems, such as discharges of naturally saline waters and acid mine wastes; and (2) the possibility that chemical wastes, poisons, bacteria, or viruses may reach objectionable levels in spite of high-level biological treatment because of inadequate dilution when dilution flows are determined wholly by residual BOD.

The model does not incorporate a large number of alternative solutions.[11] The North Atlantic Region Study Group listed legal innovations, demand constraints, education, and flood-plain management as "passive measures"; diversion, impoundment, groundwater recharge, weather modifications, offstream storage, channel improvement, clearing and cleaning, flood protection, bank protection, watershed management, tidal flood protection, and beach erosion control as "active common measures"; and waste treatment, water renovation, reaeration, desalination, groundwater return, offstream cooling, and drainage as "active separable facilities." Each "device" is characterized by its own cost function, so that selection of the combination of devices that meets a particular objective – e.g., minimum aggregate cost – is likely to be a more complicated process than our own two-dimensional model implies.[12]

In our model scant attention is paid to hydroelectric power, navigation, and sport fish habitat and other instream recreational uses of water. We have merely assumed that hydroelectric power requirements would passively adjust to other demands for water. Where hydropower output is built into a basin or project repayment plan, however, and where reregulatory capacity is not available, requirements for hydropower may limit other uses of water. How extensive this possibility is we do not know. Navigation and recreational uses of rivers were ignored on the assumption that the maintenance of stipulated dilution flows and the assurance of a minimum dissolved oxygen content of 4 mg/l would mean that the requirements for both uses would be met automatically. Furthermore, recreational benefits, in-

cluding fish habitat, would be supplied by projected new reservoirs. It is quite possible, however, that recreational flows (and usable recreational lake volume) will decline on a per capita basis.

Several other limitations of the model should be kept in mind as the reader compares our results with those of other, more detailed studies for particular regions.

1. Regional estimates of water supply and demand sometimes conceal important differences within regions. The most extreme example is the Western Gulf region where the High Plains area is already short of water although the region as a whole is not.

2. By ignoring groundwater as a resource that can be mined we fail to account for the activity of a region like the High Plains of Texas and New Mexico. We consequently understate the importance attached by such regions to interbasin transfers of water, fail to consider the local economic effects of prospective declines in physical supply, and ignore the possibilities of water use in other regions in which groundwater supplies might be developed.

3. By failing to account systematically for likely conflicts in water use and the need for reconciliation, either by revision of projected uses or by additional regulatory and treatment capacity, we may understate required treatment and storage or overstate the level of production consistent with a specified flow-treatment combination, or both.

4. All separable costs – e.g., hydroelectric power plants, canals and other conveyances for irrigation and municipal water supplies, local distribution systems, etc. – are ignored. Hence total required investment in water-related activity is understated.

5. By failing to account systematically for the quality of water in estuaries and lakes (except for specifying that coastal and lacustrine wastes receive primary treatment before discharge), we may have understated, perhaps seriously, the level of required treatment and required flows discharged into lakes and estuaries.[13]

The foregoing exclusions and omissions imply that we have probably understated rather than overstated the foreseeable pressures on our water supply, and that we have understated the prospective "costs of water" even within our own limited definition of "costs."

To all these reservations must be added the usual criticisms directed against any model for which technical coefficients – physical inputs per unit of physical output – are set independently of solutions yielded by the analysis. Benefit-cost models, usually developed for specific projects, are intended to yield partial equilibrium solutions. General or partial equilibrium solutions, in contrast to a "requirements" approach, are designed to reveal "uneconomically" high marginal costs of water as well as economically justified opportunities for further water use. The most impres-

---

[11] The Coordinating Committee of the North Atlantic Regional Study Group, U.S. Army Corps of Engineers, calls a solution a "device." In an analytical table of "needs, resources, and devices" prepared in 1968, the Committee lists thirty devices.

[12] See Allen V. Kneese and Blair T. Bower, *Managing Water Quality: Economics, Technology, Institutions* (The Johns Hopkins Press for Resources for the Future, 1968), table 1, p. 42, and fig. 7, p. 43, for methods of dealing with the problem of man-made wastes and improving the quality of receiving waters.

[13] See Davis, *Range of Choice*, for a discussion of the upper Potomac estuary.

sive deficiency of a requirements model is its failure to allow for the substitutions that high costs of water would evoke.

Uses of the Study

In spite of these deficiencies, which are amplified and supplemented elsewhere in these pages, a requirements model serves several useful ends.

1. It incorporates many discrete bits of information into a decision framework.

2. At least to a limited degree, it incorporates quality considerations into a consistent set of statistics on regional requirements.

3. While recognizing that the region is the most significant area for analysis, it permits us to view water both as a national and a regional resource.

4. In spite of a restricted framework, it reveals a range of possible behavior and various bases for action regarding water resource use and supply.

5. Under specific assumptions of water use it forecasts the location and magnitude of water deficits and surpluses and the impediments to growth of regional and national product.

6. It similarly forecasts magnitudes of investment likely to be required as a result of growing pressure on water resources and allows us to consider their merits in relation to alternative economic adjustments.

7. It will, the authors hope, point the way to more comprehensive and more refined projections of water supply and demand — a work that is being carried on by many hands, notably, in agencies of the government, the Water Resources Council, the National Water Commission, the Office of Water Resources Research, and the federal-state-local collaborative river basin studies and programs.

Chapter 3

A SUMMARY OF THE FINDINGS

As the preceding chapter has shown, the forward estimates in this study rest on a fragile base. It is unlikely that the fundamental assumptions of growth in population and economic activity will be borne out over a fifty-year period, that regional trends will be consistent with national trends, or that progress in technology will occur as we now expect. Not all of the alternative lines of action are considered. And our model takes no account of the effects of changes in the cost of water that are sure to occur, or of regional shifts in population and industrial location in response to the adequacy of water supplies.

Consequently our findings are not predictions, nor even full-scale projections. They are an attempt to portray — in specific terms like billions of gallons or dollars — the problems likely to arise if current trends continue. The chief value of this study may lie in its stimulus to actions that would head off some of the situations it projects.

The selected findings presented here are drawn from Part II of the study where methods, results, and qualifications are discussed in detail. In this chapter we give the greatest attention to the basic model and to Medium projections of economic growth. Variations will be clearly identified.

Population and Economic Activity

The population of the forty-eight contiguous states was 178 million in 1960; according to our Medium projections, it will reach 233 million in 1980, 303 million in 2000, and 393 million in 2020. High and Low levels are also projected for each of the three years with, naturally, a widening range as one moves further into the future. (See chapter 5.) By the year 2000 the spread between Low and High is 45 percent, and by 2020 it is 55 percent — 335 million as against 520 million. Our estimates take account of the de-

cline in the U.S. birth rate over the past decade and are generally in line with the projections modified in 1966 by the Bureau of the Census.

Since the increase in population will not be distributed evenly, growth rates in some areas will be far above national estimates. In the South Pacific region the number of people (Medium estimate) is projected to double between 1960 and 1980 and to double again by 2020. A larger proportion of the total U.S. population will be concentrated in cities. In 1960, 65 percent of the people were in standard metropolitan statistical areas; by 2020 this percentage is projected to rise to 84.

By 2020 the gross national product is projected to reach (in constant dollars) eight times its 1960 level. Some industries that are heavy users or polluters of water, or both, are expected to grow even more rapidly. A tenfold increase is projected for chemicals, twelvefold for steam-electric generation, and eighteenfold for rubber and plastics. On the other hand, other water-using industries — notably food processing, petroleum refining, and primary metals — are expected to increase less rapidly than GNP. Irrigated agriculture, currently the largest single user of water, is projected to grow far more slowly (40 percent between 1960 and 2020).

The projected patterns of population and economic activity, in conjunction with appropriate coefficients of water use, are the basis of our estimates of water requirements.

Projected Water Requirements

Withdrawals of water by the year 2020 are expected to be about three and a half times larger than in 1960. Although withdrawals are not a satisfactory measure of requirements – the same water can often be used several times during its passage down a river – estimates of withdrawals are useful in revealing a pattern of water use, serving as crude indicators of waste loads, and providing the base from which losses can be computed.

Withdrawals in 1960, totalling 250 bgd, were apportioned as follows: agriculture, 139; steam-electric power, 66; manufacturing, 23; municipal, 20; and mining, 3. (The slight discrepancy is due to rounding.)

For selected projections, total withdrawals are:

	(bgd)
1980 Low	333
1980 Medium	405
2000 Medium	563
2020 Medium	897
2020 High	1,632

Within these totals, the pattern of withdrawals is expected to change. Mining remains the smallest use. Steam-electric power withdrawals gradually gain on agriculture and according to our projections would overtake agricultural diversions by 2020 High. In these projections we assume a rate of recirculation high enough to avoid the need for thermal dilution flows in excess of those required for BOD dilution. If past trends in recirculation rates were followed, withdrawals for power production would exceed irrigation withdrawals by 1980 under the Medium projection.

Growth in total loss, including onsite losses after 1960, is projected as follows:

	(bgd)
1960	104
1980 Low	115
1980 Medium	126
2000 Medium	148
2020 Medium	185
2020 High	259

Onsite losses constitute about 3 to 4 percent of the totals for Medium projections and about 6 percent for High projections. (Onsite losses charged against runoff are measured as the increase over 1960 losses. Also, Medium projections call for no change in the area devoted to swamps and wetlands.)

Estimated losses reveal a pattern different from that of withdrawals. In 1960, agriculture accounted for 87 percent of estimated losses from withdrawal uses; by 2020, Medium projection, agriculture will account for only 52 percent, but it will continue to be the largest consumer of water. Aggregate losses grow more slowly than withdrawals, even when withdrawals are computed at revised rates of recirculation. The explanation lies in the relatively slow rate of growth of irrigation. Agricultural losses are projected at an almost unchanged rate – a mere 9 percent increase in 2020 over 1960. Other losses grow rapidly: between 1960 and 2020, Medium projection, a fivefold increase for municipal use;

more than a sevenfold increase for manufacturing; and a tenfold increase for steam-electric power.

Roughly 10 percent of annual average runoff is now lost to the atmosphere or mingled with the water of the sea, and by 2020, High projection, this figure rises to 25 percent. Although evapotranspiration and estuarine discharges can be reduced in some measure – especially losses from irrigation – it is likely that the slack is relatively small when compared with the other component of water requirement, waste dilution. Projected losses represent a hard core of water requirements and are subject to fairly small absolute reduction by improved technology. When losses are viewed in terms of national totals, it appears that the water supply of the United States could support four times the High level of activity projected for 2020; this should carry us well into or beyond the twenty-second century. But within a number of regions the outlook is very different.

Although evapotranspiration losses portend no threat when measured against total runoff, the relatively low inter-basin mobility of water draws attention to what happens in each region. In three regions – Rio Grande–Pecos, Colorado, and South Pacific – the amount of water required today to meet evapotranspiration losses or municipal discharge into the sea exceeds average annual net flow. (In the first two of these regions as well as in a third, the Upper Missouri, storage now in existence or under construction is even greater than the amount specified by Löf and Hardison[1] for maximum physical regulation.) The deficiency is met by a draw-down of groundwater, importation from other basins, or rationing of water use to a less-than-optimum amount. Projected deficiencies grow in these regions. The 2020 High projection shows that a fourth region, the Upper Arkansas–White–Red, is faced with prospective losses in excess of maximum net regulated flow and another region, the Great Basin, reaches a condition of approximate balance.

Dilution Flow

Streamflow to cover net losses from withdrawal and onsite uses is only a part of required flow as defined in our model. To attain desired levels of water quality the basic model stipulates an instream dissolved oxygen content of 4 mg/l and the option of reducing biochemical oxygen demanding substances in waste discharges to within 2½ percent of their original potential. Larger amounts of water are involved in meeting the dissolved oxygen requirements than in making up for net losses, costs of alleviation are higher, and a larger area of the country is affected.

Needs for dilution flow depend on levels of waste treatment. The variations are wide; in the Medium projections for 1980 and 2000, for example, dilution requirements with a treatment level of 70 percent BOD removal from municipal organic wastes and 50 percent BOD removal from manufacturing wastes are nearly twenty times as great as those with 97½ percent treatment.

[1] George O. G. Löf and Clayton H. Hardison, "Storage Requirements for Water in the United States," *Water Resources Research*, vol. 2, no. 3 (Third Quarter 1966), table 7, p. 340.

Selected estimates of required dilution flow (U.S. aggregates) are as follows:

	Treatment (percent)	(bgd)
1980 Low	97½	66
1980 Medium	70/50	1,423
	95	231
	97½	78
2000 Low	97½	105
2000 Medium	70/50	2,857
	95	413
	97½	154
2020 Low	97½	189
2020 Medium	70/50	5,569
	95	740
	97½	295
2020 High	97½	650

When these alternative requirements are combined with projected losses, the implications are clear. At a level of treatment no higher than 70 percent for municipal wastes and 50 percent for industrial wastes, average annual runoff could not sustain a standard of 4 mg/l in 1980 (Medium projection) without an additional 60 percent of mean net annual flow. If, however, the level of treatment is raised to 95 percent, required flow would be 357 bgd (including losses), far under maximum regulated flow. The figures also indicate that waste dilution flows would exceed losses for all levels of treatment in the years 2000 and 2020 and for all levels of treatment except 97½ percent in 1980. As the projected level of activity rises, required dilution flows mount more rapidly than losses.

In seeking to measure quality requirements we did not consider dissolved solids. Our projected BOD dilution flows may be enough to take care of salinity, too, but we cannot be sure, especially as levels of treatment rise. Thus, our dilution requirements may be understated.

Throughout most of the study, the water supply with which requirements are matched is regulated flow that can be counted on 98 percent of the time. The maximum volume — 956 billion gallons a day — represents top physical availability (ignoring possible additions to supply from desalination or other methods), regardless of cost. (The present dependable flow is 400 bgd.) A moderate ceiling on costs of storing water would not greatly affect the available supply. If costs of new storage were limited to 2 cents per 1,000 gallons the maximum dependable flow would be 854 bgd; at a 10-cent limit the maximum would be 926 bgd.

Adequacy of Total Supply

Since there are many combinations of treatment and storage by which the stipulated quality standards can be met, there is a wide range in the estimates of total requirements that could be made for 1980, 2000, and 2020 at the three projected levels of economic growth. We have limited ourselves to three projections based on minimum flow, minimum treatment, and minimum cost programs. When the dilution requirements of each of these are added to the losses (which are the same for all three) the required flows for selected projections are estimated as follows:

	Minimum flow	Minimum cost	Minimum treatment
	(billion gallons per day)		
1980 Low	181	386	752
1980 Medium	205	426	776
2000 Medium	303	525	879
2020 Medium	480	679	1,004
2020 High	909	948	1,210

An idea of the adequacy of national supply can be obtained by comparing these projections with the 956 bgd maximum flow figure and its variants. These estimates for the whole country conceal great differences among the twenty-two regions. For instance, the Medium projection for 1980 (minimum flow program) shows a national surplus of 751 bgd, but a gross deficit (the sum of deficits projected for individual regions) of 15 bgd. For the year 2000 the national surplus is 653 bgd and the gross deficit 30 bgd; for 2020 the respective figures are 476 and 78 bgd. The 2020 High projection shows a national surplus of 45 bgd and a gross deficit of 255 bgd. Although the national estimates have their own uses, it is the regional situations that will determine what kinds of water programs are needed and how much they will cost.

Regional Prospects

As we have noted, the three regions that comprise the Southwest already lack the water to cover their losses, let alone their required dilution flows. According to the 2020 High projection, the Upper Arkansas-White-Red region would be in the same straits, with the Great Basin region just on the edge. As one might expect, the Southwest would remain the country's hard-core area of water shortage. At the other end of the scale, New England and the Lower Arkansas-White-Red region have dependable flows with present storage that are larger than the requirements of the 2020 High projection for a minimum flow program. In most regions high treatment levels plus new storage can bring supplies up to projected requirements, but as the projections move further into the future an increasing number of them show deficits.

This is best illustrated by the estimates of required flow for selected minimum flow program projections, drawn from table 82 and shown on page 21 (underlined figures indicate deficits).

Although ceilings on storage costs would affect the size of surpluses or deficits in some regions, no region would shift for that reason to a deficit position by 2020 High if the limit were 10 cents per 1,000 gallons, and only one more region — Eastern Great Lakes — would show a deficit if the limit were 2 cents.

A regional deficit, as projected in our basic model, assumes that treatment has been carried to 97½ percent and that storage has brought flow up to the maximum that can be expected 98 percent of the time. A deficit thus implies that the stipulated bill of goods will not be met, or that the deficit will be overcome, at extra cost, by methods not considered in the model — importation of water from another region, for example, or interregional shifts of population or economic activity.

	Max. regulated flow	Medium			High
		1980	2000	2020	2020
		(billion gallons per day)			
New England	60,895	3,177	4,522	6,474	9,935
Delaware and Hudson	28,629	6,486	9,785	14,627	25,907
Chesapeake Bay	46,657	6,025	10,410	17,767	39,329
Ohio	99,457	4,154	6,748	11,055	23,041
Eastern Great Lakes	33,278	4,800	7,995	13,482	30,471
Western Great Lakes	30,283	10,639	17,502	*30,641*	*71,965*
Upper Mississippi	46,125	3,350	5,321	8,275	16,133
Lower Missouri	16,211	957	1,657	2,896	5,703
Southeast	186,030	25,451	48,176	87,941	*186,781*
Cumberland	14,647	1,810	4,280	9,088	*23,529*
Tennessee	40,389	3,019	5,742	10,381	24,493
Lower Mississippi	35,207	3,130	5,311	8,536	16,732
Lower Arkansas-White-Red	57,661	3,099	4,463	6,064	10,114
Upper Missouri	25,600	15,912	18,179	24,084	*38,553*
Upper Arkansas-White-Red	7,053	6,730	*7,486*	*8,969*	*14,550*
Western Gulf	25,900	17,235	*26,747*	*44,441*	*98,408*
Upper Rio Grande-Pecos	3,000	*5,507*	*6,529*	*8,921*	*12,901*
Colorado	11,400	*16,950*	*25,204*	*42,643*	*65,373*
Great Basin	6,934	*6,251*	*7,011*	*10,046*	*18,038*
South Pacific	815	*8,135*	*12,278*	*18,055*	*26,098*
Central Pacific	45,478	26,834	30,309	37,267	*54,872*
Pacific Northwest	134,570	25,068	36,886	58,005	96,342
United States	956,219	204,719	302,541	470,658	909,268

Alternative Programs Compared

The minimum flow, minimum cost, and minimum treatment programs come closer together as estimated requirements rise from the 1980 Low to the 2020 High projection. Unless a region's maximum regulated flow is greater than that required with maximum treatment, there is no room for choice; a minimum flow program is the only course. Consequently, the national estimates for the minimum treatment and minimum cost programs include an increasing number of minimum flow figures from water-short regions.

For 2020, High projection, with the highest dissolved oxygen requirement we considered — 6 mg/l — only six regions have enough flow to be able to exercise choice. They are New England, Ohio, Upper Mississippi, Lower Missouri, Lower Mississippi, and Lower Arkansas-White-Red. For other projections and lower dissolved oxygen levels the opportunities for choice are, of course, greater.

The significant bases of comparison among the three programs are: (1) required volume of new storage capacity; (2) required levels of waste treatment; and (3) program costs, including the division of the costs between storage and treatment, and the distribution of projected outlays among regions. We also compare the costs of storage and waste treatment (depending on choice of program) with the costs of sewerage (collection) and recirculation. The latter costs, though not dependent on type of program and not included as elements of choice in our model, are significant items. We also take note of the industrial origin of flow and treatment requirements. Finally, we consider briefly the costs of storage already built and the estimated levels and costs of treatment to which waste is now subjected.

The difference in required flow among the three programs has already been noted. For all Medium projections of required flow the ratio of minimum cost to minimum flow, which in 1960 was 2.6 to 1, is estimated at 2.1 to 1 in 1980, 1.7 to 1 in 2000, and 1.4 to 1 in 2020. The spread between minimum flow and minimum treatment programs is, of course, higher.

When the difference among programs is expressed in required new storage capacity, contrasts are greater because of the rapid decline in marginal physical productivity of storage. For the 1980 Low projection, required storage is 6 million acre-feet, 42 million acre-feet, and 1,421 million acre-feet, respectively, for minimum flow, minimum cost, and minimum treatment programs. For the 2020 High projection the figures are 813 million acre-feet, 839 million acre-feet, and 2,493 million acre-feet. The converging of minimum flow and minimum cost programs is clear; the minimum treatment program remains in a class by itself. For Medium projections, required new storage for minimum cost programs is about twice the amount required for minimum flow programs. For example, for the year 2000 the figures are 99 million acre-feet and 180 million acre-feet, respectively.

Obviously, the choice among the three alternative programs[2] will have a substantial effect on the regimen of rivers and on land use in river valleys. While differences between minimum cost and minimum flow programs are relatively small compared with differences between either of these and minimum treatment programs, they are none-

[2] One can conceive of other guides but not within the fairly simple economic model that was used. If, for example, total U.S. population and economic activity were allowed to vary as a consequence of changes in the "water economy," alternative policy goals might be related to changes in size or composition of GNP or distribution, geographical or otherwise, of population or income.

theless significant until the level of population and economic activity reaches that of the 2020 High projection.

Another physical attribute of the water resource economy is the level of treatment given to waste. If a minimum flow policy is followed, treatment is always extended to 97½ percent BOD removal. Minimum cost and minimum treatment programs are less predictable. If streams had been regulated in 1960 in accordance with a minimum treatment program, thirteen regions would not have required more than the minimum level, 70/50 percent; a fourteenth, Central Pacific, would have required 70/55 percent. Four regions would have required 97 or 97½ percent. The 2020 Medium projection shows that, for a minimum treatment program, only three regions would have enough water to keep treatment at 70/50 percent; fourteen regions would have to treat at 90 percent or higher.

The average level of treatment required for different programs and projections is approximated by comparing the program cost of treatment with aggregate U.S. expenditure on treatment if all regions are treating at the same level. For example, according to the 1980 Medium projection, if each region averaged 70 percent treatment, costs would be $743 million; if the average were 80 percent, costs would be $819 million. Aggregate U.S. costs of treatment for the minimum treatment program, 1980 Medium projection, are $810 million, which by straight-line interpolation implies 79 percent average treatment for the United States. If instream dissolved oxygen of 4 mg/l is the standard, by 1980 treatment at the very minimum must be more than double the estimated present national average of about 35 percent.

Two important qualifications of the basic model and its variants could lead to underestimation of costs. Estimated costs of flow regulation assume perfect basinwide operation of reservoir capacity. Needs for reregulation or for compensating inevitable imperfections of systemic operation will require additional capacity. We have no way of estimating how much allowance should be made for additional capacity. A second deficiency is the omission of the problem raised by estuarine water quality. We allowed the levels of treatment by conventional means to vary between 50 and 97½ percent BOD removal for upstream points but restricted treatment to 35 percent for wastes discharged into estuaries or the ocean. By this restriction we may have implicitly accepted an unsatisfactory level of water quality in the estuaries of the country.

Treatment costs and costs of recirculation apparently will be much higher than costs of new storage unless minimum treatment (maximum flow) programs are adopted, in which case not only is the reverse true, but also total costs are at their highest. Very high marginal costs of flow implied by the synthetic schedules come into play when treatment is kept to a minimum. An idea of their magnitude is given by the response of maximum sustained flow and cumulative annual equivalent costs of new storage as successively higher marginal cost constraints are removed. The figures, aggregated for the United States, are given in table 1. Over the entire range, sustained flow rises 50 percent with a 23-fold increase in the cost of storage. At the upper end of the table – a marginal cost of 30 cents and above – a 100 percent increase in cost induces a 1 percent increase in flow.

In the basic model existing storage is assumed to be free. But the life of existing storage is an uncertain quantity. At some stage of our analysis, we should take cognizance of the cost of existing storage. Minimum cost programs are calculated as the sum of *total* treatment plus *new* storage on the grounds that investments made in existing storage will not be recovered over the projection period, 1960–2020. Almost half of the storage capacity estimated to be in place or under construction in 1964 was built or begun after 1954. When we know more about the usable life of a reservoir, we can adjust our calculations to reflect the costs of total reservoir capacity.

On the basis of the same method of cost estimation that was applied to new storage, annual cost of existing storage is estimated at about $1 billion for a total capacity of about 500 million acre-feet, of which 433 million are estimated to be usable as regulatory capacity and the remainder as flood control capacity. (As total storage increases in volume a correspondingly larger fraction of existing storage will be considered usable as regulatory capacity.) On the basis of 433 million acre-feet of regulatory capacity, we have assumed that minimum flows can now be set at 399 bgd, net of reservoir losses, or at about 42 percent of net maximum regulated flow.

A large amount of existing storage capacity is composed of small reservoirs, which cost more per acre-foot of capacity than the relatively large reservoirs postulated for the early steps of the synthetic schedules in table 1. This explains the apparent anomaly of the cost per unit of existing regulated flow being higher than the costs of the first few steps of future regulated flow.

If the aggregate social costs of water for a specified national bill of goods are to be minimized, virtually all municipal and industrial waste must be subjected to secondary treatment by 1980. Even if treatment is minimized, but a standard of 4 mg/l is maintained, an average level of 79 percent implies that secondary treatment is given to three-fourths or more of all waste.

The 1980 Medium projection shows annual costs of new storage and treatment for alternative programs as follows:

	($ million)
Minimum treatment	5,013
Minimum flow	1,252
Minimum cost	992

The difference in costs between minimum treatment and minimum flow or minimum cost programs grows in absolute terms for later projections, but relatively it declines. For example, the figures for the 2020 Medium projection are:

	($ million)
Minimum treatment	7,502
Minimum flow	3,562
Minimum cost	3,383

The absolute difference between the costs of minimum flow and minimum cost programs remains on the order of $200–300 million per year for most projections. As absolute requirements for minimum flow programs increasingly press on maximum net regulated flow, the difference between the two programs diminishes. For the 2020 High projection the absolute difference in annual costs is $113 million, or about 1½ percent of either total (about $7 billion), a distinction that can scarcely be considered significant in light of the probable error accumulated by the succession of estimates that went into its calculation.

Costs of recirculation and of waste collection would not vary with choice of program and therefore are not incorporated in our model. But they are important enough to warrant side calculations.

Recirculation costs were estimated for steam-electric power plants at recirculation rates required to avoid thermal pollution (assuming the required BOD dilution flow for the minimum cost program). Annual recirculation costs turn out to be a relatively large component of total water quality control costs. For Medium projections they were estimated as follows:

	($ million)
1960 (Est. actual)	67
1980	874
2000	1,572
2020	3,295
2020 High	6,450

For the year 2020, Medium projection, the costs of recirculation[3] are approximately the same as the combined annual costs of new storage and treatment; for other projections they are 10 to 13 percent less. Whether lower treatment levels and lower amounts of recirculation, coupled with larger volumes of storage capacity and higher minimum flows, would cost less in the aggregate than the calculated minimum program was not examined but should be. It is likely, however, that because of the relatively high marginal costs of storage, savings would be relatively slight.

Sewerage costs, estimated at a uniform annual cost per urban resident and without supplementation for additional costs where existing combined storm and sanitary sewers must be separated, were estimated as follows for selected projections:

	($ million)
1960	513
1980 Medium	746
2000 Medium	1,035
2020 Medium	1,385
2020 High	1,832

These costs, like those for recirculation, are not subject to variation by choice of program. A final cost element, also fixed, is the annual equivalent cost of existing storage, estimated at $958 million.

Aggregate annual costs of existing storage, recirculation, and collection (non-programmatic), plus costs of new storage and treatment under a minimum cost program, amount to the following:

[3] About 10 percent should be added to indicated costs for manufacturing recirculation at the same rates.

	($ million)
1960 (Est. actual)	1,838
1980 Medium	3,571
2000 Medium	5,369
2020 Medium	9,020
2020 High	16,309

When related to projected GNP these figures indicate that no undue economic burden ought to be anticipated at Medium rates of growth. These costs apparently would continue to be about one-quarter of 1 percent of GNP; a little more or a little less, depending on the level of water quality that is maintained and the method of adjusting to deficits. When a high growth rate is coupled with 6 mg/l of dissolved oxygen, however, the High projection for 2020 indicates vastly larger expenditure.

Breakdown by Purpose and Area

The costs of storage can be divided between those for evapotranspiration flows and those for waste dilution flows. The costs of waste dilution flows plus treatment plus recirculation are incurred specifically to maintain quality. The division of total flows between evapotranspiration (and other losses) and waste dilution is on the order of one to two. Thus, two-thirds of total storage (new and old) plus waste treatment plus recirculation constitute expenditures for quality maintenance. Aggregate expenditures for storage, including existing storage, treatment, recirculation, and the share attributable to quality maintenance are estimated as follows:

	Total	Quality maintenance
		($ million)
1980 Medium	2,825	2,517 (89% of total)
2000 Medium	4,335	3,998 (92% of total)
2020 Medium	7,642	7,218 (94% of total)
2020 High	14,485	13,798 (95% of total)

The prospect for quality maintenance costs is that they will become an increasingly larger share of the national total.

Up to now expenditures for reservoir capacity have been larger in the West (Mid-continent, Southwest, and North Pacific divisions) than in the East by the ratio of 1.6 to 1, measured by estimated costs of existing storage.[4] The 2020 Medium projection, minimum cost program, shows cumulative expenditures on storage capacity to be equal for the two halves of the country; under the 2020 High projection, annual expenditures in the East are 1.5 times those in the West. This shift is somewhat slower for minimum flow programs and very much faster for minimum treatment programs. Should the latter policy be followed, outlays between now and 1980 for new reservoirs in the East alone would exceed those incurred up to now for the country as a whole.

[4] Part of existing regulatory storage consists of natural lakes whose outlets are subjected to control. For this reason, estimated costs of existing storage may be too high and may be improperly divided between East and West.

Expenditures for new storage plus recirculation would be about twice as large in the East as in the West under the projected minimum cost programs. About half of the total projected costs of storage, treatment, and recirculation are found in the regions that contain the three future megalopolises of "Boswash" (New England, Delaware and Hudson, Chesapeake Bay); "Chipitts" (Ohio, Eastern Great Lakes, Western Great Lakes); and "Sansan" (Central Pacific, South Pacific).[5]

Costs by Industry

If the "cost of water" is divided among industries, classifying municipal use as one of the "industries" and comprehending within cost the items of flow regulation — including the cost of existing storage — treatment, and recirculation, the assignments are as follows (2000 Medium projection, 4 mg/l, 98 percent, 0.0425, minimum cost programs):

	Percentage of total
Manufacturing[6]	47
Steam-electric power	35
Municipal	13
Agriculture	5
Mining and land treatment	½

If "cost" is limited to flow regulation and treatment, the assignments are:

	Percentage of total
Manufacturing	70
Municipal	21
Agriculture	8
Steam-electric power, mining, and land treatment	1

(The reader will recall that for Medium projections no change in swamps and wetlands was projected.) For higher projections the relative importance of manufacturing and steam-electric increases.

For the year 2000, Medium projection, minimum cost program, the production of chemicals and pharmaceuticals accounts for two-fifths of the total of storage and treatment costs. When foods and kindred products and pulp and paper are added, their production accounts for two-thirds of projected storage and treatment costs.

The other large single projected class of expenditures is the cost of recirculation. Under the 2000 Medium projection about three-fourths of the cost of maintaining water quality and supplying required flow is assigned to the industries mentioned above, plus electric power. Out of projected annual costs of $4.5 billion these industries would account for $3.5 billion.

Costs of Meeting Deficits

As already noted, requirements for water-deficit regions are always estimated on the basis of a minimum flow program. To meet projected deficits, water must either be imported into deficit regions or activity must be transferred to surplus regions, the national bill of goods must be modified, or a new technology that reduces water inputs must be developed. The costs of such activities, which are not included in our model, could be considerable.

If it is assumed that activity moves from water-deficit to water-surplus regions, required flows for the whole country would presumably be no more than originally projected, and probably would be less.[7] Most reduction in water requirements would come from transferring agriculture from arid to humid regions, or from transferring industrial polluting activity from inland to coastal locations. For other activities, the best way to approximate the cost of overcoming the gross water deficit is to estimate by how much the costs of storage would rise in regions that received the shifted activity. (Costs of treatment are already fully accounted for, except for the possibility of a change in treatment level as activity moves.) The estimates cannot be precise because storage costs of redirected activity would, of course, not be known until the identity of the receiving region was fixed.

Total required flows for minimum cost programs are below 600 bgd up to the 2020 Medium projection, which shows required flow to be 679 bgd. Under the 2020 High projection, required flow is 948 bgd. Flow-cost curves indicate that net flows of 631 bgd in the United States can be provided at storage costs per 1,000 gallons ranging between zero and one-half cent. If an average of one-quarter cent per 1,000 gallons is adopted, all deficits except those shown under the 2020 Medium and High projections can be met at a cost of slightly under $1 million per year per bgd. Thus, supplementary storage costs would amount to about $16 million under the 1980 Medium projection and $30 million under the 2000 Medium projection. These additions would raise costs of new storage for 1980 by almost 50 percent; costs of new storage plus treatment would rise by 3 percent. In the year 2000, costs of new storage would rise by 12 percent; costs of new storage plus treatment would rise by less than 2 percent. The gross deficit of 78 bgd shown in the 2020 Medium projection could be met by marginal flows having an average cost of three to four cents per 1,000 gallons, or about $3 million annually per bgd, or an aggregate of $234 million. Storage costs would rise by about 40 percent; costs of new storage plus treatment, by 7 percent. Thus, for all Medium projections, costs of new storage and treatment reflect an understatement, which appears to be on the order of 5 percent, resulting from relocation of deficit activity to water surplus regions.

As projected economic and population levels rise, the deficits and the marginal cost of water are both greater. The cost of overcoming the deficit of 255 bgd shown under the 2020 High projection is many times greater than the cost of

---

[5] Herman Kahn and Anthony J. Wiener, *Toward the Year 2000: A Framework for Speculation* (Macmillan Co., 1967).

[6] An amount equal to 10 percent of steam-electric costs of recirculation was added to costs of water used in manufacturing.

[7] The opposite is possible. A shift of urban population from inland to coastal locations in the same region would increase losses.

meeting the deficit under the 2020 Medium projection because flow must be regulated to the point where marginal costs of flow are between 50 cents and 75 cents per 1,000 gallons. Minimum aggregate costs of providing the required flow of 948 bgd, by distributing water use among all regions so that marginal costs of flow are approximately equal in all regions, would require annual expenditures of about $4.4 billion. This can be compared with the projected cost of flow, before taking deficits into account, of $1.6 billion (minimum cost program). Costs of storage would rise by a factor of three. Total costs — new storage and treatment — would rise by 40 percent. To ignore the cost of meeting flow deficits is to understate seriously the full cost of water for the 2020 High projections.

Capital Costs

To this point, costs have been measured as the equivalent annual outlays of capital expenditures, plus current operating expenses for flow regulation and treatment, augmented when so indicated by costs of recirculation and sewerage. Conversion of annual costs to capital costs yields the cumulative capital investment for each projection.

By the year 2000, Medium projection, capital additions to storage are estimated at $5.5 billion, *total* treatment facilities are estimated at $39 billion, and steam-electric recirculation capital facilities are estimated at $5.5 billion. If it is assumed that existing treatment and recirculation facilities will have to be replaced between now and the year 2000, but existing storage facilities will not, total cumulative new investment for the period 1960–2000 amounts to $50 billion, or about $1.25 billion per year. To this would be added annual operating and maintenance costs — something on the order of $200–300 million. Cash outlay, therefore, amounts to about $1.5 billion annually if the economy follows the Medium growth path. (In addition to the costs of storage, treatment, and recirculation, costs of abating pollution engendered by combined storm and sanitary sewers and costs of abating other forms of pollution, such as surface drainage and acid mine drainage, will have to be incurred if high-quality water is to be maintained in streams and rivers. These additional costs, not known with much precision, may fall in the range of $20 billion to $60 billion — perhaps more, perhaps less.)

If the High growth path is followed, average annual investment between now and the year 2020 would be approximately twice as much, with a corresponding level of average annual operating expenses. These figures should be corrected by subtracting the value of existing treatment and circulation facilities that do not require replacement during the projection period and by adding the value of existing storage capacity that does. Without further research it is not possible to estimate the magnitude of the correction.

Coupling the Basic Model with Short-Term Chemical Treatment

Waste treatment within the basic model is a constant twelve-month activity at the same level of BOD removal. It is a high capital-cost, low current-cost operation. Minimum flows during the period of low flow are adequate for the stipulated quality standard. This means that storage is built

to maximum certainty, namely, to a 2 percent chance of deficiency.

An alternative scheme is to build reservoir capacity to a lower degree of certainty and to meet the period of deficiency by a short-term increase in the level of treatment designed to reduce residual BOD by 50 percent. Two objectives might be gained: (1) the river's natural regimen would be subjected to less interference and less valley land would be inundated; and (2) the total cost would be reduced if the savings in the cost of reservoir capacity exceeded the cost of supplementary short-term treatment. Another kind of tradeoff would consist of reducing permanent treatment to a level consistent with flows during the months in which flows exceeded the design minimum, and supplying supplementary short-term treatment during the period of minimum flow.

Several subsidiary considerations come into play. Since maximum net regulated flow is greater at 90 percent availability (10 percent chance of deficiency) than at 98 percent availability (2 percent chance of deficiency) a region might be water-short at 98 percent availability but not at 90 percent availability. But to assure the larger regulated flow at 90 percent availability might require as much storage capacity as the regulated flow at 98 percent availability, or more, depending on the synthetic schedule of storage increments coupled with evaporation rates and the behavior of gross flow. The effect of supplementary chemical treatment in water-short regions would be to reduce the shortage but not save money.

Another possibility is the continuous use of supplementary chemical treatment on a twelve-month basis, with a corresponding reduction in storage for required flow with a 2 percent chance of deficiency. Still another that we examined is the effect of a double layer of supplementary chemical treatment: one layer twelve months of the year and the other layer for one month. The first layer would reduce required flow on an all-year basis, correspondingly reducing storage requirements along the 98 percent availability curve. Because of the additional decrease in waste dilution flows made possible by the second layer, required flow would be further reduced for one month. As a result, reservoir capacity would be reduced along the 98 percent availability curve in accordance with the reduction in required flow from the first layer, and reduced again by selecting the required storage from the 90 percent availability curve.

Flow yielded 98 percent of the time from storage designed to yield a larger flow 90 percent of the time must equal or exceed required flow after short-term chemical treatment if water quality is to be maintained at the specified level. For most regions this condition was met. In the remainder, storage could not be reduced to the amount indicated by the 90 percent curve, but only to some larger capacity. Another qualification is the capability of chemical treatment to reduce plant nutrients. Required flows would not fall in accordance with a 50 percent reduction in residual BOD if plant nutrients were ruling and a corresponding adjustment in required flow had to be made.

For the year 2000, Medium projection, basic model, required new storage with 98 percent availability is 180 million acre-feet for the minimum cost program. To yield the same flow (525 bgd) 90 percent of the time requires 86 million acre-feet. But in several regions in which ruling dilution flows are fixed by phosphorus, or where at the storage level for 90 percent certainty the flow available 98 percent of the time is less than that required after short-term treatment, some storage has to be restored, leaving the final amount of 104 million acre-feet. Savings in storage costs are $118 million annually; but allowing $22 million for chemical treatment for one month, annual net savings are $96 million. For other projections, comparable savings are estimated.

If chemical treatment were undertaken on a twelve-month basis, reducing the flow required 98 percent of the time, the savings in the cost of storage would be less than the additional costs of chemical treatment. If a one-month second layer of chemical treatment were added, and storage were built to a 10 percent chance of deficiency instead of to 2 percent, total costs would rise, but by a smaller amount; there would be a reduction in required storage. Our figures indicate that minimum storage can be achieved at less cost by the use of supplementary chemical treatment superimposed on the minimum cost program than by direct choice of the minimum flow program. The addition of two-layer chemical treatment to the *minimum flow program* would reduce required storage to the low figure of 9 million acre-feet, with a 10 percent chance of deficiency being offset by the second layer of treatment. The net increase in costs over the basic costs of the minimum flow program would be about $155 million.

In short, supplementary chemical treatment for one month per year, coupled with construction of storage to a 10 percent chance of deficiency, promises to save both money and required reservoir capacity. Permanent chemical one-layer treatment superimposed on the minimum cost program would save storage but cost money. Two-layer chemical treatment (one layer all year and a second layer for one month) would save even more storage and not cost as much, net, as one-layer treatment, since storage would be built to 90 percent security. The greatest saving in required storage would result from superimposing two-layer chemical treatment on the minimum *flow* program, but would cost about $471 million more than the basic minimum cost program (2000 Medium projection, 4 mg/l). For those to whom new lakes add a net amount of utility, the additional costs are clearly a waste of money; the information required for drawing a net social balance is not yet available.

Variations of the Basic Model

The sensitivity of the basic model was tested by changing instream dissolved oxygen from 4 mg/l to 1 mg/l and 6 mg/l, the chance of deficiency of flow from 2 percent to 5 percent and 10 percent, and the annual factor for storage costs from 0.0425 to 0.0200 and 0.0525.

In other sensitivity tests the projected output of industrial waste per unit of product was reduced by 10 percent for 1980, 20 percent for 2000, and 30 percent for 2020; and also by 20 percent, 40 percent, and 60 percent, respectively. Downstream municipal water was assumed to be recirculated instead of being discharged after one use to the

sea; and lakes were augmented in volume beyond regulatory reservoir capacity previously computed by assuming that 25 percent of reservoir capacity was kept as a recreational pool. Required flow, new storage, level of treatment, costs of flow, and costs of treatment were estimated for each variation.

In estimating the effect of these modifications a few implicit conditions must be kept in mind. A change in unit costs of storage induced by raising or lowering the annual factor will have no effect on the quantity of storage required for minimum flow or minimum treatment programs but will affect the minimum cost combination of storage and treatment. Costs of storage, as distinct from quantity, are, of course, affected. An increase or decrease in chance of deficiency will leave required flow for the minimum treatment program unchanged but can change the treatment-flow combination of the minimum treatment program. A change in dissolved oxygen will have no effect on the level of treatment for the minimum flow program but will induce changes in other characteristics. Changes in dissolved oxygen and output of waste per unit of product, recirculation of municipal coastal discharge, and reservation of recreational pools affect the "demand" for water. Changes in the chance of deficiency and the annual factor affect the "supply" of water.

Response to changes in the annual factor, to dissolved oxygen content and to percentage chance of deficiency follows a predictable path, but sensitivity tends to vary from one projection to another. Hence, summarizing statements should be checked against detailed tables found elsewhere in this book.

The reader will recall that a change in the factor used to convert capital costs of storage to annual costs induces a change in the flow-treatment combination of minimum cost programs. In the basic model the annual factors for both storage and treatment are based on an interest rate of 4 percent, which probably understates the interest cost of industrial treatment. By lowering the annual factor from 0.0425 to 0.0200, the effect of a comparatively higher cost of treatment is revealed. When expressed as a percentage of required flow for the basic model, the effect on required flow for selected projections is as follows:

1980 Medium	109
2000 Medium	103
2020 Low	108
2020 Medium	115
2020 High	101

When the annual factor for storage costs is raised to 0.0525, again leaving unchanged the costs of treatment, the effects on required flow are as follows:

1980 Medium	100
2000 Medium	99
2020 Low	96
2020 Medium	78
2020 High	100

The explanation of the high sensitivity for the 2020 Medium projection is that the marginal costs of flow are high and there is a considerable range of choice of flow-treatment combinations that are physically still available. By 2020, High projection, this leeway has disappeared almost completely.

When required flows are translated into amounts of new storage capacity, the effect of changes in the annual factor on the minimum cost program is noticeably heightened. For example, the 1980 Medium projection shows that 84 percent more storage is required if the annual factor is 0.0200 instead of 0.0425. On the other hand, if the annual factor is 0.0525 instead of 0.0425 required storage falls by 3 percent. The corresponding variations for the 2000 Medium projection are 118 percent and 95 percent; for the 2020 Medium projection, 152 percent and 69 percent; and for the 2020 High projection, 103 percent and 100 percent. We can conclude, therefore, that use of a conversion factor for treatment that is low in relation to the factor for storage may substantially understate the amount of storage appropriate for the minimum cost program, while a relatively high factor for treatment would have an opposite effect.

By restricting the change in the annual factor to storage costs alone, the effect is greater than if the annual factor applicable to treatment costs were also allowed to change. Current costs, as distinct from investment costs, are more important for treatment than for storage, so that a change in interest rates will affect the annual cost of treatment less than that of storage.

If the annual factor were allowed to vary for treatment costs and treatment were at a high level (e.g., between secondary and tertiary), an increase in the annual factor from 0.0425 to 0.0525 would raise treatment costs per mgd by about 15 percent compared with an increase of 23.5 percent in storage costs.[8] A reduction of the annual factor from 0.0425 to 0.0200[9] reduces storage costs by 53 percent but reduces treatment costs by about 30 percent. Hence, the push toward higher treatment when the annual factor is raised and toward lower treatment when the annual factor is lowered, as shown by our model, is greater than would occur if the upward or downward movements of interest rates applied equally to storage and treatment.

The major effect of accepting a higher chance of deficiency is the saving of storage capacity and costs of storage. Although required flows for the minimum cost program are 3 percent *less* if the chance of deficiency falls from 10 percent to 2 percent, the amount of required new storage capacity virtually doubles — going from 94 million acre-feet to 180 million acre-feet — and the costs of storage more than double. Differences between a 2 percent chance of deficiency and a 5 percent chance are much less: a 13 percent savings in volume and 15 percent in costs of storage. Dollar savings in accepting a 10 percent chance of deficiency, rather than 2 percent, are $143 million annually at

Medium projected levels for 2000. If, instead of merely accepting the higher chance of deficiency, a program of short-term treatment were instituted, savings would be only $96 million annually when measured in dollars, but almost the full saving in storage capacity would be retained. Since the depth of the deficiency is not given, it is possible that the shortage might be greater than could be handled by a single layer of short-term chemical treatment. The threat remains, therefore, that projected outputs could not be supported by available flows, or, if more than one layer of chemical treatment is required, that money savings would not be realized.

Dissolved Oxygen

Another parametric change is variation in dissolved oxygen. Although 4 mg/l and 5 mg/l are frequently encountered standards, the maintenance of high-quality aquatic life usually requires more dissolved oxygen. At the other end of the spectrum, the waste-carrying capacity of the stream is most fully utilized — albeit at the expense of aquatic life — if dissolved oxygen falls to a level that is barely aerobic. Hence, alternatives of 6 mg/l and 1 mg/l of dissolved oxygen were examined.

Required flows vary for minimum flow and minimum cost programs, but not for minimum treatment programs except where treatment is 70/50 percent. When reliability of flow is held constant at 98 percent and the annual factor at 0.0425, required flows for minimum cost programs swing above and below required flows for 4 mg/l as follows (4 mg/l = 100):

	1 mg/l	6 mg/l
1980 Medium	93	104
2000 Medium	93	111
2020 Medium	85	123
2020 High	82	166

For 2020, High projection, required flow is 66 percent greater for 6 mg/l than for 4 mg/l — an amount that exceeds by 60 percent the aggregate flow for the United States with full regulation. Such a deficiency could be overcome only by desalination or the importation of a vast quantity of water, at a cost that is severalfold higher than the cost of meeting a standard of 4 mg/l.[10] For nearer projections the difference in costs is very much less. As an example, the cost of new storage and treatment, 2000 Medium projection, minimum cost program, is $1.8 billion annually for 4 mg/l and $2 billion for 6 mg/l, plus the additional costs of storage needed to overcome deficiencies.[11]

How much is 6 mg/l of dissolved oxygen "worth" in comparison with 4 mg/l; or how much is 4 mg/l "worth" in comparison with 1 mg/l? The drop from 4 mg/l to 1/mg/l probably introduces severe restrictions on recreational use

---

[8] By contrast, for our model we assumed that the change in treatment costs was zero in order to get a response of maximum sensitivity to changes in interest rates.

[9] Representing a decline in interest rate from 4 percent to 2 percent, coupled with an increase in the life of the asset from 50 years to 100 years.

[10] Theoretically the deficiency might also be met by weather modification or by practices that convert a larger fraction of precipitation into runoff.

[11] Some readers of this study were skeptical. They felt that an increase in instream D.O. would entail substantially higher costs than revealed by our model. Only field research will settle the issue.

and aesthetic satisfaction, and may intuitively be avoided unless cost differences become greater than they appear to be. For the 2000 Medium projection, minimum cost program, annual costs of new storage and treatment are $1.6 billion for 1 mg/l and $1.8 billion for 4 mg/l. (Added to these totals would be the costs of storage required to overcome deficiencies.) Hence, again, two uncertainties creep in that might affect the choice of policy: (1) Does added reservoir capacity yield net positive utility? (2) Are the costs of *water* treatment (as opposed to waste treatment) significantly affected as instream dissolved oxygen moves from one level to another? Available information suggests that the effect would be small.

Our findings that costs increase relatively slowly with increases in dissolved oxygen do not conform with instances that have been reported elsewhere.[12] Studies of the Potomac and Delaware estuaries indicate that costs rise rapidly as the level of dissolved oxygen is raised by the use of flow regulation and conventional treatment. There are, however, some important differences among the studies. For one thing, there is no way of comparing the absolute amounts of estimated costs. Also, the two cited studies are concerned with estuaries, whereas we are concerned wholly with streams above the estuary. Upstream treatment is not carried as far in the cited studies as we have assumed it would be under minimum flow or minimum treatment programs. It is also important to note that meaningful comparisons among the different studies can be made only for projections that do not imply water shortages.

Annual Factor

The choice of the annual factor is important chiefly as a test of the importance of selecting the economically appropriate interest rate. Even if the interest rate has no effect on the mix of products and services, a change in the relationships between the annual factors applied to storage and treatment changes their relative importance. From the physical standpoint, however, the effect (2000 Medium projection, 4 mg/l, 98 percent) of lowering or raising the annual factor to 0.0200 or 0.0525 is plus 15 percent and minus 5 percent respectively, an unimpressive swing in light of the probable range of error in the underlying computations. (The spread between 0.0200 and 0.0525 is 42 million acre-feet of capacity for the country as a whole.)

For the 2000 Medium projection, 0.0425, 98 percent, minimum cost program, the change in cost above and below the basic model for 6 mg/l and 1 mg/l dissolved oxygen, respectively, is about $200 million. The spread in new storage capacity between 1 mg/l and 6 mg/l is 117 million acre-feet.

Simultaneous Changes

What happens when two or three parameters are changed simultaneously? One model — 90 percent, 0.0200,

1 mg/l — minimizes storage capacity and cost of storage and total cost.[13] Using the 2000 Medium projection, compared with the basic model, annual treatment cost would decline from $1.6 billion to $1.4 billion; new storage cost would decline from $246 million to $72 million; required storage would decline from 180 million acre-feet to 112 million acre-feet; but required flow would *rise* from 525 bgd to 544 bgd.

The opposite pole is given by 98 percent, 0.0525, 6 mg/l, although required storage for the minimum cost program would be higher (even though costs of storage would be less) if an annual factor of 0.0200 were used. The minimum cost program for this model compares with that of the basic model as follows (2000 Medium projection):

	98%, 0.0525, 6 mg/l	98%, 0.0425, 4 mg/l
Flow *(bgd)*	539	525
Storage *(million acre-feet)*	198	180
Cost of storage *($ million)*	353	246
Cost of treatment *($ million)*	1,757	1,558

Changes in parametric values are roughly additive in their impact on total costs of new storage and treatment for minimum cost programs. Table 2 shows the effects on total costs of the three parametric changes in the 2000 Medium projection. Not revealed by the chart are the average implicit treatment levels for the United States as a whole. The highest level is 96 percent, for 98 percent, 0.0525, 6 mg/l. The lowest is 85 percent, for 90 percent, 0.0200, 1 mg/l. Next to the lowest is 90⅔ percent for 98 percent, 0.0425, 1 mg/l. Next to the highest is 95¾ percent, for 98 percent, 0.0425, 6 mg/l. The remainder falls between 93½ and 94 percent. Thus, compared with prevailing levels of treatment, the difference between what is required for the least demanding and for the most demanding of the postulated conditions is relatively insignificant.

Impact of Technology

The possible impact of technological changes that reduce the output of waste products for a given bill of goods promises to be much greater than any of the parametric changes discussed above. We tested the response to a reduction in organic waste per unit of product. By one hypothesis, output of waste was less than in the basic model by 10 percent, 20 percent, and 30 percent, respectively, for 1980, 2000, and 2020. By another hypothesis the corresponding percentages were 20, 40, and 60. All changes were built on the basic model — 98 percent, 0.0425, 4 mg/l.

For the 2000 Medium projection, the effect of a 40 percent reduction per unit of product has the same effect on total cost as the combined effects of going to 90 percent, 0.0200, 1 mg/l with the original output of waste products; storage requirements for 4 mg/l would be less than for 1 mg/l under the original conditions. By the year 2020, Medium projections show that savings in total costs over

[12] Robert K. Davis, *The Range of Choice in Water Management: A Study of Dissolved Oxygen in the Potomac Estuary* (The Johns Hopkins Press for Resources for the Future, 1968); and Allen V. Kneese and Blair T. Bower, *Managing Water Quality: Economics, Technology, Institutions* (The Johns Hopkins Press for Resources for the Future, 1968), table 15, p. 233.

[13] The physical quantity of storage would be further reduced by the use of 0.0525 as the annual factor, but the cost of storage would be higher.

the basic model would be $850 million annually if industrial wastes were reduced by 30 percent, and $1.5 billion annually if the reduction were 60 percent. Furthermore, with a 60 percent reduction in the output of industrial wastes, 2020 High, 6 mg/l water requirements fall within maximum net regulated flow instead of 60 percent beyond. Total costs – new storage and treatment – fall from $9.7 billion (98 percent, 0.0425, 6 mg/l) to about half that sum. A substantial reduction in the output of waste products could extend the range of options open to us.

Another test performed on the basic model was the introduction of the assumption that the intake of municipalities located on the coast or on estuaries was recirculated. This did not necessarily mean that recirculated water was introduced into the municipal system; it could be used to meet intake requirements of manufacturing or agriculture. The question asked was: How would the *cost of flow* be affected if total requirements were reduced to correspond with downstream municipal losses computed in the same way as upstream municipal losses instead of being equal to downstream municipal intake? The effect, for the 2000 Medium projection, minimum cost program, basic model, was to reduce the total cost of flow for all coastal municipalities by $13 million. More than offsetting this, but not computed, would be the higher level of treatment required; in the basic model, waste discharged into estuaries was given primary treatment only.

The last variant explored was an assumption that reservoir capacity would be increased by 25 percent to provide a recreational pool.[14] The effect on required storage to assure specified flows plus the recreational reservation varied from region to region depending on the flow-storage curve and evaporation rates. For 2000, Medium projection, basic model, minimum cost program, total storage rose from $246 million to $326 million; in some regions treatment levels rose in response to the increase in evaporation losses, thereby restraining the increase in required new storage. Total costs (new storage and treatment) rose from $1,804 million to $1,920 million.

All of the foregoing solutions for the 2000 Medium projections were based on unconstrained maximum net regulated flows. If a maximum marginal cost of flow of 2 cents per 1,000 gallons is introduced, the effect on the basic model is quite small and is limited to two regions: Western Gulf and South Pacific. Flow in the former would be restricted by 4 bgd and in the latter by 1 bgd, raising gross deficiency from 30 bgd to 35 bgd out of a total requirement of 525 bgd. From this it seems reasonable to infer that the costs of regulation should not impose an undue burden on the economy as a whole, provided there is sufficient flexibility of regional relocation. The same observation may also apply to the Medium projection for 2020, since aggregate required flow of 679 bgd falls within aggregate regulated flow of 854 bgd as constrained by a maximum marginal cost of storage of 2 cents per 1,000 gallons ($6.52 per acre-foot), but since the gross deficit of 79 bgd

implies a greater stress of interregional relocation, it cannot be asserted that other restrictions may not become binding.

Comparison with Committee Print No. 32

Eight years intervened between the writing of this study and its antecedent, Committee Print No. 32. Therefore, a brief comparison is in order.

The important changes were: (1) storage requirements for flows in excess of 50 percent of mean annual flow were substantially increased; (2) credit was taken for storage already in place or under construction so that estimates for new storage fall despite the increase in total storage required for a specified flow; (3) intake and loss of water in production of steam-electric power was reduced by shifting from "flow-through" figures to estimates of actual intake after stipulated degrees of recirculation; (4) projected swamp and wetland areas were substantially lowered; (5) municipal losses were increased by charging as loss all intake by municipalities at coastal or estuarine locations; (6) intake of brackish and fresh water for manufacturing was more carefully distinguished; and (7) dilution flows and costs of treatment per p.e. produced were lowered by the new equations developed by George Reid and his associates.[15]

The estimates of water requirements for swamps and wetlands in Committee Print No. 32 could still prove closer to reality than the far lower estimates used in the present study; the full strength of recreational demands may not yet be appreciated. It is not implausible to postulate a demand for outdoor recreation that will impose requirements for new rivers and lakes, as well as habitat for ducks and geese, substantially beyond the facilities implied by our cost-minimizing or flow-minimizing models. Because of the growth in the demand for outdoor recreation and the demand for higher water quality than is realized by dilution-treatment combinations to yield 6/mg/l of dissolved oxygen, the optimum program for 2000 or 2020 might be the level of treatment specified for the minimum flow program and the quantity of flow specified for the minimum treatment program. Further investigation is needed to establish with reasonable accuracy what the net per capita change in supply of water for recreation is likely to be, as well as to establish ways of measuring the demand for recreational water. Analogously, further study is needed to determine the compatibility of projected navigational flow requirements with projected dilution flows.

In spite of the differences between the two studies, several of the original conclusions still hold: (1) the Southwest is projected to be a hard-core water shortage area; (2) costs of treatment will dominate future outlays for water if streams are to be kept aerobic; (3) a relatively large amount of flow is required to dilute wastes after treatment has been carried to levels that are twice or more the present level, measured by the percentage of BOD removed; (4) because of required dilution flows, water shortage will spread east-

---

[14] For computational purposes it was assumed that 80 percent of storage capacity was available for flow regulation, and total capacity was estimated accordingly.

[15] For original estimates used in the preparation of Committee Print No. 32, see George W. Reid, *Water Requirements for Pollution Abatement*, Committee Print No. 29, Senate Select Committee on National Water Resources, 86th Cong., 2d sess. (1960).

ward; and (5) unless large-scale transbasin movements of water are undertaken in the West, most of the expenditures on water from now on will be for waste treatment and flow regulation in the East.

The conclusions of the current study, however, differ from those of its antecedent in a number of particulars. The following stand out when equivalent programs and projections are compared: (1) new storage is less and the amount spent on new storage falls even more; (2) treatment costs in the aggregate are less because of lower unit costs of treatment; (3) water shortage is less even though maximum net regulated flow is less, because of reductions in water required for swamps and wetlands and steam-electric power; (4) the Upper Missouri and Western Great Lakes regions, which were projected as being water-short by 2000 Medium, are not now projected as water-short regions until higher levels of population and economic activity are attained; (5) the costs of sewerage – i.e., the collection of wastes for delivery to treatment plants – are estimated as a substantially larger sum; (6) thermal pollution, ignored in the earlier study, is likely to pose a major problem in the future unless the discharge of heated effluent is substantially reduced below amounts extrapolated along a current-trend line; and (7) costs of recirculation needed to avoid heat pollution by steam-electric power plants promise to be a major part of the future costs of maintaining stream quality.

Under the Medium projections, the pressure on water resources – measured by required flow, new storage, and treatment costs – for 2020 is now expected to be less than that projected for 2000 in Committee Print No. 32. (The gross deficit for the 2020 Medium projection is equal to the gross deficit originally shown in the 2000 Medium projection, hence the cost of alleviating it by transfer of water or transfer of activity would be about the same for each projection.)

The effect of all changes on annual costs (98 percent, 0.0425, 4 mg/l) is shown at the top of the next column. That the totals are so little changed is purely fortuitous. Obviously the two patterns of projected expenditures are quite different. Since our information about costs rests

| | 1980 Medium | | 2000 Medium | |
	Committee Print No. 32	This study	Committee Print No. 32	This study
	($ million)			
Cost of new storage	537	67	799	246
Treatment	1,621	926	3,263	1,558
Collection	251	746	363	1,035
Recirculation	Not computed	874	Not computed	1,572
Totals	2,409	2,613	4,425	4,411

heavily on hypothetical conditions it would not be surprising if future studies were to lead to further corrections.

Comparison with Water Resources Council Assessment

The first National Assessment of the Water Resources Council benefits from more carefully developed economic projections than those in this study and provides a richer source of detailed information regarding the uses of water and the specific water resource problems of each region. On the other hand, the assessment is not built around, nor does it culminate in, an economic model dependent on an optimizing criterion. It is intended that this will come later.

The fact that projections of economic variables and water inputs in the National Assessment differ from our own is not a matter of serious concern at the moment. In a number of instances the two sets of estimates come very close together. Part of the difference may be attributed to the expected role of ocean or brackish water, especially for cooling purposes. Another reflects different assumptions regarding the discharge of municipal water at coastal or estuarine locations. Still another part of the difference reflects different guesses regarding changes in technical coefficients, future composition of the national bill of goods, and changes in regional location. As time goes on, the quality of projections will undoubtedly improve along with the detailed information from which projections are made. Even straightforward historical measures, such as manufacturing water intake, are likely to contain substantial errors at present, but we can anticipate fairly rapid improvement under stimulus of the national assessment.

Table 1. U.S. FLOWS AND COSTS AT VARIOUS MARGINAL COSTS
PER 1,000 GALLONS

Marginal cost/ 1,000 gallons equal to or less than: (cents)	Minimum flow (bgd)	Annual cost of storage[a] ($ million)
0.5	631	306
0.99	693	461
1.99	838	1,175
4.99	909	2,054
9.99	927	2,451
14.99	936	2,880
19.99	941	3,210
29.99	943	3,435
49.99	947	4,016
74.99	949	4,431
99.99	954	6,068
199.99	956.2	6,899
200 and up	956.3	7,110

[a]At 1964 prices.

Table 2. EFFECT OF PARAMETRIC CHANGES ON U.S. TOTAL COSTS OF NEW STORAGE AND TREATMENT,
MINIMUM COST PROGRAMS: 2000 MEDIUM

($ billion annually)

D.O. (mg/l)	90% Availability			95% Availability			98% Availability		
	Annual factor: 0.0200	0.0425	0.0525	Annual factor: 0.0200	0.0425	0.0525	Annual factor: 0.0200	0.0425	0.0525
6								2.0	2.1
4		1.6			1.8		1.7	1.8	1.9
1	1.4							1.6	

Chapter 4

CONCLUSIONS, POLICY ISSUES, AND RESEARCH PRIORITIES

Our findings can be briefly summarized as follows:

1. The study not only reinforces the conclusion of earlier investigations that degradation of water quality and the related environment is a serious threat to well-being but also poses the possibility that a serious physical limitation will prevent achieving a high-quality water environment — e.g., 6 mg/l of dissolved oxygen. We are given a clear signal that high-quality water is likely to be available only if the output of raw waste per unit of GNP is reduced by either changing the nation's product mix or by changing production processes.[1] Because of the great deficiency of water when a standard of 6 mg/l of dissolved oxygen is combined with 2020 High projections, it seems reasonable to conclude that even if this standard were to be adopted over the next forty years or so, it would be abandoned at a later date. But this tentative conclusion could be proven wrong by an evolution of use for which high quality water would be necessary, or by a dramatic decline in the costs of desalination and transportation or other methods of augmenting surface flow, or by a large-scale shift of waste-producing activity to coastal regions. The stringencies indicated by our projections will become more severe with the passage of time and will be greatly aggravated if the growth of population and economic activity follows the High projections.

2. Over the next half-century the Southwest will remain the nation's hard-core area of absolute water shortage, to be joined later in the period by the Upper Arkansas-White-Red region. Deficiencies in these and a few other areas by 2020,

under High projections, cannot be met under the assumptions of our model; large-scale importation of water, shifts of population or industrial activity, or increases in supply through advances in technology beyond those stipulated in our model would be required.

3. From a national viewpoint, problems of water quality apparently will be larger and more difficult than those of quantity. Aggregate needs for higher levels of waste treatment and new storage to provide dilution flow will become greater in the East than in the West.

In sum, between now and the year 2000, assuming that adequate measures are taken in time, no serious threat to the welfare, comfort, and productivity of the United States economy is posed by impending water shortage; nor do prospective costs of adjustment promise to absorb more than a nominal fraction of the nation's resources. Furthermore, assuming that projected population and economic activity is not unduly wide of the mark, the period in which the outlook is relatively favorable can be extended to 2020 under the Medium projections. But by the time that the 2020 High projections are realized, the strain on water resources will be acute, unless technological innovation to reduce the effect of pollution has advanced by great strides. In the absence of new techniques of production and waste treatment, the strain will be relieved only by substantial changes in the product mix between water-related and non-water-related activity; mere interregional redistribution of activity or water will not suffice because the blight of water shortage will cover large parts of the country.

On the other hand, the technological possibilities for maintaining quality have scarcely been explored. Only within the last decade has the machinery of state and federal governments been seriously involved in the question of

---

[1] The impairment of freshwater quality can also be reduced by relocating activity to coastal regions. However, protection of coastal areas will probably require comparably high levels of treatment.

water pollution. During that period the Water Pollution Control Administration was created out of a division of the Public Health Service and transferred from the Department of Health, Education, and Welfare to the Department of the Interior; the Office of Water Resources Research and the Office of Saline Water were created to foster and lend financial assistance to research; and federal legislation was enacted that either established water quality standards or stimulated the states to establish standards. It thus seems reasonable to anticipate new techniques of water use and water and waste treatment that go far beyond present knowledge and practices. There still remains the danger that, despite the fairly large effort now under way, the lag between initiation of interest, discovery and invention, and diffusion of practice may be so long that the serious situation presaged by our projections may not be avoided. There is considerable interest in large-scale diversions from water-surplus to water-deficit regions, but high costs of diversion relative to the productivity of water in agriculture make it unlikely that recipients of imported water can afford to pay its full costs so long as the present price structure for agricultural products prevails. Other factors, such as substantial changes in population distribution, may bolster the case for large-scale importation, but the facts are still cloudy.

Institutional obstacles may be as great as those of physical or economic origin, or greater. An assortment of adaptations to restrictions on activity imposed by the limited supply of low-cost water is slowly becoming apparent; but it is not equally apparent that the political processes on which the solution to water resource problems largely rest are sufficiently adaptable to take full advantage of what is offered.

For example, there is the problem of cost allocation, which we have avoided in this study. When we speak of costs of storage as costs incurred to provide water of adequate quality, we do not necessarily imply that all such costs should be "assigned" to water quality. Since provision of regulated flow by surface storage constitutes an investment that yields a number of outputs jointly, the allocation of costs among specific beneficiaries and society in general depends on policies that presumably reflect local economic, social, and political forces within a framework of national objectives. Without more knowledge of income effects and the objectives of rationing or augmenting supplies in each water resource system, specific rules of cost allocation cannot be formulated. Present procedures for dividing water resource costs between federal and local governments lead to decisions that are socially wasteful. This is primarily because of insufficient flexibility in legal and institutional arrangements for handling the growing pressures on water resources.

The subdued optimism with which we can view conditions within the country as a whole, *assuming that remedial action is taken as required*, is not intended to imply that regional and local problems, some quite severe, will not demand solution before 2000. A sample of regional problems that face us today includes: the draft of groundwater on the high plains of Texas and the Salt River Valley of Arizona, the pollution of Lake Erie, the warmed water of the Mahoning River, the polluted tidal basin of the Potomac, the acid mine wastes in Pennsylvania, the high salinity of the lower Colorado, and the pollution of Puget Sound by the wastes of paper mills. No part of the country is free, but in the context of the national economy these problems impose no severe strain because there is still room to maneuver — at costs that are still reasonable. By 2020 all maneuvering room will be lost except that afforded by technology and population control. If water requirements can be reduced to the quantity dissipated by evaporation and transpiration, the pressure that is now on the horizon will recede, at Medium rates of growth, more than 200 years into the future. At the Low rate of growth this period will almost double; at the High rate of growth it will take somewhat over 100 years.

Qualifications and Omissions

In connection with these and other conclusions drawn from our study, we must remind the reader once more of the danger of treating projections as authoritative statements of required action. Nothing in this study can be used to justify a particular program unless it is first demonstrated that the assumed levels of activity and technical coefficients are real and that other possible solutions have been studied and found to be inferior.

The evaluation of alternatives is often a formidable task and when properly conducted may encompass an awesome number of possibilities, especially in the context of a multiregional equilibrium. Programs that extend twenty years into the future, to say nothing of forty and sixty years, are dangerously oversimplified when the possible mode of adjustment is limited to four or five alternatives. There is no certainty that the most reasonable choices are, in fact, included among the few that may have been examined.

But even without taking into account the inscrutability of the future, our analysis suffers serious deficiencies. For one thing, the optimizing model is only two dimensional: waste treatment plus regulated flow. (Other dimensions are introduced to a limited extent by changes in parameters.)

Our basic projections also fail to reflect prospective changes in the regional distribution of population and economic activity unless such changes have been at work in the past. Our model is a series of static pictures rather than a dynamic analysis that adequately accounts for different time sequences of inputs and outputs. It is possible that more complete recognition of the passage of time would change the nature of cost-minimizing solutions.

While our study is cast in the form of an economic model that relates treatment level to required flows, the reader must continually be reminded that marginal costs of flow are estimated from synthetic schedules of storage, costs of treatment are estimated by the use of generalized cost functions that reflect expected economies, regional aggregate dilution flows have never been subjected to verification in the field, and basic economic projections were made in a somewhat naive fashion. We hope that our figures will not be used rashly and that with the appearance of successive National Assessments, errors can be promptly corrected.

We have had relatively little experience with multidimensional models and are unable to compare their potentials

34

THE OUTLOOK FOR WATER

for identifying savings or increments in net benefits (including those difficult to evaluate, such as aesthetic characteristics) with those of a two-dimensional model. Clearly, much detailed information would have to be acquired before one could rely on regional averages or aggregates.

To take account of changes in demand for water or for water-related goods and services, one must introduce new technical coefficients or adjust the basic economic projections. Changes in water input per unit of output (including per capita usage of municipalities) is a fairly uncomplicated problem since "basic" projections need not be altered.[2] If benefits that are not accounted for in the original projections of water-related goods and services accrue to water resource projects, the need for revision of projections must also be examined. Will the benefits raise GNP, or are they intangibles that can be augmented or diminished without interfering with the composition and aggregate value of regional and national product? If the benefits comprise outputs of goods and services that should be added to GNP, either the composition of the bill of goods has been altered or a higher productivity has been realized than was projected. In either event the model must be adjusted to maintain internally consistent relations. Such adjustment would most likely include a redistribution of activity among water resource regions.

Some Issues of Policy

All of the important decisions on future water development and use will, by definition, involve policy considerations. Many of these choices will be influenced largely by the facts in the case — both those that are available and those that will become available through research along the lines indicated in the preceding section. But for other choices, physical, biological, and economic data will not provide enough guidance; the taste and the scale of values of individuals are likely to be the controlling factors. The more deeply understood and widely debated these subjective issues are, the sounder the decisions are likely to be.

Our study brings out a number of issues of this kind. Those that seem the most significant are discussed briefly below.

Is High Growth Always a Good Thing?

In our model three rates of growth are projected simply as a hedge against uncertainty. Should there be a conscious effort to attain either the High, Medium, or Low level? Since one of the main purposes of this study is to show where the tight spots may occur, High-growth-rate models may generate more interest because shortages are more acute and costs of treatment and storage are higher; but the reader should not overlook the social benefits that might come from lower growth rates; nor should he fail to explore ways in which lower rates might be realized.

The cumulative effect of Low projection and high treatment versus High projection and low treatment is so great that anyone whose tastes run toward minimum disturbance

of the natural environment has no problem in making a choice. While selection of the treatment level is a decision of the kind that voters in the United States are prepared to make, determination that growth shall be along Low, Medium, or High paths is still to be left largely to chance. One might consider whether the mild persuasion undertaken now in the interests of dampening the rate of population growth and the output of polluting substances could point the way toward avoiding more stringent controls in the near future. Economists in this country have shown little interest in studying macroeconomic models in which environmental quality and the minimization of social abrasion play a prominent role.

More Lakes versus Undisturbed Flow

Some people prefer the artificial lakes that would be created by new storage dams; others prefer the natural streamflow that would be disturbed by dams. The issue is largely aesthetic, although economic and other tangible benefits can be claimed by both sides.

In this study the question comes up most strongly in connection with the minimum treatment program. Because minimum treatment would cost much more than the minimum flow or minimum cost programs, would flood more valley land, and would lead to situations of regional water shortage much sooner, one might question the merit of including it as an alternative policy guide. What is the conceivable benefit to be derived? One answer would be that many lakes are created; and if these lakes yield a net addition to welfare (by providing goods and services not otherwise available within the limits of projected GNP and subordinate categories), the policy deserves consideration.[3] Those who wish to preserve as much as possible of the natural characteristics of streamflow have the verdict of dollars on their side, at least in terms of aggregate costs. Under present arrangements that control the sharing of costs of water resource facilities between federal and local governments, the pressure is toward reservoirs, since their use minimizes local costs.

Who Should Bear the Costs?

The observation that the federal government at present bears most of the cost of water storage raises the broader question of who should pay for what. Our findings suggest that no insuperable problem would be encountered in distributing the costs of water via the price system and market processes. The form which the regulatory process might take (e.g., standards of effluent, taxes on waste discharge, fees for waste treatment) and the form which facilities for treatment, cooling, and provision of supply might take (e.g., centralized versus decentralized) are difficult questions to which a number of experts have addressed themselves.

From our finding that the needs of a few large industries would account for most of the future costs of water supply

---

[2] Assuming a reasonable degree of independence between, say, productivity per unit of labor and final bill of goods on the one hand and costs of water on the other.

[3] Another answer, which reveals the limited applicability of the basic model, might be that only a maximum flow policy will cope with conservative pollutants (e.g., dissolved solids) or other pollutants not reduced by standard treatment.

and treatment, it appears that equity might be most easily attained by assigning to consumers the costs for which these industries are responsible. The same principle can presumably be applied to the consumers of agricultural and mineral products and to the inhabitants of cities. Superficially, the principle appears to be a simple one. In putting it into operation, however, various complicating phenomena are encountered, such as parity of treatment relative to the order in which a succession of firms reduces the assimilative capacity of a river; the synergistic or compensating effects of particular pollutants in combination; the scale of priority accorded to different "rights" to make use of a river's properties (e.g., its waste disposal capability versus its capability for recreation); the impact on the competitive advantage or disadvantage of different pollution abatement standards; and the like. Rapid urbanization, suburbanization, and growth of family income have given rise to new vested interests which conflict with older vested interests in the way a river is used. This conflict is critical because the "excess capacity" of our rivers has suddenly disappeared.

In choosing systems, perhaps the two most important considerations are: (1) the relative advantages of each system in stimulating technological improvements designed to reduce waste output and improve waste treatment; and (2) equity in the distribution of costs. Of somewhat lesser importance are the ease and economy with which a system of control can be administered. A lively interest in innovation and experimentation, and a greater fund of knowledge regarding the physical, biological, and chemical processes of water-related activity are prerequisites to attaining efficiency, equity, and economy. Beyond that the question is one of citizens' preferences.

How Much Risk of Deficiency?

Available information offers a number of clues to the consequences of building storage to provide a specified dependable flow 98 percent, 95 percent, or 90 percent of the time and of the degree of short-term chemical treatment of wastes needed to further reduce the risk of deficiency. Further research can remove some of the remaining uncertainties. Under the 2000 Medium projection, for example, our basic model indicates that the choice of the 95 percent level of certainty would result in negligible money savings over the 98 percent level and a small saving (24 million acre-feet) in new storage; at the 90 percent level money savings would be $200 million a year and storage savings 86 million acre-feet. Are such gains — or savings that would result from not providing for supplementary treatment — worth the added risk of occasional water shortage? There is no certain answer at the present time; it is a matter of judgment.

What Standards of Quality?

The nature and cost of future water programs will depend to a great extent on how clean the American people want their streams and lakes to be. The choice of a 4 mg/l standard for dissolved oxygen in our basic model, though in line with much contemporary thinking, was essentially intuitive; 5 or 3 mg/l could have been used. Choice of the extremes used to test the basic model was less arbitrary: 6 mg/l would provide an undoubtedly high level of quality; 1 mg/l would barely keep streams from being putrescent. As we have noted, maintaining a 6 mg/l level of dissolved oxygen would be extremely costly and would call for larger regulated flows than most regions could muster with natural supplies. What quality levels would be worth the effort? Should standards differ among regions, or among streams within regions?

Weighing Aesthetic Values

An intractable problem is the choice between investment for production of tangible goods and services — whether water-related or not — and investment to enhance the aesthetic quality of rivers and lakes and the related landscape. There is no "market" in which a scale of consumer preference for environmental quality can be established. The "market" for a flowing stream as a commonly enjoyed resource — to walk beside or to look at — does not exist, nor can one be constructed without serious disturbance of usual propery rights. Who has prior claim to the physical attributes of a river — the manufacturer who uses it for waste disposal, the person who walks and sits on its banks, or the irrigator who withdraws its water far upstream? No institution exists to protect the interests of the person who uses a stream as a direct source of satisfaction. His interest often has been expropriated without compensation, even where a stream is legally considered to be an asset for the benefit of all. What rule shall be followed in restoring to him what once was his? One can formulate a theoretical model whereby all who contribute to the deterioration of the natural environment either pay compensation to all who suffer loss of satisfaction resulting from such deterioration or incur the costs of restoring environmental quality to an acceptable level. The larger the number of people to be compensated, the more likely it is that the costs of stream quality regeneration would be less than the costs of compensation. Rules that relate liability for damage inversely to priority of use would probably go by the board; they would be simple and effective rationing devices only so long as the total burden on streams and lakes did not foreclose any class of user from equitable access to common resource.

How should costs of assuring the specified standard of quality be distributed? If we follow the present pattern, treatment costs would be borne directly by those who produce the wastes, and flow regulation costs would be borne directly by the government. A wide range of physical devices as well as methods of cost allocation are available and should be studied before large fixed investments are committed.[4]

Some Urgent Research Needs

Most of our findings, to one degree or another, suggest further research. The need for additional information on the movement of groundwater and for other basic hydrologic data has been noted at several points in the study.

[4] See Allen V. Kneese and Blair T. Bower, *Managing Water Quality: Economics, Technology, Institutions* (The Johns Hopkins Press for Resources for the Future, 1968).

Scarcity of data on recreational demands for water also has been mentioned. Indeed, there are few aspects of water management in which more facts and better analysis will not be helpful. The examples given below represent some of the research opportunities that we believe to be especially significant and promising.

Treatment of Dissolved Solids

Our model did not take account of requirements for treatment and dilution of dissolved solids. There is little information on the probable build-up of salts, except for a presentiment that it is likely to become severe as intrabasin reuse reaches projected magnitudes. Although a stream can naturally rejuvenate its oxygen supply, it can do little with dissolved solids. Up to now salinity has been kept in bounds by dilution, and it may be that projected BOD dilution flows will be adequate for dilution of salts in water. But as treatment levels are raised in order to reduce required BOD dilution flows, the likelihood that salinity will be adequately diluted diminishes. Also, increased intraplant recirculation may present problems of highly concentrated semisolid waste. We need a more complete treatment-dilution model before we can be confident about our conclusions, and we need more research regarding the range of biophysical and biochemical responses.

Interbasin Transfers

Interregional movement of water is fairly expensive, especially if distances and lifts are great, as they would be by the year 2000. The question that cannot be answered is whether it is "cheaper" to move water or to move people and economic activity, taking into account the price one would be willing to pay for meeting one's preference for domicile. On the basis of our extrapolations, one or the other movement will have to be made. Either movement possesses elements of irreversibility and cumulative effect. There is not enough information now available to provide a basis for making a choice, even though political pressures on both sides of the issue are growing rapidly.

Waste Collection and Thermal Pollution

Of the elements treated as part of the cost of water in this study — flow regulation, waste treatment, waste collection costs, and cooling-water recirculation costs — the latter two loomed as the largest. The prospective magnitude of these costs justifies a search for new ways of collecting waste and disposing of unwanted heat. As Kneese and others have pointed out, the "waste problem" is increasingly becoming the problem of discovering ways of using what we now discard — organic material, chemicals, minerals, heat, and so forth.

Our projected expenditures for controlling thermal pollution in 1980 are many times larger than estimated actual expenditure in 1960, when the quality standard of a maximum increase of 5.4°F. over natural levels was not a restriction. Further investigation is clearly called for to evaluate the accuracy of estimated future costs of recirculation.

These outlays can be avoided by providing higher dilution flows, by achieving higher rates of thermal efficiency, by placing future power plants in locations where a greater temperature rise can be accepted, or by new technology that reduces the use of cooling water. A method deserving investigation is the possibility of using cooling towers only in the warm months. The ecological effect of the substantial warming of receiving bodies of water in winter months, as well as the effect on costs of part-year operation, should be ascertained. Technological prospects are mixed. Perhaps more attention will be given to placing new power plants on bodies of water that can tolerate or quickly dissipate substantial amounts of heat. One might speculate upon inland or coastal locations in Canada or Alaska, but in the absence of knowledge regarding ecological effects, costs of long-distance power transmission, and risks of vulnerability to hostile action, little more can be said.

Waste Treatment versus Water Treatment

An important point that remains largely unexplored is the connection between costs of water treatment and changes in instream quality. No attempt was made in this study to establish a relationship between expenditures on waste treatment and expenditures on water treatment. The matter deserves further study. Existing information suggests that the effect of changes in instream quality on water treatment costs is small.

Inputs per Unit of Output

Our definition of "requirement" is based not on intake or diversion but on loss, a parameter that is much less susceptible to changes that would affect water inputs per unit of output. There are, nonetheless, potential improvements in the technology of water use that warrant further serious study.

The use that is most likely to offer economies is irrigation. Our computation of loss was based on the assumption that about one-half of the difference between the diversion requirement per irrigated acre and the amount of water evapotranspired by the crop was lost to further use. Much of this loss might be saved by new techniques of water delivery. Changes in crop characteristics might bring further savings by reducing the evapotranspiration requirement itself.

Regional Data and Analysis

Regional studies are rich in detailed information about the small geographic units that make up a region but tend to scant the interregional economic implications of the solutions reached for each region separately. Still lacking at the regional and subregional level is information regarding surface storage potential and its costs, groundwater storage potential and its costs, and interaction among various storage elements when treated as a single system. Such information is needed not only to provide cost data as regulation proceeds beyond present levels but also to indicate physical limits.

If further efforts are made to study regions as single points in space, as we have done, some way must be developed for "calibrating" regional aggregate values to make them consistent with the subregional aggregate values. One way of doing this would be to compare results yielded by our basinwide analysis with results yielded by routing the water downstream from headwaters to point of discharge, using the same basic economic projections for both methods. Another test would be to route the water downstream from subregion to subregion on the basis of economic projections made separately for each sub-basin and not subject to regionwide controls. As the sophistication of the National Assessment increases, we shall probably be able to check different techniques of estimation against each other.

Price Elasticity of Water

Changes in the input of water per unit of product (or changes in per capita municipal water use) as a result of changes in the price (cost) per unit of water presumably can be incorporated within a more comprehensive model than ours. Studies of price elasticity have been made for munici-pal water use[5] but relatively little is known about agricultural and industrial responsiveness. A major deficiency in existing knowledge is the interaction between changes in the price of water and the levels of water use in one region when accompanied by changes in the price of water in other regions. By restricting prospective costs of flow to a marginal cost of 2 cents per 1,000 gallons, the effect of price elasticity is attenuated, but whether the remaining effect is important cannot be established without further investigation. For example, synthetic schedules of storage have to be tested for reality by establishing that the hypo-thetical inventory of sites is borne out by the facts. In the thickly settled regions of the East, it is quite conceivable that physically feasible reservoir sites that have been pre-empted by urban activity will never be inundated. Curves describing cost of flow and the effect of a marginal cost constraint would have to be corrected.

[5] See Charles W. Howe and F. P. Linaweaver, Jr., "The Impact of Price on Residential Water Demand and Its Relation to System Design and Price Structure," *Water Resources Research*, vol. 3, no. 1 (First Quarter 1967), pp. 13–32.

PART TWO
THE STUDY IN DETAIL

Population and Economic Activity Projections to the Year 2020

Coefficients of Water Use: Withdrawal Uses

Withdrawals and Losses: All Uses

Water Quality

The "Supply" of Water and the Costs of Flow

The Basic Model: The Results

Short-Term Tertiary Treatment and Reduced Storage

Variations in Selected Parameters

Chapter 5

POPULATION AND ECONOMIC
ACTIVITY PROJECTIONS TO THE YEAR 2020

The principal determinants of water use are population and the level and pattern of economic activity. Of these, population has the more direct relationship with water requirements.

Because of the decline in the U.S. birth rate during the past decade, the Bureau of the Census has lowered its population projections, and we have made corresponding changes in this study. The estimates of the total population of the 48 contiguous states that are used are as follows:

1960		1980	2000	2020
			(millions)	
	Low	219	255	335
178	Medium	233	303	393
	High	254	369	520

In the Senate Select Committee reports of 1960 (Committee Print No. 5[1] and No. 32), the Medium projection for 1980 was 244 million, and for 2000, 329 million.

The reader's attention is directed to the range of projected values. For the year 2000, the High projection is 45 percent greater than the Low; for 2020 the difference is 55 percent. Even for a date as near as 1980 the spread is equal to 16 percent of the Low estimate. In view of the long lead time required for many water resource projects, the programming of construction should be flexible enough to provide for acceleration or deceleration, as required, to match facilities with needs.

The methods used in estimating total and urban population and the populations of Standard Metropolitan Statisti-cal Areas (SMSAs) are described in the appendix. Tables 3, 4, and 5 contain the estimates of total, urban, and SMSA populations used in this study. Apart from the prospective growth indicated by the tables, the most significant aspects of the projections are: (1) the regional distribution of population compared with that of the present and (2) the dominance of relatively large urban centers.

The projections indicate that the U.S. population might double between 1960 and 2000 but probably will grow by a somewhat smaller amount. Should the population grow at the High rate — about 1¾ percent annually — it would approximately triple between 1960 and 2020. Even growth at the Low rate, 1 percent a year, will mean a doubling of the population by 2020. Either prospect means more than difficulties in meeting water requirements; a doubling or tripling of the population will be accompanied by many changes in environmental amenities. If, however, we were to become seriously concerned about urban congestion, maintenance of open spaces, preservation of wilderness areas, and similar problems stemming from increased density of population, corrective steps might include a reduction in births beyond that implied by the Low rate of growth.

According to the projections, urban population will grow more rapidly than total population but less rapidly than population in major urban centers — i.e., SMSAs.[2] In 1960, 65 percent of the total population were in SMSAs; by 2020, Medium projection, this proportion is expected to be 84 percent. Rural population, a share of which may be

[1] *Population Projections and Economic Assumptions*, Senate Select Committee on National Water Resources, 86th Cong., 2d sess. (1960).

[2] The reader's attention is called to the 2020 High population projections for particular regions: 66 million in Delaware and Hudson, 50 million in South Pacific, and 274 million in the Northeast quadrant. We may have overemphasized the concentration of population.

in SMSAs, is projected to fall from 30 percent in 1960 to about 15 percent by 2020 Medium.

Prospective increases in the urban population of certain regions are substantially greater than the national average. In the Colorado basin, for example, our Medium projection shows an urban population that by 2020 has grown to five times its size in 1960 (from 1.2 million to 6.5 million). While this may be a far more rapid rate of growth than is experienced elsewhere, it poses problems of negligible consequence compared with those implied by the absolute growth projected for the North Atlantic area, which is composed of the New England, Delaware and Hudson, and Chesapeake Bay regions. At the Medium rate of growth, by 2020 more than 81 million people are projected for the region's cities alone; at the High rate, there would be 108 million.

All projections are based on the assumption that neither war nor depression will lead to erratic changes in population growth rates, affect the trend of growth in production per man hour, or induce a change in the trend of the population-labor force ratio. Estimated labor force combined with hours worked per year and with output per man hour yields estimated gross national product.

Gross National Product

Gross national product (in real terms), at Medium rates of change in population, labor force participation, and productivity per worker, is projected to grow to eight times the 1960 level by the year 2020. Certain industries that use large quantities of water and contribute heavily to its pollution are expected to grow more rapidly: chemicals, tenfold (based on 1959); and rubber and plastics, eighteenfold. Pulp and paper is projected at the same rate as GNP; and food, petroleum refining, primary metals, and other manufacturing are expected to grow less rapidly. For 2020 Medium, output of power by steam-electric utilities is projected at twelve times 1960 production. In general, outputs of extractive industries — mining and irrigated agriculture — are expected to grow at lower rates than changes in GNP. Irrigated acreage, which today is the largest single user of water, gross and net, is projected to grow by only 40 percent by 2020 Medium, and only by 63 percent at the High rate of growth. All parts of the country share in the expansion of irrigated acreage, although the Mid-continent and North Pacific divisions account for most of the increase.

The estimated increase in man-days of fishing and hunting amounted to a tripling over the period 1954–2000,[3] but these changes were not used in projecting the water requirements of fish and wildlife habitat. Instead, a much smaller rate of expansion in habitat was projected, based mainly on increases planned by federal agencies.[4]

[3] See U.S. Senate, Select Committee on National Water Resources, Committee Print No. 18, *Fish and Wildlife and Water Resources*, 86th Cong., 2d sess. (1960).

[4] The only depleting use of recreational water that was studied was water lost by evaporation and transpiration in swamps and wetlands. Conversion of dry land to swamps and wetlands at rates proportional to projected increases of man-days of hunting seemed implausible. See later discussion.

In projecting GNP it was assumed that the fraction of population 14 years and over in 2000 and 2020 would remain at the level estimated by the Bureau of the Census for 1980. The fraction of the population that composed the labor force was estimated as 58.3 percent in 1980, 59.9 percent in 2000, and 60.0 percent in 2020. Output per worker was assumed to grow at 2.5 percent per year for the High projection, 2 percent for the Medium projection, and 1.7 percent for the Low projection. It was assumed that the rate of unemployment would be 4.5 percent of the labor force.

GNP projections yielded by these assumptions were as follows:

1960		1980	2000	2020
			($ billion, 1960)	
504	Low	1,023	1,680	3,103
	Medium	1,091	2,151	4,150
	High	1,209	2,914	6,708

The effect of compounding the High population growth rate with the High rate of growth in productivity per man-year yields a High GNP for 2020 that exceeds the Medium projection by 62 percent. One might seriously question the usability of alternative projections that differ by such a wide margin, but no better procedure is presently available to call attention to the flexibility that must be maintained. It should be noted that the High projection leads the Medium and the Medium leads the Low by about 20 years.

The relative differences between estimated GNP in this study and estimated GNP in Committee Print No. 32[5] were used to modify projected levels of production in manufacturing and steam-electric power. The comparisons of GNP estimates are as follows:

		Committee Print No. 32	This study
		($ billion, 1960)	
1980	Low	960	1,023
	Medium	1,060	1,091
	High	1,260	1,209
2000	Low	1,680	1,680
	Medium	2,200	2,151
	High	3,290	2,914

Slight differences in the rate of population growth, labor force participation rates, and the rates of change in output per man hour led, on balance, to very small changes except for the 2000 High projection.

Manufacturing

Indexes of manufacturing output were computed by adjusting the projections made earlier by RFF to correspond with revised projections of GNP, and were then extended to

[5] The estimates in Committee Print No. 32 were taken from Hans H. Landsberg, Leonard L. Fischman, and Joseph L. Fisher, *Resources in America's Future* (The Johns Hopkins Press for Resources for the Future, 1963). Hereinafter referred to as RFF.

the year 2020 in accordance with the implied ratio of the trend of value added of each industry to GNP over the period 1960–2000. Because of their importance in use of water and contribution to pollution, five industries were projected through a sequence of steps involving separate determinations of value added, water use, and water-borne waste residual coefficients. Abbreviated methods of estimation were employed for other manufacturing industries, whereby indexes of output were applied directly to measures of intake and loss for the year 1958. Each industry's output was distributed among regions in accordance with the percentage distribution used in projections prepared for the Senate Select Committee. Similar procedures were followed for mining and electric power.

Indexes of output for ten manufacturing classes are shown in table 6. The limitation that must be kept in mind for all High and Low projections, especially for manufacturing and mining where interproduct substitution is important, is illustrated by table 6. The High index for "rubber, plastics, etc.," of 7,593 (1959 = 100) for the year 2020 is based on the assumption that plastics are used in place of other materials to the maximum degree portended by present evidence. If such should turn out to be true, presumably the output of glass, aluminum foil, paper and cardboard, wood products, and other substitutes would be affected, and there would be corresponding effects on the extraction of raw materials. To aggregate all Highs or all Lows is inconsistent with the assumptions that lie behind each individual High or Low. Since some substitution is at the expense of nonwater-related production, it is theoretically possible and internally consistent for output to be simultaneously projected as "High" for various combinations of substitutes, but not for all substitutes simultaneously. The overstatement yielded by aggregating all Highs is probably greater than the understatement yielded by aggregating all Lows.

Perhaps more reasonable limits of water use and costs of water are provided by values that are about halfway between the Medium and the High and Low projections. Perhaps such adjustment should be limited only to manufacturing and mining, since for other activities, such as steam-electric power, the projections depend on growth rates for the economy as a whole. The wide range between Low and High GNP by the year 2020 is not the effect of inconsistent aggregation of industry Lows and Highs but the result of compounding High and Low population growth rates with High and Low productivity growth rates. Such compounding is logically acceptable; whether it is realized is, of course, another question.

Steam-Electric Power

While today's largest single class of water use — measured by intake — is agriculture, the time will come when the lead will shift to steam-electric power, unless, of course, unforeseen techniques of power production come to the fore. First rank seems ordained for electric power, even with a substantial increase in recirculation.

Estimates of power produced by utility steam-electric plants reflect not only the prospective increase in power consumption, but also a trend away from self-supply by major power users toward the purchase of power from utilities.

Estimates of future power production prepared for the Senate Select Committee were modified to accord with more recently prepared projections to 1980 made by the Federal Power Commission. Beyond 1980, projections were based on the trend of power production relative to GNP. The new projections constitute a slight upward revision. As can be seen in table 7, for the Medium projections, between 1960 and 1980 utility power production would triple. For each of the succeeding twenty-year periods production is projected to double. The High rate projected to 2020 is consistent with the High rate of growth of population and output per man hour, and is not subject to criticism on grounds of internal inconsistency.

Mining

Mining projections, as shown in table 8 for major classes, were made by modifying recent estimates of the Bureau of Mines to accord with our own projections of gross national product. The spread of Highs and Lows, in this industry as well as in all others, was based on RFF projections. Regional distribution was assumed to be the same as that estimated by the Bureau of Mines for the Select Committee.

The problem of internal consistency of Lows and Highs is less severe within mining than within manufacturing. Because of implied physical restrictions in the projected output of petroleum, natural gas, and natural gas liquids, the possibility of double counting vis-à-vis coal or "other minerals," which includes fissionable materials, is substantially dampened. It is also likely that relationships between copper and iron are dominated by complementarity rather than substitutability. There remains, however, the likelihood that synthetics will increasingly take the place of various natural substances, which means an unknown amount of double counting between manufacturing and mining must be assumed when Lows and Highs are aggregated.

Agriculture

Agricultural water use consists of domestic use, stock watering, and irrigation. Soil and moisture conservation activities have been treated as a separate activity in this study and, moreover, one that is independent of population and economic activity.

Rural domestic water use was modified in accordance with revised estimates of rural population (equal to the difference between total and urban population in each region; see tables 3 and 4). Requirements for water for stock watering were based on a projection of livestock population assumed to be proportional to a projection of value added by livestock. The projection of value added was based on estimated production of hay and pasture, adjusted for a projected reduction in feed consumed per livestock unit. The resulting index of livestock production is given in table 9.

The major water use in the United States today, whether measured by intake or by loss to the atmosphere, is irrigation. While there is considerable scope for change in the input of water per acre, the main determinant of water use in the foreseeable future will be the number of acres under irrigation. To estimate this number one must take into account such factors as exports, national and regional demands, crop mix, regional distribution of total agricultural activity, competing uses of land, prices paid by irrigators for irrigation water, the policies adopted by Congress for construction of water resource projects, and direct allocation of water among competing uses. In making their estimates of irrigated acreage for the Senate Select Committee, the U.S. Department of Agriculture (USDA) combined these factors, in what was ultimately an intuitive fashion, to yield Low, Medium, and High acreages.[6] A possible shortage of water was not to be taken into account, except that projected acreage could not require more water than a region's natural, fully regulated supply. A later estimate by George Pavelis of the USDA included a similar restriction but reached the values for Low, Medium, and High acreage by assuming three different upper limits to which attained acreage would move asymptotically. The largest attainable acreage was 100 percent of potentially irrigable land; the intermediate level assumed 50 percent of ultimate development; the Low estimate assumed that 25 percent of the land dependent on federal projects and 50 percent of other land would be developed. Pavelis then estimated the rate of movement toward each of these limits on the basis of historical experience.[7]

Vernon Ruttan's estimates, which appeared about the same time as Pavelis's, were based on another different method.[8] Using a statistically derived Cobb-Douglas production function, Ruttan made three types of computations. By one, which he felt was the most realistic of the three, he estimated acreage on the assumption that the 1980 demand for agricultural output would be distributed among regions according to past historical experience, but that farmers would pay the full costs of bringing new land under irrigation. By another, he estimated acreage on the assumption that irrigation water would be supplied at prices based on today's federal policies. By a third, which is not a projection, he estimated irrigated acreage by equating the marginal revenue product of irrigated land to full marginal cost.

Pavelis's estimates extended to the year 2020, although only the estimates to 2000 were published. Ruttan's study was for 1980 only. The USDA estimates for the Select Committee went to the year 2000.[9]

[6] U.S. Senate, Select Committee on National Water Resources, Committee Print No. 12, *Land and Water Potentials and Future Requirements for Water*, 86th Cong., 1st sess. (1960).

[7] George A. Pavelis, "Irrigation Policy and Long-term Growth Functions," *Agricultural Economics Research*, April 1965, and unpublished worksheets.

[8] Vernon W. Ruttan, *The Economic Demand for Irrigated Acreage: New Methodology and Some Preliminary Projections, 1954–1980* (The Johns Hopkins Press for Resources for the Future, 1965).

[9] See app. A for details on method and comparisons of results.

On a broad regional basis – "East" and "West" – the estimates for 1980 were as follows:

	U.S.	East	West
	(millions of irrigated acres)		
Ruttan, demand model	49.7	12.4	37.4
Pavelis, Medium	43.2	4.1	39.1
USDA, Medium	36.7	3.7	33.0

The major disagreement among the three estimates is Ruttan's solution for the East, vis-à-vis the other two. Table 10 shows the estimates of irrigated acreage that we have used. These are Pavelis's estimates.

Some Comparisons with Other Projections

Where information on population and economic activity was readily available, we compared our projections with others for various regions.[10] With one notable disagreement, namely pulp and paper production in the Pacific Northwest, our Medium projections tended to be lower than the single-value projections made by others. Our projections were higher than the estimates made by others for primary metals in New England, 2000 Medium; and for primary metals in Ohio, 1980 and 2000 Medium. The greatest variance was in our estimate of pulp and paper production for the Pacific Northwest. For 1980, our index of production was 648 (1960 = 100), whereas the Bonneville Power Administration estimate was 244. Our estimates of pulp and paper production in other parts of the country – the Cumberland, Tennessee, Eastern Great Lakes, Ohio, and New England regions – were substantially lower, but whether because of inadequate appreciation of an interregional shift or because of a generally lower level of projection could not be ascertained.

Since pulp and paper production is a major source of pollution, our failure to account fully for an eastward movement of the industry would, on balance, mean that we have understated the expected pressure on the nation's water resources. By insisting on our own projections, we are also guilty of downward bias stemming largely from the polluting effects of chemicals in New England; food manufacturing in the Chesapeake Bay region; petroleum refining in the Ohio region; food processing and petroleum refining in the Eastern Great Lakes region; food processing and chemicals manufacturing in the Cumberland and Tennessee regions; and food, chemicals, and petroleum in the Upper Missouri region.[11]

[10] See app. A for identification of other studies.

[11] Since the foregoing was written, the U.S. Water Resources Council has issued its first national assessment: *The Nation's Water Resources* (1968). Projections are for a single rate of growth. In general, the Council's projections fall between our Mediums and Highs. In particular instances, e.g., irrigated acreage, the Council's estimates are above our Highs.

Table 3. TOTAL POPULATION OF THE CONTERMINOUS UNITED STATES, BY REGION

(thousands)

	1960	1980			2000			2020		
		L	M	H	L	M	H	L	M	H
NORTHEAST	102,010	119,286	126,965	138,382	135,823	161,469	196,637	176,690	207,282	274,265
N Eng	10,262	12,214	13,002	14,175	13,914	16,566	20,176	18,188	21,336	28,232
D & H	23,700	28,198	30,013	32,725	32,399	38,580	46,982	42,489	49,846	65,955
Ches	10,017	12,315	13,108	14,240	14,530	17,300	21,069	19,462	22,832	30,209
Ohio	17,716	19,199	20,435	22,282	20,601	24,531	29,873	25,411	29,810	39,442
EGL	12,631	15,653	16,660	18,165	18,778	22,360	27,230	25,369	29,762	39,380
WGL	13,596	16,342	17,394	18,965	19,130	22,779	27,740	25,548	29,972	39,656
U Miss	11,783	12,931	13,763	15,006	14,077	16,763	20,413	17,691	20,754	27,461
L Mo	2,305	2,434	2,590	2,824	2,394	2,590	3,154	2,532	2,970	3,930
SOUTHEAST	32,738	40,644	43,162	47,064	46,675	55,577	67,683	61,467	72,110	95,411
SE	20,154	26,906	28,639	31,227	32,176	38,314	46,658	44,093	51,727	68,442
Cumb	1,219	1,224	1,304	1,422	1,288	1,533	1,868	1,520	1,783	2,359
Tenn	2,957	3,383	3,601	3,927	3,694	4,398	5,356	4,657	5,464	7,229
L Miss	4,427	5,117	5,451	5,944	5,778	6,880	8,379	7,444	8,733	11,555
L AWR	3,981	4,014	4,167	4,544	3,739	4,452	5,422	3,753	4,403	5,826
MID-CONTINENT	18,046	20,534	21,854	23,829	23,177	27,222	33,147	28,774	33,754	44,661
U Mo	6,022	6,781	7,216	7,868	7,558	9,000	10,960	9,656	11,326	14,986
U AWR	3,437	3,370	3,587	3,911	3,503	3,793	4,618	3,438	4,033	5,336
W Gulf	8,587	10,383	11,051	12,050	12,116	14,429	17,569	15,680	18,395	24,339
SOUTHWEST	13,245	22,650	24,108	26,285	30,286	36,064	43,920	43,456	50,982	67,457
RG-P	1,379	1,965	2,091	2,280	2,626	3,127	3,808	3,690	4,329	5,728
Colo	1,880	3,263	3,472	3,786	4,191	4,991	6,078	6,366	7,468	9,882
G Basin	1,030	1,226	1,306	1,424	1,262	1,503	1,831	1,389	1,630	2,156
S Pac	8,956	16,196	17,239	18,795	22,207	26,443	32,203	32,011	37,555	49,691
NORTH PACIFIC	12,137	15,887	16,910	18,440	19,037	22,667	27,613	24,614	28,875	38,205
C Pac	6,725	9,472	10,083	10,994	11,518	13,715	16,703	14,753	17,307	22,900
PNW	5,412	6,415	6,827	7,446	7,519	8,952	10,910	9,861	11,568	15,305
U.S.	178,176	219,001	232,999	254,000	254,998	302,999	369,000	335,001	393,003	519,999

Table 4. URBAN POPULATION OF THE CONTERMINOUS UNITED STATES, BY REGION

(thousands)

	1960	1980			2000			2020		
		L	M	H	L	M	H	L	M	H
NORTHEAST	75,433	94,205	100,260	109,299	112,333	133,553	162,643	149,533	175,424	232,109
N Eng	7,922	9,615	10,235	11,160	11,172	13,298	16,197	14,737	17,287	22,874
D & H	21,087	25,301	26,927	29,365	29,354	34,948	42,559	38,633	45,323	59,970
Ches	6,625	9,207	9,798	10,646	11,739	13,974	17,018	16,270	19,087	25,253
Ohio	10,418	12,372	13,168	14,361	14,132	16,824	20,488	17,971	21,082	27,893
EGL	10,068	13,238	14,088	15,364	16,529	19,679	23,965	22,815	26,766	35,416
WGL	10,757	13,869	14,760	16,097	17,067	20,318	24,744	23,330	27,371	36,215
U Miss	7,259	9,051	9,633	10,505	10,689	12,725	15,497	13,966	16,384	21,678
L Mo	1,297	1,552	1,651	1,801	1,651	1,787	2,175	1,811	2,124	2,810
SOUTHEAST	17,278	27,193	28,881	31,499	35,717	42,523	51,785	50,127	58,805	77,809
SE	11,138	18,993	20,215	22,046	25,771	30,682	37,364	37,428	43,908	58,097
Cumb	542	720	766	836	883	1,052	1,281	1,114	1,306	1,729
Tenn	1,149	1,704	1,813	1,978	2,153	2,563	3,121	2,892	3,393	4,490
L Miss	2,475	3,348	3,567	3,890	4,393	5,230	6,370	6,046	7,093	9,385
L AWR	1,974	2,428	2,520	2,749	2,517	2,996	3,649	2,647	3,105	4,108
MID-CONTINENT	11,937	15,678	16,684	18,195	19,284	22,658	27,589	24,927	29,243	38,691
U Mo	3,353	4,579	4,872	5,313	5,702	6,788	8,267	7,670	8,997	11,905
U AWR	2,188	2,493	2,653	2,893	2,809	3,042	3,703	2,861	3,356	4,439
W Gulf	6,396	8,606	9,159	9,989	10,773	12,828	15,619	14,396	16,890	22,347
SOUTHWEST	11,292	20,854	22,193	24,203	28,575	34,020	41,429	41,346	48,505	64,180
RG-P	1,007	1,742	1,853	2,021	2,342	2,789	3,396	3,363	3,945	5,220
Colo	1,260	2,517	2,678	2,921	3,515	4,184	5,096	5,555	6,516	8,623
G Basin	644	843	897	979	925	1,101	1,341	1,039	1,219	1,612
S Pac	8,381	15,752	16,765	18,282	21,793	25,946	31,596	31,389	36,825	48,725
NORTH PACIFIC	8,595	12,235	13,022	14,163	15,484	18,433	22,454	20,493	24,041	31,810
C Pac	5,172	7,560	8,047	8,736	9,477	11,282	13,739	12,289	14,416	19,076
PNW	3,423	4,675	4,975	5,427	6,007	7,151	8,715	8,204	9,625	12,734
U.S.	124,535	170,165	181,040	197,359	211,393	251,187	305,900	286,426	336,018	444,599

Table 5. POPULATION OF STANDARD METROPOLITAN STATISTICAL AREAS, BY REGION

(thousands)

	1960	1980			2000			2020		
		L	M	H	L	M	H	L	M	H
NORTHEAST	73,865	92,301	98,004	106,595	111,844	132,833	162,077	152,287	178,871	236,279
N Eng	7,532	9,441	10,018	10,908	11,398	13,554	16,539	15,544	18,255	24,116
D & H	21,856	25,605	27,165	29,583	29,667	35,283	43,050	39,353	46,219	61,055
Ches	7,023	9,881	10,484	11,374	12,876	15,311	18,683	18,441	21,671	28,624
Ohio	10,019	12,061	12,873	13,935	14,117	16,790	20,486	18,485	21,710	28,677
EGL	9,755	13,018	13,812	15,040	16,677	19,834	24,200	23,597	27,715	36,611
WGL	10,871	13,928	14,776	16,091	17,272	20,541	25,064	24,043	28,238	37,300
U Miss	5,625	6,871	7,289	7,937	8,192	9,742	11,886	10,952	12,864	16,992
L Mo	1,184	1,496	1,587	1,727	1,645	1,778	2,169	1,872	2,199	2,904
SOUTHEAST	13,820	22,019	23,310	25,386	29,517	35,103	42,833	42,927	50,417	66,600
SE	9,045	15,375	16,312	17,765	21,416	25,469	31,077	32,338	37,980	50,169
Cumb	464	615	653	710	732	870	1,062	935	1,098	1,450
Tenn	935	1,146	1,215	1,324	1,367	1,626	1,984	1,832	2,153	2,844
L Miss	1,897	2,814	2,988	3,254	3,686	4,384	5,350	5,222	6,133	8,103
L AWR	1,479	2,069	2,142	2,333	2,316	2,754	3,360	2,600	3,053	4,034
MID-CONTINENT	9,397	13,889	14,841	16,047	17,385	20,400	24,887	23,001	27,015	35,684
U Mo	2,148	2,985	3,167	3,449	3,840	4,567	5,572	5,373	6,311	8,335
U AWR	1,527	2,055	2,287	2,374	2,570	2,779	3,390	2,825	3,318	4,383
W Gulf	5,722	8,849	9,387	10,224	10,975	13,054	15,925	14,803	17,386	22,966
SOUTHWEST	11,429	21,244	22,594	24,626	29,273	34,849	42,459	42,348	49,697	65,730
RG-P	667	1,419	1,505	1,639	2,317	2,756	3,362	3,374	3,963	5,234
Colo	1,057	2,609	2,767	3,013	3,631	4,319	5,270	5,693	6,687	8,834
G Basin	751	1,020	1,083	1,179	1,118	1,331	1,624	1,270	1,492	1,971
S Pac	8,954	16,196	17,239	18,795	22,207	26,443	32,203	32,011	37,555	49,691
NORTH PACIFIC	7,957	11,548	12,252	13,345	14,982	17,817	21,746	20,437	24,002	31,705
C Pac	5,025	7,600	8,064	8,782	9,866	11,734	14,318	13,254	15,566	20,562
PNW	2,932	3,948	4,188	4,563	5,116	6,083	7,428	7,183	8,436	11,143
U.S.	116,468	161,001	171,001	185,999	203,001	241,002	294,002	281,000	330,002	435,998

Note: SMSAs computed in order to estimate point loadings of waste disposal.

Table 6. INDEX OF MANUFACTURING OUTPUT FOR SELECTED INDUSTRIES

(1959 = 100)

		Food	Pulp & paper	Chemicals	Petroleum, etc.	Primary metals	Textiles	Lumber, etc.	Rubber, plastics, etc.	Stone, clay, etc.	Leather, etc.
	L	145	195	183	150	131	119	97	197	144	115
1980	M	161	225	250	176	191	152	185	300	211	133
	H	217	243	379	212	253	191	278	524	307	161
	L	199	310	287	213	170	153	107	330	219	134
2000	M	254	436	518	309	327	235	332	739	443	186
	H	468	602	1,108	454	528	391	727	1,993	873	272
	L	321	565	520	372	284	195	118	551	332	156
2020	M	415	834	1,018	588	540	364	598	1,819	426	260
	H	1,015	1,401	2,810	950	1,090	802	1,896	7,593	2,488	460

Table 7. POWER GENERATED BY UTILITY STEAM-ELECTRIC PLANTS

(billion kilowatt-hours)

1960		1980	2000	2020
	L	1,630	2,716	5,120
753	M	2,230	4,520	8,964
	H	3,212	7,683	17,709

Table 8. MINING OUTPUT

		Bituminous coal	Copper ore	Iron ore	Phosphate rock	Sand & gravel	All other minerals	Petroleum	Natural gas	Natural gas liquid
		(millions of short tons)						*(bil. bbl.)*	*(tril. cu. ft.)*	*(mil. bbl.)*
1960		415	135	140	60	720	815	2.6	12.8	339
1980	L	619	196	175	104	1,717	1,884	3.9	20.1	591
	M	799	292	261	152	2,510	2,755	4.6	25.2	747
	H	1,112	414	370	221	3,645	4,000	5.9	32.3	966
2000	L	600	227	174	143	3,254	3,464	3.9	20.1	591
	M	871	449	344	290	6,587	7,013	4.6	25.2	747
	H	1,658	844	646	572	12,466	13,837	5.9	32.3	966
2020	L	581	263	173	197	6,166	6,370	3.9	20.1	591
	M	1,105	806	531	647	20,228	20,885	4.6	25.2	747
	H	2,472	1,721	1,128	1,480	46,331	47,862	5.9	32.3	966

Table 9. INDEX OF LIVESTOCK PRODUCTION

(1960 = 100)

	L	M	H
1980	150	159	173
2000	175	208	255
2020	246	289	358

Table 10. IRRIGATED ACREAGE, BY REGION

(thousand acres)

	1960	1980 L	1980 M	1980 H	2000 L	2000 M	2000 H	2020 L	2020 M	2020 H
NORTHEAST	435	840	858	934	1,120	1,159	1,330	1,336	1,388	1,654
N Eng	27	23	23	23	23	23	23	23	23	23
D & H	166	245	259	308	261	283	377	264	289	409
Ches	56	133	135	144	189	195	221	230	239	286
Ohio	33	73	73	75	109	111	116	142	145	154
EGL	29	60	61	64	83	87	96	99	106	124
WGL	50	104	104	110	145	147	163	176	178	209
U Miss	65	153	154	160	228	231	249	290	295	331
L Mo	9	49	49	50	82	82	85	112	113	118
SOUTHEAST	1,920	3,222	3,272	3,479	4,021	4,144	4,715	4,529	4,721	5,738
SE	573	782	785	773	966	978	966	1,128	1,153	1,203
Cumb	3	7	7	7	10	10	11	13	14	14
Tenn	31	62	64	68	82	86	100	94	101	125
L Miss	607	1,157	1,170	1,255	1,509	1,545	1,784	1,730	1,788	2,208
L AWR	706	1,214	1,246	1,376	1,454	1,525	1,854	1,564	1,665	2,188
MID-CONTINENT	14,053	16,191	17,315	19,262	16,492	18,203	21,606	16,536	18,431	22,670
U Mo	6,297	7,141	7,601	8,141	7,335	8,117	9,291	7,371	8,296	9,943
U AWR	2,533	3,237	3,398	4,048	3,307	3,516	4,536	3,313	3,531	4,685
W Gulf	5,223	5,813	6,366	7,073	5,850	6,570	7,779	5,852	6,604	8,042
SOUTHWEST	7,194	7,871	8,116	8,420	8,059	8,485	9,168	8,120	8,636	9,623
RG-P	1,329	1,466	1,571	1,675	1,482	1,642	1,854	1,484	1,663	1,944
Colo	3,088	3,256	3,340	3,415	3,294	3,449	3,625	3,303	3,496	3,758
G Basin	1,928	2,081	2,130	2,188	2,124	2,219	2,357	2,136	2,259	2,467
S Pac	849	1,068	1,075	1,142	1,159	1,175	1,332	1,197	1,218	1,454
NORTH PACIFIC	11,254	13,268	13,625	14,125	14,194	14,944	16,232	14,648	15,681	17,777
C Pac	6,386	7,565	7,634	7,843	8,238	8,410	8,984	8,617	8,888	9,874
PNW	4,868	5,703	5,991	6,282	5,956	6,534	7,248	6,031	6,793	7,903
U.S.	34,856	41,392	43,186	46,220	43,886	46,935	53,051	45,169	48,857	57,462

Source: Appendix A.

Chapter 6

COEFFICIENTS OF WATER USE: WITHDRAWAL USES

We distinguish among three categories of water use, the first two of which contribute to evaporation and transpiration losses: (1) withdrawal (or intake), (2) onsite, and (3) flow. Onsite uses and waste dilution flow will be discussed in later chapters.[1]

Withdrawal uses are those that involve movement of water from a natural water course or lake into a man-made hydraulic system – irrigation ditches, city water works, steam power plants, steel mills, and the like. All withdrawal uses require a larger "flow-through" than is lost to the atmosphere (or incorporated into the product). Flow-through will exceed intake if water is recirculated within a given hydraulic system; if not, flow-through and intake are the same.

All separate water users within a particular category – e.g., food processing, or in some cases the larger category, manufacturing – are aggregated and treated as a single entity.[2] Each category of intake contains an implicit industry-wide recirculation rate, which is an average for that industry, in that region, in that year.

Sometimes flow-through is described as "gross water applied" and therefore may be confused with "gross use," which we define as "intake," or "withdrawal." By "flow-through" is meant the quantity of water per unit of output that must flow through the hydraulic system in response to the fabrication, internal transport, cooling, chemical processing, and waste disposal steps in production. To the degree that manufacturing, thermal power production, and mining use the same molecule of water for more than one step in the production process, or use a given molecule of water more than once for a given step, intake is correspondingly less than the application of water per unit of product.

If it is not recirculated, a user's intake that is neither exhausted to the atmosphere nor retained in the product is discharged, usually to a surface channel and frequently to the body of water whence it came. If the discharge is sufficiently far upstream, it merges with the water supply that serves downstream users. Thus, even if there is little or no recirculation within a particular hydraulic system, there may be a large amount of inter-user reuse. A measure of basinwide recirculation is the aggregate intake of all users per unit of time divided by basin flow per unit of time.[3] For any basin, aggregate intake can be a comparatively high multiple of flow. The practical, as distinct from the theoretical, upper limit of this multiple will depend on the geographic distribution of users within the basin and on the maintenance of quality to a level that avoids prohibitively high treatment costs at the point of intake.

---

[1] Flow uses – e.g., navigation, hydroelectric power, recreation, and waste dilution – suffer loss through evaporation from the surface of the river and from transpiration by vegetation lining stream banks. In some cases the evapotranspiration is "nonbeneficial" in the sense that the vegetation may be unwanted. Such losses, for the most part, are reflected in stream gauge readings, and therefore are not to be counted separately. If flows are controlled by new reservoirs, the additional evaporation loss from the reservoir should be counted. Additional evaporation in the river induced by the discharge of heated water should be counted as a loss. It is also possible that increased regulation of streamflow will raise (or lower) average evaporation per year per mile of stream relative to unregulated flows beyond the losses incurred in new regulatory reservoirs. Such additional losses were ignored in the absence of any information regarding their occurrence or magnitude.

[2] See app. B for details.

[3] This ratio is an understatement by the amount of in-plant recirculation.

Although we make no pretense at distributing economic activity within a water resource region, one geographic location is especially crucial, namely, the point of discharge from the region. At this point the intake of all users must be matched by a flow of at least equal magnitude.[4]

While intake per unit of product may vary widely depending on the internal rate of recirculation, and while aggregate intake for a water resource region can be an indeterminate multiple of basin flow depending on the extent of intrabasin reuse, the same indeterminacy does not apply to rate of loss. With a given state of technology, loss of water per unit of output is reasonably determined, even if not accurately known.[5] Loss per unit of time, then, depends on the rate of output. It is likely that changes in recirculation rates as well as other technical changes, e.g., the method of applying irrigation water, will affect loss rates, but to the best of our knowledge these rates are reasonably stable. By postulating loss rates on the basis of known physical relationships, as in the case of water loss per kilowatt-hour produced at specified temperatures and pressures, or on the basis of known biological restrictions dependent on temperature, humidity, and type of crop, we can project loss coefficients at various assumed states of technical efficiency. How far wide of the mark our assumed states of efficiency may turn out to be is, of course, another question.

We have handled onsite losses of water (attributable to soil and moisture conservation and expansion of swamp and wetland habitat) differently from withdrawal losses. Whereas the latter are computed as aggregates measured by total production, onsite losses are computed on the basis of *changes* from the present (about 1964). It is assumed that soil and moisture conservation practices that were adopted previous to 1964 are reflected in the runoff record. If water losses incurred through such practices were treated as losses in this study, we would commit an error of double counting. The same applies to water lost through existing swamps and wetlands.

The water required for onsite uses is estimated only on a loss basis, although in the original work done by the Soil Conservation Service[6] gross and net requirements were distinguished. (Some of the water initially intercepted by onsite practices will reappear as downstream flow and should not be counted as loss to the region. A comparable phenomenon is observed in irrigation; part of the water initially diverted from its natural channel and delivered to farms reappears as surface or groundwater drainage.)

By evaporation and transpiration, agriculture and onsite uses lose a relatively large fraction of gross requirements, in contrast to the fairly small ratio of losses to withdrawals for mining, manufacturing, and steam-power production. Measurements of water use for mining are sometimes complicated by the interception of underground streams that must be pumped out of the mines, and it is not certain that anomalies of this nature have been accurately handled. Fortunately, the quantities of water are quite small.

We have made no distinction between water withdrawn from the ground and water taken from a surface source. Both were assumed to be a charge against measured surface flow. For the purpose of computing losses, however, we distinguished between withdrawals made "upstream" and those made "downstream." Loss for upstream users was computed as the difference between intake and discharge; loss for downstream users was considered to be equal to intake. This distinction was based on the assumption that water discharged at points near the coast or on estuaries mingled with salt or brackish water and therefore lost its quality of freshness. "Downstream" is defined as those counties within a region that contain maritime coasts, whether estuarine or directly on the ocean. The distinction between upstream and downstream points of use is especially critical when a major downstream metropolitan area taps a water supply that is a substantial distance upstream. The reach of river below the point of intake suffers a loss of flow equal to the intake, in spite of the fact that a relatively large fraction is discharged after use.

Agriculture

Water inputs per acre irrigated — gross and net — were taken from USDA estimates prepared for the Select Committee. After studying the information on delivery efficiency that has appeared since 1960, it was decided that no changes should be made. The USDA estimated a gross (or "diversion") requirement and a net (or "irrigation") requirement per acre, based on an average vegetative requirement for each region's crop mix and assumed rates of efficiency in delivery to the farm and on-farm delivery to the plant. Efficiencies were assumed to rise between now and 2000. We assumed they would remain at the same level for 2000 and 2020.

Net requirements are dependent on the efficiency with which water is delivered to the crop and on the recovery of water that seeps into the ground en route to the plant. The USDA estimated that in the East (Upper and Lower Mississippi, Lower Missouri, Lower Arkansas-White-Red regions, and all other drainage basins to the east) 20 percent of the difference between the plant requirement and the diversion requirement would be recovered. In the West, 55 percent was recovered; in the Pacific Northwest, 60 percent. (Delivery efficiencies were estimated to be much lower in the West.) Water lost by irrigation was therefore equal to: percentage not recovered X (diversion requirement − plant requirement) + plant requirement.

Between 1954 and 2000, efficiency in the use of water, measured by reduction in loss per acre irrigated, was projected to rise by about 30 to 35 percent for western regions and by a somewhat smaller amount for eastern regions. In

---

[4]Except for the minimum flow program for the Delaware and Hudson region (4 mg/l), required waste dilution flows are greater than coastal intake requirements for all regions and all projections. Accordingly, we assume that if waste dilution requirements are met there is no need for additional flow to satisfy intake requirements at any point.

[5]The effect of different rates of in-plant recirculation on loss rates per unit of output is not well known, but the variations are presumed to be relatively small.

[6]See U.S. Senate, Select Committee on National Water Resources, Committee Print No. 13, *Estimated Water Requirements for Agricultural Purposes and Their Effects on Water Supplies*, 86th Cong., 2d sess. (1960).

western regions the net input of water per acre remains high – projected at four to five feet per acre for the Southwest and two to two and one-half feet per acre for the Northwest. In the Southwest, the contribution to plant growth by natural precipitation is negligible, except in high mountain valleys. Table 11 shows gross and net rates of water use per acre.

Other losses accounted for by agriculture are water for livestock and rural household use. Water use for livestock was estimated by applying an index of livestock population directly to total water use by livestock as estimated for 1960. We assumed that net requirements for livestock were equal to gross, and that net requirements for rural household use equalled 20 percent of gross. Gross use by rural households was assumed to rise from 50 gallons per capita per day to 60 gpcd to reflect the assumption that by 1980 all rural households will having running water and the usual appliances.

Mining

Water coefficients for mining were computed from estimates made by the Bureau of Mines for 1962 and were extended into the future by equations relating total water use (including recirculated water), water intake, and water loss.

Unit requirements for both withdrawals and losses are expected to rise in the production of coal, copper, and iron, among the metals; and for sand and gravel, of the non-metals. Other unit requirements are assumed to remain unchanged. (See tables 12 and 13.)

The ratio of loss to intake varies substantially among types of mineral. For sand and gravel it is about 5 percent. For crude petroleum it is about 90 percent. The high loss rate for the latter reflects the contamination of water by brines and other substances in the drilling process. "Mining" requirements are distributed between actual extraction and those forms of processing that do not fall under the heading of "manufacturing."

Manufacturing

Unit water coefficients based on intake, loss, and proportion used for cooling were estimated per dollar of value added for the five major water-using manufacturing classes – food and kindred products, paper and allied products, chemicals and allied products, petroleum and coal products, and primary metals. For the other manufacturing classes, water use was estimated by directly extrapolating total intake and loss for each of five classes – textile mill products; lumber and wood products; rubber and plastics products; leather and leather products; and stone, clay, and glass products – and the aggregate of the remaining classes. All together, these accounted for 97 percent of industrial water use, the rest being accounted for by plants that withdrew less than 20 million gallons per year. Small water users probably procured their water mostly from municipal systems and presumably are included in our estimates of municipal water use.

Unit coefficients were computed to exclude brackish or saltwater intake and to account for an expected increase in the rate of recirculation. Industry-wide coefficients of in-

take and loss per dollar of value added for 1954, 1959, and 1964 are given in table 14. Because figures for 1964 were not available at the time we made our projections, our base was 1960, as estimated from the *U.S. Census of Manufactures: 1958*.[7] The rise in intake or loss coefficients for chemicals, primary metals, and paper products is not fully understood and may reflect errors of measurement or reporting. For the five major water-using industries, separate coefficients were estimated for each region, based on census data.

Unit loss coefficients were adjusted upward to incorporate instream evaporation losses resulting from the discharge of heated effluent. It was assumed that unit loss rates would remain unchanged over the projection period, regardless of projected decreases in intake per dollar of value added resulting from higher recirculation rates. It was assumed that intake coefficients for chemicals, petroleum, and primary metals would decline by 10 percent per decade; for food and paper the estimated decline was 5 percent per decade, since cooling water for these industries is less important. These are, of course, arbitrary changes in values, but they do not lead to unduly high average rates of recirculation by 2020 compared with the experience of plants that now recirculate.

The water use of other manufacturing sectors was computed by extrapolating for each region the quantities of intake and loss reported in the 1958 *Census of Manufactures*. For the five industries projected separately (textiles; lumber and wood; rubber and plastics; leather; and stone, clay, and glass) the extrapolation was by the projected index of output for the country as a whole. The category of "all other manufacturing" was projected by using the index of GNP. Withdrawal coefficients were reduced by 10 percent per decade for lumber and wood; rubber and plastics; stone, clay, and glass; and all other. Textiles and leather were reduced 5 percent per year. Loss coefficients were assumed to remain unchanged. No attempt was made to adjust for variable rates of growth among regions.

Two reductions in withdrawals and losses were made to avoid overcounting: (1) to account for industrial supply acquired from municipal systems, and (2) to account for intake of brackish water in coastal and estuarine regions.

Study of intake and loss coefficients reveals a wide variation among regions – an eight to one spread between the highest and the lowest can be found in a number of industries, even higher for primary metals. The variation might be attributable to product mix, technology, or error of measurement. An error in the loss coefficient probably does not significantly affect our results, since manufacturing losses constitute a rather small component of water requirements, but, since Reid's estimates of waste loading were computed as a function of waste discharge, an error in measurement could be serious via its effect on dilution requirements. However, even the changes in total water requirements that reflect fairly large hypothetical changes in the output of waste load per unit of product are rather small.

---

[7]U.S. Bureau of the Census, *U.S. Census of Manufactures: 1958*, "Industrial Water Use," Subject Report MC 58(1)-11 (1961).

While proof is meager, it is hard to overcome the feeling that a large share of interregional variation in loss (or intake) per unit of output is caused by inexact measurement, especially since a small swing in opposite directions of intake of water and output of product produces a fairly large change in unit coefficients.[8]

For most measurements of water use and supply, a region was considered to be a point in space to which all flow and all use were assigned. A deviation from this approach consisted of the distinction between "upstream" and "downstream" manufacturers. It was argued that if streamflow at the discharge end of the basin was less than the sum of intake requirements at that point, flow was deficient by the difference, since intrabasin reuse is impossible once the discharged water mingles with brackish or salt water. A side computation was made of aggregate manufacturing and municipal freshwater coastal (i.e., "downstream") intake and compared with required flow minus upstream losses. Except for minimum flow programs in the Delaware and Hudson regions, waste dilution flows exceeded coastal withdrawals in all regions for all projections.

It should be noted that increased stringency in downstream freshwater flows could be partially met by increasing the rate of recirculation and increasing the use of brackish or ocean water.[9] At present the recirculation of municipal water for domestic use is considered distasteful, but the use of treated municipal waste effluent for industrial purposes already takes place.

Steam-Electric Power

Steam-electric power is expected to be the largest future single user of fresh water, measured by withdrawals, although at present it is second to irrigation. Intake of fresh water per kilowatt-hour is determined by thermal efficiency, the rate of recirculation, and the degree to which brackish or ocean water is substituted for fresh water. As thermal efficiency rises, gross use (flow-through of water, including that which is recirculated) declines, hence intake for any given degree of recirculation declines.

In making our projections we assumed that thermal efficiency would rise between now and the year 2000 and remain unchanged for 2020. (This may be unduly optimistic since the thermal efficiency of nuclear plants is fairly low.) For 1980 and thereafter, fresh water as a percentage of total intake was projected to fall by 10 percent in the New England, Lower Mississippi, Western Gulf, South Pacific, and Central Pacific regions; and by about 24 percent in the Delaware and Hudson, Chesapeake Bay, and Southeast regions.

The rate of recirculation is defined as the ratio of gross water applied per kwh produced, including the water supplied by recirculation, to intake of new water per kwh. The reciprocal of the recirculation rate is the percentage of gross water applied that is procured by the intake of new water. The lower limit of this percentage is assumed to be 1.4 percent; hence the maximum recirculation rate is 70. In the

eastern half of the country (Northeast and Southeast), recirculation is comparatively low and has been increasing comparatively slowly. A single rate was used for all eastern regions, and it was projected to rise from a little over 1 at present to 1.3 by 2020, based on the recent trend. In the western half of the country (Mid-continent, Southwest, and North Pacific divisions), current rates are higher and have also been rising at varying speeds. Separate rates were estimated for each region.

The discharge of warm water into the streams of the thirteen eastern regions implied by the recirculation rates referred to above required large amounts of dilution water to prevent an undue increase in stream temperature. In order to reduce the dilution requirement to a level consistent with other pollutants, an alternative set of recirculation rates was computed. In one region, Eastern Great Lakes, the upper limit of 70 had to be postulated in order to eliminate thermal pollution. This approximates a closed system in which there is no discharge of heated water. It appears likely, therefore, that the future will bring an acceleration in the rate at which higher rates of recirculation will be introduced. (Table 15 is based on the higher rates of recirculation.)

While there is considerable uncertainty regarding intake per kwh, loss to the atmosphere and blowdown to eliminate impurities are assumed to vary over a narrow range. For 1960 the figure was taken as 0.7 gallon per kwh and for 1980, 2000, and 2020 it was assumed to be 0.5 gallon per kwh.[10] This coefficient was assumed to include instream loss as well as in-plant loss, was applied to inland as well as coastal regions, and was not modified by any assumed change in recirculation.[11]

Municipal

Municipal use of water satisfies domestic, commercial, manufacturing, and public needs in varying proportions from community to community and region to region. In the Southwest, domestic use is relatively high because of irrigated lawns and gardens. The ratio of loss to intake depends mainly on climate and whether discharge is into estuarine or coastal water. Per capita use is also a function of price charged[12] and average income.

Withdrawals per capita were projected to grow between 1960 and 1980 at the average annual rate of growth that was reported for the period 1959-63. For the period 1980-2000 this rate of growth was reduced by one-half, and for the period 2000-2020, by two-thirds.

[10] Estimates for future intake and loss were based largely on Paul H. Cootner and George O. G. Löf, *Water Demand for Steam Electric Generation: An Economic Projection Model* (The Johns Hopkins Press for Resources for the Future, 1965).

[11] No special account was taken of downstream freshwater intake by power plants, since use of brackish or ocean water can readily be increased for cooling purposes, and intake of boiler feed is roughly equal to loss and is therefore automatically computed as part of required flow at downstream points.

[12] Charles W. Howe and F. P. Linaweaver, Jr., "The Impact of Price on Residential Water Demand and Its Relation to System Design and Price Structure," *Water Resources Research*, vol. 3, no. 1 (First Quarter 1967), pp. 13-32.

[8] See app. B for evidence supplied by Blair Bower.

[9] Primarily for cooling.

Information available on municipal use reveals certain contrary tendencies. Per capita use apparently rises with income but falls with increased density of population (e.g., more apartment dwellers), but per capita industrial use tends to rise as more manufacturing firms shift from self-supply to municipal supply. There is some evidence that per capita use might rise more slowly than has been projected or might even stabilize at a level near the present.

Estimated municipal withdrawals in 1960 averaged 161 gallons per capita per day for the United States (see table 16). The range, by regions, extended from 133 gpcd in the Southeast to 266 in the Great Basin. By 1980 the U.S. average was projected to rise to 217 gpcd; by 2000, to 252; and by 2020, to 279. Although the highest rates of growth were projected for the southeastern regions, all of which reach projected levels of 315 gpcd or more by 2020, the Great Basin remains at the top of the scale with 465 gpcd by that date.

Losses in the form of evaporation and transpiration are difficult to measure. Because of leakage from lines under pressure, infiltration into sewer lines, and mingling of storm and sanitary sewers, the difference between pumpage by the water treatment plant and liquid received by the sewage treatment plant is an inexact measure by loss. Reported losses from various cities reveal unexplained variations. In San Antonio, reported loss is 6 percent; in Amarillo, 59 percent; in Provo, 15 percent; and in Portland, Oregon, 33 percent. Some measurements of domestic use have been made on an accurate basis by Linaweaver.[13] Comparable data on losses for industrial, commercial, and public uses are not available.

After taking into account the scattered bits of information on the relative importance of different uses and assumed rates of loss by type of use, the following rates of loss as a percentage of municipal intake were adopted:

13 eastern regions	— 25 percent
8 western regions	— 40 percent
Western Gulf region	— 35 percent

The loss rate in each region was further adjusted to account for discharge into estuaries or the ocean by adding to the loss rates given above a proportion of municipal intake equal to the proportion of a region's urban population projected for coastal standard metropolitan areas. Final rates of loss as a percentage of intake range between 97 percent for the South Pacific region and 25 percent for a number of inland eastern regions.

Per capita rates of loss were estimated at 85 gallons per day in 1960 for the United States as a whole, and were projected to rise to 118 gallons in 1980, to 138 gallons in 2000, and 154 gallons in 2020 (table 17). Loss rates were highest in the coastal regions, and the highest of these were in the South Pacific and Pacific Northwest regions. Loss as a percentage of intake remained unchanged for the entire projection period.

Should there be a change in the relative importance of domestic, commercial, industrial, and public uses; or in the loss rate of each type of use; or in the practice of discharging municipal water into coastal or estuarine bodies after a single use, our loss coefficients would be in error, apart from possible error in the projected rates of intake. A possible adaptation to water shortage, in addition to restricted use induced by higher prices for water, would be internal recirculation of municipal water. This practice would serve as a water-saving device only for coastal areas, since inland municipal discharge is presumed to be reused at downstream points. The effect of municipal recirculation is discussed later.

Onsite and Flow Uses

Projections of onsite and flow uses were not made on the basis of unit coefficients of water use. Instead, aggregates of gross and net use were projected directly on the basis of current usage. The results are discussed in the following chapter.

[13] See app. B.

Table 11. GROSS AND NET USE OF WATER PER ACRE FOR AGRICULTURE

(acre-feet per acre)

	1960		1980		2000		2020	
	Withdrawal	Loss	Withdrawal	Loss	Withdrawal	Loss	Withdrawal	Loss
N Eng	0.8	0.8	0.8	0.7	0.8	0.7	0.8	0.7
D & H	1.1	1.0	1.0	0.9	0.9	0.8	0.9	0.8
Ches	1.4	1.3	1.3	1.2	1.2	1.1	1.2	1.1
Ohio	1.4	1.3	1.3	1.2	1.2	1.1	1.2	1.1
EGL	1.1	1.0	1.0	0.9	0.9	0.8	0.9	0.8
WGL	1.4	1.3	1.3	1.2	1.2	1.1	1.2	1.1
U Miss	1.7	1.5	1.5	1.4	1.4	1.3	1.4	1.3
L Mo	1.7	1.5	1.5	1.4	1.4	1.3	1.4	1.3
SE	1.8	1.7	1.7	1.6	1.6	1.5	1.6	1.5
Cumb	1.1	1.0	1.0	0.9	0.9	0.8	0.9	0.8
Tenn	1.2	1.2	1.2	1.1	1.1	1.0	1.1	1.0
L Miss	1.9	1.8	1.8	1.6	1.7	1.6	1.7	1.6
L AWR	1.8	1.7	1.6	1.5	1.5	1.4	1.5	1.4
U Mo	3.2	2.0	2.5	1.8	2.1	1.5	2.1	1.5
U AWR	3.2	2.2	2.5	1.8	2.2	1.7	2.2	1.7
W Gulf	2.7	1.8	2.1	1.5	1.8	1.4	1.8	1.4
RG-P	6.4	3.9	4.8	3.2	3.8	2.8	3.8	2.8
Colo	7.2	4.7	5.5	3.9	4.8	3.6	4.8	3.6
G Basin	4.8	3.2	3.8	2.7	3.2	2.2	3.2	2.2
S Pac	5.5	3.8	4.3	3.2	3.8	3.0	3.8	3.0
C Pac	5.4	3.7	4.7	3.3	4.0	3.0	4.0	3.0
PNW	5.1	2.9	3.8	2.3	3.2	2.2	3.2	2.2

Table 12. MINING WITHDRAWAL COEFFICIENTS

	1960	1980	2000	2020
	(gallons per ton)			
Coal, metals, nonmetals				
Intercept coefficient	18	18	18	18
Slope coefficient				
Coal (bituminous)	76	86	100	114
Copper	554	566	566	566
Iron ore	717	811	845	845
Phosphate rock	2,166	2,166	2,166	2,166
Sand & gravel	331	353	377	377
Other	132	132	132	132
	(billion gallons per 1,000 barrels)			
Crude petroleum	41.4	41.4	41.4	41.4
	(gallons per barrel)			
Natural gas liquids	280	280	280	280

Table 13. MINING LOSS COEFFICIENTS

	1960	1980	2000	2020
	(gallons per ton)			
Coal, metals, nonmetals				
Intercept coefficient	6	6	6	6
Slope coefficient				
Coal (bituminous)	35	39	44	51
Copper	61	63	63	63
Iron ore	79	98	102	102
Phosphate rock	494	494	494	494
Sand & gravel	17	18	19	19
Other	24	24	24	24
	(billion gallons per 1,000 barrels)			
Crude petroleum	37.6	37.6	37.6	37.6
	(gallons per barrel)			
Natural gas liquids	60	60	60	60

Table 14. MANUFACTURING WATER USE COEFFICIENTS

(gallons per $1 value added)

	Food	Pulp & paper	Chemicals	Petroleum refinery & coal products	Primary metals
			Withdrawals (intake)		
1954	86	626	343	332	439
1959	68	460	214	288	319
1964	68	497	202	232	361
			Losses		
1954	10	63	21	58	19
1959	7	29	18	46	14
1964	7	32	18	26	23

Table 15. STEAM-ELECTRIC POWER, RATES OF WATER USE WITH RECIRCULATION HIGH ENOUGH TO AVOID THERMAL POLLUTION

(gallons per kilowatt-hour)

	Intake		
	1980	2000	2020
N Eng	2	0.7	0.3
D & H	2	1	1
Ches	7	6	6
Ohio	2	2	2
EGL	0.7	0.7	0.7
WGL	4	3	3
U Miss	12	10	9
L Mo	15	13	11
SE[a]	18	15	14
Cumb[a]	40	33	31
Tenn	15	13	11
L Miss	9	8	8
L AWR	41	31	24
U Mo[a]	23	14	12
U AWR[a]	0.7	0.6	0.6
W Gulf[a]	4	2	2
RG-P[a]	0.7	0.6	0.6
Colo[a]	0.9	0.8	0.8
G Basin[a]	0.9	0.8	0.8
S Pac[a]	0.2	0.2	0.2
C Pac[a]	0.2	0.2	0.2
PNW	21[a]	16[a]	13

Note: Loss for all regions, 1980, 2000, and 2020 is 0.5 gallons per kilowatt-hour.

[a]No change from rate originally projected.

Table 16. MUNICIPAL WITHDRAWALS, BY REGION

(gallons per capita per day)

	1960	1980	2000	2020
N Eng	135	175	199	217
D & H	139	181	206	224
Ches	139	181	206	224
Ohio	134	174	198	216
EGL	199	254	289	315
WGL	246	319	363	397
U Miss	171	221	252	275
L Mo	149	193	220	240
SE	133	213	269	315
Cumb	144	229	290	340
Tenn	156	249	315	369
L Miss	137	218	276	323
L AWR	136	216	273	320
U Mo	155	227	276	314
U AWR	135	197	239	272
W Gulf	136	199	241	274
RG-P	147	197	229	253
Colo	159	276	321	355
G Basin	266	362	421	465
S Pac	186	250	290	321
C Pac	145	161	172	178
PNW	238	263	281	291
U.S. Average	161	217	252	279

Table 17. MUNICIPAL LOSSES, BY REGION

(gallons per capita per day)

	1960	1980	2000	2020
N Eng	89	116	132	144
D & H	123	161	183	199
Ches	108	140	160	174
Ohio	34	44	50	54
EGL	50	64	72	79
WGL	62	80	91	99
U Miss	43	55	63	69
L Mo	37	48	55	60
SE	63	101	128	150
Cumb	36	57	72	85
Tenn	39	62	79	92
L Miss	70	112	141	166
L AWR	34	54	68	80
U Mo	62	91	110	126
U AWR	54	79	96	109
W Gulf	74	108	131	149
RG-P	59	79	92	101
Colo	64	110	128	142
G Basin	106	145	168	186
S Pac	180	242	281	311
C Pac	115	127	136	141
PNW	188	208	222	230
U.S.	85	118	138	154

Chapter 7

WITHDRAWALS AND LOSSES:
ALL USES

Withdrawals

Withdrawals are a common measure of water "use." Our projections reveal a sharp change in the relative importance of different withdrawal uses over the next fifty to sixty years (table 18). In 1960 agriculture accounted for slightly more than half of aggregate withdrawals. According to our Medium projection, between 1960 and the year 2020 there will be a decline in absolute withdrawals for agriculture — the only one of the five major categories of use for which a decline is indicated. (At the High rate, agricultural withdrawals grow moderately.)

Mining uses decline in relative importance, although they grow absolutely; manufacturing uses grow slightly in relative importance, as do municipal uses. The largest foreseeable growth, absolute and relative, is for steam-electric power. This growth is a function of the projected output of power coupled with assumed rates of recirculation. The prospective thermal pollution induced by intake and discharge of the magnitudes projected in table 59 presages a likelihood that recirculation rates will rise more rapidly than in the past. At originally projected rates of recirculation,[1] thermal power accounts for almost two-thirds of withdrawal uses by 2020. Furthermore, at the High rate of growth, power requirements would be so great as to require a pass-through at least once of the average annual water crop of the nation — a phenomenally large offstream use of water.

The magnitude of pumping for all withdrawal uses is indicated by the projected rise in aggregate withdrawals from 250 bgd in 1960 to 891 bgd by 2020 Medium and to 1,618 bgd by 2020 High. (Roughly speaking, withdrawals for 2040 Medium would be equal to withdrawals projected for 2020 High.) If recirculation rates for steam-electric power were raised to avoid thermal pollution (see chapter 8), intake requirements would fall by amounts ranging between one-third and one-half of withdrawals originally projected (see table 19). With higher recirculation rates, aggregate intake is almost equal to average annual runoff by 2020 High.

Onsite uses are discussed below, since their measurement was based on water lost by evapotranspiration. In order to give an idea of their magnitude relative to withdrawals, onsite uses have been included in table 19, which shows gross use; tables 20 through 23, which show detail by regions for Medium projections; and table 24, which shows aggregate withdrawals by region for all projections.

The reader will recall that gross use is not a component of the measure of water "requirements." The quantities of discharge of cooling water and discharge of process water by manufacturing are, however, elements used in the computation of thermal pollution and organic waste loadings, respectively. Our estimates of withdrawals can be fairly wide of the mark without introducing serious error in estimates of losses. If recirculation of fresh water or the substitution of brackish for fresh water proceeds more rapidly than has been anticipated, estimates of freshwater withdrawals would be excessive. Neither of these developments would of themselves imply that measures of loss are correspondingly excessive. Whether loss rates rise, fall, or remain unchanged with increased recirculation is not known. And, since brackish water is used mainly for cooling, the main source of error in the measure of loss that would emerge from greater use of brackish water than has been antici-

---

[1] Our "original" recirculation rate created a heat pollution problem and therefore was modified to the "new" recirculation rate. See app. B for a more complete explanation.

pated would be in the form of instream evaporation – an amount that is quite small.

Losses

Losses attributable to withdrawal uses grow at a much slower pace than withdrawals, since losses attributable to steam-electric power are quite low. Agriculture persists over the projection period as the dominant consumer, but the trends indicate that at some time beyond 2020 municipal losses will equal and then overtake agricultural losses. (See tables 25 and 26.) However, since municipal losses grow rapidly, in large part because of the discharge of municipal wastes into coastal waters, a fairly large reduction in municipal loss could be achieved by recirculation of municipal intake. Mining, manufacturing, and steam-electric losses together are no more than 30 bgd by 2020 Medium – or roughly 3 percent of average annual runoff. When agricultural and municipal losses are added, total losses by the year 2020 range between 15 and 25 percent of average annual runoff.

Onsite Uses

Classified as onsite uses are soil conservation programs and swamp and wetlands habitat for wildlife – mainly ducks and geese.

Total losses are only moderately increased when projected onsite losses are added to losses from withdrawal uses. Water consumption by soil conservation practices is estimated to increase by 6.5 bgd by 2020. Increased evapotranspiration projected for swamp and wetland habitat over levels now being incurred rise to 8.6 bgd by 2020 for the High projection. For the Medium projection no changes in losses were assumed to occur. For the Low projection we assumed a reduction in loss below present levels. Prospective onsite increases in evaporation do not, therefore, contribute significantly to foreseeable problems of water shortage, looked at from the national aggregate point of view.

As used here, "onsite" refers to the fact that changes in land use or land structures occurring "onsite" will affect the quantity of stream runoff and thereby constitute a release or absorption of water. Classic examples of changes contributing to erosion and sedimentation are deforestation, overgrazing, construction of new highways, and growth of cities. Changes in ground cover will affect the rate of the overland movement of water, the quantity of water that sinks into the ground, the rate of evaporation and transpiration, and the net effect on streamflow at a measuring point.

The Soil Conservation Service (SCS) is the agency most intimately concerned with restoring ground cover where it has been removed by improper or excessive agricultural practices. It fosters the extension of such practices as terracing; contour farming; planting of cover crops; and construction of stock ponds, check dams, and other anti-erosion structures. SCS engineers estimated for the Senate Select Committee the impact on stream runoff by distinguishing between "onsite" (a slightly different meaning from the one we have used) and "downstream" requirements. By "onsite," the SCS meant the "gross" use of

water by various practices and structures, including the amount infiltrated into the soil; and by "downstream," the net reduction in downstream flow reflecting the added evaporation, transpiration, and irrecoverable soil moisture induced by SCS practices.

Since SCS practices over past years are incorporated in the historical record of stream runoff, we have counted as a "use" only the estimated future losses of projected extensions of SCS programs. Our estimates of charges against stream runoff are biased downward, since streamflow *averages* may not adequately reflect losses induced by expansion of the program during the last decade or so. We conceive of the "present" as 1960, but have made no adjustment in average streamflows attributable to measures adopted in the years immediately preceding 1960.

On the basis of estimated net use per unit of land treated and evaporation from the surface of farm ponds, the SCS estimated the *increase* in future losses as a function of the percentage of needed land treatment installed.[2] The final estimates of water use, measured as evaporation-transpiration losses, are in table 27. By the year 2020, projected increases amount to less than 1 percent of fully regulated runoff. Variations among regions, however, are substantial. In the Upper Missouri region projected losses amount to 7 percent of fully regulated flow; in the Central Pacific region, 0.2 percent.

Swamps and Wetlands

In comparison with estimates of water requirements for wetland habitat in the United States made originally for the Senate Select Committee on National Water Resources,[3] the estimates in this study constitute a major change. In Committee Prints No. 18 and No. 32, water use (evapotranspiration) was projected to increase in proportion to the estimated growth in man-days of hunting (mainly for ducks and geese), adjusted for a reduction in bag limit. The net effect of prospective changes was a growth in wetland acreage by 1980 of 75 percent over 1954 and a doubling of 1954 acreage by 2000. The prospective use of water increased proportionately; the effects of growth were distributed among regions in accordance with the present acreage of wetlands and the relative importance of flyways.

On reexamining these estimates, it appeared that by the year 2000 a larger aggregate area of wetlands was projected than existed in the United States prior to any drainage and conversion to agricultural or urban use. It also appeared that the projection for 1980 implied a reconversion to swamps and wetlands of all land that had been drained for agricultural use in the past 200 years. By 2000, 20 percent of the total land area of the Southeast would have been used for wetlands; in the Western Great Lakes region, about 10 percent.

[2] See U.S. Senate, Select Committee on National Water Resources, Committee Print No. 13, *Estimated Water Requirements for Agricultural Purposes and Their Effects on Water Supplies*, 86th Cong., 2d sess. (1960). See also app. D for a discussion of estimates.

[3] Committee Print No. 32 and Committee Print No. 18, *Fish and Wildlife and Water Resources*, Senate Select Committee on National Water Resources, 86th Cong., 2d sess. (1960).

In view of the apparently exaggerated impact of these estimates, we adopted a much lower projected increase in swamps and wetlands. On the basis of information presented in appendix B, it was assumed that for the Medium rate of growth there would be no change in habitat – the projected gross increases, largely in public lands, being offset by the drainage of other lands for agricultural and urban uses. For the High rate of growth, increases over 1960 of 5 percent, 8 percent, and 10 percent were adopted for 1980, 2000, and 2020, respectively. For the Low rate of growth, *decreases* of the same percentages were adopted. These assumptions meant that wetland acreage in the country as a whole would increase over 1960 for the High projections for 1980, 2000, and 2020 by 3.7 million acres, 6 million acres, and 7.5 million acres, respectively.

Water losses charged against stream runoff for swamps and wetlands were measured in the same fashion as for land treatment and structures, namely, only the increase over 1960 counted (see table 28). Compared with Committee Print No. 32, the effect of the changed assumptions is substantial. Instead of a charge against runoff of 90 bgd for the country as a whole, the revised 2000 Medium projection is zero. The Upper Missouri region, which originally suffered losses of 18 bgd for swamps and wetlands by 2000 Medium, now is estimated to lose no more than 2 bgd by 2020 High, and none by 2020 Medium. Roughly speaking, projected losses for 2020 High amount to 10 percent of the losses originally estimated for 2000 Medium.

Regional Variation in Total Losses

Information on total losses by region and water use is given in tables 29 through 33. It is seen that our projections presage a relatively uneven draft on water supplies among regions, measured by the ratio of losses to fully regulated flow. The immediate implication of any situation in which projected losses exceed maximum regulated flow is that the projected bill of goods cannot be produced unless additional water is imported. (Alternative adjustments include: (1) change in the national bill of goods, keeping aggregate value constant; (2) displacement of activity from water-short to water-surplus regions, keeping unchanged the composition of the national bill of goods; and (3) changes in technology leading to reduced evapotranspiration per unit of output.)

In 1960 losses constituted a negligible fraction of average flow in the eastern regions of the country, in the aggregate, and region by region. In the Mid-continent regions, 1960 losses were equal to somewhat less than half of average regulated flow. When losses for 1960 were computed on the basis of water applications per unit as projected to 1980 and afterwards, they exceeded average flow in the Southwest. Within the Southwest, the Great Basin region had flow to spare, but the Rio Grande-Pecos, Colorado, and South Pacific regions ran a deficit.

The deficit was both real and fictional. It was real to the extent that there has been an overdraft of groundwater in various parts of the Southwest, e.g., the Salt River Valley of Arizona and the Roswell artesian basin of New Mexico. It was fictional to the degree that actual water applications

fell short of those specified in the models, mainly in agriculture,[4] but in amounts that cannot be determined with the knowledge at hand. The shortage in the South Pacific region has been very real and has been met by importations from the Colorado basin. Since our figures reflect neither exports nor imports, the losses in table 29 understate the losses of the Colorado basin by the amount of exports.[5] There are diversions from the upper Colorado basin into the Upper Missouri and Upper Arkansas-White-Red regions, and one is under construction into the Rio Grande-Pecos region.

By 1980 High, projected losses in the Upper Arkansas-White-Red region exceed maximum controlled flow and, of course, the disparity between losses and maximum flows widens for the Southwest. If growth follows the Medium path, the Upper Arkansas-White-Red region has a margin of supply up to 2020 – by which time losses and flows are equal. After reduction of projected losses for swamps and wetlands below the estimates made for the Select Committee, the Upper Missouri region no longer loses more water by evapotranspiration than is available. In Committee Print No. 32,[6] losses for the Upper Missouri region for the 1980 Medium projection were 29.2 bgd, including 13.1 bgd for swamps and wetlands; revised projected losses are 13.9 bgd. At no time through the 2020 High projection are revised losses as high as originally projected. The Upper Missouri region does not become a water-deficit area until quality flow requirements are taken into account (see chapter 10).

By 2020 the projected imbalance in the Southwest between losses and maximum regulated flows has become quite severe, implying: (1) a lower level of activity than projected; (2) a substantial change in product mix; (3) a substantial change in water-related technology for the projected output; or (4) a substantial augmentation of supply by importation, desalination, or from some source not now anticipated, such as weather modification. (Water quality is presumably protected by 100 percent treatment – else its dissolved oxygen content is below one part per million.)

One might assume, also, that regions for which projected losses are a significant fraction of maximum flow will suffer localized disparities of varying intensity, implying a growing program of intraregional redistribution of activity or water supply, or both. Since we have very little intraregional data, we shall be silent about this.

Under the High projection, losses for the western half of the country are 154 bgd by 2020. Fully regulated flow is 256 bgd. Whether these figures imply that the "West" as a

---

[4] Water shortages lead to a reduced allotment to irrigators. This reduction is met by reduction of acreage, by reduced applications of water per acre, by reductions in delivery losses and wastage, or by some combination of all three.

[5] In recent years California has been using 5.1 million acre-feet of Colorado River basin water, equal to 4.6 bgd. See letter of Harry W. Horton, Special Counsel, Imperial Irrigation District, *Central Arizona Project*, Part I, Hearings before the Senate Subcommittee on Irrigation and Reclamation, 88th Cong., 1st sess. (1963), pp. 719–21.

[6] P. 101.

whole has enough water to meet projected requirements cannot be ascertained until the level of water quality is taken into account (see chapters 9 and 10).

Since the largest disparity within the Southwest is for the South Pacific region, substantial alleviation of a prospective shortage may be promised by increased desalination of ocean water. Augmentation by importation from the Central Pacific region is apparently limited: by 2020, under the High projection, the Central Pacific region will *lose* 80 percent of fully regulated runoff as a consequence of internal use.

Further discussion of the projected supply-demand balance is reserved for later, after quality flows have been considered.

Table 18. U.S. WITHDRAWALS FOR WITHDRAWAL USES, ORIGINAL RECIRCULATION RATE

(million gallons per day)

		Agriculture	Mining	Manufacturing	Steam-electric	Municipal	Total withdrawal uses
1960		138,586	2,739	22,926	65,988	20,074	250,315
	L	129,713	5,017	31,452	131,396	37,028	334,606
1980	M	134,883	6,982	41,193	179,469	39,394	401,918
	H	142,911	9,770	54,300	258,054	42,936	508,571
	L	117,525	7,604	38,448	173,686	53,815	391,078
2000	M	125,585	14,230	63,998	289,203	63,957	556,971
	H	140,605	26,810	111,148	491,226	76,888	847,677
	L	121,787	12,051	55,976	302,287	81,225	573,326
2020	M	131,662	36,546	98,059	528,949	95,289	890,504
	H	153,395	81,764	211,426	1,044,886	126,081	1,617,552

Table 19. GROSS USE (WITHDRAWAL AND ONSITE USES), ORIGINAL AND REVISED RECIRCULATION RATES

(billion gallons per day)

		Steam-electric		All withdrawal uses		Withdrawal plus onsite uses	
		Original	Revised	Original	Revised	Original	Revised
1960		66	66	250	250	250	250
	L	131	30	335	234	333	232
1980	M	179	41	402	264	405	267
	H	259	59	509	309	516	316
	L	174	41	391	258	390	257
2000	M	289	70	557	338	563	344
	H	491	118	848	451	860	487
	L	302	73	573	344	571	342
2020	M	529	128	891	490	897	496
	H	1,045	253	1,618	826	1,633	841

Table 20. TOTAL WITHDRAWALS AND ONSITE GROSS USES, BY MAJOR USE AND REGION: 1960

(million gallons per day)

	Agriculture	Mining	Manufacturing	Steam-electric	Municipal	Swamps & wetlands	Land treatment	Total
NORTHEAST	2,498	1,207	16,986	48,148	12,401			81,241
N Eng	149	12	948	592	1,069	0	0	2,771
D & H	316	94	2,035	3,970	2,931	0	0	9,346
Ches	282	78	931	3,482	921	0	0	5,693
Ohio	536	372	5,454	17,605	1,396	0	0	25,364
EGL	195	183	3,221	6,488	2,004	0	0	12,090
WGL	258	139	3,315	9,362	2,646	0	0	15,720
U Miss	615	316	981	5,786	1,241	0	0	8,940
L Mo	147	13	101	863	193	0	0	1,317
SOUTHEAST	4,169	467	3,311	14,632	2,345			24,926
SE	1,501	124	1,618	7,688	1,481	0	0	12,412
Cumb	50	5	16	34	78	0	0	183
Tenn	149	48	717	4,258	179	0	0	5,350
L Miss	1,167	190	670	1,266	339	0	0	3,634
L AWR	1,302	100	290	1,386	268	0	0	3,347
MID-CONTINENT	38,561	470	1,098	2,830	1,685			44,642
U Mo	18,382	102	196	1,096	520	0	0	20,295
U AWR	7,376	100	193	452	295	0	0	8,416
W Gulf	12,803	268	709	1,282	870	0	0	15,931
SOUTHWEST	40,146	336	245	366	2,078			43,173
RG-P	7,637	61	40	175	148	0	0	8,062
Colo	19,921	129	31	96	200	0	0	20,378
G Basin	8,307	82	11	71	171	0	0	8,642
S Pac	4,281	64	163	24	1,559	0	0	6,091
NORTH PACIFIC	53,210	259	1,286	13	1,565			56,333
C Pac	30,912	150	220	13	750	0	0	32,046
PNW	22,298	109	1,066	0	815	0	0	24,287
U.S.	138,584	2,739	22,926	65,988	20,074			250,315

Table 21. TOTAL WITHDRAWALS AND ONSITE GROSS USES, BY MAJOR USE AND REGION: 1980 MEDIUM

(million gallons per day)

	Agriculture	Mining	Manufacturing	Steam-electric	Municipal	Swamps & wetlands	Land treatment	Total
NORTHEAST	3,606	3,383	26,855	142,716	21,463		1,145	199,168
N Eng	203	37	1,396	1,951	1,791	0	418	5,796
D & H	451	245	2,858	6,510	4,874	0	-102	14,836
Ches	422	213	2,075	7,836	1,773	0	113	12,432
Ohio	727	926	7,999	56,285	2,291	0	222	68,450
EGL	269	638	5,472	18,148	3,578	0	106	28,211
WGL	365	372	5,470	30,137	4,708	0	52	41,104
U Miss	915	916	1,324	18,534	2,129	0	204	24,022
L Mo	254	36	261	3,315	319	0	132	4,317
SOUTHEAST	6,222	1,063	7,095	29,488	6,254		792	50,914
SE	1,902	334	3,427	11,934	4,306	0	321	22,224
Cumb	59	11	737	110	175	0	54	1,146
Tenn	216	122	1,048	10,411	451	0	81	12,329
L Miss	2,059	421	1,378	3,041	778	0	121	7,798
L AWR	1,986	175	505	3,992	544	0	215	7,417
MID-CONTINENT	37,482	1,123	1,862	5,058	3,452		909	49,886
U Mo	17,512	303	245	3,529	1,106	0	590	23,285
U AWR	7,761	198	316	82	523	0	166	9,046
W Gulf	12,209	622	1,301	1,447	1,823	0	153	17,555
SOUTHWEST	34,866	764	592	192	5,620		141	42,175
RG-P	6,784	131	48	31	365	0	87	7,446
Colo	16,506	254	48	74	739	0	46	17,667
G Basin	7,289	150	211	39	325	0	5	8,019
S Pac	4,287	229	285	48	4,191	0	3	9,043
NORTH PACIFIC	52,707	649	4,789	2,015	2,602		153	62,915
C Pac	32,224	483	361	59	1,294	0	69	34,490
PNW	20,483	166	4,428	1,956	1,308	0	84	28,425
U.S.	134,883	6,982	41,193	179,469	39,394		3,140	405,058

Table 22. TOTAL WITHDRAWALS AND ONSITE GROSS USES, BY MAJOR USE AND REGION: 2000 MEDIUM

(million gallons per day)

	Agriculture	Mining	Manufacturing	Steam-electric	Municipal	Swamps & wetlands	Land treatment	Total
NORTHEAST	4,264	7,701	38,345	225,219	32,717		1,391	309,639
N Eng	240	90	2,139	3,395	2,646	0	462	8,971
D & H	491	515	4,079	10,411	7,199	0	-210	22,486
Ches	496	509	3,128	12,312	2,879	0	40	19,364
Ohio	852	1,908	10,363	87,830	3,331	0	352	104,636
EGL	310	1,828	8,226	30,986	5,687	0	-21	47,017
WGL	418	814	7,984	46,290	7,375	0	105	62,987
U Miss	1,134	1,964	1,809	28,932	3,207	0	464	37,509
L Mo	323	73	617	5,063	393	0	199	6,669
SOUTHEAST	7,235	1,905	12,615	49,433	11,626		1,766	84,580
SE	2,124	793	5,888	19,479	8,253	0	635	37,172
Cumb	64	19	1,375	452	305	0	86	2,301
Tenn	247	268	1,687	18,444	807	0	213	21,667
L Miss	2,530	581	2,859	4,603	1,443	0	255	12,271
L AWR	2,270	244	806	6,455	818	0	577	11,169
MID-CONTINENT	33,849	1,572	3,878	6,163	5,692		2,183	53,340
U Mo	15,879	366	906	4,641	1,873	0	1,417	25,083
U AWR	7,108	224	619	136	727	0	285	9,100
W Gulf	10,862	982	2,353	1,386	3,092	0	481	19,157
SOUTHWEST	31,140	1,289	1,309	370	9,970		218	44,296
RG-P	5,639	209	183	48	639	0	121	6,838
Colo	14,901	233	223	160	1,343	0	83	16,943
G Basin	6,412	163	376	70	464	0	11	7,495
S Pac	4,188	684	527	92	7,524	0	3	13,018
NORTH PACIFIC	49,097	1,763	7,851	8,018	3,950		245	70,924
C Pac	30,264	1,496	696	128	1,941	0	87	34,612
PNW	18,833	267	7,155	7,890	2,009	0	158	36,313
U.S.	125,585	14,230	63,998	289,203	63,957		5,803	562,774

Table 23. TOTAL WITHDRAWALS AND ONSITE GROSS USES, BY MAJOR USE AND REGION: 2020 MEDIUM

(million gallons per day)

	Agriculture	Mining	Manufacturing	Steam-electric	Municipal	Swamps & wetlands	Land treatment	Total
NORTHEAST	5,305	21,031	53,867	404,668	47,045		1,441	533,354
N Eng	297	253	3,366	5,655	3,751	0	481	13,803
D & H	567	1,303	5,759	17,877	10,152	0	-295	35,363
Ches	602	1,418	4,583	21,447	4,275	0	-2	32,323
Ohio	1,054	4,996	13,448	154,751	4,554	0	405	179,206
EGL	375	5,717	11,698	57,995	8,431	0	-87	84,128
WGL	503	2,100	11,234	84,345	10,866	0	130	109,179
U Miss	1,468	5,056	2,527	53,162	4,506	0	584	67,302
L Mo	439	188	1,252	9,436	510	0	225	12,050
SOUTHEAST	8,295	4,395	21,207	91,356	18,812		2,196	146,261
SE	2,489	2,214	9,755	35,249	13,831	0	770	64,308
Cumb	77	41	2,313	1,274	444	0	100	4,250
Tenn	296	703	2,655	35,501	1,252	0	276	40,683
L Miss	2,931	1,021	5,189	7,825	2,291	0	313	19,570
L AWR	2,502	416	1,295	11,507	994	0	737	17,450
MID-CONTINENT	34,606	2,799	7,304	11,151	8,366		2,562	66,790
U Mo	16,424	441	2,158	8,252	2,825	0	1,816	31,917
U AWR	7,192	291	1,103	258	913	0	255	10,013
W Gulf	10,990	2,067	4,043	2,641	4,628	0	491	24,860
SOUTHWEST	31,827	3,076	2,587	755	15,699		197	54,141
RG-P	5,731	423	434	92	998	0	105	7,783
Colo	15,137	221	563	351	2,313	0	100	18,685
G Basin	6,545	206	642	138	567	0	13	8,111
S Pac	4,414	2,226	948	174	11,821	0	-21	19,562
NORTH PACIFIC	51,629	5,246	13,094	21,019	5,367		107	96,461
C Pac	32,028	4,743	1,269	266	2,566	0	79	40,950
PNW	19,601	503	11,825	20,753	2,801	0	28	55,511
U.S.	131,662	36,546	98,059	528,949	95,289		6,503	897,007

Table 24. TOTAL WITHDRAWALS FOR INTAKE AND ONSITE USES AT ORIGINAL RATES OF RECIRCULATION, BY REGION

	1960	1980			2000			2020			Max. reg. flow, 98%
		L	M	H	L	M	H	L	M	H	
			(million gallons per day)									*(bgd)*
NORTHEAST	81,241	150,907	199,168	275,535	193,148	309,639	512,443	312,387	533,354	1,037,887	359
N Eng	2,771	4,884	5,796	7,164	6,370	8,971	13,322	9,294	13,803	24,613	61
D & H	9,346	12,010	14,836	19,291	15,162	22,486	35,003	22,601	35,363	64,909	29
Ches	5,693	9,678	12,432	16,863	12,346	19,364	31,796	19,375	32,323	62,891	47
Ohio	25,364	50,628	68,450	97,048	63,414	104,636	177,370	102,399	179,206	356,182	99
EGL	12,090	21,372	28,211	38,969	28,990	47,017	78,460	48,296	84,128	167,246	33
WGL	15,720	30,922	41,104	56,773	39,156	62,987	103,463	64,432	109,179	209,242	30
U Miss	8,940	18,094	24,022	33,617	23,278	37,509	62,149	38,690	67,302	130,081	43
L Mo	1,317	3,319	4,317	5,810	4,432	6,669	10,880	7,300	12,050	22,723	16
SOUTHEAST	24,926	39,243	50,914	69,343	54,290	84,580	136,802	88,952	146,261	278,098	334
SE	12,412	16,957	22,224	29,859	23,869	37,172	58,873	39,638	64,308	118,357	186
Cumb	183	950	1,146	1,604	1,476	2,301	4,152	2,572	4,250	9,368	15
Tenn	5,350	9,265	12,329	17,467	13,274	21,667	36,650	23,585	40,683	80,494	40
L Miss	3,634	6,012	7,798	10,632	7,932	12,271	19,917	11,895	19,570	38,112	35
L AWR	3,347	6,059	7,417	9,781	7,739	11,169	17,210	11,262	17,450	31,767	58
MID-CONTINENT	44,642	43,598	49,886	59,082	42,256	53,340	71,967	49,397	66,790	102,991	59
U Mo	20,295	20,209	23,285	27,238	19,523	25,083	33,322	23,322	31,917	48,203	26
U AWR	8,416	8,451	9,046	10,826	8,150	9,100	12,124	8,594	10,013	14,621	7
W Gulf	15,931	14,938	17,555	21,018	14,583	19,157	26,521	17,481	24,860	40,167	26
SOUTHWEST	43,173	40,005	42,175	44,896	39,334	44,294	51,685	45,855	54,141	70,188	22
RG-P	8,062	6,850	7,446	8,069	5,910	6,838	8,096	6,430	7,783	10,098	3
Colo	20,378	17,083	17,667	18,271	15,784	16,943	18,443	16,991	18,685	21,629	11
G Basin	8,642	7,456	8,019	8,656	6,471	7,495	8,848	6,706	8,111	10,448	7
S Pac	6,091	8,616	9,043	9,900	11,169	13,018	16,298	15,728	19,562	28,013	1
NORTH PACIFIC	56,333	59,712	62,915	67,136	60,996	70,925	87,433	74,673	96,461	143,453	175
C Pac	32,046	33,700	34,490	36,023	32,341	34,612	39,409	35,350	40,950	53,257	40
PNW	24,287	26,012	28,425	31,113	28,655	36,313	48,024	39,323	55,511	90,196	135
U.S.	250,315	333,465	405,058	515,992	390,024	562,778	860,330	571,264	897,007	1,632,617	948

Table 25. U.S. LOSSES FROM WITHDRAWAL USES

(million gallons per day)

		Agriculture	Mining	Manufacturing	Steam-electric	Municipal	Total losses from withdrawal uses
1960		89,848	698	2,001	900	10,661	104,108
1980	L	90,358	1,119	3,267	1,634	19,945	116,323
	M	93,889	1,450	4,296	2,237	21,226	123,098
	H	99,483	1,944	5,795	3,220	23,133	133,575
2000	L	87,215	1,376	4,819	2,751	29,137	125,298
	M	93,024	2,211	8,186	4,581	34,649	142,651
	H	104,158	3,801	14,792	7,781	42,195	172,727
2020	L	90,698	1,804	8,428	5,226	44,114	150,270
	M	97,865	4,481	15,339	9,144	51,750	178,579
	H	113,934	9,437	34,476	18,064	68,475	244,386

Table 26. U.S. LOSSES FROM WITHDRAWAL AND ONSITE USES

(million gallons per day)

		Land treatment & structures	Swamps & wetlands	Total onsite losses	Total losses from withdrawal uses	Total losses
1960		0	0	0	104,108	104,109
1980	L	3,140	−4,282	−1,142	116,323	115,181
	M	3,140	0	3,140	123,098	126,238
	H	3,140	4,282	7,422	133,575	140,997
2000	L	5,803	−6,855	−1,052	125,298	124,246
	M	5,803	0	5,803	142,651	148,454
	H	5,803	6,855	12,658	172,727	185,385
2020	L	6,503	−8,564	−2,061	150,270	148,209
	M	6,503	0	6,503	178,579	185,082
	H	6,503	8,564	15,067	244,386	259,453

Table 27. LAND TREATMENT AND STRUCTURES: WITHDRAWALS AND LOSSES, BY REGION, INCREASE OVER 1960

(million gallons per day)

	1980	2000	2020
NORTHEAST	1,145	1,391	1,441
N Eng	418	462	481
D & H	-102	-210	-295
Ches	113	40	-2
Ohio	222	352	405
EGL	106	-21	-87
WGL	52	105	130
U Miss	204	464	584
L Mo	132	199	225
SOUTHEAST	792	1,766	2,196
SE	321	635	770
Cumb	54	86	100
Tenn	81	213	276
L Miss	121	255	313
L AWR	215	577	737

Table 27. Continued

	1980	2000	2020
MID-CONTINENT	909	2,183	2,562
U Mo	590	1,417	1,816
U AWR	166	285	255
W Gulf	153	481	491
SOUTHWEST	141	218	197
RG-P	87	121	105
Colo	46	83	100
G Basin	5	11	13
S Pac	3	3	-21
NORTH PACIFIC	153	245	107
C Pac	69	87	79
PNW	84	158	28
U.S.	3,140	5,803	6,503

Note: For purposes of tabulation, withdrawals, or onsite gross uses, are defined as equal to losses.

Table 28. SWAMPS AND WETLANDS: WITHDRAWALS AND LOSSES, BY REGION, INCREASE OVER 1960

(million gallons per day)

	1980			2000			2020		
	L	M	H	L	M	H	L	M	H
NORTHEAST	-602		602	-964		964	-1,206		1,206
N Eng	-22	0	22	-35	0	35	-44	0	44
D & H	-63	0	63	-100	0	100	-125	0	125
Ches	-43	0	43	-69	0	69	-87	0	87
Ohio	-8	0	8	-14	0	14	-17	0	17
EGL	-51	0	51	-82	0	82	-103	0	103
WGL	-180	0	180	-288	0	288	-360	0	360
U Miss	-235	0	235	-376	0	376	-470	0	470
L Mo	0	0	0	0	0	0	0	0	0
SOUTHEAST	-1,582		1,582	-2,533		2,533	-3,164		3,164
SE	-1,005	0	1,005	-1,608	0	1,608	-2,010	0	2,010
Cumb	-2	0	2	-4	0	4	-4	0	4
Tenn	-3	0	3	-5	0	5	-6	0	6
L Miss	-476	0	476	-762	0	762	-952	0	952
L AWR	-96	0	96	-154	0	154	-192	0	192
MID-CONTINENT	-1,559		1,559	-2,497		2,497	-3,120		3,120
U Mo	-876	0	876	-1,402	0	1,402	-1,752	0	1,752
U AWR	-53	0	53	-86	0	86	-107	0	107
W Gulf	-630	0	630	-1,009	0	1,009	-1,261	0	1,261
SOUTHWEST	-342		342	-547		547	-682		682
RG-P	-69	0	69	-111	0	111	-138	0	138
Colo	-13	0	13	-20	0	20	-25	0	25
G Basin	-260	0	260	-416	0	416	-519	0	519
S Pac	0	0	0	0	0	0	0	0	0
NORTH PACIFIC	-197		197	-314		314	-392		392
C Pac	-173	0	173	-276	0	276	-345	0	345
PNW	-24	0	24	-38	0	38	-47	0	47
U.S.	-4,282		4,282	-6,855		6,855	-8,564		8,564

Note: For purposes of tabulation, withdrawals, or onsite gross uses, are defined as equal to losses.

Table 29. LOSSES, BY REGION AND TYPE OF USE: 1960

(million gallons per day)

	Agriculture	Mining	Manufacturing	Steam-electric	Municipal	Swamps & wetlands	Land treatment	Total
NORTHEAST	1,391	268	1,241	573	5,899			9,372
N Eng	56	2	129	8	705	0	0	900
D & H	196	14	176	44	2,594	0	0	3,024
Ches	141	12	99	39	716	0	0	1,006
Ohio	241	125	311	242	354	0	0	1,273
EGL	90	32	258	71	503	0	0	954
WGL	140	22	159	98	667	0	0	1,086
U Miss	422	58	102	61	312	0	0	957
L Mo	105	3	7	10	48	0	0	172
SOUTHEAST	3,382	105	284	179	1,007			4,957
SE	1,089	22	171	69	702	0	0	2,053
Cumb	22	2	0	0	20	0	0	45
Tenn	76	7	36	71	45	0	0	235
L Miss	1,036	49	49	18	173	0	0	1,326
L AWR	1,159	25	28	21	67	0	0	1,301
MID-CONTINENT	25,107	208	296	97	799			26,507
U Mo	11,526	29	25	19	208	0	0	11,807
U AWR	5,064	68	56	21	118	0	0	5,327
W Gulf	8,517	111	215	57	473	0	0	9,373
SOUTHWEST	26,161	74	68	41	1,717			28,061
RG-P	4,655	21	12	8	59	0	0	4,755
Colo	13,001	21	12	13	81	0	0	13,128
G Basin	5,536	12	0	4	68	0	0	5,621
S Pac	2,969	20	44	16	1,509	0	0	4,557
NORTH PACIFIC	33,807	43	111	9	1,239			35,209
C Pac	21,154	27	53	9	595	0	0	21,838
PNW	12,653	16	58	0	644	0	0	13,371
U.S.	89,848	698	2,000	899	10,661			104,109

Table 30. LOSSES, BY REGION AND TYPE OF USE: 1980 MEDIUM

(million gallons per day)

	Agriculture	Mining	Manufacturing	Steam-electric	Municipal	Swamps & wetlands	Land treatment	Total
NORTHEAST	2,248	588	2,433	1,408	10,165		1,145	17,990
N Eng	68	5	225	18	1,187	0	418	1,922
D & H	281	31	317	68	4,335	0	−102	4,930
Ches	251	27	264	75	1,372	0	113	2,102
Ohio	372	243	547	586	579	0	222	2,550
EGL	140	89	581	189	902	0	106	2,007
WGL	229	50	315	274	1,181	0	52	2,100
U Miss	703	137	157	168	530	0	204	1,899
L Mo	204	6	27	30	79	0	132	480
SOUTHEAST	5,141	206	716	355	2,734		792	9,946
SE	1,428	48	411	149	2,042	0	321	4,399
Cumb	33	3	37	1	44	0	54	173
Tenn	124	16	65	130	112	0	81	528
L Miss	1,760	97	139	33	400	0	121	2,550
L AWR	1,796	42	64	42	136	0	215	2,295
MID-CONTINENT	26,946	418	620	272	1,642		909	30,807
U Mo	12,647	75	37	77	443	0	590	13,870
U AWR	5,592	125	92	59	210	0	166	6,243
W Gulf	8,707	218	491	136	989	0	153	10,694
SOUTHWEST	24,607	146	227	115	4,628		141	29,864
RG-P	4,528	40	20	22	146	0	87	4,843
Colo	11,695	38	20	41	295	0	46	12,134
G Basin	5,176	20	89	22	130	0	5	5,443
S Pac	3,208	48	98	30	4,057	0	3	7,444
NORTH PACIFIC	34,947	92	300	87	2,057		153	37,634
C Pac	22,580	70	98	40	1,022	0	69	23,877
PNW	12,367	22	202	47	1,035	0	84	13,757
U.S.	93,889	1,450	4,296	2,237	21,226		3,140	126,241

Table 31. LOSSES, BY REGION AND TYPE OF USE: 2000 MEDIUM

(million gallons per day)

	Agriculture	Mining	Manufacturing	Steam-electric	Municipal	Swamps & wetlands	Land treatment	Total
NORTHEAST	2,820	1,046	4,261	2,749	15,392		1,391	27,659
N Eng	81	10	400	36	1,755	0	462	2,744
D & H	292	58	570	130	6,395	0	−210	7,235
Ches	319	57	459	147	2,236	0	40	3,257
Ohio	472	355	884	1,126	841	0	352	4,030
EGL	173	213	1,088	397	1,417	0	−21	3,268
WGL	286	97	565	526	1,849	0	105	3,428
U Miss	920	246	238	329	801	0	464	2,997
L Mo	277	10	57	58	98	0	199	700
SOUTHEAST	6,238	292	1,556	724	5,146		1,766	15,724
SE	1,670	96	886	292	3,927	0	635	7,507
Cumb	40	5	85	7	76	0	86	298
Tenn	151	30	126	279	202	0	213	1,003
L Miss	2,313	112	341	61	737	0	255	3,820
L AWR	2,064	49	118	85	204	0	577	3,096
MID-CONTINENT	25,362	461	1,330	540	2,719		2,183	32,596
U Mo	11,423	79	70	166	747	0	1,417	13,902
U AWR	5,501	128	167	114	292	0	285	6,487
W Gulf	8,438	254	1,093	260	1,680	0	481	12,207
SOUTHWEST	23,058	199	457	241	8,269		218	32,438
RG-P	4,156	48	54	40	257	0	121	4,675
Colo	11,166	34	45	100	536	0	83	11,963
G Basin	4,411	21	159	44	185	0	11	4,830
S Pac	3,325	96	199	57	7,291	0	3	10,970
NORTH PACIFIC	35,546	213	582	327	3,122		245	40,034
C Pac	22,636	179	202	80	1,534	0	87	24,718
PNW	12,910	34	380	247	1,588	0	158	15,316
U.S.	93,024	2,211	8,186	4,581	34,648		5,803	148,451

Table 32. LOSSES, BY REGION AND TYPE OF USE: 2020 MEDIUM

(million gallons per day)

	Agriculture	Mining	Manufacturing	Steam-electric	Municipal	Swamps & wetlands	Land treatment	Total
NORTHEAST	3,644	2,413	7,425	5,304	22,049		1,441	42,276
N Eng	100	26	718	71	2,489	0	481	3,886
D & H	324	137	1,019	248	9,019	0	−295	10,453
Ches	401	148	793	282	3,321	0	−2	4,943
Ohio	622	692	1,448	2,149	1,138	0	405	6,454
EGL	221	602	1,954	805	2,115	0	−87	5,610
WGL	362	228	1,012	1,004	2,710	0	130	5,446
U Miss	1,232	558	368	633	1,130	0	584	4,505
L Mo	382	22	113	112	127	0	225	982
SOUTHEAST	7,235	543	3,162	1,437	8,434		2,196	23,007
SE	2,011	240	1,763	567	6,586	0	770	11,937
Cumb	53	8	177	21	111	0	100	469
Tenn	187	73	248	573	312	0	276	1,670
L Miss	2,693	155	752	112	1,177	0	313	5,202
L AWR	2,291	67	222	164	248	0	737	3,729
MID-CONTINENT	26,007	581	2,733	1,054	4,017		2,562	36,955
U Mo	11,866	85	138	344	1,134	0	1,816	15,382
U AWR	5,583	134	297	215	366	0	255	6,851
W Gulf	8,558	362	2,298	495	2,517	0	491	14,722
SOUTHWEST	23,588	377	894	491	13,003		197	38,550
RG-P	4,227	70	124	77	398	0	103	5,002
Colo	11,345	32	104	219	925	0	100	12,724
G Basin	4,507	25	278	86	227	0	13	5,136
S Pac	3,509	250	388	109	11,453	0	−21	15,688
NORTH PACIFIC	37,391	567	1,125	858	4,247		107	44,295
C Pac	23,951	508	398	166	2,033	0	79	27,134
PNW	13,440	59	727	692	2,214	0	28	17,160
U.S.	97,865	4,481	15,339	9,144	51,750		6,503	185,083

Table 33. TOTAL LOSSES FROM WITHDRAWALS AND ONSITE USES, BY REGION

	1960	1980			2000			2020			Max. reg. flow, 98%
		L	M	H	L	M	H	L	M	H	(bgd)
	(million gallons per day)										
NORTHEAST	9,372	15,563	17,990	21,379	20,636	27,659	38,666	30,283	42,276	68,717	359
N Eng	900	1,786	1,922	2,105	2,278	2,744	3,415	3,171	3,885	5,508	61
D & H	3,024	4,489	4,930	5,588	5,771	7,235	9,418	8,305	10,452	15,341	29
Ches	1,006	1,885	2,102	2,403	2,541	3,257	4,361	3,765	4,943	7,639	47
Ohio	1,273	2,130	2,550	3,181	2,861	4,030	6,065	4,213	6,454	11,668	99
EGL	954	1,663	2,007	2,519	2,193	3,268	5,183	3,465	5,610	10,919	33
WGL	1,086	1,676	2,100	2,645	2,328	3,428	5,021	3,617	5,446	9,028	30
U Miss	957	1,484	1,899	2,412	2,051	2,997	4,336	2,939	4,505	7,277	43
L Mo	172	450	480	526	613	700	867	808	981	1,337	16
SOUTHEAST	4,960	7,778	9,946	12,612	11,032	15,724	22,384	15,796	23,007	36,665	334
SE	2,053	3,092	4,399	5,828	4,660	7,507	11,072	7,624	11,937	19,240	186
Cumb	45	157	173	201	237	298	423	347	469	834	15
Tenn	235	459	528	642	770	1,003	1,431	1,182	1,670	2,892	40
L Miss	1,326	1,961	2,550	3,295	2,669	3,820	5,527	3,504	5,202	8,507	35
L AWR	1,301	2,109	2,296	2,646	2,696	3,096	3,927	3,139	3,729	5,192	58
MID-CONTINENT	26,507	27,076	30,807	35,904	26,409	32,596	42,249	28,641	36,955	52,464	59
U Mo	11,807	12,159	13,870	15,761	11,130	13,902	17,377	11,876	15,382	20,451	26
U AWR	5,327	5,854	6,243	7,460	5,899	6,487	8,478	6,066	6,851	9,510	7
W Gulf	9,373	9,063	10,694	12,683	9,380	12,207	16,394	10,699	14,722	22,503	26
SOUTHWEST	28,061	28,372	29,864	31,709	29,029	32,438	37,263	33,702	38,550	47,876	22
RG-P	4,755	4,444	4,843	5,251	4,069	4,675	5,463	4,238	5,002	6,218	3
Colo	13,128	11,781	12,134	12,478	11,276	11,963	12,802	11,776	12,724	14,256	11
G Basin	5,621	5,016	5,443	5,904	4,090	4,830	5,722	4,153	5,136	6,576	7
S Pac	4,557	7,131	7,444	8,076	9,594	10,970	13,276	13,535	15,688	20,826	1
NORTH PACIFIC	35,209	36,396	37,634	39,391	37,143	40,034	44,828	39,785	44,294	53,734	175
C Pac	21,838	23,384	23,877	24,839	23,528	24,718	27,270	25,161	27,134	32,082	40
PNW	13,371	13,012	13,757	14,552	13,615	15,316	17,558	14,624	17,160	21,652	135
U.S.	104,109	115,185	126,241	140,995	124,249	148,451	185,386	148,207	185,082	259,456	948

Chapter 8

WATER QUALITY

The amount of required dilution flow is dependent on the standard of water quality that is to be maintained, the location and characteristics of receiving waters, the amount and character of water-borne waste produced by man's activities, and the level of treatment given to waste before it is discharged. The quantities of flow specified are those required to avoid violation of the quality standard under adverse seasonal conditions – i.e., periods of high air and water temperatures and naturally low streamflows.

Amount of Waste Produced

For every projection of population and economic activity there is a level of waste which is measured in two ways: (1) the amount of decomposable organic matter which, while undergoing the process of chemical and biological change (i.e., decomposition), utilizes the dissolved oxygen (D.O.) of water; and (2) the amount of heat added to rivers by the discharge of cooling water.[1]

Municipal and industrial waste imposes a biochemical oxygen demand (BOD) on receiving waters. The oxygen-demanding burden of industrial waste is given a common measurement with municipal waste by use of the unit "population equivalent" (p.e.) – 0.25 pounds of oxygen per day required to oxidize the waste of an average urban person.

On the basis of urban population and specified levels of production in the main waste-producing manufacturing industries (food processing, pulp and paper, chemicals, petroleum refining and coal products, textiles, and tanneries), an aggregate amount of BOD, measured in p.e.'s, is produced.

By subjecting waste to treatment, the burden of assimilation imposed on receiving waters is correspondingly reduced. By discharging waste into coastal or estuarine bodies of water, the burden on *fresh* water is reduced still further, but only at the expense of the impact on the nation's estuaries and coastal waters. (A major gap in knowledge and in our model of water use is the effect of this impact.) We estimated the amount of waste that is, and would be, discharged into estuarine and coastal waters, the Great Lakes, and the Great Salt Lake. All other discharges were assumed to be into fresh water. (See table 34.)

Waste discharged into streams was assumed to be subjected to treatment, expressed as an average percentage of BOD removed for a region, ranging between 70 percent and 97½ percent for municipal waste and between 50 percent and 97½ percent for industrial waste. Wastes discharged into other bodies of water – i.e., estuaries, etc. – were assumed to receive primary treatment, 35 percent BOD removal.[2]

This chapter is based on the study "Treatment, Dilution, and Treatment Costs of Municipal and Industrial Wastes" conducted by George W. Reid, Wesley W. Eckenfelder, Leale Streebin, Robert Nelson, and Oliver T. Love, Jr., and included herein as app. D. Our debt to them is unbounded, since without their major contribution the scope of the economic model would have been much narrower.

[1] It is assumed that pollution from bacteria, viruses, chemicals, dissolved solids, or suspended solids is reduced to acceptable levels by the dilution flows required to meet a D.O. standard after "standard" waste treatment.

[2] See table D-7, for values of the percentage of BOD, nitrogen, and phosphorus removed by primary, secondary, and tertiary levels of treatment. Primary treatment customarily refers to about 35 percent BOD removal; secondary treatment at high efficiency provides 95 percent removal, but frequently less; tertiary treatment, which may be provided by one or more methods, reduces the residual BOD, after secondary treatment, by about 50 percent. Hence, under efficient conditions tertiary treatment implies about 97½ percent BOD removal. The proportions of nitrogen and phosphorus removed by successively higher levels of treatment are different, although the percentages tend to converge for tertiary treatment.

We assumed that waste effluent discharged into streams after treatment was accompanied by a diluting flow that maintained instream water quality at specified levels. For our basic model the qualities that could not be violated were:

dissolved oxygen — not to fall below 4 mg/l of water (approximately 4 parts per million);
phosphorus — not to exceed 0.1 ppm of water; and
nitrogen — not to exceed 1 ppm of water.

The D.O. standard is usually specified as "4 mg/l" and automatically implies the associated phosphorus and nitrogen constraints. Two alternative quality standards were also examined:

(1) D.O. = 6 mg/l
Phosphorus = 0.3 ppm
Nitrogen = 3 ppm
(2) D.O. = 1 mg/l
Phosphorus = 0.3 ppm
Nitrogen = 3 ppm

They are identified as "6 mg/l" and "1 mg/l," respectively.

The response of a stream to successively higher levels of treatment is not known with certainty. Reid et al. point out that stream-response equations are both complex and dependent on values that are not firmly established for all streams or for any single stream under all possible conditions. Dilution flows also are subject to possible modification, not only by correction of stream response equations but also by changes in the quantity or quality of waste produced per unit of product or by change in the proportion of effluent discharged "upstream" or "downstream."

Dilution flows computed on the basis of Reid et al. revealed that, at rates of in-plant recirculation extrapolated from past trends, the flows required to offset thermal pollution would exceed those required to offset other pollutants. Since the recirculation of cooling water is already widely accepted, we assumed that its practice would be increased rapidly enough to avoid thermal pollution (see table B-18). This meant that the "ruling dilution flow" was the amount of streamflow needed to avoid violation of the BOD and plant nutrient constraints. The largest of the three computed flows was the "ruling" flow, since it was assumed that dilution requirements were nonadditive.

Several deficiencies and possible sources of error should be noted. First, no account is taken of deterioration in water quality as a result of an increase in the amount of material washing into streams from the surrounding land — mainly soil, chemicals, and organic material. No account is taken of the increasing concentration of dissolved solids, notably salts, in western regions as a consequence of minerals leaching from the soil, and in eastern regions as a result of intrabasin municipal and industrial reuse. No account is taken of acid mine wastes, a problem of serious consequence in old coal-mining areas, nor of threats posed by piles of radioactive rock resulting from the mining and processing of uranium. No account is taken of poisons or bacterial contamination. It should be noted,

therefore, that in some cases there are additional costs of withholding or diluting these substances that must be added to the costs we have incorporated into our model. Treatment at high levels of BOD removal will also remove other noxious substances, but there are notable exceptions, such as salts. Hence, the dilution requirements in areas where chlorides are a serious pollutant, or threaten to be, are likely to be understated. Absence of data on required flows into estuarine bodies of water to maintain requisite salinity balance and other characteristics is another deficiency.

As a result of the enumerated exclusions, it appears likely that our estimates of required flows are biased downward rather than upward for a given bill of goods and level of waste treatment. Offsetting this bias is the possibility of changes in production techniques that reduce the amount of waste per unit of product. This possibility is already visible in the production of paper.

Coefficients supplied by Eckenfelder were used to estimate the output of oxygen-demanding wastes of various manufacturing industries. These values were converted to population equivalents per dollar's worth of value added or per million gallons per day of discharge. Municipal discharge was also converted to p.e.'s on the basis of one p.e. per urban person. Industrial wastes discharged into municipal systems were counted as part of industrial wastes. No special account was taken of situations where storm and sanitary sewers were connected, hence the output of discharged waste is biased downward. (See tables 35 to 40.)

As already noted, water-borne waste was assumed to be subjected to treatment in accordance with an ascending scale of BOD removal. Treatment processes do not lend themselves to continuous variation but tend to be about 35 percent, 90-95 percent, or 97½ percent BOD removal, depending on whether the process is primary, primary plus secondary, or primary plus secondary plus tertiary. Thus, intermediate values for a region reflect varying combinations of treatment levels found within the region. The mix for each treatment level, on the basis of which dilution flows and costs of treatment were computed, is given in table 41.

In computing the percentage of decomposable organic waste removed by treatment, the percentages of table 41 were joined with the percentages of amounts removed by treatment as given in table D-7. The schedule of phosphorus removed by treatment given in table 43 serves as an example. When treatment is at 80 percent, 41 percent of phosphorus is removed. This figure is equal to the sum of the products:

primary	= 0.26 × 0.10 (% removed)	= 0.0260
secondary	= 0.54 × 0.35	= 0.1890
tertiary	= 0.20 × 0.98	= 0.1960
	Total	= 0.4110
		= 41%

The same mix of treatment was used to compute treatment costs.

The output of BOD, measured in population equivalents, was estimated for each projection. (Tables 35 to 39 give waste loads produced for selected projections.) In 1960, municipal waste accounted for about one-third of total p.e.'s produced, but in 1980, it will account for only about 26 percent. (See table 44 for percentage distributions.) Industrial activity will account for an increasingly larger fraction of the total waste load. In addition, there is a slight upward trend in the projected fraction of p.e.'s produced that is discharged to fresh water (before treatment).

The projected increase in produced wastes is substantial. At the Medium growth rate, the output of wastes produced at freshwater locations would be 6.3 times greater in the year 2020 than in 1960. At the High growth rate, the output would be 15 times the 1960 level. Our projections indicate that the output of waste grows more rapidly than total economic activity. (Adjustment of GNP to reflect the negative impact of nuisance abatement will become increasingly important whenever changes in GNP are used to measure changes in welfare.)

The output of organic wastes at freshwater locations would soon be far beyond the assimilative capacity of the country's rivers were it not for treatment of waste effluent prior to discharge. Treatment at 97½ percent BOD removal means that only 2½ percent of produced p.e.'s is discharged. If treatment were at that level for the 2020 High projection, there still would be discharged into fresh water the equivalent of raw waste produced by 80 million people. At the Medium rate of growth, by 2020 discharge after 97½ percent treatment would be equal to the raw waste of 34 million people (see tables 38 and 39).

It is difficult to describe the prospective physical impact of future waste discharge, even after treatment has proceeded to 97½ percent BOD removal, because we have no well-defined standard of comparison. We do not know what the average level of treatment is in the United States today. The assumption that it was 35 percent in 1960 would imply that the equivalent raw waste of 140 million people had been discharged into streams. High-level treatment by 2020, even at the projected High rate of economic growth, would relieve our streams of a substantial amount of the pollution to which they are now subjected.

Dilution Flows

Given the quantity of organic wastes produced, measured in p.e.'s, the amount of water needed to dilute the effluent from waste treatment plants is a function of the desired stream quality, the natural reoxygenation capacity of the river, and, of course, the amount of decomposable material removed by treatment. Our water resource economic model treats the output of wastes, stream quality, and reoxygenation capability as parameters, the first two being assigned various values, while the last is invariant. (See appendix D.)

For the basic program, the amount of waste produced in future years was assumed to vary directly with changes in the output of waste-producing activities. Urban population is the determinant of municipal waste; industrial p.e.'s are determined by the outputs of food, pulp and paper, textiles, tanneries, chemicals, and refined petroleum products.

For two variants of the basic model, the following assumptions were made:

Variant 1: output of p.e.'s per $1 million of value added would fall by 10 percent of 1960 value in 1980, by 20 percent in 2000, and by 30 percent in 2020.

Variant 2: 20 percent, 40 percent, and 60 percent, respectively, were substituted for the values used in Variant 1.

The variants, it is noted, assume a fall in the output of BOD per unit of product before treatment. No comparable variant was adopted for municipal waste. Instead, a test was made of sensitivity to the assumption that municipal water in coastal regions was recirculated. This has no effect on waste dilution, which was assumed to be zero at coastal points, but reduces intake and losses.

As noted above, the stream quality standard was defined by dissolved oxygen, phosphorus, and nitrogen in the region's streams. Given the desired levels of dissolved oxygen, phosphorus, and nitrogen, the amount of required dilution flow depends on the level of treatment in accordance with the stream response equations of appendix D. Dilution flows required to meet the D.O. constraint would fall in direct proportion to the effect on residual BOD of a given change in treatment level. For example, raising the treatment level from 80 percent to 90 percent would reduce residual BOD from 20 percent to 10 percent, and halve the required dilution flow. The same thing would happen in going from 90 percent to 95 percent and from 95 percent to 97½ percent.

When treatment rises from primary to secondary, a larger fraction of decomposable organic material is converted into inorganic nitrogen and phosphorus. This has the further effect of fertilizing the receiving waters and stimulating the growth of algae. Algae not only deplete the dissolved oxygen of water as they decay, but contribute adverse taste, odor, and physical characteristics to streams. For this reason an upper limit on allowable nitrogen and phosphorus is needed in order to maintain suitable stream quality. The higher the level of BOD removal over the range of 50–95 percent treatment, the greater is the fertilization by phosphorus and nitrogen and the greater is the dilution required to offset the effects of such fertilization. When standard treatment goes from 95 percent to 97½ percent, based on the addition of chemicals, lagooning, additional filtration, or other "polishing" techniques, the process sharply reduces the amount of plant nutrients remaining in the effluent. Hence, a treatment level of 97½ percent reverses the effect on the dilution of plant nutrients that increases in treatment level up to that point had created.

Because U.S. treatment levels at 80 percent, 90 percent, and 95 percent consist of a mix of primary, secondary, and tertiary levels of treatment, the averaging effect of the sharp reduction in dilution flows called for by 97½ percent treatment becomes increasingly felt. Required dilution to offset plant nutrients reaches a peak in most regions at 80 percent treatment for phosphorus and at 90 percent for nitrogen.

For each level of treatment, the highest required flow among BOD, phosphorus, and nitrogen is designated as the "ruling" flow.[3] Treatment levels were assumed to range between 70 and 97½ percent BOD removal for municipal wastes, and between 50 and 97½ percent for industrial wastes. The scale of treatment, therefore, was expressed in percentages as 70/50, 70/60, 70/70, 80/80, 90/90, 95/95, and 97½/97½. One could have assumed different combinations and computed dilution flows accordingly — e.g., 90 percent municipal and 50 percent industrial.

Tables 45 to 53 are summaries that indicate the behavior of dilution flows as the level of economic activity, the D.O. constraint, and the level of treatment vary. Table 45 shows detail for New England, 2000 Medium projection, 4 mg/l. In the absence of a decision that thermal dilution requirements would be ignored unless recirculation rates had reached a maximum attainable level (in contrast to the extrapolated level that is implicit in these figures for New England), it is seen that heat pollution would have been ruling at all levels of treatment in excess of 80 percent. As it is, BOD dilution rules at all levels of treatment except 95 percent, for which phosphorus is ruling. In a number of regions phosphorus rules at 90 percent, and in a few instances at lower rates. Invariably, however, at 97½ percent treatment BOD is ruling.

Based on U.S. population and production in 1960, required dilution flows for selected treatment levels for a D.O. standard of 4 mg/l are as follows (also see table 46):

Treatment (percent)	Dilution flow (mgd)
70/50	612,219
80/80	303,792
95/95	120,809
97½/97½	34,709

The absence of proportionality between the change in dilution flows and the change in residual BOD as treatment rises from 95 percent to 97½ percent reflects the fact that at 95 percent, phosphorus is the ruling flow in all except six regions.[4]

If the level of treatment is kept constant at 95 percent and dissolved oxygen is not allowed to fall below 4 mg/l, the effect of economic growth on dilution flows can be seen in table 47. For the conterminous United States, dilution requirements grow as follows:

Year	Low	Medium	High
		(bgd)	
1960	–	121	–
1980	199	231	290
2000	291	413	693
2020	487	740	1,594

Moving along the Medium path, dilution flows by 2020 would have to be six times the level that would have been required in 1960 had treatment been at 95 percent and water quality maintained at no less than 4 mg/l of dissolved oxygen.[5] The burden of assimilating prospective waste loads is perhaps more evident if it is recalled that at current levels of waste treatment (which cannot be accurately measured but are probably below 70/50 percent) there would not be enough water in the United States to assure 4 mg/l of dissolved oxygen by 1980 Medium. (See table 48.) By implication, the degradation of waters at higher levels of output would be proportionately more severe.

A D.O. standard of 4 mg/l permits the survival of most desirable aquatic life, even though it may not allow successful completion of the life cycle of all species of fish such as trout. By adopting a D.O. standard of 4 mg/l, higher oxygen levels are not precluded and, in fact, are presumed to prevail in parts of the basin. However, a standard of 4 mg/l may not necessarily be consistent with all uses, since dissolved oxygen serves as a proxy for other qualities as well. Accordingly, an alternative standard of 6 mg/l was examined. This higher standard implies that waters, especially in the lower parts of basins where temperatures are fairly high and velocities fairly low, would be close to natural levels prior to use by man. At the other extreme, a D.O. standard of 1 mg/l implies that water barely avoids being anaerobic. With dissolved oxygen never below 1 mg/l, decomposition of degradable organic material presumably reaches a state of completion, but in the process the oxygen content of water is so depleted that only inferior forms of aquatic life can survive.

The relative difference in dilution flows that result from raising D.O. standards from 1 mg/l to 4 mg/l gradually diminishes with growth in total economic activity. (See table 49.) At the 1960 level of population and production, required flow at 4 mg/l is 2.3 times the flow for 1 mg/l. Between 1960 and 2020 the relative difference slowly declines, as follows:

1980	2.1
2000	2.1
2020	2

The increase in required flow resulting from raising the D.O. standard from 4 mg/l to 6 mg/l, measured as a multiple of 4 mg/l, is:

1960	1.11
1980	1.30
2000	1.43
2020	1.53

[3] On the assumption that recirculation of cooling water is high enough to prevent thermal pollution.

[4] Whether BOD or phosphorus is the ruling factor depends, for a given level of production and treatment, on the physical–chemical characteristics of the river, namely, the "natural" level of D.O. (i.e.,

before introduction of man-made BOD) and the reaeration capabilities. The latter depend on the degree of impoundment, velocity, cross-section, length of reach, and turbidity, to name the major determinants. These physical characteristics are not, however, part of the nutritional models. See app. D.

[5] The reader will recall that no provision is made for the dilution of water discharged into estuaries.

Contrary to the effect of going from 1 mg/l to 4 mg/l, the effect of going from 4 mg/l to 6 mg/l requires an increasingly larger multiple of flow as time goes on.

It should be emphasized, however, that regionwide stream responses of variations in pollution load are still inadequately known. Further investigation may reveal different responses to specified waste loadings.

Tables 50 and 51 indicate required dilution flows if treatment is carried to the upper limit specified for the basic program — namely 97½ percent removal of BOD. Had treatment been at this level in 1960, it would have required an aggregate flow of 35 bgd to meet requirements for 4 mg/l of dissolved oxygen. Required flows along the Medium path of growth double every twenty years. BOD waste loads *produced* grow at a somewhat lower rate, as do BOD waste loads produced at freshwater sites. The difference between the two growth rates is explained by differences in the rates of growth of output of water-borne wastes discharged into fresh water among regions relative to differences in the reoxygenation capabilities of streams. On the basis of such differentials, one might construct an interregional model designed to minimize aggregate dilution flow requirements for a specified level of treatment and a specified bill of goods.

The significance of tables 50 and 51 lies in the large quantities of dilution flow that are required *even if* treatment is carried to the limit of 97½ percent BOD removal. Further reduction in required flow would be contingent on: (1) acceptance of a lower quality of water, e.g., 1 mg/l of dissolved oxygen instead of 4 mg/l or 6 mg/l; (2) changes in production processes designed to reduce output of organic waste per unit of product (tables 52 and 53); (3) a change in product mix; or (4) some combination of all three. The range of possibilities, measured by required dilution flow, is partially indicated by comparing the required dilution flows in tables 52 and 53 with those in tables 50 and 51.

Table 52, Variant 1, is constructed by assuming that the output of waste per unit of industrial product falls below 1960 levels in the projection years by 10 percent, 20 percent, and 30 percent, respectively. Variant 2 (table 53) assumes that the decline is 20 percent, 40 percent, and 60 percent. The bill of goods remains unchanged. A decline of 20 percent by the year 2000, Medium projection (table 52), would reduce required dilution for 4 mg/l by about 16 percent. A decline of 40 percent (table 53) would reduce required dilution by about 32 percent. The effect of a 40 percent decline in unit output of waste, coupled with the adoption of a D.O. standard of 1 mg/l instead of 4 mg/l, would lead to a reduction in dilution flow of about 60 percent. This, then, is one measure of the range of physical response for the economy as projected for 2000 Medium without a change in the bill of goods or a change in the regional distribution of production and population. Since losses are unaffected by changes in dilution flows, the relative change in total required flows is less. These effects are discussed in chapter 12.

The reader will note the nonlinear relationship between changes in instream dissolved oxygen and required dilution flow. To go from 1 mg/l to 4 mg/l requires an increase in dilution flow of about 70 percent; to go from 4 mg/l to 6 mg/l requires an increase of about 90 percent. Treatment levels are, of course, held constant. (See table 51.) The same relationship holds for the variants.

Costs of Treatment

Costs of treatment are derived in two ways. The "standard" progression of treatment from 50 percent to 97½ percent is based on a relatively heavy investment in fixed plant and is assumed to be operative every day of the year. Special short-term treatment was also considered; since its costs consist wholly of an outlay for chemicals no fixed charges are involved. The short-term treatment program was assumed to be used one month every year. Short-term treatment can be added at any level of long-term treatment and is designed to reduce residual BOD by 50 percent; its effect on residual nitrogen and phosphorus, however, is assumed to be negligible. This is further discussed in connection with the short-term treatment model. Unless otherwise specified, "treatment costs" refer to the standard capital-intensive twelve-month method.

For industrial wastes, treatment costs were computed on the basis of a plant having a capacity of 5 million gallons per day. The costs for a plant with this capacity are significantly lower than for a plant of 1 mgd. (Economies of scale in going from 5 to 10 mgd are much less than in going from 1 to 5 mgd. See table D–9.) Municipal treatment costs were based on a design capacity of 1 mgd for urban non-SMSA population and 50 mgd for urban SMSA population. Costs of construction, operation, and maintenance were averaged for plants of both sizes and then converted into dollars per p.e. for successively higher levels of treatment.[6]

Industrial costs of treatment were estimated separately for each of the six manufacturing industries specified below. This procedure grew out of the fact that the estimated p.e.'s per mgd discharged and the costs of treatment per mgd varied from industry to industry. P.e.'s produced per mgd of untreated discharge were as follows:

Industry	P.E.'s/mgd
Food	53,900
Textiles	21,500
Paper	13,000
Chemicals	98,200
Petroleum	14,700
Leather	39,300

The annual cost of treatment per p.e. by level of treatment was computed by converting the annual cost per mgd — the sum of the annual equivalent of capital cost plus annual operation and maintenance costs — for primary (35 percent), secondary (95 percent), and tertiary (97½ percent) into a weighted average cost for each level of treatment between 50 percent and 97½ percent in accordance with the mix given in table 41. The method is illustrated by the food processing industry.

Capital construction costs per mgd for the food processing industry were given by Reid et al. as $53,100 for primary, $674,000 for secondary, and $591,500 for ter-

---

[6]Capital costs were converted to annual costs by assuming a plant life of fifty years and an interest rate of 4 percent.

tiary treatment (the same as for municipal tertiary). Capital costs were converted to annual costs by a factor of 0.04; therefore, annual costs of fixed capital per mgd were equal to $2,124, $26,960, and $23,660, respectively. Operation and maintenance costs per mgd were estimated as $8,860, $10,000, and $26,390, for primary, secondary, and tertiary levels, respectively. Total annual costs per mgd were, therefore, equal to $10,984, $36,960, and $50,050.

These were then converted to costs of treatment per p.e. for each level of treatment. If the strength of waste for food processing is 53,900 p.e.'s per mgd, then the cost of primary treatment per p.e. is equal to 20 cents ($10,984 ÷ 53,900); the cost of secondary treatment is 69 cents per p.e. ($36,960 ÷ 53,900); and the cost of tertiary treatment is 93 cents per p.e. ($50,050 ÷ 53,900). For intermediate levels of treatment, cost per p.e. is the weighted average of primary, secondary, and tertiary as weighted by the mix in table 41. The cost of 70 percent treatment is equal to:

$$0.42 \times 20¢ = 0.08$$
$$0.48 \times 69¢ = 0.33$$
$$0.10 \times 93¢ = \underline{0.09}$$

(rounded) 0.50, i.e., 50¢ per p.e. treated.

Costs per p.e. treated are given in table 54 for six industries. Costs per p.e. for municipal treatment are given in table 55. Further details are in the appendixes.

With the costs of treatment per p.e. in hand, the total costs of treatment were computed for each region for each level of treatment for each projection of population (urban) and level of manufacturing. Wastes discharged into estuaries, coastal waters, the Great Lakes, and the Great Salt Lake were assumed to be given primary treatment only, and costs were computed at the values given for the 35 percent treatment level. (It will also be recalled that no dilution flows were supplied for such wastes.)

Tables E-4 through E-13 show total municipal and industrial costs of treatment incurred by each region as the treatment level rises. Figures for the United States for all projections are given in table 56. Absolute costs depend, of course, on the level of economic activity and the size of urban population. (Rural domestic waste was assumed to be unsewered and untreated.)

Information regarding present levels of treatment *achieved* and the relative distribution of points of discharge between streams and other points (including the Great Lakes and the Great Salt Lake) is so fragmentary that a base point representing "today's" conditions cannot be accurately established. The closest we can come is an estimate based on (1) 1959-60 figures on wastes discharged "to streams" (it is unclear whether any of the discharges were to estuarine areas);[7] and (2) a comparison of these figures with our own estimates of p.e.'s produced in 1960.[8]

		P.E.'s discharged to streams	P.E.'s produced
Industrial	1959	150	
	1960		243
Municipal	1960	75	124
Total		225	367

By comparing the figures on P.E.'s discharged into streams with the figures on P.E.'s produced, one may infer that the average level of treatment is about 39 percent — industrial, 38 percent, and municipal, 40 percent. How the "average" is distributed among zero, primary, secondary, and tertiary treatment is not known. Very little treatment is now at the tertiary level, if any.

Eighty million people, or 64 percent of the urban population in 1960, were served by waste treatment plants.[9] The reduction from 124 to 75 million p.e.'s implied that the average level of treatment was 63 percent for that portion of the urban population whose wastes were treated, and that 53 percent of the wastes received primary treatment and 47 percent received secondary treatment. These figures further imply that, of total urban population, the wastes of 34 percent received primary treatment and the wastes of 30 percent received secondary treatment. It is impossible without further data to verify the accuracy of these estimates.[10]

Regarding industrial wastes, it can be inferred from our estimates of BOD produced that the average level of treatment for all manufacturing wastes is slightly in excess of primary treatment. The severely polluted state of many rivers, lakes, and coastal regions indicates that either our estimate of the current treatment level is too high, or that very high treatment will be required in the future if pollution is to be reduced from present levels.[11]

The poor state of information regarding present treatment levels and quantities of waste discharged reflects the fact that industrial and, to a lesser degree, municipal dischargers of waste resist supplying accurate measures of waste production, treatment, and discharge. It is hoped that adequate benchmarks will be established in the near future, so that projections of waste production and its effect on rivers and streams will rest on firmer facts than we now possess.

[7] See Murray Stein, "Problems and Programs in Water Pollution," *Natural Resources Journal*, vol. 2, no. 3 (December 1962), pp. 396-98. See also *Water Pollution Control and Abatement*, Part 1A-National Survey, Hearings before a Subcommittee of the House Committee on Government Operations, 88th Cong., 1st sess. (1964).

[8] See table 35. Our estimated aggregate of P.E.'s discharged "to streams" before treatment in 1960 was 215. Figures given by Stein ("Problems and Programs") would be greater than ours if he made no deduction for discharges into the Great Lakes or into reaches of streams that we defined as "estuaries."

[9] Because industrial p.e.'s were taken out of municipal waste, we counted one urban person as equal to one p.e. Since domestic waste per person may rise, we may be understating municipal waste loads. Stein ("Problems and Programs," p. 397) used a factor of 1.75 p.e.'s per capita for 1980.

[10] Our estimates are based on an urban population of 124 million. Stein ("Problems and Programs") uses a figure of 105 million served by sewers, of which 80 million are also served by treatment plants. The raw waste of 25 million is discharged and the total population equivalent discharge is 75 million. This implies that the waste of the sewered population that is also served by treatment plants is treated to about 50 percent.

[11] It is likely that the latter inference is more correct. See letter from Thomas L. Kimball to Stewart L. Udall quoted in "Water Pollution: Officials Goaded into Raising Quality Standards," *Science*, vol. 160, no. 3823 (April 5, 1968), p. 49.

If 34 percent of total urban municipal waste had been given primary treatment at a cost of $1.71 per P.E.; if 30 percent of municipal waste had been given secondary treatment at a cost of $3.94 per P.E.; and if all industrial waste had been given primary treatment at a cost of 31 cents per P.E., total treatment costs would have been $73.5 million, plus $149.7 million, plus $75.3 million, respectively, for a total of $299 million in the composite year, 1959–60. This might be a reasonably accurate figure; who knows?

On the basis of the same system of computation, the schedule of annual costs of waste treatment for the country as a whole in 1960 would have been:

Treatment *(percent)*	Annual costs *($ million)*
70/50	422
70/60	434
70/70	453
80/80	498
90/90	544
95/95	606
97½/97½	743

If all wastes produced in 1960 had been given primary treatment, costs would have been:

$$[(125 \times 10^6) \times \$1.71] + [243 \times 10^6 \times 0.31] =$$
$$\$214 \text{ million} + 75 \text{ million} = \$289 \text{ million}.$$

This is an outlay approximately equal to that required for the combination of zero, primary, and secondary treatment that presumably was supplied. If our estimate is reasonably accurate, annual outlays would have to double to provide treatment at the 70/50 percent level for 1980 Low. If the level of treatment is kept constant at 95 percent, projected treatment costs rise by about 60 percent every twenty years along the Medium path. This is not, however, the rate of change that would be followed by the "optimum" combination of treatment and storage.

The optimum treatment level for a given bill of goods depends on the selected criterion. If the criterion is minimum cost of new storage plus treatment (constrained by a minimum treatment level of 70/50 percent), given the present level of flow regulation, the optimum level may be anywhere between 70/50 percent and 97½/97½ percent, depending on the relative movements of storage and treatment costs. If, instead, the objective is minimum interference with the river's natural physical and biotic characteristics, treatment would proceed to 97½/97½ percent. The maximum level of treatment physically attainable coincides in general with today's "conservationist" position. Movement along the 97½/97½ percent path, which falls below the maximum level theoretically attainable, indicates that the index of treatment costs would behave as follows (rounded):

1960	(as estimated above)	100
1980	Medium	400
2000	Medium	650
2020	Medium	1,050
2020	High	1,870

Apparently a change in the relative importance of municipal and industrial treatment costs is in the offing, unless there is a change in the output of waste per person or per unit of product. (Compare tables 57 and 58.) The use of garbage disposal units in the home has already contributed to a rise in BOD per person. At any rate, table 57 indicates that in 1960 about two-thirds of treatment costs would have been municipal and one-third industrial if both types of waste had been treated at the same level. By 2000 Medium, the two costs would be approximately equal. By 2020 Medium, industrial treatment costs would be 50 percent greater than municipal; and for 2020 High, they would be slightly more than twice as much. Costs do not move proportionately with BOD produced, since costs of treating industrial wastes per p.e. are lower than for municipal wastes. There are also differences in the assumed proportions discharged into coastal and estuarine waters.

The impact on the total treatment cost of changes in waste loadings incorporated in Variants 1 and 2 is indicated by comparing basic with variant models for the year 2020 for 95 percent treatment: Variant 1 would save 30 percent and Variant 2, 60 percent of industrial treatment costs, and 18 percent and 36 percent, respectively, of total treatment costs. The proportional change for 2020 High was about the same. As indicated by tables 57 and 58, when all BOD pollutants are given secondary treatment (95 percent), reduction in the output of industrial pollutants per unit of product by 30 percent (Variant 1, 2020) would save about $1 billion annually in treatment costs alone for the Medium projection, and about $2 billion at the High projection. Offsetting these savings are, of course, the net costs of changing production processes in the desired direction; reinforcing these savings is the reduction in residual BOD discharged to streams and the consequent reduction in required dilution flows.

Thermal Pollution and Recirculation Costs

Intake and discharge of cooling water for manufacturing and steam-electric power was assumed to grow in the future in proportion to increased output adjusted for an increase in the average rate of recirculation. Special attention was paid to steam-electric power, since it accounted for 83 percent of the total cooling water discharge in 1960 and under the Medium projection will account for 91 percent by the year 2020. At original recirculation rates,[12] the total cooling water discharge was estimated to rise from 79 bgd in 1960 to 1,140 bgd by 2020 High as follows (see table 59 for details):

		(bgd)
1960		79
1980	Low	147
	Medium	201
	High	287
2000	Low	191
	Medium	319
	High	546
2020	Low	325
	Medium	570
	High	1,140

[12] See table B–18 for original and revised rates.

According to estimates made by Reid and associates, the amount of dilution water required to prevent instream temperature from rising more than 5.4°F. was approximately two and a half times the discharged amount of cooling water. Table 60 shows dilution requirements based on the original projection of recirculation rates.[13]

It appears as though the rate of recirculation will have to grow much more rapidly in the future than it has up to now. For eleven regions – eight in the Northeast, plus Tennessee, Lower Mississippi, and Lower Arkansas-White-Red – dilution flows needed to prevent a temperature rise in excess of 5.4°F. exceeded dilution flows for other pollutants when treatment reached relatively high levels. In a number of regions – e.g., Ohio, Eastern Great Lakes, and Western Great Lakes – required flows by 1980 Medium would exceed maximum regulated flows, implying that temperatures would rise by more than 5.4°F. even if maximum regulation were achieved. In the remaining regions of the country, recirculation rates initially projected were high enough to avoid thermal pollution.

The heating of streams is undesirable for several reasons: (1) dissolved oxygen falls, thereby reducing the capacity of the stream to assimilate organic waste; (2) some desirable aquatic life cannot survive an increase in water temperature; (3) the stream's usefulness for cooling is reduced; and (4) the water may become warm enough to be aesthetically objectionable.[14]

Table 61 summarizes for the conterminous United States estimated intake and costs of recirculation at original and revised recirculation rates. These totals would be from 9 percent to 17 percent more if account were taken of recirculation costs of manufacturing cooling water – the additions being made in descending order beginning with 1960 and ending with 2020 High.

Our estimates indicate that the ratio of flow-through to intake ("recirculation rate") was 1.25 in 1960 and was originally projected to reach 1.70 by 2020. After revision, the recirculation rate was estimated at 6.2 for 1980 and 7.2 for 2020. The big jump to meet our thermal pollution standards should occur now.

Estimated costs of recirculation at original rates would rise from $76 million per year to $1.5 billion by 2020 Medium. At revised rates, the costs of recirculation would be a little more than twice as high. It appears that the costs of avoiding heat pollution will constitute a major share of the "costs of water."

Details for the various regions are in tables in appendix E. By the year 2000, Medium projection, costs of recirculation in the eastern half of the United States would amount to $1.2 billion annually. In the Ohio basin alone such costs would be almost $500 million annually. These are expenditures that dwarf the present estimated annual outlay of $67 million. Unless the geographic distribution of power production is substantially different from that projected (see table A-15), expenditures of this magnitude appear likely.

Collection Costs

It was estimated that the average annual costs of sanitary sewerage amounted to $4.12 per urban resident. The figure of $4.12 is the equivalent of a capital cost of $125[15] converted to an annual cost by use of 0.033 as an annual factor. (A substantially higher cost would apply to the separation of storm and sanitary sewers now needed by about 40 million people.) Whether we should consider collection costs as part of the "cost of water" any more than ordinary treatment and delivery costs depends, of course, on the objective of the analysis. The cost of removing waste from an urban area is a matter of sanitary necessity that is not *necessarily* related to water. Modern plumbing and adequate water supply make the toilet and the kitchen sink conveniences that other forms of waste disposal cannot easily compete with – either aesthetically or in cost. In order to keep a fixed cost from obtruding on our models (since sewerage cost is assumed to vary only with the size of urban population), we can show it as a separate item.

A quick comparison of collection costs, recirculation costs, and treatment costs at 95 percent BOD removal is made in table 62. Collection costs are less than treatment costs for both municipal and industrial wastes, but exceed the treatment costs for municipal wastes alone. Once everyone is hooked up to a treatment plant, the added costs of raising the level of treatment are not very much, relatively speaking. For example, for 2000 Medium, collection plus treatment plus recirculation costs for the conterminous United States vary by level of treatment as follows:

Treatment	Collection	Municipal & industrial treatment	Total collection & treatment	Recirculation costs (rev.)	Total collection, treatment, recirculation
(percent)		*($ million)*			
70/50	1,035	1,058	2,093	1,572	3,665
70/60	1,035	1,098	2,133	1,572	3,705
70/70	1,035	1,177	2,212	1,572	3,784
80/80	1,035	1,305	2,340	1,572	3,912
90/90	1,035	1,431	2,466	1,572	4,038
95/95	1,035	1,599	2,634	1,572	4,206
97½/97½	1,035	1,964	2,999	1,572	4,571

In going from 70/50 percent to 95/95 percent treatment, total costs of collection and treatment rise by about 25 percent; they rise by only 43 percent on going to 97½/97½ percent. When recirculation costs are also considered, total treatment – thermal and biological – plus collection vary by only 25 percent in going from 70/50 percent to 97½ percent.

Collection costs are assigned only to urban population. If the wastes of industrial users are sewered, an additional charge should be made. Total collection costs by region are shown in table 63.

[13] Thermal dilution flows may be understated by virtue of a probable reduction in average thermal efficiency as a result of the greater importance of nuclear power plants in the future.

[14] There may be places where an increase in water temperature might be sought – e.g., coastal waters that are now too cold for comfortable swimming.

[15] Estimated after a review of the literature. This figure is fairly low. See *A Study of Pollution – Water*, Staff Report to the Senate Committee on Public Works, 88th Cong., 1st sess. (1963).

Short-Term Tertiary Treatment

Suppose we build storage not to 98 percent security but to 90 percent security. This means that, roughly speaking, regulated flow will fall short of the specified amount 10 percent of the time instead of 2 percent of the time. The difference is one month per year, on the average. If during that one month we can provide short-term high-level treatment by a method that involves no fixed cost — only current operating expense — it may be possible to save both storage capacity and money.

According to Reid et al. the use of a microstrainer, polyelectrolites, or carbon provides a short-term onsite treatment process capable of removing an additional 50 percent of residual BOD after regular treatment. If regular treatment achieved 95 percent BOD removal, additional short-term treatment would achieve 97½ percent; if regular treatment achieved 97½ percent, short-term treatment would achieve 98¾ percent. Short-term cost computations were based on the use of polyelectrolites — $710 per mgd of waste effluent per month — converted to dollars per p.e. per month. (See appendixes D and E.)

By reducing residual BOD by 50 percent, waste dilution to offset BOD would fall by 50 percent. If the flow available 98 percent of the time from storage designed to yield a specified higher flow 90 percent of the time was enough to offset required flow after short-term treatment, the trade could presumably be made — lower storage against supplementary short-term treatment costs. If the flow available 98 percent of the time from storage computed on the 90 percent curve fell short of required flow after short-term treatment, storage had to be increased until the deficit was overcome.

A further restriction lay in the fact that supplementary short-term BOD removal did not reduce plant nutrients. Hence, the dilution flow required to offset phosphorus (usually ruling) or nitrogen at the permanent treatment level also had to be taken into account. All was satisfactory if the flow available 98 percent of the time from storage designed to yield a base flow 90 percent of the time was equal to, or more than, the larger of BOD dilution flow after supplementary treatment or phosphorus dilution flow before supplementary treatment.

The tradeoff between storage and short-term treatment is based on a specified level of "permanent" treatment. The level we have used is the standard treatment for the minimum cost program in regions not subject to water shortage and for the minimum flow program in regions that are. For the former, a lesser amount of storage (storage yielding the specified flow but with a 10 percent chance instead of a 2 percent chance of deficiency) yielded savings that could be compared with short-term treatment costs. For water-short regions, additional treatment would reduce the size of water deficits. The question to be asked is whether the saving in water requirement is worth the added outlay.

Short-Term Treatment versus Lower Permanent Treatment

Another possible tradeoff, but one that was not explored, would be to construct treatment facilities to the level required 90 percent of the time on the basis of storage designed to yield a specified flow 98 percent of the time. The flows equalled or exceeded 90 percent of the time would be higher than the flows equalled or exceeded 98 percent of the time and therefore would be compatible with a lower permanent level of treatment. During 8 percent of the time, when flows reached the minimum level consistent with the aggregate amount of shortage and administration of the storage capacity, short-term high-level treatment would be provided. The tradeoff would be the savings in the annual cost of avoiding a higher level of permanent treatment against the short-term supplemental treatment costs required during the periods of lowest flow.

Table 34. PERCENTAGE OF TOTAL WASTE
DISCHARGED TO STREAMS, BY REGION

	Municipal	Industrial		Municipal	Industrial
N Eng	45	15	L Miss	65	70
D & H	15	35	L AWR	100	100
Ches	30	70	U Mo	100	100
Ohio	100	100	U AWR	100	100
EGL	25	50	W Gulf	70	70
WGL	20	45	RG-P	100	100
U Miss	100	100	Colo	100	100
L Mo	100	100	G Basin	30	65
SE	70	75	S Pac	5	20
Cumb	100	100	C Pac	35	40
Tenn	100	100	PNW	35	55

Table 35. BOD WASTE LOADS IN POPULATION EQUIVALENTS, BY MAJOR SOURCE AND REGION: 1960

(thousands)

	Municipal	Industrial Food	Textiles	Pulp & paper	Chemicals	Petroleum	Leather	Total to fresh water before treatment	Total produced Industrial	Municipal	Total
NORTHEAST	75,433	58,886	1,385	23,824	72,865	1,279	1,124	126,402	159,363	75,433	234,796
N Eng	7,922	2,359	724	5,498	2,623	19	261	5,287	11,484	7,922	19,406
D & H	21,087	13,710	352	4,157	24,506	453	160	18,331	43,338	21,087	64,425
Ches	6,625	4,377	158	2,037	5,803	42	134	10,773	12,551	6,625	19,176
Ohio	10,418	8,247	50	2,365	14,881	179	181	36,321	25,903	10,418	36,321
EGL	10,068	5,887	55	2,078	8,212	173	0	10,720	16,405	10,068	26,473
WGL	10,757	11,020	46	4,392	11,926	264	388	14,768	28,036	10,757	38,793
U Miss	7,259	12,365	0	2,969	4,700	149	0	27,442	20,183	7,259	27,442
L Mo	1,297	921	0	328	214	0	0	2,760	1,463	1,297	2,760
SOUTHEAST	17,278	6,736	2,997	11,517	17,730	231	0	44,855	39,211	17,278	56,489
SE	11,138	4,294	2,702	7,126	7,773	10	0	24,225	21,905	11,138	33,043
Cumb	542	83	0	0	0	0	0	625	83	542	625
Tenn	1,149	424	226	1,095	4,925	0	0	7,819	6,670	1,149	7,819
L Miss	2,475	1,511	69	1,136	3,608	179	0	6,161	6,503	2,475	8,978
L AWR	1,974	424	0	2,160	1,424	42	0	6,025	4,050	1,974	6,024
MID-CONTINENT	11,937	7,233	27	819	14,560	1,170	0	29,049	23,809	11,937	35,746
U Mo	3,353	4,625	0	0	1,317	149	0	9,444	6,091	3,353	9,444
U AWR	2,188	673	0	0	771	352	0	3,983	1,796	2,188	3,984
W Gulf	6,396	1,935	27	819	12,472	669	0	15,622	15,922	6,396	22,318
SOUTHWEST	11,292	3,267	0	410	1,756	307	0	4,428	5,740	11,292	17,032
RG-P	1,007	83	0	0	0	111	0	1,201	194	1,007	1,201
Colo	1,260	164	0	0	0	0	0	1,426	164	1,260	1,424
G Basin	644	248	0	0	0	0	0	355	248	644	892
S Pac	8,381	2,773	0	410	1,756	196	0	1,446	5,135	8,381	13,516
NORTH PACIFIC	8,595	8,070	0	4,197	2,623	274	0	10,032	15,164	8,595	23,759
C Pac	5,172	5,970	0	614	1,970	232	0	5,325	8,786	5,172	13,958
PNW	3,423	2,100	0	3,583	653	42	0	4,707	6,378	3,423	9,801
U.S.	124,535	84,192	4,409	40,767	109,534	3,261	1,124	214,766	243,287	124,535	367,822

Note: One p.e. is the waste equivalent of one person, measured as 0.25 lb. of oxygen per day utilized in decomposition.

Table 36. BOD WASTE LOADS IN POPULATION EQUIVALENTS, BY MAJOR SOURCE AND REGION: 1980 MEDIUM

(thousands)

| | Municipal | Industrial | | | | | | Total to fresh water before treatment | Total produced | | Total |
		Food	Textiles	Pulp & paper	Chemicals	Petroleum	Leather		Industrial	Municipal	
NORTHEAST	100,260	89,377	2,193	34,587	170,547	2,369	1,573	223,011	300,646	100,260	400,906
N Eng	10,235	2,607	1,146	8,457	6,145	62	365	7,423	18,782	10,235	29,017
D & H	26,927	20,425	557	4,802	51,699	1,010	225	31,590	78,718	26,927	105,645
Ches	9,798	5,784	251	5,918	16,038	123	187	22,750	28,301	9,798	38,099
Ohio	13,168	13,844	79	2,734	34,441	195	253	64,713	51,546	13,168	64,714
EGL	14,088	7,688	87	3,379	22,290	212	0	20,350	33,656	14,088	47,744
WGL	14,760	20,911	73	5,068	23,189	566	543	25,610	50,350	14,760	65,110
U Miss	9,633	17,104	0	3,379	13,115	175	0	43,405	33,773	9,633	43,406
L Mo	1,651	1,014	0	850	3,630	26	0	7,170	5,520	1,651	7,171
SOUTHEAST	28,881	9,912	4,747	26,148	54,248	365	0	99,447	95,420	28,881	124,301
SE	20,215	6,322	4,279	18,561	21,412	26	0	52,101	50,600	20,215	70,815
Cumb	766	393	0	850	7,730	8	0	9,747	8,981	766	9,747
Tenn	1,813	838	358	1,679	9,047	8	0	13,742	11,930	1,813	13,743
L Miss	3,567	1,862	110	1,679	12,376	274	0	13,730	16,301	3,567	19,868
L AWR	2,520	497	0	3,379	3,683	49	0	10,127	7,608	2,520	10,128
MID-CONTINENT	16,684	10,181	42	1,679	35,918	2,095	0	52,933	49,915	16,684	66,599
U Mo	4,872	5,101	0	0	3,629	175	0	13,778	8,905	4,872	13,777
U AWR	2,653	921	0	0	3,276	412	0	7,262	4,609	2,653	7,262
W Gulf	9,159	4,159	42	1,679	29,013	1,508	0	31,893	36,401	9,159	45,560
SOUTHWEST	22,193	7,842	0	727	5,953	589	0	11,007	15,111	22,193	37,304
RG-P	1,853	186	0	0	193	130	0	2,362	509	1,853	2,362
Colo	2,678	724	0	51	193	8	0	3,654	976	2,678	3,654
G Basin	897	962	0	51	1,552	8	0	1,942	2,573	897	3,470
S Pac	16,765	5,970	0	625	4,015	443	0	3,049	11,053	16,765	27,818
NORTH PACIFIC	13,022	17,714	0	24,275	6,498	313	0	28,516	48,800	13,022	61,822
C Pac	8,047	13,161	0	1,065	4,721	264	0	10,501	19,211	8,047	27,258
PNW	4,975	4,553	0	23,210	1,777	49	0	18,015	29,589	4,975	34,564
U.S.	181,040	135,026	6,982	87,416	273,164	5,731	1,573	414,914	509,892	181,040	690,932

Note: One p.e. is the waste equivalent of one person, measured as 0.25 lb. of oxygen per day utilized in decomposition.

Table 37. BOD WASTE LOADS IN POPULATION EQUIVALENTS, BY MAJOR SOURCE AND REGION: 2000 MEDIUM

(thousands)

| | | Industrial | | | | | | Total to fresh water before treatment | Total produced | | Total |
	Municipal	Food	Textiles	Pulp & paper	Chemicals	Petroleum	Leather		Industrial	Municipal	
NORTHEAST	133,553	137,707	3,390	52,245	297,399	4,323	2,199	371,224	497,263	133,553	630,816
N Eng	13,298	3,249	1,771	14,712	9,807	116	511	10,509	30,166	13,298	43,464
D & H	34,948	30,700	862	5,836	93,228	1,889	314	51,732	132,829	34,948	167,777
Ches	13,974	9,281	387	8,180	34,516	232	262	41,193	52,858	13,974	66,832
Ohio	16,824	22,225	122	4,904	64,782	366	353	109,576	92,752	16,824	109,576
EGL	19,679	12,385	135	4,269	41,711	396	0	34,368	58,896	19,679	78,575
WGL	20,318	33,255	113	6,174	43,413	1,059	759	42,211	84,773	20,318	105,091
U Miss	12,725	25,443	0	4,904	2,459	216	0	67,880	33,022	12,725	45,747
L Mo	1,787	1,169	0	3,266	7,483	49	0	13,755	11,967	1,787	13,754
SOUTHEAST	42,523	14,879	7,338	52,296	130,517	657	0	197,892	205,687	42,523	248,210
SE	30,682	10,161	6,615	34,328	54,408	49	0	100,648	105,561	30,682	136,243
Cumb	1,052	517	0	1,638	18,361	15	0	21,583	20,531	1,052	21,583
Tenn	2,563	1,128	553	3,266	17,793	15	0	25,318	22,755	2,563	25,318
L Miss	5,230	2,494	170	6,532	33,264	512	0	33,479	42,972	5,230	48,202
L AWR	2,996	579	0	6,532	6,691	66	0	16,864	13,868	2,996	16,864
MID-CONTINENT	22,658	14,682	65	9,808	89,780	3,520	0	110,744	117,855	22,658	140,513
U Mo	6,788	6,570	0	4,904	7,483	216	0	25,962	19,173	6,788	25,961
U AWR	3,042	1,283	0	1,638	8,843	511	0	15,317	12,275	3,042	15,317
W Gulf	12,828	6,829	65	3,266	73,454	2,793	0	69,465	86,407	12,828	99,235
SOUTHWEST	34,020	14,299	0	8,927	13,158	1,019	0	25,559	37,403	34,020	71,423
RG-P	2,789	362	0	1,638	514	162	0	5,465	2,676	2,789	5,465
Colo	4,184	1,283	0	3,266	514	15	0	9,262	5,078	4,184	9,262
G Basin	1,101	1,769	0	1,638	3,854	15	0	5,060	7,276	1,101	8,377
S Pac	25,946	10,885	0	2,385	8,276	827	0	5,772	22,373	25,946	48,319
NORTH PACIFIC	18,433	31,900	0	45,958	13,715	561	0	51,291	92,134	18,433	110,567
C Pac	11,282	24,212	0	4,146	10,032	499	0	19,504	38,889	11,282	50,171
PNW	7,151	7,688	0	41,812	3,683	62	0	31,787	53,245	7,151	60,396
U.S.	251,187	213,467	10,793	169,234	544,569	10,080	2,199	756,710	950,342	251,187	1,201,529

Note: One p.e. is the waste equivalent of one person, measured as 0.25 lb. of oxygen per day utilized in decomposition.

Table 38. BOD WASTE LOADS IN POPULATION EQUIVALENTS, BY MAJOR SOURCE AND REGION: 2020 MEDIUM

(thousands)

| | Municipal | Industrial | | | | | | Total to fresh water before treatment | Total produced | | Total |
		Food	Textiles	Pulp & paper	Chemicals	Petroleum	Leather		Industrial	Municipal	
NORTHEAST	175,424	221,095	5,252	78,893	590,029	8,430	3,074	626,521	906,773	175,424	1,082,197
N Eng	17,287	4,822	2,744	26,291	15,256	227	714	15,287	50,054	17,287	67,341
D & H	45,323	48,238	1,335	6,122	162,635	3,732	439	84,674	222,501	45,323	267,824
Ches	19,087	15,314	600	11,538	68,508	458	366	73,474	96,784	19,087	115,871
Ohio	21,082	36,494	189	9,429	117,070	718	494	185,476	164,394	21,082	185,476
EGL	26,766	20,446	209	4,474	74,963	784	0	57,129	100,876	26,766	127,642
WGL	27,371	54,394	175	5,252	92,789	2,088	1,061	75,566	155,759	27,371	183,130
U Miss	16,384	39,742	0	7,361	44,441	326	0	108,255	91,870	16,384	108,254
L Mo	2,124	1,645	0	8,426	14,367	97	0	26,660	24,535	2,124	26,659
SOUTHEAST	58,805	23,881	11,366	103,138	276,461	1,297	0	377,903	416,143	58,805	474,948
SE	43,908	16,741	10,247	64,213	118,515	97	0	188,096	209,813	43,908	253,721
Cumb	1,306	704	0	3,174	38,649	30	0	43,862	42,557	1,306	43,863
Tenn	3,393	1,645	856	6,317	33,199	30	0	45,441	42,047	3,393	45,440
L Miss	7,093	3,953	263	16,821	74,407	1,010	0	72,127	96,454	7,093	103,547
L AWR	3,105	838	0	12,613	11,691	130	0	28,377	25,272	3,105	28,377
MID-CONTINENT	29,243	23,001	101	27,356	193,821	6,505	0	210,054	250,784	29,243	280,027
U Mo	8,997	9,757	0	15,787	14,367	327	0	49,236	40,238	8,997	49,235
U AWR	3,356	1,883	0	5,252	19,828	556	0	30,875	27,519	3,356	30,875
W Gulf	16,890	11,361	101	6,317	159,626	5,622	0	139,943	183,027	16,890	199,917
SOUTHWEST	48,505	25,402	0	26,802	26,508	1,871	0	53,013	80,583	48,505	129,088
RG-P	3,945	662	0	5,252	1,113	177	0	11,149	7,204	3,945	11,149
Colo	6,516	2,235	0	10,340	1,113	30	0	20,235	13,718	6,516	20,234
G Basin	1,219	3,177	0	5,088	8,351	30	0	11,185	16,646	1,219	17,865
S Pac	36,825	19,328	0	6,122	15,931	1,634	0	10,444	43,015	36,825	79,840
NORTH PACIFIC	24,041	56,205	0	87,945	26,850	1,049	0	91,856	172,049	24,041	196,090
C Pac	14,416	43,168	0	10,699	19,720	982	0	34,873	74,569	14,416	88,985
PNW	9,625	13,037	0	77,246	7,130	67	0	56,983	97,480	9,625	107,105
U.S.	336,018	349,584	16,719	324,134	1,113,669	19,152	3,074	1,359,347	1,826,332	336,018	2,162,350

Note: One p.e. is the waste equivalent of one person, measured as 0.25 lb. of oxygen per day utilized in decomposition.

Table 39. BOD WASTE LOADS IN POPULATION EQUIVALENTS, BY MAJOR SOURCE AND REGION: 2020 HIGH

(thousands)

		Industrial							Total to fresh water before treatment	Total produced		
	Municipal	Food	Textiles	Pulp & paper	Chemicals	Petroleum	Leather			Industrial	Municipal	Total
NORTHEAST	232,109	539,856	11,569	132,490	1,628,629	13,629	5,440		1,526,250	2,331,613	232,109	2,563,722
N Eng	22,874	11,775	6,045	44,146	42,117	369	1,263		26,151	105,715	22,874	128,589
D & H	59,970	117,790	2,940	10,289	448,892	6,032	777		214,348	586,720	59,970	646,690
Ches	25,253	37,384	1,322	19,381	189,089	740	648		181,570	248,564	25,253	273,817
Ohio	27,893	89,108	416	15,838	323,139	1,162	874		458,430	430,537	27,893	458,430
EGL	35,416	49,935	460	7,515	206,926	1,266	0		141,905	266,102	35,416	301,518
WGL	36,215	132,804	386	8,815	256,120	3,376	1,878		188,763	403,379	36,215	439,594
U Miss	21,678	97,045	0	12,357	122,680	526	0		254,286	232,608	21,678	254,286
L Mo	2,810	4,015	0	14,149	39,666	158	0		60,797	57,988	2,810	60,798
SOUTHEAST	77,809	58,295	25,042	173,237	763,113	2,098	0		880,578	1,021,785	77,809	1,099,594
SE	58,097	40,881	22,577	107,857	327,143	158	0		414,629	498,616	58,097	556,713
Cumb	1,729	1,707	0	5,334	106,685	49	0		115,505	113,775	1,729	115,504
Tenn	4,490	4,015	1,886	10,617	91,622	49	0		112,679	108,189	4,490	112,679
L Miss	9,385	9,643	579	28,257	205,384	1,631	0		177,947	245,494	9,385	254,879
L AWR	4,108	2,049	0	21,172	32,279	211	0		59,818	55,711	4,108	59,819
MID-CONTINENT	38,691	56,152	223	45,948	534,990	10,516	0		533,338	647,829	38,691	686,520
U Mo	11,905	23,808	0	26,516	39,666	530	0		102,426	90,520	11,905	102,425
U AWR	4,439	4,604	0	8,815	54,729	897	0		73,485	69,045	4,439	73,484
W Gulf	22,347	27,740	223	10,617	440,595	9,089	0		357,427	488,264	22,347	510,611
SOUTHWEST	64,180	62,061	0	45,017	73,177	3,024	0		102,959	183,279	64,180	247,459
RG-P	5,220	1,624	0	8,815	3,073	285	0		19,017	13,797	5,220	19,017
Colo	8,623	5,463	0	17,364	3,073	49	0		34,572	25,949	8,623	34,572
G Basin	1,612	7,771	0	8,549	23,061	49	0		26,113	39,430	1,612	41,042
S Pac	48,725	47,203	0	10,289	43,970	2,641	0		23,257	104,103	48,725	152,828
NORTH PACIFIC	31,810	137,253	0	147,694	74,097	1,697	0		182,632	360,741	31,810	392,551
C Pac	19,076	105,415	0	17,968	54,419	1,589	0		78,433	179,391	19,076	198,467
PNW	12,734	31,838	0	129,726	19,678	108	0		104,199	181,350	12,734	194,084
U.S.	444,599	853,617	36,834	544,386	3,074,006	30,964	5,440		3,225,757	4,545,247	444,599	4,989,846

Note: One p.e. is the waste equivalent of one person, measured as 0.25 lb. of oxygen per day utilized in decomposition.

Table 40. TOTAL POPULATION EQUIVALENTS TO FRESH WATER BEFORE TREATMENT, BY REGION

(thousands)

	1960	1980 L	1980 M	1980 H	2000 L	2000 M	2000 H	2020 L	2020 M	2020 H
NORTHEAST	126,402	184,762	223,011	301,985	246,939	371,224	69,306	374,799	626,521	1,526,250
N Eng	5,287	6,645	7,423	8,610	8,035	10,509	14,961	11,338	15,287	26,151
D & H	18,331	25,520	31,590	44,090	33,092	51,732	100,462	50,511	84,674	214,348
Ches	10,773	18,563	22,750	30,630	26,497	41,193	77,642	43,693	73,474	181,570
Ohio	36,321	52,969	64,713	88,880	71,531	109,576	208,086	113,159	185,476	458,430
EGL	10,720	16,554	20,350	27,945	22,243	34,368	65,378	34,555	57,129	141,905
WGL	14,768	21,381	25,610	34,861	28,561	42,211	79,465	47,401	75,566	188,763
U Miss	27,442	37,232	43,405	57,357	47,907	67,880	122,136	72,523	108,255	254,286
L Mo	2,760	5,898	7,170	9,612	9,073	13,755	24,931	1,619	26,660	60,797
SOUTHEAST	44,855	81,764	99,447	130,120	128,512	197,892	356,344	226,628	377,903	880,578
SE	24,225	43,942	52,101	65,271	68,201	100,648	171,396	118,088	188,096	414,629
Cumb	625	7,479	9,747	14,009	12,635	21,583	43,808	23,563	43,862	115,505
Tenn	7,819	10,827	13,742	19,093	15,598	25,318	48,749	25,880	45,441	112,679
L Miss	6,161	10,954	13,730	19,022	20,708	33,479	64,237	41,193	72,127	177,947
L AWR	6,025	8,562	10,127	12,725	11,370	16,864	28,154	17,904	28,377	59,818
MID-CONTINENT	29,049	43,595	52,933	71,764	71,663	110,744	207,345	130,598	220,054	533,338
U Mo	9,444	12,019	13,778	17,929	18,639	25,962	43,484	33,431	49,236	102,426
U AWR	3,983	6,082	7,262	9,537	10,235	15,317	28,002	18,363	30,875	73,485
W Gulf	15,622	25,494	31,893	44,298	42,789	69,465	135,859	78,804	139,943	357,427
SOUTHWEST	4,428	9,767	11,007	13,694	18,804	25,559	40,170	37,146	53,013	102,959
RG-P	1,201	2,168	2,362	2,726	4,178	5,465	7,670	8,122	11,149	19,017
Colo	1,426	3,366	3,654	4,265	7,132	9,262	13,084	14,872	20,235	34,572
G Basin	355	1,594	1,942	2,719	3,329	5,060	9,378	6,937	11,185	26,113
S Pac	1,446	2,639	3,049	3,984	4,165	5,772	10,038	7,215	10,444	23,257
NORTH PACIFIC	10,032	24,951	28,516	34,189	37,379	51,291	80,825	64,015	91,856	182,632
C Pac	5,325	9,260	10,501	13,619	14,447	19,504	33,831	24,802	34,873	78,433
PNW	4,707	15,691	18,015	20,570	22,932	31,787	46,994	39,213	56,983	104,199
U.S.	214,766	344,839	414,914	551,752	503,297	756,710	1,377,745	833,186	1,369,347	3,225,757

Note: One p.e. is the waste equivalent of one person, measured as 0.25 lb. of oxygen per day utilized in decomposition.

Table 41. MIX OF TREATMENT BY PERCENTAGE
OF INDUSTRIAL BOD REDUCTION

(percent)

Level of treatment	Primary	Secondary	Tertiary
35	100	0	0
50	75	25	0
60	58	42	0
70	42	48	10
80	26	54	20
90	10	60	30
95	2	48	50
97½	0	0	100

Table 42. BASIC AND VARIANT ASSUMPTIONS FOR WASTE LOADS PER UNIT OF OUTPUT

(BOD waste in p.e.'s per $1 million of value added)

Manufacturing industry	Basic: 1960 invariant for all years	Variant 1 Percent reduction below 1960: 1980 (10%)	Variant 1 2000 (20%)	Variant 1 2020 (30%)	Variant 2 Percent reduction below 1960: 1980 (20%)	Variant 2 2000 (40%)	Variant 2 2020 (60%)
Food	10,347	9,312	8,278	7,243	8,278	6,208	4,139
Textiles	1,852	1,667	1,482	1,296	1,482	1,111	741
Pulp & paper	10,238	9,214	8,190	7,167	8,190	6,143	4,095
Chemicals	10,706	9,635	8,565	7,494	8,565	6,424	4,282
Petroleum refining	1,370	1,233	1,096	959	1,096	822	548
Leather	7,039	6,335	5,631	4,927	5,631	4,223	2,816

Note: One p.e. is the waste equivalent of one person, measured as 0.25 lb. of oxygen per day utilized in decomposition.

Table 43. PERCENTAGE OF PHOSPHORUS AND
NITROGEN REMOVED BY VARIOUS
LEVELS OF TREATMENT

(percent)

Level of treatment	Phosphorus removed	Nitrogen removed
50	16.2	18.5
60	20.5	25.6
70	30.8	37.3
80	41.0	48.9
90	51.2	60.5
95	65.8	73.7
97½	97.5	99.0

Table 44. PERCENTAGE DISTRIBUTION OF TOTAL
BOD PRODUCED, BY MAJOR SOURCE

		Munic-ipal	Food	Textiles	Pulp & paper	Chem-icals	Petro-leum	Total
1960		34	23	1	11	30	1	100
1980	M	26	20	1	13	40	1	100
2000	M	21	18	1	14	45	1	100
2020	M	16	16	1	15	52	1	100
	H	9	17	1	11	62	1	100

Note: Discrepancies due to rounding.

Table 45. DILUTION FLOWS FOR NEW ENGLAND, 4 mg/l D.O.: 2000 MEDIUM

Treatment level	BOD dilution	Phosphorus dilution	Nitrogen dilution	Thermal dilution	Ruling dilution
(percent)			*(million gallons per day)*		
70/50	27,464	5,663	149	11,472	27,464
70/60	24,402	5,781	235	11,472	24,402
70/70	21,339	5,812	306	11,472	21,339
80/80	14,226	5,827	606	11,472	14,226
90/90	7,113	5,638	971	11,472	7,113
95/95	3,557	4,240	825	11,472	4,240
97½/97½	1,778	242	–	11,472	1,778

Table 46. RULING DILUTION FLOWS AT SELECTED
LEVELS OF TREATMENT, BY REGION,
4 mg/l D.O.: 1960

(million gallons per day)

	Treatment level *(percent)*			
	70/50	80	95	97½
NORTHEAST	218,088	108,687	42,814	12,000
N Eng	13,057	7,152	2,406	894
D & H	16,824	7,229	3,247	904
Ches	34,136	14,742	3,686	1,843
Ohio	15,928	16,396	11,932	900
EGL	26,594	11,740	2,935	1,468
WGL	92,739	39,391	9,848	4,924
U Miss	16,011	10,233	7,447	895
L Mo	2,799	1,804	1,313	172
SOUTHEAST	210,417	96,430	29,051	11,966
SE	170,568	78,308	19,577	9,789
Cumb	1,381	1,396	1,016	86
Tenn	26,093	11,089	5,063	1,386
L Miss	4,319	1,929	1,047	241
L AWR	8,056	3,708	2,348	464
MID-CONTINENT	81,485	47,969	32,438	4,538
U Mo	20,814	15,954	11,611	1,213
U AWR	7,767	8,113	5,904	337
W Gulf	52,904	23,902	14,923	2,988
SOUTHWEST	28,313	17,339	8,100	2,034
RG-P	3,136	2,955	2,151	236
Colo	17,224	10,658	4,782	1,332
G Basin	2,158	1,104	407	138
S Pac	5,795	2,622	760	328
NORTH PACIFIC	73,916	33,367	8,406	4,171
C Pac	25,477	11,795	3,013	1,474
PNW	48,439	21,572	5,393	2,697
U.S.	612,219	303,792	120,809	34,709

Table 47. RULING DILUTION FLOW AT 95% TREATMENT, BY REGION, 4 mg/l D.O.

(million gallons per day)

	1980			2000			2020		
	L	M	H	L	M	H	L	M	H
NORTHEAST	60,411	70,956	92,455	78,654	112,858	199,451	120,775	185,354	429,691
N Eng	2,947	3,189	3,571	3,450	4,240	5,512	4,617	5,695	8,853
D & H	4,365	5,176	6,842	5,530	8,066	14,435	8,207	12,716	29,435
Ches	6,402	7,846	10,563	9,201	14,305	26,962	15,251	25,647	63,379
Ohio	16,099	18,664	23,844	20,450	28,813	49,179	30,093	44,954	99,607
EGL	4,453	5,585	7,669	6,118	9,454	17,984	9,522	15,743	39,103
WGL	14,258	17,078	23,247	19,045	28,148	52,990	31,609	50,390	125,875
U Miss	9,813	11,030	13,725	12,243	16,251	26,342	17,643	24,292	50,521
L Mo	2,074	2,388	2,994	2,617	3,581	6,047	3,833	5,917	12,918
SOUTHEAST	51,882	61,793	78,699	78,313	116,695	202,579	132,655	214,012	482,435
SE	35,511	42,105	52,749	55,124	81,339	138,514	95,432	152,009	335,080
Cumb	4,393	5,523	7,671	6,989	11,419	22,325	12,325	22,128	56,807
Tenn	7,190	8,702	11,510	9,878	14,915	26,785	15,349	25,018	58,192
L Miss	1,677	1,991	2,588	2,730	4,107	7,347	4,855	7,979	18,688
L AWR	3,111	3,472	4,181	3,592	4,915	7,608	4,694	6,878	13,668
MID-CONTINENT	45,301	51,866	64,522	63,968	89,481	149,245	101,090	153,824	336,209
U Mo	15,096	16,681	20,082	19,744	25,577	38,445	29,643	39,380	74,325
U AWR	7,572	8,535	10,184	10,060	13,281	21,543	14,042	21,531	46,692
W Gulf	22,633	26,650	34,256	34,164	50,623	89,257	57,405	92,913	215,192
SOUTHWEST	16,578	18,024	20,774	30,665	40,106	58,510	61,604	84,580	151,010
RG-P	3,720	3,995	4,452	5,312	6,536	8,465	8,187	10,187	15,307
Colo	10,115	10,834	12,130	20,392	26,482	37,410	43,980	59,838	102,235
G Basin	1,326	1,616	2,262	2,870	4,362	8,084	6,090	9,820	22,925
S Pac	1,417	1,579	1,930	2,091	2,726	4,551	3,347	4,735	10,543
NORTH PACIFIC	24,919	28,537	33,501	39,404	54,321	83,174	70,629	101,956	194,960
C Pac	5,216	5,915	7,671	8,282	11,181	19,395	14,413	20,266	45,581
PNW	19,703	22,622	25,830	31,122	43,140	63,779	56,216	81,690	149,379
U.S.	199,091	231,176	289,951	291,004	413,461	692,959	486,753	739,726	1,594,305

Table 48. RULING DILUTION FLOWS AT SELECTED LEVELS OF TREATMENT, BY REGION, 4 mg/l D.O.: MEDIUM PROJECTIONS

(million gallons per day)

	Treatment level (percent): 1980				Treatment level (percent): 2000				Treatment level (percent): 2020			
	70/50	80	95	97½	70/50	80	95	97½	70/50	80	95	97½
NORTHEAST	402,276	189,146	70,956	21,598	685,520	311,826	112,858	36,279	1,205,600	531,677	185,354	62,936
N Eng	18,877	10,044	3,189	1,255	27,464	14,226	4,240	1,778	41,220	20,702	5,695	2,588
D & H	29,539	12,453	5,176	1,557	48,923	20,396	8,066	2,550	80,799	33,392	12,716	4,174
Ches	74,402	31,383	7,846	3,923	137,224	57,219	14,305	7,152	248,474	102,588	25,647	12,823
Ohio	29,467	25,645	18,664	1,604	51,008	39,590	28,813	2,717	87,845	61,768	44,954	4,601
EGL	51,981	22,339	5,585	2,792	89,123	37,815	9,454	4,727	150,051	62,971	15,743	7,871
WGL	162,901	68,310	17,078	8,539	270,644	112,593	28,148	14,074	489,303	201,562	50,390	25,195
U Miss	26,446	15,155	11,030	1,451	42,986	22,330	16,251	2,324	70,839	33,378	24,292	3,770
L Mo	8,663	3,817	2,388	477	18,148	7,657	3,581	957	37,069	15,316	5,917	1,914
SOUTHEAST	479,474	212,503	61,793	26,563	967,001	417,990	116,695	52,248	1,869,692	792,020	214,012	99,002
SE	375,307	168,420	42,105	21,053	743,956	325,354	81,339	40,669	1,420,730	608,034	152,009	76,004
Cumb	31,714	13,097	5,523	1,637	78,094	31,859	11,419	3,982	170,315	68,947	22,128	8,618
Tenn	47,176	19,922	8,702	2,490	90,950	37,915	14,915	4,739	169,020	69,689	25,018	8,711
L Miss	10,813	4,639	1,991	580	28,610	11,929	4,107	1,491	64,973	26,671	7,979	3,334
L AWR	14,464	6,425	3,472	803	25,391	10,933	4,915	1,367	44,654	18,679	6,878	2,335
MID-CONTINENT	166,349	86,980	51,866	9,071	370,729	169,706	89,481	19,815	776,114	336,949	153,824	40,539
U Mo	35,069	22,920	16,681	2,042	76,593	35,144	25,577	4,277	161,311	69,613	39,380	8,702
U AWR	10,967	11,727	8,535	487	18,386	18,248	13,281	999	40,509	29,584	21,531	2,118
W Gulf	120,313	52,333	26,650	6,542	275,750	116,314	50,623	14,539	574,294	237,752	92,913	29,719
SOUTHWEST	104,755	56,005	18,024	6,979	312,767	148,672	40,106	18,584	729,509	328,921	84,580	41,115
RG-P	9,114	5,489	3,995	664	29,506	14,830	6,536	1,854	67,277	31,348	10,187	3,918
Colo	68,080	38,525	10,834	4,816	216,965	105,927	26,482	13,241	521,306	239,353	59,838	29,919
G Basin	15,260	6,462	1,616	808	42,480	17,448	4,362	2,181	96,915	39,280	9,820	4,910
S Pac	12,301	5,529	1,579	691	23,816	10,467	2,726	1,308	44,011	18,940	4,735	2,368
NORTH PACIFIC	270,275	114,146	28,537	14,268	520,575	215,287	54,321	27,161	988,519	407,827	101,956	50,618
C Pac	52,802	23,659	5,915	2,957	102,757	44,725	11,181	5,591	190,935	81,066	20,266	10,133
PNW	217,473	90,487	22,622	11,311	417,818	172,562	43,140	21,570	797,584	326,761	81,690	40,485
U.S.	1,423,129	658,780	231,176	78,479	2,856,592	1,263,481	413,461	154,087	5,569,434	2,397,394	739,726	294,210

Table 49. RULING DILUTION FLOWS AT 95% TREATMENT, BY REGION: MEDIUM PROJECTIONS

(million gallons per day)

	1960			1980			2000			2020		
	1 mg/l	4 mg/l	6 mg/l	1 mg/l	4 mg/l	6 mg/l	1 mg/l	4 mg/l	6 mg/l	1 mg/l	4 mg/l	6 mg/l
NORTHEAST	19,410	42,814	41,346	33,213	70,956	73,612	53,944	112,858	122,994	90,984	185,354	213,430
N Eng	1,117	2,406	2,980	1,569	3,189	4,185	2,223	4,240	5,928	3,235	5,695	8,626
D & H	1,129	3,247	3,012a	1,946	5,176	5,189	3,187	8,066	8,498	5,218	12,716	13,913
Ches	2,250	3,686	6,416	4,789	7,846	13,657	8,731	14,305	24,901	15,655	25,647	44,645
Ohio	3,978	11,932	3,978a	6,221	18,664	6,221a	9,604	28,813	9,782a	14,985	44,954	16,565a
EGL	1,861	2,935	4,769	3,542	5,585	9,075	5,995	9,454	15,362	9,983	15,743	25,582
WGL	6,155	9,848	16,413	10,673	17,078	28,462	17,593	28,148	46,914	31,494	50,390	83,984
U Miss	2,482	7,447	3,168a	3,677	11,030	5,135a	5,417	16,251	8,222a	8,097	24,292	13,341a
L Mo	438	1,313	610a	796	2,388	1,688a	1,194	3,581	3,387a	2,317	5,917	6,774
SOUTHEAST	14,099	29,051	49,696	30,289	61,793	109,460	59,259	116,695	214,731	112,218	214,012	406,087
SE	10,940	19,577	41,329	23,529	42,105	88,888	45,454	81,339	171,714	84,946	152,009	320,907
Cumb	339	1,016	339a	1,999	5,523	5,700	4,862	11,419	13,864	10,521	22,128	30,005
Tenn	1,688	5,063	5,183	2,934	8,702	9,311	5,583	14,915	17,721	10,262	25,018	32,572
L Miss	349	1,047	942a	670	1,991	2,264	1,722	4,107	5,822	3,850	7,979	13,018
L AWR	783	2,348	1,903a	1,157	3,472	3,297a	1,638	4,915	5,610	2,639	6,878	9,585
MID-CONTINENT	10,812	32,438	21,078	17,288	51,866	42,695	29,827	89,481	92,142	51,588	153,824	187,079
U Mo	3,870	11,611	3,942a	5,560	16,681	6,638a	8,526	25,577	13,900a	13,277	39,380	28,280a
U AWR	1,968	5,904	1,968a	2,845	8,535	2,845a	4,427	13,281	4,427a	7,177	21,531	7,918a
W Gulf	4,974	14,923	15,168	8,883	26,650	33,212	16,874	50,623	73,815	31,134	92,913	150,881
SOUTHWEST	2,893	8,100	7,708	8,739	18,024	26,614	21,747	40,106	71,220	47,927	84,580	157,871
RG-P	717	2,151	944a	1,332	3,995	2,656a	2,179	6,536	7,415	4,478	10,187	15,674
Colo	1,594	4,782	5,202	5,562	10,834	18,804	15,292	26,482	51,702	34,554	59,838	116,827
G Basin	166	407	497	969	1,616	2,908	2,617	4,362	7,851	5,892	9,820	17,676
S Pac	416	760	1,065	876	1,579	2,246	1,659	2,726	4,252	3,003	4,735	7,694
NORTH PACIFIC	5,157	8,406	14,528	17,981	28,537	47,690	34,234	54,321	90,743	64,313	101,956	169,969
C Pac	1,667	3,013	6,053	3,343	5,915	12,141	6,320	11,181	22,951	11,455	20,266	41,599
PNW	3,490	5,393	8,475	14,638	22,622	35,549	27,914	43,140	67,792	52,858	81,690	128,370
U.S.	52,371	120,809	134,356	107,510	231,176	300,071	199,011	413,461	591,830	367,030	739,726	1,134,436

a6 mg/l dilution less than 4 mg/l because of an increased restriction on phosphorus at 4 mg/l.

Table 50. RULING DILUTION FLOWS AT 97½% TREATMENT, BY REGION, 4 mg/l D.O.

(million gallons per day)

	1980			2000			2020		
	L	M	H	L	M	H	L	M	H
NORTHEAST	17,932	21,598	29,129	24,218	36,279	67,887	39,096	62,936	153,766
N Eng	1,124	1,255	1,456	1,360	1,778	2,532	1,919	2,588	4,427
D & H	1,257	1,557	2,172	1,630	2,550	4,951	2,490	4,174	10,566
Ches	3,201	3,923	5,282	4,601	7,152	13,841	7,626	12,823	31,689
Ohio	1,313	1,604	2,203	1,774	2,717	5,160	2,807	4,601	11,373
EGL	2,271	2,792	3,835	3,059	4,727	8,992	4,761	7,871	19,552
WGL	7,129	8,539	11,623	9,523	14,074	26,495	15,804	25,195	62,937
U Miss	1,245	1,451	1,918	1,640	2,324	4,181	2,526	3,770	8,856
L Mo	392	477	640	631	957	1,735	1,163	1,914	4,366
SOUTHEAST	22,116	26,563	33,999	34,656	52,248	91,609	60,684	99,002	224,984
SE	17,756	21,053	26,374	27,562	40,669	69,257	47,716	76,004	167,541
Cumb	1,256	1,637	2,353	2,331	3,982	8,083	4,630	8,618	22,695
Tenn	1,962	2,490	3,460	2,920	4,739	9,126	4,961	8,711	21,601
L Miss	463	580	803	922	1,491	2,861	1,904	3,334	8,225
L AWR	679	803	1,009	921	1,367	2,282	1,473	2,335	4,922
MID-CONTINENT	7,443	9,071	12,332	12,693	19,815	37,425	23,902	40,539	99,047
U Mo	1,782	2,042	2,658	3,070	4,277	7,163	5,908	8,702	18,102
U AWR	432	487	588	667	999	1,826	1,259	2,118	5,040
W Gulf	5,229	6,542	9,086	8,956	14,539	28,436	16,735	29,719	75,905
SOUTHWEST	6,307	6,979	8,421	13,992	18,584	27,624	29,524	41,115	74,535
RG-P	610	664	766	1,417	1,854	2,602	2,854	3,918	6,683
Colo	4,436	4,816	5,621	10,196	13,241	18,705	21,990	29,919	51,118
G Basin	663	808	1,131	1,435	2,181	4,042	3,045	4,910	11,462
S Pac	598	691	903	944	1,308	2,275	1,635	2,368	5,272
NORTH PACIFIC	12,460	14,268	16,750	19,702	27,161	41,586	35,315	50,978	97,480
C Pac	2,608	2,957	3,835	4,141	5,591	9,697	7,207	10,133	22,790
PNW	9,852	11,311	12,915	15,561	21,570	31,889	28,108	40,845	74,690
U.S.	66,258	78,479	100,631	105,261	154,087	266,131	188,521	294,570	649,812

Table 51. RULING DILUTION FLOWS AT 97½% TREATMENT, BY REGION: MEDIUM PROJECTIONS

(million gallons per day)

	1960			1980			2000			2020		
	1 mg/l	4 mg/l	6 mg/l	1 mg/l	4 mg/l	6 mg/l	1 mg/l	4 mg/l	6 mg/l	1 mg/l	4 mg/l	6 mg/l
NORTHEAST	7,443	11,999	20,305	13,389	21,598	36,582	22,478	36,279	61,496	39,001	62,936	106,715
N Eng	559	893	1,490	785	1,255	2,092	1,111	1,778	2,964	1,617	2,588	4,313
D & H	565	904	1,506	973	1,557	2,594	1,593	2,550	4,249	2,609	4,174	6,957
Ches	1,125	1,843	3,209	2,394	3,923	6,829	4,366	7,152	12,450	7,827	12,823	22,322
Ohio	540	900	1,619	962	1,604	2,887	1,630	2,717	4,891	2,761	4,601	8,283
EGL	931	1,468	2,385	1,771	2,792	4,538	2,997	4,727	7,681	4,992	7,871	12,791
WGL	3,077	4,924	8,207	5,337	8,539	14,231	8,796	14,074	23,457	15,747	25,195	41,992
U Miss	542	895	1,584	878	1,451	2,567	1,406	2,324	4,111	2,289	3,770	6,670
L Mo	104	172	305	289	477	844	579	957	1,693	1,159	1,914	3,387
SOUTHEAST	6,740	11,966	24,828	15,020	26,563	54,731	29,583	52,248	107,366	56,110	99,002	203,044
SE	5,470	9,789	20,665	11,765	21,053	44,444	22,727	40,669	85,857	42,473	76,004	160,454
Cumb	53	86	150	999	1,637	2,850	2,431	3,982	6,932	5,261	8,618	15,002
Tenn	816	1,386	2,591	1,467	2,490	4,656	2,792	4,739	8,861	5,131	8,711	16,286
L Miss	139	241	471	335	580	1,132	861	1,491	2,911	1,925	3,334	6,509
L AWR	262	464	951	454	803	1,649	772	1,367	2,805	1,320	2,335	4,793
MID-CONTINENT	2,462	4,538	9,960	4,986	9,071	20,762	10,916	19,815	45,725	22,332	40,539	93,540
U Mo	769	1,213	1,971	1,295	2,042	3,319	2,712	4,277	6,950	5,518	8,702	14,140
U AWR	128	337	405	264	487	837	588	999	1,867	1,247	2,118	3,959
W Gulf	1,565	2,988	7,584	3,427	6,542	16,606	7,616	14,539	36,908	15,567	29,719	75,441
SOUTHWEST	1,195	2,034	3,854	4,083	6,979	13,307	10,844	18,584	35,610	23,963	41,115	78,936
RG-P	135	236	472	379	664	1,328	1,059	1,854	3,707	2,239	3,918	7,837
Colo	769	1,332	2,601	2,781	4,816	9,402	7,646	13,241	25,851	17,277	29,919	58,414
G Basin	83	138	248	485	808	1,454	1,309	2,181	3,926	2,946	4,910	8,838
S Pac	208	328	533	438	691	1,123	830	1,308	2,126	1,501	2,368	3,847
NORTH PACIFIC	2,578	4,171	7,263	8,991	14,268	23,844	17,117	27,161	45,371	32,156	50,978	84,985
C Pac	833	1,474	3,026	1,672	2,957	6,070	3,160	5,591	11,475	5,727	10,133	20,800
PNW	1,745	2,697	4,237	7,319	11,311	17,774	13,957	21,570	33,896	26,429	40,845	64,185
U.S.	20,148	34,708	66,210	46,469	78,479	149,226	90,938	154,087	295,568	173,562	294,570	567,220

Table 52. RULING DILUTION FLOWS AT 97½% TREATMENT, VARIANT 1, BY REGION: MEDIUM PROJECTIONS

(million gallons per day)

	1960			1980			2000			2020		
	1 mg/l	4 mg/l	6 mg/l	1 mg/l	4 mg/l	6 mg/l	1 mg/l	4 mg/l	6 mg/l	1 mg/l	4 mg/l	6 mg/l
NORTHEAST	7,444	12,000	20,303	12,280	19,808	33,553	18,606	30,026	50,897	28,531	46,048	78,075
N Eng	559	894	1,490	755	1,208	2,013	1,016	1,625	2,709	1,379	2,206	3,677
D & H	566	904	1,506	888	1,421	2,368	1,307	2,091	3,486	1,889	3,022	5,037
Ches	1,125	1,843	3,207	2,186	3,581	6,234	3,581	5,868	10,214	5,662	9,276	16,147
Ohio	540	900	1,619	886	1,476	2,657	1,354	2,257	4,063	2,027	3,378	6,080
EGL	931	1,468	2,385	1,624	2,561	4,162	2,484	3,917	6,365	3,669	5,786	9,403
WGL	3,077	4,924	8,207	4,864	7,783	12,972	7,207	11,531	19,218	11,365	18,184	30,307
U Miss	542	895	1,584	810	1,338	2,368	1,178	1,946	3,443	1,701	2,810	4,972
L Mo	104	172	305	267	440	779	479	791	1,399	839	1,386	2,452
SOUTHEAST	6,740	11,966	24,828	13,881	24,554	50,607	24,761	43,750	89,965	41,601	73,440	150,776
SE	5,470	9,789	20,665	10,908	19,519	41,206	19,152	34,272	72,351	31,813	56,928	120,182
Cumb	53	86	150	907	1,486	2,587	1,968	3,225	5,613	3,729	6,110	10,636
Tenn	816	1,386	2,591	1,339	2,274	4,251	2,290	3,888	7,268	3,707	6,293	11,765
L Miss	139	241	471	307	532	1,038	706	1,223	2,388	1,385	2,398	4,681
L AWR	262	464	951	420	743	1,525	645	1,142	2,345	967	1,711	3,512
MID-CONTINENT	2,462	4,538	9,960	4,611	8,399	19,167	9,096	16,492	37,972	16,370	29,675	68,293
U Mo	769	1,213	1,971	1,211	1,910	3,104	2,312	3,645	5,923	4,165	6,568	10,673
U AWR	128	337	405	247	470	784	494	839	1,568	914	1,551	2,900
W Gulf	1,565	2,988	7,584	3,153	6,019	15,279	6,290	12,008	30,481	11,291	21,556	54,720
SOUTHWEST	1,195	2,034	3,854	3,927	6,716	12,822	9,529	16,340	31,349	18,789	32,260	62,022
RG-P	135	236	472	371	650	1,300	956	1,672	3,344	1,805	3,159	6,318
Colo	769	1,332	2,601	2,707	4,687	9,151	6,808	11,789	23,016	13,763	23,834	46,534
G Basin	83	138	248	443	738	1,329	1,064	1,773	3,192	2,091	3,485	6,273
S Pac	208	328	533	406	641	1,042	701	1,106	1,797	1,130	1,782	2,897
NORTH PACIFIC	2,578	4,171	7,263	8,207	13,030	21,794	14,041	22,294	37,295	23,228	36,850	61,533
C Pac	833	1,474	3,026	1,549	2,741	5,626	2,656	4,699	9,645	4,258	7,533	15,463
PNW	1,745	2,697	4,237	6,658	10,289	16,168	11,385	17,595	27,650	18,970	29,317	46,070
U.S.	20,419	34,709	66,208	42,906	72,507	137,943	76,033	128,902	247,478	128,519	218,273	420,699

Table 53. RULING DILUTION FLOWS AT 97½% TREATMENT, VARIANT 2, BY REGION: MEDIUM PROJECTIONS

(million gallons per day)

	1960			1980			2000			2020		
	1 mg/l	4 mg/l	6 mg/l	1 mg/l	4 mg/l	6 mg/l	1 mg/l	4 mg/l	6 mg/l	1 mg/l	4 mg/l	6 mg/l
NORTHEAST	7,443	12,000	20,304	11,171	18,021	30,524	14,730	23,771	40,293	18,069	29,161	49,437
N Eng	559	894	1,490	725	1,160	1,934	920	1,472	2,453	1,141	1,825	3,042
D & H	565	904	1,506	803	1,285	2,142	1,021	1,633	2,722	1,169	1,871	3,118
Ches	1,125	1,843	3,208	1,977	3,240	5,639	2,797	4,583	7,977	3,497	5,729	9,972
Ohio	540	900	1,619	809	1,348	2,427	1,078	1,797	3,235	1,293	2,154	3,878
EGL	931	1,468	2,385	1,478	2,331	3,787	1,970	3,107	5,049	2,347	3,702	6,015
WGL	3,077	4,924	8,207	4,393	7,028	11,713	5,617	8,987	14,978	6,983	11,173	18,621
U Miss	542	895	1,584	742	1,225	2,168	949	1,568	2,775	1,120	1,850	3,274
L Mo	104	172	305	244	404	714	378	624	1,104	519	857	1,517
SOUTHEAST	6,740	11,966	24,828	12,743	22,544	46,487	19,940	35,248	72,562	27,091	47,876	98,507
SE	5,470	9,789	20,665	10,051	17,986	37,970	15,576	27,873	58,844	21,153	37,852	79,910
Cumb	53	86	150	815	1,335	2,325	1,506	2,467	4,295	2,198	3,601	6,268
Tenn	816	1,386	2,591	1,212	2,058	3,847	1,788	3,036	5,675	2,282	3,875	7,244
L Miss	139	241	471	279	483	944	552	955	1,865	844	1,461	2,853
L AWR	262	464	951	386	682	1,401	518	917	1,883	614	1,087	2,232
MID-CONTINENT	2,462	4,538	9,960	4,237	7,727	17,573	7,274	13,168	30,220	10,408	18,813	43,046
U Mo	769	1,213	1,971	1,128	1,778	2,890	1,911	3,013	4,897	2,812	4,435	7,206
U AWR	128	337	405	230	453	730	400	679	1,269	580	985	1,842
W Gulf	1,565	2,988	7,584	2,879	5,496	13,953	4,963	9,476	24,054	7,016	13,393	33,998
SOUTHWEST	1,195	2,034	3,854	3,771	6,453	12,335	8,212	14,097	27,088	13,615	23,404	45,103
RG-P	135	236	472	363	635	1,271	852	1,491	2,981	1,371	2,399	4,798
Colo	769	1,332	2,601	2,632	4,558	8,900	5,969	10,337	20,182	10,249	17,748	34,651
G Basin	83	138	248	401	669	1,204	819	1,366	2,458	1,236	2,060	3,708
S Pac	208	328	533	375	591	960	572	903	1,467	759	1,197	1,946
NORTH PACIFIC	2,578	4,171	7,263	7,423	11,792	19,745	10,966	17,429	29,221	14,297	22,719	38,076
C Pac	833	1,474	3,026	1,427	2,525	5,182	2,152	3,807	7,815	2,788	4,933	10,126
PNW	1,745	2,697	4,237	5,996	9,267	14,563	8,814	13,622	21,406	11,509	17,786	27,950
U.S.	20,418	34,709	66,209	39,345	66,537	126,664	61,122	103,713	199,384	83,480	141,973	274,169

Table 54. INDUSTRIAL WASTE TREATMENT COSTS PER p.e., BY LEVEL OF TREATMENT AND SELECTED
INDUSTRIES

(1964 dollars)

Treatment *(percent)*	Food	Textiles	Pulp & paper	Chemicals	Petroleum	Leather
35	0.20	0.39	0.71	0.16	1.75	0.33
50	.32	0.55	0.85	.23	2.51	0.56
60	.41	0.67	0.94	.27	3.03	0.71
70	.50	0.89	1.30	.33	3.58	0.87
80	.61	1.14	1.64	.38	4.15	1.01
90	.71	1.37	1.99	.43	4.71	1.15
95	.79	1.68	2.55	.47	5.10	1.25
97½	0.93	2.33	3.85	0.51	5.53	1.27

Note: One p.e. is the waste equivalent of one person, measured as 0.25 lb. of oxygen per day utilized in decomposition.

Table 55. MUNICIPAL WASTE TREATMENT COSTS
PER p.e., BY LEVEL OF TREATMENT

Treatment level *(percent)*	Cost *($ per p.e.)*
35	1.71
70	2.45
80	2.87
90	3.29
95	3.94
97½	5.43

Source: Appendixes D and E.

Note: One p.e. is the waste equivalent of one person, measured
as 0.25 lb. of oxygen per day utilized in decomposition.

Table 56. U.S. ANNUAL COSTS OF STANDARD
TREATMENT, BY LEVEL OF TREATMENT

($ million)

		Level of treatment *(percent)*						
		70/50	70/60	70	80	90	95	97½
1960		422	434	453	498	544	606	743
1980	L	614	632	666	734	802	896	1,099
	M	680	702	743	819	896	1,000	1,225
	H	787	817	869	958	1,048	1,166	1,417
2000	L	814	841	895	990	1,084	1,213	1,495
	M	1,057	1,098	1,177	1,303	1,431	1,600	1,964
	H	1,515	1,590	1,722	1,911	2,099	2,338	2,832
2020	L	1,219	1,267	1,363	1,513	1,663	1,868	2,310
	M	1,646	1,722	1,873	2,085	2,297	2,578	3,172
	H	2,892	3,067	3,387	3,778	4,167	4,650	5,621

Table 57. MUNICIPAL AND INDUSTRIAL COSTS FOR 95% TREATMENT, BY REGION

($ million)

	1960			1980 Medium			2000 Medium			2020 Medium			2020 High		
	Mun.	Ind.	Total	Mun.	Ind.	Total	Mun.	Ind.	Total	Mun.	Ind.	Total	Mun.	Ind.	Total
NORTHEAST	233.0	125.3	358.3	309.1	213.7	522.8	410.1	354.9	765.0	537.2	600.1	1,137.3	710.8	1,389.5	2,100.3
N Eng	24.7	11.4	36.1	31.9	17.9	49.8	41.5	29.8	71.3	53.9	51.4	105.3	71.4	95.5	166.9
D & H	56.4	27.2	83.6	72.0	45.2	117.2	93.4	73.0	166.4	121.2	118.6	239.8	160.3	287.9	448.2
Ches	19.2	10.6	29.8	28.4	24.9	53.3	40.5	41.0	81.5	55.3	68.6	123.9	73.2	155.4	228.6
Ohio	41.0	20.8	61.8	51.9	35.5	87.4	66.3	63.0	129.3	83.1	112.5	195.6	109.9	270.4	380.3
EGL	28.4	11.9	40.3	39.8	21.4	61.2	55.5	34.8	90.3	75.5	55.5	131.0	100.0	135.5	235.5
WGL	29.6	21.4	51.0	40.6	34.8	75.4	55.8	55.0	110.8	75.2	90.8	166.0	99.5	217.6	317.1
U Miss	28.6	20.3	48.9	38.0	29.2	67.2	50.1	45.3	95.4	64.6	72.7	137.3	85.4	168.5	253.9
L Mo	5.1	1.7	6.8	6.5	4.8	11.3	7.0	13.0	20.0	8.4	30.0	38.4	11.1	58.7	69.8
SOUTHEAST	61.8	45.1	106.9	102.8	100.5	203.3	151.1	203.1	354.3	208.3	399.8	608.1	275.7	825.7	1,101.4
SE	38.9	26.5	65.4	70.6	61.8	132.4	107.2	117.8	225.0	153.4	222.9	376.3	202.9	447.2	650.1
Cumb	2.1	0.1	2.2	3.0	6.2	9.2	4.1	13.3	17.4	5.1	27.0	32.1	6.8	65.3	72.1
Tenn	4.5	5.8	10.3	7.1	9.8	16.9	10.1	18.6	28.7	13.4	34.6	48.0	17.7	76.7	94.4
L Miss	8.5	6.0	14.5	12.2	11.7	23.9	17.9	32.8	50.7	24.2	76.3	100.5	32.1	164.6	196.7
L AWR	7.8	6.7	14.5	9.9	11.0	20.9	11.8	20.6	32.4	12.2	39.0	51.2	16.2	71.9	88.1
MID-CONTINENT	44.1	19.3	63.4	61.7	37.1	98.8	83.5	90.7	174.2	107.6	199.7	307.3	142.5	437.9	580.4
U Mo	13.2	5.0	18.2	19.2	6.6	25.8	26.7	22.3	49.0	35.4	56.4	91.8	46.9	107.8	154.7
U AWR	8.6	2.7	11.3	10.5	4.4	14.9	12.0	12.0	24.0	13.2	27.0	40.2	17.5	56.4	73.9
W Gulf	22.3	11.6	33.9	32.0	26.1	58.1	44.8	56.4	101.2	59.0	116.3	175.3	78.1	273.7	351.8
SOUTHWEST	32.1	4.5	36.6	62.8	10.7	73.5	96.2	37.5	133.7	137.7	93.0	230.7	182.3	178.6	360.9
RG-P	4.0	0.6	4.6	7.3	0.9	8.2	11.0	5.5	16.5	15.5	15.3	30.8	20.6	26.7	47.3
Colo	5.0	0.1	5.1	10.6	0.8	11.4	16.5	9.7	26.2	25.7	28.8	54.5	34.0	50.3	84.3
G Basin	1.9	0.2	2.1	2.6	1.5	4.1	3.2	6.4	9.6	3.5	16.6	20.1	4.7	33.3	38.0
S Pac	21.2	3.6	24.8	42.3	7.5	49.8	65.5	15.9	81.4	93.0	32.3	125.3	123.0	68.3	191.3
NORTH PACIFIC	25.6	15.5	41.1	38.7	63.1	101.8	54.7	118.2	172.9	71.4	222.9	294.3	94.5	412.2	506.7
C Pac	15.4	6.5	21.9	23.9	13.0	36.9	33.5	28.3	61.8	42.8	57.6	100.4	56.7	124.9	181.6
PNW	10.2	9.0	19.2	14.8	50.1	64.9	21.2	89.9	111.1	28.6	165.3	193.9	37.8	287.3	325.1
U.S.	396.6	209.7	606.3	575.1	425.1	1,000.2	795.6	804.4	1,600.1	1,062.2	1,515.5	2,577.7	1,405.8	3,243.9	4,649.7

Table 58. MUNICIPAL AND INDUSTRIAL COSTS FOR 95% TREATMENT, VARIANTS 1 AND 2, BY REGION

($ millions)

	2020 Medium						2020 High					
	Variant 1			Variant 2			Variant 1			Variant 2		
	Mun.	Ind.	Total	Mun.	Ind.	Total	Mun.	Ind.	Total	Mun.	Ind.	Total
NORTHEAST	537.2	419.9	957.1	537.2	240.1	777.3	710.8	972.8	1,683.6	710.8	555.8	1,266.6
N Eng	53.9	36.0	89.9	53.9	20.6	74.5	71.4	66.9	138.3	71.4	38.2	109.6
D & H	121.2	83.0	204.2	121.2	47.5	168.7	160.3	201.5	361.8	160.3	115.1	275.4
Ches	55.3	48.0	103.3	55.3	27.4	82.7	73.2	108.8	182.0	73.2	62.2	135.4
Ohio	83.1	78.7	161.8	83.1	45.0	128.1	109.9	189.3	299.2	109.9	108.1	218.0
EGL	75.5	38.8	114.3	75.5	22.2	97.7	100.0	94.9	194.9	100.0	54.2	154.2
WGL	75.2	63.5	138.7	75.2	36.3	111.5	99.5	152.3	251.8	99.5	87.1	186.6
U Miss	64.6	50.9	115.5	64.6	29.1	93.7	85.4	118.0	203.4	85.4	67.4	152.8
L Mo	8.4	21.0	29.4	8.4	12.0	20.4	11.1	41.1	52.2	11.1	23.5	34.6
SOUTHEAST	208.3	279.8	488.1	208.3	159.9	368.2	275.7	577.9	853.6	275.7	330.2	605.9
SE	153.4	156.0	309.4	153.4	89.2	242.6	202.9	313.0	515.9	202.9	178.9	381.8
Cumb	5.1	18.9	24.0	5.1	10.8	15.9	6.8	45.7	52.5	6.8	26.1	32.9
Tenn	13.4	24.2	37.6	13.4	13.8	27.2	17.7	53.7	71.4	17.7	30.7	48.4
L Miss	24.2	53.4	77.6	24.2	30.5	54.7	32.1	115.2	147.3	32.1	65.8	97.9
L AWR	12.2	27.3	39.5	12.2	15.6	27.8	16.2	50.3	66.5	16.2	28.7	44.9
MID-CONTINENT	107.6	139.8	247.4	107.6	79.9	187.5	142.5	306.5	449.0	142.5	175.2	317.7
U Mo	35.4	39.5	74.9	35.4	22.6	58.0	46.9	75.4	122.3	46.9	43.1	90.0
U AWR	13.2	18.9	32.1	13.2	10.8	24.0	17.5	39.5	57.0	17.5	22.6	40.1
W Gulf	59.0	81.4	140.4	59.0	46.5	105.5	78.1	191.6	269.7	78.1	109.5	187.6
SOUTHWEST	137.7	65.1	202.8	137.7	37.1	174.8	182.3	125.0	307.3	182.3	71.4	253.7
RG-P	15.5	10.7	26.2	15.5	6.1	21.6	20.6	18.7	39.3	20.6	10.7	31.3
Colo	25.7	20.2	45.9	25.7	11.5	37.2	34.0	35.2	69.2	34.0	20.1	54.1
G Basin	3.5	11.6	15.1	3.5	6.6	10.1	4.7	23.3	28.0	4.7	13.3	18.0
S Pac	93.0	22.6	115.6	93.0	12.9	105.9	123.0	47.8	170.8	123.0	27.3	150.3
NORTH PACIFIC	71.4	156.0	227.4	71.4	89.1	160.5	94.5	288.6	383.1	94.5	164.9	259.4
C Pac	42.8	40.3	83.1	42.8	23.0	65.8	56.7	87.5	144.2	56.7	50.0	106.7
PNW	28.6	115.7	144.3	28.6	66.1	94.7	37.8	201.1	238.9	37.8	114.9	152.7
U.S.	1,062.2	1,060.6	2,122.8	1,062.2	606.1	1,668.3	1,405.8	2,270.8	3,676.6	1,405.8	1,297.5	2,703.3

Table 59. COOLING WATER DISCHARGE AT ORIGINAL RECIRCULATION RATES, BY REGION

(million gallons per day)

	1960	1980 L	1980 M	1980 H	2000 L	2000 M	2000 H	2020 L	2020 M	2020 H
NORTHEAST	58,336	115,808	158,318	226,816	147,130	246,294	420,871	245,565	431,889	862,591
N Eng	924	1,818	2,435	3,436	2,483	4,097	6,970	3,827	6,693	13,703
D & H	4,588	5,450	7,386	10,561	6,975	11,613	19,791	11,104	19,472	38,873
Ches	3,901	6,448	8,728	12,497	8,143	13,660	23,544	13,289	23,346	47,318
Ohio	21,399	44,967	61,622	88,584	56,262	94,289	161,521	92,212	162,238	324,473
EGL	8,686	15,872	21,739	31,137	21,396	36,146	62,049	36,626	64,847	131,403
WGL	11,618	24,672	33,795	48,095	30,738	51,480	87,381	51,956	91,367	180,739
U Miss	6,313	14,080	19,185	27,684	17,850	29,713	50,531	30,880	54,062	106,682
L Mo	907	2,501	3,428	4,822	3,283	5,296	9,084	5,671	9,864	19,400
SOUTHEAST	16,256	24,440	33,023	47,543	33,189	55,458	95,516	57,503	100,732	203,620
SE	8,352	9,800	13,271	18,898	13,109	21,686	36,940	22,145	38,601	77,024
Cumb	34	516	655	1,024	845	1,461	2,908	1,633	2,927	6,962
Tenn	4,682	8,115	11,002	15,876	11,513	19,294	33,189	20,879	36,632	73,347
L Miss	1,675	2,874	3,878	5,652	3,680	6,246	10,984	5,980	10,635	22,598
L AWR	1,513	3,135	4,217	6,093	4,042	6,771	11,495	6,866	11,937	23,689
MID-CONTINENT	3,348	4,240	5,733	8,162	4,422	7,294	12,622	7,336	12,785	25,853
U Mo	1,217	2,666	3,622	5,167	2,987	4,903	8,328	5,092	8,818	17,341
U AWR	543	155	210	301	206	359	691	330	598	1,443
W Gulf	1,588	1,419	1,901	2,694	1,229	2,032	3,603	1,914	3,369	7,069
SOUTHWEST	387	176	234	318	278	434	700	518	815	1,537
RG-P	194	27	34	43	48	71	106	94	144	252
Colo	97	39	53	75	88	136	213	198	312	575
G Basin	75	81	109	147	102	161	268	159	244	493
S Pac	21	29	38	53	40	66	113	67	115	217
NORTH PACIFIC	431	2,516	3,299	4,413	6,025	9,873	16,470	13,661	23,692	46,573
C Pac	52	72	95	131	105	169	300	174	296	588
PNW	379	2,444	3,204	4,282	5,920	9,704	16,170	13,487	23,396	45,985
U.S.	78,758	147,180	200,607	287,252	191,044	319,353	546,176	324,583	569,913	1,140,174

Table 60. THERMAL DILUTION REQUIREMENTS AT ORIGINAL RECIRCULATION RATES, 98% AVAILABILITY, 0.0425 ANNUAL FACTOR, 4 mg/l D.O.

(million gallons per day)

	1960	1980			2000			2020		
		L	M	H	L	M	H	L	M	H
NORTHEAST	135,400	265,175	362,470	518,993	337,910	565,951	967,004	564,573	993,315	1,985,281
N Eng	2,588	5,091	6,819	9,621	6,953	11,472	19,515	10,715	18,739	38,367
D & H	12,112	14,389	19,500	27,880	18,414	30,658	52,248	29,316	51,407	102,626
Ches	9,401	15,540	21,035	30,118	19,624	32,921	56,740	32,026	56,265	114,035
Ohio	41,086	86,336	118,315	170,081	108,023	181,035	310,120	177,046	311,497	622,987
EGL	25,796	47,140	64,564	92,477	63,546	107,355	184,284	108,778	192,594	390,268
WGL	30,672	65,134	89,218	126,971	81,150	135,908	230,686	137,164	241,208	477,151
U Miss	12,057	26,893	36,643	52,877	34,093	56,752	96,515	58,980	103,258	203,763
L Mo	1,688	4,652	6,376	8,968	6,107	9,850	16,896	10,548	18,347	36,084
SOUTHEAST	17,714	28,042	37,884	54,664	38,563	64,560	111,576	67,636	118,644	240,508
SE	6,765	7,938	10,749	15,307	10,618	17,566	29,921	17,938	31,267	62,389
Cumb	57	862	1,094	1,709	1,411	2,440	4,856	2,727	4,888	11,627
Tenn	7,818	13,552	18,373	26,512	19,227	32,221	55,426	34,867	61,175	122,489
L Miss	1,909	3,276	4,421	6,444	4,195	7,120	12,522	6,817	12,123	25,762
L AWR	1,165	2,414	3,247	4,692	3,112	5,213	8,851	5,287	9,191	18,241
MID-CONTINENT	4,092	7,862	10,673	15,219	8,728	14,334	24,431	14,808	25,674	50,751
U Mo	3,370	7,386	10,034	14,312	8,279	13,582	23,069	14,104	24,426	48,036
U AWR	277	79	107	153	105	183	353	168	305	736
W Gulf	445	397	532	754	344	569	1,009	536	943	1,979
SOUTHWEST	166	103	137	187	159	250	412	288	463	877
RG-P	54	8	10	12	14	20	30	26	40	71
Colo	50	20	27	38	45	69	109	101	159	293
G Basin	34	37	50	68	47	74	123	73	112	227
S Pac	28	38	50	69	53	87	150	88	152	286
NORTH PACIFIC	1,408	8,747	11,468	15,330	21,094	34,577	57,638	47,975	83,213	163,562
C Pac	68	95	126	173	139	224	395	230	391	776
PNW	1,340	8,652	11,342	15,157	20,955	34,353	57,243	47,745	82,822	162,786
U.S.	158,780	309,929	422,632	604,393	406,454	679,672	1,161,061	695,280	1,221,309	2,440,979

Table 61. STEAM-ELECTRIC POWER INTAKE AND COSTS OF RECIRCULATION AT ORIGINAL AND REVISED RECIRCULATION RATES

Year		Original average recirculation rate	Production (bil. kwh)	Original recirculation rate					Revised recirculation rate					Revised average recirculation rate
				Intake (bgd)	Intake (bgy)	Flow-through (bgy)	Amount of recirculation (bgy)	Cost of recirculation ($ mil.)	Intake (bgd)	Intake (bgy)	Flow-through[a] (bgy)	Amount of recirculation (bgy)	Cost of recirculation ($ mil.)	
1960		1.25	610	66	24,216	30,201	5,985	67	66	24,216	30,201	5,985	67	1.25
1980	L		1,631											
	M	1.39	2,269	179	65,432	90,890	25,458	288	41	14,881	92,241	77,360	874	6.2
	H		3,212											
2000	L		2,716											
	M	1.51	4,522	289	105,561	159,584	54,023	610	70	25,371	164,474	139,103	1,572	6.4
	H		7,682											
2020	L		5,124											
	M	1.70	8,966	529	193,127	328,210	135,083	1,526	131	47,820	339,379	291,559	3,295	7.1
	H	1.70	17,714	1,045	381,323	641,821	260,498	2,944	253	92,315	663,063	570,748	6,450	7.2

[a]Theoretically, there should be no difference between original and revised flow-through. Differences are about 3%.

Table 62. PROJECTED U.S. COLLECTION,
TREATMENT, AND RECIRCULATION
COSTS FOR 95% TREATMENT

($ million)

		Costs of treatment	Costs of collection	Costs of recirculation (rev.)
1980	M	998	746	874
2000	M	1,599	1,035	1,572
2020	M	2,577	1,384	3,295
2020	H	4,640	1,832	6,450

Table 63. ANNUAL URBAN WASTE COLLECTION COSTS AT $4.12 PER CAPITA,[a] BY REGION

($ thousand)

	Equivalent costs for 1960	1980 L	1980 M	1980 H	2000 L	2000 M	2000 H	2020 L	2020 M	2020 H
NORTHEAST	310,784	388,125	413,071	453,312	462,812	550,238	670,089	616,076	722,747	956,289
N Eng	32,639	39,613	42,168	45,979	46,028	54,788	66,732	60,716	71,222	94,241
D & H	86,878	104,240	110,939	120,984	120,938	143,986	175,343	159,168	186,731	247,076
Ches	27,295	37,933	40,368	43,862	48,365	57,573	70,114	67,032	78,638	104,042
Ohio	42,922	50,973	54,252	59,167	58,224	69,315	84,411	74,041	86,858	114,919
EGL	41,480	54,541	58,043	63,300	68,099	81,077	98,736	93,998	110,276	145,914
WGL	44,319	57,140	60,811	66,320	70,316	83,710	101,945	96,120	112,769	149,206
U Miss	29,907	37,290	39,688	43,281	44,039	52,427	63,848	57,540	67,502	89,313
L Mo	5,344	6,394	6,802	7,420	6,802	7,362	8,961	7,461	8,751	11,577
SOUTHEAST	71,186	112,035	118,990	129,776	147,154	175,195	213,354	206,523	242,277	320,573
SE	45,889	78,251	83,286	90,830	106,177	126,410	153,940	154,203	180,901	239,360
Cumb	2,233	2,966	3,156	3,444	3,638	4,334	5,278	4,590	5,381	7,123
Tenn	4,734	7,020	7,470	8,149	8,870	10,560	12,859	11,915	13,979	18,499
L Miss	10,197	13,794	14,696	16,027	18,099	21,548	26,244	24,910	29,233	38,666
L AWR	8,133	10,003	10,382	11,326	10,370	12,344	15,034	10,906	12,793	16,925
MID-CONTINENT	49,181	64,593	68,738	74,963	79,450	93,351	113,666	102,699	120,481	159,407
U Mo	13,814	18,865	20,073	21,890	23,492	27,967	34,060	31,600	37,068	49,049
U AWR	9,015	10,271	10,930	11,919	11,573	12,533	15,256	11,787	13,827	18,289
W Gulf	26,352	35,457	37,735	41,155	44,385	52,851	64,350	59,312	69,587	92,070
SOUTHWEST	46,523	85,918	91,435	99,716	117,729	140,162	170,688	170,346	199,841	264,422
RG-P	4,149	7,177	7,634	8,327	9,649	11,491	13,992	13,856	16,253	21,506
Colo	5,191	10,370	11,033	12,035	14,482	17,238	20,996	22,887	26,846	35,527
G Basin	2,653	3,473	3,696	4,033	3,811	4,536	5,525	4,281	5,022	6,641
S Pac	34,530	64,898	69,072	75,322	89,787	106,898	130,176	129,323	151,719	200,747
NORTH PACIFIC	35,412	50,408	53,651	58,352	63,794	75,944	92,510	84,431	99,049	131,057
C Pac	21,309	31,147	33,154	35,992	39,045	46,482	56,605	50,631	59,394	78,593
PNW	14,103	19,261	20,497	22,359	24,749	29,462	35,906	33,800	39,655	52,464
U.S.	513,068	701,079	745,855	816,120	870,939	1,034,890	1,260,308	1,180,075	1,384,395	1,831,748

[a]$125 capital cost per capita × 0.033 based on 75-year life and 4 percent interest rate. See *A Study of Pollution–Water*, Staff Report to the Senate Committee on Public Works (June 1963), pp. 28–30.

Chapter 9

THE "SUPPLY" OF WATER
AND COSTS OF FLOW

The most important single difference between the data in this study and in its predecessor, Committee Print No. 32, is in the amount of storage required for high-level flows and, consequently, in the cost of flow when flow approaches full regulation. Revised flow-storage relationships are taken from the paper by George O. G. Löf and Clayton H. Hardison, "Storage Requirements for Water in the United States.[1]

While we have adopted the Löf-Hardison storage requirements for specified minimum gross flows, our computations of net flows, the maximum physical limit to which net flow can be raised, and the costs of flow are different. The differences grow out of several circumstances: (1) subsequent to the Löf-Hardison article we modified the size distribution of new storage; (2) Löf-Hardison applied the "synthetic" schedule of increments of storage to total reservoir capacity, whereas we applied it only to new capacity; (3) costs per unit of storage used by Löf and Hardison were based on 1960 prices, whereas we adjusted ours to 1964; and (4) Löf and Hardison made a relatively precise determination of the maximum physical limit by using a continuously varying flow-storage relationship, whereas our determination rests on a step function and is therefore subject to over- or under-assessment.

For the hydrologist, the "supply" of water is a physical measurement. Usually it is a frequency distribution of measured flows of rivers at specified points on the rivers. (Where appropriate, account is taken of water that is underground.) The average of flows over a period of time is the maximum sustained gross flow that could have been attained over that period of time, provided adequate capacity had been available to hold water when natural flow was higher than the average and to release water when natural flow was lower than the average.

A distinction is made between "gross" and "net" flow because of the additional evaporation suffered when aggregate water surface is increased as a result of reservoir construction.

The amount of storage required for a specified regulated flow is dependent on the natural history of a region: (1) the amount of precipitation and its chronological variation; (2) geologic and geographic characteristics — soil and rock, topography, elevation, temperature, etc.; and (3) biotic characteristics — mainly type and density of vegetation. These factors are, of course, interrelated and, to some degree, are subject to manipulation by man. In some regions precipitation will run off rapidly; flood flows are very high and low flows are very low. In other regions the same amount of precipitation may be associated with lower peaks and shallower troughs. The amount of storage needed to raise existing minimum flow to some higher level will be less in the latter regions than in the former.

The flow that is equalled or exceeded 95 percent of the time under virgin or unregulated conditions is considered to be the present minimum flow. Quantities of storage can be expressed as multiples or fractions of mean annual flow — i.e., a "dimensionless" measurement, since it is a ratio — or as an absolute physical quantity, such as acre-feet. We have followed the practice of measuring flows in millions or billions of gallons per day and storage in millions of acre-feet.

Regionwide flows are the aggregates of discharges from unrelated rivers, e.g., New England or the Southeast, or the discharge at the low point of the basin measured on the

---

[1] *Water Resources Research*, vol. 2, no. 3 (Third Quarter 1966), pp. 323–54.

main stem of a single river system. Some estimation by the U.S. Geological Survey went into the determination of regionwide figures, since complete measurements were not available in all regions. Quantities of flow and storage are, of course, nonduplicative. For example, flows for the Lower Mississippi region do not include contributions from water resource regions upstream.

No special account is taken of groundwater. It is assumed that measures of surface flow include contributions from ground storage. To the degree that water can be mined, or to the degree that groundwater leaves the region underground, our figures understate physical supply. Coastal regions are likely to have aquifers that do not contribute to surface flow but discharge directly to the sea. Inland, such as in the high plains of Texas, Oklahoma, and New Mexico, there are quantities of groundwater that can be mined. No account is taken of interbasin movements that already take place; flows of originating basins are not reduced nor flows of receiving basins increased.

In handling both the requirement for flow and the supply of flow, no account was taken of a possibility that flow would be regulated in an uneven time pattern because of seasonal peaks or troughs in requirements. Regulation to meet a particular seasonal pattern might require more or less storage than to raise minimum flow from its natural level to some higher figure depending on the seasonal patterns of unregulated and regulated flow. In the preparation of Committee Print No. 32, it was acertained that the approximate frequency with which more storage would be required was about the same as the approximate frequency for less. Accordingly, it was decided to ignore the effect of seasonality on storage requirements.

In the tables prepared by Löf and Hardison, regulated gross flow is given with a chance of deficiency equal to 2 percent, 5 percent, or 10 percent of the time. These percentages refer to the relative number of years in a reasonably long sequence in which flow will fall short of the specified amount for an unspecified period of time within the year and by an unspecified quantity. The sequential character of the deficiency is also unspecified — e.g., for a 2 percent chance of deficiency it is not known whether there will be four years in which minimum flow falls below the stated figure followed by 196 years of sufficiency, or one year of deficiency followed by 49 years of sufficiency in fifty-year cycles.

We have assumed, following Löf and Hardison, that a 2 percent chance of deficiency (98 percent availability) is the highest attainable degree of certainty; in our models we have treated 98 percent as tantamount to 100 percent, since we have made no provision for shortage in 2 percent of the years. (Presumably some draw-down of surface storage beyond the normal annual variation is possible, where water is stored for hydraulic head. Another adjustment would be temporary cessation or reduction of water-related activity.)

We also assumed that a 10 percent chance of deficiency can be treated as a deficiency of one month's duration out of every year, given a relatively long run of years. We then compared the difference in costs of storage requirements with additional short-term (i.e., thirty-day) treatment costs.

Cost of Flow

The cost of flow, or, in the economist's term, a supply curve of water, is the schedule of successively higher quantities of sustained flow associated with the successively higher annual costs required for the financing and amortization of the reservoirs.[2] The supply curve (referred to more frequently as the cost curve) was constructed for each water resource region in the following fashion:

1. Based on present and planned reservoirs, a percentage distribution of reservoirs by size class was computed for each region. The assumption was that future reservoirs would repeat the pattern of the past, except that the anticipated aggregate capacity assigned to reservoirs of the smallest and largest size classes was usually reduced from present figures when these appeared to be large. This adjustment was done intuitively.

2. A percentage distribution of reservoirs by physiographic zone was computed on the basis of existing and planned reservoirs, tempered in some instances by the relative area of each physiographic zone within a region.

3. Evaporation rates per surface acre of water and average depths for each size class served as the basis for computing evaporation from new reservoirs to be charged against gross runoff.

4. Capital costs per unit of storage capacity, based on size class and physiographic zone, were adapted from curves that had been prepared by the Corps of Engineers for the Senate Select Committee. Costs per unit were adjusted from 1960 prices to 1964 prices.

5. Capital costs were converted to annual equivalents by the following alternative factors:

   (a) 0.0200: equal to a life of 100 years, an annual interest charge of 2 percent, and zero costs for operation and maintenance.
   (b) 0.0425: equal to a life of 50 years, an interest rate of 4 percent, and one-quarter of 1 percent of capital cost for operation and maintenance.
   (c) 0.0525: equal to a life of 50 years, an interest rate of 5½ percent, and one-half of 1 percent for operation and maintenance.

The rate of 4¼ percent was treated as "basic" with the others serving as variants.

6. "Costs of flow," for the purpose of computing minimum cost programs, consisted only of the costs of storage in excess of the capacity now in place or under construction. In estimating the required amount of new storage for a specified gross flow, existing flood control storage was assumed to be available only to the extent of a fraction equal to the following ratio:

$$\frac{\text{specified flow}}{\text{maximum attainable flow}}$$

---

[2] The textbook supply curve refers to costs per unit of output. Our supply curves are usually in the form of cumulative costs for specified minimum flows. They can, however, be translated into costs per unit of minimum flow.

Thus, when the specified flow equalled the maximum attainable flow, all existing flood control storage was assumed to be available for flow regulation.[3]

On the basis of the foregoing elements, a flow-cost curve was constructed for each region. The curve was a step function, each step constituting a specified aggregate amount of storage assigned to a size class. Successive steps went from the largest to the smallest size class; for each class an average cost and average rate of evaporation were estimated, based on the distribution between physiographic zones if more than one was involved.[4]

By converting capital costs to annual costs and subtracting the increment in evaporation from the increment in gross flow, a cost-of-flow schedule was constructed. For the purpose of this schedule, the costs of existing storage were assumed to be zero on the ground that any minimum cost program should be computed by comparing increments in costs of successively higher levels of treatment with increments in costs of successively higher levels of flow. The costs of existing storage are "sunk" costs — i.e., the cost of existing storage is assumed to be zero.

Maximum physical capacity is fixed at the point where the increase in gross flow — "marginal flow" — is equal to the increase in evaporation — "marginal evaporation" — per unit increase in reservoir capacity. This equality was only approximately determined, since, by using a step function which implied an average rate of evaporation and an average rate of added flow per unit of storage, the precise marginal equality could not be ascertained. Our figures may be short of, or exceed, the "true" maximum.

Another point that should be kept in mind is the arbitrary quality of the schedule of increments of storage and the assumed characteristics of percentage distribution by size (volume), average depth (and therefore surface area), location (and therefore physiographic zone and evaporation rate), and sequence of construction. A change in any of these characteristics would induce a change in net marginal flow, the physical maximum, and costs of flow.

Costs of storage can be expressed as either capital or annual and as total, average, or marginal costs of flow. Schedules showing these computations are in appendix F.

Table 64 shows the differences among maximum physical regulatory storage capacities as given in Committee Print No. 32, in Löf and Hardison, and in this study. In Committee Print No. 32, storage was computed on the assumption that existing storage was reflected in existing flow records, and that "storage" referred only to net additions beyond the present. In Löf-Hardison and in this study "storage" refers to total requirements, including capacity already in place. Löf and Hardison give total requirements as 3,587 million acre-feet; we give them as 2,923 million acre-feet. The difference originates in our changes in the

percentage distributions by size class and in the coarse determination of the physical limit resulting from the relatively large steps by which increments of storage were added.

Required storage for sustained flows beyond 50 percent of mean annual flow is now estimated to be much greater than shown in Committee Print No. 32. At full regulation, required storage is about three times as much as originally estimated. Because of the increase in water surface and evaporation loss, maximum net flow is now estimated to be 14 percent less.

Table 64 also reveals that storage in existence or under construction in 1964 amounted to 17 percent of maximum physical capacity.[5] In table 65, two columns indicate the cost of storage in existence or under construction when valued at the same unit costs used for future storage. While existing capacity is 17 percent of the projected maximum, the estimated cost of existing capacity is 12 percent of the projected total. We have, therefore, tended to use relatively low-cost sites in comparison with those implied at full regulation in the synthetic schedules. Total magnitudes are impressive and raise the question of how far we are properly to proceed with construction of reservoirs if at each step the decision rests on a benefit-cost ratio that is properly conceived and accurately measured. As our analysis proceeds, we see that projected national bills of goods are consistent with widely varying flow requirements, depending on the water resource policy that is adopted. Movement along the High path of growth, however, restricts our options to a high level of regulation, given the specified bill of goods and projected technology. We must therefore accept the possibility that 2 billion acre-feet of storage capacity may be in place within the next fifty years, compared with the present 500 million.

Capital costs of full regulation with a 2 percent chance of deficiency is about $191 billion, of which $23 billion has already been spent or committed. Measured as the annual equivalent, the cost of full regulation would be about $8.1 billion. If we were to reach maximum development by 2020, we would spend an average of $3.4 billion in new capital outlays every year; the annual equivalent cost that is now estimated at about $1 billion would grow to $8.1 billion.

These expenditures, relative to present and prospective GNP, are not especially burdensome. They do, however, reveal — only partially, since treatment costs have not yet been discussed — that what was treated as a free good not many years ago, except in certain western regions, has quite suddenly acquired status on a national scale as an economic good.

What is of more interest than the absolute quantities of flow, capacity, and dollars is the sensitivity of all three to possible variants of policy. According to table 66, an increase in the chance of deficiency from 2 percent to 5 percent (i.e., from a chance that there will be a deficiency one year out of fifty to a chance of deficiency two and a half years out of fifty) lowers total required storage for

---

[3] This procedure rests on the assumption that at maximum regulation, assuming perfect efficiency in the administration of all reservoirs, there is no need for separate flood control storage capacity. In the absence of other information it was assumed that if, for example, regulation reached 10 percent of maximum, 10 percent of existing flood control storage would be available for flow regulation.

[4] See details in app. F.

[5] Maximum physical capacity refers to the amount of storage associated with maximum net flow, given the synthetic schedule of storage capacity that was adopted.

maximum regulation by 17 percent and raises maximum regulated flow 4 percent. Adopting a 10 percent chance of deficiency rather than a 2 percent chance implies a saving of 23 percent in storage capcity for maximum regulation and a further increase in maximum regulated flow. The relative savings in money are slightly greater than the relative savings in storage capacity.

Three alternative annual factors induce changes in annual costs but not in capital costs. Annual costs are directly proportional to the annual factor selected; use of three alternatives reflects uncertainty over the interest rate, the life of the facility, and the level of operation and maintenance costs. We examined the effects of variations in the annual cost of storage on the combination of storage and treatment that minimizes costs. These combinations are discussed in a later chapter.

Table 66 and several that follow show the effects of introducing a marginal cost constraint on maximum flow and the costs of flow.[6]

Introduction of a marginal cost constraint of 50 cents[7] per 1,000 gallons does not impose a restriction on flow in the Central Pacific region or in any of thirteen other regions. For the country as a whole, regulated flow would be reduced by 1 percent. The greatest restriction is in the Ohio region where the 50-cent marginal cost constraint reduces regulated flow by 4 percent. For the country as a whole, unrestricted costs of new storage up to the physical limit are $7,140 million annually; with a 50-cent marginal cost constraint, total annual costs are $4,038 million, or a reduction of 43 percent (table 67). It is clear, therefore, that our synthetic schedules imply very high marginal costs for a relatively insignificant fraction of total regulated flow.

The point is perhaps even clearer with a marginal cost constraint of 10 cents per 1,000 gallons. Referring again to sustained flow with a 2 percent chance of deficiency, such constraint reduces total flow by 3 percent and total costs of flow by 66 percent (table 67). When the same constraint is applied to storage providing 90 percent availability, flow is reduced by 7 percent and costs by 54 percent (table 68).

Imposition of a marginal cost constraint of 10 cents per 1,000 gallons reduces costs by relatively large sums, but what is perhaps of greater ultimate concern is its effect on required reservoir capacity (table 68). The constraining strength diminishes with the increased chance of deficiency,

but at 98 percent availability total reservoir capacity would be limited to 69 percent of the physical limit. The total effect of a cost constraint of 10 cents per 1,000 gallons and an increased chance of deficiency from 2 percent to 10 percent would imply that maximum reservoir capacity would grow by no more than 3.7 times present capacity instead of by about 6 times as implied by the unconstrained physical limit.

The very great difference between marginal and average costs of regulation at relatively high levels of regulation implies that "real" marginal costs might be concealed by an "improper" sequence of reservoir construction.[8] Because of the systemic interaction of reservoirs on a given river, a newly constructed reservoir can render useless a reservoir built at an earlier date, or at least substantially reduce its usefulness. During the early development of a region, inadequate appreciation of future requirements may result in the construction of small, high-unit-cost reservoirs. By the time a fairly high degree of regulation is achieved for these reservoirs, implicit marginal costs of flow could be very high. Costs would be high not only in money but also in water, since a relatively high implicit marginal cost usually reflects a relatively high evaporation loss relative to added regulatory control.

High implicit marginal costs may be concealed not only by the order in which reservoirs of different sizes are added to a system, but also by the scale to which any given reservoir is developed. The cost per unit of flow rises as the degree of regulation rises because increasingly larger amounts of storage capacity must be idle for long periods of time. Because of this problem and the likelihood of capital budget limitations, smaller reservoirs are more attractive. The economic problem is to achieve the proper tradeoff between ultimately higher implicit marginal costs induced by too many small reservoirs and the burden of excess capacity associated with large reservoirs. This problem is further complicated by the possibility that the size of a given reservoir may be extended beyond a reasonable marginal cost level if attention is focused only on average cost per unit of regulated flow. For the conterminous United States the spread between marginal and average costs of our synthetic schedules is very wide; at 98 percent availability and an annual factor of 0.0425, the average annual cost per mgd is $2,647 when a marginal cost of 10 cents per 1,000 gallons is imposed. This constraint is equal to a marginal cost of $36,500 per mgd, or fourteen times as high.

The need for fixing marginal costs project by project has been pointed out by others[9] and is only repeated here by virtue of the implications of our synthetic schedules. If a river basin were to behave like the United States taken as a

---

[6] Marginal cost per 1,000 gallons is computed as follows (using the Central Pacific region, 98 percent availability, 0.0425 annual factor): An increase in cumulative storage from 121,016,000 acre-feet to 122,000,000 acre-feet raises net flow from 45,409 mgd to 45,478 mgd, or by 69 mgd. Annual cumulative cost rises from $245.3 million to $253.5 million, or by $8.2 million per year. Sixty-nine mgd equals 25,185 mgy, or 25,185,000 thousands of gallons per year at a marginal cost of $8.2 million per year, or to 33 cents per 1,000 gallons. By implication, there is enough storage to allow for some daily, weekly, or monthly variation in the delivery of the 1,000 gallons, since storage capacity is large enough for it to be delivered at a constant daily rate. In 2 percent of the years there would be a shortage that would impede its delivery, especially since it is the "final" increment of sustained flow whose costs we have computed.

[7] The choice of 50 cents, 10 cents, and 2 cents per 1,000 gallons roughly coincides with a range of prices commonly encountered in agricultural and municipal uses.

[8] "Real" marginal costs can be defined as equal to the savings in outlays per marginal unit of flow that would result if the least productive storage unit were withdrawn at any time and, magically, all unamortized capital costs of that unit were recovered. "Marginal costs" in the context of water resources refer to capital costs; the implicit period of time to which the analysis refers is long enough for us to treat new capital costs as variable costs.

[9] Irving K. Fox and Orris C. Herfindahl, "Attainment of Efficiency in Satisfying Demands for Water Resources," *American Economic Review*, May 1964, pp. 198–206.

whole, an average cost of 1.2 cents per 1,000 gallons of regulated flow would be associated with a marginal cost of 50 cents per 1,000 gallons (98 percent availability; 0.0425 annual factor; see tables 69 and 70). In going from a 10-cent marginal cost constraint to a 50-cent marginal cost constraint (98 percent, 0.0425), aggregate regulated flow rises 2.3 percent, but total costs rise 64 percent. By looking only at average costs as the river's system of dams is gradually brought to full capacity, this "fact" could be missed. The word "fact" is in quotes because our costs all depend on the synthetic schedules of storage that were adopted. With available data, there is no way to test the reasonableness of these schedules.

As previously noted, costs of flow in three regions — Upper Missouri, Rio Grande–Pecos, and Colorado (plus Upper Arkansas-White-Red at 90 percent availability) — are given as zero. In these regions, present installed capacity plus capacity under construction exceed the amounts given for full regulation. Some capacity goes for provision of hydraulic head, flow regulation, and flood control in tandem, and minimum pools for recreation. These purposes add to capacity beyond the amounts specified for flow regulation. We have ignored the problem of "overregulation" because we had no way of estimating its probable magnitude; further research might provide a basis for measurement.

Table 64.   ESTIMATES OF MAXIMUM PHYSICAL DEVELOPMENT, 98% AVAILABILITY, BY REGION

	Löf and Hardison		This study		Committee Print No. 32[a]		Storage	
	Storage *(mil. af)*	Net flow *(bgd)*	Storage *(mil. af)*	Net flow *(bgd)*	Storage *(mil. af)*	Net flow *(bgd)*	Existing, 1964 *(mil. af)*	Added for physical maximum, this study *(mil. af)*
NORTHEAST	1,268	360	1,229	362	415	416	51	1,178
N Eng	172	57	180	61	86	65	11	169
D & H	79	28	82	29	31	31	3	79
Ches	174	46	174	47	55	51	2	172
Ohio	394	98	495	100	76	108	16	479
EGL	107	33	84	33	37	39	2	82
WGL	113	32	70	30	48	40	1	69
U Miss	118	48	81	46	65	59	10	71
L Mo	111	18	63	16	17	23	6	57
SOUTHEAST	1,256	341	882	334	382	391	130	752
SE	640	189	412	186	219	210	54	358
Cumb	57	14	38	15	14	17	14	24
Tenn	158	40	192	40	43	43	16	176
L Miss	143	37	83	35	41	46	5	78
L AWR	258	61	157	58	65	75	41	116
MID-CONTINENT	238	52	175	59	74	83	161	14
U Mo	68	23	68	26	27	28	102	−34
U AWR	31	6	19	7	12	12	17	2
W Gulf	139	23	88	26	35	43	42	46
SOUTHWEST	63.2	21.7	50.9	22.1	38	26.5	90	−39
RG-P	6.4	2.6	6.4	3.0	15	2.3	8	−1.6
Colo	28.7	11.0	28.7	11.4	15	12.7	75	−46.3
G Basin	22.2	7.4	11.3	6.9	6.5	10.0	5	6.3
S Pac	5.9	0.7	4.5	0.8	1.5	1.5	2	2.5
NORTH PACIFIC	762	184	586	180	167	200	74	512
C Pac	298	51	122	45	37	58	26	96
PNW	464	133	464	135	130	142	48	416
U.S.	3,587.2	958.7	2,922.9	956	1,076	1,117	506	2,417

Note: Figures partially rounded.

[a]Physical maximum not shown for all regions in Committee Print No. 32; some of the above are unpublished figures from that study.

Table 65. MAXIMUM REGULATED FLOW, STORAGE, AND COSTS OF STORAGE, BY REGION: 98%, 95%, AND 90% AVAILABILITY

	Maximum regulated flow (mgd)			Quantity of storage for maximum regulated flow (mil. af)			Costs of existing storage ($ million)		Costs of storage (including existing) ($ million)					
									Capital			Annual		
	98%	95%	90%	98%	95%	90%	Capital	Annual	98%	95%	90%	98%	95%	90%
NORTHEAST	361,535	375,867	399,192	1,229.8	967.9	862.2	4,265.0	181.3	106,366.8	80,430.0	72,525.5	4,520.5	3,418.2	3,081.8
N Eng	60,895	61,856	65,100	180.0	120.0	129.7	1,600.6	68.0	18,000.6	12,174.6	13,120.6	765.0	517.4	557.6
D & H	28,629	29,171	30,319	81.9	57.8	49.4	365.5	15.5	9,478.9	6,688.5	5,720.6	402.8	284.2	243.1
Ches	46,657	47,341	50,077	174.0	131.0	122.4	248.2	10.5	18,300.2	13,800.2	12,910.7	777.7	586.5	548.2
Ohio	99,457	101,632	107,168	495.0	307.0	260.7	1,267.3	53.9	40,290.3	24,977.3	21,203.3	1,712.4	1,061.6	901.2
EGL	33,278	34,057	36,070	83.8	60.3	59.9	106.0	4.5	7,602.0	5,456.0	5,422.0	323.1	231.9	230.4
WGL	30,283	33,527	36,315	70.4	90.3	76.0	66.5	2.8	4,150.5	5,326.5	4,479.5	176.4	226.3	190.4
U Miss	46,125	50,548	54,477	81.4	118.0	100.9	434.9	18.5	4,591.3	6,715.9	5,724.9	195.1	285.4	243.3
L Mo	16,211	17,735	19,666	63.3	83.5	63.2	176.0	7.5	3,953.0	5,291.0	3,944.0	168.0	224.9	167.6
SOUTHEAST	333,934	343,065	368,433	881.4	708.0	767.0	4,253.1	180.8	37,873.1	28,224.1	30,985.8	1,609.6	1,199.5	1,316.9
SE	186,030	187,225	202,204	412.0	326.0	454.2	1,811.8	77.0	16,254.8	12,781.8	17,959.8	690.8	543.2	763.3
Cumb	14,647	14,968	15,904	37.5	26.0	22.9	410.9	17.5	1,316.9	871.9	752.6	56.0	37.1	32.0
Tenn	40,389	40,566	42,805	192.0	119.0	101.7	759.9	32.3	12,634.9	7,519.9	6,385.9	537.0	319.6	271.4
L Miss	35,207	41,623	40,976	82.9	110.0	65.9	100.2	4.3	1,820.2	2,417.2	1,446.2	77.4	102.7	61.5
L AWR	57,661	58,683	66,544	157.0	127.0	122.3	1,170.3	49.7	5,846.3	4,633.3	4,441.3	248.4	196.9	188.7
MID-CONTINENT	58,553	60,712	65,985	174.9	171.9	149.9	4,287.7	182.2	6,000.7	6,550.7	6,251.7	255.0	278.4	265.7
U Mo	25,600	25,600	25,600	68.0	50.8	34.5	2,195.1	93.3	2,195.1	2,195.1	2,195.1	93.3	93.3	93.3
U AWR	7,053	8,428	9,100	18.5	23.4	17.7	612.1	26.0	689.1	911.1	612.1	29.3	38.7	26.0
W Gulf	25,900	26,684	31,285	88.4	97.7	97.7	1,480.5	62.9	3,116.5	3,444.5	3,444.5	132.4	146.4	146.4
SOUTHWEST	22,149	23,119	24,273	50.9	44.2	40.7	4,392.1	186.7	4,908.1	5,046.1	5,078.1	208.6	214.5	215.8
RG-P	3,000	3,000	3,000	6.4	4.8	3.4	354.6	15.1	354.6	354.6	354.6	15.1	15.1	15.1
Colo	11,400	11,400	11,400	28.7	21.1	18.3	3,540.5	150.5	3,540.5	3,540.5	3,540.5	150.5	150.5	150.5
G Basin	6,934	7,761	8,749	11.3	13.5	14.3	271.2	11.5	580.2	695.2	735.2	24.6	29.5	31.2
S Pac	815	958	1,124	4.5	4.8	4.7	225.8	9.6	432.8	455.8	447.8	18.4	19.4	19.0
NORTH PACIFIC	180,048	190,955	195,019	586.0	568.9	425.0	5,349.8	227.4	35,410.1	34,757.8	26,246.8	1,504.8	1,477.2	1,115.4
C Pac	45,478	51,148	53,775	122.0	208.7	164.0	1,662.2	70.6	7,626.5	12,990.2	10,227.2	324.1	552.1	434.6
PNW	134,570	139,807	141,244	464.0	360.2	261.0	3,687.6	156.7	27,783.6	21,767.6	16,019.6	1,180.7	925.1	680.8
U.S.	956,219	993,718	1,052,902	2,923.0	2,460.9	2,244.8	22,547.7	958.3	190,558.8	155,008.7	141,087.9	8,098.5	6,587.8	599.6
Excluding existing									168,011.1	132,461.0	118,540.2	7,140.2	5,629.5	5,037.3

Source: Appendix F.

Note: All costs are in 1964 dollars.

Table 66. U.S. STORAGE REQUIREMENTS AT FULL
AND CONSTRAINED CAPACITY

Availability (percent)	Maximum physical flow (mil. af)	Marginal cost ⩽ 10¢/1,000 gals. (mil. af)	Reduction of capacity induced by marginal cost constraint (percent)
98	2,923	2,026	31
95	2,461	1,987	19
90	2,245	1,865	17

Table 67. REGIONAL COMPARISON OF PHYSICAL MAXIMUM NET FLOW WITH NET FLOW LIMITED BY
MARGINAL COST: 98% AVAILABILITY, 0.0425 ANNUAL FACTOR

	Physical maximum net flow	Net flow if marginal cost is not more than 50¢/1,000 gals.	Net flow if marginal cost is not more than 10¢/1,000 gals.	Net flow as a percentage of physical maximum attainable:		Annual cost:	
				when MC ⩽ 50¢	when MC ⩽ 10¢	when MC ⩽ 10¢	when MC ⩽ 50¢
		(bgd)		*(percent)*		*($ million)*	
NORTHEAST	361.5	354.9	344.7			1,209.0	1,933.2
N Eng	60.9	59.7	59.4	98	98	125.6	183.8
D & H	28.6	28.4	26.3	99	92	141.8	275.4
Ches	46.7	45.3	42.3	97	91	93.8	256.6
Ohio	99.5	95.8	95.8	96	96	431.7	431.7
EGL	33.3	33.1	30.8	99	92	98.0	275.0
WGL	30.3	30.3	29.3	100	97	119.2	173.6
U Miss	46.1	46.1	45.4	100	98	143.0	176.6
L Mo	16.2	16.2	15.4	100	95	55.9	160.5
SOUTHEAST	333.9	333.0	329.1			861.2	1,198.8
SE	186.0	186.0	184.7	100	99	518.3	613.8
Cumb	14.6	14.6	14.5	100	99	23.5	38.5
Tenn	40.4	39.5	38.0	98	94	111.7	274.7
L Miss	35.2	35.2	35.0	100	99	60.2	73.1
L AWR	57.7	57.7	56.9	100	99	147.5	198.7
MID-CONTINENT	58.6	58.6	58.1			63.0	72.6
U Mo[a]	25.6	25.6	25.6	100	100	0	0
U AWR	7.1	7.1	7.0	100	99	1.7	3.1
W Gulf	25.9	25.9	25.5	100	98	61.3	69.5
SOUTHWEST	22.12	22.11	21.3			11.1	16.9
RG-P[a]	3.0	3.0	3.0	100	100	0	0
Colo[a]	11.4	11.4	11.4	100	100	0	0
G Basin	6.9	6.9	6.9	100	100	11.1	11.1
S Pac	0.82	0.81	0	99	0	0	5.8
NORTH PACIFIC	180.1	178.6	172.4			317.2	816.3
C Pac	45.5	45.5	43.3	100	95	118.4	253.5
PNW	134.6	133.1	129.1	99	96	198.8	562.8
U.S.	956.2	947.2	925.6	99	97	2,461.5	4,037.8

[a]No new storage needed.

Table 68. MARGINAL COST CONSTRAINT: SELECTED STORAGE FLOWS AND COSTS, BY REGION, 0.0425 ANNUAL FACTOR

	95% Availability Marginal cost ≤ 10¢		90% Availability Marginal cost ≤ 10¢		Storage with Marginal cost ≤ 10¢/1,000 gallons		
	Net flow (bgd)	Annual cost ($ mil.)	Net flow (bgd)	Annual cost ($ mil.)	98% Availability (mil. af)	95% Availability (mil. af)	90% Availability (mil. af)
NORTHEAST	361.5	1,257.6	387.5	1,196.0	646.4	636.4	595.8
N Eng	59.8	118.5	63.2	129.1	93.9	75.2	81.0
D & H	28.3	167.9	29.4	142.2	33.8	38.2	32.7
Ches	45.8	192.6	47.7	179.8	70.1	78.9	73.8
Ohio	97.9	429.3	104.6	361.0	225.5	216.5	184.0
EGL	32.3	112.3	34.6	111.6	46.6	45.5	45.2
WGL	31.8	89.6	35.4	100.0	60.0	59.2	57.3
U Miss	48.1	95.6	53.6	116.6	77.6	78.6	81.8
L Mo	17.5	51.8	19.0	55.7	38.9	44.3	40.0
SOUTHEAST	338.7	697.9	363.4	675.8	735.7	632.4	623.7
SE	185.6	393.6	199.2	399.3	393.6	312.0	351.8
Cumb	14.9	17.0	15.8	11.1	32.2	25.3	21.9
Tenn	39.0	111.0	41.3	92.4	82.9	75.8	65.4
L Miss	41.2	67.1	41.0	57.2	78.8	99.0	65.9
L AWR	58.0	109.2	66.1	115.8	148.2	120.3	118.7
MID-CONTINENT	60.4	74.9	65.8	73.6	205.9	215.9	213.2
U Mo	25.6	0	25.6	0	101.8[b]	101.8[b]	101.8[b]
U AWR	8.4	8.6	9.1[a]	0	18.3	22.6	16.8[b]
W Gulf	26.4	66.3	31.1	73.6	85.8	91.5	94.6
SOUTHWEST	23.0	15.6	24.1	16.4	93.4	98.4	99.0
RG-P	3.0	0	3.0	0	7.8[b]	7.8[b]	7.8[b]
Colo	11.4	0	11.4	0	74.6[b]	74.6[b]	74.6[b]
G Basin	7.7	11.0	8.6	12.0	11.0	12.3	12.9
S Pac	0.9	4.6	1.1	4.4	0	3.7	3.7
NORTH PACIFIC	182.5	432.0	191.8	362.2	346.1	403.9	333.3
C Pac	47.8	150.2	52.7	170.0	97.4	125.3	128.9
PNW	134.7	281.8	139.1	192.2	248.7	278.6	204.4
U.S.	966.1	2,478.0	1,032.6	2,324.0	2,027.5	1,987.0	1,865.0

[a] No new storage needed.
[b] Amount in existence or under construction, 1964.

Table 69. U.S. MARGINAL AND AVERAGE COSTS FOR SELECTED FLOWS

	Average annual costs per mgd (dollars)	Average costs per million gallons (dollars)
Maximum physical flow		
98%	7,469	20.46
95%	5,664	15.52
90%	4,783	13.10
Marginal cost constraint		
98%, MC ≤ 50¢	4,264	11.68
98%, MC ≤ 10¢	2,647	7.25
95%, MC ≤ 10¢	2,565	7.02
90%, MC ≤ 10¢	2,250	6.16

Table 70.   SELECTED FLOWS AND AVERAGE COSTS
OF FLOW, U.S. AGGREGATES: 0.0425
ANNUAL FACTOR

	Flow (bgd)	Annual total costs ($ mil.)	Average annual costs per mgd (dollars)	Percentage of physical capacity
Maximum physical flow				
98%	956	7,140	7,469	
95%	994	5,630	5,664	
90%	1,053	5,037	4,783	
Flow constrained by M.C.				
98%, MC ≤ 50¢	947	4,038	4,264	99
98%, MC ≤ 10¢	930	2,462	2,647	97
95%, MC ≤ 10¢	966	2,478	2,565	97
90%, MC ≤ 10¢	1,033	2,324	2,250	93

Note: Costs are for storage in addition to what is now in existence (in place and under construction).

Chapter 10

THE BASIC MODEL:
THE RESULTS

When projected losses are added to projected waste dilution requirements, the resulting total requirements, expressed as a function of treatment level, can be compared with availability of flows at successively higher levels up to the physically attainable maximum. The combination of treatment and flow, yielding the costs of treatment and flow, can be selected in accordance with one or another of the various criteria and restrictions already discussed. If the chance of deficiency is 2 percent, the annual factor is 0.0425, and the standard of stream quality is set at 4 mg/l of dissolved oxygen, 0.1 parts per million of phosphorus, and 1 ppm of nitrogen, we have the "basic" model. This chapter is a description of the implications of the basic model regarding required storage, required levels of treatment, required flows relative to maximum available flows, and costs of treatment and flow regulation for Low, Medium, and High projections for the years between 1960 and 2020.[1] Subsequent chapters deal with variants of the basic model.

Although any combination of flow and storage within the specified limits could be adopted, we examine only three combinations, each of which is designated as a "program":

1. The program that minimizes storage (required flow)
2. The program that minimizes level of treatment
3. The program that minimizes the combined cost of new storage and treatment

[1] The problem of dynamics — i.e., the adaptation of each year's level of investment in water resource facilities to what has gone before and to what follows — is ignored. In this sense our analysis is wholly static.

In several regions — the number depends on the year and the projection — losses exceed maximum regulated flow. For these regions no options are available, and we have constructed only minimum flow programs for them. When national aggregates of minimum treatment or minimum cost programs are tabulated, they automatically include the minimum flow program for water-short regions.

Unless the regional activity mix has been changed or its level has been lowered in response to water shortage, aggregates of flow and treatment costs fall short of the full costs of the projected national aggregate of activity by the cost of overcoming water shortage. Another inconsistency created by water shortage is implicit violation of the quality standard because of the deficiency of waste dilution.

Minimum Treatment Program

If every region had enough water the minimum treatment program would combine 70/50 percent treatment with the minimum flow needed to maintain water quality at the specified level. This flow might not require additional storage, since required flow at 70/50 percent treatment might be less than existing regulated flow. Under this condition the minimum treatment and minimum cost programs would coincide.

For some regions and some projections the minimum treatment program might require less water than existing regulated flow. The effect of raising treatment to 70/50 percent is therefore equivalent to an improvement in water quality beyond the stipulated standard. (The present level of treatment and the present quality of water might be below standard.) This phenomenon occurs in two regions: New England, 1980 Low and Medium; and Lower Arkansas-White-Red, through 2000 Low. We made no attempt to adjust for the implicit higher water quality of the minimum treatment programs in these two regions. (The same effect, but even more exaggerated, would be observed if treatment were raised to 97½ percent.)

If total requirements are sufficiently high, the minimum treatment program becomes the minimum level of treatment (equal to or more than 70/50 percent) consistent with maximum physical regulation. As noted above, by 1980 High all regions except the Lower Arkansas-White-Red would require storage beyond 1964 capacity to meet a D.O. standard of 4 mg/l, and by 2000 Medium new storage would also be needed in the Lower Arkansas-White-Red.

The minimum treatment program implies maximum regulation in all except six regions by 1980 Medium; in all except four regions by 2000 Medium; in all except three regions by 2020 Medium; and in all by 2020 High. For the 2020 High projection the minimum treatment level is above 70/50 percent in every region (70/68 percent in New England, which is the lowest of all regions) and regulation is at its physical maximum in every region. Treatment levels are below 97½ percent in all regions that are not water short — eleven of them — and are at 97½ percent in the remaining eleven regions that are water short. This means that, because of the constrained definitions of "minimum flow," "minimum cost," and "minimum treatment" programs, there is no distinction among these programs in eleven regions; all are minimum flow programs, and required flow in all exceeds maximum regulated flow.

As the level of economic activity and population rises, the range of choice regarding water resource policy narrows. This is shown in table 71. For 1980 Low the minimum flow program uses one-fourth the water required for minimum treatment and one-half the water required for minimum cost. By 2020 High the minimum flow program requires 96 percent of total U.S. regulated flow and 75 percent of the flow required for minimum treatment.[2]

In 1960, if water had been used on the same basis as projected — i.e., giving to land its optimum ration — three regions would have shown deficits, and probably did anyway, when required flow for the minimum flow program is compared with maximum net flow. Five regions (add Lower Mississippi and Great Basin to Rio Grande–Pecos, Colorado, and South Pacific) showed lower sustained flows on the basis of 1964 storage than required flows for the minimum flow program. If treatment had been at 70/50 percent in all regions, if available storage (in 1964) had been used for low-flow augmentation in accordance with the rules specified in chapter 9, and if flows had been equalized *within* the basin, quality standards would not have been violated in seventeen regions.

[2] Aggregate required flow for minimum treatment exceeds U.S. regulated flow because the total of required flow for the minimum flow program, plus the total of available flow in regions of water shortage, is greater than aggregate regulated flow. That is, required flows for the minimum flow program exceed available flow in several regions. Since the minimum treatment program uses all the available flow by the later projection periods, aggregate required flow for the minimum treatment program exceeds available flow.

Using maximum net regulated flow (98 percent) as the upper limit of water supply, there are three water-short regions for 1980 Low, five for 1980 High, four for 2000 Medium, seven and a borderline case for 2000 High, the same for 2020 Medium, and eleven for 2020 High (see table 72). If water supply is limited by a regulatory (i.e., storage) cost of 10 cents per 1,000 gallons, an additional region, Delaware and Hudson, is on the borderline by 2020 High.

It is most interesting to note that an upper limit of 10 cents per 1,000 gallons for cost of flow has virtually no effect on determining whether a region is water short within the horizon of our projections. If the marginal cost limit is lowered from 10 cents to 2 cents (i.e., $6.52 per acre-foot in the reservoir), the Central Pacific region is barely at the limit by 2000 Medium; by 2020 High the Eastern Great Lakes region is well over the line and the Delaware and Hudson region has come up to it. No other restrictive effects are noted.

Table 71 shows that if dissolved oxygen is kept at 4 mg/l we have some choice of policy in the United States until economic activity and population reach the level of 2020 High. At that projection, there is little difference among flow-minimizing, cost-minimizing, and treatment-minimizing programs.

There is no difference between the number of water-short regions under a minimum treatment program and under a minimum flow program unless the minimum treatment level is kept fixed at a specified percentage of BOD removal. (Otherwise, we automatically adjust treatment levels to maximum regulated flow, except that minimum treatment cannot be reduced below 70/50 percent.) If treatment were kept constant at 70/50 percent, by the 2020 High projection no region would have adequate water supplies; for the Medium and Low projections only the New England, Ohio, and Lower Arkansas-White-Red regions could meet requirements. At this level of treatment, required flows in several regions are equal to or more than the total regulated flow for the United States. It is because the minimum treatment program is always defined relative to available flow that the flows do not reach the magnitudes given in table 73. By 2020 Medium, if treatment were 70/50 percent and the D.O. content were 4 mg/l, required flows for the United States would be six times greater than maximum net regulated flow; at the High projection required flows would be equal to twelve times maximum net regulated flow.

Required Storage

A question of concern to all who hope to minimize the effect of man's activities on nature is the required amount of storage. Figures for the United States, by program and projection, are in table 74. Until the projection reaches the level of 2020 High the differences in aggregate storage among all three programs is significant. Minimum flow programs require half the storage required for minimum cost programs, or less. The minimum treatment program builds up rapidly. By 2020 High all streams are fully regulated.

One might look at a different relationship — the cost in dollars to the cost in interference with streams. How much is it worth not to build dams? The differences between the minimum flow and minimum cost programs in the annual costs of new storage plus treatment are as follows:

		Minimum flow	Minimum cost
		($ million)	
1980	Medium	1,252	992
2000	Medium	2,120	1,804
2020	Medium	3,562	3,383
2020	High	7,183	7,070

For 1980 Medium, at an additional cost of $260 million per year we can avoid construction of 37 million acre-feet of reservoir capacity. For 2020 Medium, at an additional cost of $179 million annually we save 181 million acre-feet of capacity. Why is there such a difference between the dollar-storage capacity tradeoffs in the two years? The explanation lies in the absolute levels of storage and treatment. In 1980, in going from minimum flow to minimum cost solutions, storage costs rise from $27 million to $67 million, but treatment costs fall from $1.2 billion to $926 million. By 2020 Medium, treatment costs for the minimum flow program are $3.2 billion and fall to $2.8 billion when costs are minimized. Storage costs rise from $390 million to $605 million – the saving of $400 million in treatment costs being partially offset by the added expenditure of $200 million in storage costs. In 1980 a small increase in sustained flow offsets a fairly large drop in treatment costs. By 2020 the fall in treatment costs associated with the minimum cost program is great enough to warrant quite a large increase in reservoir capacity.

Projected increases in storage volume and storage investment indicate that by 2020 Medium, minimum cost program, East and West will account for approximately equal total amounts in place (table 75). By 2020 High (or what would be 2040 Medium if trends are extrapolated) the East would account for 60 percent of the total, including existing storage. When output is expanded from 2020 Medium to 2020 High, our projections indicate an increase in storage volume that is disproportionately great when compared with the change in required flow or GNP. This is a reflection of movement along the flat tail of the flow-storage curve.

Level of Treatment

The prospective outflow of wastes is so great that by 1980 Medium the level of treatment for the minimum treatment program will have to exceed 70/50 percent for all except six regions in the United States. By 2000 Medium only five regions can be at the constrained minimum – New England, Ohio, Upper Mississippi, Lower Mississippi, and Lower Arkansas-White-Red. By 2020 Medium, the New England, Ohio, and Lower Arkansas-White-Red regions are all that are left and by 2020 High no region can treat as low as 70/50 percent. What is probably of greater interest is the number of regions for which the *minimum* level is 90 percent or above: fourteen by 2020 Medium; all but New England and Lower Arkansas-White-Red by 2020 High. By

1980 Medium the minimum level of treatment must be 90 percent or above in eight regions (table 76).

As already noted, minimum flow programs call for 97½ percent treatment in all regions for every projection. Minimum cost programs are the same as minimum flow programs in nine regions for 1980 and 2000 Medium, in thirteen regions for 2020 Medium, and in nineteen regions for 2020 High. By 2020 Medium, minimum cost program, the lowest treatment level is 70 percent (Ohio) followed by 80 percent (New England and Lower Arkansas-White-Red); elsewhere treatment is 90 percent and above.

Expenditures for Quality Standards and Flow Regularity

Elsewhere we estimated 1960 treatment costs as about $300 million annually. The annual equivalent cost of existing storage capacity at 1960 prices was estimated at $958 million, although much of this capacity was not used for flow regulation.[3] If we assume that 60 percent is available for flow regulation, the 1964 annual estimated outlay of regulated water supply (instream) was about $900 million ($300 million for treatment; $575 million for reservoir capacity rounded to $600 million). This figure could be compared with the costs of treatment and flow if the standard of 4 mg/1 had been applied in all regions and the postulated coefficients of loss had been met. The figures are given in table 77.

Without counting any deficiency in collection or recirculation costs relative to conditions postulated in the basic model for 1980 and thereafter – and there are deficiencies[4] – an instream D.O. standard of 4 mg/1 plus specified losses could have been met in 1960 by the expenditure, on an annual equivalent basis, of $247 million more than the estimated actual costs for that year. Most of the $247 million would have represented additional treatment cost ($216 million); the remainder, the annual costs of storage capacity. The equivalent capital investment would have been about $5.4 billion – an amount that presumably

[3]The capacity in 1964 was distributed by function as follows (app. F):

	Acre-feet (mil., rounded)
Flood control	119
Irrigation	92
Power	197
Multiple use and other	130
Total	537

The total of 537 million acre-feet seems to be excessive. We adopted 506 million acre-feet as the best estimate.

[4]Some streams now suffer thermal pollution. Many cities have sewers that combine sanitary and storm runoff, which must be separated in order to control pollution. The estimated cost of complete separation is $30 billion or more. See *Separating Storm and Sanitary Sewers in Urban Renewal*, H. Rept. 1648, Thirty-second Report by the Committee on Government Operations (June 23, 1966). Recent estimates of the capital cost of dealing with the problem created by combined sewers range between $15 billion and $49 billion, depending on the solution chosen. See Federal Water Pollution Control Administration, *The Cost of Clean Water and Its Economic Impact*, vol. 1, *The Report* (1969), p. 131.

would have been accumulated over a number of years. Additional annual costs imposed by the separation of sewers would be, perhaps, a billion dollars. Additional re-circulation costs might be about $134 million.[5] It appears, therefore, that the total additional costs of reaching the specified quality standard in recent years would have been somewhere in the neighborhood of $2 billion annually above outlays actually incurred, of which the largest single component would have been the costs of sewer separation and construction.

If the costs of achieving the specified quality standard in 1960 were computed on the basis of a minimum increase in 1964 flow regulation, costs would have been about $450 million above estimated outlays. Of this amount, only $10 million would have been for added storage. The remainder would have been divided roughly equally between munici-pal and industrial treatment facilities. We conclude, there-fore, that given the state of flow regulation in 1964, treat-ment levels in 1960 averaged only 40 percent of what was needed to meet the specified D.O. quality standard. In addi-tion, there would have been the costs of recirculation designed to avoid thermal pollution plus the costs of elimi-nating the pollution caused by combined sewers.

Future Costs

For the moment consider only the costs of treatment (other than thermal) and the costs of additional storage to meet flow requirements. Collection costs, the annual costs of existing storage, and the costs of recirculation are ignored because they are treated as constants for any given projection. By considering *total*, rather than *additional* costs of treatment, we have introduced an asymmetry that overstates the costs of treatment facilities that must be added over the projection period relative to the *total* costs of storage, including costs of storage now in place. The main reason for this asymmetry is uncertainty over the facts: the present (1960) worth and the projected life of existing treatment facilities. Were the asymmetry to be eliminated by assuming that present storage facilities will be replaced within the projection period and thereby give rise to costs, cost minimizing programs would put greater stress on treatment and less on storage. If, on the other hand, the asymmetry is eliminated by giving credit for existing treat-ment facilities, incremental costs of treatment (or the total of treatment plus storage) can be estimated by mentally subtracting $300 million (annual costs) from the figure given.

Storage plus treatment costs prospectively vary over a wide range depending on the policy that is selected. Between the minimum cost and minimum treatment pro-grams the spread is 5 to 1 for 1980 Medium, and 1.7 to 1 for 2020 High (table 78).

Growth of the minimum cost column, including present (1960 for treatment, 1964 for storage) outlays, on the basis of 1960 being equal to 100[6], is as follows (1960 = 100):

1980	Medium	139
2000	Medium	210
2020	Medium	348
2020	High	669

The High projection for 1980 and the Low projection for 2000 require comparable outlays for water. The 2000 Medium projection is roughly comparable to 2020 Low; 2000 High is roughly comparable to 2020 Medium. If this comparability extends into the future, 2020 High is equiva-lent to 2040 Medium. Thus, if planning is based on high projections but growth follows Medium projections, excess capacity would be burdensome for about twenty years. If growth follows the High path but investment follows the Low path, the effect on water quality and the constriction imposed on water-related activity would be severe.

The most useful way of viewing the "cost of water" as part of aggregate social costs is not always clear. Are the costs of waste removal — e.g., a city's sanitary system — part of the "costs of water," or are they costs of nuisance abatement along with garbage and rubbish removal? Indus-trial and power cooling processes can be based on the move-ment of air or water through a heat exchange system. If water is used, are the costs to be assigned to water or to production of a good or service? The answer is neither clear nor necessarily the same in all contexts. Furthermore, the costs are usually not for water per se but for equipment used to convey water from one place to another. This is true of dams, aqueducts, pumps, etc. Treatment plants and cooling towers are designed to change the chemical, physi-cal, and biological properties of water and so are more intimately connected with water as such.

Local distribution systems have been wholly ignored on the ground that their costs are part of the city's plumbing system and are no more a part of the "cost of water" than are the pipes and spigots of a residence. The exclusion is arbitrary, but it is based on the belief that local distribution costs are not an object of water resource policy even though "water shortage," in the United States at least, is exacerbated by the fact that the costs of local distribution and treatment are comparatively low.

For selected projections, tables 80 and 81 give figures based on our postulation that the costs of water are equal to the total costs of required storage, including the costs of reservoirs now in place, plus the costs of required waste treatment to abate BOD and plant nutrients, plus the costs of steam-electric recirculation to avoid heat pollution, plus the costs of sewerage. The results reveal a slowly declining relationship with projected gross national product. These figures understate the full cost of water because account was not taken of the costs of overcoming water shortage. Were these additional costs to be incurred rather than a shift in product mix, they probably would not raise total water costs beyond the fraction of GNP they accounted for in 1960.[7]

---

[5]This is a guess based on the estimated increase in recirculation required to eliminate thermal pollution in 1980.

[6]In this, we assume that 1960 required outlays were in fact met. Estimated 1960 actual outlays were not $1,147 million but were about $900 million.

[7]It is improper to assume that "costs of water" accounted for 0.3 percent of GNP as computed by the Department of Commerce for 1960. No account is taken of capital consumption allowances for government property in official measurements of GNP; hence a large fraction of the annual costs of water as we have computed them are excluded from present GNP and also from projected GNP.

Of total projected costs for regulatory storage, treatment, and recirculation (ignoring sewage collection costs), storage costs recede in relative importance from about 64 percent in 1960 to 36 percent for the minimum cost program for 1980 Medium, to 28 percent for 2000 Medium, to 21 percent for 2020 Medium, and to 18 percent for 2020 High. If treatment for BOD and plant nutrients reaches projected levels in future years, expenditures for 2000 Medium will be about five times the estimated 1960–64 outlays, whereas projected regulatory storage costs will grow by 88 percent. The disparity in growth rates becomes greater as we move into the future and regulated flow approaches the physical net maximum. Of the total cost of water for 2000 Medium, almost three-fourths will consist of treatment and recirculation and the remainder, flow regulation.

If flow regulation costs are divided in the same proportion that required flows are divided between losses and waste dilution and waste dilution costs are added to costs of treatment and recirculation, the resulting sum is a measure of "quality maintenance" costs. Such costs account for 80 percent of total water costs for 1960 (1964 for costs of storage), 89 percent for 1980 Medium, 92 percent for 2000 Medium, 94 percent for 2020 Medium, and 95 percent for 2020 High. (See table 79.)

Since costs of existing storage, recirculation, and collection are the same regardless of program (but depend on the projection), a simple view of the differences among options is revealed by comparing only the costs of new storage and treatment (table 80). The first line of figures for 1960 shows not "actual" but required outlays to meet the quality standard of 4 mg/l. The difference in cost between the minimum treatment program and either of the others grows as the level of economic activity and the size of population grows, while the difference between the other two narrows. Annual costs of new storage plus treatment compare as follows:

		Minimum flow	Minimum treatment	Minimum cost
		($ million)		
1960		753	1,476	546
1980	Medium	1,252	5,013	993
2000	Medium	2,120	5,986	1,804
2020	Medium	3,562	7,503	3,382
2020	High	7,182	12,321	7,069

The message is clear: Reliance on dilution rather than on treatment to maintain water quality not only involves much higher regulated flows — i.e., is costly in terms of regulatory capacity and flow — but also is more expensive in aggregate real cost than either of the alternative policies. The unfavorable cost situation of the minimum flow program relative to the minimum cost program, by contrast, diminishes to the point that by 2020 High the difference is negligible. For the Medium projections during the period 1960–2020, the average difference in annual cost between minimum flow and minimum cost programs is about $240 million. This, then, is the price that would have to be paid to keep regulation to a minimum.

Regional Shortages and Aggregate Gross Deficits

By 1980, Medium projection, the gross deficit[8] will be 16 bgd (table 82). Gross deficits projected thereafter are:

2000	Medium	30 bgd
2020	Medium	78 bgd
2020	High	255 bgd

Should the regional distribution of population growth and economic activity remain unaffected by water shortage, we would see some 25 percent of average aggregate annual runoff redistributed by 2020 High, or supplies would be augmented by desalination or other means.

If each region were developed to the limit fixed by marginal costs of flow equal to, or less than, 10 cents per 1,000 gallons, there would be more than enough flow to meet projected 2020 High requirements for the minimum flow program, assuming that activities could be shifted from water-deficit to water-surplus regions at no increase in required flow. (See table 83.) Aggregate annual costs of flow constrained by marginal costs of 10 cents per 1,000 gallons are about $2.5 billion, an amount equal to unconstrained costs of flow of the minimum cost program. One might assume, therefore, that if land supply and transportation costs do not impose serious restrictions on interregional relocation of activity, the projected bill of goods can be met. Water requirements in general would be reduced if activities were transferred from the regions in which they were originally projected to regions of water surplus. There is the unanswered question of whether land would be available in regions of comparable climate to receive activity dislocated by water shortage. However, increases in productivity per acre, such as those resulting from the extension of irrigation in the eastern half of the United States, would serve to offset reductions in agricultural acreage induced by water shortages.[9]

If flow regulation were constrained by a marginal cost limit of 2 cents per 1,000 gallons, the gross shortage of water by 2020 High would amount to 298 bgd and the country itself would be on a deficit basis. Thirteen regions would show deficits or be barely in balance (see table 84). A gross deficit of 298 bgd represents 35 percent of maximum regulated flow as constrained by marginal costs of 2 cents per 1,000 gallons. A redistribution of water among regions in the amount indicated (298 bgd) but subject to the marginal cost constraint would still leave a deficit of 55 bgd and is not likely to be undertaken.

A marginal cost constraint of 10 cents per 1,000 gallons implies that eleven regions cannot meet projected requirements for 2020 High, compared with thirteen regions if

[8] "Gross deficit" is the aggregate deficit of all regions suffering a deficit measured as the difference between required flow and maximum regulated flow. "Net deficit" is the difference between the gross deficit and the aggregate surplus of regions having surpluses. The size of the gross deficit is not affected by choice of program, since it is assumed that any region encountering a deficit adopts a minimum flow program. Net deficits and surpluses are affected by choice of program.

[9] The assumption is that agricultural uses of water would feel the pinch of shortage first in most regions.

marginal costs are limited to 2 cents per 1,000 gallons. The difference in the aggregate cost of water between the lower and higher marginal cost constraint is about $1.2 billion annually. It is difficult, however, to reach any conclusion regarding the binding effect of $1.2 billion in annual costs of water some fifty years hence.

The regional distribution of projected deficits poses no surprises regarding the Southwest, for which the deficit would have been greater had not the known shortage of water inhibited projected growth of agriculture. The Pacific Northwest, to which other parts of the West may look for additional water, remains a surplus region even for 2020 High; the surplus is 39 bgd if regulation is not constrained by marginal cost, and 33 bgd if so constrained. (Reducing the limit from 10 cents to 2 cents per 1,000 gallons apparently has little effect on regulated flow.) For 2020 Medium the West (the three western divisions) shows a surplus of 9 bgd if regulation is unconstrained; is in approximate balance (deficit of 1 bgd) if flow is limited by a 10-cent marginal cost; and is short by 10 bgd if flow is limited by marginal costs of 2 cents per 1,000 gallons. Thus, even if the Pacific Northwest shares its surplus, the West faces absolute restriction by 2020.

California – defined as the sum of the Central Pacific and South Pacific regions – is faced with the following projected requirements (minimum cost, 4 mg/l):

	(bgd)
1980 Medium	35
2000 Medium	42
2020 Medium	55
2020 High	81
Unconstrained maximum flow	46
Marginal cost ≤ 10¢/1,000 gals.	43
Marginal cost ≤ 2¢/1,000 gals.	37

Up to 1980 Medium, California can make ends meet within a marginal cost constraint of 2 cents per 1,000 gallons without importation from the Colorado basin or the Pacific Northwest; by 2000 Medium the constraint must be raised to 10 cents per 1,000 gallons. By 2020 Medium, aggregate unconstrained flow must be supplemented by 9 bgd. By 2020 High the deficit is in the neighborhood of 40 bgd, its exact amount depending on whether there is a limit imposed on marginal costs.

The prospect is for California, Texas, the rim around the Western Great Lakes, and the Rio Grande–Pecos and Colorado basins to be the areas in which water shortage will press most heavily against projected population and economic activity.

Regional Variation in Costs

Tables 86, 87, 88, and 89 divide the costs of storage, treatment, and collection of sewage between East and West. Although information is incomplete, for 1960 the regional division of total costs between East and West for the minimum cost program would have been roughly equal if the D.O. standard of 4 mg/l had been met and losses had been incurred at specified rates.

As the projections move through time, the expenditures mount more rapidly in the East than in the West for all purposes – storage, BOD, and thermal. Annual expenditure (and cumulated total investment) on storage capacity is evenly divided between East and West by 2020 Medium; expenditures on treatment and recirculation are, of course, much greater in the East than in the West. If we were to minimize treatment instead of costs, the regional difference would be even greater, since shortage of water in the West prevents exercise of an option. The differences between minimum cost and minimum flow programs are relatively small. (Recirculation costs for 1960 are estimated as those actually incurred rather than those that would have been required to avoid thermal pollution. Expenditures for recirculation would have been higher in the East had thermal pollution been avoided.)

Table 89 shows the division of outlays between East and West classified according to whether or not they vary by program. A determination that expenditures on recirculation and sewerage are invariant by program merely reveals that not all conceivable alternatives have been included in our analysis. We have not considered an alternative to water cooling in the production of power, nor have we considered the possibility of relocating steam-electric power plants in order to avoid the need for freshwater cooling. We have also assumed that a sewerage collection system much as we now have will be required in the future without thought of any alternative disposition of liquid wastes. As a consequence, rigidities have been introduced into the projected cost structure that future technological innovations may invalidate. The reader will note that projected nonprogrammatic expenditures for the 2000 Medium projection constitute about two-thirds of total expenditures for the minimum cost program. The possibilities of reducing seemingly inevitable and substantial outlays for nonprogrammatic activities offer larger possibilities of savings than are promised by research in the commonly recognized area of waste treatment and flow regulation.

Table 71. REQUIRED FLOWS FOR THE UNITED STATES, BY PROGRAM, 98% AVAILABILITY, 0.0425 ANNUAL FACTOR, 4 mg/l D.O.

(billion gallons per day)

		Minimum flow program	Minimum treatment program	Minimum cost program
1960		139	576	360
1980	L	181	751	393
	M	205	776	426
	H	242	818	497
2000	L	230	805	468
	M	303	879	525
	H	451	995	586
2020	L	337	901	570
	M	480	1,004	679
	H	909	1,210	948

Table 72. DEFICITS (−) OF FLOWS, BY REGIONS, MINIMUM FLOW PROGRAMS, 98% AVAILABILITY, 4 mg/l D.O.

(billion gallons per day)

	Maximum regulated flow—98%	Required 1980 M	Deficit[a] 1980 M	Required 2000 M	Deficit 2000 M	Required 2020 M	Deficit 2020 M	Required 2020 H	Deficit 2020 H	Deficit, 2020 High when marginal cost is limited to		Maximum regulated flows	
										10¢/1,000 gal.	2¢/1,000 gal.	2¢ limit	10¢ limit
NORTHEAST	362	40	+322	64	+298	105	+257	222	+140	+121	+86	310	345
N Eng	61	3		5		6		10		+49	+46	56	59
D & H	29	6		10		15		26		0	0	26	26
Ches	47	6		10		18		39		+3	+3	42	42
Ohio	99	4		7		11		23		+73	+56	79	96
EGL	33	5		8		13		30		+1	−4	26	31
WGL	30	11		18		31		72	−42	−43	−47	25	29
U Miss	46	3		5		8		16		+29	+24	40	45
L Mo	16	1		2		3		6		+9	+8	14	15
SOUTHEAST	334	37	+297	68	+266	122	+212	262	+72	+68	+41	303	329
SE	186	25		48		88		187	−1	−2	−20	167	185
Cumb	15	2		4		9		24	−9	−9	−11	13	15
Tenn	40	3		6		10		24		+14	+10	34	38
L Miss	35	3		5		9		17		+18	+18	35	35
L AWR	58	3		4		6		10		+47	+44	54	57
MID-CONTINENT	59	40	+19	52	+7	77	−18	152	−93	−93	−97	55	58
U Mo	26	16		18		24		39	−13	−13	−13	26	26
U AWR	7	7		7		9	−2	15	−8	−8	−8	7	7
W Gulf	26	17		27	−1	44	−18	98	−72	−72	−76	22	26
SOUTHWEST	22	37	−15	51	−29	80	−58	122	−100	−101	−101	21	21
RG-P	3	6	−3	7	−4	9	−6	13	−10	−10	−10	3	3
Colo	11	17	−6	25	−14	43	−32	65	−54	−54	−54	11	11
G Basin	7	6		7	0	10	−3	18	−11	−11	−11	7	7
S Pac	1	8	−7	12	−11	18	−17	26	−25	−26	−26	0	0
NORTH PACIFIC	180	52	+128	67	+113	95	+85	151	+29	+21	+15	166	172
C Pac	45	27		30		37		55	−10	−12	−18	37	43
PNW	135	25		37		58		96		+33	+33	129	129
U.S.	956	205	+751	303	+653	480	+476	909	+45	+16	−55[a]	854	926
Gross Deficit			−15		−30		−78		−255	−260	−298		

Note: Plus sign indicates surplus; minus sign indicates deficit.
[a]Discrepancy due to rounding.

Table 73. REQUIRED FLOWS AT 70/50% TREAT-
MENT, 4 mg/l D.O., BY REGION: 2020

(billion gallons per day)

	98% maximum regulated flow	2020		
		L	M	H
N Eng	61	33	45	80
D & H	29	56	91	223
Ches	47	149	253	631
Ohio	99	57	94	234
EGL	33	92	156	392
WGL	30	307	495	1,248
U Miss	46	50	75	178
L Mo	16	23	38	87
SE	186	877	1,433	3,239
Cumb	15	91	171	452
Tenn	40	96	171	428
L Miss	35	40	70	171
L AWR	58	31	48	101
U Mo	26	119	177	366
U AWR	7	30	47	108
W Gulf	26	329	589	1,514
RG-P	3	52	72	125
Colo	11	386	534	935
G Basin	7	64	102	234
S Pac	1	43	60	122
C Pac	45	159	218	472
PNW	135	560	815	1,490
U.S.	956	3,644	5,754	12,830

Table 74. U.S. NEW STORAGE, 98% AVAILABILITY,
0.0425 ANNUAL FACTOR, 4 mg/l D.O.

(million acre-feet)

		Minimum flow program	Minimum treatment program	Minimum cost program
1960		4	546	24
1980	L	6	1,421	42
	M	21	1,582	58
	H	59	1,638	140
2000	L	29	1,615	101
	M	99	1,769	180
	H	194	2,295	287
2020	L	110	1,801	212
	M	195	2,026	376
	H	813	2,493	839

Table 75. NEW STORAGE, EAST AND WEST, FOR
THE MINIMUM COST PROGRAM, 0.0425
ANNUAL FACTOR, 4 mg/l D.O.: 1960
AND PROJECTIONS

		East	West	Total	Required flow
		(million acre-feet)			*(bgd)*
Existing: total		181	325	506	
Existing: regulatory		127	220	347	386
1960		21	3	24	360
1980	L	39	3	42	393
	M	45	13	58	426
	H	94	46	140	497
2000	L	83	18	101	468
	M	113	67	180	525
	H	176	111	287	586
2020	L	134	84	212	570
	M	245	137	376	679
	H	646	200	839	948

Note: East = Northeast and Southeast Divisions; West = Mid-
continent, Southwest, and North Pacific Divisions.

Table 76. TREATMENT LEVELS FOR ALTERNATIVE PROGRAMS, BY REGION, 98% AVAILABILITY, 0.0425 ANNUAL FACTOR, 4 mg/l D.O.

(percentage of BOD removed)

	Minimum flow program	Minimum treatment program					Mimimum cost program				
		1960	1980 M	2000 M	2020 M	2020 H	1960	1980 M	2000 M	2020 M	2020 H
N Eng	97.5	70/50	70/50	70/50	70/50	70/68	70/50	70/50	70	80	90
D & H	97.5	70/50	70/61	79	89	97.1	90	97.5	97.5	97.5	97.5
Ches	97.5	70/50	72	85	92	96.9	90	95	95	95	97.5
Ohio	97.5	70/50	70/50	70/50	70/50	95.3	70/50	70/60	70/60	70	97.5
EGL	97.5	70/50	72	84	91	97.1	95	95	95	97.5	97.5
WGL	97.5	85	92	95	97.5	97.5	95	97.5	97.5	97.5	97.5
U Miss	97.5	70/50	70/50	70/50	73.1	95.7	70/50	70	70	95	97.5
L Mo	97.5	70/50	70/50	70/58	80.1	92.8	70/50	70	90	90	97.5
SE	97.5	70/50	78	89	94	97.5	80	90	95	97.5	97.5
Cumb	97.5	70/50	78	91.7	96	97.5	70/50	90	95	97.5	97.5
Tenn	97.5	70/50	70/59	79	88.9	96.4	70/60	80	90	95	97.5
L Miss	97.5	70/50	70/50	70/50	77.5	92.2	70/60	70/60	80	90	95
L AWR	97.5	70/50	70/50	70/50	70/50	73.3	70/50	70/50	70/60	80	90
U Mo	97.5	92	96	96.6	97.4	97.5	92	96	96.6	97.4	97.5
U AWR	97.5	96.9	97.4	97.5	97.5	97.5	97.5	97.5	97.5	97.5	97.5
W Gulf	97.5	93	96.4	97.5	97.5	97.5	97.5	97.5	97.5	97.5	97.5
RG-P	97.5	97.5	97.5	97.5	97.5	97.5	97.5	97.5	97.5	97.5	97.5
Colo	97.5	97.5	97.5	97.5	97.5	97.5	97.5	97.5	97.5	97.5	97.5
G Basin	97.5	76	95.4	97.5	97.5	97.5	97.5	97.5	97.5	97.5	97.5
S Pac	97.5	97.5	97.5	97.5	97.5	97.5	97.5	97.5	97.5	97.5	97.5
C Pac	97.5	70/55	81.7	90.7	95.5	97.5	95	97.5	97.5	97.5	97.5
PNW	97.5	70/50	73	86	92.8	96.2	70/50	90	95	95	97.5

Table 77. COSTS OF ALTERNATIVE PROGRAMS, 98% AVAILABILITY, 0.0425 ANNUAL FACTOR, 4 mg/l D.O.: 1960

($ million)

	Existing (wild estimate)	Costs to meet 4 mg/l D.O., plus losses		
		Minimum flow program	Minimum treatment program	Minimum cost program
Storage	600[a]	610[b]	1,614[b]	631[b]
Treatment	300	743	462	515
Collection	n.a.	(513)	(513)	(513)
Thermal	67	(201)[c]	(201)[c]	(201)[c]
Total[d]	900	1,353	2,076	1,146

[a]Based on storage in place or under construction in 1964.
[b]Existing plus new.
[c]Estimated at same multiple of "existing" that "revised" was of "original" for 1980.
[d]Excludes collection and thermal.

Table 78. ANNUAL COSTS OF NEW STORAGE PLUS TREATMENT, 98% AVAILABILITY, 0.0425 ANNUAL
FACTOR, 4 mg/l D.O.

($ millions)

		Minimum flow program	Minimum treatment program	Minimum cost program	Minimum cost minus estimated 1960 treatment cost[a]	Minimum cost plus estimated 1960 storage cost[b]
1960		753	1,476	546	246	1,146
	L	1,111	4,356	867	567	1,467
1980	M	1,252	5,013	992	692	1,592
	H	1,496	5,252	1,247	947	1,847
	L	1,529	5,255	1,248	948	1,848
2000	M	2,120	5,987	1,804	1,504	2,404
	H	3,219	8,486	3,084	2,784	3,684
	L	2,485	6,316	2,139	1,839	2,739
2020	M	3,562	7,502	3,383	3,083	3,983
	H	7,183	12,320	7,070	6,770	7,670

[a]Equals added storage plus added treatment costs over 1960 levels.
[b]Equals total treatment and storage costs, including annual equivalent costs of storage in place or under construction in 1964.

Table 79. U.S. "COSTS OF QUALITY," MINIMUM COST PROGRAM, 98% AVAILABILITY, 0.0425 ANNUAL
FACTOR, 4 mg/l D.O.

($ million)

		Storage[a]		Treatment	Recirculation	Total	Total cost of quality[b]
		Losses	Waste dilution				
1960		198	442	300[c]	67	1,007	809
1980	M	308	717	926	874	2,825	2,517
2000	M	337	867	1,559	1,572	4,335	3,998
2020	M	424	1,146	2,777	3,295	7,642	7,218
	H	687	1,857	5,491	6,450	14,485	13,798

[a]Includes cost of existing regulatory storage.
[b]Waste dilution, treatment, recirculation (revised rates).
[c]Estimated actual.

Table 80.   U.S. ANNUAL TOTAL COSTS, BY PROGRAM, 98% AVAILABILITY, 0.0425 ANNUAL FACTOR, 4 mg/l D.O.

($ million)

	Total "all program" items	All programs			Minimum flow program			Minimum treatment program			Minimum cost program		
		Existing storage	Recirculation[a]	Collection	New storage	Treatment	Total[b]	New storage	Treatment	Total[b]	New storage	Treatment	Total[b]
1960 estimated	1,538	958	67	513	10	743	2,291	1,014	462	3,014	31	515	2,084
1960 actual		958	67	513		300	1,838		300	1,838		300	1,838
1980 M	2,578	958	874	746	27	1,225	3,830	4,203	810	7,591	67	926	3,571
2000 M	3,565	958	1,572	1,035	156	1,964	5,685	4,591	1,395	9,551	246	1,558	5,369
2020 M	5,638	958	3,295	1,385	390	3,172	9,200	5,054	2,449	13,141	605	2,777	9,020
H	9,240	958	6,450	1,832	1,561	5,621	16,422	7,111	5,210	21,561	1,578	5,491	16,309

Note: No costs shown for manufacturing recirculation.

[a]Revised rates (except 1960) based on estimated recirculation needed to avoid heat pollution.
[b]Includes existing storage, recirculation, and collection.

Table 81.   COSTS OF WATER RELATED TO GNP, MINIMUM COST PROGRAMS

		GNP ($ mil. 1960)	Total costs[a] ($ mil. 1964)	Total costs as a percentage of GNP	Total costs exclusive of collection ($ mil. 1964)	Total costs exclusive of collection costs as a percentage of GNP
1960		503,000	1,838	0.37	1,325	0.26
1980	M	1,091,000	3,571	0.33	2,825	0.26
2000	M	2,151,000	5,369	0.25	4,334	0.20
2020	M	4,150,000	9,020	0.22	7,635	0.18
	H	6,708,000	16,309	0.24	14,477	0.22

[a]Existing storage, recirculation (steam-electric power) required treatment (standard), new storage, and collection.

Table 82. TOTAL REQUIRED FLOWS (LOSSES PLUS DILUTION) FOR MINIMUM FLOW PROGRAMS, BY REGION, 0.0425 ANNUAL FACTOR, 4 mg/l D.O.

	98% Maximum regulated flow	1960	1980			2000			2020			Present regulated flow (98%)
			L	M	H	L	M	H	L	M	H	(bgd)
			(million gallons per day)									
NORTHEAST	361,535	21,370	33,497	39,588	50,509	44,854	63,940	106,191	69,379	105,217	222,484	
N Eng	60,895	1,793	2,910	3,177	3,562	3,638	4,522	5,946	5,090	6,474	9,935	22.4
D & H	28,629	3,928	5,747	6,486	7,760	7,401	9,785	14,369	10,795	14,627	25,907	7.5
Ches	46,657	2,849	5,086	6,025	7,685	7,141	10,410	17,842	11,391	17,767	39,329	3.4
Ohio	99,457	2,173	3,443	4,154	5,384	4,635	6,748	11,225	7,020	11,055	23,041	10.0
EGL	33,278	2,421	3,935	4,800	6,353	5,252	7,995	14,175	8,226	13,482	30,471	3.5
WGL	30,283	6,010	8,805	10,639	14,269	11,851	17,502	(31,516)	19,421	(30,641)	(71,965)	8.8
U Miss	46,125	1,852	2,729	3,350	4,330	3,691	5,321	8,516	5,465	8,275	16,133	15.8
L Mo	16,211	344	842	957	1,166	1,245	1,657	2,602	1,971	2,896	5,703	5.4
SOUTHEAST	333,934	16,924	29,894	36,509	46,613	45,688	67,972	113,988	76,482	122,010	261,649	
SE	186,030	11,841	20,848	25,451	32,203	32,222	48,176	80,329	55,340	87,941	(186,781)	95.0
Cumb	14,647	131	1,413[a]	1,810	2,554	2,568	4,280	8,506	4,977	9,088	(23,529)	11.1
Tenn	40,389	1,621	2,421	3,019	4,102	3,690	5,742	10,556	6,144	10,381	24,493	20.8
L Miss	35,207	1,567	2,424	3,130	4,098	3,591	5,311	8,388	5,409	8,536	16,732	1.5
L AWR	57,661	1,764	2,788	3,099	3,656	3,617	4,463	6,209	4,612	6,064	10,114	23.9
MID-CONTINENT	58,553	31,045	34,518	39,877	48,235	39,104	52,412	79,673	52,545	77,494	151,511	
U Mo	25,600	13,020	13,941	15,912	18,419	14,201	18,179	24,540	17,784	24,084	(38,553)	25.6
U AWR	7,053	5,664	6,285	6,730	(8,047)	6,567	(7,486)	(10,303)	(7,326)	(8,969)	(14,550)	6.7
W Gulf	25,900	12,361	14,292	17,235	21,769	18,336	(26,747)	(44,830)	(27,435)	(44,441)	(98,408)	15.4
SOUTHWEST	22,149	30,095	34,678	36,843	40,130	43,021	51,022	64,886	63,227	79,665	122,410	
RG-P	3,000	(4,991)	(5,053)	(5,507)	(6,017)	(5,486)	(6,529)	(8,065)	(7,092)	(8,921)	(12,901)	3.0
Colo	11,400	(14,460)	(16,217)	(16,950)	(18,099)	(21,472)	(25,204)	(31,507)	(33,766)	(42,643)	(65,373)	11.4
G Basin	6,934	5,759	5,679	6,251	7,035	5,525	7,011	9,763	7,198	10,046	18,038	5.4
S Pac	815	(4,885)	(7,729)	(8,135)	(8,979)	(10,538)	(12,278)	(15,551)	(15,171)	(18,055)	(26,098)	0.7
NORTH PACIFIC	180,048	39,379	48,855	51,902	56,142	56,845	67,195	86,414	75,100	95,272	151,214	
C Pac	45,478	23,312	25,991	26,834	28,675	27,669	30,309	36,967	32,368	37,267	(54,872)	26.2
PNW	134,570	16,067	22,864	25,068	27,467	29,176	36,886	49,447	42,732	58,005	96,342	62.8
U.S.	956,219	138,813	181,442	204,719	241,629	229,512	302,541	451,152	336,733	479,658	909,268	

Note: Figures in bold type and parentheses indicate required flows in excess of maximum regulated flow.

[a] Projected growth of the chemical industry accounts for the large increase over 1960.

Table 83. MINIMUM FLOW REQUIREMENTS EXCEEDING CONSTRAINED MAXIMUM NET FLOW, BY REGION

(billion gallons per day)

| | 98% Availability | | Minimum flow requirements | | | | | |
| | Maximum net flow when marginal cost ≤ 10¢/1,000 gals. (0.0425) | Maximum net flow unconstrained by marginal cost | 1980 | | 2000 | | 2020 | |
			M	H	M	H	M	H
NORTHEAST	344.7	361.5						
N Eng	59.4	60.9						
D & H	26.3	28.6						
Ches	42.3	46.7						
Ohio	95.8	99.5						
EGL	30.8	33.3					(30.6)	(30.5)
WGL	29.3	30.3				31.5	30.6	72.0
U Miss	45.4	46.1						
L Mo	15.4	16.2						
SOUTHEAST	329.1	333.9						
SE	184.7	186.0						186.8
Cumb	14.5	14.6						23.5
Tenn	38.0	40.4						
L Miss	35.0	35.2						
L AWR	56.9	57.7						
MID-CONTINENT	58.1	58.6						
U Mo	25.6	25.6				(24.5)	(24.1)	38.6
U AWR	7.0	7.1		8.0	7.5	10.3	9.0	14.6
W Gulf	25.5	25.9			26.7	44.8	44.4	98.4
SOUTHWEST	21.3	22.1						
RG-P	3.0	3.0	5.5	6.0	6.5	8.1	8.9	12.9
Colo	11.4	11.4	17.0	18.1	25.2	31.5	42.6	65.4
G Basin	6.9	6.9	(6.3)	7.0	7.0	9.8	10.0	18.0
S Pac	0.0	0.8	8.1	9.0	12.3	15.6	18.1	26.1
NORTH PACIFIC	172.4	180.1						
C Pac	43.3	45.5						54.9
PNW	129.1	134.6						
U.S.	925.6	956.2						

Note: Figures in parentheses indicate minimum flow requirements that come close to but do not yet exceed maximum net flow.

Table 84. DEFICIT REGIONS WITH A MAXIMUM MARGINAL COST OF 2 CENTS PER 1,000 GALLONS, 98% AVAILABILITY

Table 84. – Continued

| | Maximum net flow when marginal cost ≤ 2¢/1,000 gals. (bgd) | Annual cost ($ mil.) | Required flow: minimum flow program | | |
			2000 H (bgd)	2020 M (bgd)	2020 H (bgd)
NORTHEAST	309.5	646.4			
N Eng	55.9	61.0			
D & H	26.3	142.0			(25.9)
Ches	42.3[a]	93.8			
Ohio	79.3	156.8			
EGL	26.4	54.8			X
WGL	25.4	48.5		X	X
U Miss	40.2	63.3			
L Mo	13.7	26.2			
SOUTHEAST	302.9	393.0			
SE	166.9	183.9			X
Cumb	13.4	6.6			X
Tenn	34.2	47.0			
L Miss	34.6[a]	49.9			
L AWR	53.8[a]	105.6			
MID-CONTINENT	54.6	27.8			
U Mo	25.6	–		(24.1)	X
U AWR	6.9[a]	1.2	X	X	X
W Gulf	22.1	26.6	X	X	X
SOUTHWEST	20.9	4.1			
RG-P	3.0	–	X	X	X
Colo	11.4	–	X	X	X
G Basin	6.5	4.1	X	X	X
S Pac	0.0	0.0	X	X	X
NORTH PACIFIC	166.2	237.1			
C Pac	37.1	38.1		(37.3)	X
PNW	129.1	199.0			
U.S.	854.1	1,308.4			

Note: Near-deficits are shown in parentheses.

[a] $0.021/1,000 gallons.

Table 85. PROJECTED WATER-SHORT REGIONS: MINIMUM FLOW PROGRAM, MAXIMUM MARGINAL COST OF 2 CENTS PER 1,000 GALLONS, 98% AVAILABILITY, 4 mg/l D.O.

(million gallons per day)

	1960	1980 L	1980 M	1980 H	2000 L	2000 M	2000 H	2020 L	2020 M	2020 H	Maximum flow
NORTHEAST											310
N Eng											56
D & H										X	26
Ches											42
Ohio											79
EGL										X	26
WGL							X		X	X	25
U Miss											40
L Mo											14
SOUTHEAST											303
SE										X	167
Cumb										X	13
Tenn											34
L Miss											35
L AWR											54
MID-CONTINENT											55
U Mo										X	26
U AWR				X	X	X	X	X	X	X	7
W Gulf				X		X	X	X	X	X	22
SOUTHWEST											21
RG-P	X	X	X	X	X	X	X	X	X	X	3
Colo	X	X	X	X	X	X	X	X	X	X	11
G Basin				X	X	X	X	X	X	X	7
S Pac	X	X	X	X	X	X	X	X	X	X	0
NORTH PACIFIC											166
C Pac						X			X	X	37
PNW											129
U.S.											854

Table 86. EAST AND WEST STORAGE, TREATMENT, AND COLLECTION COSTS FOR MINIMUM FLOW PROGRAMS, 98% AVAILABILITY, 0.0425 ANNUAL FACTOR, 4 mg/l D.O.

($ million)

		East						West					
		Storage		Treatment				Storage		Treatment			
		Existing	New	BOD	Thermal	Collection	Total	Existing	New	BOD	Thermal	Collection	Total
1960		362	0.1	572	19	382	1,335	596	10	171	49	131	957
1980	M	362	8	891	686	532	2,479	596	19	334	188	214	1,351
2000	M	362	46	1,372	1,210	725	3,715	596	110	592	362	310	1,969
2020	M	362	255	2,135	2,382	965	6,100	596	135	1,037	912	419	3,100
	H	362	1,161	3,842	4,716	1,277	11,358	596	400	1,780	1,733	555	5,064

Note: East = Northeast and Southeast; West = Mid-continent, Southwest, and North Pacific.

Table 87. EAST AND WEST STORAGE, TREATMENT, AND COLLECTION COSTS FOR MINIMUM TREATMENT PROGRAMS, 98% AVAILABILITY, 0.0425 ANNUAL FACTOR, 4 mg/l D.O.

($ million)

| | | East | | | | | | West | | | | | |
| | | Storage | | Treatment | | | | Storage | | Treatment | | | |
		Existing	New	BOD	Thermal	Collection	Total	Existing	New	BOD	Thermal	Collection	Total
1960		362	665	327	19	382	1,755	596	348	135	49	131	1,259
1980	M	362	2,831	535	686	532	4,947	596	1,372	275	188	214	2,645
2000	M	362	3,219	876	1,210	725	6,392	596	1,372	519	362	310	3,159
2020	M	362	3,681	1,500	2,382	965	8,891	596	1,372	949	912	419	4,249
	H	362	5,738	3,483	4,716	1,277	15,576	596	1,372	1,727	1,733	555	5,984

Note: East = Northeast and Southeast; West = Mid-continent, Southwest, and North Pacific.

Table 88. EAST AND WEST STORAGE, TREATMENT, AND COLLECTION COSTS FOR MINIMUM COST PROGRAM, 98% AVAILABILITY, 0.0425 ANNUAL FACTOR, 4 mg/l D.O.

($ million)

| | | East | | | | | | West | | | | | |
| | | Storage | | Treatment | | | | Storage | | Treatment | | | |
		Existing	New	BOD	Thermal	Collection	Total	Existing	New	BOD	Thermal	Collection	Total
1960		362[a]	21	365[b]	19	382	1,148	596[a]	10	150[b]	49	131	936
1980	M	362	48	625	686	532	2,254	596	19	300	188	214	1,317
2000	M	362	136	1,007	1,210	725	3,440	596	110	552	362	310	1,929
2020	M	362	415	1,804	2,382	965	5,928	596	191	974	912	419	3,092
	H	362	1,178	3,712	4,716	1,277	11,245	596	400	1,779	1,733	555	5,064

Note: East = Northeast and Southeast; West = Mid-continent, Southwest, and North Pacific. Minor discrepancies due to rounding.

[a]Total storage, not only regulatory.
[b]Required, not estimated actual.

Table 89. EAST AND WEST COSTS VARIABLE BY PROGRAM, 98% AVAILABILITY, 0.0425 ANNUAL FACTOR, 4 mg/l D.O.

($ million)

| | | | | BOD treatment and new storage | | | | | |
| | | Outlays common to all programs | | Minimum flow program | | Minimum treatment program | | Minimum cost program | |
		East	West	East	West	East	West	East	West
1960		763	776	572	181	992	483	386	160
1980	M	1,580	998	899	353	3,366	1,647	673	319
2000	M	2,297	1,268	1,418	702	4,095	1,891	1,143	662
2020	M	3,709	1,927	2,390	1,172	5,181	2,321	2,219	1,165
	H	6,355	2,884	5,003	2,180	9,221	3,099	4,890	2,179

Note: East = Northeast and Southeast; West = Mid-continent, Southwest, and Pacific Northwest.

Chapter 11

SHORT-TERM TERTIARY TREATMENT AND REDUCED STORAGE

Without changing the D.O. standard, the postulated economic projections, or the output of pollution per unit of product, the amount of required storage can be reduced by accepting a greater risk of deficiency of flow. A higher frequency of shortage can be met with stoicism, makeshift rationing, acceptance of quality deterioration, or by countermeasures. One countermeasure is the impoundment of liquid wastes for release during periods of greater flow. Another is short-term chemical treatment of wastes to reduce required dilution water. According to Reid et al.,[1] short-term chemical treatment will reduce residual BOD by about 50 percent and can be used to augment the level of treatment achieved by standard (continuous) methods. Thus, if regular treatment is carried to 97½ percent, short-term treatment will raise the level to 98¾ percent. Required BOD dilution flow would be halved, but dilution for plant nutrients would remain at the level given for 97½ percent treatment. If short-term tertiary were added to 90 percent treatment, residual BOD would fall to 5 percent, but plant nutrients would remain at the level given by 90 percent treatment.[2]

The steps in our analysis of the effect of short-term chemical treatment on water resource policy are as follows:

1. For a specified flow (to meet requirements as projected for losses and waste dilution for 4 mg/l of D.O.), construct storage to provide flow 90 percent of the time.

---

[1] See app. D.

[2] Short-term tertiary treatment could also be substituted for a higher level of permanent treatment. (See fig. 3. Standard treatment could be set at a level consistent with flow OD. During periods of shortage, short-term treatment would lower the BOD dilution requirement to OC.)

Ascertain the difference in capacity and in dollar savings between storage to provide flow 90 percent of the time and storage to provide the same flow 98 percent of the time.

2. Compare savings in storage costs with additional short-term treatment costs. Short-term treatment costs were assumed to be incurred on the average of one month per year, in accordance with the increased frequency of shortage from 2 percent of the time to 10 percent of the time.

3. Storage yielding a specified flow 90 percent of the time will yield a smaller flow 98 percent of the time (OE in figure 3). Ascertain this flow and compare it with required flow after reduction in BOD by short-term tertiary treatment. (The flow equalled or exceeded 98 percent of the time presumably is dependent on the way storage is administered. We made no computations to ascertain the degree of incompatibility, if any, between administering storage to yield a given flow 90 percent of the time and the likelihood that the same administration would yield a smaller given amount 98 percent of the time. Furthermore, the amount and duration of shortage within any given year cannot be ascertained without further analysis of flow data. To simplify matters, we have assumed that the measurement "90 percent of the time" means eleven months out of twelve, since we assumed that "98 percent of the time" meant all the time.)

Savings Yielded by Short-Term Chemical Treatment

An occasional anomaly appears in detailed flow-storage and cost tables. In some regions the maximum net flow physically attainable with a 10 percent chance of deficiency is higher than that attainable with a 2 percent chance of deficiency and, moreover, is associated with a larger volume of storage capacity. Thus, in water-short regions where

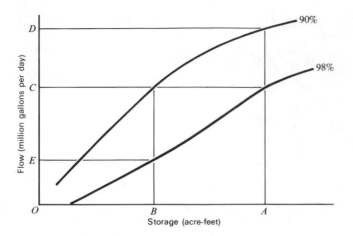

Figure 3. Comparison of flow and storage requirements with short-term tertiary treatment.

OA = required storage, basic model, for required flow *OC*.

OB = storage to yield flow *OC* 90% of the time instead of 98% of the time.

OE = flow available 98% of the time from storage *OB*.

OD = flow available 90% of the time from storage *OA*. If we had so chosen, we could have reduced permanent treatment to a level consistent with this flow and superimposed short-term tertiary on that level for one month of the year during which flow would be *OC*. Note: The period "one month" is an approximation over a long period of time of the average additional deficiency per year if storage is built to meet a 10% chance of deficiency instead of a 2% chance of deficiency. As noted in the text, it is not necessarily true that when a deficiency occurs with storage *OB*, the flow will fall to *OE* for a period not exceeding 2% of the time. First of all, the storage may not be administered toward such an objective; second, the depth and duration within a given year of shortage is not known. The "chance of deficiency" applies to the number of years over a long period of time that a deficiency is expected, but says nothing of the number of days or weeks within the year that the deficiency will persist, nor of the amount of deficiency below the level for which flow is expected 98% of the time.

short-term tertiary treatment could not substitute for reservoir capacity, since maximum flow was required in any event, the only effect of short-term treatment would be the reduction (or elimination) of the shortage. Total costs in those regions would rise by the aggregate of short-term tertiary costs *and* additional storage physically feasible along the 90 percent flow-storage curve. This anomaly is apparent, for example, in the Western Great Lakes region.

When flow yielded 98 percent of the time from storage designed to meet basic required flow[3] with 90 percent certainty was less than required flow after short-term treatment, storage was adjusted upward if the physical capacity was present.

Using the 2000 Medium projection for the minimum cost program as the basis for estimates, short-term chemical treatment for one month would cost $22.3 million. (See table 90.) The saving in storage, after adjusting for deficiencies that would otherwise appear in the Ohio, Cumberland, Upper Arkansas-White-Red, Great Basin, and Central

[3] That is, requirements given by the minimum cost program with permanent waste treatment.

Pacific regions, would amount to about 76 million acre-feet,[4] representing a saving in annual costs of storage of $118 million. Net dollar savings would be the difference, or about $96 million annually.

The geographic distribution of net savings is unevenly divided. In the Upper Missouri, Rio Grande-Pecos, and Colorado regions no offset in storage costs is possible, since storage for maximum net regulation is already in place. For these regions "net savings" is a negative amount equal to the cost of short-term chemical treatment. In the Lower Missouri, Southeast, Cumberland, Tennessee, Lower and Upper Arkansas-White-Red, and Pacific Northwest regions, storage in place exceeds required storage on the 98 percent curve or offers no saving when accepted uncertainty is changed from 2 percent to 10 percent. Here, also, no storage savings are enjoyed. In New England a saving in storage costs is overbalanced by the short-term treatment costs because of the relatively low marginal cost of flow.

There are ten regions in which savings in storage costs exceed additional treatment costs. Savings in the regions that enjoy savings amount to $106.8 million. Whether short-term chemical treatment would be used in regions where it contributes to a net increase in cost would depend on the desirability of reducing required storage capacity.

Approximately half of the savings occurs in one region — Western Gulf; about one-third of the savings occurs in the Northeast outside of New England.

Table 91, which shows dollar savings for all projections, indicates that the higher the level of projected activity is, the greater the expected saving from short-term chemical treatment will be.[5] Savings for 2020 Medium are about double the savings for 2000 Medium, and double again for 2020 High. About 75 percent of total savings for 2020 High occurs in one region — Southeast. In constructing table 91 it was assumed that short-term chemical treatment was not employed in regions in which water shortage persists at 90 percent, since no savings in storage costs would be enjoyed.

According to Reid et al., short-term chemical treatment does not reduce the need for the dilution of plant nutrients. When, therefore, dilution flows for phosphorus at standard treatment exceed dilution flows for BOD after short-term chemical treatment, the former rather than latter would rule. This circumstance is critical when flow available 98 percent of the time from storage designed to yield 90 percent security is less than required flow after short-term treatment. If we were to assume that the technology of waste treatment improved so that short-term chemical treatment reduced plant nutrients in the same proportion it reduced BOD, the upward adjustment in required storage would be smaller in the Ohio and Cumberland regions but unchanged in the Upper Arkansas-White-Red, Great Basin,

[4] Shortages beyond maximum net regulated flow persisted in the Rio Grande–Pecos, Colorado, and South Pacific regions.

[5] At 2020 High there is only one region — Lower Mississippi — in which an increase in storage is both feasible and needed to meet requirements 98 percent of the time after chemical treatment.

[6] Q_p is the symbol for flow required to dilute the concentration of phosphorus in a stream. The phosphorus constraint associated with 4 mg/l of D.O. is a level equal to, or less than, 0.1 mg/l of water.

or Central Pacific regions. (See table 90, columns "Q_p unresponsive" and "Q_p responsive.")[6]

The benefits yielded by chemical treatment can be measured by savings in required storage capacity, savings in required flow in regions of water shortage (provided the chemical treatment is utilized twelve months of the year), as well as by savings in dollar costs. Those who put a higher value on an undisturbed river than on a chain of reservoirs presumably are willing to pay something for the realization of their preference. We do not have enough information at present to know whether there is a net social preference for the one or the other. It can be noted (table 90), however, that savings in storage capacity for 2000 Medium amount to 94 million acre-feet, unadjusted, and 76 million acre-feet, adjusted. (In the absence of short-term treatment, new storage would be 180 million acre-feet.) By 2020 High the saving in storage would be 247 million acre-feet, most of it in the Southeast.

Continuous Chemical Treatment

A saving in required flow per se is of no advantage under our model unless the region is water short, or unless the specified level of water quality – e.g., 4 mg/l of D.O. – is too low for the realization of the projected bill of goods. Unless chemical treatment were continuous (instead of short term), it would not save flow. Continuous chemical treatment would be one way of raising the level of treatment from 97½ percent to 98¾ percent BOD removal. An increase in the level of treatment in water-short regions eases the required adjustment to water shortage. Relief could take the form of a reduced need for water importation, or for displacement of activity to water-surplus regions, or for changes in the bill of goods away from water-related to nonwater-related goods and services. For the 2000 Medium projection of economic activity, continuous chemical treatment would cost more on a twelve-month basis than a uniform increase in the level of standard treatment from 90 percent to 95 percent but would cost less than a uniform increase from 95 percent to 97½ percent. We made no estimates of the cost on a "permanent," or capital intensive, basis, i.e., of raising treatment levels from 97½ percent to 98¾ percent (halving residual BOD), but presumably these costs would be equal to, or more than, the costs incurred in going from 95 percent to 97½ percent. Direct comparability is uncertain because plant nutrients are unaffected by short-term chemical treatment; but at 97½ percent standard treatment, required flows to dilute plant nutrients are much lower than flows required for BOD; hence they are not likely to be ruling until BOD removal is above 98¾ percent.

The level of standard treatment for the minimum cost program for 2000 Medium falls just short of 95 percent removal of BOD as measured by cost. (If all regions treated their wastes at 95 percent, aggregate treatment costs would be $1,600 million annually; the aggregate for the minimum cost program, 98 percent, 0.0425, 4 mg/l, would be $1,558 million. For the country as a whole, continuous chemical treatment, as an alternative to a one-step rise in the level of standard treatment, would cost about $268 million annually for 2000 Medium. The cost of a uniform rise for all regions from a standard level of 95 percent to a standard level of 97½ percent would be $364 million annually.[7]

Continuous chemical treatment would reduce required total flow (losses plus dilution) by an amount equal to half the required dilution flow if BOD were ruling, but there would be no reduction if plant nutrients were ruling. Assuming that short-term chemical treatment would have no effect on plant nutrients, required flow for 2000 Medium would fall from 525 bgd to 395 bgd. If technology improved to the extent of inducing a proportionately equal reduction in plant nutrient dilution, required flow would fall to 337 bgd. The savings in storage costs would not be enough to warrant expenditure on full-time chemical treatment. Storage costs would fall by $165 million if plant nutrients were responsive and by $129 million if they were not. The annual cost of chemical treatment would be $268 million (table 92).

The reduction in storage costs was computed on the basis of 98 percent reliability of flow. In this situation, chemical treatment is an alternative to an increase in the level of standard treatment. In seven regions, standard treatment under the minimum cost program is 90 percent or less and presumably could be raised at lower cost by increasing the number of plants operating at 95 percent than by increasing those at 35 percent. In eleven regions, however, treatment levels are 95 percent or 97½ percent and could be raised at less cost by the continuous use of chemicals, except in regions where plant nutrients are ruling.

For 2000 Medium, table 92 shows estimated savings in the costs of storage and estimated costs of continuous chemical treatment. The columns headed "Q_p unresponsive" are based on the assumption that chemical treatment does not reduce the required flow for plant nutrients; the columns headed "Q_p responsive" are based on the assumption that a technology will be developed whereby plant nutrients respond in the same way as residual BOD.

Although the increase in treatment costs in eleven regions would be less for the use of chemicals than for the use of capital intensive methods, only in four regions would positive savings accrue – Western Great Lakes, Western Gulf, Great Basin, and Central Pacific. In these regions, aggregate savings in storage costs would exceed the cost of continuous chemical treatment by $52 million annually. It also happens that BOD, rather than phosphorus, determines waste dilution flow; hence a new technology of waste treatment is unnecessary in order to realize such savings.

The cost of continuous chemical treatment in six water-short regions (Upper Arkansas-White-Red, Western Gulf, and the four regions of the Southwest) for 2000 Medium would be $42 million per year. Required flow would fall from 85 bgd to 69 bgd, reducing the projected deficit in flow from 31 bgd to 14 bgd. Furthermore, the reduction in

---

[7]An ambiguity in this statement should be noted, since "90 percent" refers to a weighted average of plants that are treating at 35 percent, 95 percent, and 97½ percent, respectively. We can presumably conclude that if the average level is raised by increasing the number of plants that treat at 95 percent rather than at 35 percent, the standard – i.e., capital intensive – method is cheaper than chemical treatment, but not if the average is raised by raising the number of firms that go from 95 percent to 97½ percent.

required flow would mean that neither Western Gulf or Great Basin would be a deficit region, nor would Upper Arkansas-White-Red if phosphorus could be reduced by chemical treatment.

If added reservoir capacity is viewed as a negative utility of sufficient negative value, we might willingly accept the added costs of continuous chemical treatment. It should be noted, however, that if minimization of required flow is a desired social objective, it would be proper to base a continuous chemical treatment program on a basic minimum flow program rather than on a basic minimum cost program. For the country as a whole, the results would be as follows (Q_p responsive, 2000 Medium, 4 mg/1, 0.0425):

	Basic programs		Basic plus continuous chemical treatment	
	Minimum flow	Minimum cost	Minimum flow	Minimum cost
Flow *(bgd)*	303	525	226	337
Losses *(bgd)*	148	148	148	148
Dilution *(bgd)*	155	376	78	188
Storage *(mil. af)*	99	180	36	63
Storage costs *($ mil.)*	156	246	50	81
Basic treatment costs *($ mil.)*	1,964	1,558	1,964	1,558
Chemical treatment costs *($ mil.)*	–	–	268	268
Total costs *($ mil.)*	2,120	1,804	2,282	1,907
Increase in costs *($ mil.)*			162	103

For the basic minimum flow program, at a cost of $2.3 billion per year for treatment and new storage, required new storage could be reduced from 99 million acre-feet to 36 million acre-feet. For the basic minimum cost program, at a cost of $1.9 billion, new storage could be reduced from 180 million acre-feet to 63 million acre-feet.

One might speculate on the effects of improving waste treatment to the point at which dilution flows would be unnecessary. For 2000 Medium, such an improvement would reduce new storage required to offset losses to 5 million acre-feet for both the basic minimum cost program and the minimum flow program. For 2020 High, storage to meet losses would be 84 million acre-feet; required new storage would be 839 million acre-feet for the minimum cost program, or 813 million acre-feet for the minimum flow program. The total cost of new storage would be about $149 million annually, compared with storage costs of $1,578 million to meet the minimum cost program.

Continuous chemical treatment under present technology would afford net savings of about $207 million annually for 2020 High, largely as a result of net savings amounting to $580 million in two regions – Southeast and Central Pacific. (Elsewhere savings are small or negative.) The closer that required flows of basic programs approach maximum regulation, the greater is the likelihood that savings in the cost of storage will exceed the additional cost of continuous chemical treatment.

Should waste treatment techniques advance enough to eliminate the need for dilution flows, the number of water-short regions for 2020 High would fall from ten to four. The regions for which losses alone would exceed maximum

regulated flow would be Upper Arkansas-White-Red, Rio Grande-Pecos, Colorado, and South Pacific.[8]

What is the effect of superimposing two layers of chemical treatment on the basic minimum cost program?

By using two layers of chemical treatment – one layer continuously and one layer on a short-term basis – storage may be planned for 90 percent reliability for required flows which have been reduced by the effect of a halving of residual BOD. Treatment costs would rise above those of the basic program by an amount equal to thirteen times the cost for one month's chemical treatment. Based on the 2000 Medium projection, this would be $290 million annually. (See table 93, the case for which phosphorus is assumed to respond.) If phosphorus were assumed responsive, storage amounting to 25 million acre-feet would meet required flow of 337 bgd with a 10 percent chance of deficiency. Required flow during the "one month" of deficiency after the second layer of chemical treatment – the short-term layer – would be 243 bgd. Except for the regions that would be in short supply anyway – Western Gulf, Rio Grande-Pecos, Colorado, Great Basin, and South Pacific – shortages during the period of deficient flow, measured as the excess of required flow after short-term treatment over flow available 98 percent of the time from storage designed to afford 90 percent security, would appear only in the Lower Mississippi region. The Upper Arkansas-White-Red region, which is water short under the basic minimum flow program, is just able to meet requirements with two-layer chemical treatment and storage on the 90 percent curve.

The net cost of two-layer treatment, reduced as it is by building storage to a 10 percent chance of deficiency, is less than the net cost of continuous one-layer treatment with storage built to a 2 percent chance of deficiency. Net costs for 2000 Medium could be reduced further if treatment levels were raised by standard, capital intensive methods rather than by the use of chemicals in those regions for which average treatment levels were 90 percent or less – New England, Ohio, Upper Mississippi, Lower Missouri, Tennessee, Lower Mississippi, and Lower Arkansas-White-Red.

If short-term treatment to which phosphorus will respond cannot be developed, the net cost of two-layer chemical treatment would be $103 million annually rather than $84 million if phosphorus were responsive. The entire difference in costs originates in the Northeast – mostly the Ohio region, which suffers a $16 million swing.

Table 94 summarizes the effects on storage and costs of the various alternatives we have just described. In comparison with the basic minimum cost program, if a double layer of chemical treatment were used – one layer continuously and one layer intermittently – total new storage would fall from the 180 million acre-feet required by the minimum

---

[8] Because we have ignored pollution by dissolved solids – mainly salts – this may be an understatement of the occurrence of shortage. Regions such as Upper Missouri, Western Gulf, and Great Basin, for which losses came to within 80 percent or more of maximum regulated flow, may in fact suffer shortage because of the necessity of diluting dissolved solids.

cost program to 25 million acre-feet. But this change would be associated with a net additional annual cost of $84 million, provided that phosphorus could be made responsive to chemical treatment at no increase in cost.

Single-layer short-term chemical treatment in conjunction with accepting a 10 percent chance of deficient flow would apparently be economical in dollars and allow a saving in new storage of about 42 percent even if phosphorus were not responsive to chemical treatment. Net savings in the cost of water, for 2000 Medium, appear to be in the neighborhood of $100 million annually. Money savings could be further increased by using short-term chemical treatment only in those regions that experience positive savings.

The importance of this chapter lies mainly in the idea that various alternatives and combinations ought to be systematically explored and tested. The use of short-term chemical treatment was emphasized because it lent itself readily to analysis within the framework of our model. Other alternatives might yield comparably suggestive results: changes in the technology of production designed to reduce waste output per unit of product, storage of wastes for discharge during periods of high flow, direct oxygenation of receiving waters, rearrangement of waste collection and effluent distribution systems, and the like. In his study of the Potomac estuary, Robert Davis examined a number of techniques that could be used to meet water quality objectives and pointed out that the optimum solution might be a combination of several systems.[9] If minimum social cost is the criterion of optimization, the optimum combination cannot be chosen without knowledge of the cost functions of all the alternatives and knowledge of interdependencies. Even if some other guide is used, knowledge of the cost functions is essential.

A further observation ought to be inserted at this point. Once we embark on attempts at "fine tuning" (a phrase borrowed in this context from Davis), the efficiency with which a system of reservoirs is used to achieve control over flow is critical, and the simplifying assumption of treating a region as a point in space must be abandoned. When this is done, it is likely that storage capacity for flow regulation will be greater than the quantities we have used, that marginal changes will also be greater, and that we have understated the amount of storage and costs of storage for any specified flow. We also may have overstated the relative importance of flow regulation for cost-minimizing programs.

[9]*The Range of Choice in Water Management: A Study of Dissolved Oxygen in the Potomac Estuary* (The Johns Hopkins Press for Resources for the Future, 1968).

Table 90. SHORT-TERM TREATMENT, MINIMUM COST BASE, 0.0425 ANNUAL FACTOR, 4 mg/l D.O.: 2000 MEDIUM

	Required flow (bgd)			Storage: standard required flow (mil. af)			Need for adjustment if Q_p responsive	Flow available 98% of the time from 90% storage (bgd)	Costs of storage: standard flow ($ mil.)			Cost, one-month chemical treatment ($ mil.)	Net savings, short-term treatment ($ mil.)
	Standard	Q_p unresponsive	Q_p responsive	98% Availability	90% Availability	90% Adjusted			98% Availability	90% Adjusted	Savings storage		
NORTHEAST	163.9	124.2		94.5	54.4	54.4		130.2	129.4	87.6	41.8	9.5	32.3
N Eng	24.1	13.4		1.9	1.5	1.5		23.7	1.5	1.2	0.3	0.7	-0.4
D & H	9.8	8.5		4.5	2.7	2.7		8.9	20.4	12.0	8.4	1.1	7.3
Ches	17.6	10.4		10.4	7.7	7.7		13.8	9.7	7.2	2.5	1.0	1.5
Ohio	45.8	42.6	24.9	34.7	22.1	31.5	no	32.8	51.6	46.5	5.1	2.7	2.4
EGL	12.7	8.0		7.2	5.7	5.7		10.7	11.7	9.2	2.5	0.9	1.6
WGL	17.5	10.5		13.5	6.1	6.1		12.7	16.1	7.2	8.9	0.9	8.0
U Miss	30.9	25.3		22.2	8.6	8.6		22.2	18.4	4.3	14.1	1.8	12.3
L Mo	5.5	5.5		0.1	0	0		5.4	0	0		0.4	-0.4
SOUTHEAST	191.0	111.8		17.7	9.6	9.6		164.2	9.9	6.5	3.4	6.2	-2.8
SE	88.8	56.0		0	0	0		95.0	0	0	0	3.8	-3.8
Cumb	11.7	11.7	6.0	1.7	0	1.7	no	11.2	1.6	1.6	0	0.4	-0.4
Tenn	20.8	20.8		0	0	0		24.0	0	0	0	0.6	-0.6
L Miss	15.7	9.8		16.0	9.6	9.6		10.1	8.3	4.9	3.4	0.7	2.7
L AWR	54.0	13.5		0	0	0		23.9	0	0	0	0.7	-0.7
MID-CONTINENT	59.8	52.4		48.1	19.3	19.3		53.0	72.8	20.8	52.0	3.2	48.8
U Mo	25.6	25.6		0	0	0		25.6	0	0	0	1.0	-1.0
U AWR	7.5	7.3	7.0	1.7	0	1.7	yes	6.7	3.3	3.3	0	0.5	-0.5
W Gulf	26.7	19.5		46.4	19.3	19.3		20.7	69.5	17.5	52.0	1.7	50.3
SOUTHWEST	51.0	41.7		8.1	2.5	2.5		20.7	21.9	10.8	11.1	1.3	9.8
RG-P	6.5	5.6		0	0	0		3.0	0	0	0	0.4	-0.4
Colo	25.2	18.6		0	0	0		11.5	0	0	0	0.6	-0.6
G Basin	7.0	5.9	5.9	5.9	0.1	1.5	yes	5.4	13.1	1.4	11.7	0.1	11.6
S Pac	12.3	11.6		2.2	2.4	2.4		0.8	8.8	9.4	-0.6	0.2	-0.8
NORTH PACIFIC	88.8	64.4		11.4	0	0		88.7	15.1	5.4	9.7	2.1	7.6
C Pac	30.3	27.5	27.5	11.4	0	4.2	yes	25.9	15.1	5.4	9.7	0.6	9.1
PNW	58.5	36.9		0	0	0		62.8	0	0	0	1.5	-1.5
U.S.	554.5	394.5	336.5	179.8	85.8	104.2	93.1	456.8	249.1	131.1	118.0	22.3	95.7

Table 91. DOLLAR SAVINGS WITH SHORT-TERM TERTIARY TREATMENT, 90% AVAILABILITY, 0.0425 ANNUAL FACTOR, 4 mg/l D.O.

($ million; WS = water shortage)

	1960	1980			2000			2020		
		L	M	H	L	M	H	L	M	H
N Eng	-0.4	-0.4	-0.5	-0.5	-0.5	-0.4	-0.4	-0.1	-0.6	-1.1
D & H.	0.9	-0.6	-0.8	1.7	0.9	7.3	19.9	10.4	21.0	51.2
Ches	0.5	1.5	0.6	1.0	0.8	1.5	5.5	1.7	4.8	18.4
Ohio	2.8	6.0	7.7	2.1	8.9	16.0/2.4	-2.9	16.6	33.2	-0.4
EGL	-0.2	0.2	0.5	1.2	0.7	1.6	1.7	1.6	1.5	29.2
WGL	3.5	-0.5	2.8	7.0	5.0	8.0	125.0	8.6	130.7	WS
U Miss	-0.1	1.3	0.9	4.9	1.7	12.3	10.4	6.4	8.0	-4.4
L Mo	-0.2	-0.2	0.6	0	-0.7	-0.4	1.6	0.1	1.3	-1.1
SE	-1.1	-2.0	-2.3	0.1	6.3	-3.8	-5.4	-3.8	-6.4	410.1
Cumb	0	-0.1	-0.2	-0.2	-0.3	1.2/-0.4	-0.7	3.9	-0.7	23.4
Tenn	-0.2	-0.2	-0.4	-0.4	0	-0.6	10.0	-0.7	6.5	-0.4
L Miss	0.5	1.5	1.9	2.1	2.2	2.7	3.3	1.0	4.8	7.5
L AWR	-0.3	-0.4	-0.4	-0.5	-0.5	-0.7	-0.9	2.1	-1.0	-0.4
U Mo	-	-	-	-	-	-1.0	-	-	-	-
U AWR	-0.3	-0.2	-0.1	2.9	-0.5	3.1/-0.5	WS	2.7	2.5	WS
W Gulf	-0.6	-0.8	3.8	23.5	-	-	-	-	-	-
RG-P	-	-	-	-	-	0/-0.4	-	-	-	-
Colo	-	-	-	-	-	0/-0.6	-	-	-	-
G Basin	1.0	0.8	2.7	12.9	0.3	12.9/11.6	WS	12.1	WS	WS
S Pac	WS	WS	WS	WS	WS	-0.8	WS	WS	WS	WS
C Pac	-0.2	0.1	2.8	9.1	5.6	14.5/9.1	16.3	16.6	17.4	WS
PNW	-0.2	-0.7	-0.8	2.1	-1.0	-1.5	8.2	3.6	14.6	13.1
U.S.	4.7	4.4	18.1	68.2	35.1	122.2/95.7	180.6	129.7	243.4	545.1

Source: Appendixes D and E.

Note: Dual figures for 2000 Medium show unadjusted savings and savings after increase in storage to meet required flows 98% of the time after short-term chemical treatment. For 2020 High, where required flow was less than maximum net regulated flow, 90% storage was adequate for flow required 98% of the time after short-term treatment, except in Lower Mississippi. No savings are shown when water shortage persists at 90% availability unless maximum storage is significantly less for 90% availability than for 98%.

Table 92. CONTINUOUS CHEMICAL TREATMENT (Q_p UNRESPONSIVE AND RESPONSIVE), MINIMUM COST BASE, 98% AVAILABILITY, 0.0425 ANNUAL FACTOR, 4 mg/l D.O.: 2000 MEDIUM

	Required flow (bgd)			Storage, 98% (mil. af)			Cost of Storage ($ mil.)			Savings, storage ($ mil.)		Costs, 12 months continuous chemical treatment ($ mil.)	Net Savings ($ mil.)	
	Standard	Q_p unresponsive	Q_p responsive	Standard	Q_p unresponsive	Q_p responsive	Standard	Q_p unresponsive	Q_p responsive	Q_p unresponsive	Q_p responsive		Q_p unresponsive	Q_p responsive
NORTHEAST	163.9	124.2	95.7	94.5	58.6	29.8	126.2	79.4	47.2	46.8	79.0	114.0	-67.2	-35.0
N Eng	24.1	13.4	13.4	1.9	0	0	1.5	1.5		1.5	1.5	8.4	-6.9	
D & H	9.8	8.5	8.5	4.5	2.4	2.4	17.2	11.1	11.1	6.1	6.1	13.2	-7.1	
Ches	17.6	10.4	10.4	10.4	5.2	5.2	9.7	4.9	4.9	4.8	4.8	12.0	-7.2	
Ohio	45.8	42.6	24.9	34.7	31.5	14.5	51.6	46.5	21.5	5.1	30.1	32.4	-27.3	
EGL	12.7	8.0	8.0	7.2	3.5	3.5	11.7	5.7	5.7	6.0	6.0	10.8	-4.8	
WGL	17.5	10.5	10.5	13.5	2.5	2.5	16.1	3.1	3.1	13.0	13.0	10.8	2.2	
U Miss	30.9	25.3	16.9	22.2	13.3	1.7	18.4	8.1	0.9	10.3	17.5	21.6	-11.3	
L Mo	5.5	5.5	3.1	0.1	0.1	0	0	0	0	0	0	4.8	-4.8	
SOUTHEAST	161.0	111.8	88.4	17.7	10.8	9.2	9.8	6.3	4.7	3.5	5.1	74.4	-70.9	-69.3
SE	88.8	56.0	48.2	0	0	0	0	0	0	0	0	45.6	-45.6	
Cumb	11.7	11.7	6.0	1.7	1.6	0	1.6	1.6	0	0	1.6	4.8	-4.8	
Tenn	20.8	20.8	10.9	0	0	0	0	0	0	0	0	7.2	-7.2	
L Miss	15.7	9.8	9.8	16.0	9.2	9.2	8.2	4.7	4.7	3.5	3.5	8.4	-4.9	
L AWR	24.0	13.5	13.5	0	0	0	0	0	0	0	0	8.4	-8.4	
MID-CONTINENT	59.8	52.4	46.2	48.1	15.8	15.4	72.8	15.2	13.5	57.6	59.3	38.4	19.2	20.9
U Mo	25.6	25.6	19.8	0	0	0	0	0	0	0	0	12.0	-12.0	
U AWR	7.5[a]	7.3[a]	7.0	1.7	1.7	1.3	3.3	3.3	1.6	0	1.7	6.0	-6.0	
W Gulf	26.7[a]	19.5	19.5	46.4	14.1	14.1	69.5	11.9	11.9	57.6	57.6	20.4	37.2	
SOUTHWEST	51.0	41.7	41.7	8.1	3.8	3.8	21.9	10.2	10.2	11.7	11.7	15.6	-3.9	-3.9
RG-P	6.5[a]	5.6[a]	5.6[a]	0	0	0	0	0	0	0	0	4.8	-4.8	
Colo	25.2[a]	18.6[a]	18.6[a]	0	0	0	0	0	0	0	0	7.2	-7.2	
G Basin	7.0[a]	5.9	5.9	5.9	1.6	1.6	13.1	1.4	1.4	11.7	11.7	1.2	10.5	
S Pac	12.3[a]	11.6[a]	11.6[a]	2.2	2.2	2.2	8.8	8.8	8.8	0	0	2.4	-2.4	
NORTH PACIFIC	88.8	64.4	64.4	11.4	4.2	4.2	15.1	5.4	5.4	9.7	9.7	25.2	-15.5	-15.5
C Pac	30.3	27.5	27.5	11.4	4.2	4.2	15.1	5.4	5.4	9.7	9.7	7.2	2.5	
PNW	58.5	36.9	36.9	0	0	0	0	0	0	0	0	18.0	-18.0	
U.S.	524.6	394.5	336.5	179.8	93.2	62.5	245.9	116.5	81.0	129.3	164.8	267.6	138.3	-102.8

Source: Appendixes D and E.

[a] Exceeds maximum net regulated flow, 98% availability.

Table 93. TWO-LAYER TREATMENT WITH Q_p RESPONSIVE, MINIMUM COST BASE, 90% AVAILABILITY, 0.0425 ANNUAL FACTOR, 4 mg/l D.O.: 2000 MEDIUM

	Required flow after chemical treatment (bgd)	Storage, 90% (mil. af)	Flow, 98% (bgd)	Required flow after second layer of treatment[a] (bgd)	Cost of storage ($ mil.) Basic flow, 98%	After continuous chemical treatment 98%	After continuous chemical treatment 90%	Savings; storage[b] ($ mil.)	Cost: 13-month chemical treatment ($ mil.)	Net savings[c] ($ mil.)
NORTHEAST	95.7	16.9	94.9	61.7	126.2	47.2	27.7	98.5	123.5	-25.0
N Eng	13.4	0	22.4	8.1	1.5	0		1.5	9.1	-7.6
D & H	8.5	1.4	7.9	7.9	17.2	11.1	6.3	10.9	14.3	-3.4
Ches	10.4	3.8	8.6	6.8	9.7	4.9	3.5	6.2	13.0	-6.8
Ohio	24.9	9.0	19.2	14.5	51.6	21.5	13.4	38.2	35.1	3.1
EGL	8.0	2.8	7.0	5.6	11.7	5.7	4.5	7.2	11.7	-4.5
WGL	10.5	0	8.8	6.9	16.1	3.1	0	16.1	11.7	4.4
U Miss	16.9	0	15.5	10.0	18.4	0.9	0	18.4	23.4	-5.0
L Mo	3.1	0	5.4	1.9	0	0	0	0	5.2	-5.2
SOUTHEAST	88.4	5.6	160.5	52.1	9.8	4.7	2.8	7.0	80.6	-73.6
SE	48.2	0	95.0	27.8	0	0	0	0	49.4	-49.4
Cumb	6.0	0	11.2	3.2	1.6	0	0	1.6	5.2	-3.6
Tenn	10.9	0	24.0	6.0	0	0	0	0	7.8	-7.8
L Miss	9.8	5.6	6.4	6.8[d]	8.2	4.7	2.8	5.4	9.1	-3.7
L AWR	13.5	0	23.9	8.3	0	0	0	0	9.1	-9.1
MID-CONTINENT	46.2	0	47.7	39.4	72.8	13.5	0	72.8	41.6	31.2
U Mo	19.8	0	25.6	16.8	0	0	0	0	13.0	-13.0
U AWR	7.0	0	6.7	6.7	3.3	1.6	0	3.3	6.5	-3.2
W Gulf	19.5	0	15.4	15.8[d]	69.5	11.9	0	69.5	22.1	47.4
SOUTHWEST	41.7	2.4	20.7	37.1	21.9	10.2	9.4	12.5	16.9	-4.4
RG-P	5.6	0	3.0	5.1[d]	0	0	0	0	5.2	-5.2
Colo	18.6	0	11.5	15.3[d]	0	0	0	0	7.8	-7.8
G Basin	5.9	0	5.4	5.4[d]	13.1	1.4	0	13.1	1.3	11.8
S Pac	11.6	2.4	0.8	11.3[d]	8.8	8.8	9.4	-0.6	2.6	-3.2
NORTH PACIFIC	64.4	0	88.7	52.2	15.1	5.4	0	15.1	27.3	-12.2
C Pac	27.5	0	25.9	26.1[d]	15.1	5.4	0	15.1	7.8	7.3
PNW	36.9	0	62.8	26.1	0	0	0	0	19.5	-19.5
U.S.	336.5	24.9	412.6	242.5	245.9	81.0	39.9	206.0	289.9	-83.9

[a] Losses plus dilution flow equal to one-quarter standard dilution flow.
[b] Standard storage for 98% availability minus storage for 90% availability after continuous chemical treatment.
[c] Storage savings minus chemical treatment costs.
[d] Deficiency of available flow.

Table 94. SUMMARY: CHEMICAL TREATMENT ALTERNATIVES BASED ON THE STANDARD MINIMUM COST PROGRAM, 98% AVAILABILITY, 0.0425 ANNUAL FACTOR, 4 mg/l D.O.: 2000 MEDIUM

	Required flow (bgd)	Storage (mil. af) Avail-ability (%)		Cost of storage ($ mil.) Avail-ability (%)		Cost of standard treatment ($ mil.)	Cost of chemical treatment ($ mil.)			Total cost ($ mil.)	Net savings[a] ($ mil.)
		98	90	98	90		1 mo.	12 mos.	13 mos.		
Standard	525	180		246		1,558				1,804	
Short-term											
Q_p unresponsive-unadjusted	395		86		106	1,558	22			1,686	118
Q_p unresponsive-adjusted	395		104		131	1,558	22			1,711	93
Q_p responsive-adjusted	337		97		116	1,558	22			1,696	108
Continuous chemical treatment											
Q_p unresponsive	395	93		117		1,558		268		1,943	−138
Q_p responsive	337	63		81		1,558		268		1,907	−103
Two-layer chemical treatment											
Q_p unresponsive[b]	355		41		59	1,558			290	1,907	−103
Q_p responsive[c]	243		25		40	1,558			290	1,888	−84

[a]Disparities due to rounding.

[b]Unadjusted; storage would have to be increased in Ohio, Upper Mississippi, Lower Missouri, Cumberland, Lower Mississippi, Upper Arkansas-White-Red, Western Gulf, and Central Pacific.

[c]Unadjusted; storage would have to be increased slightly in Lower Mississippi.

Chapter 12

VARIATIONS IN SELECTED PARAMETERS

The basic model is based on a 2 percent chance of flow deficiency, an annual factor of 0.0425, and an instream quality standard of 4 mg/l of dissolved oxygen. We first examine the effects of changing one or more of these parameters, and later we shall introduce still other variations. The underlying economic projections are kept unchanged. The costs of existing storage, recirculation, and collection (sewerage) are considered to be invariant. Hence, "total costs" in this chapter always refer to costs of treatment (BOD) plus new storage, unless otherwise defined.

Change in Certainty of Flow

A change in the accepted chance of deficiency, 5 percent or 10 percent instead of 2 percent (95 percent or 90 percent availability instead of 98 percent), will lower required storage for minimum flow, minimum treatment, and minimum cost programs; will lower the costs of storage and total costs; and in some instances will reduce prospective water shortages in regions that are developed to the physical maximum.[1] Required flows for the minimum flow program are unaffected, but required flows for the minimum treatment program will increase (since maximum regulated flow is greater) except in regions for which the minimum treatment program is already at the 70/50 percent treatment level. Since the costs of storage for any given flow are changed, there may be a change in the minimum cost combination of flow and treatment, thereby inducing a change in treatment costs. Treatment costs for the minimum flow

program remain unaffected, but storage costs are reduced.

While the usual effect of a reduction in security is a reduction in required storage for the minimum cost program, the opposite result is theoretically possible. As a consequence of a change in the slope of the flow-storage curve, a particular step in the storage-cost function may encourage a substitution of flow for treatment and lead to a minimum cost combination with more, rather than less, storage. This result is rare but occurs in the Lower Missouri region in going from 95 percent availability to 90 percent and in the Western Gulf region in going from 98 percent availability to 95 percent – for 2000 Medium, 0.0425, 4 mg/l.[2] In some regions, reduced security may be associated with a higher maximum net flow and larger maximum volume of regulatory capacity. If the region is water short, so that storage volume is extended to maximum net flow, aggregate outlay on storage may increase for a lower degree of security for minimum flow, minimum treatment, and minimum cost programs, since they are one and the same.

Table 95 summarizes for the United States the effect on required new storage of changes in the chance of deficiency, keeping constant the annual factor at 0.0425 and the standard of water quality at 4 mg/l of dissolved oxygen.

Relative effects are greatest for the minimum flow program for low economic projections – e.g., 1980 Medium and High – and are least for the minimum cost program for high projections – e.g., 2020 Medium – for which the difference in aggregate storage capacity between 2 percent and

---

[1] A higher chance of deficiency implies a smaller quantity of storage for a given flow, hence implies lower evaporation losses and greater maximum regulated net flow.

[2] An alternative possibility is that the result is spurious and rests on an inaccurate determination of the position of the flow-storage curve, especially at its lower end.

10 percent chances of deficiency are negligible. If one looks at *costs of storage*, however, the effect of a change in security is substantial — reflecting a rearrangement of inter-regional distribution of capacity in the face of rising marginal costs of storage. (See table 96.)

The effect of a change in the accepted chance of deficiency on the costs of storage tends to be greater than the effect on the volume of storage, regardless of whether minimum flow, minimum treatment, or minimum cost programs are examined. A rough generalization for minimum cost programs is that the costs of storage fall by about 20–25 percent when security falls from 98 percent to 95 percent, and by about 25–50 percent when security falls from 98 percent to 90 percent. As a part of *total* costs (new storage plus treatment), however, the impact is much less. For example, for 2000 Medium, 0.0425, 4 mg/l, the total cost falls by 2½ percent if certainty is reduced from 98 percent to 95 percent, and by 8 percent if certainty is reduced from 98 percent to 90 percent.

Table 97 shows that a change in availability has no effect on treatment costs for minimum flow programs but induces a fall with a decline in certainty for minimum treatment and minimum cost programs, albeit one of negligible consequence — e.g., less than 1 percent for 2000 Medium, minimum cost program.

In general, it appears as though the savings in total dollar costs (table 98) in comparison with 98 percent security are not likely to be impressive enough to offset the inconvenience, and possibly the net aggregate social loss, of accepting higher frequencies of deficiency. The conclusion is both tentative and intuitive, since no study has been made of the net costs of adjusting to different probabilities of deficiency. It is equally difficult to draw any conclusion regarding a tradeoff between the cost of accepting a higher uncertainty of flow and the benefit, if any, associated with a reduced volume of reservoir capacity.

Variation in Annual Factor

By postulating annual factors of 0.0200 and 0.0525 as alternatives to 0.0425, we simulate the effect of higher or lower interest rates and, in the case of 0.0200, a longer period of amortization. Treatment costs for minimum flow and minimum treatment programs are unaffected. A lower annual cost factor induces a substitution of storage for treatment in minimum cost programs and the reverse for a higher annual cost factor. For most projections, however, the effect of either change is negligible. (See table 99.)

Required flows and quantity of storage for minimum flow and minimum treatment programs also are unaffected. Changes in the quantity of storage for minimum cost programs can be large, relatively as well as absolutely. While an increase in the annual factor from 0.0425 to 0.0525 has a negligible effect in 1980 and 2000, by 2020 Medium, the difference in storage volume is 31 percent. The volume of storage is sensitive to a change in the annual factor when demand for regulated flow brings regulation close to the physical limit but is not great enough to induce a shortage. By 2020 High, changes in the annual factor have little effect, whether the change is up or down (table 100).

The reader will recognize that an annual factor of 0.0525 reflects the approximate level of the long-run "social cost" of capital.[3] By raising the annual cost of storage and keeping unchanged the annual cost of treatment, the substitution of treatment for flow is stimulated in order to minimize costs. (See tables 101 and 102.) The differences between 0.0425 and 0.0525 in total costs of minimum cost programs are hardly apparent in 1960 or 1980, when the physical possibilities of substitution are greatest. The differences in the *physical quantity* of storage are 5 percent or less for 1980 Medium and 2000 Medium, and the differences in treatment costs (a proxy for the change in the physical level of treatment) are of roughly equal magnitude but opposite in sign. The response of the total cost of storage to the higher annual factor is positive — i.e., the reduction in physical quantity is relatively less than the increase in unit cost. The only significant exception to this "inelasticity" is the solution for 2020 Medium.

The reader will note that where the demand for storage capacity is fixed by other objectives — i.e., minimum flow or minimum treatment programs — changes in the annual factor yield a directly proportional change in the costs of storage. Tables 100 and 102 also indicate that a decline in the annual factor from 0.0425 to 0.0200, while having a negligible effect on the total cost, would lead to relatively large increases in the use of storage capacity until 2020 High, at which point physical constraints inhibit response to changes in relative cost.

In general, an increase to 0.0525 from 0.0425 in the annual equivalent cost of reservoir capacity would have little effect on the flow-treatment minimum cost mix; a decline to 0.0200 would have a somewhat greater effect. For the country as a whole, the changes in storage quantity for 2000 Medium would be as follows, specifying 0.0425 as equal to 100:

Annual factor		Storage quantity
0.0200	=	118
.0425	=	100
0.0525	=	95

However, in seventeen regions the quantity of storage for the minimum cost program, 2000 Medium, 4 mg/l, remains the same over the range 0.0200–0.0525. Virtually all of the response is found in four regions: Upper Mississippi, Lower Mississippi, Lower Missouri, and Central Pacific.

Although variation in interest rates and in the speed of amortization had relatively little effect on the physical combination of flow and treatment, a more comprehensive test of the sensitivity of policy to interest rates would be constructed differently. Such a test would allow the bill of goods to vary, provide for different time paths of inputs and outputs, and compare a range of measures that vary more widely than those we used with respect to capital intensity.

[3]Compare John V. Krutilla and Otto Eckstein, *Multiple Purpose River Development: Studies in Applied Economic Analysis* (The Johns Hopkins Press for Resources for the Future, 1958), chap. 4.

By lowering the annual factor for storage costs to 0.0200, keeping unchanged the costs of treatment, we get an idea of the effect of having possibly understated the annual costs of treatment. If treatment costs are influenced by the private costs of capital, and if the life of treatment facilities is less than has been assumed, the annual factor applicable to treatment costs might be on the order of 0.06 instead of the value of 0.04 that has been used. While the higher value would not change the minimum treatment or minimum flow combination of treatment and storage, it would induce greater reliance on dilution flow for the minimum cost program. A comparable effect is approximated by reducing the annual factor for storage to 0.0200, holding treatment costs constant. Should industrial treatment take place via the use of municipal systems, and should the interest rate for municipal systems reflect the tax advantage given to municipal bonds, the relationship could be reversed. An approximation of the effects is given by raising the annual factor for storage, holding constant that for treatment.

If the change in the annual factor were also applied to treatment costs, the direction of shifts as indicated above would persist but in smaller amount. Because treatment incurs a larger component of current charges relative to long-term investment charges than does storage, the two forms of expenditure do not respond equally to a change in interest rates. Minimum cost combinations of treatment and storage, if interest rates moved for both, would fall somewhere between the basic model and the variants described above.

Variation in Dissolved Oxygen

The effect on policy of variations in dissolved oxygen is examined by holding constant the likelihood of deficiency at 2 percent and the annual factor at 0.0425, but allowing D.O. to fall from 4 mg/l to 1 mg/l or to rise from 4 mg/l to 6 mg/l. Minimum flow, minimum treatment, and minimum cost programs are affected. The level of treatment is untouched for minimum flow programs and is only moderately responsive for minimum treatment programs (table 103). The higher the projected level of population and activity is, the less responsive the level of treatment is to a change in D.O. for either minimum treatment or minimum cost programs. In a number of regions there is no response, since the range of behavior is restricted at both the upper and the lower limits. However, even by 2020 Medium, the level of treatment in most regions can respond to a change in D.O. for minimum treatment programs. By 2020 High, 6 mg/l, the lowest level of treatment computed for any region is 81 percent in New England. Sixteen regions by then are treating at 97½ percent under the minimum treatment program. For the same projection, if D.O. is set at 1 mg/l, New England's minimum treatment program calls for 70/50 percent and only nine regions must be at 97½ percent.

The 2000 Medium projections show that if D.O. is 1 mg/l, six regions can treat at 70/50 percent; four must treat at 97½ percent; and the remainder fall in between. The change in the required level of treatment for the

United States as a whole is roughly indicated by the index of treatment costs (4 mg/l = 100):

		Minimum treatment D.O. *(mg/l)*			Minimum cost D.O. *(mg/l)*		
		1	4	6	1	4	6
1980	Medium	92	100	105	92	100	107
2000	Medium	93	100	107	93	100	110
2020	Medium	93	100	110	91	100	106
2020	High	89	100	101	93	100	98

For the minimum treatment program, a given region will remain at the minimum level of 70/50 percent so long as regulated flow can be raised to offset either a higher D.O. standard or a larger amount of pollution-inducing activity, or both. After regulation reaches its physical maximum, the response can only be in the level of treatment. If water shortage appears at, say, 4 mg/l, a rise in the D.O. standard to 6 mg/l will have no effect on required treatment levels or costs of treatment, since by postulation standard treatment cannot exceed 97½ percent BOD removal.[4] For this reason, there is only a 1 percent difference between costs of treatment at 4 mg/l and 6 mg/l for 2020 High.

In general, the cost-minimizing level of treatment falls with a lower D.O. standard and rises with a higher, except for 2020 High. The apparent anomaly for 2020 High stems from the fact that for 6 mg/l of D.O. the phosphorus and nitrogen constraints were relaxed relative to their specification for 4 mg/l. This meant that dilution requirements were dominated by plant nutrients (phosphorus) at 95 percent treatment in the Ohio and Upper Mississippi regions for 4 mg/l but by BOD at 6 mg/l. The change in required flow relative to treatment costs shifted the minimum cost combination in these regions from 97½ percent for 4 mg/l to 95 percent for 6 mg/l. Dilution flows, of course, were higher for 6 mg/l than for 4 mg/l.

A D.O. standard of 6 mg/l imposes a strain on aggregate water resources for higher economic projections that appears to be unreasonable. Table 104 indicates that if the standard of water quality is 1 mg/l or 4 mg/l of D.O., aggregate requirements do not exceed aggregate maximum net regulated flow for any projection provided a minimum cost or minimum flow program is followed. This means that if water is shipped from surplus to deficit regions, or if water use is transferred from deficit to surplus regions, all requirements can be met without resort to desalination or importation from a foreign country. If a minimum treatment program is followed, there is a net national deficit for 2000 Medium for 6 mg/l, for 2000 High for 4 mg/l, and for 2020 High for 1 mg/l.

If D.O. is set at 6 mg/l, neither the minimum flow nor minimum cost programs for 2020 High are within the limit of maximum net regulated flow. Furthermore, they are beyond this limit by an amount equal to about 60 percent of maximum net regulated flow. None of the plans that have been discussed for importation of water to the continental

---

[4] The only response under these circumstances will be a greater water shortage (or failure to reach the stipulated standard).

United States from Canada and Alaska come remotely close to matching such a deficit.[5]

Desalination to meet the deficit, at 10 cents per 1,000 gallons, would cost $21 billion annually — an expenditure that seems high considering current attitudes regarding water quality. (Ten cents per 1,000 gallons is, of course, a lower cost than has been considered feasible. Targets of 50 cents per 1,000 gallons have been discussed; present experience is in the neighborhood of $1 per 1,000 gallons.) The $21 billion would be added to the costs of storage and treatment ($9.7 billion) shown in table 106, to which also would be added the costs of moving water from the six surplus regions to the sixteen deficit regions plus the costs of going to full regulation in the six surplus regions. For the minimum cost program, 2020 High, 6 mg/l, 98 percent, 0.0425, the costs of new storage, treatment, and desalination would be $30 billion annually, to which would have to be added the costs of interregional water transportation and storage if the water were transported. If transportation costs were no more than 1 cent per 1,000 gallons for the average required distance plus lift, this would amount to $2.5 billion per year for the total movement of water, including that which is desalinated. Costs of 10 cents per 1,000 gallons for desalination and 1 cent per 1,000 gallons for transportation are lower than they are likely to be in the immediate future. An estimate of $36 billion annually to meet the water bill — storage, waste treatment, desalination, and interbasin transportation (including transportation inland from the coast) — seems reasonably conservative.[6]

The justification of a policy to provide 6 mg/l of D.O. can be determined only by a cost-benefit analysis. For the minimum cost program, if a standard of 4 mg/l for 2020 High is adopted, total costs — as defined above for 6 mg/l — would be equal to $7,070 million for storage and treatment plus the cost of transporting the gross deficit of 255 bgd plus the costs of storage of 255 bgd (since only the costs of intraregional storage have been taken into account thus far). Transportation costs would be almost $1 billion annually at 1 cent per 1,000 gallons. Storage costs — roughly — would be about $5.5 billion higher.[7] Total costs would be about $13.5 billion. The saving of $22–23 billion annually would have to be compared with the loss of satisfaction engendered by a reduction of water quality from a minimum of 6 mg/l of D.O. to a minimum of 4 mg/l. At present such a comparison cannot be made.

For years closer at hand, the differences in costs and required flows between 4 mg/l and 6 mg/l are relatively small. The differences between 1 mg/l and 4 mg/l are cor-respondingly small. For example, total costs (before adjusting for deficits) for 1980 Medium are as follows:

1 mg/l	$910 million annually
4 mg/l	$992 million annually
6 mg/l	$1,149 million annually

Table 106, which shows total costs for the United States, is somewhat deceptive in that for 2020 High the difference shown between the annual costs for maintaining a 4 mg/l standard ($7,070 million) and a 6 mg/l standard ($9,695 million) does not take into account the large costs that would be incurred in meeting the deficits of flow. So long as aggregate required flows are within the limit of maximum net regulation, or maximum net regulation subject to a marginal cost constraint, these additional costs can be limited to additional storage costs in water-surplus regions provided that activity can be transferred from water-deficit to water-surplus areas. (Waste treatment costs are included in the total of costs whether flows are available or not.) An approximation of full costs to meet all activity is indicated by the fact that the costs of storage for 2020 High, 4 mg/l, 98 percent, 0.0425, are $1.6 billion annually (minimum cost program) without taking into account the added costs required to overcome deficits. The costs of maximum regulation, subject to a limit of 50 cents per 1,000 gallons for the cost of storage, would be $4 billion annually with a flow of 947 bgd.[8] Hence relocation — assuming that no other factor, such as land, impeded relocation — would imply about $2.4 billion in additional costs of water to meet all deficits.

The merit of 4 mg/l of D.O. over 1 mg/l as an appropriate quality standard is commonly accepted in the United States, as well as in other countries. The difference in costs is on the order of 10 to 15 percent (apart from the added costs of overcoming shortage). The added costs in going from 4 mg/l to 6 mg/l are about the same, except that water requirements mount much more rapidly and the costs of overcoming deficits dominate the total costs of water. The merit of 6 mg/l over 4 mg/l is less evident, perhaps because it has not been the subject of study. As our society becomes more aware of the existence of environmental deterioration, and as it becomes more willing to invest resources in environmental enhancement, the commonly demanded standard of water quality may rise. We cannot say that expenditures to yield 6 mg/l are not (or will not be) justified, regardless of how high, until we know what satisfactions are rendered by 6 mg/l over those yielded by 4 mg/l. Research on this question — more generally, over the whole scale of water qualities — is needed.[9]

Combined Variations

Having briefly surveyed the effects of changes made separately in the chance of deficiency, the annual factor,

---

[5] The North American Water and Power Alliance would transport 110 million acre-feet of water, an amount equal to 98 bgd. It is not clear whether all of this would be imported.

[6] Equal to 9.7 billion for storage and treatment before transfers, plus $21 billion for desalination, plus $2.5 billion for transportation, plus $3 billion for storage up to maximum net regulated flow.

[7] Costs of new storage to achieve maximum net regulated flow, 98 percent, 0.0425, would be about $7.1 billion annually. Costs of storage to meet 2020 High requirements without taking into account storage of water that is surplus to the region is $1.6 billion.

[8] Relocation would probably reduce aggregate requirements since unit requirements in agriculture would fall and unit requirements for other uses would remain about the same.

[9] It was observed in chap. 2 that costs in our model responded more gently to changes in D.O. than they did in two other studies of

and dissolved oxygen, what is the effect of simultaneously changing all three? Certain combinations have mixed effects relative to the basic combination of 98 percent, 0.0425, 4 mg/l. For example, 90 percent, 0.0200, 1 mg/l implies that storage capacity is reduced by accepting an increased chance of deficiency coupled with less D.O., but increased because of the lower annual factor. The cost of storage, however, would fall in response to the lower annual factor; hence from the point of view of total costs, 90 percent, 0.0200, 1 mg/l represents one extreme. The other extreme would be 98 percent, 0.0525, 6 mg/l, although the quantity of storage would be inhibited by the relatively high annual factor. (Compare tables 107 and 108.)

Those who find dams to be an undesirable interference with a river's natural flow (but who also are likely to want high-quality water) will be interested in the comparison of 90 percent, 0.0200, 1 mg/l with 90 percent, 0.0425, 4 mg/l in table 107. For a number of projections the amount of storage required for the higher water quality standard, when coupled with the higher annual factor, is less than storage requirements for the lower quality and lower annual factor for the minimum cost programs.

If an objective of minimizing required storage were adopted, however, we would presumably accept the costs of minimum flow programs. The difference in cost between the minimum flow and minimum cost programs would be the cost of minimizing the volume of storage. The range in new required storage covered by minimum flow programs, as both the chance of deficiency and dissolved oxygen are varied, is as follows:

		90%, 1 mg/l	98%, 4 mg/l	98%, 6 mg/l
		(million acre-feet)		
1960		2	4	10
1980	Low	3	6	52
	Medium	4	21	88
	High	6	59	116
2000	Low	3	29	99
	Medium	10	99	153
	High	97	194	447
2020	Low	13	110	214
	Medium	85	195	548
	High	256	813	1,596

The absolute differences between 90 percent, 1 mg/l, and 98 percent, 6 mg/l, which cannot be reduced further within the limits of the assumed technology of water use, waste production, and standard waste treatment, mount rapidly with increased population and economic activity. Required storage for 98 percent, 4 mg/l, minimum flow falls roughly between the selected extremes. Added to these figures, on the assumption that the bill of goods is unaffected by regional shortage, would have to be the additional storage in water-surplus regions on receipt of displaced activity.

The range of total costs expressed in index form (exclusive of additional storage needed to offset receipt of activity from deficit regions) covering the parametric changes along with alternative programs is given in table 109. The base is 98 percent, 0.0425, 4 mg/l, minimum cost program.

Minimum treatment programs, beginning with 1980 Medium, exceed the costs of other programs, even when parameters are fixed at 90 percent, 0.0200, 1 mg/l. Thus, the adoption of low water quality standards cannot be a money-saving device if a minimum treatment (maximum dilution) policy is adopted.

The more important policy question is likely to turn on the choice of minimum flow versus minimum cost policies. Since we have defined both of these programs as being subject to the same physical constraint, the water deficit in a particular region — but not in the United States as a whole — for a minimum cost program is no greater than the water deficit for a minimum flow program to provide the same water quality. But added costs of storage to provide for relocated activity would be somewhat greater for a minimum cost program than for a minimum flow program (since marginal costs of water would be higher); hence the cost differential after meeting deficits would be less.

If we adopt a minimum cost policy at the outset, the differences in cost between 1 mg/l and 4 mg/l are never more than 20 percent — plus the added difference in the costs of offsetting deficits. (See table 110.) But these added differences are not very great, at least not for 1980 and 2000 Medium.[10]

Given the uncertainties that surround all estimates, the differences in costs between 1 mg/l and 4 mg/l may not be significant as a basis for planning at the present time. Similarly, the difference in costs between minimum flow and minimum cost programs may not be great enough, in light of probable errors of estimates, to provide the basis of a choice of policy. One is tempted to argue intuitively in favor of a general policy of minimizing flow rather than minimizing cost, and for 4 mg/l rather than 1 mg/l. The estimated total difference in costs between minimum cost, 1 mg/l, and minimum flow, 4 mg/l, is about 34 percent. The absolute difference would be $547 million per year (including an $8 million difference in the cost of meeting the water deficit), as follows:

estuarine water quality and devices for its improvement. See Robert K. Davis, *The Range of Choice in Water Management: A Study of Dissolved Oxygen in the Potomac Estuary* (The Johns Hopkins Press for Resources for the Future, 1968); and Allen V. Kneese and Blair T. Bower, *Managing Water Quality: Economics, Technology, Institutions* (The Johns Hopkins Press for Resources for the Future, 1968), for further discussion of Potomac and Delaware estuary studies.

[10] For 2000 Medium, total required flow for 1 mg/l is 487 bgd with a gross deficit of 23 bgd; total required flow for 4 mg/l is 525 bgd, with a gross deficit of 32 bgd. If displaced activity goes into the regions with relatively low marginal costs of water, storage could be provided for the deficit at a cost per 1,000 gallons of $0.005 or less. If we adopt an average of $0.0025 per 1,000 gallons, the total cost of additional storage to accommodate the deficit would be $21 million for 1 mg/l and $29 million for 4 mg/l. Hence, the total cost of new storage plus treatment, including storage in water-surplus regions to accommodate the activity displaced from water-deficit regions would be $1,611 million for 1 mg/l and $1,833 million for 4 mg/l — a 14 percent difference.

2000 Medium *($ million)*	
Minimum cost, 1 mg/l, new storage and treatment	$1,590
Plus cost of overcoming deficit	21
Total	$1,611
Minimum flow, 4 mg/l, new storage and treatment	$2,129
Plus cost of overcoming deficit	29
Total	$2,158

Reduction in Industrial Waste Output

Two industrial waste variants were examined. Waste Variant 1 was based on the hypothesis that the output of waste per unit of product would fall from the 1960 level by 10 percent in 1980, 20 percent in 2000, and 30 percent in 2020. Variant 2 was based on declines of 20 percent, 40 percent, and 60 percent, respectively, for the same dates.

There is evidence that by changing production processes the output of waste per unit of product can be substantially reduced. One of the most recent studies to deal with this problem is *The Economics of Water Utilization in the Beet Sugar Industry* by George O. G. Löf and Allen V. Kneese.[11] Löf and Kneese said of beet sugar production that

> some processes such as pulp drying, the use of continuous diffusers accompanied by recirculation of pulp screen and press water, and the productive use of Steffens house residuals have reached a point where they are profitable, or nearly so, even in terms of the internal economics of the plant. . . . it would require only a comparatively small external stimulus . . . to induce the further use of these procedures that by themselves eliminate some 70 percent of the BOD which would be contained in the waste water from a factory using no recirculating or treatment process.[12]

The implications of Variants 1 and 2 are set forth in table 111. They are compared with the basic programs for the year 2000, Medium projection. Major leverage is exerted on the quantity and the cost of storage, provided a minimum flow or minimum cost program is followed. A 20 percent reduction of industrial BOD induces a 10 percent saving in treatment cost and an 11 percent saving in total cost; but these percentages conceal the fact that required new storage capacity is less by 20 percent and the costs of new storage are less by 29 percent.

We could "afford," if necessary, to pay industry about $500 million annually to induce a 40 percent reduction in the output of BOD at the level of production represented by 2000 Medium.[13] On the basis of 1963 prices and indexes used to project output in food manufacturing, pulp and paper, chemicals, petroleum and coal products, leather and leather products, and textiles, the value added by these manufacturing industries for 2000 Medium would be about $220 billion. If, therefore, the reduction in BOD of Variant 2 could be acquired at a cost of about 0.25 percent of value

added, the benefits of Variant 2 would, in effect, be costless.

The spread between the basic projection and Variants 1 and 2 widens considerably for 2020, in part because of a large percentage saving in the output of BOD, and in part because of the effect of a higher level of economic activity. For 2020 High, storage requirements for the basic minimum flow program are 813 million acre-feet; they are 255 million acre-feet for Variant 2. Thus, a 60 percent decline in industrial BOD induces a 69 percent decline in required reservoir capacity. Savings in the cost of water (new storage and treatment) are about $3.4 billion annually, which is approximately 0.25 percent of projected value added in the six BOD-producing manufacturing industries.

The concern that Löf and Kneese express regarding the possibility of adopting policies that concentrate exclusively on final treatment at the expense of changes in process bear repeating here. The leverage effect on storage requirements could itself justify a full-scale attack on reduction of BOD in the production process, even at the expense of a net increase in the aggregate cost of production, treatment, and provision of flow.

Recirculation of Municipal Coastal Intake

In adjusting to increased stringency of water supply, one response could be to reuse municipal water that otherwise would be discharged into coastal waters.[14] Such water could be put to uses that did not require high quality, or, if the need were great enough, the treatment of waste waters could be extended to the point where the effluent could be used for domestic purposes. The buildup of salts would probably pose the main problem, apart from the repugnance that might be encountered.

The overall effect on water requirements would be negligible, based on the level of water use projected for 2000 Medium. On the assumption of once-through municipal use (basic program, 2000 Medium), aggregate municipal intake would be 64 bgd; with recirculation at coastal locations, municipal withdrawals would fall to 58 bgd. Losses would fall from 34.5 bgd to 28.7 bgd.

National aggregates respond less than coastal regions, since the withdrawals and losses of interior regions remain unchanged. In coastal regions, such as New England and Delaware and Hudson, where major metropolitan areas are coastal or estuarine, the relative effect is still only moderate. Even in a region such as South Pacific, where the main loss consists of the discharge of municipal water to the sea, the effect is only moderate:

standard total loss   11 bgd
total loss with municipal intake recirculated   9.2 bgd

The estimated effects for each region are shown in table 112. In interior regions, there is no saving in water "use" by municipal recirculation, since we counted as part of re-

---

[11] The Johns Hopkins Press for Resources for the Future, 1968.
[12] P. 86.
[13] This is the approximate difference in the cost of storage and treatment between Variant 2 and the basic minimum flow program. The difference between minimum cost programs is less.

[14] See Richard J. Frankel, "Viewing Water Renovation and Reuse in Regional Water Systems," *Water Resources Research*, vol. 3, no. 1 (First Quarter 1967), pp. 57–61 for discussion related to Washington, D.C.

quired flow only the water that was lost by evaporation and transpiration. Relative to the U.S. average, losses are high in the Southwest for interior cities; hence the effect of municipal recirculation on total losses in the South Pacific region is small.

One can only speculate on the increase in treatment costs that would be required if municipal water were recirculated, since the level of treatment would be fixed by the form of reuse. In the basic model all waters discharged to the sea were assumed to receive primary treatment. A uniform increase to secondary and tertiary levels would involve a doubling or tripling of the costs of treating these waters, or more. If the water were used for certain types of irrigation or industrial activities, water of a fairly poor quality would suffice. We can be more specific about the effect on the costs of storage. For the minimum cost program, total costs (new storage and treatment) for 2000 Medium would fall from $1,804 million annually to $1,791 million annually, a decline of about 1 percent.

Reservation of Water for Recreation

We also examined how flow, storage, and costs would be affected if 25 percent of the total storage called for in the basic model were reserved for recreation. For computational purposes this meant that 80 percent of total reservoir capacity (existing plus added) became available for flow regulation. The impact on required storage to provide a designated flow varied from one region to another, depending on the shape of the flow-storage curve and the region's position on the curve, the effect of additional storage on evaporation losses, and the effect of movement along the synthetic schedule of increments of storage.

The required amount of new storage for the basic minimum cost program for 2000 Medium was 180 million acre-feet. With a 25 percent reservation, new storage rose to 224 million acre-feet – but not by a proportionately equal amount in each region. (No new storage was added in the Upper Missouri, Rio Grande–Pecos, and Colorado regions. Storage only up to the amount required for maximum physical net flow was added in the Western Gulf, Great Basin, and South Pacific regions.) This implied that somewhat more than 44 million acre-feet in new storage capacity constructed between now and the year 2000 would serve as a dead pool for recreational uses. The costs of storage – computed by moving along the synthetic schedule for each region – rose from a $246 million annual equivalent to $326 million, a difference of $80 million for the minimum cost program.

In some regions the new minimum cost combination required a higher level of treatment – otherwise required storage would have risen even further. As a consequence, total costs (new storage plus treatment) rose from $1,804 million annually to $1,920 million, a difference of $116 million. This, then, is the full cost of the recreational pool. Without the possibility of substituting higher treatment levels in some regions for added dead storage, the cost would have been higher. For example, if a policy of reserving 25 percent of reservoir capacity was based on a minimum treatment program, the cost of new storage and treatment would have risen from $5,987 annually to $7,153 annually, since virtually the entire response would be the addition of high-cost storage. On the other hand, had the reservation for recreation been based on a minimum flow program, the increase in the cost of storage would have been only $68 million annually, and this would have constituted the total increase in costs, since treatment was fixed at 97½ percent. For the minimum flow program, eight regions would not have required additional storage beyond the 1964 level (exclusive of Upper Missouri, Rio Grande–Pecos, and Colorado) under the basic program, and therefore would not have contributed new recreational capacity. This explains the smaller increase in the costs of a reservation for recreation based on a minimum flow program.

Regional Characteristics

Although the impact of parametric or policy changes are well described by changes in U.S. aggregates, some regions occasionally perform in anomalous or idiosyncratic fashion. For example, the level of treatment for minimum cost programs falls in the Upper Missouri region with an elevation of D.O. from 4 mg/l to 6 mg/l. This phenomenon is the result of a looser phosphorus constraint at 6 mg/l than at 4 mg/l coupled with the fact that the ruling dilution flow is fixed by phosphorus rather than BOD. Elsewhere, the impact on treatment levels of a change in D.O. follows the path that one would expect, whether the program is minimum cost or minimum treatment. Special interest attaches to table 114, which shows the minimum treatment levels compatible with alternative levels of D.O.[15] If D.O. is set at 6 mg/l, by 2000 Medium only three regions – New England, Ohio, and Lower Arkansas-White-Red – can remain at a 70/50 percent treatment level. By 2020 High, 6 mg/l requires that treatment be at 90 percent or above in all except the same three regions. If D.O. is set at 1 mg/l, the minimum cost program for 2020 High calls for treatment at 90 percent or above in all except these three regions.

The effect on required treatment levels of industrial waste Variants 1 and 2 for minimum cost programs, 2000 Medium, 98 percent, 0.0425, 4 mg/l is relatively small. In the Northeast division, for Variant 2, two regions (New England and Lower Missouri) can reduce treatment; in the Southeast division, three regions (Cumberland, Lower Mississippi, and Lower Arkansas-White-Red) can reduce treatment; elsewhere the only other change occurs in the Upper Missouri region, where treatment falls from 97 percent to 96 percent. For Variant 1, treatment falls only in the Lower Missouri and Lower Arkansas-White-Red.

Of greater interest than the level of treatment is the impact of parametric changes on the region's ability to meet required flows. Tables 115 and 116 reveal that the effects on required flows or on the balance between required flow and available supply (constrained or unconstrained by a marginal cost limit) or parametric changes other than D.O. is negligible. The 25 percent reservation for recreation, by inducing an increase in treatment levels for the minimum cost program, reduces total required flow, based on the basic program, by 6 percent. This is a greater

---

[15] Ignoring the problem of deficits in water-short regions.

effect than is caused by a change in the chance of deficiency or a change in the annual factor.

Tables 116 and 117 show how projected deficits spread across the country as population and the level of economic activity increase, even if D.O. is set at 1 mg/l. The projected gross deficit for 2020 Medium, 1 mg/l, is greater than the projected gross deficit for 2000 Medium, 4 mg/l. (The projected gross deficit for 2020 High, 6 mg/l, has already been discussed.) The reader will note that for 1980 and 2000 the area of deficit is limited to the Southwest and some regions of the Mid-continent. As late as 2020, under the Medium projection for 1 mg/l and 4 mg/l, deficits, other than those in the Southwest and Mid-continent, are limited to 1 bgd in the Western Great Lakes region. The jump to 2020 High, 4 mg/l, indicates that an entirely new order of magnitude of stringency would be encountered. It is impossible to imagine the shock effect of shortages of the size indicated for 2020 High. As history unfolds, the scarcity of water will be gradually felt and each region's activities will be accommodated to the supplies that are made available. But the response implies a significantly different regional distribution of activity, or a significantly different national bill of goods, or a significantly new technology, or a large outlay of funds on the provision of new water supplies.

Of total projected deficits for 2020 High, 4 mg/l, the Mid-continent and Southwest divisions account for about four-fifths. Three regions — Western Gulf, Colorado, and Western Great Lakes — account for two-thirds of the total deficit. The geographic distribution of deficits changes with a change in D.O. from 4 mg/l to 6 mg/l; the Southeast region appears in the deficit column.

A final observation — of total required flow projected for 2020 High, the division between losses and waste dilution would be as shown at the top of the opposite column. If the need for dilution flows could be eliminated by the development of new production techniques, shortages for 1, 4, or 6 mg/l for 2020 High would persist only in the Upper Arkansas-White-Red, Rio Grande–Pecos, Colorado,

D.O.	Total flow	Losses	Dilution
	(billion gallons per day)		
1 mg/l	775	259	516
4 mg/l	948	259	689
6 mg/l	1,572	259	1,313

and South Pacific regions — where shortages exist in one fashion or another today.

The projected gross national water deficit for 2020 High, 4 mg/l, minimum flow program (table 72), is about 255 bgd, or about 25 percent of the average runoff of the continental United States. In an earlier chapter, costs of offsetting deficits were estimated on the assumption of a sharp reduction from present and foreseeable costs of desalination and transbasin movement. If, in fact, the costs of desalination and transbasin movement declined to a combined level of 50–60 cents per 1,000 gallons (about $150 per acre-foot) — which would be a remarkable decline from present levels — the cost of overcoming the deficit in 2020 would be about $42 billion per year, plus the cost of fully regulating and treating to 97½ percent BOD removal practically all (909 bgd) of the nation's regular runoff. The aggregate outlay for storage, treatment, desalination, and transportation would be about $50 billion annually. This figure can be compared with present outlays for treatment and storage of some $1–2 billion per year.

Rather than become engaged in the monster projects of freshwater manufacture and movement implied by a projection of 2020 High, it would be better to direct our attention to other adjustments: (1) stabilization of population; and (2) redirection of the national bill of goods away from water-using, water-polluting goods and services to other kinds of goods and services, preferably those that not only avoid polluting our waters but avoid fouling our air and land — chemically, biologically, visually, and aurally. The environmental pinch is just beginning to be felt. If present trends continue, easing the pressure will cost a lot of money.

Table 95. REQUIRED NEW STORAGE, BY PROGRAM AND AVAILABILITY VARIANTS, 0.0425 ANNUAL FACTOR, 4 mg/l D.O.

(million acre-feet)

		Minimum flow program			Minimum treatment program			Minimum cost program		
		Availability (%)			Availability (%)			Availability (%)		
		98	95	90	98	95	90	98	95	90
1960		4	3	2	546	507	376	24	15	21
	L	6	5	4	1,421	1,234	1,151	42	38	36
1980	M	21	7	6	1,582	1,328	1,244	58	41	39
	H	59	41	11	1,638	1,371	1,271	140	107	74
	L	29	11	7	1,615	1,351	1,256	101	72	66
2000	M	99	92	40	1,769	1,512	1,354	180	156	94
	H	194	179	143	2,295	1,930	1,648	287	423	336
	L	110	101	52	1,801	1,594	1,416	212	186	122
2020	M	195	172	141	2,026	1,800	1,565	376	327	374
	H	813	784	595	2,493	2,063	1,866	839	823	633

Table 96. ANNUAL COSTS FOR NEW STORAGE, BY PROGRAM AND AVAILABILITY VARIANTS, 0.0425 ANNUAL FACTOR, 4 mg/l D.O.

($ million)

		Minimum flow program			Minimum treatment program			Minimum cost program		
		Availability (%)			Availability (%)			Availability (%)		
		98	95	90	98	95	90	98	95	90
1960		10	10	9	1,014	873	621	31	25	27
	L	12	12	11	3,646	3,143	2,823	48	46	50
1980	M	27	14	13	4,203	3,480	3,149	67	48	45
	H	79	51	21	4,277	3,521	3,176	161	116	87
	L	35	20	15	4,237	3,498	3,161	104	78	73
2000	M	156	145	56	4,591	3,809	3,282	246	208	111
	H	387	310	234	6,300	5,093	4,008	475	606	442
	L	175	164	74	4,645	3,942	3,448	286	247	147
2020	M	390	297	230	5,054	4,414	3,798	605	479	494
	H	1,561	1,586[a]	1,120	7,111	5,630	5,037	1,578	1,617[a]	1,151

[a]In some cases a larger maximum physical quantity of storage was allowed at 95% than at 98% and therefore costs of storage in water-short regions would rise for all programs. Whether U.S. aggregate costs would rise or fall would depend on which magnitude was greater—costs of increased storage in water-short regions or savings in costs of storage in nonwater-short regions. The reader will note that *volume* of storage for the United States as a whole is always less at 95% than at 98% and always less at 90% than at 95%.

Table 97. ANNUAL COSTS FOR TREATMENT, BY PROGRAM AND AVAILABILITY VARIANTS, 0.0425 ANNUAL FACTOR, 4 mg/l D.O.

($ million)

		Minimum flow program			Minimum treatment program			Minimum cost program		
		Availability (%)			Availability (%)			Availability (%)		
		98	95	90	98	95	90	98	95	90
1960		743	743	743	462	460	456	515	513	501
	L	1,099	1,099	1,099	710	706	698	819	808	788
1980	M	1,225	1,225	1,225	810	805	796	926	917	905
	H	1,417	1,417	1,417	975	971	962	1,086	1,078	1,064
	L	1,495	1,495	1,495	1,018	1,013	1,003	1,145	1,133	1,117
2000	M	1,964	1,964	1,964	1,395	1,389	1,379	1,558	1,554	1,550
	H	2,832	2,832	2,832	2,187	2,154	2,128	2,609	2,355	2,339
	L	2,310	2,310	2,310	1,671	1,658	1,656	1,854	1,835	1,829
2020	M	3,172	3,172	3,172	2,449	2,428	2,412	2,777	2.742	2,595
	H	5,621	5,621	5,621	5,210	4,927	5,127	5,491	5,467	5,456

Table 98. ANNUAL TOTAL COSTS FOR NEW STORAGE AND TREATMENT, BY PROGRAM AND AVAILABILITY VARIANTS, 0.0425 ANNUAL FACTOR, 4 mg/l D.O.

($ million)

		Minimum flow program			Minimum treatment program			Minimum cost program		
		Availability (%)			Availability (%)			Availability (%)		
		98	95	90	98	95	90	98	95	90
1960		753	753	752	1,475	1,332	1,076	546	537	529
1980	L	1,111	1,111	1,110	4,356	3,849	3,520	867	854	838
	M	1,252	1,238	1,237	5,013	4,285	3,946	992	965	950
	H	1,496	1,468	1,438	5,252	4,492	4,138	1,247	1,194	1,151
2000	L	1,529	1,515	1,509	5,255	4,511	4,164	1,248	1,211	1,191
	M	2,120	2,109	2,019	5,987	5,198	4,661	1,804	1,762	1,661
	H	3,219	3,143	3,054	8,486	7,247	6,136	3,084	2,962	2,781
2020	L	2,485	2,474	2,386	6,316	5,600	5,104	2,139	2,082	1,976
	M	3,562	3,469	3,402	7,503	6,842	6,210	3,383	3,220	3,089
	H	7,183	7,208	6,742	12,320	10,557	10,165	7,070	7,083	6,606

Table 99. ANNUAL TREATMENT COSTS, BY PROGRAM AND ANNUAL FACTOR VARIANTS, 98% AVAILABILITY, 4 mg/l D.O.

($ million)

		Minimum flow program			Minimum treatment program			Minimum cost program		
		Annual factor			Annual factor			Annual factor		
		0.0200	0.0425	0.0525	0.0200	0.0425	0.0525	0.0200	0.0425	0.0525
1960		743	743	743	462	462	462	512	515	517
1980	L	1,099	1,099	1,099	710	710	710	788	819	825
	M	1,225	1,225	1,225	810	810	810	884	926	927
	H	1,417	1,417	1,417	975	975	975	1,067	1,086	1,086
2000	L	1,495	1,495	1,494	1,018	1,018	1,018	1,109	1,145	1,186
	M	1,964	1,964	1,964	1,395	1,395	1,395	1,542	1,558	1,569
	H	2,832	2,832	2,832	2,187	2,187	2,186	2,280	2,609	2,623
2020	L	2,310	2,310	2,310	1,671	1,671	1,671	1,877	1,854	1,866
	M	3,172	3,172	3,172	2,449	2,449	2,449	2,602	2,777	2,964
	H	5,621	5,621	5,621	5,210	5,210	5,210	5,467	5,491	5,491

Table 100. NEW STORAGE, BY PROGRAM AND ANNUAL FACTOR VARIANTS, 98% AVAILABILITY, 4 mg/l D.O.

(million acre-feet)

		Minimum flow program			Minimum treatment program			Minimum cost program		
		Annual factor			Annual factor			Annual factor		
		0.0200	0.0425	0.0525	0.0200	0.0425	0.0525	0.0200	0.0425	0.0525
1960		4	4	4	546	546	546	27	24	21
1980	L	6	6	6	1,421	1,421	1,421	75	42	35
	M	21	21	21	1,582	1,582	1,582	107	58	56
	H	59	59	59	1,638	1,638	1,638	167	140	140
2000	L	29	29	29	1,615	1,615	1,615	153	101	75
	M	99	99	99	1,769	1,769	1,769	213	180	171
	H	194	194	194	2,295	2,295	2,295	482	287	276
2020	L	110	110	110	1,801	1,801	1,801	298	212	188
	M	195	195	195	2,026	2,026	2,026	571	376	258
	H	813	813	813	2,493	2,493	2,493	864	839	839

Table 101. ANNUAL COSTS FOR NEW STORAGE, BY PROGRAM AND ANNUAL FACTOR VARIANTS, 98% AVAILABILITY, 4 mg/l D.O.

($ million)

		Mininum flow program			Minimum treatment program			Minimum cost program		
		Annual factor			Annual factor			Annual factor		
		0.0200	0.0425	0.0525	0.0200	0.0425	0.0525	0.0200	0.0425	0.0525
1960		5	10	12	476	1,014	1,249	16	31	35
	L	6	12	15	1,716	3,646	4,504	44	49	53
1980	M	13	27	34	1,978	4,203	5,192	64	67	81
	H	38	79	98	2,013	4,277	5,283	90	161	199
	L	16	35	43	1,994	4,237	5,234	78	104	103
2000	M	73	156	193	2,161	4,591	5,672	130	246	292
	H	182	387	478	2,964	6,300	7,782	342	475	571
	L	82	175	216	2,186	4,645	5,738	187	286	340
2020	M	184	390	482	2,387	5,054	6,243	395	605	546
	H	731	1,561	1,920	3,346	7,111	8,784	755	1,578	1,941

Table 102. ANNUAL TOTAL COSTS, BY PROGRAM AND ANNUAL FACTOR VARIANTS, 98% AVAILABILITY, 4 mg/l D.O.

($ million)

		Minimum flow program			Minimum treatment program			Minimum cost program		
		Annual factor			Annual factor			Annual factor		
		0.0200	0.0425	0.0525	0.0200	0.0425	0.0525	0.0200	0.0425	0.0525
1960		748	753	755	938	1,475	1,711	528	546	552
	L	1,099	1,111	1,114	2,425	4,356	5,213	832	867	878
1980	M	1,225	1,252	1,258	2,788	5,013	6,003	948	992	1,008
	H	1,454	1,496	1,515	2,988	5,252	6,258	1,158	1,247	1,285
	L	1,511	1,529	1,538	3,012	5,255	6,251	1,186	1,248	1,288
2000	M	2,037	2,120	2,156	3,556	5,987	7,067	1,672	1,804	1,861
	H	3,015	3,219	3,311	5,151	8,486	9,968	2,623	3,084	3,193
	L	2,392	2,485	2,526	3,857	6,316	7,409	2,065	2,139	2,206
2020	M	3,356	3,562	3,654	4,836	7,503	8,692	2,997	3,383	3,510
	H	6,353	7,183	7,541	8,556	12,320	13,993	6,221	7,070	7,432

Table 103. ANNUAL TREATMENT COSTS, BY PROGRAM AND D.O. VARIANTS, 98% AVAILABILITY, 0.0425 ANNUAL FACTOR

($ million)

		Minimum flow program			Minimum treatment program			Minimum cost program		
		D.O. *(mg/l)*			D.O. *(mg/l)*			D.O. *(mg/l)*		
		1	4	6	1	4	6	1	4	6
1960		743	743	743	433	462	474	479	515	556
	L	1,099	1,099	1,099	660	710	750	748	819	876
1980	M	1,225	1,225	1,225	743	810	854	848	926	995
	H	1,417	1,417	1,417	897	975	1,029	1,053	1,086	1,178
	L	1,495	1,495	1,495	936	1,018	1,073	1,087	1,145	1,225
2000	M	1,964	1,964	1,964	1,303	1,395	1,487	1,454	1,558	1,710
	H	2,832	2,832	2,832	2,047	2,187	2,433	2,294	2,609	2,665
	L	2,310	2,310	2,310	1,555	1,671	1,804	1,728	1,854	2,069
2020	M	3,172	3,172	3,172	2,280	2,449	2,705	2,531	2,777	2,934
	H	5,621	5,621	5,621	4,627	5,210	5,259	5,120	5,491	5,406

Table 104. REQUIRED FLOWS, BY PROGRAM AND D.O. VARIANTS, 98% AVAILABILITY, 0.0425 ANNUAL FACTOR

(billion gallons per day)

		Minimum flow program			Minimum treatment program			Minimum cost program		
		D.O. *(mg/l)*			D.O. *(mg/l)*			D.O. *(mg/l)*		
		1	4	6	1	4	6	1	4	6
1960		125	139	170	409	576	708	312	360	373
1980	L	154	181	241	667	751	834	379	394	403
	M	173	205	275	713	776	870	396	426	445
	H	201	242	333	756	818	930	377	497	502
2000	L	186	230	325	737	805	914	383	468	515
	M	239	303	444	796	879	1,008	487	525	581
	H	342	451	697	900	995	1,116	543	586	749
2020	L	259	337	509	817	901	1,044	505	570	604
	M	359	480	752	902	1,004	1,144	576	679	834
	H	641	909	1,515	1,083	1,210	1,717	775	948	1,572

Table 105. ANNUAL STORAGE COSTS, BY PROGRAM AND D.O. VARIANTS, 98% AVAILABILITY, 0.0425 ANNUAL FACTOR

($ million)

		Minimum flow program			Minimum treatment program			Minimum cost program		
		D.O. *(mg/l)*			D.O. *(mg/l)*			D.O. *(mg/l)*		
		1	4	6	1	4	6	1	4	6
1960		10	10	16	384	1,014	3,174	17	31	32
1980	L	10	12	64	2,174	3,646	4,314	34	49	90
	M	12	27	130	3,436	4,203	4,538	62	67	154
	H	33	79	176	4,002	4,277	4,718	69	161	232
2000	L	12	35	145	3,481	4,237	4,675	46	104	202
	M	60	156	243	4,225	4,591	5,147	136	246	328
	H	204	387	836	4,667	6,300	7,111	282	475	856
2020	L	70	175	384	4,257	4,645	6,217	160	286	443
	M	206	390	983	4,642	5,054	7,111	306	605	1,047
	H	727	1,561	4,210	6,460	7,111	7,111	873	1,578	4,290

Table 106. TOTAL ANNUAL COSTS, BY PROGRAM AND D.O. VARIANTS, 98% AVAILABILITY, 0.0425 ANNUAL FACTOR

($ million)

		Minimum flow program			Minimum treatment program			Minimum cost program		
		D.O. *(mg/l)*			D.O. *(mg/l)*			D.O. *(mg/l)*		
		1	4	6	1	4	6	1	4	6
1960		753	753	759	827	1,475	3,647	496	546	588
1980	L	1,109	1,111	1,163	2,834	4,356	5,064	782	867	966
	M	1,237	1,252	1,354	4,179	5,013	5,392	910	992	1,149
	H	1,450	1,496	1,593	4,899	5,252	5,747	1,122	1,247	1,410
2000	L	1,507	1,529	1,640	4,417	5,255	5,747	1,133	1,248	1,427
	M	2,023	2,120	2,207	5,528	5,987	6,634	1,590	1,804	2,038
	H	3,036	3,219	3,668	6,714	8,486	9,544	2,576	3,084	3,521
2020	L	2,379	2,485	2,693	5,812	6,316	8,021	1,888	2,139	2,512
	M	3,378	3,562	4,155	6,922	7,503	9,816	2,838	3,383	3,981
	H	6,349	7,183	9,831	11,089	12,320	12,369	5,993	7,070	9,695

Note: Excludes costs of overcoming shortages.

Table 107. TOTAL REQUIRED NEW STORAGE FOR MINIMUM COST PROGRAMS, BY SELECTED VARIANTS

(million acre-feet)

		0.0425 annual factor, 4 mg/l D.O.			98% availability, 0.0425 annual factor			98% availability, 4 mg/l D.O.			90% availability, 0.0200 annual factor, 1 mg/l D.O.	98% availability, 0.0525 annual factor, 6 mg/l D.O.
		Availability (%)			D.O. (mg/l)			Annual factor				
		90	95	98	1	4	6	0.0200	0.0425	0.0525		
1960		21	15	24	12	24	30	27	24	21	20	22
	L	36	38	42	28	42	74	75	42	35	52	71
1980	M	39	41	58	58	58	115	107	58	56	48	113
	H	74	107	140	59	140	172	167	140	140	80	167
	L	66	72	101	43	101	161	153	101	75	77	161
2000	M	94	156	180	115	180	232	213	180	171	112	198
	H	336	432	287	196	287	471	482	287	276	286	471
	L	122	186	212	135	212	271	298	212	188	176	263
2020	M	374	327	376	216	376	609	571	376	258	224	573
	H	633	823	839	487	839	1,651	864	839	839	410	1,651

Table 108. TOTAL ANNUAL COSTS FOR NEW STORAGE, MINIMUM COST PROGRAMS, BY SELECTED VARIANTS

($ million)

		0.0425 annual factor, 4 mg/l D.O.			98% availability, 0.0425 annual factor			98% availability, 4 mg/l D.O.			90% availability, 0.0200 annual factor, 1 mg/l D.O.	98% availability, 0.0525 annual factor, 6 mg/l D.O.
		Availability (%)			D.O. (mg/l)			Annual factor				
		90	95	98	1	4	6	0.0200	0.0425	0.0525		
1960		27	25	31	17	31	32	16	31	35	15	30
	L	50	46	48	34	48	90	44	48	53	30	100
1980	M	45	48	67	62	67	154	64	67	81	29	189
	H	87	116	161	69	161	232	91	161	199	48	277
	L	73	78	104	46	104	202	76	104	103	44	250
2000	M	111	208	246	136	246	328	130	246	292	72	353
	H	442	607	475	282	475	856	342	475	571	174	1,056
	L	147	247	286	160	286	443	187	286	340	104	533
2020	M	494	479	605	306	605	1,047	395	605	546	132	1,240
	H	1,151[a]	1,617[a]	1,578	873	1,578	4,290	755	1,578	1,941	368	5,299[a]

[a]Treatment increases in some cases as we go from 90% to 95% to 98%. Offsetting this is a possibility of greater total storage in water-short regions as availability goes from 98% to 95% and 90%.

Table 109. ANNUAL TOTAL COSTS FOR NEW STORAGE AND TREATMENT, ALTERNATIVE PROGRAMS, AS A PERCENTAGE OF MINIMUM COST PROGRAMS FOR 98% AVAILABILITY, 0.0425 ANNUAL FACTOR, 4 mg/l D.O.

		Minimum flow program					Minimum treatment program					Minimum cost program					
		98% availability, 0.0425 annual factor			90% availability, 0.0200 annual factor, 1 mg/l	98% availability, 0.0200 annual factor, 6 mg/l	98% availability, 0.0425 annual factor			90% availability, 0.0200 annual factor, 1 mg/l	98% availability, 0.0200 annual factor, 6 mg/l	98% availability, 0.0425 annual factor			90% availability, 0.0200 annual factor, 1 mg/l	98% availability, 0.0525 annual factor, 6 mg/l	98% availability, 0.0425 annual factor, 4 mg/l D.O. ($ mil.)
		D.O. (mg/l)					D.O. (mg/l)					D.O. (mg/l)					
		1	4	6			1	4	6			1	4	6			
1960		138	138	139	137	140	151	270	668	110	802	91	100	108	86	109	546
1980	L	128	128	134	111	136	327	502	584	119	696	90	100	111	85	114	867
	M	125	126	136	124	139	421	505	544	181	646	92	100	116	85	119	992
	H	116	120	128	114	131	393	421	461	182	550	90	100	113	82	117	1,247
2000	L	121	123	131	120	134	354	421	461	178	549	91	100	114	84	118	1,248
	M	112	118	122	109	125	306	332	368	153	430	88	100	113	80	117	1,804
	H	98	104	119	94	125	218	323	309	118	363	84	100	114	76	121	3,084
2020	L	111	116	126	109	130	272	295	375	141	443	88	100	117	80	122	2,139
	M	100	105	123	96	130	205	222	290	114	332	84	100	118	76	125	3,383
	H	90	102	139	83	153	157	174	175	94	198	85	100	137	75	151	7,070

Note: Excludes costs of overcoming shortages.

Table 110. ANNUAL TOTAL COSTS FOR NEW STORAGE AND TREATMENT, MINIMUM COST PROGRAMS, BY SELECTED VARIANTS

($ million)

		0.0425 annual factor, 4 mg/l D.O. Availability (%)			0.0425 annual factor, 98% availability D.O. (mg/l)			98% availability, 4 mg/l D.O. Annual factor			90% availability, 0.0200 annual factor, 1 mg/l D.O.	98% availability, 0.0525 annual factor, 6 mg/l D.O.
		90	95	98	1	4	6	0.0200	0.0425	0.0525		
1960		529	537	546	496	546	588	528	546	552	468	595
1980	L	838	854	867	782	867	966	832	867	878	736	985
	M	950	965	992	910	992	1,149	948	992	1,008	840	1,185
	H	1,151	1,194	1,247	1,122	1,247	1,410	1,158	1,247	1,285	1,023	1,464
2000	L	1,191	1,211	1,248	1,133	1,248	1,427	1,186	1,248	1,288	1,051	1,475
	M	1,661	1,762	1,804	1,590	1,804	2,038	1,672	1,804	1,861	1,442	2,110
	H	2,781	2,962	3,084	2,576	3,084	3,521	2,623	3,084	3,193	2,337	3,721
2020	L	1,976	2,082	2,139	1,888	2,139	2,512	2,065	2,139	2,206	1,713	2,614
	M	3,089	3,220	3,383	2,838	3,383	3,981	2,995	3,383	3,510	2,562	4,221
	H	6,606	7,083	7,070	5,993	7,070	9,695	6,221	7,070	7,432	5,284	10,704

Note: Costs of eliminating greater shortages as D.O. level is raised are not included.

Table 111. MAJOR CHARACTERISTICS OF ALTERNATIVE PROGRAMS, BY INDUSTRIAL WASTE VARIANTS, 98% AVAILABILITY, 0.0425 ANNUAL FACTOR, 4 mg/l D.O.

	Minimum flow					Minimum treatment					Minimum cost				
	Flow (bgd)	Storage (mil. af)	Cost storage ($ mil.)	Cost treatment ($ mil.)	Cost total ($ mil.)	Flow (bgd)	Storage (mil. af)	Cost storage ($ mil.)	Cost treatment ($ mil.)	Cost total ($ mil.)	Flow (bgd)	Storage (mil. af)	Cost storage ($ mil.)	Cost treatment ($ mil.)	Cost total ($ mil.)
1980 M															
Standard	205	21	27	1,225	1,252	776	1,582	4,203	810	5,013	426	58	67	926	992
Variant 1	198	17	23	1,173	1,196	767	1,573	4,194	771	4,965	408	55	61	885	946
Variant 2	193	13	19	1,121	1,140	757	1,493	3,887	733	4,620	391	45	52	846	899
2000 M															
Standard	303	99	156	1,964	2,120	879	1,769	4,591	1,395	5,987	525	180	246	1,558	1,804
Variant 1	277	79	111	1,766	1,877	846	1,682	4,212	877	5,089	472	141	178	1,401	1,579
Variant 2	252	55	73	1,569	1,642	811	1,618	4,237	1,091	5,328	422	103	125	1,241	1,366
2020 M															
Standard	480	195	390	3,172	3,562	1,004	2,026	5,054	2,449	7,503	679	376	605	2,777	3,383
Variant 1	403	140	230	2,611	2,841	942	1,845	4,709	1,953	6,661	641	298	402	2,131	2,534
Variant 2	327	109	182	2,050	2,232	876	1,744	4,445	1,482	5,927	525	179	258	1,646	1,903
2020 H															
Standard	909	813	1,561	5,621	7,183	1,211	2,493	7,111	5,210	12,320	948	839	1,578	5,491	7,070
Variant 1	730	449	879	4,452	5,331	1,133	2,493	7,111	3,922	11,033	766	477	900	4,330	5,230
Variant 2	551	255	511	3,282	3,793	1,044	2,297	6,301	2,616	8,917	659	353	605	3,074	3,680

Table 112. WITHDRAWALS AND LOSSES, MUNICIPAL COASTAL INTAKE RECIRCULATED, BY REGION: 2000 MEDIUM

(billion gallons per day)

| | Standard | | | | Coastal intake recirculated | | | |
| | Withdrawals | | Losses | | Withdrawals | | Losses | |
	Municipal	Total	Municipal	Total	Municipal	Total	Municipal	Total
NORTHEAST	32.7	309.7	15.3	27.6	30.4	307.2	12.9	25.3
N Eng	2.6	9.0	1.8	2.7	2.3	8.6	1.4	2.4
D & H	7.2	22.5	6.4	7.2	5.7	20.9	4.9	5.7
Ches	2.9	19.4	2.2	3.3	2.4	18.9	1.7	2.8
Ohio	3.3	104.6	0.8	4.0	3.3	104.6	0.8	4.0
EGL	5.7	47.0	1.4	3.3	5.7	47.0	1.4	3.3
WGL	7.4	63.0	1.8	3.4	7.4	63.0	1.8	3.4
U Miss	3.2	37.5	0.8	3.0	3.2	37.5	0.8	3.0
L Mo	0.4	6.7	0.1	0.7	0.4	6.7	0.1	0.7
SOUTHEAST	11.6	84.7	5.1	15.7	10.8	83.9	4.4	15.0
SE	8.3	37.2	3.9	7.5	7.6	36.6	3.3	6.9
Cumb	0.3	2.3	0.1	0.3	0.3	2.3	0.1	0.3
Tenn	0.8	21.7	0.2	1.0	0.8	21.7	0.2	1.0
L Miss	1.4	12.3	0.7	3.8	1.3	12.1	0.6	3.7
L AWR	0.8	11.2	0.2	3.1	0.8	11.2	0.2	3.1
MID-CONTINENT	5.7	53.4	2.7	32.6	5.5	53.1	2.4	32.4
U Mo	1.9	25.1	0.7	13.9	1.9	25.1	0.7	13.9
U AWR	0.7	9.1	0.3	6.5	0.7	9.1	0.3	6.5
W Gulf	3.1	19.2	1.7	12.2	2.9	18.9	1.4	12.0
SOUTHWEST	9.9	44.2	8.3	32.5	8.1	42.4	6.5	30.7
RG-P	0.6	6.8	0.3	4.7	0.6	6.8	0.3	4.7
Colo	1.3	16.9	0.5	12.0	1.3	16.9	0.5	12.0
G Basin	0.5	7.5	0.2	4.8	0.5	7.5	0.2	4.8
S Pac	7.5	13.0	7.3	11.0	5.7	11.2	5.5	9.2
NORTH PACIFIC	3.9	70.9	3.1	40.0	3.3	70.3	2.5	39.4
C Pac	1.9	34.6	1.5	24.7	1.6	34.3	1.2	24.4
PNW	2.0	36.3	1.6	15.3	1.7	36.0	1.3	15.0
U.S.	63.8	562.9	34.5	148.4	58.1	556.9	28.7	142.8

Table 113. TREATMENT LEVELS FOR MINIMUM COST PROGRAMS, BY REGION AND SELECTED VARIANTS: 2000 MEDIUM, 2020 HIGH

(percent)

| | 2000 Medium | | | | | | | | | | | 2020 High | | 2000 Medium |
	0.0425 annual factor, 4 mg/l D.O. Availability (%)			98% availability, 0.0425 annual factor D.O. (mg/l)			98% availability, 4 mg/l D.O. Annual factor			90% availability, 0.0200 annual factor, 1 mg/l D.O.	98% availability, 0.0525 annual factor, 6 mg/l D.O.	98% availability, 0.0525 annual factor, 6 mg/l D.O.	98% availability, 0.0425 annual factor, 1 mg/l D.O.	25% reservation, 98% availability, 0.0425 annual factor, 4 mg/l D.O.
	90	95	98	1	4	6	0.0200	0.0425	0.0525					
N Eng	70	70	70	70/50	70	90	70	70	70	70/50	90	95	80	80
D & H	97.5	97.5	97.5	95	97.5	97.5	97.5	97.5	97.5	90	97.5	97.5	97.5	97.5
Ches	95	95	95	90	95	95	95	95	95	90	95	97.5	97.5	95
Ohio	70/60	70/60	70/60	70	70/60	90	70/60	70/60	70/60	70/50	90	95	80	70/60
EGL	95	95	95	95	95	95	95	95	95	90	97.5	97.5	97.5	95
WGL	97.5	97.5	97.5	97.5	97.5	97.5	97.5	97.5	97.5	95	97.5	97.5	97.5	97.5
U Miss	70	70	70	70/60	70	90	70	70	80	70/50	90	97.5	90	80
L Mo	80	90	90	80	90	90	80	90	90	70/60	90	95	95	90
SE	95	95	95	90	95	97.5	95	95	95	90	97.5	97.5	97.5	95
Cumb	95	95	95	90	95	97.5	95	95	95	90	97.5	97.5	97.5	97.5
Tenn	90	90	90	80	90	95	90	90	90	80	95	97.5	95	90
L Miss	70	70	80	70/60	80	90	70	80	80	70/50	90	97.5	90	90
L AWR	70/50	70/60	70/60	70/50	70/60	80	70/60	70/60	70/60	70/50	80	95	80	70
U Mo	97	97	97	90	97[a]	96[a]	97	97	97	90	96	97.5	97.5	97
U AWR	97	97.5	97.5	97.5	97.5	97.5	97.5	97.5	97.5	96	97.5	97.5	97.5	97.5
W Gulf	97.5	97.5	97.5	97.5	97.5	97.5	97.5	97.5	97.5	95	97.5	97.5	97.5	97.5
RG-P	97.5	97.5	97.5	97.5	97.5	97.5	97.5	97.5	97.5	97.5	97.5	97.5	97.5	97.5
Colo	97.5	97.5	97.5	97.5	97.5	97.5	97.5	97.5	97.5	97.5	97.5	97.5	97.5	97.5
G Basin	97.5	97.5	97.5	97.5	97.5	97.5	97.5	97.5	97.5	95	97.5	97.5	97.5	97.5
S Pac	97.5	97.5	97.5	97.5	97.5	97.5	97.5	97.5	97.5	97.5	97.5	97.5	97.5	97.5
C Pac	97.5	97.5	97.5	97.5	97.5	97.5	95	97.5	97.5	95	97.5	97.5	97.5	97.5
PNW	95	95	95	90	95	95	95	95	95	90	97.5	97.5	97.5	95

[a] Apparent anomaly caused by fact that phosphorus is ruling.

Table 114. TREATMENT LEVELS FOR MINIMUM TREATMENT PROGRAMS, BY REGION AND D.O. VARIANTS, 98% AVAILABILITY

(percent)

	1960 D.O. (mg/l)			1980 M D.O. (mg/l)			2000 M D.O. (mg/l)			2020 M D.O. (mg/l)			2020 H D.O. (mg/l)		
	1	4	6	1	4	6	1	4	6	1	4	6	1	4	6
N Eng	70/50	70/50	70/50	70/50	70/50	70/50	70/50	70/50	70/50	70/50	70/50	70/64	70/50	70/68	81
D & H	70/50	70/50	70/55	70/50	70/61	77	70/66	79	87	83	89	94	95	97	97.5
Ches	70/50	70/50	70/63	70/51	72	84	75	85	91	87	92	95	95	97	97.5
Ohio	70/50	70/50	70/50	70/50	70/50	70/50	70/50	70/50	70/50	70/50	70/50	72	70/68	95	89
EGL	70/50	70/50	70/65	70/53	72	83	75	84	90	86	91	95	96	97	97.5
WGL	76	85	91	87	92	95	92	95	97	96	97.5	97.5	97.5	97.5	97.5
U Miss	70/50	70/50	70/50	70/50	70/50	70/53	70/50	70/50	74	70/52	73	84	82	96	94
L Mo	70/50	70/50	70/50	70/50	70/50	70/50	70/50	70/58	77	70/67	80	89	86	93	95
SE	70/50	70/50	78	70/58	78	90	80	89	95	90	94	97	96	97.5	97.5
Cumb	70/50	70/50	70/50	70/63	78	87	85	92	95	93	96	97.5	97.5	97.5	97.5
Tenn	70/50	70/50	70/60	70/50	70/59	79	70/64	79	89	81	89	94	93	96	97.5
L Miss	70/50	70/50	70/50	70/51	70/50	70/50	70/50	70/50	73	70/60	78	89	86	92	96
L AWR	70/50	70/50	70/50	70/50	70/50	70/50	70/50	70/50	70/50	70/50	70/50	72	70/52	73	87
U Mo	95	92a	83a	77	96	91	90	97a	96a	96	97	97.5	97.5	97.5	97.5
U AWR	97.5	97a	95a	97	97.4	97.5	97.5	97.5	97.5	97.5	97.5	97.5	97.5	97.5	97.5
W Gulf	74	93a	95a	89	96	97.5	96	97.5	97.5	97.5	97.5	97.5	97.5	97.5	97.5
RG-P	97.5	97.5	97.5	97.5	97.5	97.5	97.5	97.5	97.5	97.5	97.5	97.5	97.5	97.5	97.5
Colo	97.5	97.5	97.5	97.5	97.5	97.5	97.5	97.5	97.5	97.5	97.5	97.5	97.5	97.5	97.5
G Basin	70/50	76	87	92	95.4	97.4	96	97.5	97.5	97.5	97.5	97.5	97.5	97.5	97.5
S Pac	97.5	97.5	97.5	97.5	97.5	97.5	97.5	97.5	97.5	97.5	97.5	97.5	97.5	97.5	97.5
C Pac	70/50	70/55	81	70/67	82	91	84	91	96	92	96	97.5	97	97.5	97.5
PNW	70/50	70/50	70/50	70/58	73	83	79	86	91	89	93	95	94	96	97.5

aTreatment level set by phosphorus dilution requirement. At 6 mg/l the phosphorus constraint is less binding than at 4 mg/l.

Table 115. REQUIRED FLOWS FOR MINIMUM COST PROGRAMS, BY REGION AND SELECTED VARIANTS: 2000 MEDIUM

(billion gallons per day)

	0.0425 annual factor, 4 mg/l D.O. Availability (%)			98% availability, 0.0425 annual factor D.O. (mg/l)			98% availability, 4 mg/l D.O. Annual factor			90% availability, 0.0200 annual factor, 1 mg/l D.O.	98% availability, 0.0525 annual factor, 6 mg/l D.O.	Maximum regulated flow, 98%, no M.C. constraint 4 mg/l D.O.	25% reservation, 98% availability, 0.0425 annual factor, 4 mg/l D.O.
	90	95	98	1	4	6	0.0200	0.0425	0.0525				
NORTHEAST	167	164	164	126	164	150	167	164	158	164	143	362	151
N Eng	24	24	24	20	24	15	24	24	24	20	15	61	17
D & H	10	10	10	10	10	11	10	10	10	14	11	29	10
Ches	18	18	18	21	18	28	18	18	18	21	28	47	18
Ohio	46	46	46	24	46	24	46	46	46	35	24	99	46
EGL	13	13	13	9	13	19	13	13	13	15	11	33	13
WGL	18	18	18	12	18	27	18	18	18	21	27	30	18
U Miss	31	31	31	24	31	19	31	31	25	29	19	46	25
L Mo	8	5	5	5	5	7	8	5	5	10	7	16	5
SOUTHEAST	172	167	161	166	161	160	167	161	161	170	160	334	143
SE	89	89	89	98	89	93	89	89	89	98	93	186	89
Cumb	12	12	12	10	12	7	12	12	12	10	7	15	4
Tenn	21	21	21	23	21	19	21	21	21	23	19	40	21
L Miss	22	22	16	17	16	15	22	16	16	20	15	35	10
L AWR	28	24	24	17	24	26	24	24	24	17	26	58	19
MID-CONTINENT	61	60	60	52	60	83	60	60	60	64	83	59	60
U Mo	26	26	26	26	26	26	26	26	26	26	26	26	26
U AWR	9	7	7	7	7	8	7	7	7	9	8	7	7
W Gulf	27	27	27	20	27	49	27	27	27	29	49	26	27
SOUTHWEST	51	51	51	43	51	68	51	51	51	45	68	22	51
RG-P	7	7	7	6	7	8	7	7	7	6	8	3	7
Colo	25	25	25	20	25	38	25	25	25	20	38	11	25
G Basin	7	7	7	6	7	9	7	7	7	7	9	7	7
S Pac	12	12	12	12	12	13	12	12	12	12	13	1	12
NORTH PACIFIC	89	89	89	99	89	119	94	89	89	102	85	180	89
C Pac	30	30	30	28	30	36	36	30	30	31	36	45	30
PNW	58	58	58	71	58	83	58	58	58	71	49	136	58
U.S.	540	531	525	487	525	581	539	525	519	544	539	956	494

Note: Discrepancies between totals and details due to rounding.

Table 116. REQUIRED FLOWS FOR MINIMUM COST PROGRAMS, BY REGION AND SELECTED VARIANTS, 98% AVAILABILITY, 0.0425 ANNUAL FACTOR

(billion gallons per day)

	98% availability, 0.0425 annual factor				1960	1980 L			2000 M		2020 M			2020 H		
	No constraint	Marginal cost			4 mg/l D.O.	D.O. (mg/l)			D.O. (mg/l)		D.O. (mg/l)			D.O. (mg/l)		
		50¢	10¢	2¢		1	4	6	1	4	1	4	6	1	4	6
NORTHEAST	362	355	345	310	82	78	103	105	126	164	171	220	210	251	236	373
N Eng	61	60	59	56	14	12	18	24	20	24	23	25	21	28	23	20
D & H	29	28	26	26	7	8	6	9	10	10	13	15	17	22	26	(33)
Ches	47	45	42	42[a]	8	10	15	13	21	18	21	31	27	27	39	(63)
Ohio	99	96	96	79	17	14	24	12	24	46	49	68	40	66	23	53
EGL	33	33	31	26	4	5	6	9	9	13	16	13	18	23	30[b]	(43)
WGL	30	30	29	25	11	11	9	14	12	18	21	(31)	(47)	(48)	(72)	(114)
U Miss	46	46	45	40	17	15	20	19	24	31	23	29	31	30	16	39
L Mo	16	16	15	14	3	5	5	6	5	5	6	9	8	7	6	9
SOUTHEAST	334	333	329	303	118	130	131	130	166	161	175	165	247	211	287	(507)
SE	186	186	185	167	80	82	74	78	98	89	97	88	172[b]	113	(187)	(373)
Cumb	15	15	15	13	1	9	10	9	10	12	11	9	15[b]	15	(24)	(40)
Tenn	40	40	38	34	22	22	24	15	23	21	22	27	18	28	24	(43)
L Miss	35	35	35	35[a]	5	7	9	6	17	16	21	19	18	28	27	25
L AWR	58	58	57	54[a]	9	9	14	23	17	24	24	22	23	27	25	25
MID-CONTINENT	59	59	58	55	44	48	46	54	52	(60)	(64)	(79)	(130)	(107)	(152)	(284)
U Mo	26	26	26	26	26	26	26	26	26	26	26	26	(30)	(32)	(39)	(50)
U AWR	7	7	7	7[a]	6	6	6	7	7	7	(8)	(9)	(11)	(12)	(15)	(19)
W Gulf	26	26	26	22	12	17	14	22	20	(27)	(30)	(44)	(90)	(62)	(98)	(215)
SOUTHWEST	22	22	21	21	(30)	(32)	(35)	(40)	(43)	(51)	(63)	(80)	(117)	(91)	(122)	(190)
RG-P	3	3	3	3	(5)	(5)	(5)	(6)	(6)	(7)	(7)	(9)	(13)	(10)	(13)	(20)
Colo	11	11	11	11	(14)	(14)	(16)	(20)	(20)	(25)	(30)	(43)	(71)	(44)	(65)	(114)
G Basin	7	7	7	7	6	5	6	6	6	7	(8)	(10)	(14)	(13)	(18)	(27)
S Pac	1	1	0	0	(5)	(8)	(8)	(8)	(12)	(12)	(17)	(18)	(20)	(24)	(26)	(29)
NORTH PACIFIC	180	179	172	166	87	90	78	73	99	89	103	136	129	115	151	(218)
C Pac	45	45	43	37	25	26	26	29	28	30	33	37	(48)	45	(55)	(79)
PNW	135	133	129	129	62	64	52	44	71	58	70	99	81	70	96	(139)
U.S.	956	947	926	854	360	379	394	403	487	525	576	679	834	775	948	1,572
Gross Deficit					11				23	32	45	79	188	134	255	760

Note: Figures in bold type and parentheses indicate required flow, excluding unconstrained maximum net flow.

[a] $0.021 per 1,000 gallons.
[b] Exceeds 2¢/1,000 gallon marginal cost constraint.

Table 117. GROSS DEFICITS OF FLOW UNDER MINIMUM COST PROGRAMS, BY REGION AND D.O. VARIANTS, 98% AVAILABILITY, 0.0425 ANNUAL FACTOR

(billion gallons per day)

	2000 M		2020 M			2020 H		
	D.O. *(mg/l)*		D.O. *(mg/l)*			D.O. *(mg/l)*		
	1	4	1	4	6	1	4	6
NORTHEAST				1	17	18	42	114
N Eng								
D & H								4
Ches								16
Ohio								
EGL								10
WGL				1	17	18	42	84
U Miss								
L Mo								
SOUTHEAST							10	215
SE							1	187
Cumb							9	25
Tenn								3
L Miss								
L AWR								
MID-CONTINENT		1	5	20	72	47	93	225
U Mo					4	6	13	24
U AWR			1	2	4	5	8	12
W Gulf		1	4	18	64	36	72	189
SOUTHWEST	23	31	40	58	96	69	100	168
RG-P	3	4	4	6	10	7	10	17
Colo	9	14	19	32	60	33	54	103
G Basin			1	3	7	6	11	20
S Pac	11	11	16	17	19	23	25	28
NORTH PACIFIC					3		10	38
C Pac					3		10	34
PNW								4
U.S.	23	30	45	79	188	134	255	760

Note: Deficits computed against maximum net flows.

APPENDIXES

Basic Economic Projections

Water Use Coefficients and Selected Aggregates

Aggregate Withdrawals and Losses by Major Use

Treatment, Dilution, and Treatment Costs of
    Municipal and Industrial Wastes

Estimation of Waste Loads and Treatment Costs

Flow-Storage Relationships and the Cost of Flow

Appendix A

BASIC ECONOMIC PROJECTIONS

Population

The population projections of this study are based on projections prepared by the U.S. Bureau of the Census and published in the *Statistical Abstract: 1966* and in *Current Population Reports*, Series P-25, Nos. 326 and 329.[1] The Medium projection of this study is the Census Series C from No. 329. Distribution by state and water resource region is based on migration assumption II in No. 326. The range between High and Low was based on the RFF projections but modified in accordance with the formula

$$\frac{\dfrac{R'_{Ht}}{R'_{Mt}}}{\dfrac{C'_{Ht}}{C'_{Mt}}} = \frac{\dfrac{R_{Ht}}{R_{Mt}}}{\dfrac{C_{Ht}}{C_{Mt}}},$$

where

R'_{Ht} = High population projection, this study, at time t;

R'_{Mt} = Medium population projection, this study, at time t;

C'_{Ht} = Census projection, Series A, *Statistical Abstract: 1966*, time t;

C'_{Mt} = Census projection, Series C, *Statistical Abstract: 1966*, time t;

R_{Ht} = High population projection, RFF study, time t;

R_{Mt} = Medium population projection, RFF study, time t;

C_{Ht} = Census projection, Series I, *Current Population Reports*, Series P-25, No. 187[2] (the Census projections on which the RFF projections are based);

C_{Mt} = Census projection, Series III, *Current Population Reports*, Series P-25, No. 187.

This procedure yielded a ratio of High to Medium and Low to Medium projections which has the same relation to the 1966 Census projections as the RFF study had to the Census projections on which it was based. The Census range was accepted for 2020 and projections for that year were obtained from those given in the *Statistical Abstract: 1966* by extrapolating Series A, C, and D from 2015 to 2020, based on the rate of growth in the series from 2000 to 2015.

The population projections derived from these methods are given below:

	1980	2000	2020
		(millions)	
Low	220	256	337
Medium	234	304	395
High	255	371	523

For purposes of comparison, other projections for the year 1980 are listed in table A-1. Note that the 1966 Cen-

---

[1] U.S. Bureau of the Census, "Illustrative Projections of the Population of States: 1970 to 1985," *Current Population Reports*, Series P-25, No. 326 (February 7, 1966); and "Revised Projections of the Population of the United States by Age and Sex to 1985," Series P-25, No. 329 (March 10, 1966).

[2] "Illustrative Projections of the Population of the United States, by Age and Sex: 1960 to 1980" (November 10, 1958).

155

sus projections are lower than the earlier ones, reflecting birth rates lower than those assumed earlier. A comparison of the projections for 2000 would show a similar development. Thus, for the Medium projections, this study implicitly assumes the lower birth rates of the 1966 Census projections.

To obtain the population projections relevant to this study – those of the conterminous United States – the population of Alaska and Hawaii had to be deducted. In 1960 these two states contained 0.47 percent of the U.S. population; in 1980, according to Census estimates, they will contain 0.49 percent.[3] We assumed that for all projections and all years 0.49 percent of the U.S. population would reside in Alaska and Hawaii. Thus, the projections for the conterminous United States are:

	1980	2000	2020
		(millions)	
Low	219	255	335
Medium	233	303	393
High	254	369	520

In order to project population by water resource region, the following procedure suggested in Committee Print No. 5[4] was followed:

Let

$$X_t^i = \frac{a_t^i}{b_t^i},$$

where

a_t^i = population in water resource region i, time t;

b_t^i = population in states contained, wholly or partly, in water resource region i, time t.

Thus, given projections of state population, b_t^i can be found and when it is combined with X_t^i, projections of population by water resource region are obtained.

Projections of state populations were found by projecting the percentage distribution of U.S. population by states and then applying the percentages to the projections of U.S. population. Only one such distribution was projected for each target year (1980, 2000, 2020). The 1980 distribution was taken from Bureau of the Census state projections in *Current Population Reports*, Series P–25, No. 326. Projection Series I–B was used because it allowed for more population redistribution than Series II–B, and we wished to allow for considerable interstate migration. The resulting percentage distribution of population by states was compared with that given in Committee Print No. 5, and, with a few exceptions, there were no large differences. Therefore, it was decided to use the 1966 projected percentage distribution for all states. In order to project a

percentage distribution for the year 2000, it was assumed that

$$X_i^{2000} = X_i^{1980} + 1/2 \ (X_i^{1980} - X_i^{1960}),$$

where

X_i^t = percentage of U.S. population in state i, time t.

This assumption corresponds with that made by the Bureau of the Census in Committee Print No. 5 that "the change in the proportion of population in each state between 1980 and 2000 would be the same as the change in the proportion that occurred between 1970 and 1980, as implied by the projections for these dates."[5]

As projected in Committee Print No. 5 for 1980, the percentage of U.S. population in a few states moved in a direction opposite to that of the 1966 Census state projections. For example, Indiana in 1960 had 2.61 percent of the U.S. population; Committee Print No. 5 gives a 1980 projection of 2.73 percent, while the 1966 Census projection is 2.46 percent. For states where this was the case, we adopted the 1966 Census projection for 1980 but kept the proportion constant rather than projecting a further increase or decrease. There were only seven states – Ohio, Indiana, Michigan, Georgia, Idaho, Washington, and Oregon – for which this procedure was necessary.

For the year 2020, it was assumed that:

$$X_i^{2020} = X_i^{2000} + 2/3 \ (X_i^{2000} - X_i^{1980})$$
$$= X_i^{2000} + 2/3 \ [(X_i^{1980} + 1/2 \ (X_i^{1980} - X_i^{1960})) - X_i^{1980}]$$
$$X_i^{2020} = X_i^{2000} + 1/3 \ (X_i^{1980} - X_i^{1960}),$$

where X_i^t is as previously defined. This assumption means that the rate of change in the percentage of U.S. population in a state was assumed to decline from half the 1960–80 change to only a third of that change. Except for the seven states listed above, we have used the change in the percentage distribution of U.S. population as given in the 1966 Census projections for 1960–80 and have then assumed that this change is dampened to half the 1960–80 rate for 1980–2000 and to one-third for 2000–2020. Thus, it is assumed that the regional pattern of population will become increasingly stabilized over the next decades with a corresponding decrease in the rates of interstate migration.

The general nature of the projected regional pattern of population is shown in table A–2. The Northeast and North Central proportion of the U.S. population is projected to decline from 54 percent in 1960 to 47 percent in 2020; the West's proportion is projected to grow from about 15 percent in 1960 to 21 percent in 2020. Thus, the main projected shift in population is from the East to the West, a trend which has held for numerous decades in U.S. history. This shift is important from the point of view of water resource development because it represents movement from generally humid areas to arid or, at least, less humid areas.

For Census geographic divisions, table A–3 presents a comparison of the Census population projections for 1980

[3] *Current Population Reports*, Series P–25, No. 326. Reference is made to Projection Series I–B.

[4] U.S. Senate, Select Committee on National Water Resources, *Population Projections and Economic Assumptions*, 86th Cong., 2d sess. (1960), p. 42.

[5] P. 30.

adopted in this study and projections for 1975 made by the National Planning Association (NPA).[6] For the West South Central and Mountain divisions, the projections appear to be similar in the percentage distribution of populations. For all other divisions except East South Central, the NPA projections display less rapid change in the division shares than the Census projections. Although this may result partly from different assumptions about state changes in fertility rates, the major cause is the difference in assumptions concerning the rates of interstate migration. The Bureau of the Census assumed that gross out-migration rates and in-migration distributions for the 1955–60 period would remain constant throughout the projection period. The NPA made initial projections of interstate migration using 1950–60 net migration rates and then reconciled state population projections with independent projections of state employment. The result of the reconciliation was that "the final projections of net interstate migration are quite different from the migration of the last decade."[7] In sum, NPA projections indicate a more stabilized regional pattern of population than the Census projections. The Census projections, therefore, were used in this report in order to allow for greater changes in population redistribution. As noted above, we assumed that the regional population pattern would become increasingly stable after 1980.

The next step was to project the ratio of water resource region population to the combined population of states contained wholly or partly in the region. The method was similar to that used by the Bureau of the Census in Committee Print No. 5.[8] The ratio was computed for 1940, 1950, and 1960. The projected ratio for 1970 was obtained by adding to the 1960 ratio the change in the ratio between 1950 and 1960. The 2000 ratio was projected by adding to the projected 1970 ratio the change in the ratio from 1940 to 1960. The projected ratio for 1980 was then obtained by linear interpolation. For 2020, the 1950–60 change in the ratio was added to the projected ratio for 2000. Thus, we have assumed that the ratio of population living in the water resource region to the population of all states contained in the region will continue to change in the direction followed in the past, but that the magnitude of the change will diminish over time.

Given the projections of state population and of the relation between water resource region and state population, projections of water resource region population can be derived. For three regions — Lower Missouri and Upper and Lower Arkansas-White-Red — there was some revision of the derived projections because these regions showed declines in population, especially for the Low projection, which were thought to be too large. Although a decline in population in some of the regions is not improbable — for example, Lower Arkansas-White-Red underwent a small decline between 1940 and 1960 — a large decline is unlikely. Accordingly, the projections for these regions were

revised upward. Finally, small changes were made for all regions in order to reconcile the regional totals with the national projections.

Urban Population

In order to determine water losses and pollution loadings for municipalities, it was necessary to project urban population. The projections of U.S. urban population are those of the NPA.[9] The latest Census projections of urban population are those in Committee Print No. 5. Figure A–1 shows

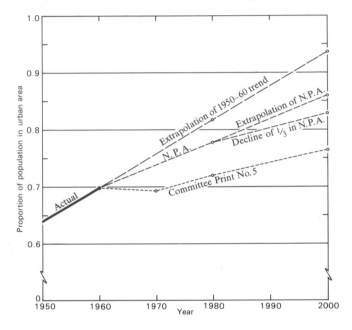

Figure A-1. Comparative population trends.
Sources: National Planning Association, *State Projections to 1975*, Regional Economic Projection Series-Report No. 65-II (October 1965); and U.S. Senate, Select Committee on National Water Resources, *Population Projections and Economic Assumptions*, 86th Cong., 2d sess. (1960), p. 42.

the change in the percentage of population living in urban areas from 1950 to 1960,[10] the Committee Print No. 5 projection, the NPA projection to 1975, a linear extrapolation of the 1950–60 trend, a linear extrapolation of the NPA projection to 2000, and an extrapolated decline of one-third in the NPA projection for years after 1980.

Note that the projections to 1970 of Committee Print No. 5 had already been exceeded by 1960: the actual urban ratio in 1960 was 69.9 percent whereas the projection in Committee Print No. 5 for 1970 was 69.2 percent. Therefore, the urban population projections in Committee Print No. 5 are not used in this study. On the other hand, a linear extrapolation of the 1950–60 trend gives an urban ratio of 81.7 percent for 1980 and 93.5 percent for 2000. Although it is possible that urbanization will continue at the 1950–60 rate and that the above ratios will be attained, it

---

[6] National Planning Association, *State Projections to 1975*, Regional Economic Projection Series Report No. 65-II (October 1965).

[7] NPA, *State Projections to 1975*, p. 93.

[8] P. 31.

[9] NPA, *State Projections to 1975*, p. 111.

[10] For earlier years, the definition of urban areas is noticeably different from that for 1950 and 1960, so it is not possible to obtain a longer time trend.

was decided that the more moderate increase projected by the NPA was more probable. Therefore, the NPA projection for 1975 was extrapolated linearly to obtain a 1980 urban ratio of 77.7 percent. For the period 1980–2000, the NPA rate of increase was decreased by one-third, yielding a projected urban ratio for 2000 of 82.9 percent. This decrease reflects the view that the urban ratio will increase in an asymptotic fashion, the asymptote being equal to one minus the ratio of the farm population necessary to provision urban areas and the rural nonfarm population needed to service the farm population to total population. For the period 2000–2020, the NPA rate was decreased by another one-third, giving a 2020 projected urban ratio of 85.5 percent.

The procedure to obtain the urban populations of water resource regions employed the equation

$$y_t^i = \frac{c_t^i}{d_t^i},$$

where

c_t^i = urban ratio of water resource region i, year t;

d_t^i = urban ratio of states representative of water resource region i, year t.

The method was to project the urban population of all states, obtaining thereby d_t^i, and then to project the ratios, y_t^i. The c_t^i were obtained as the product of the projected d_t^i and y_t^i, following the same projection method used in Committee Print No. 5. We also used the same criterion to determine "representative" states, namely, "all of the states for which a significantly large part was located within the region and for which the urban–rural division would be expected to conform roughly to what would be expected in the water resource region."[11] The representative states of the twenty-two water resource regions are as follows:

New England: Maine, New Hampshire, Massachusetts, Vermont, Rhode Island, Connecticut
Delaware–Hudson: New York, New Jersey, Delaware, Pennsylvania
Chesapeake Bay: Maryland, Virginia (also D.C.)
Ohio: Ohio, Pennsylvania, Kentucky, Indiana, West Virginia
Eastern Great Lakes: Ohio, Michigan
Western Great Lakes: Wisconsin, Illinois
Upper Mississippi: Minnesota, Iowa, Wisconsin, Missouri
Lower Missouri: Missouri, Iowa
Southeast: North Carolina, South Carolina, Georgia, Florida, Alabama, Mississippi
Cumberland: Kentucky, Tennessee
Tennessee: Tennessee
Lower Mississippi: Louisiana, Mississippi
Lower Arkansas-White-Red: Arkansas, Oklahoma
Upper Missouri: North Dakota, South Dakota, Nebraska, Wyoming, Montana, Colorado
Upper Arkansas-White-Red: Oklahoma, Kansas

[11] Committee Print No. 5, p. 13.

Western Gulf: Texas
Upper Rio Grande–Pecos: New Mexico
Colorado: Arizona, Wyoming
Great Basin: Utah, Nevada
South Pacific: California
Central Pacific: California
Pacific Northwest: Oregon, Washington, Idaho

State urban populations were projected in the same manner as the national urban population: NPA state urban ratios for 1975 were projected linearly to 1980; for 1980–2000 the NPA rates of change in the urban ratios were decreased by a third and by another third for the 2000–2020 period. Multiplying the projected state urban ratios by the previously projected state population yielded projected urban population. The projected ratio of urban to total population for the representative states was adopted as the ratio for each region.

It was assumed that the ratios of the water resource region urban ratio to the representative states of the region urban ratio would remain constant at the 1960 level. This assumption was made because these proportions were all clustered around unity and it did not seem profitable to try to project them. Multiplication of these proportions by the projected urban ratio for representative states gave projections of urban ratios for water resource regions. In two cases, however, the procedure resulted in projections of urban ratios exceeding one; consequently they had to be revised. For the South Pacific region, the urban ratio was 91.1 percent in 1950, 93.6 percent in 1960, and was projected to 98.1 percent for 1980. Projections for the South Pacific region exceeded one for 2000 and 2020; the revised projection of 99 percent was then used. This seems to be in line with the trend toward complete urbanization of the region which has occurred in the past. For the Rio Grande-Pecos region, the 1950 urban ratio was 50 percent and the 1960 ratio was 73 percent, indicating rapid urbanization of the area as "desert oases" bloomed. For 1980, the projection procedure yielded a ratio of 89.4 percent, but the 2000 and 2020 projections exceeded one. It is thought that urbanization in this region will not rise much beyond the projected 1980 level — by then, all the possible desert oases will have been developed — and, consequently, our "judgment" projections of the urban ratio are 90 percent for 2000 and 92 percent for 2020.

Multiplication of the projected urban ratios by the projected total population gave projected urban population. A slight revision was necessary in order to make the total for all regions equal the U.S. total.

Standard Metropolitan Statistical Area Population

In 1960 there were 212 Standard Metropolitan Statistical Areas (SMSAs) in the conterminous United States. They contained a population of 116.5 million — 64 percent of the total U.S. population. Note that the projection from Committee Print No. 5 has already been equalled. The reason for this appears to be that the projections of Committee Print No. 5 actually refer only to those areas classified as SMSAs in 1950; no allowance was made for new SMSAs.

Our projections were made by assuming that SMSA population will continue to grow relatively to the population of the United States but at a declining rate. In particular, it was assumed that in 1960-80, 1980-2000, and 2000-2020 the proportion of the U.S. population living in metropolitan areas would grow at 66⅔ percent, 45 percent, and 30 percent, respectively, of the 1940-60 rate. The resulting projections of the percentage of the population residing in metropolitan areas are considerably above those of Committee Print No. 5 and are somewhat lower than the "high metropolitanization" projections in Staff Working Paper No. 9 of the Outdoor Recreation Resources Review Commission (ORRRC). It should be stressed that these projections refer to total metropolitan population, not to the population of areas defined as SMSAs in 1950 and 1960.

Projections of metropolitan area populations for water resource regions were made in the same manner as those for the United States: 67 percent, 45 percent, and 30 percent were applied to the 1940-60 growth rate of metropolitan population as a percentage of the region's total population in order to obtain projections for 1980, 2000, and 2020 respectively. For a few regions — Western Gulf, Rio Grande-Pecos, Colorado, and the Great Basin — by 2000 or 2020 the fractions derived exceeded unity because of the exceptionally fast pace of metropolitanization in these areas in the past twenty-five years. For these regions, revisions were made on a judgmental basis. Finally, the regional projections were reconciled with the national projection.

Gross National Product

Projections of GNP were obtained by projecting the size of the labor force and then applying rates of productivity increase. The size of the labor force was found by applying projected labor force participation rates to projections of the population 14 years old and over. For 1980, the latter are given in the 1966 Bureau of the Census population projections,[12] and for 2000 and 2020 it was assumed that the proportion of the population 14 years old and over would be similar to the proportions given in the 1964 Census projections for 2000.[13] The 1980 labor force participation rate was taken to be that projected by Cooper and Johnston in 1965, 58.3 percent.[14] Because the Bureau of Labor Statistics projections of participation rates to 1970 and 1980 coincide more closely with the RFF High participation rates than with RFF Mediums, the RFF 2000 High — 59.9 percent — was chosen to be the 2000 participation rate. The rate was assumed to increase to 60 percent by 2020.

Projected increases in GNP per worker were those used by RFF for 1960-2000: High, 2.5 percent per year; Medium, 2 percent; Low, 1.7 percent. These rates of increase were applied to the 1965 GNP per worker of $8,027 (1960 dollars) to obtain projections of GNP per worker in 1980, 2000, and 2020. Multiplying by the previously described labor force projections, one obtains GNP projections. The assumption about unemployment is that the 1965 rate — about 4½ percent of the labor force — will be maintained.

Table A-4 presents our projections of GNP, along with others. Most of the other projections are contained within the Lows and Highs of this study. The reader is referred to the sources for the table for an explanation of the differences in projections. For example, the difference between our Low and the NPA Low is that the latter assumes an unemployment rate of 7½ percent; the difference between the 2000 RFF High and our High is explained by the former's higher rate of population growth.

Agriculture: Irrigated Acreage

Projections of irrigated acreage were made for the Senate Select Committee by the U.S. Department of Agriculture (USDA).[15] The first step was to project the future demand for food and fiber products. After allowing for the conversion of farmland to nonfarm (i.e., urban) uses, an estimate of additional acreage necessary to meet future demands was obtained. On the basis of the latter, estimates of additional irrigated acreage were made.

More recent projections have been made by Vernon Ruttan and George A. Pavelis.[16] Ruttan's "demand model" projections are based on a statistically derived Cobb-Douglas production function for farm output, a projection of demand for each region's farm output, and a determination of demand for irrigated land found by equating the marginal product of irrigated land with the cost of the land.[17] The "equilibrium model" is not really a projection model but serves "as a check on the results of procedures aimed at providing acreage projections for specific dates."[18]

Pavelis's projections are based on equations of the form

$$L - A_t = (L - A_{1959}) e^{-Bt},$$

where

L = upper limit of irrigated acreage,

A_t = irrigated acreage in year t,

B = statistically determined constant.

---

[12] *Current Population Reports*, Series P-25, No. 326.

[13] Actually, the somewhat lower population growth rates of the 1966 Census projections mean that the proportion of the population 14 years of age and over would be somewhat higher than that of the 1964 Census projections. However, the degree of change is indeterminate and probably small.

[14] Sophia Cooper and Denis F. Johnston, "Labor Force Projections for 1970-80," *Monthly Labor Review*, February 1965. These projections were based on 1964 Census population projections; adjustments to coincide with 1966 Census projections would cause little change in the overall rate.

[15] U.S. Senate, Select Committee on National Water Resources, Committee Print No. 12, *Land and Water Potentials and Future Requirements for Water*, 86th Cong., 1st sess. (1960).

[16] Vernon W. Ruttan, *The Economic Demand for Irrigated Acreage: New Methodology and Some Preliminary Projections, 1954-1980* (The Johns Hopkins Press for Resources for the Future, 1965). George A. Pavelis, "Irrigation Policy and Long-Term Growth Functions," *Agricultural Economics Research*, April 1965, and unpublished worksheets.

[17] "Cost" is taken here to be "full cost," i.e., including full amortization and operation-maintenance costs of irrigation project costs.

[18] Ruttan, *Economic Demand*, p. 25.

There are three specified values of L. The total remaining potential irrigable acreage is "construed to be the maximum acreage of soils feasibly irrigated (i.e., costs $\leq$ benefits at the extensive margin), given prevailing notions of natural moisture and yearly moisture deficiencies, future irrigation returns in relation to costs, and foreseen limits on water supplies."[19] The total remaining potentially irrigable acreage is divided into that which is susceptible to development by nonfederal efforts and that which will be developed in connection with federal projects. The first value of L (L_{100}) rests on the assumption of 100 percent development of both the remaining federal and nonfederal potential; the second (L_{50}) is based on the assumption that both federal and nonfederal development will be at 50 percent of potential; and the third represents 25 percent development of the federal potential and 50 percent of the nonfederal. Thus, Pavelis obtains three patterns of projected irrigated acreage which we call "High," "Medium," and "Low" and which represent alternative policies concerning the growth of irrigated acreage.

We believe that both the Ruttan and the Pavelis studies represent advances over the USDA study for the Select Committee, although both remain subject to limitations; for example, the Ruttan study does not incorporate a land constraint into the projections, while the Pavelis study does not consider demand factors. Pavelis's projections were adopted for this study because he provided projections to 2020 for the same regions we have specified; Ruttan's study contains projections only to 1980 and for somewhat differently defined regions.

The three projections are summarized in tables A-5 and A-6. As shown in table A-5, the projections for the western regions are roughly similar; however, for the eastern regions, Pavelis's projections are considerably below Ruttan's figure for 1980 and the USDA High for 1980; they are also well below the USDA Medium and High projections for 2000.

Projections of water required for agricultural domestic use and stock watering were made by directly extrapolating water use. The method of extrapolation is described elsewhere.

Mining

Projections of mining output were made for bituminous coal, copper ore, iron ore, phosphate rock, sand and gravel, crude petroleum, natural gas, natural gas liquids, and "all other minerals." The projections are given in table 8.

The 1980 projections for bituminous coal, copper ore, iron ore, phosphate rock, sand and gravel, and all other minerals are based on projections of the Bureau of Mines.[20] The 1980 Medium projections were found by: (1) interpolating to 1980 the Bureau's projections for 1975 and 1985, and (2) multiplying the interpolated projection by the ratio of GNP as projected in this study to the Bureau's projected GNP ($929 billion, 1960 prices), in order to

account for the higher rate of economic growth projected in this study than in the Bureau's. The 1980 Lows and Highs were found by utilizing the RFF projections of the mining sectors of the Federal Reserve Board's (FRB's) index of industrial production. The ratios of RFF Low to Medium and High to Medium projections were computed and multiplied by our Medium projections to yield Lows and Highs. The projections used were: for bituminous coal, coal mining; for copper and iron ore, metal mining; for phosphate rock, sand and gravel; and for all other minerals, stone and earth materials.

The 2000 Medium projections were obtained by adjusting the 1980-2000 RFF Medium growth rates for the above sectors by the 1960-80 growth rates of the Bureau of Mines projections. It was assumed that

$$\frac{Y_{2000}}{Y_{1980}} = \frac{Y_{1980}/Y_{1960}}{X_{1980}/X_{1960}} \left(\frac{X_{2000}}{X_{1980}}\right),$$

where

Y_t = Bureau of Mines projection, year t;

X_t = RFF Medium projection, year t.

Thus in those sectors for which the Bureau of Mines projected a higher growth rate for 1960-80 than did RFF, the RFF 1980-2000 Medium growth rate was adjusted upward to obtain Medium projections for 2000 and vice versa when the Bureau's 1960-80 growth rates were lower. The 2000 Low and High projections were found by the same method used for 1980 Highs and Lows.

Low, Medium, and High projections for 2020 were found by keeping the 1980-2000 growth rate constant for all sectors and for Low, Medium, and High.

The 1980 Medium projections of crude petroleum and natural gas production were taken from a paper presented by the Bureau of Mines at the 1966 World Power Congress. The 1980 Medium projection for the output of natural gas liquids was taken from the RFF study; Lows and Highs were estimated on the same basis as that used for the sectors described above. It was assumed that because of the exhaustion of reserves[21] the production of crude petroleum, natural gas, and natural gas liquids would reach a peak between 1980 and 2000 and that by 2000 production would return to the 1980 levels, remaining at these levels over the period 2000-2020. Additional projections were based on the assumption that the output of the three oil and gas sectors would decline after 1980.

Table A-7 presents a comparison of the 1980 mining projections of this study with the mining projections of other authors. It can be seen that our mining output projections represent a fairly high range of growth, but one which is not at all improbable when compared with the projections of other authors.

---

[19] Pavelis, "Irrigation Policy."

[20] Alvin Kaufman and Mildred Nadler, *Water Use in the Mineral Industry*, U.S. Bureau of Mines Information Circular 8285 (1966).

[21] For a discussion of the probable course of the output of the oil and gas sectors see Sam H. Schurr et al., *Energy in the American Economy, 1850-1975* (The Johns Hopkins Press for Resources for the Future, 1960).

No regional allocation of mining output was projected. Instead, projections were made directly of the regional distribution of water use, as described in appendix B.

Manufacturing

Projections of value added were made for five two-digit[22] manufacturing sectors: food and kindred products, paper and allied products, chemicals and allied products, petroleum and related products, and primary metals. The projections are given on an index number basis in table 6. The base is 1959 value added.

The projections for 1980 and 2000 were obtained by multiplying the RFF projections of the FRB indexes of industrial production by the ratio of GNP projected in this study to the GNP projected by RFF; thus, they are RFF projections as modified by differences in projections of the aggregate rate of economic growth, assuming a unitary GNP elasticity of production in all sectors.[23]

Projections of value added for 2020 were obtained by computing the ratio of value added by each sector to GNP for 1960, 1980, and 2000 along each of the growth paths. It was noted that this ratio tended to increase or decrease at a declining rate, and it was assumed that this tendency would continue through 2020. Therefore, letting X_t = ratio of value added to GNP, year t, we assumed that

$$X_{2020} - X_{2000} = (X_{2000} - X_{1980}) \frac{X_{2000} - X_{1980}}{X_{1980} - X_{1960}} .$$

That is, the ratio of the change between 2000 and 2020 to that between 1980 and 2000 would equal the ratio of the change between 1980 and 2000 to that between 1960 and 1980, which means that the ratio would continue to decrease or increase at a declining rate. The 2020 projected ratio of value added by each of the sectors to GNP was multiplied by projected GNP for 2020 to obtain the projections of value added.

Table A–8 presents a comparison of the 1980 manufacturing projections of this study with those of three other studies. Of the twelve projected figures compared with those of this study, six fall within 10 percent of our Medium projections; of the remaining six, only two — those of ORRRC for paper and pulp products and for chemical products — fall outside the range of our Highs and Lows. The ORRRC projections, under current conditions, are somewhat high: these projections were made by NPA with a projected 1976 GNP of $1,018 billion (1959 dollars), but the NPA projection made in 1966 implies a 1976 GNP projection of $942 billion in 1959 prices.[24] This reduction

of 7.5 percent in the projection of GNP supports a downward revision of the projections of manufacturing output. Such a reduction would still leave the ORRRC projections for chemicals and for paper closer to our Highs than to our Mediums, however. The reduction in ORRRC projections would probably bring the primary metals and the petroleum projections within 10 percent of our Medium projections for these sectors.

Although four out of five of the projections inferred from Almon's growth rates of output[25] are within 10 percent of our projections, they all are higher than ours. This is partly because Almon used the 1964 Census population projections which are higher than the 1966 Census projections used in this study. Use of the latter would bring the projections inferred from Almon's growth rates even closer to the projections of this study.

The method for projecting water use was to relate use to value added by means of a "water coefficient" giving water use per dollar of value added. Because our coefficients were derived from the *U.S. Census of Manufactures*, they refer to water use per dollar of value added by establishments using 20 million gallons or more of water per year. (Such establishments account for about 97 percent of all water intake by manufacturing industries.) Thus the projections needed are those of value added, not by the entire industry but by establishments using 20 million gallons or more per year.[26] In order to obtain such projections it was assumed that the percentage of value added in an industry by users of 20 million gallons and more would be the same as the 1959 percentages. That this assumption misses the mark somewhat is shown by the following Census data:[27]

	Percentage of industry value added by users of 20 mgy and over	
	1959	1963
Food products	43.3	44.0
Paper products	59.6	49.4
Chemicals	68.5	76.8
Petroleum & coal products	86.4	81.2
Primary metals	78.5	68.7

[22] As classified in the *Standard Industrial Classification Manual*, U.S. Technical Committee on Industrial Classification, Office of Statistical Standards, Bureau of the Budget (1957).

[23] For the food products sector, the RFF projections were modified by multiplying by the ratio of population as projected in this study to that projected by RFF. That is, a unitary population elasticity was assumed for production of food products.

[24] This is an extrapolation to 1976 of NPA's projection of GNP in 1975, based on the projected 1964–75 growth rate.

[25] Clopper Almon, Jr., *The American Economy to 1975* (Harper & Row, 1966). See table A–10.

[26] Assume, for example, the following data:

Year	Freshwater intake *(mil. gals.)*	Value added by establishments using 20 mgy and over *($ mil.)*	Intake coefficient	Value added, entire industry *($ mil.)*
1959	10,000	100	100	200
1980	–	–	80	400

It is desired to project freshwater intake for 1980. If we say that this equals 80 × 400 = 32,000 million gallons, then by the same logic 1959 intake = 100 × 200 = 20,000 million gallons whereas, in fact, the latter is 10,000 million = 100 × 100. Therefore, we must project not only total industry value added, but that for establishments using 20 million gallons and more per year.

[27] *U.S. Census of Manufactures: 1958*, "Industrial Water Use," (1961); and *U.S. Census of Manufactures: 1963*, "Water Use in Manufacturing" (1966). Water use data in the former are for 1959.

However, it seems to us that these data probably reflect random variations rather than systematic time trends. Therefore, the assumption mentioned above was maintained.

Committee Print No. 8 – *Future Water Requirements of Principal Water-Using Industries*[28] – was used to distribute the national projections of value added by water resource region for the five major water-related manufacturing classes. (A different procedure, described below, was used for all other manufacturing classes.) From appendix tables in Committee Print No. 8, percentage distributions of value added by water resource region as projected by the Business and Defense Services Administration of the Department of Commerce were calculated for 1980 and 2000. These percentage distributions were then applied to our projections of national value added for 1980 and 2000 to obtain projections by water resource regions. For 2020 it was assumed that

$$X^{ij}_{2020} = X^{ij}_{2000} + 2/3 \, (X^{ij}_{2000} - X^{ij}_{1980})$$

where

X^{ij}_t = percent of national value added by industry originating in region i at time t.

That is, we assumed that the regional percentage distribution of value added would tend to stabilize, thereby changing at, say, only two-thirds of the 1980–2000 change. Tables A–9 to A–13 give the projections of value added for establishments with a water intake of 20 million gallons and over by region.

All other manufacturing classes were assumed to grow in accordance with the indexes of output shown in table 6. It was also assumed that the growth rate would be uniform in all regions, based on the level of activity reported in each region in the *Census of Manufactures: 1958*.

Steam-Electric Power

Projections of steam-electric power production were based on a study made by the Federal Power Commission (FPC) in 1964.[29] The Commission's projections extended only to 1980; consequently, a variety of techniques were used to extrapolate these to 2000 and 2020.

The 1980 Medium projection of public utility steam-electric power is the FPC 1980 projection modified slightly to account for differences between the GNP projections of the FPC and those in this study. The 1980 High and Low projections were obtained by multiplying the 1980 Medium projection by the ratios of the RFF High and Low projections of 1980 kilowatt-hours generated to the RFF 1980 Medium projections. Thus, our Low and High have the same relationship to our Medium projection as the RFF Low and High have to the RFF Medium.

To obtain a Medium projection for 2000, the FPC projection for 2000 that appeared in Committee Print No. 10 was multiplied by the ratio of the FPC 1980 projection appearing in the *National Power Survey* to the FPC 1980 projection appearing in Committee Print No. 10.[30] Low and High projections for 2000 were obtained in the same manner as for 1980.

Low, Medium and High projections for steam-electric power output in 2020 were found from projections of kilowatt-hours produced per dollar of GNP. The following table shows the rather rapid increase in the production of kilowatt-hours by steam-electric power per dollar of GNP in recent years and the projected production for future years:

1940	1950	1960		1980	2000	2020
			Low	1.59	1.62	1.65
0.45	0.61	1.21	Medium	2.04	2.10	2.16
			High	2.66	2.64	2.64

The Medium projection of steam-electric power output for 1980 implies a rate of increase in this ratio which is less than the rate of increase in 1950–60, while there is almost no increase between 1980 and 2000 implied by the 2000 projections. To conform with the projected slowdown, the 2020 projections were extrapolated from 2000 at the 1980–2000 rate of increase. Multiplication of these projections by 2020 GNP projections gave 2020 projections of power output.

Table A–14 gives the projections of steam-electric power generation used in this report and also those of earlier studies. The increase in our projections over those of the 1960 FPC and 1962 RFF studies result from the upward revision of FPC projections made in 1964.

In order to distribute national steam-electric power generation by water resource region, a regional percentage distribution of the FPC projections for the Senate Select Committee was used.[31] For 1980 and 2000 the national projections were distributed by region in accordance with the FPC distribution. For the 2020 regional distribution, it was assumed that

$$X^i_{2020} = X^i_{2000} + 2/3 \, (X^i_{2000} - X^i_{1950}),$$

where

X^i_t = percentage of national steam-electric power output in region i at time t.

This assumption corresponds with that used elsewhere in this report — that the regional distribution of outputs tends to stabilize over time.

Table A–15 gives the regional projections of utility steam-electric power output.

---

[28] Senate Select Committee on National Water Resources, 86th Cong., 2d sess. (1960).

[29] Federal Power Commission, *National Power Survey: A Report* (1964).

[30] *Electric Power in Relation to the Nation's Water Resources*, Senate Select Committee on National Water Resources, 86th Cong., 2d sess. (1960).

[31] In Committee Print No. 10, the FPC projections were divided into projections for power supply regions. FPC materials prepared for the Senate Select Committee's use contained projections by water resource regions for 1980 and 2000.

Comparisons with Other Projections of Economic Activity

Over the past few years, several economic studies of individual water resource regions have been made.

1. New England: *Projective Economic Studies of New England*, Arthur D. Little, Inc., for the U.S. Army Corps of Engineers (1964).

2. Chesapeake Bay: Preliminary summary tables of the Chesapeake Bay-Susquehanna River Basin, National Planning Association, 1966.

3. Ohio: *Ohio River Comprehensive Study*, appendix B, "Projective Economic Study of the Ohio River Basin," Arthur D. Little, Inc. for the U.S. Army Corps of Engineers (1964).

4. Eastern Great Lakes: *Preliminary Economic Projections for the Great Lakes Area*, Office of Business Economics, Department of Commerce (1965).

5. Cumberland and Tennessee: *Preliminary Economic Projections for the Appalachia Region*, Office of Business Economics, Department of Commerce (1965).

6. Upper Missouri: *Preliminary Economic Projections for the Missouri River Basin Area*, Office of Business Economics, Department of Commerce (1965).

7. Western Gulf: *Water for Texas – A Plan for the Future*, Texas Water Development Board (1966).

8. Pacific Northwest: *Pacific Northwest Economic Base Study*, Bonneville Power Administration, U.S. Department of the Interior (1965).

Other studies – for example, the Delaware River Commission's study of the Delaware River Basin, the Battelle Institute's study of the Susquehanna Basin, and studies conducted by various states – are not referred to because they cover regions that are not comparable to those of this report. Even for the studies listed, the precise area covered is generally somewhat different than in this report, as can be seen from the comparison of 1960 population estimates. The Cumberland–Tennessee and the Pacific Northwest studies were undertaken in reference to problems other than water. The former is a study of the Appalachia region, from which projections for the Cumberland–Tennessee region were extracted for our study, and the latter is a survey of the demand for power.

Finally, many of the regional studies projected industrial growth by means of employment, while the projections of this report are in terms of value added. In order to compare these magnitudes, we put the employment projections on an index number basis and also converted the NPA's projections of GNP (value added plus depreciation) originating per employee[32] to an index number basis, then computed the product of these to give an index of value added. For example, the Office of Business Economics (OBE) gives employment in the paper and allied products industry in the Eastern Great Lakes region as 39,000 in 1960 and projects this to 42,000 in 1980. Thus, the 1980 employment

index (1960 = 100) is 108. The NPA estimates the GNP originating per employee in the paper and products industry to be $8,900 in 1959 and projects this to $15,400 in 1976. With appropriate adjustments the 1980 index of GNP originating per employee, with 1960 as base, is 182. The product of 1.08 and 1.82 is 1.97, or the index of value added for the paper and products industry in the Eastern Great Lakes region is implicitly projected by the OBE and NPA to be 197 in 1980 (1960 = 100).

Brief summaries and tables comparing the projections of the regional studies with those of this report are given below. Of the eight studies considered, three contained both higher and lower projections than those in this report; the projections of the other five studies were all higher. Part of the difference between our projections and the others is explained by the fact that the regional projections were tied to earlier and higher Census projections of population than those in this study. To the extent that this accounts for the size of the regional projections, there is no problem of consistency among them. However, even after allowing for this factor, the regional projections are still rather high and pose the problem of interregional consistency and consistency with national aggregates. None of the cited studies contained information on consistency with national projections.

It was attempted to ascertain whether the projections of population were consistent with the economic base represented by the industrial projections. No readily available answer could be obtained because, even after allowing for high base multipliers, the industrial projections represented only a small amount of the total employment. In the brief summaries below, the projections of the regional studies are compared with those of this study. (Also see tables A-16 to A-23.)

1. *New England* – Population projections made by Arthur D. Little, Inc., for New England are tied to national population projections made by the Bureau of the Census in 1962 which, as pointed out above, are higher than the 1966 Census projections. The New England population projections fall between the Mediums and Highs of this report. The projections of output of the New England chemical industry also fall between our Mediums and Highs, the pulp and paper industry is higher than our Highs, and the primary metals industry falls between our Lows and Mediums. Because the latter industry is less important than the other two, the Little industrial projections can be said to be, on the whole, between our Mediums and Highs.

2. *Chesapeake Bay* – The NPA Chesapeake Bay population projections are tied to the national population projections made by the Census Bureau in 1964. These are higher than our national population projections, so it is not surprising that the NPA Chesapeake Bay population projections are between our Mediums and Highs. The NPA paper, chemicals, and primary metals projections fall between our Lows and Mediums; the petroleum projection is below our Low, while the food products projection is between our Medium and High. Thus, the NPA Chesapeake Bay industrial projections are, on the whole, lower than those of this report.

[32] Outdoor Recreation Resources Review Commission, *Projections to the Years 1976 and 2000: Economic Growth, Population, Labor Force and Leisure, and Transportation*, Study Report 23 (1962), p. 224. These projections were prepared by NPA.

3. *Ohio* – The Arthur D. Little Ohio population projections, tied to the 1964 Census national projections, fall between our Medium and High. The paper and petroleum projections are above our Highs, while the food products projection falls between our Medium and High. The primary metals projection falls between our Lows and Mediums.

4. *Eastern Great Lakes* – The OBE's population projection for 1980 falls between our Medium and High, while those for 2000 and 2020 fall between our Low and Medium. The projections for the paper and petroleum industries are above our Highs; the food industry, between our Mediums and Highs. The chemicals and primary metals industries are, for 1980, at our Medium, and for 2000 are between our Medium and High. Thus, while the population projections are somewhat lower than ours, the industrial projections are higher.

5. *Cumberland and Tennessee* – The projections were taken from the OBE's study of the Appalachia region. The population projections are above our Highs. From 1920–40, the population of the region grew 28 percent, from 2.9 to 3.7 million and, from 1940–60, 19 percent, from 3.7 to 4.2 million. OBE assumes a higher rate of population growth than has prevailed at any time in the last forty years. The industrial projections for the region display a corresponding rate of growth.

6. *Upper Missouri* – The OBE's population projections for the Upper Missouri region fall between our Medium and High, while all industrial projections are higher than our Highs. The chemicals sector is projected to expand seventeenfold and the petroleum sector, eightfold over a forty-year period. This would imply an annual increase of about 7½ percent in the chemicals sector and about 5½ percent in petroleum refining.

7. *Western Gulf* – The only projection available was that for population, which lies along or above our High projection. A tripling rather than a doubling of the population of this region by 2020 is a possibility and should not be ruled out.

8. *Pacific Northwest* – The population projections lie above or along our Highs, while the industrial projections are distinctly lower than ours, except for petroleum refining which is insignificant in the region. Our estimated output of pulp and paper for 1980 Medium is about 2.7 times greater than the Bonneville Power Administration's (BPA's) estimate. Because of the polluting effects of pulp and paper a difference of this magnitude is critical. If production grows at the slower rate projected by BPA, either we have underestimated the output of pulp and paper in other regions or we have overestimated the national level of production. The estimates made by others of pulp and paper production for 1980 in the New England, Ohio, Eastern Great Lakes, Cumberland, and Tennessee regions, all show greater rates of growth than those we have used, indicating the possibility of a greater interregional shift than we have taken into account. Should such a shift occur, the net effect would be to increase the pressure on water supplies, since our High projections for the Eastern Great Lakes and Cumberland regions indicate relatively little margin by the year 2020. The Southeast is also projected as a shortage region for 2020 High.[33]

[33] Since the foregoing was written, the First National Assessment of the Water Resources Council, *The Nation's Water Resources*, has appeared. Time did not permit any comparisons.

Table A-1. COMPARATIVE PROJECTIONS OF THE U.S. POPULATION FOR 1980

(millions)

	Census (1958)	ORRRC (1962)	RFF (1963)	Census (1964)	NPA (1965)	Census (1966)
L	231 (Series IV)	231[a]	226	233 (Series D)		226 (Series D)
M	245 (Series III)	245[a]	245	236 (Series C)	245[b]	234 (Series C)
H	273 (Series I)	259[a]	279	252 (Series A)		249 (Series A)

Sources: U.S. Bureau of the Census, *Current Population Reports*, Series P-25, No. 187 (November 10, 1958), No. 286 (July 10, 1964), and No. 329 (March 10, 1966); Outdoor Recreation Resources Review Commission, Working Paper No. 8 (1962); Hans H. Landsberg, Leonard L. Fischman, and Joseph L. Fisher, *Resources in America's Future* (The Johns Hopkins Press for Resources for the Future, 1963); and National Planning Association, *State Projections to 1975*, Regional Economic Projection Series-Report No. 65-II (October 1965).

[a]Obtained by extrapolating the 1976 projection to 1980, using the 1960-76 rate of growth.

[b]Obtained by extrapolating the 1975 projection to 1980, using the 1960-75 rate of growth. The NPA projection is based on the Census projection of 1964 (above), Series B (not listed above).

Table A-2. POPULATION OF SELECTED REGIONS AS A PERCENTAGE OF THE POPULATION OF THE CONTERMINOUS UNITED STATES

	1960	1980	2000	2020
Northeast	25.03	23.35	22.41	21.84
North Central	28.91	26.82	26.00	25.46
South	30.79	31.28	31.33	31.41
West	15.23	18.59	20.24	21.35

Note: Regions are aggregates of states as defined by the U.S. Bureau of the Census.

Table A-3. POPULATION OF SELECTED DIVISIONS AS A PERCENTAGE OF THE POPULATION OF THE CONTERMINOUS UNITED STATES

	Census (1960)	NPA[a] (1975)	This study[b] (1980)
New England	5.89	5.80	5.59
Mid-Atlantic	19.14	18.49	17.76
East North Central	20.29	19.76	19.30
West North Central	8.62	8.10	7.52
South Atlantic	14.55	15.00	15.56
East South Central	6.75	6.13	6.22
West South Central	9.49	9.49	9.50
Mountain	3.83	4.35	4.57
Pacific	11.40	12.84	14.02

Note: U.S. Bureau of the Census geographic divisions.

[a]National Planning Association, *State Projections to 1975*, Regional Economic Projection Series-Report No. 65-II (October 1965).

[b]Our medium projections put into Bureau of the Census divisions.

Table A-4. COMPARATIVE PROJECTIONS OF GNP

($ billion, 1960)

		This study	Knowles[a] (1960)	RFF (1963)	Little (1964)	NPA[b] (1965)	OBE (1965)
1980	L	1,023	1,009	965		968	
	M	1,091	1,116	1,060	1,068	1,079	1,142
	H	1,209	1,260	1,250		1,140	
2000	L	1,680		1,680			
	M	2,151		2,200	2,174		2,450
	H	2,914		3,290			
2020	L	3,103					
	M	4,150			4,401		5,357
	H	6,708					

Sources: James W. Knowles, *The Potential Economic Growth in the United States*, Study Paper No. 20, Joint Economic Committee (1960); Hans H. Landsberg, Leonard L. Fischman, and Joseph L. Fisher, *Resources in America's Future* (The Johns Hopkins Press for Resources for the Future, 1963); *Projective Economic Studies of New England*, prepared for the U.S. Army Corps of Engineers by Arthur D. Little, Inc. (1964); National Planning Association, *State Projections to 1975*, Regional Economic Projection Series-Report No. 65-II (October 1965); and *Preliminary Economic Projections for the Missouri River Basin Area*, prepared for the ad hoc Water Resources Council by the Office of Business Economics, U.S. Department of Commerce (1965).

[a]Projections represent the extension of Knowles's projections to 1980 on the basis of projected 1959-75 growth rates.

[b]Projections for 1980 represent extrapolations of NPA 1975 projections based on 1964-75 growth rates.

Table A–5. COMPARATIVE PROJECTIONS OF IRRI-GATED ACREAGE, EAST AND WEST

(thousand acres)

		Pavelis (Medium)	Ruttan (Demand model)	USDA (Medium)
U.S.				
	L	41,392		35,042
1980	M	43,236	49,733	36,700
	H	46,220		50,601
	L	43,886		34,823
2000	M	46,935		55,512
	H	53,051		78,491
EAST:				
	L	4,062		3,245
1980	M	4,130	12,343	3,707
	H	4,413		11,322
	L	5,141		3,281
2000	M	5,303		15,067
	H	6,045		30,661
WEST:				
	L	37,330		31,797
1980	M	39,106	37,390	32,943
	H	41,807		39,279
	L	38,745		31,543
2000	M	41,632		40,445
	H	47,006		47,830

Sources: George A. Pavelis, "Irrigation Policy and Long-Term Growth Functions," *Agricultural Economics Research* (April 1965); Vernon W. Ruttan, *The Economic Demand for Irrigated Acreage* (The Johns Hopkins Press for Resources for the Future, 1965); and Committee Print No. 12, *Land and Water Potentials and Future Requirements for Water*, prepared by the U.S. Department of Agriculture for the Senate Select Committee on National Water Resources, 86th Cong., 1st sess. (1960).

Note: East = Northeast and Southeast divisions; West = Mid-continent, Southwest, and North Pacific divisions.

Table A–6. COMPARATIVE PROJECTIONS OF IRRI-GATED ACREAGE, BY REGION: 1980

(thousand acres)

	USDA (Medium)	Pavelis (Medium)	Ruttan (Demand model)
N Eng	80	23	
D & H	195	259	3,390[a]
Ches	78	135	
Ohio	93	73	
EGL	42	61	
WGL	71	104	876[b]
U Miss	101	154	215[c]
L Mo	21	49	
SE	1,079	785	
Cumb	7	7	4,299[d]
Tenn	34	64	
L Miss	918	1,170	901
L AWR	990	1,246	2,672
U Mo	6,287	7,601	4,668
U AWR	1,681	3,398	1,698
W Gulf	5,126	6,366	7,137
RG-P	1,416	1,571	1,955
Colo	3,280	3,340	1,674
G Basin	2,257	2,130	1,229
S Pac	816	1,075	2,257
C Pac	6,869	7,634	10,928
PNW	5,262	5,991	5,844
U.S.	36,700	43,236	49,733

Sources: Committee Print No. 12, *Land and Water Potentials and Future Requirements for Water*, prepared by the U.S. Department of Agriculture for the Senate Select Committee on National Water Resources, 86th Cong., 1st sess. (1960); George A. Pavelis, "Irrigation Policy and Long-Term Growth Functions," *Agricultural Economics Research* (April 1965); and Vernon W. Ruttan, *The Economic Demand for Irrigated Acreage* (The Johns Hopkins Press for Resources for the Future, 1965).

[a]Total for Delaware-Hudson, New England, and Chesapeake Bay.
[b]Total for Western and Eastern Great Lakes.
[c]Total for Upper Mississippi, Ohio, and Lower Missouri.
[d]Total for Cumberland, Southeast, and Tennessee.

Table A–7. COMPARATIVE PROJECTIONS OF MINING PRODUCTION FOR 1980

(1960 = 100)

		ORRRC[a] (1962)	RFF (1963)	Almon[b] (1966)		This study
Coal mining[c]	L		112		149	
	M	196	145	155	193	
	H		202		268	
Oil and gas[d]	L		142		89	157
	M	222	177	176	107	197
	H		228		136	253
Metals[e]	L		93		125	
	M	168	138	194	186	
	H		196		264	
Stone and earth minerals[f]	L		139		238	
	M	271	204	179	349	
	H		296		506	

Sources: Outdoor Recreation Resources Review Commission, *Projections to the Years 1976 and 2000: Economic Growth, Population, Labor Force and Leisure, and Transportation*, Study Report 23 (1962); Hans H. Landsberg, Leonard L. Fischman, and Joseph L. Fisher, *Resources in America's Future* (The Johns Hopkins Press for Resources for the Future, 1963); Clopper Almon, Jr., *The American Economy to 1975* (Harper & Row, 1966).

[a]Projections for 1976 (prepared for ORRRC by the National Planning Association) were extrapolated to 1980 on the basis of the 1957–76 growth rate.

[b]Represents an extrapolation of Federal Reserve Board indexes of production for 1963 to 1980 based on Almon's 1963–75 rates of growth in gross output.

[c]Figures for this study for bituminous coal only.

[d]Figures for this study — on the left, crude petroleum only; on the right, natural gas only.

[e]Figures for this study for iron ore only.

[f]Figures for this study for sand and gravel only.

Table A-8. COMPARATIVE PROJECTIONS OF
MANUFACTURING OUTPUT FOR 1980
(1960 = 100)

		ORRRC[a] (1962)	Almon[b] (1966)	Little[c] (1964)	This study
Food	L				145
	M	162	190		161
	H				217
Paper and pulp	L				195
	M	273	229		225
	H				243
Chemicals	L				183
	M	446	264	269	250
	H				379
Petroleum	L				150
	M	202	192		176
	H				212
Primary metals	L				131
	M	222	203	160	191
	H				253

Sources: Outdoor Recreation Resources Review Commission, *Projections to the Years 1976 and 2000: Economic Growth, Population, Labor Force and Leisure, and Transportation,* Study Report 23 (1962); Clopper Almon, Jr., *The American Economy to 1975* (Harper & Row, 1966); and *Projective Economic Studies of New England*, prepared for the U.S. Army Corps of Engineers by Arthur D. Little, Inc. (1964).

[a]National Planning Association projections for ORRRC of Federal Reserve Board indexes of production extrapolated to 1980 on the basis of the 1957–75 growth rate.

[b]Represents extrapolation to 1980 of the 1963 FRB indexes based on Almon's 1963–75 growth rates in gross output in the industries. To obtain two-digit sectors from some of Almon's three-digit sectors the latter were weighted by 1963 percentages of two-digit value added.

[c]Represents the index of A.D. Little projections of U.S. value added.

Table A-9. VALUE ADDED BY FOOD AND KINDRED PRODUCTS, BY REGION

($ million, 1960)

	1960	1980 L	1980 M	1980 H	2000 L	2000 M	2000 H	2020 L	2020 M	2020 H
NORTHEAST	5,692	7,823	8,638	11,666	10,435	13,309	24,535	16,487	21,368	52,175
N Eng	228	228	252	340	246	314	578	360	466	1,138
D & H	1,325	1,788	1,974	2,667	2,326	2,967	5,469	3,597	4,662	11,384
Ches	423	506	559	754	704	897	1,654	1,141	1,480	3,613
Ohio	797	1,211	1,338	1,807	1,684	2,148	3,959	2,721	3,527	8,612
EGL	569	673	743	1,003	938	1,197	2,206	1,525	1,976	4,826
WGL	1,065	1,831	2,021	2,730	2,520	3,214	5,926	4,056	5,257	12,835
U Miss	1,195	1,497	1,653	2,233	1,928	2,459	4,534	2,964	3,841	9,379
L Mo	89	89	98	132	89	113	209	123	159	388
SOUTHEAST	650	867	958	1,293	1,128	1,438	2,651	1,780	2,307	5,634
SE	415	553	611	825	770	982	1,810	1,249	1,618	3,951
Cumb	8	34	38	51	39	50	91	52	68	165
Tenn	41	73	81	109	86	109	202	123	159	388
L Miss	146	163	180	243	189	241	445	295	382	932
L AWR	41	44	48	65	44	56	103	63	81	198
MID-CONTINENT	699	891	984	1,329	1,113	1,419	2,616	1,715	2,223	5,428
U Mo	447	447	493	666	498	635	1,171	727	943	2,301
U AWR	65	80	89	120	97	124	228	141	182	445
W Gulf	187	364	402	543	518	660	1,217	847	1,098	2,681
SOUTHWEST	317	687	758	1,024	1,082	1,382	2,549	1,895	2,456	5,997
RG-P	8	17	18	25	27	35	65	50	64	157
Colo	16	64	70	95	97	124	228	167	216	528
G Basin	24	84	93	125	134	171	316	237	307	751
S Pac	268	522	577	779	824	1,052	1,940	1,441	1,868	4,562
NORTH PACIFIC	781	1,550	1,712	2,312	2,416	3,083	5,682	4,191	5,432	13,264
C Pac	577	1,152	1,272	1,718	1,834	2,340	4,313	3,219	4,170	10,188
PNW	203	398	440	594	582	743	1,369	972	1,260	9,077
U.S.	8,139	11,818	13,050	17,624	16,174	20,631	38,033	26,066	33,783	82,498

Table A-10. VALUE ADDED BY PULP AND PAPER PRODUCTS, BY REGION

($ million, 1960)

	1960	1980 L	1980 M	1980 H	2000 L	2000 M	2000 H	2020 L	2020 M	2020 H
NORTHEAST	2,326	2,925	3,378	3,646	3,633	5,103	7,051	5,222	7,706	12,941
N Eng	537	715	826	891	1,023	1,437	1,985	1,740	2,568	4,312
D & H	406	406	469	506	406	570	788	405	598	1,005
Ches	199	500	578	624	568	799	1,103	764	1,127	1,893
Ohio	231	231	267	288	341	479	662	624	921	1,547
EGL	203	286	330	357	297	417	576	296	437	734
WGL	429	429	495	534	430	603	834	348	513	861
U Miss	290	286	330	357	341	479	662	487	719	1,207
L Mo	32	72	83	89	227	319	441	558	823	1,382
SOUTHEAST	1,125	2,211	2,554	2,756	3,636	5,108	7,060	6,826	10,074	16,921
SE	696	1,569	1,813	1,956	2,387	3,353	4,633	4,250	6,272	10,535
Cumb	–	72	83	89	114	160	222	210	310	521
Tenn	107	142	164	177	227	319	441	418	617	1,037
L Miss	111	142	164	177	454	638	882	1,113	1,643	2,760
L AWR	211	286	330	357	454	638	882	835	1,232	2,068
MID-CONTINENT	80	142	164	177	682	958	1,325	1,811	2,672	4,488
U Mo	–	–	–	–	341	479	662	1,045	1,542	2,590
U AWR	–	–	–	–	114	160	222	348	513	861
W Gulf	80	142	164	177	227	319	441	418	617	1,037
SOUTHWEST	40	60	71	77	621	872	1,207	1,774	2,618	4,397
RG-P	–	–	–	–	114	160	222	348	513	861
Colo	–	4	5	6	227	319	441	684	1,010	1,696
G Basin	–	4	5	6	114	160	222	337	497	835
S Pac	40	52	61	65	166	233	322	405	598	1,005
NORTH PACIFIC	409	2,052	2,371	2,558	3,195	4,489	6,202	5,820	8,590	14,426
C Pac	60	90	104	112	288	405	560	708	1,045	1,755
PNW	350	1,962	2,267	2,446	2,907	4,084	5,642	5,112	7,545	12,671
U.S.	3,980	7,390	8,538	9,213	11,767	16,530	22,845	21,453	31,660	53,173

Table A-11. VALUE ADDED BY CHEMICALS AND ALLIED PRODUCTS, BY REGION

($ million, 1960)

	1960	1980 L	1980 M	1980 H	2000 L	2000 M	2000 H	2020 L	2020 M	2020 H
NORTHEAST	6,807	11,678	15,928	24,157	16,541	29,851	63,859	28,148	55,113	152,122
N Eng	245	421	574	871	507	916	1,960	728	1,425	3,934
D & H	2,289	3,542	4,829	7,325	4,825	8,708	18,632	7,758	15,191	41,929
Ches	542	1,098	1,498	2,271	1,786	3,224	6,898	3,268	6,399	17,662
Ohio	1,390	2,359	3,217	4,879	3,353	6,051	12,946	5,585	10,935	30,183
EGL	767	1,527	2,082	3,158	2,159	3,896	8,336	3,576	7,002	19,328
WGL	1,114	1,588	2,166	3,285	2,247	4,055	8,676	4,426	8,667	23,923
U Miss	439	898	1,225	1,857	1,273	2,297	4,916	2,120	4,151	11,459
L Mo	20	249	339	514	387	699	1,495	685	1,342	3,705
SOUTHEAST	1,656	3,716	5,067	7,685	6,755	12,191	26,085	13,189	25,824	71,280
SE	726	1,467	2,000	3,034	2,816	5,082	10,874	5,654	11,070	30,557
Cumb	–	529	722	1,095	950	1,715	3,670	1,844	3,610	9,965
Tenn	460	619	845	1,281	921	1,662	3,557	1,584	3,101	8,558
L Miss	337	848	1,156	1,753	1,722	3,107	6,649	3,550	6,950	19,184
L AWR	133	253	344	522	346	625	1,337	558	1,092	3,015
MID-CONTINENT	1,359	2,460	3,355	5,088	4,649	8,386	17,941	9,246	18,104	49,970
U Mo	123	249	339	515	387	699	1,495	685	1,342	3,705
U AWR	72	225	306	464	458	826	1,767	946	1,852	5,112
W Gulf	1,165	1,987	2,710	4,109	3,802	6,861	14,679	7,615	14,910	41,154
SOUTHWEST	164	408	556	844	681	1,228	2,628	1,265	2,476	6,835
RG-P	–	13	18	27	26	48	102	53	104	287
Colo	–	13	18	27	26	48	102	53	104	287
G Basin	–	107	145	221	199	360	770	399	780	2,154
S Pac	164	275	375	569	428	773	1,654	760	1,488	4,107
NORTH PACIFIC	245	445	607	921	710	1,281	2,741	1,281	2,507	6,921
C Pac	184	324	441	669	519	937	2,005	941	1,842	5,083
PNW	61	122	166	252	191	344	736	340	666	1,838
U.S.	10,231	18,707	25,513	38,695	29,333	52,937	113,266	53,139	104,024	287,128

Table A-12. VALUE ADDED BY PETROLEUM REFINING, BY REGION

($ million, 1960)

	1960	1980 L	1980 M	1980 H	2000 L	2000 M	2000 H	2020 L	2020 M	2020 H
NORTHEAST	935	1,476	1,729	2,086	2,174	3,156	4,629	3,892	6,153	9,947
N Eng	14	39	45	55	58	85	124	105	166	269
D & H	331	629	737	889	950	1,379	2,023	1,723	2,724	4,403
Ches	31	77	90	109	117	169	248	211	334	540
Ohio	131	121	142	171	184	267	392	332	524	848
EGL	126	132	155	187	199	289	424	362	572	924
WGL	193	353	413	498	532	773	1,133	964	1,524	2,464
U Miss	109	109	128	154	109	158	232	150	238	384
L Mo	–	16	19	23	25	36	53	45	71	115
SOUTHEAST	169	228	267	324	332	480	703	599	947	1,532
SE	7	16	19	23	25	36	53	45	71	115
Cumb	–	5	6	8	8	11	16	14	22	36
Tenn	–	5	6	8	8	11	16	14	22	36
L Miss	131	171	200	241	258	374	548	466	737	1,191
L AWR	31	31	36	44	33	48	70	60	95	154
MID-CONTINENT	854	1,306	1,530	1,845	1,770	2,570	3,769	3,005	4,749	7,676
U Mo	109	109	128	154	109	158	232	151	239	387
U AWR	257	257	301	363	257	373	547	257	406	655
W Gulf	488	940	1,101	1,328	1,404	2,039	2,990	2,597	4,104	6,634
SOUTHWEST	224	367	430	520	513	744	1,091	864	1,366	2,208
RG-P	81	81	95	115	81	118	173	81	129	208
Colo	–	5	6	8	8	11	16	14	22	36
G Basin	–	5	6	8	8	11	16	14	22	36
S Pac	143	276	323	389	416	604	886	755	1,193	1,928
NORTH PACIFIC	200	196	229	277	282	409	600	485	766	1,239
C Pac	169	165	193	233	251	364	534	454	717	1,160
PNW	31	31	36	44	31	45	66	31	49	79
U.S.	2,382	3,573	4,185	5,052	5,071	7,359	10,792	8,845	13,981	22,602

Table A-13. VALUE ADDED BY PRIMARY METALS, BY REGION

($ million, 1960)

	1960	1980 L	1980 M	1980 H	2000 L	2000 M	2000 H	2020 L	2020 M	2020 H
NORTHEAST	9,054	11,227	16,386	21,705	14,048	27,057	43,656	22,288	42,308	85,483
N Eng	425	425	620	822	424	817	1,318	426	808	1,633
D & H	967	957	1,397	1,850	1,339	2,580	4,162	2,353	4,466	9,024
Ches	574	960	1,401	1,855	1,345	2,590	4,179	2,286	4,340	8,770
Ohio	3,348	3,756	5,483	7,263	3,964	7,634	12,318	5,564	10,561	21,339
EGL	1,637	2,182	3,184	4,218	3,085	5,941	9,586	5,331	10,120	20,447
WGL	1,615	2,458	3,588	4,752	3,402	6,553	10,573	5,754	10,923	22,069
U Miss	383	383	559	741	383	737	1,189	468	889	1,796
L Mo	106	106	154	204	106	205	331	106	201	405
SOUTHEAST	659	1,096	1,599	2,119	1,621	3,122	5,036	3,222	6,117	12,362
SE	393	624	910	1,206	969	1,867	3,012	1,764	3,348	6,765
Cumb	–	–	–	–	–	–	–	–	–	–
Tenn	202	201	294	389	211	407	656	492	935	1,889
L Miss	–	115	168	223	206	396	639	483	917	1,854
L AWR	64	156	227	301	235	452	729	483	917	1,854
MID-CONTINENT	329	464	677	897	706	1,360	2,193	1,395	2,649	5,352
U Mo	–	14	20	27	18	35	56	45	86	174
U AWR	138	140	205	271	170	327	527	266	505	1,019
W Gulf	191	310	452	599	518	998	1,610	1,084	2,058	4,159
SOUTHWEST	276	639	933	1,236	891	1,718	2,771	1,569	2,976	6,012
RG-P	–	28	41	54	36	70	112	85	161	324
Colo	43	43	63	83	43	83	135	79	149	301
G Basin	–	196	286	379	238	459	740	384	728	1,471
S Pac	234	372	543	720	574	1,106	1,784	1,021	1,938	3,916
NORTH PACIFIC	298	463	675	894	783	1,509	2,434	1,731	3,285	6,638
C Pac	64	99	144	191	155	299	482	281	533	1,077
PNW	234	364	531	703	628	1,210	1,952	1,450	2,752	5,561
U.S.	10,616	13,889	20,270	26,851	18,049	34,766	56,090	30,205	57,335	115,847

Table A-14. COMPARATIVE PROJECTIONS OF
POWER GENERATED BY UTILITY
STEAM-ELECTRIC PLANTS

(billion kilowatt-hours)

		FPC (1960)	RFF (1963)	FPC (1964)	This study
1960					753
1980	L		1,423		1,630
	M	1,843	1,446	2,316	2,230
	H		2,805		3,212
2000	L		2,611		2,716
	M	4,149	4,348		4,520
	H		6,404		7,683
2020	L				5,120
	M				8,964
	H				17,709

Sources: "Federal Power Commission Report on Electric Power as Related to the Nation's Water Problem," in Senate Select Committee on National Water Resources, *Electric Power in Relation to the Nation's Water Resources*, Committee Print No. 10, 86th Cong., 2d sess. (1960); Hans H. Landsberg, Leonard L. Fischman, and Joseph L. Fisher, *Resources in America's Future* (The Johns Hopkins Press for Resources for the Future, 1963); and Federal Power Commission, *National Power Survey: A Report* (1964).

Table A-15. UTILITY STEAM-ELECTRIC POWER GENERATION, BY REGION

(billion killowatt-hours)

	1960	1980 L	1980 M	1980 H	2000 L	2000 M	2000 H	2020 L	2020 M	2020 H
NORTHEAST	375	957	1,308	1,885	1,531	2,549	4,329	2,809	4,915	9,711
N Eng	24	65	89	129	106	177	300	197	344	680
D & H	69	145	198	286	228	380	646	414	725	1,433
Ches	31	81	110	158	128	214	363	236	412	815
Ohio	126	313	428	617	494	822	1,397	896	1,569	3,099
EGL	37	101	138	199	174	290	492	336	588	1,162
WGL	51	146	200	287	231	384	652	419	733	1,449
U Miss	32	90	123	178	144	240	407	264	462	912
L Mo	5	16	22	31	26	42	72	47	82	161
SOUTHEAST	120.3	293	439	577	480	801	1,361	900	1,574	3,109
SE	61	177	242	349	285	474	806	525	919	1,815
Cumb	0.3	1	1	2	3	5	9	9	15	30
Tenn	37	70	95	137	122	204	347	239	418	825
L Miss	11	22	70	44	33	56	94	58	102	202
L AWR	11	23	31	45	37	62	105	69	120	237
MID-CONTINENT	57	169	231	333	275	457	776	508	890	1,759
U Mo	10	41	56	80	73	121	206	143	251	496
U AWR	11	32	43	63	50	83	141	90	157	310
W Gulf	36	96	132	190	152	253	429	275	482	953
SOUTHWEST	42	108	149	213	181	301	512	342	597	1,180
RG-P	4	11	16	22	18	29	50	32	56	110
Colo	7	22	30	44	44	73	124	92	160	317
G Basin	2	11	16	22	19	32	54	36	63	124
S Pac	29	64	87	125	100	167	284	182	318	629
NORTH PACIFIC	16	104	142	204	249	414	704	565	990	1,955
C Pac	16	79	108	155	141	234	398	277	485	958
PNW	0	25	34	49	108	180	306	288	505	997
U.S.	610	1,631	2,269	3,212	2,716	4,522	7,682	5,124	8,966	17,714

Table A-16. NEW ENGLAND REGION: COMPARATIVE PROJECTIONS OF POPULATION, URBAN RATIO, AND VALUE ADDED, BY SELECTED INDUSTRIES

| | | Population *(mil.)* | | Urban ratio *(percent)* | | Value added (1960 = 100) | | | | | |
| | | | | | | Chemicals | | Primary metals | | Pulp & paper | |
		This study	Little	This study	Little	This study	Little	This study	Little	This study	Little
1960		10.3	10.5	77.2	76.4	100	100	100	100	100	100
1980	L	12.2				177		100		133	
	M	13.0	13.8	78.7	80.8	234	244	146	135	154	202
	H	14.2				356		193		166	
2000	L	13.9				207		100		190	
	M	16.6	18.7	80.3	84.1	374	522	192	166	268	456
	H	20.2				800		310		370	
2020	L	18.2				297		100			
	M	21.3	25.2	81.0	86.5	582	1,082	190	200		
	H	28.2				1,606		384			

Source: Projective Economic Studies of New England, Arthur D. Little, Inc., for the U.S. Army Corps of Engineers.

Table A-17. CHESAPEAKE BAY REGION: COMPARATIVE PROJECTIONS OF POPULATION AND OF VALUE ADDED, BY SELECTED INDUSTRIES

| | | Population *(mil.)* | | Value added (1960 = 100) | | | | | | | | | |
| | | | | Food | | Pulp & paper | | Chemicals | | Petroleum | | Primary metals | |
		This study	NPA	This study	NPA	This study	NPA	This study	NPA	This study	NPA	This study	NPA
1960		10.0	10.8	100	100	100	100	100	100	100	100	100	100
1980	L	12.3		120		251		203		248		167	
	M	13.1	14.6	132	161	290	277	276	227	290	242	244	174
	H	14.2		178		314		419		352		323	
2000	L	14.5											
	M	17.3	20.7										
	H	21.1											
2020	L	19.5											
	M	22.8	28.7										
	M	30.2											

Source: National Planning Association, Preliminary and Summary Tables of the Chesapeake-Susquehanna River Basin (1966).

Table A-18. OHIO REGION: COMPARATIVE PROJECTIONS OF POPULATION, URBAN RATIO, AND VALUE ADDED, BY SELECTED INDUSTRIES

| | | Population *(mil.)* | | Urban ratio *(percent)* | | Value added (1960 = 100) | | | | | | | |
| | | | | | | Food | | Pulp & paper | | Petroleum | | Primary metals | |
		This study	Little	This study	Little	This study	Little	This study	Little	This study	Little	This study	Little
1960		17.7	17.8	58.8	58.5	100	100	100	100	100	100	100	100
1980	L	19.2				152		100		92		112	
	M	20.4	21.5	64.4	65.2	168	184	116	205	108	213	164	122
	H	22.3				227		125		131		217	
2000	L	20.6				211		148		140		118	
	M	24.5	26.6	68.6	70.2	270	332	207	381	204		228	161
	H	29.9				497		287		299		368	

Source: Ohio River Comprehensive Study, app. B, "Projective Economic Study of the Ohio River Basin," Arthur D. Little, Inc., for the U.S. Army Corps of Engineers (1964).

Table A-19. EASTERN GREAT LAKES: COMPARATIVE PROJECTIONS OF POPULATION AND OF VALUE ADDED, BY SELECTED INDUSTRIES

| | | Population (mil.) | | Value added (1960 = 100) | | | | | | | | | | |
| | | | | Food | | Pulp & paper | | Chemicals | | Petroleum | | Primary metals | |
		This study	OBE	This study	OBE	This study	OBE	This study	OBE	This study	OBE	This study	OBE
1960		12.6	12.7	100	100	100	100	100	100	100	100	100	100
1980	L	15.7		118		141		199		105		133	
	M	16.7	17.0	131	166	163	197	271	267	123	201	194	191
	H	18.2		176		176		412		148		258	
2000	L	18.8		165		146		281		158		188	
	M	22.4	22.0	210	315	205	421	508	716	229	464	363	424
	H	27.2		388		284		1,087		337		586	
2020	L	25.4											
	M	29.8	28.6										
	H	39.4											

Source: *Preliminary Economic Projections for the Great Lakes Area*, prepared for the ad hoc Water Resources Council by the Office of Business Economics, U.S. Department of Commerce (1965).

Table A-20. CUMBERLAND AND TENNESSEE REGIONS: COMPARATIVE PROJECTIONS OF POPULATION AND OF VALUE ADDED, BY SELECTED INDUSTRIES

| | | Population (1960 = 100) | | Value added[a] (1960 = 100) | | | | | | | |
| | | | | Food | | Pulp & paper | | Chemicals | | Primary metals | |
		This study	OBE	This study	OBE	This study	OBE	This study	OBE	This study	OBE
1960		100	100	100	100	100	100	100	100	100	100
1980	L	110		218		168		234		168	
	M	117	131	243	197	194	291	326	348	194	291
	H	128		327		209		495		209	
2000	L	119		255		268		389		268	
	M	142	183	324	405	377	839	703	1,145	377	839
	H	173		598		522		1,506		522	
2020	L	148									
	M	174	257								
	H	230									

Source: *Preliminary Economic Projections for the Appalachia Region*, prepared for the ad hoc Water Resources Council by the Office of Business Economics, Department of Commerce (1966).

[a]OBE inferred.

Table A-21. UPPER MISSOURI REGION: COMPARATIVE PROJECTIONS OF POPULATION AND OF VALUE ADDED, BY SELECTED INDUSTRIES

| | | Population (mil.) | | Value added (1960 = 100) | | | | | |
| | | | | Food | | Chemicals | | Petroleum | |
		This study	OBE	This study	OBE	This study	OBE	This study	OBE
1960		6.0	5.6	100	100	100	100	100	100
1980	L	6.8		100		202		100	
	M	7.2	7.4	110	167	276	424	117	275
	H	7.9		149		419		141	
2000	L	7.6		111		315		100	
	M	9.0	10.2	142	327	568	1,748	145	790
	H	11.0		262		1,215		213	
2020	L	9.7							
	M	11.3	14.3						
	H	15.0							

Source: *Preliminary Economic Projections for the Missouri River Basin Area*, prepared for the ad hoc Water Resources Council by the Office of Business Economics, Department of Commerce (1965).

Table A-22. WESTERN GULF REGION: COMPARA-
TIVE POPULATION PROJECTIONS

(1960 = 100)

		This study	Texas water plan[a]
1960		100	100
1980	L	121	
	M	129	
	H	140	
2000	L	141	190[b]
	M	168	
	H	205	
2020	L	183	
	M	214	320
	H	283	

Source: Water for Texas – A Plan for the Future, Texas Water Development Board (1966).

[a]Figures are for Texas only.
[b]Estimate for 1990.

Table A-23. PACIFIC NORTHWEST REGION: COMPARATIVE PROJECTIONS OF POPULATION, IRRIGATED ACREAGE, AND VALUE ADDED, BY SELECTED INDUSTRIES

		Population *(mil.)*		Irrigated acreage *(1,000 acres)*		Value added (1960 = 100)						
						Pulp & paper		Primary metals	Steel in-got prod.	Petroleum refining	Refining capacity
		This study	BPA	This study	BPA	This study	BPA[a]	This study	BPA	This study	BPA
1960		5.4	5.5	4,868	5,605	100	100	100	100	100	100
1980	L	6.4		5,703		561		156		100	279
	M	6.8	8.4	5,991	7,758	648	244	227	213	116	
	H	7.4		6,282		700		300		142	392
2000	L	7.5									
	M	9.0									
	H	10.9		7,428							
2020	L	9.9									
	M	11.6	13.4[b]								
	H	15.3		7,903							

Source: Pacific Northwest Economic Base Study, Bonneville Power Administration, U.S. Department of the Interior (1965).

[a]Adjusted.
[b]Estimate for 2010.

Appendix B

WATER USE COEFFICIENTS
AND SELECTED AGGREGATES

Agriculture

Projections of water withdrawals and losses for irrigated agriculture were obtained as the product of the projections of irrigated acreage in each region multiplied by projected water withdrawals and losses per irrigated acre in each region. The withdrawal coefficient refers to the gross amount of water diverted from streams or pumped from groundwater per acre irrigated. The loss coefficient is the withdrawal coefficient less the return flow to streams and aquifers.

Coefficients are taken from Committee Print No. 12.[1] The U.S. Department of Agriculture's (USDA's) procedure in that document was to estimate for each region the amount of irrigation water required for evapotranspiration by the plant and, by dividing the latter first by an application efficiency (the fraction of water delivered to the farm which reached the plant) and then by a delivery efficiency (the fraction of diversions reaching the farm), to derive a total withdrawal coefficient. The loss coefficient was calculated by adding to the amount of water evapotranspired by the plant an estimate of loss between the point of diversion and the plant; this loss was estimated at 80 percent withdrawals above plant requirements in the East and 45 percent in the West (40 percent in the Pacific Northwest). The lower figure for the western regions is the result of large seepage in conveyance, much of which is ultimately recovered for reuse.

It must be emphasized that the irrigation coefficients refer to "ideal water use" in the sense that they are the amounts which would be withdrawn and lost in the absence of water scarcity. "Actual water use" coefficients in most western regions — parts of the Pacific Northwest, Western Gulf, and Upper Missouri regions being exceptions — are less than the "ideal use" coefficients because of inadequate water supplies in most of these areas.

Because the concept of "ideal use" was adopted in this study, it is not possible to check the USDA estimates of farm application efficiencies from existing empirical data. There are no data concerning the amount of water actually reaching the plant, and we cannot assume that the amount is that given by the USDA "ideal plant requirement." It is possible, however, to obtain data relating to "delivery" or "distribution" efficiency from data on the irrigation of western lands in the *Census of Agriculture*.[2] Computations of delivery efficiencies, derived by dividing water delivered to farms by water delivered to farms plus conveyance losses, show the following:

Region	Census of Agriculture 1949	Census of Agriculture 1959	Committee Print No. 12
	(percent)		
Upper Missouri	71	72	40
Upper Arkansas–White–Red	80	81	55
Western Gulf	84	85	60
Upper Rio Grande–Pecos	72	69	55
Colorado	70	79	55
Great Basin	80	84	55
South Pacific	92	94	50
Central Pacific	78	80	50
Pacific Northwest	75	78	60

---

[1]*Land and Water Potentials and Future Requirements for Water*, Senate Select Committee on National Water Resources, 86th Cong., 1st sess. (1960), tables 39, 40, and 41.

[2]U.S. Bureau of the Census, *Census of Agriculture: 1959*, vol. 3, *Irrigation of Agricultural Lands* (1962); and *Census of Agriculture: 1950*, vol. 3, *Irrigation of Agricultural Lands* (1952).

Thus, the data of the *Census of Agriculture* show that delivery efficiencies in western regions average around 80 percent.

Additional empirical data were available concerning water diversions and deliveries on Bureau of Reclamation projects.[3] Delivery efficiencies were computed from this data with the following results:

Region	Bureau of Reclamation 1963–65 average	Committee Print No. 12
	(percent)	
Upper Missouri	50	40
Upper Rio Grande–Pecos	62	55
Colorado	79	55
Great Basin	68	55
Central Pacific	67	50
Pacific Northwest	69	60

With the exception of the Rio Grande–Pecos region, delivery efficiencies computed from both Census and Bureau of Reclamation data were higher than those of Committee Print No. 12. However, with the exception of the Colorado region, the efficiencies computed from Bureau of Reclamation data were lower than those computed from the *Census of Agriculture*.

One would expect delivery efficiencies on Bureau of Reclamation projects to be lower than those on non-Bureau projects. Bureau projects often involve long-distance transmission; moreover, diversion is typically from surface water rather than from wells located close to irrigation areas. Thus, it follows that the efficiencies given in the *Census of Agriculture* are not far off the mark, for, except for the Colorado region, they are higher than efficiencies on Bureau projects for which data are available. Pavelis notes some reasons for the apparent downward bias in the efficiencies of Committee Print No. 12. The USDA water use coefficients (1) include storage as well as diversion in efficiencies, (2) do not fully consider groundwater usage, and (3) were developed with Bureau projects in mind. The delivery efficiencies used in this report were prepared by Pavelis from the Census data and from MacKichan and Kammerer's *Estimated Use of Water in the United States, 1960.*[4] The efficiencies are given in table B–1. Application efficiencies are the same as those in Committee Print No. 12.

Both application and delivery efficiencies were projected to increase to 2000. Since they are already high by that date, it was assumed they would not change by 2020. Whether technological change in irrigated agriculture will be sufficient to bring about the projected increase in efficiencies is, of course, an open question. Available data are inadequate for determining the amount of increase in irrigation efficiency in recent years.[5]

Two additional categories for agricultural water use were specified: rural domestic use and stock watering. Withdrawals for rural domestic use were estimated at 50 gallons per capita per day in 1960. MacKichan and Kammerer as well as the Public Health Service (in Committee Print No. 7)[6] estimate that persons living in homes with running water use about 60 gpcd, while the former points out that about one-fourth of rural Americans live in homes without running water and their water use is about 10 gpcd. Weighting domestic use in homes with and without running water by the respective proportions of rural populations yields an estimate of about 50 gpcd for rural domestic use. It is assumed that by 1980 all rural homes will have running water and rural domestic withdrawals will rise to 60 gpcd. The same estimate is projected to 2000 and 2020. Losses from rural domestic use are estimated to be 20 percent of withdrawals.

Withdrawals for water use by farm animals were projected on the basis of USDA's projection of product added by livestock (Committee Print No. 12, table 6). The USDA projections were adjusted, first, for differences in population projections assumed in Committee Print No. 12 and in this study. Second, an adjustment was made for increases in the efficiency of feed conversion by livestock. Thus, value added by livestock was projected as follows:

	1980	2000	2020
		(1960 = 100)	
Low	149.7	174.5	246.1
Medium	158.9	208.0	288.5
High	172.5	254.7	358.4

These index numbers were then multiplied by MacKichan and Kammerer's[7] estimates of 1960 water withdrawals for farm animals in each region. It was assumed that the value added by livestock would increase at the same rate in every region. Losses of water for livestock watering are assumed to equal withdrawals. The projections are given in table B–2.[8]

Mining

Estimates of water use by the mining sectors in 1960 were obtained by using the Bureau of Mines estimates of water intake and losses for 1962[9] and adjusting these by the ratio of output in the various sectors in 1960 to that in 1962. Projections of water withdrawals and losses in six of the nine mining sectors — bituminous coal, copper ore, iron

---

[3] U.S. Bureau of Reclamation, *Statistical Appendix to Crop Report and Related Data.*

[4] K. A. MacKichan and J. C. Kammerer, U.S. Geological Survey Circular 456 (1961).

[5] Irrigation efficiencies may be improved by various means: lining of canals, cultivation to reduce nonbeneficial water transpiration in the field, use of underground watering systems, land coating,

practices designed to prevent overirrigation, better field distribution systems, utilization of tailwater, and the like.

[6] *Future Water Requirements for Municipal Use*, Senate Select Committee on National Water Resources, 86th Cong., 2d sess. (1960).

[7] *Estimated Use of Water*, table 4.

[8] The procedure used for projecting water use by livestock was originally developed by Karl Gertel of the USDA in a memorandum of January 1960.

[9] Alvin Kaufman and Mildred Nadler, *Water Use in the Mineral Industry*, U.S. Bureau of Mines Information Circular 8285 (1966).

ore, phosphate rock, sand-gravel, and all other — were obtained from the Bureau of Mines projection equations. The equations for these six sectors are

$$T_i = 25 + 0.644\,(a_i\,b_i\,x_i) = \text{total water use,}$$
$$I_i = 18 + 0.245\,(a_i\,c_i\,x_i) = \text{water intake,}$$
$$L_i = 5 + 0.11\,R_i = \text{water loss,}$$

where

$T, I,$ and L are in billions of gallons per year, and where

x_i = total output, millions of tons, sector i;

a_i = percentage of output processed, sector i;

b_i = total water process requirement factor, sector i;

c_i = water intake process requirement factor, sector i;

R_i = water recirculated, billions of gallons per year.

By noting that $R_i = T_i - I_i$, we have

$$L_i = 6 + (0.071\,b_i - 0.027\,c_i)\,a_i\,x_i.$$

For 1980, the a_i were found by interpolating the values given by the Bureau of Mines for 1975 and 1985; for 2000 and 2020, the a_i were obtained by extrapolating the projected 1962–85 growth rate, with the restriction that $a_i \leqslant 1$. The b_i and c_i were taken to be the values given by the Bureau of Mines and were not subject to change over time.

As an example of the use of the equations, consider iron ore mining: for this sector, a_i was projected to be 0.96 for 1980, i.e., 96 percent of the iron ore mined was actually processed; b_i was 2.75 and c_i was 3.45, reflecting the amount of water required per ton of product processed to be fairly high. Substituting these values into the equations, one obtains:

$$I_i = 18 + 0.811\,x_i,$$
$$L_i = 6 + 0.098\,x_i.$$

Equations for other projection dates and for the other five sectors mentioned above were derived in the same manner. The slope of the equations (0.811 and 0.098) are, of course, the water use coefficients of the iron ore sector, except for the constant term.

For the crude petroleum and natural gas sectors, a somewhat different method was used. The equations of the Bureau of Mines did not apply to these sectors, but water use for 1962 by the two sectors together were given: withdrawals were 121.5 billion gallons and losses were 110.6 billion gallons. These figures were extrapolated to 1980, 2000, and 2020 by using the projected indices of production for crude petroleum and natural gas and weighting them in accord with their weights in the Federal Reserve Board (FRB) index of production. That is, the weight of crude petroleum production in the FRB index is 4.33 and that of natural gas is 0.32; or, crude petroleum has 93.1 percent of the total weight of crude petroleum and natural gas. Water withdrawals were then estimated as

$$(0.931\,P_t + 0.069\,G_t)\,W_o$$

and losses as

$$(0.931\,P_t + 0.069\,G_t)\,L_o,$$

where

P_t = index of crude petroleum, as projected to year t;

G_t = index of natural gas output, as projected to year t;

W_o = withdrawals in the base year;

L_o = losses in the base year.

Thus, we assumed that total withdrawals and losses in these sectors would rise proportionately with output. The same assumption was made with respect to the production of natural gas liquids.

For all mining sectors the above techniques gave projections of withdrawals and losses for the United States. The allocation by region was based on the percentage of national water intake as given in Committee Print No. 8[10] for bituminous coal, metals, nonmetals, crude petroleum, and natural gas liquids. (See tables B–3 and B–4.) For bituminous coal the same distribution was used for 2000 and 2020 as for 1980. For metals and nonmetals the Bureau of Mines had prepared projections for water intake to 2000 as well as to 1980; these were used to find regional percentage distributions for 1980 and 2000. The 2020 regional distributions for metals and nonmetals were found by assuming

$$x^i_{2020} = x^i_{2000} + 2/3\,(x^i_{2000} - x^i_{1980}),$$

where

x^i_t = percentage of national water use in region i at time t.

The distribution for metals was applied to the copper ore and iron ore sectors; that for nonmetals was applied to the phosphate rock, sand and gravel, and other minerals sectors. For crude petroleum, natural gas, and natural gas liquids, it was assumed that the same percentage distribution given in Committee Print No. 8 for 1980 would obtain for 2000 and 2020. For all mining sectors, it was assumed that the regional distribution of losses would be the same as that for withdrawals. One should note that this technique involves the assumption that losses constitute the same percentage of withdrawals in all regions.

No estimates for shale oil were incorporated in the model. In 1959 the Colorado Water Conservation Board estimated that water withdrawals in Colorado for the production of oil from shale would be 250,000 acre-feet per year and losses would be 160,000 acre-feet per year, when production reaches a stable level.

[10] *Future Requirements of Principal Water-using Industries*, Senate Select Committee on National Water Resources, 86th Cong., 2d sess. (1960).

Manufacturing

Water withdrawals and losses for the five major water-using manufacturing sectors (food and kindred products, paper and pulp products, chemical and allied products, petroleum and coal products, and primary metals) were computed as the product of value added projected for these sectors and the projections of water withdrawal and loss coefficients. The latter refer to the amount of freshwater intake and loss per dollar of value added. In estuarine regions, some industries withdrew fairly substantial amounts of brackish water. These are not withdrawals from the water supply — surface runoff as it is defined in this report — nor does evaporation of brackish water diminish the water supply so defined. Therefore, the coefficients refer to freshwater withdrawals and losses.

The water coefficient approach outlined above is, of course, subject to many shortcomings. The coefficients depend on a whole range of factors, among which are:

1. The degree of recirculation of water within the plant — With an increase in recirculation, intake per unit of product will fall; losses per unit of product may either rise or fall, although a slight fall may occur because the plant's internal water use is subject to more scrutiny.

2. The substitution of brackish water for fresh — This action, possible in coastal areas, will cause a decrease in the withdrawal and loss coefficients as defined here. The reverse type of substitution, which has perhaps occurred in some petroleum refineries in the San Francisco Bay area, will cause an opposite movement in the coefficients.

3. The scale of plant — Fragmentary data collected by Blair Bower indicate that in petroleum refining, for example, water intake per unit of product is higher in the larger refineries.[11]

4. The product mix of the sector — Changes in the pulp and paper sector, for example, in the relative importance of mill versus finishing operations or of the output of "bleached" versus "unbleached" paper will change the coefficients.

5. The price of water relative to other input prices — Increases in the relative price of water, for example, are likely to cause increased recirculation, i.e., a substitution of capital equipment for water intake.

Many other variables, particularly industrial technology, also have an influence on the water coefficients.[12]

The withdrawal and loss coefficients for the manufacturing sectors were obtained by computing coefficients for 1960 from the 1958 *Census of Manufactures*.[13] The coefficients were then projected for the later dates.

There are, of course, many sources of industrial coefficients other than the *Census of Manufactures*.[14] However, some give coefficients in terms of the physical product, e.g., per barrel of crude oil refined; others cover only a few industries within the two-digit classifications; still others refer only to withdrawals. The most complete source of data which maintains some degree of internal consistency is the Bureau of the Census,[15] although there appear to be some errors of reporting and of measurement. For example, the data for the largest water-using industry in the primary metals sector, Standard Industrial Classification 3312, blast furnaces and steel mills, show value added of $4.9 billion and withdrawals of 3,152 billion gallons for 1954. For 1959, value added is given as $6.6 billion and water intake as 2,994 billion gallons. That is, value added increased 25 percent and water intake decreased 5 percent. This cannot be attributed solely to recirculation, for the recirculation ratio only increased from 1.3 to 1.5. The possibility that these "changes" reflect errors in reporting and measurement is confirmed by Bower's observations:

> In some cases not even the water intake to an industrial plant is measured, particularly where a plant has its own water supply. More often waste water discharge is not metered, the exceptions being where sewer charges are paid on the basis of quantity. With respect to data on recirculated water, virtually all such data are estimates usually based on pump capacities and hours of operation.[16]

As stated above, the coefficients for the base year (1960) were taken from the 1958 *Census of Manufactures*. Table 14 presents the coefficients for the United States as a whole for 1954, 1959, and 1963. The decision to base the 1960 coefficients on the 1958 *Census of Manufactures* was initially made because the 1963 *Census of Manufactures* was not available and the 1959[17] data appeared to be better than that for 1954. The 1963 data showed that the 1959 coefficients may, for unknown reasons, have a downward bias in two industries.

Separate coefficients were computed for each region based on Census Bureau data for water resource regions. In some cases the Census Bureau's regional classification is less detailed than that used here. For example, for Census the Arkansas-White-Red is a region, while we have distinguished between the Upper and the Lower Arkansas-White-Red. In this case, we assumed that the coefficients for the Census region would hold also for the two component regions.

An increase in loss coefficients computed from the *Census of Manufactures* was made to account for instream losses due to the discharge of heated effluent and the subse-

---

[11] Blair T. Bower, "Water Utilization in Petroleum Refining" (preliminary report, Resources for the Future, 1966, mimeo.).

[12] For a more complete discussion of the variables determining water use, see Blair T. Bower, "The Economics of Industrial Water Utilization," in Allen V. Kneese and Stephen C. Smith (eds.), *Water Research* (The Johns Hopkins Press for Resources for the Future, 1966).

[13] U.S. Bureau of the Census, *U.S. Census of Manufactures: 1958*, "Industrial Water Use," Subject Report MC (1)–11 (1961).

[14] See, for example, National Association of Manufacturers, *Water in Industry* (January 1965); and U.S. Geological Survey Water-Supply Papers 1330–A to 1330–D. There are also numerous estimates in the engineering literature.

[15] *U.S. Census of Manufactures: 1958*, "Industrial Water Use."

[16] Bower, "Water Utilization in Petroleum Refining," p. 10.

[17] All water-use data in the *Census of Manufactures: 1958* are for 1959.

quent increase of instream evaporation. Instream losses due to the discharge of heated effluent were calculated at the following percentages of discharge coefficients (the withdrawal coefficient minus the loss coefficient):[18]

	(percent)
Food	2
Chemicals	2
Petroleum	3.7
Primary metals (average of ferrous and nonferrous)	2.5

No instream losses due to the discharge of heated effluent were computed for the pulp and paper sector because, as Landsberg, Fischman, and Fisher observe, "the [pulp and paper] industry uses comparatively little cooling water — only about 20 percent of total intake."[19]

Projections of withdrawal coefficients were based on the assumption that the main factor influencing these coefficients would be an increase in water recirculation. Thus, the coefficients are expected to fall over a period of time. The extent of the decrease will depend to a great degree on the relative price of water and recirculation equipment; it is also influenced by the relative importance of cooling and process water, because the possibilities of recirculating are generally greater where the former is more important. It was assumed that in the chemicals, petroleum and coal products, and primary metals sectors, the coefficients would decline by 10 percent per decade; and that in the food products and paper products sectors, where cooling water is somewhat less important, the decline would be 5 percent per decade. These rates were applied uniformly to all regions. Available data are not sufficient to estimate past trends; therefore, the magnitude of the change in the projections is arbitrary, although the direction is probably correct.

One can judge the implications of these projections by their impact on recirculation rates. Assuming that gross water applied per dollar of value added is constant, then the projections imply a shift from intake to recirculated water. Under this assumption, the change in recirculation would be as follows (I = intake water; R = recirculated water; $G = R + I$ = total water applied):

		G/I	R/G
Food products	1960	2.1	52%
	2020	2.8	65%
Paper products	1960	3.1	68%
	2020	4.3	77%
Chemicals	1960	1.6	38%
	2020	3.2	68%
Petroleum	1960	4.4	77%
	2020	8.6	88%
Primary metals	1960	1.5	35%
	2020	3.0	67%

These rates appear reasonable, even for the petroleum sector in which water recirculation is projected to be quite

high. For example, preliminary data on petroleum refining collected by Bower[20] indicate that some refineries have a recirculation ratio, measured by R/I, exceeding 13. R/I implied by the above projection for the entire petroleum and coal products sector would rise to 7.6 in 2020. Thus, what is projected is a movement of recirculation rates within plants that either recirculate in a modest amount, or not at all, toward recirculation rates that have already been achieved in some plants.

The loss coefficients were assumed to remain unchanged over the entire projection period. This assumption was made in view of a lack of knowledge concerning the probable direction of movement of the coefficients. Increased water recirculation will result in increased in-plant evaporation; however, the evaporation in streams caused by the discharge of heated effluent will decrease with recirculation. Because the instream evaporation due to heat dissipation is included in our loss coefficients, there should be no *net* change in loss coefficients attributable to recirculation, although there would be a change from instream to in-plant losses. It can also be maintained that recirculation will decrease loss coefficients, apart from evaporation from cooling towers, because of the general "tightening up" and more careful management of the plant's water system which generally accompanies high recirculation rates. However, it is unlikely that such an effect would substantially change the loss coefficients, although small declines might occur.

Projections of water withdrawals and losses were also made for manufacturing other than the five major sectors specified earlier. For the textiles, lumber and wood, rubber and plastics, leather products, and stone-clay-glass sectors, the procedure was to use the RFF projections of the FRB index of production for 1980 and 2000 (the indexes were extended to 2020 using the 1980–2000 rate of change); withdrawals and losses by a given sector in a given region for 1959 were multiplied by the projected index of production for that sector. This gave projections of water use for the three target dates for each region for each of the sectors based on the assumption that water use per unit of output would be unchanged. The projections of withdrawals were then reduced to allow for a 10 percent decline per decade in the withdrawal coefficient for lumber and wood, rubber and plastics, and stone-clay-glass. Reductions to allow for a 5 percent decline per decade in withdrawals per unit of output were made for textiles and leather products. The use of water for cooling is not as important for textiles and leather products as for the other three sectors. Loss coefficients were assumed to remain unchanged. Note that the method — multiplication of an index of national production by regional water use in a base year — is based on the assumption that all regions share equally in the increase in national output. Finally, there remained a residual water use in manufacturing accounted for by sectors other than the ten which had been projected. Total withdrawals and losses accounted for by the residual sectors in each region were multiplied by the index of our GNP projections. That is, it was assumed that the growth of

[18] Based on RFF, pp. 820–22.

[19] Ibid., p. 822.

[20] Bower, "Water Utilization in Petroleum Refining."

output in these residual sectors would parallel the growth in GNP. Withdrawals were once again reduced by 10 percent per decade below what they would have been if withdrawal coefficients remained unchanged.

Total water use of plants covered by the *Census of Manufactures* accounts for about 97 percent of manufacturing water use. The other 3 percent is used by establishments that withdraw less than 20 million gallons per year. Most, if not all, of these establishments probably withdraw water from public supplies; therefore their water use is probably included in the estimates of municipal water use and need not be considered further. On the other hand, some of the withdrawals of industrial users of 20 million gallons and more per year are also from public systems. Such withdrawals, and the losses associated with them, are consequently included twice, once in the estimates of municipal water use and again in the estimates of industrial water use. In order to eliminate this source of double counting, industrial water use was reduced by the amount of withdrawals and losses estimated to have been made from municipal water systems (table B–5). Thus, for example, if projected withdrawals for the chemicals sector are 1,000 billion gallons per year and losses are 200 bgy, then both of these are reduced by 10 percent because that fraction of withdrawals and losses is already included in the projections of municipal use. It is assumed that the fraction of industrial withdrawals and losses from municipal systems remains at the levels indicated in the last column of table B–5.[21]

Water discharged into salt or brackish water should be counted as a loss. This is equivalent to saying that all intake by plants that discharge into estuaries or into the ocean should be counted as loss. Although losses were computed in this fashion for municipal use, this procedure was not followed for other withdrawal uses, on the assumption that in-plant recirculation could be increased, and probably would be.[22]

A somewhat different concern was expressed for manufacturing intake (and other withdrawal uses) in coastal areas: Is enough water coming downstream to meet intake requirements? As a way of answering this question a comparison was made between "downstream" intake for all uses and required flow minus "upstream" losses.

Downstream intake for withdrawal uses — agriculture, manufacturing, steam power, and mining — was estimated from the ratio of value added in coastal SMSAs to value added for all SMSAs in the region. It was then assumed that total water intake — fresh plus brackish — in estuarine areas would equal the product of the above ratio and total water intake in the entire region. Because all brackish withdrawals would occur in a region's coastal areas (the use of inland brackish water has been ignored), fresh withdrawals in estuarine areas were assumed to be

$$F_c = c\,(F + B) - B,$$

where

F_c = fresh withdrawals, estuarine areas;

c = percentage of region's value added originating in estuarine areas;

F = total regional fresh withdrawals;

B = total regional brackish withdrawals.

In some cases, the estimates of F_c were negative; when this occurred, it was assumed that all withdrawals of the sector in estuarine areas were brackish water. Estimated fresh withdrawals in estuarine areas were summed up for all sectors, and the ratio of the sum to total fresh withdrawals in the region was computed. The results of the computation are shown in table B–6. The estimates represent, of course, rather crude guesses based on available data. Moreover, the percentages given are subject to the possibility of sizable decreases over time, if recirculation of water by industry in estuarine areas proceeds at a faster rate than recirculation in inland areas, or if estuarine manufacturers substitute additional amounts of brackish water for fresh.

Withdrawal and loss coefficients expressed as gallons per dollar of value added are given in tables B–7 through B–15. Table B–16 shows the values estimated for cooling water as a percentage of discharge.

Steam-Electric Power

The amount of fresh water withdrawn per kilowatt-hour for utility steam-electric power generation depends principally on:

1. The amount of "once-through" water use or gross water applied, i.e., the amount of intake plus the amount of water recirculated. This amount is primarily a function of the thermal efficiency of the power plant — the higher the thermal efficiency, the less heat to be dissipated, and, hence, the smaller the amount of cooling water to be passed through the condenser.

2. The amount of gross water applied which is withdrawn from brackish sources.

3. The rate of recirculation which, in turn, is a function of the price and availability of water as compared with the cost of recirculation equipment.[23]

[21] A comparable adjustment for mining was not made because withdrawals from municipal systems by mining are very low: 6 percent of mining withdrawals in 1954 (*Census of Mineral Industries*, "Energy, Water, and Selected Supplies," Bulletin MI–F) and 4 percent of mining withdrawals in 1962 (Kaufman and Nadler, *Water Use*). For the same reason, no adjustment for withdrawals from municipal systems by steam-electric utilities are made. The *Census of Manufactures: 1958* shows that less than 1 percent of withdrawals by steam-electric utilities were from municipal systems.

[22] In-plant recirculation is deemed an equivalent of in-basin recirculation for computation of a region's water requirements. Drainage from coastal irrigated land is likely to be irrecoverable; hence we probably have understated agricultural losses in coastal regions. In some coastal areas the source of supply is groundwater that may have escaped measurement as surface flow. For such cases the errors are compensating insofar as net impact on a region's water resources are concerned. We need greater fineness of detail to be confident of generalities regarding coastal and estuarine areas.

[23] For a full discussion of these and other factors, see Paul H. Cootner and George O. G. Löf, *Water Demand for Steam Electric Generation: An Economic Projection Model* (The Johns Hopkins Press for Resources for the Future, 1965).

For this report, the gross amount of water applied per kilowatt-hour for 1960 was determined from the data for water use by steam-electric utilities in the 1958 *Census of Manufactures*. Because the gross application coefficient is primarily a function of thermal efficiency, projection of the coefficients depends on assumed increases in thermal efficiency. Cootner and Löf project the coefficient for the West South Central region to decline to 46 gallons per kwh by about 1980, and the FPC projected the coefficient for Power Supply Area V[24] (geographically similar to the West South Central) to be 53 gallons per kwh in 1980. We assumed that the FPC coefficient would obtain in 1980 and that of Cootner-Löf in 2000. Thus, we assume that the increase in thermal efficiency is smaller than that assumed by Cootner and Löf. All 1980 gross application coefficients were those of the FPC; for 2000, the coefficients were determined by the formula

$$y^i_{2000} = \frac{X^G_{1980}}{y^G_{1980}} y^i_{1980},$$

where

X^G = Cootner-Löf projection for the West South Central;

y^G = FPC projection for Power Supply Area V;

y^i_t = projection of this report, year t, region i.

Further increases in thermal efficiency after 2000 are likely to be small, and the gross application coefficients for 2020 were assumed to remain at their 2000 levels.

The product of the gross application coefficient and projected kilowatt-hours generated gave projected gross applications for each region. However, part of this total is met through the use of brackish water. From the 1958 *Census of Manufactures* ("Industrial Water Use") the percentage of gross water applied coming from brackish sources was computed for each region (zero for inland regions), and total applications were reduced by this amount in order to find freshwater applications. Freshwater withdrawals were found as the product of the latter and the reciprocal of the recirculation rate (defined as gross applications divided by withdrawals).

Data from the 1954 *Census of Manufactures*, "Industrial Water Use Supplement," show an average recirculation rate for the eastern area (all regions in the Northeast and Southeast divisions) of 1.04 with a range from 1.00 to 1.79 (the Cumberland figure was 2.15). In 1959, the average rate in the East was 1.06 with a range of 1.02 to 1.47. Because of the limited amount of recirculation in the East, one recirculation rate was used for all eastern regions. The recirculation rate was assumed to increase at the 1954–59 rate yielding values of 1.14 for 1980, 1.22 for 2000, and 1.30 for 2020.[25]

Recirculation is more important in the West than in the East; the 1954 average recirculation rate in the West was 2.56 with a low of 1.48 (Upper Missouri) and a high of 5.96 (Colorado). By 1959 the average for the West was 4.08 with a range of 1.70 (Upper Missouri) to 11.89 (Colorado). Because of the variation in recirculation rates in the West, different rates were projected for various regions. The South Pacific, Central Pacific, Colorado, Great Basin, Rio Grande–Pecos, and Upper Arkansas-White-Red regions appear to be those in which recirculation is greatest. It is assumed that recirculation in these regions will be almost complete by 1980 and that the recirculation rate will rise to 70 in 1980 and remain at that level for 2000 and 2020. This is based on (1) the estimate of Cootner and Löf that where recirculation is complete withdrawals will be about 1.4 percent of gross use,[26] and (2) data for a southwestern power plant with extensive recirculation;[27] the design recirculation rate of all three power units in the plant is 68, and the actual rates vary from somewhere around 55 to 95, depending on the season and the operating rate. For the Upper Missouri, Western Gulf, and Pacific Northwest regions, recirculation rates were projected to increase at the 1954–59 rates of change.

Losses were computed at the rate of 0.7 gallons per kwh generated in 1960 and 0.5 gallons per kwh for 1980, 2000, and 2020. According to Cootner and Löf,

> . . . at a current average efficiency in U.S. central station power plants of about 33 percent . . . , corresponding to a heat rate of 10,300 btu per kilowatt-hour, approximately 0.7 gallons of water evaporate into the atmosphere per kilowatt-hour generated. . . . As average power plant efficiencies increase toward 40 percent during the next two decades, minimum consumptive water requirements will decrease from the present 0.7 toward 0.5 gallon per kilowatt-hour, and practical estimates of net water use, or disappearance, can be based on these figures.[28]

Because it is likely that average efficiencies will not increase much after 1980, the projected loss coefficient was maintained at 0.5 gallon per kwh for 2000 and 2020. Also, as Cootner and Löf point out, the above figure refers to evaporation per kwh generated, *irrespective of whether the evaporation occurs in the plant or in the stream*. Therefore,

---

[24] The FPC projections (from Committee Print No. 10 and unpublished data prepared for the Senate Select Committee) were taken as projections of withdrawal coefficients in Committee Print No. 32. However, they appear to refer to gross application coefficients: the average of the FPC "water requirement" coefficients for 1980 is about 55 gallons per kwh. Cootner and Löf (*Steam Electric Generation*, p. 86) give a 1980 projection for the West South Central region of "unrecycled" water use, i.e., gross application, of 46 gallons per kwh. Thus, it seems apparent that the FPC projections refer to the gross application coefficient, not the intake coefficient.

[25] This is the "original" recirculation rate, which turned out to create a problem of heat pollution and therefore was modified to the "new" recirculation rate. It should also be noted that thermal efficiency of nuclear power plants is relatively low. For this reason we may have overstated the expected average increase in thermal efficiency.

[26] *Steam Electric Generation*, p. 82.

[27] Data are for the New Mexico Public Service Company's Reeves Plant in Albuquerque. Mr. Karl Lang, chief engineer at the Reeves Plant, furnished the data and provided some helpful suggestions.

[28] *Steam Electric Generation*, pp. 74–75.

no adjustment to account for instream loss due to the discharge of heated effluent is necessary.

The "original" rates of recirculation are those produced by the procedure just described. When withdrawals (table B-17) are translated into discharge of warm water and a consequent need for dilution to offset an undue (greater than 5.4°F.) rise in stream temperature, the required dilution flows exceeded those required to offset other forms of pollution (BOD, nitrogen, phosphorus). On the assumption that recirculation would be raised to the level required to offset thermal pollution, a new set of recirculation rates were computed. Both sets are shown in table B-18.

Municipal Water Use

Total municipal withdrawals in each region were estimated as the product of urban population and average per capita use. Rates of change in per capita use were estimated from pumpage figures reported by the U.S. Public Health Service (USPHS) in the *Survey of Municipal Water Facilities* for 1958, 1960, 1962, and 1964. Because in many instances the reported figures appear to reflect estimates rather than metered readings, and in some cases seem to vary without clear cause, an average of 1958 and 1960 was used for the initial period and an average for 1962 and 1964 was used for the final period. These averages approximate the experience of the four-year period 1959-63. Random error in growth rates was further reduced by grouping cities into five divisions: Northeast, Southeast, Mid-continent, Southwest, and North Pacific. The average rate of growth in per capita use was computed separately for each division and then used for the water resource regions in that division.

The computed annual rate of increase in per capita water withdrawals for the United States was 1.75 percent. Linaweaver,[29] however, indicated that the thirty-year period from 1924 to the mid-fifties saw the U.S. municipal average rise from 100 gallons per capita per day to 155 gpcd, a growth rate of about 1.5 percent compounded annually. In order to reflect the lower average rate estimated by Linaweaver, per capita gallonage in each division was reduced by the proportion 1.5/1.75. The resulting annual growth rates are given in table B-19. These rates were then applied to the figures reported by the USPHS for 1954,[30] to obtain 1960 and 1980 per capita intakes. For the period 1980-2000 the rate of increase was assumed to be half the 1954-80 rate, and for the period 2000-2020 the rate of increase was assumed to be one-third of the 1954-80 rate.

There are sufficient uncertainties regarding future water use to require that one use projected per capita intake rates with circumspection. "Municipal" use is a composite of four different classifications of use: domestic, commercial, industrial, and public. Each category is subject to its own underlying trend, and in some cases the trends may be con-

[29] F. P. Linaweaver, Jr., "Report II, Phase Two, Residential Water Use" (The Johns Hopkins University, June 1965, mimeo.), pp. 2-3.

[30] Committee Print No. 7, p. 5, table 5, except that figures for New England and Rio Grande-Pecos were revised as follows: New England, reduced from 142 to 125 gpcd; and Rio Grande-Pecos, increased from 120 to 134 gpcd.

trary. Domestic use rises with higher incomes and greater use of appliances and air conditioning but probably falls with increased density of population and apartment living. Industrial water use is likely to increase on a per capita basis as industrial users switch from their own systems to municipal systems. Per capita trends of public and commercial uses are not clear. The variation in per capita municipal use that is visible from region to region is the result of differences in income levels, climate, and the mix of the four categories of municipal use. Variations in the relative importance of the four categories as revealed by thirty-three cities divided between "East" and "West" are as follows:

	Total (33 cities)	East (21 cities)	West (12 cities)
	(percentage of total use)		
Domestic	43	37	55
Commercial	20	19	22
Industrial	23	28	15
Public	13	16	7

There is some slight evidence, based on the experience of particular communities between particular dates, that per capita use might decline in the future or might at least stabilize at a level not greatly higher than the present. These are alternative possibilities that should not be excluded; existing information, however, does not lend them a high degree of probability.

Municipal Losses

Losses from municipal uses are poorly measured. If all pipes were leakproof and sanitary and storm sewers were separate, losses in general would be equal to the difference between water pumped to consumers and the quantity of liquid discharged from the sewage treatment plant. But because water leaks out of pipes under pressure (water lines) and into pipes not under pressure (sewage lines) and because many systems have linked sanitary and storm sewers, measurements of losses tend to be somewhat impressionistic. Some reported figures appear to be implausible. For example, in San Antonio, reported loss is 6 percent; in Amarillo, 59 percent; in Provo, 15 percent; and in Portland (Oregon), 33 percent. Questionnaires on water use were sent to a number of western cities. The list of cities and the reported loss (measured as water pumped minus sewage received divided by water pumped) for which usable figures were supplied is as follows (all refer to 1964 or 1965):

	Loss as a percentage of water pumped
San Antonio	6
El Paso	64
Fresno	55
Provo	15
Albuquerque	50
Tucson	49
Amarillo	59
Sacramento	25
Portland	33

Data collected by F. P. Linaweaver and associates[31] on the basis of measuring the flows delivered to residential areas reveal differences based on location, type of residence, and whether metered or flat rate. The major factor contributing to variation was the relative importance of sprinkling in the areas. Estimated percentages of water lost are as follows:

10 metered areas in the west	54 percent
11 metered areas in the east	42 percent
8 flat rate areas in the west	71 percent
5 apartment areas, east and west	28 percent

Comparable data for losses from industrial, commercial, and public uses are not available. We can infer that losses from industrial and commercial uses are likely to be comparatively low, since sprinkling is unimportant. Losses from public uses are likely to be high.

We assumed that in eastern regions the use of water was evenly divided between domestic and public uses on the one hand and industrial and commercial on the other. In the West we assumed that domestic and public uses accounted for 65 percent, with industrial and commercial accounting for the remainder. On the basis of these assumptions and the scattered measurements we had of intake (pumpage) and loss, we estimated loss as a percentage of intake as follows:

13 eastern regions (Northeast and Southeast)	25 percent
8 western regions	40 percent
Western Gulf	35 percent

The Western Gulf region was handled separately because of the wide climatic variation between the eastern and western halves of the region. A comparable variation exists in the Central Pacific and Pacific Northwest regions, where the coastal areas tend to be humid and the inland areas tend to be dry. However, because special consideration was given to discharge from coastal municipalities, these regions were treated as the others of the West.

Another special factor to be accounted for is the use of stabilization ponds (lagoons) in waste treatment. On the basis of data supplied by Blair Bower, a preliminary estimate of additional municipal losses was made. The amounts appeared to be small relative to those already estimated, even in the Upper Missouri region where stabilization ponds were most common. Accordingly, no further adjustment was made to account for such losses. Should the use of waste lagoons increase materially, they should be given specific consideration.

Discharge of Coastal Cities

Cities that discharge wastes into coastal or estuarine water should be treated as though all intake into the municipal system is lost to further use. The impact on water supplies is especially acute where points of intake are located well upstream, as in New York, San Francisco, and Los Angeles.[32]

Adjustment for coastal and estuarine points of discharge was accomplished by calculating the percentage of a region's total urban population that lived in coastal SMSAs in 1960, and counting that percentage of municipal intake as discharged into coastal waters and therefore lost to reuse. In the Central Pacific region, for example, it was estimated that 65 percent of the urban population would be at coastal or estuarine points of discharge in 1980, 2000, and 2020. (The 1960 percentage was kept the same for each of these years.) The inland loss rate was estimated at 40 percent of intake. Total municipal losses, as a percentage of intake, were equal to $C + L (1 - C)$, where C is the percentage of total urban population in coastal SMSAs (65 percent) and L is the inland loss rate (40 percent). For the Central Pacific, therefore, municipal losses were equal to $0.65 + 0.40 (0.35)$, or 79 percent of municipal intake. (See table B-20 for municipal loss rates.)

This technique fails to account for urban population in coastal counties that is not part of SMSAs, but it counts as urban the rural population in SMSAs. We were forced to use SMSAs because it was in this form that we had information on those municipal systems that discharged into tidal water but had their intakes at upland locations. The tabulation of cities and points of discharge was prepared by Blair Bower.

In some instances (table B-21) the upland point of intake is shown as "groundwater." We assumed that groundwater withdrawn upstream was a loss of surface flow, just as a withdrawal directly from the river would have been. We have no way of knowing to what degree this assumption may lead to an overestimation of loss.

Land Treatment and Structures

Soil conservation practices use water mainly by increasing the amount of evapotranspiration. Soil conservation measures classified as "land treatment," e.g., terracing, contour farming, and additional cover crops, result in additional retention of moisture by the soil, thereby contributing to greater evapotranspiration and a decline in surface runoff. Practices classified as "structural measures" are the construction of stock ponds and watershed structures which are designed to retard surface runoff and prevent flood damage. Structural measures decrease streamflow because of evaporation from the surface of the reservoirs and ponds.[33]

---

[31] Tabulated by Charles W. Howe, Resources for the Future, for presentation here. See various reports of F. P. Linaweaver, Jr. and associates on "Residential Water Use," Phases One and Two, The Johns Hopkins University.

[32] No account was taken of the fact that in some instances water comes from another region, e.g., from the Colorado River basin to meet part of the requirements of Los Angeles. In the case of New York, water is diverted from the Delaware River basin into the Hudson River basin, but this is accounted for by the aggregation of the two basins into a single water resource region.

[33] In U.S. Senate, Select Committee on National Water Resources, Committee Print No. 13, *Estimated Water Requirements for Agricultural Purposes and Their Effects on Water Supplies*, 86th Cong., 2d sess. (1960), the SCS included, in addition to the loss of streamflow from land treatment and structural measures, losses resulting from the use of ponds and reservoirs by farm animals and for domestic use. Because the latter have already been included under "Agriculture," above, they were excluded from this section.

In Committee Print No. 13, the Soil Conservation Service (SCS) reported both an "onsite" water requirement and a "downstream" requirement. The "onsite" requirement refers to the amount of water absorbed by the soil or transpired by vegetation in a drainage area of one-tenth of a square mile. Part of this amount will eventually return to the stream via underground movements or will be reused through wells. Thus, the onsite requirement corresponds to withdrawals, not losses. The part of the onsite requirement which is evapotranspired and does not return to the stream is the "downstream" requirement and represents losses. In order to determine losses due to soil conservation, several assumptions were made:

1. It was assumed that the losses estimated by the SCS to have occurred in 1954 due to land treatment and structural measures are reflected in stream runoff records. Because of the nature of water losses from soil conservation measures, i.e., precipitation is intercepted before reaching the stream rather than diverted from the stream, it is not possible to determine what runoff would have been in the absence of such measures, and it is assumed that streamflow data already reflect these losses. By an unknown but probably small amount, this assumption underestimates losses due to soil conservation, because stream runoff data reflect the *average* losses from soil conservation over the period of record. However, soil conservation practices have been increasing in magnitude and, consequently, the 1954 losses are probably in excess of the historical average. Therefore, not all 1954 losses are reflected in historical streamflow data.

2. It was assumed that the losses occurring in 1960 were not significantly different from those in 1954. This assumption misses the mark because it is known that both the amount of land subject to conservation treatment and the number of structural measures increased between 1954 and 1960. Thus, water losses also increased. However, the degree to which land treatment and structural measures were extended in the 1954–60 period was not ascertainable; rather than make an adjustment which would be only a guess, we preferred to assume that losses in 1960 were not far above those of 1954.

3. From the two assumptions above it follows that the estimates for this report on water losses due to soil conservation (1) for 1960, are zero because it is assumed that 1954 losses are included in streamflow data and that 1954 losses equal 1960 losses; and (2) for 1980, 2000, and 2020, are the *increase* in losses on these dates over those prevailing in 1960.

4. For 1980 and 2000, the projections of water losses in Committee Print No. 13 are used in this report. Implicitly this involves at least three assumptions, the first being that the extension of land treatment practices will proceed along the lines projected by the SCS and as shown in table B–22. A more recent SCS publication[34] contains the following estimates of the percentage of land in need of treatment in 1965:

Region	Cropland	Pasture & range	Forest & woodland
Northeast	61	65	38
Lake States	67	72	58
Corn Belt	60	69	74
Northern Plains	65	58	27
Appalachian	64	69	54
Southeast	63	75	81
Delta States	60	74	70
Southern Plains	62	85	39
Mountain	60	74	33
Pacific	60	73	41

The Northeast region of this table corresponds roughly to New England plus the Delaware-Hudson region. About 60 percent of the Northeast region is indicated as in need of treatment. Table B–22 showed that approximately an additional 30 percent of the land in this area would be brought under land treatment by 2000. Thus, even though the 1965 figures may be overestimates of the amount of land needing treatment,[35] two conclusions emerge:

(a) the projections of Committee Print No. 13 are not impossibly high;

(b) even after 2000, there will be a need for extending land treatment practices.

The second implicit assumption is that the pattern of land use will not be too different from that projected in Committee Print No. 13. The following table shows some alternative projections of the pattern of land use:

	Committee Print No. 13 (1980 Medium)	USDA Land & Water Policy Committee[36]	SCS[37] (to 1975)
	(millions of acres)		
Cropland	480	407	436
Pasture–range	589	641	497
Forest–woodland	601	741	440
Miscellaneous	234	472	60
Total	1,904	2,261	1,433

Although the projections are not comparable, the USDA projection shows less cropland and more land in the other three categories. If we accept the assumptions made in Committee Print No. 13, then a shift in land use away from cropland and toward other uses will mean that streamflow will be augmented to some degree. However, because the table does not indicate a really major shift from that projected in Committee Print No. 13, it is assumed that no adjustment need be made for this factor.

The third implicit assumption is that the construction of ponds, watershed structures, and other small reservoirs will proceed on the path projected in Committee Print No. 13.

---

[34] U.S. Department of Agriculture, *Soil and Water Conservation Needs – A National Inventory*, Miscellaneous Publication No. 971 (1965).

[35] There are reasons for believing these are overestimated. See R. Burnell Held and Marion Clawson, *Soil Conservation in Perspective* (The Johns Hopkins Press for Resources for the Future, 1965), pp. 166–67.

[36] U.S. Department of Agriculture, *Land and Water Resources: A Policy Guide* (1962). Includes Hawaii and Alaska.

[37] U.S. Department of Agriculture, *Soil and Water Conservation Needs*, p. ix. Excludes all federal land, and the projection date is 1975.

Because of the scarcity of data, this assumption was not altered.

5. For 2020, it was assumed that the pattern of land use would continue to change in the same direction as for 1980–2000 and that land treatment practices would continue to be extended. However, it is thought that both of these factors would begin to stabilize, so that water losses after 2000 would increase by only half the amount of the increase from 1980 to 2000. Similarly the construction of structural measures was assumed to continue to increase, but at only a third of the 1980–2000 rate, so that losses in 2020 would be only a third higher than in 2000.

Swamps and Wetlands

Lands used primarily for wildlife habitat, especially for waterfowl, frequently consist of swamps, lowlands, marshes, and bogs. The water surfaces of these lands and the vegetation — cattails, willows, wild rice, etc. — evapotranspire fairly large amounts of water. Since the settlement of the United States by Europeans, land area in wetlands has undergone continuous contraction because of drainage. In the future this trend may be reversed because of the growing demand for recreation, including waterfowl hunting, and the growing concern about the maintenance and expansion of waterfowl habitat.

Evapotranspiration from existing wetlands is incorporated into data on streamflow. An expansion of wetlands, by increasing evapotranspiration, would decrease stream runoff and, similarly, a reduction of the acreage in wetlands would increase runoff. Therefore, the current evapotranspiration from swamps and wetlands is not counted as loss in this report; increases or decreases in evapotranspiration from wetlands are counted as losses or gains, respectively.

In Committee Print No. 18,[38] the procedure of the Fish and Wildlife Service for estimating and projecting water use for wetlands was, first, to determine the acreage in wetlands in 1954 for each water resource region as set forth in the National Wetlands Inventory.[39] Second, a water use factor (evapotranspiration per acre) computed by the U.S. Geological Survey was applied to the acreage figures to obtain losses. Third, the Fish and Wildlife Service assumed that because of increased demand for waterfowl hunting acreage in wetlands will increase 75 percent by 1980 and will double by 2000 with evapotranspiration rising by the same amounts.

According to the National Wetlands Inventory, there were 74.4 million acres of wetlands in the continental United States in 1954. Thus, the Fish and Wildlife Service assumed that there would be 130 million acres in 1980 (a 75 percent increase) and 149 million acres in 2000 (a doubling over 1954). We believe that this is an overestimate for the following reasons:

1. The Inventory indicates that the original wetlands area of the United States prior to any drainage and conversion to agricultural use was 127 million acres. Thus, the projection implies that an amount of land equivalent to all that converted from wetlands to agricultural use during the past 200 years will be reconverted from its present use to wetlands between 1954 and 1980.

2. In some areas, the magnitude of the change required is very large. In the Western Great Lakes region, the 1954 data show one of every ten acres to be wetlands; doubling this by 2000 would require that 10 percent of the region be converted to wetlands. In the Southeast, in 1954 about one of every five acres was classed as wetlands; doubling this would require that 20 percent of the land area of the Southeast region be converted into wetlands by 2000.

In view of this, the projections of the Fish and Wildlife Service were abandoned.

The only other projections available are those of Clawson, Held, and Stoddard.[40] Their projections refer to land "primarily for wildlife" which apparently consists of land in federal and state wildlife refuges. There were 14 million acres of these lands in 1950, which are projected to increase to 18 million acres in 1980 and 20 million acres in 2000. Landsberg, Fischman, and Fisher say, "About 15 million acres of public land . . . are now given over to wildlife. The additions that seem likely in the next four decades — perhaps on the order of 5 million acres — will probably be almost entirely wetlands set aside for the benefit of waterfowl."[41] Against the increase in wetlands held by the government must be set the possibility of further drainage of wetlands for agriculture and, especially in the future, for urban uses. It is therefore assumed that, as a Medium projection, there will be no *net* increase in wetlands. The High projection assumes increases of 5 percent, 8 percent and 10 percent in wetlands acreage for 1980, 2000, and 2020, respectively. This means that the assumed absolute increase in wetlands is 3.7 million acres by 1980, 6 million acres by 2000, and 7.5 million acres by 2020. The Low projections assume decreases in acreage in wetlands of 5 percent, 8 percent and 10 percent, for 1980, 2000, and 2020, respectively. Because of lack of knowledge, it is assumed that these rates of increase and decrease apply to all regions. It is also assumed that water losses increase or decrease proportionately.

Table B–23 gives the estimated amount of evapotranspiration from wetlands in 1960. Estimates for 1980, 2000, and 2020 were obtained by raising or lowering the 1960 figures in accordance with the percentages indicated above. The resulting figures were treated both as a measure of gross use (withdrawals) and as net use (loss).

---

[38] *Fish and Wildlife and Water Resources*, Senate Select Committee on National Water Resources, 86th Cong., 2d sess. (1960).

[39] U.S. Fish and Wildlife Service, *Wetlands of the United States*, Circular 39 (1956).

[40] Marion Clawson, R. Burnell Held, and Charles H. Stoddard, *Land for the Future* (The Johns Hopkins Press for Resources for the Future, 1960).

[41] RFF, p. 372.

Table B-1. DELIVERY EFFICIENCIES (PERCENTAGE
OF DIVERSIONS REACHING FARMS), BY
REGION

	1960	1980	2000	2020
N Eng	100	100	100	100
D & H	100	100	100	100
Ches	100	100	100	100
Ohio	100	100	100	100
EGL	100	100	100	100
WGL	100	100	100	100
U Miss	100	100	100	100
L Mo	100	100	100	100
SE	100	100	100	100
Cumb	100	100	100	100
Tenn	100	100	100	100
L Miss	95	95	95	95
L AWR	90	95	95	95
U Mo	75	80	85	85
U AWR	85	90	95	95
W Gulf	80	85	90	90
RG-P	75	80	85	85
Colo	80	85	90	90
G Basin	80	85	90	90
S Pac	85	90	95	95
C Pac	80	85	90	90
PNW	70	75	80	80

Sources: Delivery efficiencies prepared by George A. Pavelis
from data in the *Census of Agriculture* and in K. A. MacKichan and
J. C. Kammerer, *Estimated Use of Water in the United States*, 1960,
U.S. Geological Survey Circular 456 (1961).

Table B-2. WITHDRAWALS (AND LOSSES) FOR LIVESTOCK, BY REGION

(million gallons per day)

	1960	1980			2000			2020		
		L	M	H	L	M	H	L	M	H
NORTHEAST	672	1,006	1,068	1,159	1,173	1,398	1,712	1,654	1,939	2,408
N Eng	13	19	21	22	23	27	33	32	38	47
D & H	22	33	35	38	38	46	56	54	63	79
Ches	42	63	67	72	73	87	107	103	121	151
Ohio	130	195	207	224	227	270	331	320	375	466
EGL	38	57	60	66	66	79	97	94	110	136
WGL	54	81	86	93	94	112	138	133	156	194
U Miss	290	434	461	500	506	603	739	714	837	1,039
L Mo	83	124	132	143	145	173	211	204	239	297
SOUTHEAST	275	412	437	474	480	572	700	677	793	986
SE	129	193	205	223	225	268	329	317	372	462
Cumb	13	19	21	22	23	27	33	32	38	47
Tenn	25	37	40	43	44	52	64	62	72	90
L Miss	41	61	65	71	72	85	104	101	118	147
L AWR	67	100	106	116	117	139	171	165	193	240
MID-CONTINENT	423	633	672	730	738	880	1,077	1,041	1,220	1,516
U Mo	251	376	399	433	438	522	639	618	724	900
U AWR	74	111	118	128	129	154	188	182	213	265
W Gulf	98	147	156	169	171	204	250	241	283	351
SOUTHWEST	158	237	251	273	276	329	402	389	456	566
RG-P	22	33	35	38	38	46	56	54	63	79
Colo	32	48	51	55	56	67	82	79	92	115
G Basin	22	33	35	38	38	46	56	54	63	79
S Pac	82	123	130	141	143	171	209	202	237	294
NORTH PACIFIC	59	88	94	102	103	123	150	145	170	211
C Pac	35	52	56	60	61	73	89	86	101	125
PNW	24	36	38	41	42	50	61	59	69	86
U.S.	1,587	2,376	2,522	2,738	2,769	3,301	4,042	3,906	4,578	5,688

Source: Projection procedures originally developed by Karl Gertel, U.S. Department of Agriculture.

Table B-3. MINING OUTPUT BY REGION AS A PERCENTAGE OF THE U.S. TOTAL, SELECTED MINERALS

	Non-metals (phosphate rock, sand & gravel, other)				Metals (copper ore, iron ore)			
	1960	1980	2000	2020	1960	1980	2000	2020
N Eng	0.0085	0.0083	0.0080	0.0078	0.0001	0	0	0
D & H	.0529	.0469	.0411	.0373	.0293	0.0310	0.0343	0.0363
Ches	.0474	.0434	.0425	.0419	.0149	.0161	.0200	.0225
Ohio	.1209	.1276	.1341	.1384	.0083	.0119	.0157	.0181
EGL	.1162	.1356	.1585	.1735	.0137	.0170	.0251	.0303
WGL	.0566	.0548	.0532	.0522	.0949	.1099	.1347	.1569
U Miss	.1637	.1672	.1528	.1431	.0932	.1104	.1273	.1376
L Mo	.0072	.0070	.0061	.0056	0	0	0	0
SE	.0730	.0668	.0663	.0659	.0119	.0128	.0161	.0182
Cumb	.0012	.0012	.0011	.0010	0	0	0	0
Tenn	.0311	.0263	.0233	.0213	.0032	.0033	.0037	.0039
L Miss	.0479	.0384	.0296	.0238	0	0	0	0
L AWR	.0220	.0145	.0102	.0074	.0873	.0684	.0605	.0549
U Mo	.0372	.0401	.0218	.0096	.0459	.0594	.0408	.0282
U AWR	.0078	.0065	.0046	.0034	.0128	.0125	.0110	.0099
W Gulf	.0645	.0604	.0554	.0520	.0116	.0137	.0158	.0171
RG-P	.0118	.0100	.0090	.0084	.0309	.0312	.0357	.0384
Colo	.0076	.0063	.0031	.0010	.1982	.1917	.1182	.0687
G Basin	.0055	.0042	.0025	.0013	.1282	.1146	.0839	.0631
S Pac	.0317	.0437	.0580	.0676	.0001	0	0	0
C Pac	.0745	.0843	.1134	.1327	.0544	.0758	.1286	.1627
PNW	0.0107	0.0065	0.0055	0.0049	0.1612	0.1202	0.1285	0.1332

Source: Derived from *Future Water Requirements of Principal Water-Using Industries*, Committee Print No. 8, Senate Select Committee on National Water Resources, 86th Cong., 2d sess. (1960).

Table B-4. MINING OUTPUT BY REGION AS A PERCENTAGE OF THE U.S. TOTAL

	Bituminous coal		Crude petroleum & natural gas		Natural gas liquids	
	1960	1980-2020	1960	1980-2020	1960	1980-2020
N Eng	0	0	0	0	0	0
D & H	0	0	0	0	0	0
Ches	0.0014	0.0014	0.0003	0.0003	0	0
Ohio	.7567	.7567	.1694	.1480	0.1410	0.1360
EGL	0	0	.0208	.0206	0	0
WGL	0	0	.0051	.0050	.0003	.0002
U Miss	.1080	.1080	.0306	.0306	0	0
L Mo	.0129	.0129	.0015	.0020	0	0
SE	.0682	.0682	.0025	.0027	.0040	.0050
Cumb	.0205	.0205	.0020	.0013	0	0
Tenn	.0036	.0036	.0001	.0001	0	0
L Miss	0	0	.0575	.0565	.3930	.3790
L AWR	.0086	.0086	.0414	.0409	.0130	.0130
U Mo	.0033	.0033	.0580	.0797	.0100	.0190
U AWR	.0028	.0028	.2193	.2193	.0500	.0530
W Gulf	0	0	.2787	.2791	.3100	.3110
RG-P	0	0	.0482	.0478	.0420	.0420
Colo	0.0141	0.0141	.0048	.0064	0	.0040
G Basin	0	0	.0001	.0002	0	.0020
S Pac	0	0	.0414	.0412	.0190	.0180
C Pac	0	0	0.0183	.0183	0.0180	.0170
PNW	0	0	0	0.0003	0	0.0010

Source: Derived from *Future Water Requirements of Principal Water-Using Industries*, Committee Print No. 8, Senate Select Committee on National Water Resources, 86th Cong., 2d sess. (1960).

Table B-5. FRESHWATER WITHDRAWALS FROM MUNICIPAL SYSTEMS BY USERS OF 20 MGY AND OVER AS A PERCENTAGE OF THE USERS' TOTAL FRESHWATER WITHDRAWALS

	1959	1964	Estimate used in this study
Food	27.7	28.2	28
Paper	12.4	12.0	12
Chemicals	6.3	10.7	10
Petroleum	18.2	18.3	18
Primary metals	8.2	4.0	5
Textiles	29.6	31.5	30
Lumber & wood	7.8	4.8	5
Rubber & plastics	22.1	17.9	20
Stone, clay, glass	10.2	15.3	12
Leather products	41.7	37.5	40
All other manufacturing (Other than ten above)	67.7	50.4	60

Source: Census of Manufactures.

Table B-6. ESTIMATED INDUSTRIAL FRESHWATER WITHDRAWALS IN ESTUARINE AREAS AS A PERCENTAGE OF TOTAL REGIONAL FRESHWATER WITHDRAWALS BY INDUSTRY

	Reported 1963[a]	Estimate used in this study
New England	14	15
Delaware-Hudson	49	50
Chesapeake Bay	14	20
Southeast	2	5
Lower Mississippi	17	15
Western Gulf	5	10
South Pacific	74	85
Central Pacific		60
Pacific Northwest	30	30

[a]*Census of Manufactures.*

Table B-7. WITHDRAWAL COEFFICIENTS FOR FOOD AND KINDRED PRODUCTS, BY REGION

(gallons per $1 value added)

	1960	1980	2000	2020
N Eng	41	37	33	30
D & H	35	32	28	26
Ches	50	45	40	36
Ohio	59	53	48	43
EGL	32	29	26	23
WGL	46	41	37	34
U Miss	84	76	68	61
L Mo	95	86	77	69
SE	88	79	71	64
Cumb	91	82	74	66
Tenn	51	46	41	37
L Miss	215	194	174	157
L AWR	69	62	56	50
U Mo	95	86	77	69
U AWR	69	62	56	50
W Gulf	26	23	21	19
RG-P	26	23	21	19
Colo	63	57	51	46
G Basin	227	204	184	166
S Pac	48	43	39	35
C Pac	48	43	39	35
PNW	122	110	99	89

Source: Computed from Census of Manufactures.

Table B-8. WITHDRAWAL COEFFICIENTS FOR PULP AND PAPER, BY REGION

(gallons per $1 value added)

	1960	1980	2000	2020
N Eng	472	425	382	345
D & H	432	389	350	315
Ches	607	546	492	443
Ohio	260	234	211	190
EGL	464	418	376	339
WGL	371	334	301	271
U Miss	367	330	297	268
L Mo	625	562	506	456
SE	494	445	400	361
Cumb[a]	716	644	580	523
Tenn	716	644	580	523
L Miss	302	272	245	220
L AWR	308	277	249	225
U Mo	625	562	506	456
U AWR	308	277	249	225
W Gulf	402	362	326	293
RG-P	402	362	326	293
Colo[b]	271	244	220	198
G Basin[b]	271	244	220	198
S Pac	271	244	220	198
C Pac	271	244	220	198
PNW	746	671	604	545

Source: Computed from the Census of Manufactures.

[a]Coefficient for Tennessee.
[b]Coefficient for California.

Table B-9.   WITHDRAWAL COEFFICIENTS FOR
CHEMICALS, BY REGION

(gallons per $1 value added)

	1960	1980	2000	2020
N Eng	72	58	46	37
D & H	72	58	46	37
Ches	294	235	188	150
Ohio	458	366	293	234
EGL	389	311	249	198
WGL	157	126	100	80
U Miss	94	75	60	48
L Mo	110	88	70	56
SE	178	142	114	91
Cumb[a]	418	334	268	213
Tenn	418	334	268	213
L Miss	381	305	244	194
L AWR	251	201	161	128
U Mo	110	88	70	56
U AWR	251	201	161	128
W Gulf	119	95	76	61
RG-P	119	95	76	61
Colo[b]	49	39	31	25
G Basin[b]	49	39	31	25
S Pac	49	39	31	25
C Pac	49	39	31	25
PNW	333	266	213	170

Source: Computed from the *Census of Manufactures*.

[a]Coefficient for Tennessee
[b]Coefficient for California.

Table B-11.   WITHDRAWAL COEFFICIENTS FOR
PRIMARY METALS, BY REGION

(gallons per $1 value added)

	1960	1980	2000	2020
N Eng	69	55	44	35
D & H	234	187	150	119
Ches	92	74	59	47
Ohio	389	311	249	198
EGL	413	330	264	211
WGL	428	342	274	218
U Miss	225	180	144	115
L Mo	45	36	29	23
SE	187	150	120	95
Cumb[a]	50	40	32	26
Tenn	50	40	32	26
L Miss	187[b]	150	120	95
L AWR	199	159	127	101
U Mo	45	36	29	23
U AWR	199	159	127	101
W Gulf	52	42	42[d]	42[d]
RG-P	52	42	42[d]	42[d]
Colo	263	210	168	134
G Basin[c]	263	210	168	134
S Pac	41	33	26	21
C Pac	41	33	26	21
PNW	195	156	125	99

Source: Computed from *Census of Manufactures*.

[a]Coefficient for Tennessee.
[b]Coefficient for Southeast.
[c]Coefficient for Colorado.
[d]Coefficient for Western Gulf and Rio Grande-Pecos left at 1980
level to avoid assumption that intake is exceeded by loss.

Table B-10.   WITHDRAWAL COEFFICIENTS FOR
PETROLEUM AND COAL PRODUCTS,
BY REGION

(gallons per $1 value added)

	1960	1980	2000	2020
N Eng	67	54	43	34
D & H	362	290	232	185
Ches	32	32	32	32
Ohio	343	274	220	175
EGL	519	415	332	265
WGL	755	604	483	385
U Miss	132	106	84	67
L Mo	270	216	173	138
SE[a]	681	545	436	347
Cumb[a]	681	545	436	347
Tenn[a]	681	545	436	347
L Miss	681	545	436	347
L AWR	107	86	68	68
U Mo	270	216	173	138
U AWR	107	86	68	68
W Gulf	213	170	136	109
RG-P	213	170	136	109
Colo[b]	80	64	51	51
G Basin[b]	80	64	51	51
S Pac	80	64	51	51
C Pac	80	64	51	51
PNW	97	78	62	49

Source: Computed from *Census of Manufactures*.

[a]Coefficient for Lower Mississippi.
[b]Coefficient for California.

Table B-12. WITHDRAWALS FOR SELECTED MANUFACTURING INDUSTRIES, BY REGION: 1960

(million gallons per year)

	Textiles	Lumber & wood	Rubber & plastics	Stone, clay, glass	Leather	All other
N Eng	25,920	0	21,000	2,970	2,850	81,600
D & H	15,360	0	7,000	40,590	1,900	100,980
Ches	2,880	0	7,000	9,900	1,900	16,320
Ohio	960	940	8,000	22,770	950	70,380
EGL	0	0	51,000	27,720	0	123,420
WGL	960	0	6,000	76,230	2,850	67,320
U Miss	0	940	4,000	41,580	0	52,020
L Mo	0	0	2,000	4,950	0	2,040
SE	69,120	2,820	6,000	15,840	0	10,200
Cumb	0	0	0	0	0	0
Tenn	6,720	0	5,000	990	0	2,040
L Miss	960	940	3,000	0	0	0
L AWR	0	940	0	990	0	0
U Mo	0	0	1,000	3,960	0	1,020
U AWR	0	0	0	1,980	0	1,020
W Gulf	960	1,880	1,000	2,970	0	4,080
RG-P	0	0	0	0	0	1,020
Colo	0	0	0	0	0	0
G Basin	0	0	0	0	0	0
S Pac	0	0	1,000	11,880	0	9,180
C Pac	0	15,980	0	8,910	0	6,120
PNW	0	83,660	0	1,980	0	2,040

Source: Census of Manufactures.

Table B-13. INDEX OF WITHDRAWALS AND LOSSES PER DOLLAR OF VALUE ADDED, BY SELECTED INDUSTRIES

(1960 = 100)

		Textiles	Lumber & wood	Rubber & plastics	Stone, clay, glass	Other manufacturing	
1960		100	100	100	100	100	100
1980	L M H	90	80	80	80	90	80
2000	L M H	81	64	64	64	81	64
2020	L M H	73	51	51	51	73	51

Table B-14. TOTAL LOSS COEFFICIENTS FOR
SELECTED INDUSTRIES FOR ALL
YEARS, BY REGION

(gallons per $1 value added)

	Food	Paper	Chemicals	Petroleum	Primary metals
N Eng	6	56	14	7	7
D & H	6	15	9	40	21
Ches	6	84	18	32	14
Ohio	6	23	20	75	21
EGL	5	26	61	53	21
WGL	5	22	11	48	15
U Miss	9	25	9	38	39
L Mo	6	10[a]	17	59	6
SE	7	19	31	58	42
Cumb	7	29[b]	17	58	6
Tenn	6	29	17	58	6
L Miss	11	9	29	58	42
L AWR	11	10	36	62	29
U Mo	6	10[a]	17	59	6
U AWR	11	10	36	62	29
W Gulf	5	65	36	66	36
RG-P	5	65	36	66	36
Colo	9	21[c]	24	44	104
G Basin	12	21[c]	24	44	104
S Pac	9	21	24	44	11
C Pac	9	21	24	44	11
PNW	7	21	43	34	21

Note: Total loss coefficients = in-plant and in-stream losses.

[a]Arbitrary figure; 1959 loss coefficient insignificant.
[b]Coefficient for Tennessee.
[c]Coefficient for California.

Table B-15. LOSSES FROM SELECTED MANUFACTURING INDUSTRIES: 1960

(million gallons per year)

	Textiles	Lumber & wood	Rubber & plastics	Stone, clay, glass	Leather	All other
N Eng	2,880	0	1,000	0	950	25,500
D & H	1,920	0	1,000	1,980	0	2,040
Ches	0	0	1,000	990	0	2,040
Ohio	0	0	1,000	1,980	0	7,140
EGL	0	0	3,000	2,970	0	5,100
WGL	0	0	0	3,960	0	2,040
U Miss	0	0	0	1,980	0	1,020
L Mo	0	0	0	990	0	0
SE	7,680	940	0	6,930	0	1,020
Cumb	0	0	0	0	0	0
Tenn	960	0	1,000	0	0	1,020
L Miss	0	940	0	0	0	0
L AWR	0	0	0	990	0	0
U Mo	0	0	0	0	0	0
U AWR	0	0	0	990	0	0
W Gulf	0	940	1,000	990	0	1,020
RG-P	0	0	0	0	0	0
Colo	0	0	0	0	0	0
G Basin	0	0	0	0	0	0
S Pac	0	0	0	1,980	0	2,040
C Pac	0	2,820	0	990	0	1,020
PNW	0	6,580	0	0	0	0

Table B-16. COOLING WATER AS A PERCENTAGE
OF DISCHARGE, MANUFACTURING
SECTORS, ALL YEARS

Food	73
Paper	37
Chemicals	87
Petroleum refining	93
Primary metals	76
Textiles	34
Lumber and wood	81
Rubber and plastics	83
Stone, clay, glass	79
Leather	17
All other	77

Table B-17. WITHDRAWALS FOR STEAM-ELECTRIC
POWER AT ORIGINAL RECIRCULATION
RATES, BY REGION

(gallons per kilowatt-hour)

	1960	1980	2000	2020
N Eng	9	8	7	6
D & H	21	12	10	9
Ches	41	26	21	19
Ohio	51	48	39	36
EGL	64	48	39	36
WGL	67	55	44	42
U Miss	66	55	44	42
L Mo	63	55	44	42
SE	46	18	15	14
Cumb	41	40	33	31
Tenn	42	40	33	31
L Miss	42	37	30	28
L AWR	46	47	38	35
U Mo	40	23	14	12
U AWR	15	0.7	0.6	0.6
W Gulf	13	4	2	2
RG-P	16	0.7	0.6	0.6
Colo	5	0.9	0.8	0.8
G Basin	13	0.9	0.8	0.8
S Pac	0.3	0.2	0.2	0.2
C Pac	0.3	0.2	0.2	0.2
PNW	66	21	16	15

Table B-18. ORIGINAL AND REVISED RECIRCULATION RATES FOR STEAM-ELECTRIC POWER, BY REGION

	Withdrawals: percentage of total that is fresh		Recirculation rates[a]						
				Original projection			Revised projection		
	1960	1980–2020	1960	1980	2000	2020	1980	2000	2020
N Eng	17	15	1.25	1.14	1.22	1.30	3.5	10.1	29.0
D & H	33	25	1.08	1.14	1.22	1.30	8.8	8.8	8.8
Ches	65	50	1.04	1.14	1.22	1.30	4.3	4.3	4.3
Ohio	100	100	1.05	1.14	1.22	1.30	27.6	27.6	27.6
EGL	100	100	1.02	1.14	1.22	1.30	70.0	70.0	70.0
WGL	100	100	1.02	1.14	1.22	1.30	16.6	16.6	16.6
U Miss	100	100	1.08	1.14	1.22	1.30	5.1	5.2	6.3
L Mo	100	100	1.06	1.14	1.22	1.30	4.1	4.1	5.1
SE	59	45	1.13	1.14	1.22	1.30	1.14	1.14	1.14
Cumb	100	100	1.11	1.14	1.22	1.30	1.14	1.14	1.14
Tenn	100	100	1.09	1.14	1.22	1.30	3.1	3.1	3.7
L Miss	87	80	1.11	1.14	1.22	1.30	5.6	5.6	5.6
L AWR	100	100	1.47	1.14	1.22	1.30	1.3	1.5	1.9
U Mo	100	100	1.70	2.58	3.46	4.34			
U AWR	100	100	4.49	70.00	70.00	70.00			
W Gulf	82	75	4.77	10.21	15.65	21.09			
RG-P	100	100	4.77	70.00	70.00	70.00			
Colo	100	100	11.89	70.00	70.00	70.00		Unchanged from	
G Basin	100	100	6.72	70.00	70.00	70.00		original projection	
S Pac	28	25	70.00[b]	70.00	70.00	70.00			
C Pac	28	25	70.00[b]	70.00	70.00	70.00			
PNW	100	100	2.19	2.51	2.83	3.15			3.50

Source: 1960 estimated from 1959 Bureau of the Census data.

[a]Gross application divided by intake. "Gross application" is total flow-through including recirculated water.
[b]Actual data for California shows 79. This may be an overstatement.

Table B–19. ANNUAL GROWTH RATES OF
                  MUNICIPAL PER CAPITA WATER IN-
                  TAKE, BY DIVISION

(percent)

	I 1954–1980	II 1980–2000 (Col. I ÷ 2)	III 2000–2020 (Col. I ÷ 3)
Northeast	1.29	0.65	0.43
Southeast	2.36	1.18	.79
Mid-Continent	1.93	0.97	.64
Southwest	1.50	0.75	.50
North Pacific	0.50	0.25	.17
U.S.	1.50	0.75	0.50

Sources: F. P. Linaweaver, Jr., "Report II, Phase Two, Residential Water Use" (The Johns Hopkins University, June 1965, mimeo.), and U.S. Public Health Service, *Survey of Municipal Water Facilities* (1958, 1960, 1962, 1964).

Table B–20. MUNICIPAL LOSSES AS A PERCENTAGE
                  OF INTAKE, BY REGION

	Fraction of regional urban population in coastal SMSAs	Fraction of municipal intake lost in upstream areas	Fraction of municipal intake lost for region
N Eng	55	25	66¼
D & H	85	25	88¾
Ches	70	25	77½
Ohio		25	25
EGL		25	25
WGL		25	25
U Miss		25	25
L Mo		25	25
SE	30	25	47½
Cumb		25	25
Tenn		25	25
L Miss	35	25	51¼
L AWR		25	25
U Mo		40	40
U AWR		40	40
W Gulf	30	35	54½
RG-P		40	40
Colo		40	40
G Basin		40	40
S Pac	95	40	97
C Pac	65	40	79
PNW	65	40	79

Table B-21.   MAJOR COASTAL CITIES WITH AN UPLAND WATER SUPPLY (INCLUDING GROUNDWATER) AND OCEAN DISCHARGE

	Discharge to:	Comments
Everett, Wash.	Puget Sound	
Seattle, Wash.	Puget Sound	
Tacoma, Wash.	Puget Sound	
Vancouver, Wash.	Tidal Columbia River	Groundwater
Portland, Oreg.	Tidal Columbia River	
Oakland, Berkeley, etc., Calif. (East Bay Municipal Utility District)	San Francisco Bay	
San Francisco, Calif.	San Francisco Bay, Pacific Ocean	
San Jose, Calif.	San Francisco Bay	Groundwater
San Diego, Calif.	Pacific Ocean	
Los Angeles, Calif.	Pacific Ocean	Some groundwater
Metropolitan Water District of S. Calif.	Pacific Ocean	
Santa Barbara, Calif.	Pacific Ocean	Some groundwater
San Luis Obispo, Calif.	Pacific Ocean	
Riverside, Calif.	Pacific Ocean	Some groundwater
Santa Ana, Calif.	Pacific Ocean	Some groundwater

Note: Essentially all of San Francisco Bay and Southern California areas are supplied from upland and groundwater sources and discharge to Pacific Ocean or adjacent bays.

Corpus Christi, Tex.	Gulf of Mexico	
Galveston-Texas City, Tex.	Gulf of Mexico	Groundwater
Houston, Tex.	Gulf of Mexico	Some groundwater
Beaumont-Port Arthur, Tex.	Gulf of Mexico	Some groundwater
New Orleans, La.	Tidal Mississippi River	
Mobile, Ala.	Gulf of Mexico	
Pensacola, Fla.	Gulf of Mexico	Groundwater
Saint Petersburg, Fla.	Tampa Bay	Groundwater
Tampa, Fla.	Tampa Bay	Some groundwater
Miami, Miami Beach, Fla.	Atlantic Ocean	Groundwater

Note: Apparently the East coast of Florida from Palm Beach to Coral Gables obtains water from wells and/or surface sources and discharges to the ocean.

Savannah, Ga.	Tidal Savannah River	Some groundwater
Charleston, S.C.	Tidal Cooper River	
Wilmington, N.C.	Tidal Cape Fear River	
Norfolk-Newport News, Va.	Tidal James River	
Washington, D.C. (metro. area)	Potomac estuary	Some groundwater
Baltimore, Md.	Chesapeake Bay	
Wilmington, Del.	Tidal Delaware River	
Philadelphia, Pa. (Schuylkill)	Tidal Delaware River	
Chester, Pa.	Tidal Delaware River	
Camden, N.J.	Tidal Delaware River	Groundwater
Northeastern New Jersey (Hackensack, Newark, Middlesex, etc.)	Essentially Atlantic Ocean	Some groundwater
New York City, N.Y.	Atlantic Ocean	
Atlantic City, N.J.	Atlantic Ocean	Groundwater
Bridgeport, Conn.	Atlantic Ocean	
New Haven, Conn.	Atlantic Ocean	Some groundwater
Providence, R.I. (metro. area)	Naragansett Bay	Some groundwater
Fall River, Mass.	Naragansett Bay	
New Bedford, Mass.	Atlantic Ocean	
Boston, Mass. (metro. area)	Atlantic Ocean	
Portland, Maine	Atlantic Ocean	

Note: Table prepared by Blair T. Bower, Resources for the Future, October 1966.

Table B-22.   ESTIMATED PERCENTAGE OF LAND
              UNDER TREATMENT, BY REGION

	1960	1980	2000
N Eng	16	31	46
D & H	17	34	49
Ches	17	37	54
SE	25	45	72
EGL	19	38	54
WGL	14	26	45
Ohio	18	38	56
Cumb	22	40	58
Tenn	22	40	59
U Miss	16	35	55
L Miss	20	36	58
L Mo	23	36	55
L AWR	19	34	56
U Mo	21	34	54
U AWR	13	24	38
W Gulf	16	28	52
RG-P	6	21	35
Colo	14	26	47
G Basin	7	16	30
PNW	27	40	58
C Pac	18	35	48
S Pac	11	20	34

Note: Percentages relate to the total of areas designated as crop-
land, open pasture and grazing land, and woodland and forest in
*Estimated Water Requirements for Agricultural Purposes and Their
Effects on Water Supplies*, Committee Print No. 13, Senate Select
Committee on National Water Resources, 86th Cong., 2d sess.
(1960), table 4.

Table B-23.   ESTIMATED LOSSES FOR SWAMPS AND
              WETLANDS, BY REGION: 1960

(million gallons per day)

Region	Value	Region	Value
N Eng	494	L Miss	10,661
D & H	1,400	L AWR	2,152
Ches	969	U Mo	19,615
Ohio	190	U AWR	1,197
EGL	1,151	W Gulf	14,115
WGL	4,027	RG-P	1,547
U Miss	5,263	Colo	280
L Mo	0	G Basin	5,816
SE	22,500	S Pac	8
Cumb	50	C Pac	3,867
Tenn	72	PNW	529

Source: Estimates represent updating of 1954 acreages given in
Fish and Wildlife and Water Resources, Committee Print No. 18,
Senate Select Committee on National Water Resources, 86th Cong.,
2d sess. (1960).

Appendix C

AGGREGATE WITHDRAWALS AND LOSSES BY MAJOR USE

Table C-1. WITHDRAWALS FOR AGRICULTURE, BY REGION

(million gallons per day)

	1960	1980			2000			2020		
		L	M	H	L	M	H	L	M	H
NORTHEAST	2,498	3,431	3,606	3,947	3,743	4,264	5,101	4,682	5,305	6,640
N Eng	149	192	203	225	204	240	288	255	297	385
D & H	316	426	451	515	431	491	624	498	567	767
Ches	282	404	422	479	449	496	587	541	602	754
Ohio	536	689	727	787	732	852	1,019	919	1,054	1,324
EGL	195	255	269	291	268	310	370	326	375	474
WGL	258	350	365	393	373	418	492	455	503	624
U Miss	615	872	915	985	994	1,134	1,345	1,300	1,468	1,800
L Mo	147	243	254	272	292	323	376	388	439	512
SOUTHEAST	4,169	6,074	6,222	6,646	6,846	7,235	8,335	7,795	8,295	10,180
SE	1,501	1,855	1,902	1,947	1,990	2,124	2,267	2,329	2,489	2,802
Cumb	50	56	59	64	55	64	77	67	77	96
Tenn	149	205	216	233	217	247	296	260	296	377
L Miss	1,169	2,028	2,059	2,212	2,446	2,530	2,934	2,812	2,931	3,630
L AWR	1,302	1,930	1,986	2,190	2,138	2,270	2,761	2,327	2,502	3,275
MID-CONTINENT	38,561	35,000	37,482	41,550	30,632	33,849	40,256	31,015	34,606	42,659
U Mo	18,382	16,453	17,512	18,764	14,307	15,879	18,227	14,562	16,424	19,734
U AWR	7,376	7,391	7,761	9,227	6,669	7,108	9,156	6,727	7,192	9,525
W Gulf	12,803	11,156	12,209	13,559	9,656	10,862	12,873	9,726	10,990	13,400
SOUTHWEST	40,146	33,788	34,866	36,166	29,534	31,140	33,642	29,880	31,827	35,457
RG-P	7,637	6,331	6,784	7,234	5,085	5,639	6,373	5,110	5,731	6,707
Colo	19,921	16,087	16,506	16,883	14,218	14,901	15,681	14,288	15,137	16,301
G Basin	8,307	7,119	7,289	7,491	6,129	6,412	6,822	6,180	6,545	7,162
S Pac	4,281	4,251	4,287	4,558	4,102	4,188	4,766	4,302	4,414	5,287
NORTH PACIFIC	53,210	51,420	52,707	54,602	46,770	49,097	53,271	48,415	51,629	58,459
C Pac	30,912	31,924	32,224	33,119	29,615	30,264	32,363	31,019	32,028	35,631
PNW	22,298	19,496	20,483	21,483	17,155	18,833	20,908	17,396	19,601	22,828
U.S.	138,586	129,713	134,883	142,911	117,525	125,585	140,605	121,787	131,662	153,395

195

Table C-2. WITHDRAWALS FOR MINING, BY REGION

(million gallons per day)

	1960	1980			2000			2020		
		L	M	H	L	M	H	L	M	H
NORTHEAST	1,207	2,400	3,383	4,786	3,997	7,701	14,811	6,718	21,031	47,574
N Eng	12	26	37	53	45	90	176	78	253	578
D & H	94	170	245	350	260	515	1,001	406	1,303	2,959
Ches	78	148	213	305	256	509	991	439	1,418	3,227
Ohio	372	685	926	1,282	1,059	1,908	3,576	1,705	4,996	11,181
EGL	183	444	638	914	920	1,828	3,565	1,770	5,717	13,033
WGL	139	260	372	528	416	814	1,562	666	2,100	4,715
U Miss	316	642	916	1,304	1,003	1,964	3,798	1,594	5,056	11,454
L Mo	13	25	36	50	38	73	142	60	188	427
SOUTHEAST	467	772	1,063	1,478	1,051	1,905	3,514	1,514	4,394	9,711
SE	124	235	334	477	404	793	1,541	694	2,214	5,042
Cumb	5	8	11	15	11	19	35	15	41	92
Tenn	48	85	122	175	135	268	524	217	702	1,602
L Miss	190	318	421	569	365	581	971	437	1,021	2,085
L AWR	100	126	175	242	136	244	443	151	416	890
MID-CONTINENT	470	847	1,123	1,525	964	1,572	2,695	1,146	2,799	5,819
U Mo	102	218	303	423	204	366	670	168	441	937
U AWR	100	158	198	260	163	224	332	171	291	505
W Gulf	268	471	622	842	597	982	1,693	807	2,067	4,377
SOUTHWEST	336	544	764	1,063	689	1,289	2,408	1,014	3,076	6,847
RG-P	61	97	131	179	123	209	367	160	423	895
Colo	129	179	254	352	126	233	426	80	221	463
G Basin	82	105	150	208	87	163	300	71	206	437
S Pac	64	163	229	324	353	684	1,315	203	2,226	5,052
NORTH PACIFIC	259	454	649	918	903	1,763	3,382	1,659	5,246	11,813
C Pac	150	338	483	687	762	1,496	2,887	1,489	4,743	10,733
PNW	109	116	166	231	141	267	495	170	503	1,080
U.S.	2,739	5,017	6,982	9,770	7,604	14,230	26,810	12,051	36,546	81,764

Table C-3. WITHDRAWALS FOR MANUFACTURING, BY REGION

(million gallons per day)

	1960	1980			2000			2020		
		L	M	H	L	M	H	L	M	H
NORTHEAST	16,986	19,987	26,855	36,123	22,105	38,345	67,816	29,405	53,867	119,377
N Eng	948	1,163	1,396	1,665	1,439	2,139	3,385	2,087	3,366	6,984
D & H	2,035	2,232	2,858	3,748	2,487	4,079	7,022	3,255	5,759	12,585
Ches	931	1,620	2,075	2,742	1,887	3,128	5,717	2,553	4,583	10,743
Ohio	5,454	5,725	7,999	11,110	5,703	10,363	19,085	7,133	13,448	31,576
EGL	3,221	3,973	5,472	7,535	4,536	8,226	14,968	6,063	11,698	27,959
WGL	3,315	4,016	5,470	7,239	4,507	7,984	13,437	6,065	11,234	22,302
U Miss	981	1,049	1,324	1,747	1,140	1,809	3,198	1,464	2,527	4,869
L Mo	101	209	261	337	406	617	1,004	785	1,252	2,359
SOUTHEAST	3,311	5,596	7,095	9,325	7,818	12,615	22,528	12,313	21,207	47,502
SE	1,618	2,777	3,427	4,204	3,804	5,888	9,648	5,927	9,755	19,816
Cumb	16	559	737	1,058	801	1,375	2,765	1,251	2,313	5,940
Tenn	717	801	1,048	1,468	1,006	1,687	3,256	1,473	2,655	6,508
L Miss	670	1,062	1,378	1,946	1,704	2,859	5,511	2,885	5,189	12,605
L AWR	290	397	505	649	503	806	1,348	777	1,295	2,633
MID-CONTINENT	1,098	1,460	1,862	2,542	2,417	3,878	6,923	4,305	7,304	15,725
U Mo	196	200	245	337	623	906	1,423	1,418	2,158	3,919
U AWR	193	236	316	441	366	619	1,149	622	1,103	2,512
W Gulf	709	1,024	1,301	1,764	1,428	2,353	4,351	2,265	4,043	9,294
SOUTHWEST	245	455	592	781	845	1,309	2,104	1,630	2,587	4,738
RG-P	40	40	48	59	127	183	266	288	434	751
Colo	31	35	48	63	152	223	326	374	563	984
G Basin	11	154	211	283	229	376	617	399	642	1,294
S Pac	163	226	285	376	337	527	895	569	948	1,709
NORTH PACIFIC	1,286	3,954	4,789	5,529	5,263	7,851	11,777	8,323	13,094	24,804
C Pac	220	282	361	484	446	696	1,215	769	1,264	2,549
PNW	1,066	3,672	4,428	5,045	4,817	7,155	10,562	7,554	11,825	21,535
U.S.	22,926	31,452	41,193	54,300	38,448	63,998	111,148	55,976	98,059	211,426

Table C–4. WITHDRAWALS FOR STEAM-ELECTRIC POWER AT ORIGINAL RECIRCULATION RATES, BY REGION

(million gallons per day)

	1960	1980 L	1980 M	1980 H	2000 L	2000 M	2000 H	2020 L	2020 M	2020 H
NORTHEAST	48,148	104,379	142,716	205,535	135,360	225,219	382,514	231,244	404,668	799,402
N Eng	592	1,425	1,951	2,827	2,033	3,395	5,753	3,238	5,655	11,178
D & H	3,970	4,767	6,510	9,403	6,247	10,411	17,699	10,208	17,877	35,334
Ches	3,482	5,770	7,836	11,255	7,364	12,312	20,885	12,285	21,447	42,425
Ohio	17,605	41,162	56,285	81,140	52,784	87,830	149,268	88,373	154,751	305,655
EGL	6,488	13,282	18,148	26,170	18,592	30,986	52,570	33,140	57,995	114,608
WGL	9,362	22,000	30,137	43,247	27,847	46,290	78,597	48,214	84,345	166,734
U Miss	5,786	13,562	18,534	26,822	17,359	28,932	49,063	30,378	53,162	104,942
L Mo	863	2,411	3,315	4,671	3,134	5,063	8,679	5,408	9,436	78,526
SOUTHEAST	14,632	21,702	29,488	42,099	29,577	49,433	83,968	52,265	91,356	780,454
SE	7,688	8,729	11,934	17,211	11,712	19,479	33,123	20,137	35,249	69,616
Cumb	34	110	110	219	271	452	814	764	1,274	2,548
Tenn	4,258	7,671	10,411	15,014	11,030	18,444	31,373	20,299	35,501	70,068
L Miss	1,266	2,230	3,041	4,460	2,712	4,603	7,726	4,449	7,825	15,496
L AWR	1,386	2,962	3,992	5,195	3,852	6,455	10,932	6,616	11,507	22,726
MID-CONTINENT	2,830	3,697	5,058	7,244	3,715	6,163	10,484	6,356	11,151	22,039
U Mo	1,096	2,584	3,529	5,041	2,800	4,641	7,901	4,701	8,252	16,307
U AWR	452	61	82	121	82	136	232	148	258	510
W Gulf	1,282	1,052	1,447	2,082	833	1,386	2,351	1,507	2,641	5,222
SOUTHWEST	366	137	192	272	223	370	628	434	755	1,493
RG-P	175	21	31	42	30	48	82	53	92	181
Colo	96	54	74	108	96	160	272	202	351	695
G Basin	71	27	39	54	42	70	118	79	138	272
S Pac	24	35	48	68	55	92	156	100	174	345
NORTH PACIFIC	13	1,481	2,015	2,904	4,811	8,018	13,632	11,988	21,019	41,498
C Pac	13	43	59	85	77	128	218	152	266	525
PNW	0	1,438	1,956	2,819	4,734	7,890	13,414	11,836	20,753	40,973
U.S.	65,988	131,396	179,469	258,054	173,686	289,203	491,226	302,287	528,949	1,044,886

Table C–5. WITHDRAWALS FOR STEAM-ELECTRIC POWER AT REVISED RECIRCULATION RATES, BY REGION

(billion gallons per day)

	1960	1980 L	1980 M	1980 H	2000 L	2000 M	2000 H	2020 L	2020 M	2020 H
NORTHEAST	48.3	10.0	13.4	19.4	12.6	21.2	36.1	22.0	38.7	76.4
N Eng	0.6	0.4	0.5	0.7	0.2	0.3	0.6	0.2	0.3	0.6
D & H	4.0	0.8	1.1	1.6	0.6	1.0	1.8	1.1	2.0	3.9
Ches	3.5	1.6	2.1	3.0	2.1	3.5	6.0	3.9	6.8	13.4
Ohio	17.6	1.7	2.3	3.4	2.7	4.5	7.7	4.9	8.6	17.0
EGL	6.5	0.2	0.3	0.4	0.3	0.6	0.9	0.6	1.1	2.2
WGL	9.4	1.6	2.2	3.1	1.9	3.2	5.4	3.4	6.0	11.9
U Miss	5.8	3.0	4.0	5.9	3.9	6.6	11.1	6.5	11.4	22.5
L Mo	0.9	0.7	0.9	1.3	0.9	1.5	2.6	1.4	2.5	4.9
SOUTHEAST	14.7	14.8	20.1	29.2	20.1	33.8	57.3	33.9	59.2	117.0
SE	7.7	8.7	11.9	17.2	11.7	19.5	33.1	20.1	35.2	69.6
Cumb	0	0.1	0.1	0.2	0.3	0.5	0.8	0.8	1.3	2.5
Tenn	4.3	2.9	3.9	5.6	4.3	7.3	12.4	7.2	12.6	24.9
L Miss	1.3	0.5	0.7	1.1	0.7	1.2	2.1	1.3	2.2	4.4
L AWR	1.4	2.6	3.5	5.1	3.1	5.3	8.9	4.5	7.9	15.6
MID-CONTINENT	2.9	3.8	5.0	7.2	3.7	6.1	10.5	6.3	11.2	22.0
U Mo	1.1	2.6	3.5	5.0	2.8	4.6	7.9	4.7	8.3	16.3
U AWR	0.5	0.1	0.1	0.1	0.1	0.1	0.2	0.1	0.3	0.5
W Gulf	1.3	1.1	1.4	2.1	0.8	1.4	2.4	1.5	2.6	5.2
SOUTHWEST	0.4	0.1	0.1	0.3	0.2	0.4	0.7	0.5	0.8	1.5
RG-P	0.2	0	0	0	0	0	0.1	0.1	0.1	0.2
Colo	0.1	0.1	0.1	0.1	0.1	0.2	0.3	0.2	0.4	0.7
G Basin	0.1	0	0	0.1	0	0.1	0.1	0.1	0.1	0.3
S Pac	0	0	0	0.1	0.1	0.1	0.2	0.1	0.2	0.3
NORTH PACIFIC	0	1.4	2.1	2.9	4.8	8.0	13.6	10.5	18.3	36.0
C Pac	0	0	0.1	0.1	0.1	0.1	0.2	0.2	0.3	0.5
PNW	0	1.4	2.0	2.8	4.7	7.9	13.4	10.3	18.0	35.5
U.S.	66.3	30.1	40.7	59.0	41.4	69.5	118.2	73.2	128.2	252.9

Table C-6. WITHDRAWALS FOR MUNICIPAL USES, BY REGION

(million gallons per day)

	1960	1980 L	1980 M	1980 H	2000 L	2000 M	2000 H	2020 L	2020 M	2020 H
NORTHEAST	12,401	20,167	21,463	23,400	27,516	32,718	38,844	40,102	47,046	62,248
N Eng	1,069	1,683	1,791	1,953	2,223	2,646	2,223	3,198	3,751	4,964
D & H	2,931	4,579	4,874	5,315	6,047	7,199	8,767	8,654	10,152	13,433
Ches	921	1,666	1,773	1,927	2,418	2,879	3,506	3,644	4,275	5,657
Ohio	1,396	2,153	2,291	2,499	2,798	3,331	4,057	3,882	4,554	6,025
EGL	2,004	3,362	3,578	3,902	4,777	5,687	6,926	7,187	8,431	11,156
WGL	2,646	4,424	4,708	5,135	6,195	7,375	8,982	9,262	10,866	14,377
U Miss	1,241	2,000	2,129	2,322	2,694	3,207	3,905	3,841	4,506	5,961
L Mo	193	300	319	348	363	393	479	435	510	674
SOUTHEAST	2,345	5,889	6,254	6,822	9,766	11,627	14,160	16,036	18,812	24,891
SE	1,481	4,046	4,306	4,696	6,932	8,253	10,051	11,790	13,831	18,301
Cumb	78	165	175	191	256	305	371	379	444	588
Tenn	179	424	451	493	678	807	983	1,067	1,252	1,657
L Miss	339	730	778	848	1,212	1,443	1,758	1,953	2,291	3,031
L AWR	268	524	544	594	687	818	996	847	994	1,315
MID-CONTINENT	1,685	3,243	3,452	3,751	4,841	5,692	6,931	7,131	8,366	11,069
U Mo	520	1,039	1,106	1,206	1,574	1,873	2,282	2,408	2,825	3,738
U AWR	295	491	523	558	671	727	885	778	913	1,207
W Gulf	870	1,713	1,823	1,988	2,596	3,091	3,764	3,945	4,628	6,123
SOUTHWEST	2,078	5,281	5,619	6,129	8,374	9,970	12,141	13,382	15,699	20,772
RG-P	148	343	365	398	536	639	778	851	998	1,321
Colo	200	695	739	806	1,128	1,343	1,636	1,972	2,313	3,061
G Basin	171	305	324	354	389	464	565	483	567	750
S Pac	1,559	3,938	4,191	4,571	6,320	7,524	9,163	10,076	11,821	15,641
NORTH PACIFIC	1,565	2,447	2,604	2,834	3,318	3,950	4,812	4,575	5,367	7,101
C Pac	750	1,217	1,296	1,407	1,630	1,941	2,363	2,187	2,566	3,396
PNW	815	1,230	1,308	1,427	1,688	2,009	2,449	2,387	2,801	3,706
U.S.	20,074	37,028	39,394	42,936	53,815	63,957	76,888	81,225	95,289	126,081

Table C-7. WITHDRAWALS FOR ALL USES AT REVISED RECIRCULATION RATES, BY REGION

(million gallons per day)

	1960	1980 L	1980 M	1980 H	2000 L	2000 M	2000 H	2020 L	2020 M	2020 H
NORTHEAST	81,392	55,985	68,707	87,656	69,961	104,228	151,684	102,907	165,949	312,239
N Eng	2,778	3,464	3,927	4,596	4,111	5,415	6,672	5,818	7,967	13,511
D & H	9,376	8,207	9,528	11,528	9,825	13,284	19,214	13,913	19,781	33,644
Ches	5,712	5,438	6,583	8,453	7,110	10,512	16,801	11,077	17,678	33,781
Ohio	25,358	10,952	14,243	19,078	12,992	20,954	35,437	18,539	32,652	67,106
EGL	12,103	8,234	10,257	13,042	10,801	16,651	26,729	15,946	27,321	54,822
WGL	15,758	10,650	13,115	16,395	13,391	19,791	29,873	19,848	30,703	53,918
U Miss	8,953	7,563	9,284	12,258	9,731	14,714	12,357	14,699	24,957	46,584
L Mo	1,354	1,477	1,770	2,307	1,999	2,906	4,601	3,068	4,889	8,872
SOUTHEAST	24,994	33,131	40,734	53,471	45,581	67,182	105,837	71,558	111,908	209,284
SE	12,424	17,613	21,869	28,524	24,830	36,558	56,607	40,840	63,489	115,561
Cumb	149	888	1,082	1,528	1,423	2,263	4,048	2,512	4,175	9,216
Tenn	5,393	4,415	5,737	7,969	6,336	10,309	5,183	10,217	17,505	35,044
L Miss	3,668	4,638	5,336	6,675	6,427	8,613	13,274	9,387	13,632	25,751
L AWR	3,360	5,577	6,710	8,775	6,564	9,438	14,448	8,602	13,107	23,713
MID-CONTINENT	44,714	44,350	48,919	56,568	42,554	51,091	67,305	49,897	64,275	97,272
U Mo	20,300	20,510	22,666	25,730	19,508	23,624	30,502	23,256	30,148	44,628
U AWR	8,464	8,376	8,898	10,586	7,969	8,778	11,722	8,398	9,799	14,249
W Gulf	15,950	15,464	17,355	20,253	15,077	18,688	25,081	18,243	24,328	38,394
SOUTHWEST	43,205	40,168	41,941	44,439	39,642	44,108	50,995	46,406	53,989	69,314
RG-P	8,086	6,811	7,328	7,870	5,871	6,670	7,884	6,509	7,686	9,874
Colo	20,381	17,096	17,647	18,204	15,724	16,900	18,369	16,914	18,634	21,509
G Basin	8,671	7,683	7,974	8,436	6,834	7,515	8,404	7,233	8,060	9,943
S. Pac	6,067	8,578	8,992	9,929	11,212	13,023	16,339	15,750	19,609	27,989
NORTH PACIFIC	56,320	59,675	62,849	66,783	61,054	70,661	86,842	73,472	93,636	137,457
C Pac	32,032	33,761	34,464	35,797	32,553	34,497	39,028	35,664	40,906	52,809
PNW	24,288	25,914	28,385	30,986	28,501	36,164	47,814	37,807	52,730	84,649
U.S.	262,436	233,309	263,150	308,917	258,792	337,270	450,386	344,239	489,756	825,566

Table C-8. LOSSES FROM AGRICULTURE, BY REGION

(million gallons per day)

	1960	1980 L	1980 M	1980 H	2000 L	2000 M	2000 H	2020 L	2020 M	2020 H
NORTHEAST	1,391	2,152	2,248	2,443	2,511	2,820	3,351	3,259	3,644	4,468
N Eng	56	65	68	74	70	81	95	88	100	125
D & H	196	265	281	326	261	292	378	289	324	443
Ches	141	243	251	275	294	319	372	368	401	491
Ohio	241	355	372	400	412	472	558	549	622	756
EGL	90	134	140	151	153	173	205	195	221	272
WGL	140	222	229	245	261	286	334	332	362	440
U Miss	422	672	703	754	811	920	1,087	1,095	1,232	1,493
L Mo	105	196	204	218	249	277	322	343	382	448
SOUTHEAST	3,382	5,037	5,141	5,475	5,961	6,238	7,151	6,845	7,235	8,821
SE	1,089	1,406	1,428	1,437	1,596	1,670	1,734	1,909	2,011	2,198
Cumb	22	31	33	35	35	40	48	46	53	64
Tenn	76	118	124	133	135	151	180	167	187	234
L Miss	1,036	1,736	1,760	1,889	2,245	2,313	2,678	2,590	2,693	3,328
L AWR	1,159	1,746	1,796	1,981	1,950	2,064	2,511	2,133	2,291	2,997
MID-CONTINENT	25,107	25,164	26,946	29,870	22,948	25,362	30,206	23,310	26,007	32,077
U Mo	11,526	11,883	12,647	13,552	10,287	11,423	13,119	10,517	11,866	14,257
U AWR	5,064	5,325	5,592	6,648	5,159	5,501	7,087	5,219	5,583	7,389
W Gulf	8,517	7,956	8,707	9,670	7,502	8,438	10,000	7,574	8,558	10,431
SOUTHWEST	26,161	23,861	24,607	25,521	21,873	23,058	24,924	22,150	23,588	26,294
RG-P	4,655	4,226	4,528	4,828	3,748	4,156	4,697	3,769	4,227	4,947
Colo	13,001	11,398	11,695	11,961	10,655	11,166	11,749	10,709	11,345	12,213
G Basin	5,536	5,056	5,176	5,320	4,216	4,411	4,693	4,255	4,507	4,933
S Pac	2,969	3,181	3,208	3,412	3,254	3,325	3,785	3,417	3,509	4,201
NORTH PACIFIC	33,807	34,144	34,947	36,174	33,922	35,546	38,526	35,134	37,391	42,274
C Pac	21,154	22,372	22,580	23,204	22,159	22,636	24,197	23,205	23,951	26,628
PNW	12,653	11,772	12,367	12,970	11,763	12,910	14,329	11,929	13,440	15,646
U.S.	89,848	90,358	93,889	99,483	87,215	93,024	104,158	90,698	97,865	113,934

Table C-9. LOSSES FROM MINING, BY REGION

(million gallons per day)

	1960	1980 L	1980 M	1980 H	2000 L	2000 M	2000 H	2020 L	2020 M	2020 H
NORTHEAST	268	443	588	803	604	1,046	1,912	871	2,413	5,300
N Eng	2	3	5	7	5	10	19	8	26	59
D & H	14	22	31	43	30	58	111	44	137	307
Ches	12	19	27	38	30	57	110	47	148	334
Ohio	125	191	243	324	232	355	611	299	692	1,458
EGL	32	65	89	124	113	213	404	196	602	1,354
WGL	22	37	50	69	52	97	180	77	228	502
U Miss	58	101	137	189	136	246	457	192	558	1,237
L Mo	3	5	6	9	6	10	19	8	22	49
SOUTHEAST	105	158	206	277	184	292	495	227	543	1,125
SE	22	35	48	67	52	96	183	80	240	541
Cumb	2	3	3	5	3	5	8	4	8	16
Tenn	7	11	16	22	16	30	58	23	73	166
L Miss	49	76	97	128	80	112	169	86	155	278
L AWR	25	33	42	55	33	49	77	34	67	124
MID-CONTINENT	208	337	418	543	346	461	663	361	581	973
U Mo	29	59	75	100	55	79	123	50	85	148
U AWR	68	103	125	160	104	128	168	104	134	186
W Gulf	111	175	218	283	187	254	372	207	362	639
SOUTHWEST	74	113	146	194	125	199	338	153	377	784
RG-P	21	32	40	52	35	48	73	38	70	127
Colo	21	29	38	51	21	34	58	14	32	62
G Basin	12	15	20	27	12	21	37	10	25	51
S Pac	20	37	48	64	57	96	170	91	250	544
NORTH PACIFIC	43	68	92	127	117	213	394	192	567	1,254
C Pac	27	52	70	97	98	179	334	170	508	1,130
PNW	16	16	22	30	19	34	60	22	59	124
U.S.	698	1,119	1,450	1,944	1,376	2,211	3,801	1,804	4,481	9,437

Table C-10. LOSSES FROM MANUFACTURING, BY REGION

(million gallons per day)

	1960	1980			2000			2020		
		L	M	H	L	M	H	L	M	H
NORTHEAST	1,241	1,844	2,433	3,276	2,501	4,261	7,632	4,088	7,425	16,644
N Eng	129	193	225	264	280	400	603	475	718	1,364
D & H	176	244	317	432	339	570	1,029	562	1,019	2,336
Ches	99	209	264	336	280	459	797	446	793	1,777
Ohio	311	397	547	749	496	884	1,593	780	1,448	3,282
EGL	258	424	581	830	601	1,088	2,113	1,001	1,954	4,887
WGL	159	236	315	418	327	565	970	553	1,012	2,025
U Miss	102	121	157	208	145	238	418	212	368	747
L Mo	7	20	27	39	33	57	109	59	113	226
SOUTHEAST	284	537	716	989	897	1,556	2,937	1,682	3,162	7,361
SE	171	308	411	557	510	886	1,632	937	1,763	3,889
Cumb	0	28	37	54	49	85	173	95	177	461
Tenn	36	49	65	92	74	126	252	129	248	666
L Miss	49	104	139	197	196	341	663	401	752	1,856
L AWR	28	48	64	89	68	118	217	120	222	489
MID-CONTINENT	296	483	620	845	794	1,330	2,473	1,502	2,733	6,335
U Mo	25	30	37	50	45	70	124	83	138	299
U AWR	56	72	92	122	99	167	304	159	297	664
W Gulf	215	381	491	673	650	1,093	2,045	1,260	2,298	5,372
SOUTHWEST	68	170	227	302	273	457	760	521	894	1,740
RG-P	12	16	20	25	36	54	81	80	124	223
Colo	12	14	20	27	27	45	71	64	104	197
G Basin	0	62	89	120	86	159	266	152	278	589
S Pac	44	78	98	130	124	199	342	225	388	731
NORTH PACIFIC	111	233	300	383	354	582	990	635	1,125	2,396
C Pac	53	76	98	135	124	202	371	225	398	882
PNW	58	157	202	248	230	380	619	410	727	1,514
U.S.	2,001	3,267	4,296	5,795	4,819	8,186	14,792	8,428	15,339	34,476

Table C-11. LOSSES FROM STEAM-ELECTRIC POWER, BY REGION

(million gallons per day)

	1960	1980			2000			2020		
		L	M	H	L	M	H	L	M	H
NORTHEAST	573	1,030	1,408	2,030	1,652	2,749	4,670	3,031	5,304	10,481
N Eng	8	13	18	27	22	36	62	40	71	140
D & H	44	50	68	98	78	130	221	142	248	491
Ches	39	55	75	108	88	147	249	162	282	558
Ohio	242	429	586	845	677	1,126	1,914	1,227	2,149	4,245
EGL	71	138	189	273	238	397	674	460	805	1,592
WGL	98	200	274	393	316	526	893	574	1,004	1,985
U Miss	61	123	168	244	197	329	558	362	633	1,249
L Mo	10	22	30	42	36	58	99	64	112	221
SOUTHEAST	179	262	355	516	434	724	1,231	822	1,437	2,836
SE	69	109	149	215	176	292	497	324	567	1,119
Cumb	0	1	1	3	4	7	12	12	21	41
Tenn	71	96	130	188	167	279	475	327	573	1,130
L Miss	18	24	33	48	36	61	103	64	112	221
L AWR	21	32	42	62	51	85	144	95	164	325
MID-CONTINENT	97	199	272	391	324	540	916	602	1,054	2,083
U Mo	19	56	77	110	100	166	282	196	344	679
U AWR	21	44	59	86	68	114	193	123	215	425
W Gulf	57	99	136	195	156	260	441	283	495	979
SOUTHWEST	41	82	115	163	145	241	409	281	491	970
RG-P	8	15	22	30	25	40	68	44	77	151
Colo	13	30	41	60	60	100	170	126	219	434
G Basin	4	15	22	30	26	44	74	49	86	170
S Pac	16	22	30	43	34	57	97	62	109	215
NORTH PACIFIC	9	61	87	120	196	327	555	490	858	1,694
C Pac	9	27	40	53	48	80	136	95	166	328
PNW	0	34	47	67	148	247	419	395	692	1,366
U.S.	900	1,634	2,237	3,220	2,751	4,581	7,781	5,226	9,144	18,064

Table C-12. LOSSES FROM MUNICIPAL USES, BY REGION

(million gallons per day)

	1960	1980 L	1980 M	1980 H	2000 L	2000 M	2000 H	2020 L	2020 M	2020 H
NORTHEAST	5,899	9,550	10,165	11,080	12,939	15,393	18,746	18,796	22,049	29,176
N Eng	705	1,115	1,187	1,295	1,475	1,755	2,138	2,122	2,489	3,294
D & H	2,594	4,073	4,335	4,728	5,372	6,395	7,788	7,688	9,019	11,934
Ches	716	1,289	1,372	1,490	1,878	2,236	2,723	2,831	3,321	4,394
Ohio	354	544	579	632	707	841	1,024	970	1,138	1,506
EGL	503	847	902	983	1,190	1,417	1,725	1,802	2,115	2,798
WGL	667	1,110	1,181	1,288	1,553	1,849	2,252	2,310	2,710	3,585
U Miss	312	498	530	578	673	802	976	964	1,130	1,496
L Mo	48	74	79	86	91	98	120	109	127	169
SOUTHEAST	1,007	2,571	2,734	2,982	4,323	5,146	6,268	7,191	8,434	11,162
SE	702	1,918	2,042	2,227	3,299	3,927	4,783	5,614	6,586	8,715
Cumb	20	41	44	48	64	76	92	95	111	147
Tenn	45	106	112	123	170	202	247	266	312	413
L Miss	173	375	400	436	619	737	898	1,004	1,177	1,558
L AWR	67	131	136	148	171	204	248	212	248	329
MID-CONTINENT	799	1,543	1,642	1,786	2,308	2,719	3,310	3,423	4,017	5,314
U Mo	208	417	443	483	627	747	909	966	1,134	1,500
U AWR	118	197	210	224	270	292	355	312	366	484
W Gulf	473	929	989	1,079	1,411	1,680	2,046	2,145	2,517	3,330
SOUTHWEST	1,717	4,349	4,628	5,047	6,944	8,269	10,067	11,084	13,003	17,204
RG-P	59	138	146	160	215	257	312	340	398	527
Colo	81	277	295	321	450	536	652	789	925	1,224
G Basin	68	122	130	142	155	185	225	193	227	300
S Pac	1,509	3,812	4,057	4,424	6,124	7,291	8,878	9,762	11,453	15,153
NORTH PACIFIC	1,239	1,932	2,057	2,238	2,623	3,122	3,804	3,620	4,247	5,619
C Pac	595	960	1,022	1,109	1,289	1,534	1,869	1,733	2,033	2,690
PNW	644	972	1,035	1,129	1,334	1,588	1,935	1,887	2,214	2,929
U.S.	10,661	19,945	21,226	23,133	29,137	34,649	42,195	44,114	51,750	68,475

Table C-13. LOSSES FROM LAND TREATMENT AND STRUCTURES, BY REGION: INCREASE OVER 1960

(million gallons per day)

	1960	1980 L	1980 M	1980 H	2000 L	2000 M	2000 H	2020 L	2020 M	2020 H
NORTHEAST	0	1,145	1,145	1,145	1,391	1,391	1,391	1,441	1,441	1,441
N Eng	0	418	418	418	462	462	462	481	481	481
D & H	0	-102	-102	-102	-210	-210	-210	-295	-295	-295
Ches	0	113	113	113	40	40	40	-2	-2	-2
Ohio	0	222	222	222	352	352	352	405	405	405
EGL	0	106	106	106	-21	-21	-21	-87	-87	-87
WGL	0	52	52	52	105	105	105	130	130	130
U Miss	0	204	204	204	464	464	464	584	584	584
L Mo	0	132	132	132	199	199	199	225	225	225
SOUTHEAST	0	792	792	792	1,766	1,766	1,766	2,196	2,196	2,196
SE	0	321	321	321	635	635	635	770	770	770
Cumb	0	54	54	54	86	86	86	100	100	100
Tenn	0	81	81	81	213	213	213	276	276	276
L Miss	0	121	121	121	255	255	255	313	313	313
L AWR	0	215	215	215	577	577	577	737	737	737
MID-CONTINENT	0	909	909	909	2,183	2,183	2,183	2,562	2,562	2,562
U Mo	0	590	590	590	1,417	1,417	1,417	1,816	1,816	1,816
U AWR	0	166	166	166	285	285	285	255	255	255
W Gulf	0	153	153	153	481	481	481	491	491	491
SOUTHWEST	0	141	141	141	218	218	218	197	197	197
RG-P	0	87	87	87	121	121	121	105	105	105
Colo	0	46	46	46	83	83	83	100	100	100
G Basin	0	5	5	5	11	11	11	13	13	13
S Pac	0	3	3	3	3	3	3	-21	-21	-21
NORTH PACIFIC	0	153	153	153	245	245	245	107	107	107
G Pac	0	69	69	69	87	87	87	79	79	79
PNW	0	84	84	84	158	158	158	28	28	28
U.S.	0	3,140	3,140	3,140	5,803	5,803	5,803	6,503	6,503	6,503

Table C-14. LOSSES FROM SWAMPS AND WETLANDS, BY REGION: INCREASE OVER 1960

(million gallons per day)

	1960	1980			2000			2020		
		L	M	H	L	M	H	L	M	H
NORTHEAST	0	−602	0	602	−964	0	964	−1,206	0	1,206
N Eng	0	−22	0	22	−35	0	35	−44	0	44
D & H	0	−63	0	63	−100	0	100	−125	0	125
Ches	0	−43	0	43	−69	0	69	−87	0	87
Ohio	0	−8	0	8	−14	0	14	−17	0	17
EGL	0	−51	0	51	−82	0	82	−103	0	103
WGL	0	−180	0	180	−288	0	288	−360	0	360
U Miss	0	−235	0	235	−376	0	376	−470	0	470
L Mo	0	0	0	0	0	0	0	0	0	0
SOUTHEAST	0	−1,582	0	1,582	−2,533	0	2,533	−3,164	0	3,164
SE	0	−1,005	0	1,005	−1,608	0	1,608	−2,010	0	2,010
Cumb	0	−2	0	2	−4	0	4	−4	0	4
Tenn	0	−3	0	3	−5	0	5	−6	0	6
L Miss	0	−476	0	476	−762	0	762	−952	0	952
L AWR	0	−96	0	96	−154	0	154	−192	0	192
MID-CONTINENT	0	−1,559	0	1,559	−2,497	0	2,497	−3,120	0	3,120
U Mo	0	−876	0	876	−1,402	0	1,402	−1,752	0	1,752
U AWR	0	−53	0	53	−86	0	86	−107	0	107
W Gulf	0	−630	0	630	−1,009	0	1,009	−1,261	0	1,261
SOUTHWEST	0	−342	0	342	−548	0	548	−683	0	683
RG-P	0	−69	0	69	−111	0	111	−138	0	138
Colo	0	−13	0	13	−20	0	20	−25	0	25
G Basin	0	−260	0	260	−416	0	416	−519	0	519
S Pac	0	0	0	0	−1	0	1	−1	0	1
NORTH PACIFIC	0	−197	0	197	−314	0	314	−392	0	392
C Pac	0	−173	0	173	−276	0	276	−345	0	345
PNW	0	−24	0	24	−38	0	38	−47	0	47
U.S.	0	−4,282	0	4,282	−6,856	0	6,855	−8,564	0	8,564

Appendix D

TREATMENT, DILUTION, AND TREATMENT COSTS OF MUNICIPAL AND INDUSTRIAL WASTES

By George W. Reid, W. W. Eckenfelder, Leale E. Streebin, Robert Y. Nelson, and Oliver Thomas Love, Jr.*

One of the important results of the studies of the Senate Select Committee on National Water Resources was the development of methods for approximating the amount of water required to dilute waste effluents. In Committee Print No. 29,[1] written by the senior author of this appendix, models were presented that could be used to determine dilution requirements and the costs associated with treatment. The basic models responded to biodegradable, nutritional, and persistent chemical loadings. Stream characteristics used in the models, such as stream velocity, length, discharge, rate of biological degradation (k_1), reaeration coefficient (k_2), etc., were the best estimates of the participating federal agencies. It was recognized in 1959 that these projections had several limitations and should be used primarily to provide planning guidelines and to ascertain the effects on the system of changing any of the decision variables. Since 1959 considerable progress has been made in the development of mathematical models and in better definition of input parameters.

Because much of the application of models to water resource problems has been for particular points on a stream with little attention to regions, the regional model developed in Committee Print No. 29 appears to have been misunderstood and improperly used. The present models are at a regional level, and the problem is essentially the same as it was in the initial study; that is, given aggregate economic projections, physical stream characteristics, and instream water quality standards, to develop dilution water requirements as a function of municipal and industrial waste treatment levels. Several additional ideas have been incorporated, such as the effects of short-term treatment, the effects of location and scale on treatment costs, and thermal pollution. Originally, a basin was treated as an entity, but a requirement of this study was to develop a means of providing internal disaggregation of the loadings. Another result of the 1959 study was the discovery of the important role in establishing dilution flows of nutritional pollution at advanced treatment levels. Both nutritional pollution, which is the cause of accelerated eutrophication, and reaeration, which is so essential to the biodegradable model, depend heavily on the percentage of the river impounded. As before, the basic loadings and stream characteristics were obtained from other workers, the intent of this study being to develop the basic models, unit loadings, and costs of treatment.

Development of Stream Responses

Water pollution can be generally defined as the addition of deleterious material to natural waters. These pollutants can be categorized as follows:

1. Biodegradable (L) — *organic oxygen-demanding substances*, such as sewage and certain types of industrial wastes.
2. Bacterial (B) — *infectious agents*; bacteria, viruses, parasites, etc.

*George Reid is Chairman of the Department of Civil Engineering at the University of Oklahoma. Leale Streebin is Associate Professor of Sanitary Engineering and Robert Nelson is Assistant Professor of Water Resources, both in the Department of Civil Engineering at the University of Oklahoma. Oliver Love is a water supply engineer with the U.S. Public Health Service. W. W. Eckenfelder is Professor of Civil Engineering at Vanderbilt University.

[1] George W. Reid, *Water Requirements for Pollution Abatement*, Senate Select Committee on National Water Resources, 86th Cong., 2d sess. (1960).

3. Aggravated eutrophication (E) – *plant nutrients*, particularly nitrogen (N) and phosphorus (P).

4. Conserved (C) – *persistent chemicals*; brines, certain toxic metallic ions, and radioactive substances that are largely unaffected by conventional waste treatments or natural stream recovery processes.

5. Thermal (T) – *heat* from cooling-water discharges.

6. Sediments (S) – *primarily waste-suspended solids* incorporated in sludges.

Group one substances are usually classed as biodegradable; that is, they are oxidized biologically in the receiving waters while consuming oxygen, or by treatments utilizing primarily biological processes. In the receiving waters, biodegradation can be tolerated so long as it does not lower the oxygen content below acceptable levels. The dissolved oxygen (D.O.) level is usually set at 4 mg/l to meet the required quality standards (RQS_{DO}), and is a level that will support most aquatic life. Through sensitivity analyses, other D.O. levels can be explored. Sewage and industrial waste treatment plants combined with water dilution and natural stream assimilation can cope with this type of pollutant.

Infectious agents can usually be destroyed with chlorine. In the past, typhoid, dysentery, and cholera have been the most dangerous water-borne diseases. The U.S. Public Health Service Water Quality Standard was initially designed primarily with these diseases in mind. This standard is in terms of the most probable number of *E. coli* (an index of microorganisms) per 100 ml of water (RQS_B).

Nutrients, primarily phosphorus and nitrogen, promote excessive algal growth with attendant taste and odor problems. These pollutants have become increasingly important as the conventional processes of waste disposal remove primarily the carbonaceous material and not nitrogen and phosphorus. An analysis of raw domestic sewage, for example, indicated an average ratio of C/N/P of 60/7/1 until recently, but due to the increasing discharge of detergents containing polyphosphates, the C/N/P ratio now is more like 14/2/1. Biological treatment utilizing autotrophic and heterotrophic bacteria as well as grazing microorganisms generally require these three elements in combining C/N/P of 60/10/1. The significance of these observations is that in conventionally treated effluent (wherein the primary objective is the removal of carbon) there will be a considerable excess of nitrogen and phosphorus causing eutrophication in the receiving water. Nutrient removal and pollution control can be accomplished by tertiary treatment processes and subsequent dilution. Algae grown under controlled conditions will remove the nutrients, and this process is undergoing intensive study today. Denitrification processes and phosphorus removal techniques are also available. Eutrophication is evaluated in terms of standards pertaining to algal growth potential (RQS_{AGP}) or nutrients themselves $(RQS_N$ or $RQS_P)$.

The persistent chemical group is one that is not a growth promoter like nitrogen and phosphorus nor a pollutant like sewage that can be assimilated by nature, but one that is essentially unchanged and, as it accumulates, becomes detrimental to water quality. This group includes radioactivity,

alkyl benzine sulfonate (ABS), carbon column extractibles (CCE), and brines. ABS refers to material from detergents and CCE to substances primarily from the petrochemical industry. Both have permissible levels at 0.2–0.3 mg/l (RQS_C). The only economical solution at present is exclusion or dilution to acceptable levels. This grouping actually could be further separated into conserved inorganics and refractory organics.

Ninety percent of the water withdrawn for industry is returned to the receiving stream as waste, having been used for cooling purposes. Of the 900–1,000 gallon per capita per day water withdrawal, half is subsequently returned with no alteration other than that of being heated. Heat alters the aquatic environment and can be handled by off-stream cooling and dilution. Heat is evaluated in terms of maximum summer temperature or degrees increased over normal summer temperature (RQS_T).

The sediments in a receiving stream are composed of wash load, living organisms (mostly microscopic forms), dead organisms, detritus and colloidal substances. By quenching light penetration these substances cause a decrease in phytoplankton. Depending on the hydrography of the stream, suspended matter is carried along with the water or removed to the bottom by sedimentation. The bottom (benthic) deposits cover fish-spawning beds and may result in a secondary oxygen demand due to anaerobic decomposition of the organic components.

Of prime concern in water quality management is the response of the receiving stream to the discharged waste. Water quality standards, in terms of either effluent or in-stream values (RQS_i), constitute the main objective of this problem in systems analysis. In planning for future population increases and the concomitant increased use of water, it is possible to build mathematical models depicting the optimum treatments and streamflows necessary to meet the RQS_i.

There are three stream response equations: biodegradable, nutritional, and thermal. Persistant chemicals, sediments, and bacteria are considered as constraints or minimums. The low-flow augmentation, Q_i, associated with each treatment level (TL_i), will be Q_L, Q_N, Q_P, and Q_T. This is a terminal basin flow in millions of gallons per day. TL_i is a fraction where i refers to specific criteria such as BOD, N, and P.

Biodegradable Model (L)

$$Q_L = \left[\frac{Y}{\epsilon} + (1 - Y) \right] \frac{PE}{C_s - RQS_{DO}} A \cdot \mathbb{P},$$

where

Y = fraction of total population residing in SMSAs;

ϵ = efficiency term, point load/uniform load (see below);

PE = waste discharge, prior to treatment, in terms of millions of population equivalents;

$\mathbb{P}$ = percentage of waste discharged to rivers, expressed as a fraction = $1 - TL_i$;

CS = D.O. saturation level at given temperature in milligrams per liter (see table D-1);

$$A = \frac{942,900}{k_2 \dfrac{nl}{V}} \text{ (see below).}$$

In the development of the biodegradable model, the waste assimilation capacity was based on the maximum utilization of each segment of the stream. The model thus obtained assumes a continuously applied load along the river to keep the D.O. content depressed to the required quality standard (RQS_{DO}).

The basin load on a stream is expressed as the total basin load in terms of the population equivalents (p.e.'s) generated times the fraction of the load discharged after treatment (P). As explained later, the total oxygenation capacity of the stream in pounds per day is as follows:

$$2.3 \times k_2 \times D \times 8.3 \times Q_L \times \frac{n}{3} \times \frac{l}{V}.$$

The values of K_2 (reoxygenation coefficient) used are the best field estimates adjusted to the worst temperature conditions. The quantity $Q_L \dfrac{n}{3} \dfrac{l}{V}$ represents the volume of water available to the reoxygenation process. This volume can be visualized as a pyramid, its peak representing the source or origin of the stream or tributaries with a height equal to the average stream length (l) in miles. The base is equal to the terminal flow (Q_L) in millions of gallons per day divided by the velocity (V) in miles per day. The values of velocity for each basin were supplied by the U.S. Geological Survey. The number of reoxygenation volumes or the effect of branching on aeration capacity is represented by (n). This term is calculated from

$$n = \frac{R}{l} + \frac{x-1}{x},$$

in which R is the reach of the main stem and l the average length of the total stream $\left(\dfrac{\epsilon li}{x}\right)$. The number of discrete tributaries used to calculate l is denoted by x. The value of x, determined by computation, must be used as a guide with considerable judgment exercised in the final establishment of n. The maximum oxygen deficit (D) in mg/l depends on both the maximum D.O. saturation level (CS) at the appropriate temperature and the minimum D.O. level necessary to meet the required quality standards. The terms that were constants, not decision parameters for each basin, were aggregated into one value (A) which is recorded in table D-1.

Since in practice it is not probable that actual BOD loadings would be completely spread along the river in the manner necessary to attain the maximum assimilation efficiency of the river, the model was expanded to account for the nonuniformity of the loading. As the biodegradable pollution load is directly related to the population of an area, the grouping of the population into urban areas should be representative of the nonuniformity of the stream loading in a basin. The model then is composed of two portions: (Y) that fraction of the load from population centers, or point loads, determined as the fraction of the total basin population located in SMSAs, and the remaining portion assumed to be uniformly distributed throughout the basin.

When a point load is impressed on a river the total load must be reduced to prevent a depression of the dissolved oxygen below the RQS values; that is, as indicated in Committee Print No. 29 and developed in greater detail by Hann,[2] the total assimilative capacity of the stream is reduced. The ratio of the point loading to the continuous loading capacity, ϵ, is dependent on the time necessary for the river to recover from the impressed load.

Accelerated Eutrophication Model

Nitrogen: $$Q_N = \frac{Z \cdot PE}{F_N \cdot RQS_N}$$
$$[(1 - TL_N) - 1.44 (1 - TL_L)] (3,250 \, TL_L)$$

Phosphorus: $$Q_P = \frac{Z \cdot PE}{F_P \cdot RQS_P}$$
$$[(1 - TL_P) - 0.27 (1 - TL_L)] (1,080 \, TL_L),$$

where

Q_P and Q_N = nutritional dilution required, mgd;

Z = portion of streams impounded and affected by RQS_{AGP} level (see table D-3);

PE = waste discharged, prior to treatment, in terms of millions of population equivalents;

TL_P or TL_N = phosphorus or nitrogen removal level expressed as a decimal (see table D-7);

F_P or F_N = BOD/P or BOD/N ratio divided by optimum combining ratio (see table D-2);

TL_L = BOD removal level expressed as a decimal (table D-7);

RQS_P or RQS_N = acceptable level, RQS, determined by RQS_{AGP};

AGP = algal growth potentials.

Excessive enrichment or eutrophication of receiving waters by nutrient-rich wastes has emerged as a major problem.[3] Experience has shown that the degree of eutrophication and the severity of subsequent water quality problems due to stimulated undesirable algal growth is largely de-

[2] Roy W. Hann, Jr., "Procedure for Estimating the Waste Assimilation Capacity of a River System" (Ph.D. thesis, University of Oklahoma, 1962).

[3] "Nutrient Associated Problems in Water Quality and Treatment," Task Group 2610P Report, *Journal American Water Works Association*, vol. 58 (October 1966), p. 1317.

pendent on the presence of phosphorus and nitrogen; however, other factors may also be critical.

The selection of ruling criteria (RQS_N) is very difficult. Pollution is assessed in terms of the presence of objectionable algal concentrations. Algal levels, of course, are related primarily to nutrient levels. A great deal of evidence was explored to assist in establishing these levels (see appendix B). In many instances, so-called optimum conditions in terms of mg/l of nitrogen and phosphorus were exceeded with no adverse effects, so it is possible to have rich water with little algal growth or, conversely, nutrient-poor water with intense growth.

There is also the question of whether nitrogen or phosphorus is the main determinant of algal growth. The controlling nutrient should be the one in short supply. This too, was studied in terms of the N/P ratio for optimum development. Unfortunately, nitrogen can be fixed from the atmosphere and phosphorus regenerated, clouding both issues. Oswald has indicated that adverse algal conditions can be measured in terms of algal growth potentials (AGP), which are generally related to N and P as follows: $AGP = 10\,N$ or $100\,P$; and that acceptable levels of AGP are 10 mg/l for industrial and universal waters, and 30–40 mg/l for recreational waters. This assumes an N/P ratio of 10/1, and possibly a C/N/P ratio of 50/10/1. These AGP values are designated for healthy (optimal environment) conditions – with levels perhaps three times higher being tolerated under adverse conditions. In using RQS_N values, conditions were deemed healthy for effluents previously subjected to a high level of treatment and adverse for those having lesser treatment and still containing a large fraction of the biodegradable organics; that is, the AGP was scaled from 30 to 10, from primary to tertiary levels of pretreatment.

Originally, this category was referred to as "nutritional pollution"; however, because of the complexity of, and the difficulty in, defining nutritional pollution, it was renamed "accelerated eutrophication." This characterization appears to the authors to be more realistic in terms of the goals sought in general, and particularly in that nitrogen and phosphorus values of 1 mg/l and 0.1 mg/l, respectively, have certain field validity.[4]

The bacterial utilization of nitrogen and phosphorus in the process of assimilation of the biodegradable materials during sewage treatment and in the receiving water can be formulated in terms of treatment levels and the original waste strength. The total quantity of nitrogen or phosphorus requiring dilution equals the total production of these in pounds per day multiplied by one minus that portion removed by treatment ($1 - TL_n$) minus that portion removed by bacterial action in the receiving stream (1.44 $(1 - TL_L)$ or 0.27 $(1 - TL_L)$ for N or P respectively).

If nuisance algal blooms are to be prevented in a river basin, the upper level of permissible concentration of available phosphorus and nitrogen will be controlled by the most sensitive portion of the system. The impounding of water in lakes and reservoirs allows sufficient time for the buildup, or concentration, of nutrients and thus for algal growth; therefore, this part of the stream becomes most important in accelerated eutrophication.

The controlling RQS as determined by AGP applies then to only a portion of the total volume of water. The percentage of the river flow impounded (Z or Z') in each basin was based on the existing storage as estimated by Wollman and Bonem, divided by either the median or mean flow. The decision whether to use Z (median flow base) or Z' (mean flow base) or a combination of the two depends on the potential storage capacity of the region.

This model was developed for the BOD/N/P ratio of a domestic waste. It was modified to include industrial wastes by inserting the factor F_P or F_N, where F_P is the BOD/P ratio of the industrial waste divided by the BOD/P ratio of the domestic waste.

Thermal Model

$$Q_T = \frac{\Delta T_W - G}{\Delta T_Q + G} \cdot \Delta Q,$$

where

Q_T = thermal dilution required, mgd;

ΔT_W = allowable temperature difference between added flow and RQS_T ($T - RQS_T$);

ΔT_Q = allowable temperature change ($RQS_T - T_o$);

G = ratio of K/V_s where K = geometric mean of Bowmen's ratio, and V_s = subsidence velocity (values for G may be found in table D-14);

ΔQ = waste flow, mgd.

(For values of $\dfrac{\Delta T_W - G}{\Delta T_Q + G}$ see table D-14)

Temperature alterations of the aquatic environment by the addition of a thermal load (hot or cold) in quantities detrimental to beneficial activity constitutes thermal pollution. Approximately 80 percent of all water used by U.S. industry is used in cooling operations, so that large quantities of heat are discharged into the streams and lakes. In the future, industry is expected to double its excess heat production each decade, causing a greatly increased water demand. Nuclear power will require even more than thermal power.

The thermal load imposed on surface waters must not impede the maintenance of desirable aquatic species in acceptable numbers. The beneficial or adverse effects of heated or cooled effluents on stream ecology prevent any attempt to define allowable temperatures within one specific range – the allowable temperatures fluctuate with the season and other natural environmental factors.

The impact of thermal pollution on water conditions is exemplified by at least four distinct reactions:[5]

---

[4]W. J. Oswald and C. G. Golueke, "Eutrophication Trends in the United States – A Problem?" *Journal Water Pollution Control Federation*, vol. 38 (June 1966), p. 964.

[5]B. Davidson and R. W. Bradshaw, "Thermal Pollution of Water Systems," *Environmental Science and Technology*, vol. 1, no. 8 (August 1967), pp. 618–30.

1. death or displacement of aquatic species
2. environmental modifications
3. activity reduction
4. impairment of stream self-purification

Lethal temperature levels for different species of fish vary markedly, in some instances as much as 31°F.[6] Even within species, this may vary depending on acclimation. Stream temperatures which consistently exceed 70°F. favor warm-water fish rather than cold-water species such as the salmonoids.[7] Increases in temperature of 2–3°F. above the 70°F. level have been observed to cause depopulation of salmonoids by 90 percent. Minnows, suckers, and other warm-water species gradually replace them under this condition.[8]

While the change of temperature may be within the thermal tolerance of a particular fish, it may make environmental conditions unfavorable for essential food organisms and for certain developmental stages of fish life. It is known that the trout will not hatch if incubated above 14.4°C.[9] The higher temperatures may favor competitors or predators of desirable species. Many other organisms go through resting periods at specific stages of development during certain seasons. Furthermore, certain diatoms are abundant only at temperatures below 50°F. Hypolimnion water from the bottom of Fontana Reservoir in North Carolina has altered once-productive warm-water fisheries in the Little Tennessee River.[10] Thus, by modifying the temperature of a stream, the biota distribution may be changed and the entire food chain seriously disrupted.[11]

The observation was made in 1947 that water temperature affects aquatic activity through the process of metabolism in the life form.[12] Experiments were made to determine the effects of temperature on the cruising speed of the sockeye to demonstrate this relationship.[13] The maximum sustained swimming speed of sockeyes at 10°C. and 19°C. are approximately equal. However, because of increased metabolic demand at the higher temperature, the energy reserves of the fish were found to be exhausted one

and a half to two times as quickly at 19°C. Oxygen consumption by aquatic vertebrates doubles for every 10°C. rise in stream temperature.[14]

The D.O. content of water decreases as temperature increases, for example, 10 parts per million at 59°F. to 7.6 ppm at 86°F. It should be stressed that these conditions relate to equilibrium conditions and rarely occur in vivo, but algal respiration and benthic BOD are also influenced by temperature and their subsequent demand on dissolved oxygen is increased as the temperature of the stream increases.

All biologicial processes are to some extent thermochemically controlled, with the bacterial growth rate being maximum at 86°F. As a consequence, higher or lower stream temperatures decrease the self-purification capacity of the stream. The addition of heat to surface waters increases the possibility of septic conditions and tends to make the water unsuitable for industrial reuse or for drinking purposes without expensive treatment. Furthermore, the use of a stream for recreational purposes may be reduced by excessive thermal alterations.

Estimating the Anticipated Pollution Loadings

The pollution loadings due to municipalities are based on amounts per person times the number of people per basin, as projected by Wollman and Bonem for the years 1980, 2000, and 2020.

The industrial pollution loadings for the twenty-two river basins were estimated and grouped into six categories: food and kindred products, textiles, pulp and paper, chemicals, petroleum refining and coal products, and leather. To determine the waste strength of each main category, several industries within each category were chosen and their strengths were weighted according to the total waste flows produced by the industry. The waste strengths in terms of BOD per production unit and the corresponding flows were determined by Chow et al. and are reported in table D-4[15] as the mean discharge and strengths of various pollutants per unit of production. In addition, high and low strengths and discharges, which would occur less than 16 percent (one sigma) of the time, were reported.

It was first proposed to project waste strengths from the present mean to the low value in the year 2020. The idea was that the entire industry could be expected to progress in technology to the level of the best or upper 16 percent. However, through recirculation, advanced technology also tends to reduce wastewater discharged; this tends to increase waste strengths. Consequently, upon closer scrutiny it was felt that technological advances will at best maintain the present waste strengths with the proposed increased recirculation rates. The data provided by Chow et al. were then used to compute waste discharge for six two-digit

[6] J. R. Brett, "Thermal Requirements of Fish – Three Decades of Study, 1940–1970" (R. A. Taft Sanitary Engineering Center, T. Rep. W60-3, 1960), pp. 110–16.

[7] D. L. Belding, "Water Temperature and Fish Life," *Transactions of the American Fishery Society*, vol. 58 (1928), pp. 98–105.

[8] M. C. Tarzwell and A. R. Gaufin, *Some Important Biological Effects of Pollution Often Disregarded in Stream Surveys*, Department of Health, Education, and Welfare (1953), pp. 295–98.

[9] E. E. MacNamara, "A Primary Rendition of an Annotated Bibliography on Thermal Alterations in the Aquatic Environment" (State of New Jersey Department of Conservation and Economic Development, 1966).

[10] Ibid.

[11] M. C. Tarzwell, *Water Quality Criteria for Aquatic Life* (Department of Health, Education, and Welfare, 1957), pp. 248–51.

[12] F. E. J. Fry, "Effects of the Environment on Animal Activity" (Student Biology Service, Public Ontario Fish Research Laboratory, University of Toronto, 1947).

[13] J. R. Brett et al., "Effect of Temperature on Cruising Speed of Young Sockeye and Coho Salmon," *Journal Fish Research Board*, vol. 15, no. 5 (Canada, 1958).

[14] E. G. Fruh, "The Overall Picture of Eutrophication," *Journal Water Pollution Control Federation*, vol. 39 (September 1967), pp. 1449–63.

[15] C. S. Chow, W. W. Eckenfelder, and J. F. Malina, "A Summary Report on Costs of Municipal Wastewater Treatment and Estimation of Industrial Wastewater Characteristics and Cost of Treatment" (University of Texas, 1965).

industrial categories. This was done by finding a weighted average of the wastes per unit of output for the four-digit industries in table D-4. The weights used were the proportion of total two-digit wastewater discharged by the total four-digit industry in question.[16] The reader will recall that one variant in chapter 12 was based on the assumption of a reduced amount of waste per unit of output.

A number of assumptions are inherent in the estimated waste strengths. These include:

1. The importance of various industries within a category remains the same throughout the United States, i.e., # BOD/gal. is constant for each major group. This could vary, but there is insufficient basic data to delineate the change of mix.

2. The waste concentration for each industry remains constant throughout time. However, this assumption is altered for variants of the basic model.

3. The waste concentration is based on the mean as determined by Chow et al.[17]

4. P.E.'s are based on the average flow, i.e., daily

$$\text{flow} = \frac{yearly\ flow}{365}.$$

Treatment

The estimated pollution loadings used in the models are based on the raw waste, i.e., prior to treatment for removal of the pollutants. The models were developed to determine the minimum cost of treatment plus dilution. Four levels of treatment were considered. These are: raw, primary, secondary, and tertiary. Raw implies lack of treatment. Primary treatment refers to those processes which remove a portion of the suspended solids, thereby reducing the organic and nutritional loads that reach the final receiving waters. Plain sedimentation, Imhoff tanks, and lagoons have been defined as primary treatment devices. Secondary treatment employs biological processes which satisfy the oxygen demands. The most prominent aerobic processes are activated sludge, minimum solids, and standard and high-rate trickling filters. Tertiary devices provide a "polishing" by further stabilizing or removing the pollutants. The conventional activated sludge process is combined with various systems in table D-6 to give tertiary levels. The particular design criteria used in these various processes is shown in table D-15.

Table D-6 shows characteristics of municipal wastewater after various degrees of treatment. Consideration has been given to physical, chemical, and biological methods now used for waste treatment as well as to the dilution of raw wastes without subsequent treatment.

The removal efficiencies for these various methods of treatment are presented in table D-6 and are summarized in table D-7. Although discrete levels of treatment are employed, it is possible to arrive at any desired treatment level for a basin by choosing different levels of treatment for the various industries and municipalities within the

basin. Therefore, the percentage of the various kinds of wastes removed is a continuous function rather than a step function, as it would be if only one industry were being considered, because it is a composite of all the various levels of treatment within a basin. Consequently, generalized treatment values are used in the model and are given in table D-7. These values are not explicitly identified with any particular treatment process.

Treatment Cost Data

Reliable cost data for various treatment systems capable of providing an effluent quality required to maintain some minimum quality stream standard were essential in this study. These cost data, compiled from various sources, are reported in table D-8.

All costs were converted to the *Engineering News Record* Cost Index base of 970, consistent with 1965 dollar prices. For certain desired flows the cost data were not available. To arrive at values for these flows, the available data were plotted on a logarithmic plot and the line of best fit extrapolated to these flows. These cost data are expressed as dollars per million gallons discharged per day, and as dollars per capita for waste treatment plants processing 1, 5, 10, 50, and 100 mgd. To arrive at the cost per capita, the flows per capita were graduated according to the size of the treatment plant. A flow of 100 gallons per capita per day was chosen for a 1 mgd waste treatment plant, 110 gpcd for a 5 mgd plant, 120 gpcd for a 10 mgd plant, 130 mgcd for a 50 mgd plant, and 140 gpcd for a 100 mgd plant. The flow in gallons per day was divided by gpcd to give the number of people. Dividing the cost of the treatment plant by the number of people resulted in the cost per person.

The costs for industrial waste treatment, expressed as dollars per million gallons discharged per day, are presented in table D-9. Costs at secondary and tertiary levels are cumulative, i.e., they include primary and secondary, as the case may be.

Effects of Waste Treatment on Water Treatment Costs

All pollutants from municipal or industrial wastes affect the quality of water. Whether or not these pollutants affect the cost of water treatment depends on the type and concentration of these various pollutants. Dissolved inorganic solids and mineral constituents usually are not present in high enough concentrations to affect the water treatment process, and generally they are not removed. The organics, however, are significant to the water treatment plant. The organic matter and the inorganic nutrients serve as a food for bacteria, algae, and other aquatic organisms and are responsible for tastes and odor, foaming, and other aesthetic nuisances associated with polluted waters. The prime pollutants affecting water treatment plants are (1) suspended and dissolved organic matter; (2) surface-active agents; (3) pathogenic microorganisms; and (4) nutrients, such as nitrogen and phosphorus.[18]

---

[16] Tarzwell and Gaufin, *Important Biological Effects of Pollution.*

[17] Chow, Eckenfelder, and Malina, "Summary Report on Costs."

[18] R. J. Frankel, P. H. McGauhey, and G. T. Orlob, "Economic Evaluation of Water Quality: An Engineering-Economic Model for Water Quality Management," 1st Annual Report, SERL Rep. No. 65-3 (University of California, Berkeley, January 1965).

Assuming conventional water treatment plants (coagulation, sedimentation, filtration, and chlorination) are used for treating the water supply, the capital costs are relatively little affected unless additional units are required to remove certain pollutants, e.g., activated carbon to remove taste and odors. However, in going from relatively clean to polluted water there are additional operation and maintenance costs to the water treatment plant. These added costs are due to (1) additional chemicals required to treat adequately the poorer quality raw water; (2) additional supervision to determine the suitability efficiency; and (3) additional laboratory tests required to determine the suitability of the treated water for drinking purposes.

Additional equipment and operation costs estimated to be the minimum requirements are given in a report on the economic evaluation of water quality by Frankel.[19] They are not considered in this study.

Comments on the Model

Model building is an art and must be treated as one in the interpretation of the numerical results. The model builder may choose to use a micro model and by a process of consolidation provide a model of the project scale, or he can build a macro model and disaggregate it to project level. In the case of a micro model, the builder starts with maximum fineness and selectively drops variables to obtain a workable model. In the case of a macro model, a general or coarse model, disaggregation produces fineness. The authors consider a macro model more in keeping with the objectives of the study; in addition, such models do not suffer the dangers of double counting and overrefinement.

The models in this study are macro and deterministic. Unfortunately, there are few basins that provide detailed data for a proper verification. The biodegradable model and the conserved model were operated on field data. The nutritional and thermal models were tested against limited point data. Most of the concurrence with the real world resides with the judgment of best-qualified professionals.

A large group of engineers, chemists, biologists, and other professionals associated with water quality management were consulted as to the reasonableness of the results. This process implies a great deal of sensitivity analysis because of the need for impartial techniques in model building.

On the other hand, in developing the unit loads, unit costs, and treatment effectiveness, it was possible to use a probabilistic modeling technique. All models and projections of loading and costs were responsive to technological changes over time.

The limitations of the models are obvious, of course. For example, stream-characteristic data are not probabilistic but are minimums and averages. Despite their limitations, the models can help to give decision makers a feel for the future, as well as some understanding of the possible consequences of their decisions. Since engineers often must use inadequate and poorly understood data to design and build structures that have never been built before and are too large to experiment with, the models can also serve as guides in designing water pollution control and water quality management systems.

Nonquantifiable Considerations

There are many unpredictables in terms of metrics that will occur in all probability before the year 2020. The most important are concerned with technological and socioeconomic changes.

The cities are filling up and the rural areas emptying. By the year 2020, the United States is envisioned as massive clusters of population groups. These apparently will grow into a system of independent urban areas limited only by physical problems, of which water and wastewater are important ones. The demand of the population centers for goods and services will change; the custom services of today will become the necessities of tomorrow. There already is evidence that water considered usable today for municipal purposes will be wholly unsuitable in the future. In the plains states, local water supplies frequently contain 1,500–2,000 ppm of total dissolved solids, and while people may consider this water satisfactory now, they may not in the future. Cities in western Oklahoma, for example, are looking to the newer treatment processes, such as electrodialysis and reverse osmosis to improve water quality. This is simply a matter of the new generation refusing to accept the taste levels of its parents.

Supply-demand studies indicate that in certain regions, particularly the Southwest, water will be in short supply. In isolated cases shortages have already occurred. A recent state-of-the-art paper[20] points to the need for water recycling, that is, a completely self-contained system for which the only water input would be that for consumptive use. This system could serve a household or a complete city.

Water pollution sources can be classified as either organized or dispersed. The magnitude of the total pollutional load from each classification is essentially the same at present. The organized loadings are those from sewer systems and they are amenable, at least physically, to treatment. Dispersed pollution consists of flushings from rural and urban lands and cannot be controlled by treatment. Included in dispersed pollution is also agricultural nutrient return flow. Data on the return flow are lacking, but return flow is one important source of nitrogen. The only technique available for dispersed pollution control is low-flow augmentation, source control, or both. Consequently, as the total waste generation increases, the handling of dispersed loadings may well force cities to use closed systems.

Of course, there is always the problem of recognizing technological change and its direct effect in wastewater processing and its indirect effect on waste generation. The present models have implicitly built-in provisions for treatment process improvements and for waste and water in-plant "save alls," or recirculation. Finally, it should be

[19] Frankel, McGauhey, and Orlob, "Economic Evaluation of Water Quality."

[20] David G. Stephan, "Water Renovation – Some Advanced Treatment Processes," *Civil Engineering*, September 1965 (reprint, Federal Water Pollution Control Administration, Department of Health, Education, and Welfare).

pointed out that as shortages occur, interbasin transfers, both large- and small-scale, are feasible.

Nationally, we are using only a fraction of the potentially available water, but in some areas the demand is approaching the supply. As regional and national shortages develop, low-flow augmentation and tertiary treatment will be used first. Next, as the gap between supply and demand narrows, staged use will be employed. By staged use is meant reuse sequentially so as not to offend the user, beginning with domestic use and going in turn to high-grade industrial use, low-grade industrial use, agricultural use, and so on. As the demand increases for urban use, the water and waste management will become a closed cycle, the demand for new water being the makeup to the system; the pollutional load downstream being nil. Finally, as every other loophole is plugged, interbasin transfers on a regional basis will be undertaken.

The onset of any practice will of course vary with the need and the cost. At present, the costs generally follow the suggested ordering.

Using the costs of delivered municipal water, the cheapest water is that from wells at a cost of approximately 5 cents per 1,000 gallons, followed by surface waters at a cost of from 5 to 15 cents per 1,000 gallons. The next step in the cost scale is to reclaim sewage at an incremental addition of 15 cents per 1,000 gallons or by tertiary treatment at 30 to 50 cents per 1,000 gallons. Desalting follows with estimated possible incremental costs of from 10 cents per 1,000 gallons for brackish water to 50 cents per 1,000 gallons for seawater. Finally, the most expensive water is that obtained by interbasin transfers. Generally, these transfers can be made by canals or through large- or small-quantity pipelines. The large-quantity pipelines are considerably cheaper on a unit basis. It is impossible to evaluate transfers except in terms of quantity, mileage, and lift. Recent canal studies indicate a cost of 5 cents per 1,000 gallons at the 1 bgd level, over 163 miles, and for a 600-foot lift; 20 cents per 1,000 gallons at 120 mgd, 163 miles, 600-foot lift; and 16 cents per 1,000 gallons at 60 mgd, 100 miles, 600-foot lift. Treatment costs, depending on the quality of water being transferred, would, of course, be added.

Assuming average conditions of upstream movement, this would be approximately 3 cents per 1,000 gallons per 100 miles for a canal, and 16 cents per 1,000 gallons per 100 miles for a pipeline. It might be noted that canals have the additional benefits of recreation and water transport.

Detailed Model Development

Biodegradable Model

The objective of this model is to determine the amount of dilution water required to maintain an RQS, in terms of dissolved oxygen, for various levels of treatment.

The stream assimilative capacity can be represented in differential form by:

$$\frac{dD}{dt} = K_1 L_u - K_2 D;$$

D = oxygen deficiency in mg/l;

L_u = oxygen demand in mg/l (u refers to ultimate value);

K_1 = decomposition reaction coefficient, to base e (k_1 to base 10);

K_2 = reaeration reaction coefficient, to base e (k_2 to base 10);

t = time in days.

In the above equation $\frac{dD}{dt}$ is the change in oxygen concentration with time. Assuming the D.O. concentration remains constant with time (i.e., $\frac{dD}{dt} = 0$) then

$$K_1 L_u = K_2 D,$$

where

$K_1 L_u$ = rate of oxygen depletion,

$K_2 D$ = rate of oxygen supply.

Replacing K_2 by 2.3 k_2, the rate of oxygen supply in mg/l per day is:

$$\text{mg/l of } O_2/\text{day} = (D)(2.3). \qquad (1)$$

It follows that

$$\text{lbs. } O_2 = (2.3k_2)(D)(8.3)(Q_L), \qquad (2)$$

where

Q = stream flow in mgd.

Of more importance than a discrete flow measurement is the volume of water effectively operative in the reoxygenation process. This volume is visualized as a pyramid with its peak representing the source of the stream, and having a height equal to the average stream length (l) in miles. The base equals the terminal flow of the stream (Q_t) expressed in million gallons per day divided by the velocity (V) expressed in miles per day.

With this consideration, the model will appear:

$$\text{lbs. } O_2/\text{day} = (2.3k_2) D \frac{Q_t}{3} \frac{l}{V} (8.3). \qquad (3)$$

All streams, in general, are composed of a main stem and one or more discrete contributing tributaries. For each basin the terminal flow is influenced by the number of reoxygenation volumes, represented by n, which is a multiplier for long systems to account for the fact that the same water may purify more than one waste discharge. (See table D–11 for values of n. Table D–10 shows other stream characteristics that were used to measure assimilative capacity.)

A stream's capability for natural regeneration may be expressed by the following equation:

$$\text{lbs. } O_2/\text{day} = (2.3k_2) D \frac{Q_t}{3} \frac{l}{V} \frac{8.3}{24} n. \qquad (4)$$

It is obviously more efficient to put in a given load in many small doses, vis-à-vis a slug (one big dose); hence we need to be able to make an adjustment to represent the regenerative capacity of the receiving water in terms of the way the waste load is imposed. The basic equation assumed a uniform loading. If the waste is to use all of the oxygen generated, the incremental additions should equal the incremental oxygenations. On the other hand, if waste discharges are spread at greater distances than the stream requires for recovery, an increment of the regenerative capacity is lost, and the dilution requirement for a fixed load is increased. The spacing for full utilization (t_r) is equal to

$$\frac{l}{V} \div \frac{\#SMSA}{X+1}.$$

Hann and Reid had previously developed the relative effectiveness (ϵ), in terms of t_r and K_2. Essentially, t_r is the time for the sag curve to recover to its original position. Where the spacing of loads is equal to t_r the sag curves are one right after another: 〰〰〰 . If the loadings are spaced greater than t_r, then the time between the end of one sag curve and the beginning of another is wasted. (See Figure D-1.) The formula was developed in terms of stream velocity, length (time) and number of population centers ($SMSAs$) and tributaries (x).

ϵ is defined to be less than or equal to one. Thus, it increases the rate of oxygen depletion.

$$\#BOD/\text{day} = k_2 Q_t D \frac{l}{V}\left[\frac{(8.3)(2.3)}{24(3)}\right]\epsilon. \qquad (5)$$

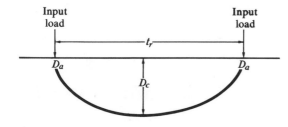

Input load   **Input load**

Figure D-1. Relationship of point loading to continuous loading.

$$t_r = \frac{l}{V(24)} \div \left[\frac{\#SMSA}{(x+1)}\right]$$

$$= \frac{l(x+1)}{24(V)} \, \frac{1}{(\#SMSA)}$$

where

    t_r = travel time, days;

    V = velocity, mph;

$\#SMSA$ = number of Standard Metropolitan Statistical Areas;

    x = number of discrete tributaries;

    D_a = initial deficit;

    D_c = critical deficit = $(CS - RQS_{DO})$.

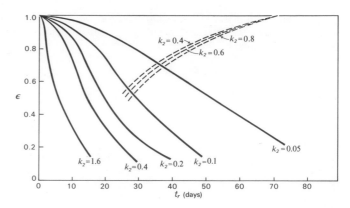

Figure D-2. Efficiency term-ratio of point loading to uniform loading. Adapted from Roy William Hann, Jr., "Procedure for Estimating the Waste Assimilative Capacity of a River System" (Ph.D. thesis, University of Oklahoma, 1962).

Assuming a population equivalent (p.e.) equal to 0.25#BOD/day, then population equivalents in millions (P.E.'s) would equal 250,000 #BOD/day.

By rearranging equation (5)

$$Q_{point\ load} = \frac{PE}{\dfrac{k_2 D\ l_n(\epsilon)}{V}}\left[\frac{(250,000)(24)(3)}{(8.3)(2.3)}\right]$$

$$\qquad\qquad\qquad\qquad\qquad\qquad\qquad (6)$$

$$Q_{point\ load} = \frac{PE}{\dfrac{k_2 D\ l_n(\epsilon)}{V}}[942,900].$$

For uniform load:

$$Q_{uniform\ load} = \frac{PE}{\dfrac{k_2 D\ nl}{V}}[942,900]. \qquad (7)$$

The total required terminal flow is obtained by taking a weighted average of the flows required for point loads and those for uniform loads. Because point loading occurs primarily in metropolitan areas and uniform loading occurs in nonmetropolitan areas, the weights used were the fraction of the region's population residing in SMSAs (Y) and the fraction not residing in such areas ($1 - Y$).

Thus,

$$Q_t = \frac{Y}{\epsilon}\left[\frac{PE}{Dk_2 n\dfrac{l}{V}}\right]942,900 + (1-Y)\frac{PE}{Dk_2\dfrac{l}{V}}942,900$$

combining: (8)

$$Q_t = \left[\frac{Y}{\epsilon} + (1-Y)\right]\frac{PE}{Dk_2\dfrac{nl}{V}}(942,900).$$

The D.O. deficit (D_c) may be expressed as the saturation level (C_s) minus the required quality standard for dissolved oxygen (RQS_{DO}); i.e.,

$$D = (CS - RQS_{DO}).$$

The low-flow augmentation associated with each treatment level is given by Q_t ($I\!P$), where $I\!P$ is defined to be the percentage of waste discharged to the stream, expressed as a fraction.

Q_t ($I\!P$) $= Q_L$ (low-flow augmentation, biodegradable stream response equation). From equation (8), it follows that:

$$Q_L = \left[\frac{Y}{\epsilon} + (1 - Y)\right] \frac{PE\,(I\!P)}{(C_s - RQS_{do})}\,A, \quad (9)$$

where

$$A = \frac{942{,}900}{k_2\,\dfrac{nl}{V}}, \text{ a parameter for each river basin.}$$

Nutritional model – accelerated eutrophication model

The nutritional model was developed by considering the amounts of excessive nutrients.

The model developed will be for phosphorus (P). A similar approach was used for nitrogen (N).

The flow (mgd) required for phosphorus at an acceptable RQS_p level is

$$\text{Flow (mgd)} = \frac{\text{lbs. phos/day}}{RQS_P\,(8.3)}. \quad (10)$$

The total phosphorus is arrived at indirectly from the amount of BOD. Raw sewage is assumed to have a BOD/P ratio of 27/1 at a per capita contribution of 0.25 lbs. On this basis the per capita contribution of phosphorus is 0.009 lbs/day.

The phosphorus of interest is the amount remaining after treatment. This amount in terms of population in millions (P) would be

$$\text{lbs. phos/day} = [(1 - TL_P)\,0.009\,(10^6)]\,(P). \quad (11)$$

Some of this phosphorus is consumed in the biodegradation process, and this amount is related to the BOD available. By assuming a BOD to phosphorus combining ratio of 100/1 the amount consumed is

$$\text{lbs. phos. consumed/day} = \frac{0.25\,(1 - TL_L)}{100}\,(P). \quad (12)$$

Subtracting equation (12) from equation (11) gives the excessive phosphorus for which dilution is required.

Excessive phos. $= P$ (13)

$$\left[(1 - TL_P)\,(0.009) - \frac{(1 - TL_L)\,(0.25)}{100}\right](10^6)$$

$$= P(0.009)\left[(1 - TL_P) - \frac{0.25\,(1 - TL_L)}{100\,(0.009)}\right]10^6.$$

Substituting into equation (10) gives the required flow:

$$\text{Flow (mgd)} = \frac{P(0.009)\,(10^6)}{8.3\,(RQS_P)} \quad (14)$$

$$[(1 - TL_P) - 0.27\,(1 - TL_L)]\,Z$$

$$= \frac{P(1080)\,Z}{RQS_P}\,[(1 - TL_P) - 0.27\,(1 - TL_L)],$$

where Z is the relative portion impounded as affected by the RQS level.[21]

Since this model was developed using nutritional ratios for domestic waste, a scale factor is necessary so that it may also be used for industrial wastes. The scale factor (F) is the BOD/P ratio for the industrial waste in question divided by the BOD/P ratio for municipal waste. This bases the industrial nutritional ratios on a municipal level. It was also considered that when wastes are discharged raw, the pollution problem is not from the nutrients but from the organics; however, when the organics are removed through primary and secondary treatment processes, then the nutrients must be considered. TL_L accounts for the fact that in wastes of high organic content, algae production is limited. The final form for the accelerated eutrophication model is:

$$Q_N = \frac{Z}{(F)\,(RQS_N)}\,(Pop)$$

$$[(1 - TL_N) - 1.44\,(1 - TL_L)]\,3250\,(TL_L),$$

$$Q_P = \frac{Z}{(F)\,(RQS_P)}\,(Pop)$$

$$[(1 - TL_P) - 0.27\,(1 - Tl_L)]\,1080\,(TL_L),$$

where

Q_N, Q_P = nutritional dilution required, mgd, for nitrogen and phosphorus, respectively;

Z = relative portion impounded and affected by RQS level (see table D–3);

F[22] = scale factor introduced to base industrial nutritional ratios on a municipal level (see table D–2);

Pop = population, millions;

TL_N, TL_P = nitrogen and phosphorus removal, respectively, expressed as a decimal (see table D–6);

---

[21] Z is number of days retention now over retention possible when flow is regulated to median flow. See table D–13.

[22] Existing BOD/N and BOD/P ratios for the categorized industrial wastes (Chow, Eckenfelder, and Malina, "Summary Report on Costs") divided by the BOD/N and BOD/P ratios for municipal wastes.

TL_L = BOD removal level expressed as a decimal (see table D–7);

RQS = acceptable quality level, use 1 ppm (N), 0.1 ppm (P).

Thermal Model

Diagramatically the conservation of thermal energy can be depicted in the following manner:

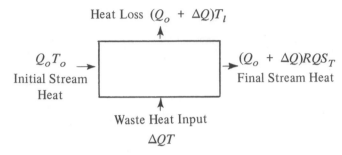

Heat Loss $(Q_o + \Delta Q) T_l$

$Q_o T_o$ → Initial Stream Heat

→ $(Q_o + \Delta Q) RQS_T$ Final Stream Heat

Waste Heat Input

ΔQT

From the diagram, it can be seen that the final temperature or RQS temperature for the stream times the total volume is equal to the initial heat flow of the stream plus the added heat of the waste portion minus the heat loss to the atmosphere:

Final Heat Load = Initial Heat Load + Waste Heat Load – Heat Loss to Atmosphere or,

$$(Q_o + \Delta Q) RQS_T = Q_o T_o + \Delta QT - (Q_o + \Delta Q) T_l, \quad (1)$$

where

Q_o = initial flow,

ΔQ = added flow (waste flow),

T_o = initial temperature,

RQS_T = quality standard for river temperature,

T_l = temperature loss,

T = temperature of added flow.

The heat loss to the atmosphere can be expressed symbolically as[23]

$$H_{Loss} = EL (1 + \sqrt{RR'}) , \quad (2)$$

where

H_{Loss} = heat loss per unit area;

E = quantity of water evaporated in cm of depth per day;

R = ratio of convection-evaporation (Bowen's ratio) @ T_o; R' @ T_1

$$= \frac{0.46 (T_o - T_a) p}{(p_1 - p_2) 760} ;$$

T_o = temperature of water, °C.;

T_a = temperature of air, °F.;

[23] Davidson and Bradshaw, "Thermal Pollution."

p_1 = vapor pressure of sat. vapor @ T_o – mmHg;

p_2 = partial pressure of actual vapor in air – mmHg;

p = atmospheric pressure.

L = heat of vaporization of water at given temperature = 1/2 ($T_o - RQS_T$).

If

A = unit surface area of stream;

and

Vs = subsidence velocity (= Q/A);

then

$$A = \frac{Q + \Delta Q}{Vs}.$$

If

$$K = EL (1 + \sqrt{RR'})$$

and

$$\text{Heat loss} = (Q_o + \Delta Q) T_L = K \frac{Q_o + \Delta Q}{Vs}. \quad (3)$$

Then from equation (1)

$$(Q_o + \Delta Q) RQS_T = Q_o T_o + \Delta QT - K \frac{Q_o + \Delta Q}{Vs} \quad (4)$$

or $\qquad (5)$

$$\Delta Q (T - RQS_T) = Q_o (RQS_T - T_o) + K \frac{Q_o + \Delta Q}{Vs}.$$

If

$$\Delta T_W = T - RQS_T$$

and

$$\Delta T_o = RQS_T - T_o$$

and

$$\Delta Q \left(\Delta T_W - \frac{K}{Vs} \right) = Q_o \left(\Delta T_o + \frac{K}{Vs} \right), \quad (6)$$

then

$$\frac{Q_o}{\Delta Q} = \frac{\Delta T_W - \dfrac{K}{Vs}}{\Delta T_o + \dfrac{K}{Vs}}. \quad (7)$$

If G is set = K/Vs,

then

$$\frac{Q_o}{\Delta Q} = \frac{\Delta T_W - G}{\Delta T_o + G}. \quad (8)$$

Equation (8) is the working expression for calculating the effects on water thermal conditions from the addition of wastes.

Table D-1. VALUES OF SELECTED PARAMETERS,
            BY REGION

	ϵ	A	CS (mg/l)
N Eng	0.99	33,565	9.0
D & H	0.98	9,676	9.0
EGL	0.96	27,588	9.2
WGL	1.0	66,684	9.0
Ches	0.92	30,310	8.7
Ohio	0.99	4,433	8.5
Cumb	0.15	8,228	8.7
Tenn	0.39	20,401	8.3
SE	1.0	61,419	7.8
U Miss	0.62	4,644	8.6
L Miss	0.52	4,599	8.1
U Mo	0.15	8,842	9.2
L Mo	0.50	7,592	8.6
U AWR	0.50	6,472	8.3
L AWR	0.81	11,040	7.9
W Gulf	0.65	18,578	7.3
RG-P	0.06	3,665	8.0
Colo	0.01	2,705	8.1
G Basin	0.42	34,900	8.5
PNW	0.17	34,577	9.5
C Pac	0.70	32,718	7.9
S Pac	0.99	46,678	9.2

Note: ϵ = efficiency term, point load/uniform load.

$$A = \frac{942,900}{K_2 \frac{nl}{V}}.$$

CS = D.O. saturation level in mg/l.

Table D-2. F SCHEDULE USED TO MODIFY A
            FORMULA BASED ON DOMESTIC WASTE
            TO ACCOMMODATE NUTRIENTS FROM
            INDUSTRIAL WASTES

	F_N	F_P
Food	0.389	3.08
Text	2.34	2.74
Pulp and paper	5.55	8.15
Chemicals	2.22	3.7
Petroleum	0.29	1.67
Leather	0.7	1.07
Municipal	1.0	1.0

Note: $F_N = \dfrac{BOD}{N}$

$F_P = \dfrac{BOD}{P}$

Table D-3. VALUES OF SELECTED PARAMETERS,
            BY REGION

	Z	Z'	$\dfrac{\Delta T_W - G}{\Delta T_Q + G}$
N Eng	0.31	0.18	2.80
D & H	0.22	0.13	2.64
Ches	0.08	0.05	2.41
SE	0.60	0.36	0.81
EGL	0.13	0.06	2.97
WGL	0.06	0.04	2.64
Ohio	0.47	0.20	1.92
Cumb-Tenn	0.88	0.53	1.67
U Miss	0.26	0.17	1.91
L Miss	0.25	0.11	1.14
U Mo	1.33	0.65	2.77
L Mo	0.91	0.23	1.86
U AWR	1.51	0.62	0.51
L AWR	0.96	0.25	0.77
W Gulf, RG-P	1.88	0.58	0.28
Colo	2.06	1.08	0.51
G Basin	0.87	0.49	0.46
PNW	0.64	0.34	3.54
C & S Pac	0.96	0.31	1.32

Note: Z = proportion of streams impounded based on median flow.

Z' = proportion of streams impounded based on mean flow.

$\dfrac{\Delta T_W - G}{\Delta T_Q + G}$, see text.

Table D-4. CHARACTERISTICS OF INDUSTRIAL WASTEWATERS, SELECTED INDUSTRIES

Industry	Unit	Flow (gal./unit) Mean	16%	84%	BOD (lb/unit) Mean	16%	84%	Suspended solids (lb/unit) Mean	16%	84%	Total solids (lb/unit) Mean	16%	84%
Sugar beet	Ton	2,700	1,750	4,000	13.0	4.0	42	-	-	-	-	-	-
Cannery	Case[a]	37	12	75	0.365	0.135	9.80	0.105	0.024	0.46	-	-	-
Milk	1,000 lb intake	163	90	295	1.16	0.75	1.81	-	-	-	-	-	-
Tannery	100 lb hides	680	445	1,025	4.55	2.0	10.25	12.0	4.90	29.5	-	-	-
Poultry	1,000 chickens, processed[b]	6,600	3,800	9,300	26.1	23.5	28.8	13.3	11.8	14.75	-	-	-
Paper & pulp	Ton product	24,000	11,200	52,000	53	10	290	42	14	125	-	-	-
Refinery	bbl[c]	140[d]	68	215	-	-	-	-	-	-	-	-	-
	bbl[e]	775[e]	710	840	-	-	-	-	-	-	-	-	-
Synthetic fibers	1,000 lb product	13,000	6,200	25,500	77	23	260	-	-	-	-	-	-
Brewery	bbl[f]	325	220	575	2.6	1.2	4.6	1.50	0.45	2.7	-	-	-
Textile	100 lb each[g]	670	270	17,000	2.45	0.62	9.50	0.93	0.38	2.25	18.5	9.4	-
Explosive	100,000 lb TNT process	36,000	-	-	320	-	-	210	-	-	-	-	-
Meat packing[h]	1,000 lb live wt.	1,045	625	3,100	12.0	6.7	20.0	11.0	7.3	16.8	-	-	35.0

[a] #2 can, 24 cans per case
[b] Assume 1 chicken = 2.5 lb; 1 duck = 4 lb
[c] 1 bbl = 42 gal.
[d] Oil field
[e] Refinery
[f] 1 bbl = 31 gal.
[g] These values are derived from a probability plot of all reported textile mills. These mills include different combinations of the following unit processes: Boiler, Kier, Silk soiling, Dyeing, Pulling, Desizing, Printing, Bleaching, Scouring, Mercerizing. Therefore, the values represent an average of all textile mills processing wool, cotton, and silk, regardless of the particular unit processes used by a given mill.
[h] Grease produced: mean, 1.32 lb/1,000 lb live wt.; 16%, 0.50 lb/1,000 lb live wt; 84%, 3.5 lb/1,000 lb live wt. NH_4 as N produced: mean, 1.5 lb/1,000 lb live wt; 16%, 0.97 lb/1,000 lb live wt; 84%, 2.3 lb/1,000 lb live wt.

Table D-5. POPULATION EQUIVALENT CONSTANTS, SELECTED INDUSTRIES

	lbs BOD/1,000 gals. discharged	H (10^6)
Food and kindred	8.76	0.1406
Textiles	3.65	.05366
Pulp and paper	2.21	.0355
Chemical	16.70	.268
Petroleum	2.50	.0450
Leather	6.69	0.1074

Note:

$$P.E. = \frac{\text{flow bgy} \times 10^9 \times \#BOD/\text{gal.}}{365\,(0.17)}$$

$$= 16.05 \times 10^6\,(\text{flow bgy}) \times \#BOD/\text{gal.}$$

$$P.E. = H\,(\text{flow}) = K\,(\text{bgy})$$

where

$$H = 16.05 \times 10^3 \times \#BOD/1{,}000\text{ gal.}$$

To determine P.E.'s for each industry multiply H times the process water discharged in bgy. Process water discharge = Total − cooling except for food and kindred where process water is equal to total discharge.

Table D-6. TREATMENT EFFICIENCY SCHEMES

(Strength applies to municipal sewages (ppm), percentages removed (T_L) to processes)

Process	Solids (S) Total dissolved solids		Solids (S) Suspended solids		Organic (L) BOD		Organic (L) COD		Nutritional (N) N		Nutritional (N) PO$_4$	
	T_L	ppm	T_L	ppm	T_L	ppm	T_L	ppm	T_L	ppm	T_L	ppm
Raw	0	620	0	250	0	200	0	550	0	50	0	40
Sedimentation	-	-	-	-	35	130	-	-	-	-	-	-
Imhoff tank	-	-	-	-	40	120	-	-	-	-	-	-
Lagoon	-	-	-	-	82	41	-	-	-	-	-	-
Primary	0	620	59	103	34	132	50	275	8	46	10	36
Activated sludge	14	435	92	20	95	12	82	100	50	25	35	26
Extended aeration	-	-	-	-	99	2	-	-	-	-	-	-
Minimum solids	-	-	-	-	60	80	-	-	-	-	-	-
Standard rate trickling filter	-	-	-	-	90	20	-	-	-	-	-	-
High rate trickling filter	-	-	-	-	80	40	-	-	-	-	-	-
Secondary	10	558	90	25	95	10	82	100	50	25	35	26
Activated sludge & a, b	-	435	92	20	94	12	82	100	90	5	35	26
Activated sludge & a, b, c	-	-	98	5	95	10	93	40	90	-5	98	-1
Activated sludge & a, b, c, d, h	-	-	0	0	99	-1	98	12	98	-5	98	-1
Activated sludge & a, b, e	92	-50	-	0	99	-2	99	-5	98	-2	98	-1
Activated sludge & a, b, i	10	560	99	2	93	-3	85	75	50	25	95	2
Activated sludge & f	5	600	92	20	93	-3	85	75	50	25	10	36
Activated sludge & lagoon	-	-	-	-	98	-4	-	-	-	-	-	-
Tertiary	92	50	99	0-5	98	0-5	99	0-5	99	0-2	98	1

Note: Minus sign (–) means less than BOD_5 = 5 day BOD. COD = chemical oxygen demand. T_L = percentage removed by treatment.

a – Nitrification   f – Foam
b – Denitrification   g – Alum
c – Lime treatment   h – Sand filtration
d – Activated carbon   i – Coagulation, sedimentation, and filtration
e – Distillation

Sources: C. S. Chow, W. W. Eckenfelder, and J. F. Malina, "A Summary Report on Costs of Municipal Wastewater Treatment and Estimation of Industrial Wastewater Characteristics and Cost of Treatment" (University of Texas, 1965); and R. J. Frankel, P. H. McGauhey, and G. T. Orlob, "Economic Evaluation of Water Quality: An Engineering-Economic Model for Water Quality Management," 1st Annual Report, SERL Report No. 65–3 (Berkeley, University of California, January 1965).

Table D-7. AVERAGE PERCENTAGE REMOVAL OF WASTES BY MUNICIPAL SEWAGE PROCESSES (T_L)

Process	BOD	COD	N	PO$_4$
Raw	0	0	0	0
Primary	34	50	8	10
Secondary	95	82	50	35
Tertiary	98	99	99	98

Sources: C. S. Chow, W. W. Eckenfelder, and J. F. Malina, "A Summary Report on Costs of Municipal Wastewater Treatment and Estimation of Industrial Wastewater Characteristics and Cost of Treatment" (University of Texas, 1965); and R. J. Frankel, P. H. McGauhey, and G. T. Orlob, "Economic Evaluation of Water Quality: An Engineering-Economic Model for Water Quality Management," 1st Annual Report, SERL Report No. 65–3 (Berkeley, University of California, January 1965).

Table D–8. CAPITAL COSTS AND OPERATION AND MAINTENANCE COSTS, MUNICIPAL SEWAGE TREATMENT PROCESSES

(1965 dollars)

Treatment process	Plant size: 100 gpcd (1 mgd) — Capital cost per mgd	per cap.	O & M per mgd	per cap.	110 gpcd (5 mgd) — Capital cost per mgd	per cap.	O & M per mgd	per cap.	120 gpcd (10 mgd) — Capital cost per mgd	per cap.	O & M per mgd	per cap.
Lagoon	93,800	9.38	3,750	0.38	55,600	6.12	2,100	0.19	–	–	–	–
Primary	253,000	25.30	10,150	1.00	167,000	18.40	8,350	0.92	134,000	16.10	10,200	1.23
Activated sludge	417,700	41.70	16,700	1.67	309,800	34.00	15,450	1.70	267,400	32.10	15,400	1.85
Extended aeration	500,000	50.00	20,000	2.00	375,000	41.40	16,900	1.86	334,500	40.00	14,600	1.75
Minimum solids	490,000	49.00	19,600	1.96	348,000	38.40	15,700	1.73	284,700	34.20	11,600	1.40
Standard rate trickling filter	520,000	52.00	20,800	2.08	485,000	53.60	14,500	1.60	422,000	50.50	11,600	1.40
High rate trickling filter	310,000	31.00	16,800	1.68	240,000	26.50	12,000	1.32	220,000	26.40	10,200	1.23
Activated sludge + a, b, c	–	–	–	–	–	–	–	–	487,000	58.50	28,100	3.38
Activated sludge + a, b, e, d, h	670,000	67.00	26,800	2.68	304,000	33.50	13,700	1.50	530,000	64.00	26,600	3.20
Activated sludge + a, b, e	1,590,000	159.00	63,500	6.35	1,035,000	114.00	46,600	5.10	815,000	98.00	40,800	4.90
Activated sludge + a, b, i	648,000	64.80	44,100	4.41	585,000	64.40	36,800	4.05	515,000	61.80	33,100	3.96
Activated sludge + f	600,000	60.00	24,000	2.40	465,000	51.00	20,600	2.26	396,600	47.60	17,700	2.12
Activated sludge + Lagoon	640,000	64.00	25,600	2.56	470,000	51.60	22,000	2.42	408,600	49.00	18,400	2.20

Treatment process	130 gpcd (50 mgd) — Capital cost per mgd	per cap.	O & M per mgd	per cap.	140 gpcd (100 mgd) — Capital cost per mgd	per cap.	O & M per mgd	per cap.
Lagoon	–	–	–	–	–	–	–	–
Primary	116,600	15.15	8,300	1.08	108,600	15.25	7,600	1.06
Activated sludge	206,000	26.80	10,400	1.35	202,000	28.30	10,100	1.42
Extended aeration	225,600	29.30	11,400	1.48	204,000	28.60	10,400	1.45
Minimum solids	175,800	22.80	8,900	1.15	160,000	22.40	8,000	1.12
Standard rate trickling filter	328,000	42.50	8,300	1.08	300,000	42.00	7,350	1.02
High rate trickling filter	184,200	23.90	8,300	1.08	167,000	23.40	7,150	1.00
Activated sludge + a, b, c	342,900	44.50	21,200	2.75	312,000	43.80	19,100	2.67
Activated sludge + a, b, e, d, h	460,000	59.60	23,500	3.05	440,000	61.50	21,200	2.96
Activated sludge + a, b, e	695,000	90.00	35,800	4.65	625,000	87.50	32,600	4.56
Activated sludge + a, b, i	368,900	48.00	24,200	3.14	320,000	45.00	21,900	3.07
Activated sludge + f	274,700	35.70	12,000	1.56	220,000	31.00	10,500	1.47
Activated sludge + Lagoon	290,700	37.80	12,900	1.68	260,000	36.40	11,600	1.62

Note:
a – nitrification
b – denitrification
c – lime treatment
d – activated carbon
e – distillation
f – foam extraction
g – alum
h – sand filtration
i – coagulation, sedimentation, filtration

Sources: C. S. Chow, W. W. Eckenfelder, and J. F. Malina, "A Summary Report on Costs of Municipal Wastewater Treatment and Estimation of Industrial Wastewater Characteristics and Cost of Treatment" (University of Texas, 1965); R. J. Frankel, P. H. McGauhey, and G. T. Orlob, "Economic Evaluation of Water Quality: An Engineering-Economic Model for Water Quality Management," 1st Annual Report, SERL Report No. 65–3 (University of California, Berkeley, January 1965); and personal records of the senior author of this appendix.

Table D-9. INDUSTRIAL WASTE TREATMENT COSTS

($ per million gallons per day)

		Plant size: 1 mgd		5 mgd		10 mgd	
		Capital cost	O & M	Capital cost	O & M	Capital cost	O & M
Pulp & paper	Primary	54,000	11,400	37,000	7,400	35,300	7,100
	Secondary	301,000	12,000	194,000	8,750	157,900	7,850
	Tertiary[a]						
Tannery	Primary	92,000	11,000	80,400	9,650	83,400	10,000
	Secondary	630,000	18,900	553,000	16,600	517,000	15,500
	Tertiary[a]						
Food & kindred	Primary	73,200	12,200	53,100	8,860	51,500	8,500
	Secondary	832,000	14,200	674,000	10,000	606,000	7,900
	Tertiary[a]						
Petroleum	Primary	–	–	–	–	–	–
	Secondary	175,000	52,000	430,000	53,000	620,000	53,000
	Tertiary[a]						
Chemical	Primary	–	–	–	–	–	–
	Secondary	580,000	62,000	420,000	26,000	360,000	17,500
	Tertiary[a]						
Textiles	Primary	–	–	–	–	–	–
	Secondary	407,000	14,000	312,000	10,000	283,000	8,000
	Tertiary[a]						

Source: C. S. Chow, W. W. Eckenfelder, J. F. Malina, "A Summary Report on Costs of Municipal Wastewater Treatment and Estimation of Industrial Wastewater Characteristics and Cost of Treatment" (University of Texas, 1965).

[a]Use municipal schedule in table D-8.

Table D-10. STREAM CHARACTERISTICS, BY REGION

	Total miles (R)	Average width (ft)	Average depth (d) (ft)	Average length (l) $(miles)$	Mean velocity (V) (mph)
N Eng	5,000	200	4	100	1½
D & H	2,500	100	3	75	1½
EGL	4,000	150	3	50	1½
WGL	7,000	150	3	50	1½
Ches	5,000	250	5	75	1½
Ohio	12,500	250	4	100	1
Cumb	1,500	100	3	100	1½
Tenn	3,500	150	4	75	1½
SE	25,000	250	5	150	1½
U Miss	13,000	100	3	150	1
L Miss	4,500	150	4	150	1½
U Mo	31,000	100	3	250	1½
L Mo	4,500	200	3.5	125	1
U AWR	7,500	100	2	200	1½
L AWR	8,000	150	3.5	175	1½
W Gulf	14,000	250	4	300	1
RG-P	7,000	50	1.5	150	1½
Colo	12,000	100	2	150	1
G Basin	6,000	50	1	100	1
PNW	21,000	250	4	150	1
C Pac	8,000	200	4	100	1½
S Pac	800	20	0.5	50	1

Table D-11. TEMPERATURE AND RELATED STREAM CHARACTERISTICS, BY REGION

	k_2/k_1 estimates at 68°F.	(T_o) Summer temperature °F.	k_2 estimates	n
N Eng	2.8	70	0.28	1.0
D & H	3.5	70	.36	2.5
EGL	2.7	68	.27	2.0
WGL	2.0	70	.20	1.7
Ches	2.0	73	.22	3.0
Ohio	2.5	75	.30	7.0
Cumb	2.8	73	.31	2.0
Tenn	1.5	78	.16	4.0
SE	2.0	83	.24	2.0
U Miss	1.5	74	.17	4.6
L Miss	2.8	80	.32	3.3
U Mo	2.5	68	.25	1.0
L Mo	2.5	74	.29	3.2
U AWR	2.0	78	.23	0.75
L AWR	2.0	82	.24	2.0
W Gulf	2.0	85	.25	1.0
RG-P	2.0	83	.24	1.0
Colo	2.5	80	.29	2.0
G Basin	1.7	75	.25	1.0
PNW	2.5	65	.25	2.0
C Pac	4.0	68	.40	3.0
S Pac	1.3	83	0.16	1.0

Note: For k_1, k_2, and n, see text.

Table D-12. DISCRETE POINT ANALYSIS, BY REGION

	No. of SMSAs	SMSA population (mil.)	Total (mil.)	Col. 2 ÷ Col. 3 (percent)
N Eng	23	7.5	10.2	73
D & H	12	21	24.0	87
EGL	8	9	12.6	71
WGL	17	11	13.6	80
Ches	14	7	9.2	76
Ohio	24	11	17.7	62
Cumb	1	.4	1.2	33
Tenn	5	1.6	2.9	55
SE	29	8.8	20.0	44
U Miss	12	5.5	11.8	46
L Miss	4	1.4	4.4	31
U Mo	8	2.0	6.0	33
L Mo	3	1.3	2.3	56
U AWR	6	1.4	3.4	41
L AWR	8	1.5	3.98	37
W Gulf	18	5.6	8.6	65
RG-P	2	.6	1.4	42
Colo	2	.9	1.9	47
G Basin	5	.9	1.0	90
PNW	7	2.9	5.4	53
C Pac	7	5.0	6.7	74
S Pac	6	8.9	8.9	100
Total	221	116.0	177.4	65

Source: Census of population, 1960.

Note: All populations in 10^6.

Table D-13. USABLE RESERVOIR CAPACITY AND CAPACITY WHEN REGULATED TO MEDIAN FLOW, BY REGION

	Usable capacity gallons (mil.)	Total capacity median flow (mg)	Z (%)
New Eng	2,898,000	11,400,000	25
D & H	992,400	4,600,000	21
Ches	309,100	6,800,000	5
S Atlantic-E Gulf	5,334,000	30,700,000	18
EGL	543,300	4,100,000	13
WGL	419,500	6,900,000	6
Ohio	1,875,000	11,300,000	17
Cumb-Tenn	6,957,000	11,000,000	63
U Miss	1,138,000	9,600,000	8
L Miss	1,455,000	6,100,000	24
U Mo-Hudson Bay	24,720,000	26,600,000	99
L Mo	406,000	2,100,000	18
U AWR	2,472,000	3,600,000	68
L AWR	7,275,000	14,500,000	52
W Gulf-RG-P	4,667,000	8,600,000	54
Colo	11,326,000	11,700,000	96
G Basin	1,659,000	2,000,000	82
PNW	9,082,000	24,400,000	37
C Pac-S Pac	5,512,000	9,100,000	58
Total or mean	89,040,000	205,000,000	22

Note: Z = usable capacity as a percentage of median flow.

Table D-14. SELECTED PARAMETERS RELATED TO THERMAL POLLUTION, BY REGION

where $T_o = T_{air}$

$T = 100$

$RQS_T - T_o = 5.4°F.$

	RQS_T	$T - T_{air}$	K/E	E (in/year)	$T = 95°F.$ G	$\dfrac{(T - RQS_T) - G}{(RQS_T - T_o) + G}$
N Eng	75.4	25.0	869	30	0.50	2.80
D & H	75.4	25.0	869	40	0.90	2.64
EGL	73.4	27.0	877	35	0.80	2.97
WGL	75.4	25.0	869	35	0.79	2.64
Ches	78.4	22.0	856	45	0.59	2.41
Ohio	80.4	20.0	846	45	0.73	1.92
Cumb	78.4	22.0	856	48	1.07	2.00
Tenn	83.4	17.0	830	50	0.80	1.34
SE	88.4	12.0	805	57	0.70	0.81
U Miss	79.4	21.0	851	44	0.98	1.91
L Miss	85.4	15.0	821	56	0.87	1.14
U Mo	73.4	27.0	877	60	1.00	2.77
L Mo	79.4	21.0	851	55	1.05	1.86
U AWR	83.4	17.0	830	91	2.90	0.51
L AWR	87.4	13.0	811	60	1.05	0.77
W Gulf	90.4	10.0	791	85	1.37	0.28
RG-P	88.4	12.0	805	90	3.80	0
Colo	85.4	15.0	821	80	2.49	0.51
G Basin	80.4	20.0	846	70	4.50	0.46
PNW	70.4	30.0	889	40	0.68	3.54
C Pac	73.4	27.0	877	70	1.27	2.65
S Pac	88.4	17.0	830	110	10.01	0

Note: For K, see text. E = quantity of water evaporated.

Table D-15. DEFINITIONS OF TREATMENT PROCESSES

Process	Design criteria	Reference
Raw	No treatment	1, 2, 3
Sedimentation	2 hr settling or 650 gal/(ft^2)/(day)	1, 3, 4
Imhoff tank	2 hr retention or 600 gal/(ft^2)/(day)	2, 3
Lagoon	Primary settling or 20 lb/(acre)/(day)	1
Activated sludge	5 hr aeration or 950 gal/(ft^2)/(day)	1, 5, 6
Extended aeration	24 hr aeration or 60 lb BOD/1,000 ft^3/day	4
Minimum solids	2 hr aeration	4, 7
Standard rate trickling filter	2 hr settling or 12.5 lb/(1,000 ft^3)/(day)	1, 2, 3, 4
High rate trickling filter	2 hr settling or 40 lb/(1,000 ft^3)/(day)	1, 2, 3, 4
Activated sludge plus nitrification & denitrification	5 hr aeration (nitrification), 2–5 hrs denitrification	1
Activated sludge plus:		
activated carbon	Carbon columns, regeneration units	1
sand filtration	5 gal./ft^2 sand bed	1
distillation	Fourteen-effect, LTV, multiple-effect evaporator	1
Coagulation, sedimentation, & filtration	2 hr settling, 200 mg/l alum 5 gal/ft^2 sand bed	1, 3
Foam exchange	Induced frothing, minimum surfactant concentration 1 mg/l	8

References:

1. C. S. Chow, W. W. Eckenfelder, J. F. Malina, "A Summary Report on Costs of Municipal Wastewater Treatment and Estimation of Industrial Wastewater Characteristics and Cost of Treatment" (University of Texas, 1965).

2. G. M. Fair and J. C. Geyer, *Water Supply and Waste-water Disposal* (Wiley & Sons, Inc., 1954).

3. E. W. Steel, *Water Supply and Sewerage* (Wiley & Sons, Inc., 1954).

4. W. W. Eckenfelder and D. J. O'Connor, *Biological Waste Treatment* (Pergamon Press, 1964).

5. T. R. Haseltine, "A Rational Approach to the Design of Activated Sludge Plants," *Biological Treatment of Sewage and Industrial Wastes* (Reinhold Publishing Corporation, 1956).

6. J. R. Brett, "Thermal Requirements of Fish—Three Decades of Study, 1940–1970" (R. A. Taft Sanitary Engineering Center, T. Rep. W60-3, 1960).

7. L. N. Nemerow, *Theories and Practices of Industrial Waste Treatment* (Reading, Mass.: Addison-Wesley Publishing Co., Inc., 1963).

8. U.S. Public Health Service, *Contaminant Removal from Sewage Plant Effluents by Foaming*, Advanced Waste Treatment Research Publication AWTR-5 (Cincinnati: December 1963).

Appendix E

ESTIMATION OF WASTE LOADS AND TREATMENT COSTS

BOD Waste Loads

In appendix D, Reid, Eckenfelder, and their associates, supplied data on industrial waste loads in terms of pounds of BOD per 1,000 gallons of process water discharged (except for food and kindred products for which the estimate was based on total water discharge — both process and cooling water). The estimates are given below:

Industry	Pounds of BOD per 1,000 gallons of process water discharged
Food and kindred	9.16
Textiles	3.65
Pulp and paper	2.21
Chemicals	16.70
Petroleum	2.50
Leather	6.69

The data were then converted into population equivalents (p.e.'s)[1] discharged per dollar of value added and multiplied by an estimate of the gallons of process water discharged per dollar of value added. The following estimates were obtained:

Industry	P.e.'s discharged per $ million of value added
Food and kindred	10,347
Textiles	1,852
Pulp and paper	10,238
Chemicals	10,706
Petroleum	1,370
Leather	7,039

Using these estimates, total industrial P.E.'s discharged in 1960 were computed to be as follows:

Industry	Millions of p.e.'s discharged, 1960
Food and kindred	84.3
Textiles	4.6
Pulp and paper	40.8
Chemicals	109.5
Petroleum	3.3
Leather	1.1
Total	243.6

An alternative estimate of industrial wastes was derived from unpublished data developed by Bower and Bonem.[2] The estimation procedure was, first, to obtain data on the pounds of BOD produced per unit of physical product in selected four-digit SIC industries (these data were taken from the existing literature). Second, the data were converted to p.e.'s and an estimate of physical product per employee was used to estimate p.e.'s per employee. The latter estimate was multiplied by 1960 employment to obtain total p.e.'s discharged in the selected four-digit industries. An estimate for the two-digit industry was then obtained by multiplying the four-digit total by the ratio of water discharged in the two-digit industry to that discharged in the four-digit classifications.

---

[1] One "population equivalent" (p.e.) is equal to the amount of BOD discharged by one person in one day; i.e., that amount of waste that exhausts from the stream 0.25 lb. of oxygen per day in the process of decomposition. When capitalized, the letters (P.E.) stand for one million population equivalents.

[2] See also Blair T. Bower, Gordon P. Larson, Abraham Michaels, and Walter M. Philips in Richard T. Anderson (ed.), *Waste Management*, Report of the Second Regional Plan, New York Region, Regional Plan Association (1968), table A–18, p. 95.

The resulting estimate of 1960 industrial wastes is given below:

Industry	Millions of p.e.'s discharged, 1960
Food and kindred	21.1
Textiles	14.7
Pulp and paper	43.8
Chemicals	(no estimate)
Petroleum	6.4
Leather	2.1

As can be seen, the biggest discrepancy between the above estimates and those of Reid and Eckenfelder is in the food and kindred products sector. It was decided that the Bower-Bonem estimate in this sector was too low and, accordingly, the Reid-Eckenfelder estimate was used.

Municipal wastes were estimated on the basis of one urban person = one p.e. No addition for industrial wastes discharged to municipal systems needed to be made because all industrial wastes are included in the above estimates.

A portion of the wastes produced by industry and by persons is discharged to oceans, estuarine waters, and lakes. These wastes do not affect the level of instream water quality in a region, although they can and do cause serious quality problems in lakes, bays, and beaches. It is to be hoped that the latter effect is offset by fairly high levels of waste treatment.

The percentage of municipal wastes discharged to points other than streams was taken to be the ratio of population residing in SMSAs which discharge to such points to total population in the region. The percentage of industrial wastes discharged to oceans, bays, and lakes was estimated to be the ratio of manufacturing value added in SMSAs adjacent to such points to total manufacturing value added in the region. The estimates are as follows:

Region	Municipal	Industrial
	(percent)	
New England	55	85
Delaware–Hudson	85	65
Chesapeake Bay	70	30
Eastern Great Lakes	75	50
Western Great Lakes	80	55
Southeast	30	25
Lower Mississippi	35	30
Western Gulf	30	30
Great Basin	70	35
South Pacific	95	80
Central Pacific	65	60
Pacific Northwest	65	45

Thermal Waste Loads

In order to determine the amount of dilution flow necessary to offset the industrial thermal waste load, it was necessary to compute the amount of industrial cooling water discharged. These amounts were computed by (1) determining total industrial discharge by deducting losses from withdrawals and (2) estimating the percentage of total discharge which is cooling water. The latter was assumed to be equal to cooling intake as a percentage of total intake; i.e., it was assumed that the same percentage

of intake is lost from cooling as from process water. Although this assumption misses the mark (generally, it is believed that the percentage of process intake lost is larger than the percentage of cooling intake lost), it provided a convenient way of segregating cooling from process water discharge. (See appendix D for equations used for the computation of thermal dilution flows.) The percentage of cooling discharge to total discharge is as follows:

Industry	
Food and kindred	73
Pulp and paper	37
Chemicals	87
Petroleum	93
Primary metals	76
Textiles	34
Lumber and wood	81
Rubber and plastics	83
Stone, clay, and glass	79
Leather	17
All other mfg.	77
Steam–electric power	100

Waste Treatment Costs

Industrial Waste Treatment Costs

Data on the costs of industrial waste treatment were supplied by Reid and Eckenfelder for plants with different design capacities. The plant size selected for incorporation into the model was that of 5 mgd design capacity. Estimates of primary (35 percent BOD removal) and secondary (95 percent BOD removal) treatment costs for plants of this size in the six industries with major waste loads are given below:

	Treatment level	Construction cost	Operation & maintenance costs
		($ per mgd)	
Food and kindred	Primary	53,100	8,860
	Secondary	674,000	10,000
Textiles	Primary	–	–
	Secondary	312,000	10,000
Pulp and paper	Primary	37,000	7,400
	Secondary	194,000	8,750
Chemicals	Primary	–	–
	Secondary	420,000	26,000
Petroleum	Primary	–	–
	Secondary	430,000	53,000
Leather	Primary	80,400	9,650
	Secondary	553,000	16,600

Data were unavailable for industrial tertiary treatment (97½ percent BOD removal) costs; consequently, it was assumed that in all industries tertiary treatment costs would be the same as the municipal tertiary treatment cost for a 5 mgd plant.[3] Annual costs were computed on the assumptions of a plant life of fifty years and an interest rate of 4 percent.

---

[3] Construction costs = $591,500 per mgd; annual equivalent = $23,660 per mgd. Annual operation and maintenance costs = $26,390 per mgd. Total annual cost = $50,050 per mgd.

Treatment levels between 35 percent and 95 percent are assumed to be attained by mixtures of primary, secondary, and tertiary treatment. Specifically, it was assumed that intermediate treatment levels were attained by the mixtures given in table 41. By taking an average of primary, secondary, and tertiary treatment costs, using the percentages in table 41 as weights, industrial waste treatment cost schedules were found for each industry.

Industrial waste treatment costs were in terms of dollars per mgd of waste treated. For computational purposes, it was desirable to translate this into dollars per year per p.e. of waste treated per day. The data used in this transformation are given below:

Industry	P.e.'s per mgd discharged
Food and kindred	53,900
Textiles	21,500
Pulp and paper	13,000
Chemicals	98,200
Petroleum	14,700
Leather	39,300

The estimates of industrial waste treatment costs are given in table 54. The variation between industries in costs is due to (1) variations in costs per mgd treated and (2) the variation in p.e.'s produced per mgd of discharge.

Municipal Waste Treatment Costs

Reid and Eckenfelder provided estimates (table E-1) of municipal waste treatment costs for various plant design capacities. Capital costs have been converted to annual equivalent costs on the basis of a 4 percent interest rate and a plant life of fifty years. In order to select plants of the appropriate size, a tabulation made by Bower of design capacities in municipal waste treatment plants from the *1962 Inventory of Municipal Waste Facilities*[4] was utilized. For non-SMSA areas, the mean design capacity for various states falls beween 0.1 mgd and 2.3 mgd (table E-2). Mean design capacity for SMSAs ranged from 8 mgd to 160 mgd, depending on the size of the city (table E-3). The larger SMSAs — those with a population of 500,000 or more — had mean design capacities exceeding 40 mgd. On the basis of these computations, a design capacity of 1 mgd was used for urban non-SMSA areas and 50 mgd for urban SMSA areas. The proportion of U.S. urban population living in each of the two categories was estimated, and treatment costs at the primary, secondary, and tertiary treatment levels were computed as a weighted average of the costs in a 1 mgd plant and those of a 50 mgd plant.

It was assumed that the percentage of plants in each of the categories of primary, secondary, and tertiary treatment at the various treatment levels was the same as in the distribution previously given for industrial treatment plants. Treatment costs at each level of treatment were then computed as a weighted average of primary, secondary, and tertiary treatment costs.

Equivalent annual costs, computed as noted above, for each level of treatment for projected urban population and industrial activity for each region are shown in tables E-4 through E-13.[5]

Recirculation Costs

The initial calculations of this study showed that in some regions dilution flows required to offset thermal waste loads would exceed dilution flows required to offset BOD, phosphorus, and nitrogen waste loads. Moreover, as the level of waste treatment increases, dilution flows to provide adequate thermal quality become more important because higher levels of waste treatment reduce BOD, phosphorus, and nitrogen without reducing the magnitude of thermal wastes.

However, a form of "treatment" can be provided for thermal wastes: by increasing in-plant recirculation of water, the dissipation of heat in cooling towers or other devices is substituted for the dissipation of heat in rivers. Therefore, a determination was made of the degree of in-plant recirculation necessary to reduce thermal dilution flows to levels that would be less than BOD, phosphorus, and nitrogen dilution flows. It was assumed, furthermore, that increased recirculation to substitute for dilution flows would occur only in steam-electric power plants because they are by far the major sources of thermal waste loads.

Projected amounts of recirculation by steam-electric power plants have been noted previously. But the amount of recirculation necessary to reduce thermal dilution flows to levels less than BOD, phosphorus, and nitrogen dilution flows is greater than that originally projected to occur. Table E-14 gives the recirculation rates necessary for the required reduction in thermal dilution flows. These are the ratios of G/I where

$$G = \text{total application of water},$$
$$I = \text{water intake}.$$

Also, $G = R + I$

where

$$R = \text{amount of water recirculated}.$$

As noted elsewhere, it is assumed that the maximum recirculation rate is 70.

In eleven regions, primarily in the West, no increase in recirculation over that previously projected was necessary, because the normal operation of technological and economic factors will result in high recirculation rates in these regions.

Reid provided data on the costs of recirculation.[6] His estimates are:

EAST

Annual capital cost: 2.8 mills/1,000 gallons
Annual operating cost: 8.5 mills/1,000 gallons
Annual total cost: 11.3 mills/1,000 gallons

---

[4] U.S. Public Health Service Publication No. 1065.

[5] Total treatment costs for any region in which waste is discharged into estuaries, large lakes, or the ocean would be greater than shown if treatment of such wastes had not been limited to the primary level or if a smaller fraction of population and activity had been assigned to downstream (and lacustrine) points of discharge.

[6] In a separate memorandum to the authors.

WEST

Annual capital cost: 1.7 mills/1,000 gallons
Annual operating cost: 6.4 mills/1,000 gallons
Annual total cost: 8.1 mills/1,000 gallons

Here "1,000 gallons" refers to thousands of gallons put through the cooling tower. Reid's data coincide closely with those of Cootner and Löf[7] who calculated that in the eastern (humid) section of the West South Central region (Arkansas, Louisiana, Oklahoma, and Texas) costs would be 10.7 mills per thousand gallons and in the western (dry section) of this region, 6.2 mills per thousand gallons. It is assumed that the above costs hold for a complete recirculation system, i.e., when the recirculation rate is 70.

Tables E–15 through E–18 show estimated quantities of discharged cooling water for 1960 and the Medium projections for 1980, 2000, and 2020. Tables E–19 through E–27 contain information used in computing costs of recirculation at original and revised rates.

Short-term Treatment Costs

Calculations were made of the costs of substituting short-term, high-level treatment for reservoir storage. Data

[7]Paul H. Cootner and George O. G. Löf, *Water Demand for Steam Electric Generation: An Economic Projection Model* (The Johns Hopkins Press for Resources for the Future, 1965).

concerning the costs of short-term, high-level treatment were supplied by Reid and associates:

	Annual capital cost ($'s per mgd capacity)	Annual operating cost ($'s per mgd capacity 1 month)
Microstrainer	313[8]	60
Polyelectrolites	–	710
Carbon	–	750

It was assumed that the relevant process in our analysis was polyelectrolites and that the same cost would apply to both municipal and industrial waste. In addition, Reid's data were converted to costs per p.e. by estimates of p.e.'s per mgd given above. The results are given below:

	Short-term treatment cost ($ per month per p.e.)
Municipal	0.09
Food and kindred	.01
Textiles	.02
Paper and pulp	.03
Chemicals	.05
Petroleum	.01
Leather	0.05

[8]Amortized over 15 years at 4 percent interest.

Table E–1. CAPITAL COSTS AND OPERATION AND MANAGEMENT COSTS, MUNICIPAL WASTE TREATMENT
($ per P.E. treated)

Treatment level	Plant size: 1 mgd Capital cost	O & M	5 mgd Capital cost	O & M	10 mgd Capital cost	O & M	50 mgd Capital cost	O & M	100 mgd Capital cost	O & M
Primary (35%)	25.30	1.00	18.40	0.92	16.10	1.23	15.15	1.08	15.25	1.06
Secondary (95%)	41.70	1.67	34.00	1.70	32.10	1.85	26.80	1.35	28.30	1.42
Tertiary (97½%)	67.00	2.68	65.00	2.90	64.00	3.20	59.60	3.05	61.50	2.96

Table E-2. MEAN DESIGN CAPACITIES OF MUNICIPAL WASTE TREATMENT PLANTS IN NON-SMSA AREAS

	Mean design capacity *(mgd)*
Montana	0.42
Colorado	2.28
Nevada	1.52
North Dakota	0.21
South Dakota	0.29
Nebraska	0.14
Kansas	0.42
Maine	0.79
New Hampshire	1.21
Oklahoma	0.63
New Mexico	0.74
Idaho	1.10
Wyoming	1.16
Vermont	1.67
Mississippi	0.60

Table E-3. MEAN DESIGN CAPACITY OF MUNICIPAL WASTE TREATMENT PLANTS IN SMSA AREAS

Population of SMSA	Mean design capacity *(mgd)*
50,000– 100,000	8
100,000– 250,000	10
250,000– 500,000	24
500,000–1,000,000	41
1,000,000–5,000,000	77
5,000,000 & over	160

Table E-4. COST OF STANDARD TREATMENT, BY LEVEL OF TREATMENT AND REGION: 1960

($ million)

	Treatment level *(percent)*:						
	70/50	70/60	70	80	90	95	97½
NORTHEAST	258.5	265.1	276.2	300.7	325.3	358.3	430.3
N Eng	29.0	29.1	29.5	31.4	33.3	36.1	42.7
D & H	71.5	72.5	74.1	77.0	79.9	83.6	91.3
Ches	21.7	22.3	23.4	25.3	27.2	29.8	35.3
Ohio	34.2	35.8	38.5	45.4	52.4	61.8	82.3
EGL	32.2	32.8	33.7	35.7	37.7	40.3	46.1
WGL	40.4	41.3	42.9	45.4	47.8	51.0	57.8
U Miss	25.7	27.4	29.9	35.6	41.3	48.9	65.6
L Mo	3.8	3.9	4.2	4.9	5.7	6.8	9.2
SOUTHEAST	62.5	64.7	70.0	80.7	91.2	106.9	141.5
SE	39.5	40.7	43.7	50.0	56.1	65.4	85.9
Cumb	1.4	1.4	1.4	1.6	1.8	2.2	3.0
Tenn	5.1	5.5	6.3	7.5	8.7	10.3	13.9
L Miss	9.3	9.6	10.2	11.4	12.7	14.5	18.3
L AWR	7.2	7.5	8.4	10.2	11.9	14.5	20.4
MID-CONTINENT	39.5	41.1	43.1	49.2	55.4	63.4	81.0
U Mo	10.4	10.9	11.5	13.5	15.6	18.2	24.0
U AWR	6.7	7.0	7.3	8.5	9.7	11.3	14.9
W Gulf	22.4	23.2	24.3	27.2	30.1	33.9	42.1
SOUTHWEST	31.2	31.4	31.5	32.9	34.4	36.6	41.2
RG-P	2.8	2.9	2.9	3.4	3.9	4.6	6.2
Colo	3.2	3.2	3.2	3.7	4.2	5.1	7.0
G Basin	1.7	1.7	1.7	1.8	1.9	2.1	2.4
S Pac	23.5	23.6	23.7	24.0	24.4	24.8	25.6
NORTH PACIFIC	30.5	31.2	32.5	34.9	37.4	41.1	49.0
C Pac	17.2	17.6	18.0	19.1	20.3	21.9	25.3
PNW	13.3	13.6	14.5	15.8	17.1	19.2	23.7
U.S.	422.2	433.5	453.3	498.4	543.7	606.3	743.0

Table E-5. COST OF STANDARD TREATMENT, BY LEVEL OF TREATMENT AND REGION: 1980 LOW

($ million)

	Treatment level *(percent)*:						
	70/50	70/60	70	80	90	95	97½
NORTHEAST	335.8	346.0	361.5	393.7	425.8	468.2	558.9
N Eng	36.2	36.5	37.0	39.3	41.6	45.2	53.2
D & H	89.3	90.7	92.8	96.5	100.1	104.6	113.8
Ches	32.9	34.2	36.4	39.7	43.0	47.5	57.2
Ohio	42.7	45.2	48.8	57.6	66.3	77.7	102.2
EGL	43.6	44.4	45.8	48.5	51.3	54.9	62.6
WGL	53.5	54.9	57.0	60.2	63.5	67.5	75.8
U Miss	32.2	34.4	37.5	44.5	51.5	60.7	80.5
L Mo	5.4	5.7	6.2	7.4	8.5	10.1	13.6
SOUTHEAST	104.2	108.3	118.1	136.1	154.1	180.2	238.7
SE	70.2	72.5	78.5	89.9	101.3	118.2	156.5
Cumb	3.9	4.2	4.8	5.7	6.6	7.7	10.0
Tenn	7.4	7.9	8.9	10.6	12.3	14.6	19.7
L Miss	13.3	13.9	14.8	16.6	18.4	20.8	26.0
L AWR	9.4	9.8	11.1	13.3	15.5	18.9	26.5
MID-CONTINENT	54.6	57.0	60.0	68.6	77.0	88.1	111.4
U Mo	13.7	14.3	14.9	17.6	20.2	23.7	31.4
U AWR	7.8	8.2	8.6	10.1	11.5	13.4	17.4
W Gulf	33.1	34.5	36.5	40.9	45.3	51.0	62.6
SOUTHWEST	57.9	58.3	58.8	61.4	64.1	68.1	76.6
RG-P	4.7	4.7	4.8	5.6	6.4	7.7	10.3
Colo	6.5	6.6	6.7	7.8	8.9	10.6	14.6
G Basin	2.8	2.9	3.0	3.2	3.4	3.6	4.1
S Pac	43.9	44.1	44.3	44.8	45.4	46.2	47.6
NORTH PACIFIC	61.1	62.8	67.8	74.4	81.1	91.1	113.3
C Pac	26.4	26.9	27.6	29.5	31.3	33.8	38.9
PNW	34.7	35.9	40.2	44.9	49.8	57.3	74.4
U.S.	613.6	632.4	666.2	734.2	802.1	895.7	1,098.9

Table E-6. COST OF STANDARD TREATMENT, BY LEVEL OF TREATMENT AND REGION: 1980 MEDIUM

($ million)

	Treatment level *(percent)*:						
	70/50	70/60	70	80	90	95	97½
NORTHEAST	372.9	384.8	403.4	439.7	475.7	522.8	622.6
N Eng	40.2	40.4	41.0	43.5	46.0	49.8	58.5
D & H	99.5	101.2	103.8	108.0	112.2	117.2	127.4
Ches	36.8	38.1	40.7	44.4	48.3	53.3	64.3
Ohio	47.6	50.7	55.1	65.0	74.7	87.4	114.0
EGL	48.2	49.2	50.9	54.1	57.2	61.2	69.7
WGL	59.3	61.0	63.5	67.2	70.8	75.4	84.6
U Miss	35.4	37.9	41.5	49.3	57.0	67.2	88.9
L Mo	5.9	6.3	6.9	8.2	9.5	11.3	15.2
SOUTHEAST	116.1	121.1	133.1	153.4	174.1	203.3	268.1
SE	77.9	80.6	87.8	100.6	113.4	132.4	175.0
Cumb	4.5	5.0	5.8	6.8	7.9	9.2	11.8
Tenn	8.4	9.0	10.3	12.3	14.4	16.9	22.5
L Miss	15.1	15.8	17.0	19.1	21.2	23.9	29.5
L AWR	10.2	10.7	12.2	14.6	17.2	20.9	29.3
MID-CONTINENT	60.9	63.7	67.5	77.0	86.4	98.8	124.1
U Mo	14.8	15.5	16.3	19.2	22.0	25.8	34.1
U AWR	8.6	9.0	9.5	11.1	12.7	14.9	19.2
W Gulf	37.5	39.2	41.7	46.7	51.7	58.1	70.8
SOUTHWEST	62.3	62.8	63.3	66.2	69.2	73.8	82.7
RG-P	4.9	5.0	5.1	6.0	6.9	8.2	11.1
Colo	6.9	7.0	7.1	8.3	9.5	11.4	15.5
G Basin	3.1	3.2	3.3	3.5	3.8	4.1	4.6
S Pac	47.4	47.6	47.8	48.4	49.0	49.8	51.5
NORTH PACIFIC	67.8	69.9	75.6	83.0	90.7	101.8	127.0
C Pac	28.7	29.4	30.2	32.2	34.3	36.9	42.5
PNW	39.1	40.5	45.4	50.8	56.4	64.9	84.5
U.S.	680.0	702.3	742.9	819.3	896.1	1,000.2	1,224.5

Table E-7. COST OF STANDARD TREATMENT, BY LEVEL OF TREATMENT AND REGION: 1980 HIGH

($ million)

	Treatment level (percent):						
	70/50	70/60	70	80	90	95	97½
NORTHEAST	435.9	451.7	477.0	519.8	562.6	617.0	729.8
N Eng	45.0	45.2	46.9	48.7	51.5	55.7	65.3
D & H	117.7	120.1	123.5	128.8	133.9	139.9	151.7
Ches	42.4	44.1	47.3	51.8	56.2	62.0	74.2
Ohio	56.5	60.7	66.8	78.7	90.4	105.2	135.3
EGL	56.1	57.5	59.7	63.5	67.2	71.9	81.5
WGL	69.9	72.1	75.3	80.0	84.4	89.7	100.3
U Miss	41.3	44.6	49.3	58.6	67.8	79.4	103.9
L Mo	7.0	7.4	8.2	9.7	11.2	13.2	17.6
SOUTHEAST	133.6	140.1	154.4	178.1	201.6	234.8	306.6
SE	88.2	91.6	99.9	114.5	129.0	150.2	197.2
Cumb	5.7	6.3	7.4	8.7	10.0	11.6	14.6
Tenn	10.1	11.0	12.7	15.1	17.5	20.6	26.8
L Miss	18.1	19.1	20.6	23.1	25.7	28.8	35.2
L AWR	11.5	12.1	13.8	16.7	19.4	23.6	32.8
MID-CONTINENT	71.7	75.7	80.6	92.0	103.3	117.2	145.5
U Mo	17.0	18.0	19.0	22.4	25.8	30.0	39.2
U AWR	9.7	10.3	10.9	12.8	14.7	17.1	21.8
W Gulf	45.0	47.4	50.7	56.8	62.8	70.1	84.5
SOUTHWEST	69.8	70.6	71.2	74.6	77.9	82.5	93.0
RG-P	5.5	5.7	5.8	6.7	7.7	9.0	12.3
Colo	7.7	7.8	7.9	9.3	10.6	12.6	17.3
G Basin	3.6	3.8	3.9	4.2	4.5	4.9	5.6
S Pac	53.0	53.3	53.6	54.4	55.1	56.0	57.8
NORTH PACIFIC	76.4	78.9	85.3	93.7	102.1	114.4	142.0
C Pac	33.4	34.2	35.3	37.7	40.1	43.1	49.4
PNW	43.0	44.7	50.0	56.0	62.0	71.3	92.6
U.S.	787.4	817.0	868.5	958.2	1,047.5	1,165.9	1,416.9

Table E-8. COST OF STANDARD TREATMENT, BY LEVEL OF TREATMENT AND REGION: 2000 LOW

($ million)

	Treatment level (percent):						
	70/50	70/60	70	80	90	95	97½
NORTHEAST	415.8	429.0	449.9	490.6	530.7	583.2	694.2
N Eng	44.8	45.0	45.7	48.5	51.3	55.5	65.3
D & H	107.2	109.1	111.7	116.3	120.7	126.0	136.7
Ches	43.0	44.4	47.3	51.4	55.6	61.3	73.3
Ohio	52.2	55.7	60.9	72.0	82.8	97.0	126.6
EGL	55.1	56.2	58.0	61.4	64.9	69.4	78.7
WGL	67.1	69.0	71.6	75.8	79.9	84.8	94.7
U Miss	39.1	41.8	45.7	54.4	62.9	73.9	97.8
L Mo	7.3	7.8	9.0	10.8	12.6	15.3	21.1
SOUTHEAST	149.1	155.4	171.7	197.8	224.2	262.4	346.6
SE	100.0	103.5	112.8	129.2	145.7	170.1	224.6
Cumb	5.7	6.2	7.3	8.6	9.9	11.6	14.9
Tenn	10.1	10.8	12.4	14.8	17.1	20.4	27.4
L Miss	22.0	23.0	25.3	28.5	31.8	36.2	45.6
L AWR	11.3	11.9	13.9	16.7	19.7	24.1	34.1
MID-CONTINENT	76.8	80.9	87.3	100.7	113.0	130.0	165.9
U Mo	19.9	21.0	23.0	27.5	31.9	38.2	52.2
U AWR	10.2	10.8	11.8	14.0	16.0	19.0	25.2
W Gulf	46.7	49.1	52.5	59.2	65.1	72.8	88.5
SOUTHWEST	85.5	86.4	88.8	94.2	99.4	107.1	124.6
RG-P	7.1	7.3	7.8	9.4	10.9	13.1	18.2
Colo	11.0	11.3	12.3	14.7	17.1	20.7	29.2
G Basin	4.6	4.8	5.3	5.8	6.3	7.1	8.6
S Pac	62.8	63.0	63.4	64.3	65.1	66.2	68.6
NORTH PACIFIC	86.4	89.3	96.8	106.5	116.4	130.7	163.3
C Pac	37.3	38.3	39.6	42.4	45.2	48.8	56.4
PNW	49.1	51.0	57.2	64.1	71.2	81.9	106.9
U.S.	813.6	841.0	894.5	989.8	1,083.7	1,213.4	1,494.6

Table E-9. COST OF STANDARD TREATMENT, BY LEVEL OF TREATMENT AND REGION: 2000 MEDIUM

($ million)

	Treatment level *(percent)*:						
	70/50	70/60	70	80	90	95	97½
NORTHEAST	538.9	558.5	589.8	643.7	697.4	765.0	906.4
N Eng	57.7	58.0	59.0	62.5	66.0	71.3	83.4
D & H	140.1	143.0	147.1	153.3	159.4	166.4	180.2
Ches	55.8	58.0	62.3	68.1	74.0	81.3	97.3
Ohio	68.6	73.9	81.8	96.5	111.1	129.3	166.7
EGL	70.8	72.5	75.2	79.9	84.5	90.3	102.3
WGL	86.8	89.5	93.3	98.9	104.4	110.8	123.6
U Miss	49.7	53.5	59.2	70.3	81.3	95.4	125.4
L Mo	9.4	10.1	11.9	14.2	16.7	20.0	27.5
SOUTHEAST	197.6	207.7	231.5	267.2	303.3	354.2	465.2
SE	130.2	135.4	148.9	170.8	192.8	225.0	296.4
Cumb	8.4	9.4	11.1	13.0	15.1	17.4	21.9
Tenn	13.9	15.1	17.5	20.9	24.2	28.7	38.0
L Miss	30.4	32.1	35.5	40.0	44.7	50.7	63.1
L AWR	14.7	15.7	18.5	22.5	26.5	32.4	45.8
MID-CONTINENT	101.9	108.0	117.9	135.2	152.3	174.2	219.3
U Mo	25.1	26.6	29.5	35.3	41.0	49.0	66.9
U AWR	12.6	13.5	15.0	17.7	20.4	24.0	31.3
W Gulf	64.2	67.9	73.4	82.2	90.9	101.2	121.1
SOUTHWEST	105.4	106.9	110.1	116.9	123.7	133.7	155.8
RG-P	8.8	9.1	9.9	11.8	13.7	16.5	22.9
Colo	13.6	14.1	15.4	18.4	21.5	26.2	36.8
G Basin	6.1	6.4	7.0	7.8	8.6	9.6	11.7
S Pac	76.9	77.3	77.8	78.9	80.1	81.4	84.4
NORTH PACIFIC	112.9	116.7	127.3	140.4	153.6	172.9	217.0
C Pac	47.1	48.4	50.2	53.8	57.4	61.8	71.5
PNW	65.8	68.3	77.1	86.6	96.2	111.1	145.5
U.S.	1,056.7	1,097.8	1,176.6	1,303.4	1,430.5	1,600.0	1,963.7

Table E-10. COST OF STANDARD TREATMENT, BY LEVEL OF TREATMENT AND REGION: 2000 HIGH

($ million)

	Treatment level *(percent)*:						
	70/50	70/60	70	80	90	95	97½
NORTHEAST	782.7	819.4	875.4	958.1	1,040.1	1,137.1	1,330.5
N Eng	77.9	78.4	79.9	84.3	88.9	95.7	111.1
D & H	207.4	212.8	220.5	230.5	240.7	251.0	270.5
Ches	80.1	84.1	91.4	100.4	109.4	120.4	142.5
Ohio	102.7	112.9	127.8	150.6	173.0	199.2	250.2
EGL	101.3	104.6	109.5	116.7	123.8	132.2	148.6
WGL	127.9	132.8	139.7	148.7	157.5	167.1	185.4
U Miss	71.7	78.8	88.8	105.6	121.9	141.8	182.4
L Mo	13.7	15.0	17.8	21.3	24.9	29.7	39.8
SOUTHEAST	284.1	302.0	341.0	393.3	445.8	517.0	667.7
SE	180.9	189.8	211.0	242.1	273.3	317.4	413.5
Cumb	14.4	16.3	19.6	23.0	26.4	30.1	36.7
Tenn	21.4	23.7	28.0	33.3	38.5	45.0	57.9
L Miss	47.0	50.2	56.1	63.1	70.3	79.0	96.2
L AWR	20.4	22.0	26.3	31.8	37.3	45.5	63.4
MID-CONTINENT	152.4	163.5	180.9	206.6	232.4	263.3	323.9
U Mo	34.4	36.9	41.6	49.6	57.7	68.6	92.2
U AWR	18.0	19.6	22.2	26.1	30.1	35.0	44.8
W Gulf	100.0	107.0	117.1	130.9	144.6	159.7	186.9
SOUTHWEST	138.1	140.4	145.4	154.6	163.9	177.2	206.3
RG-P	11.3	11.7	12.8	15.2	17.8	21.4	29.6
Colo	17.4	18.1	20.0	23.9	28.0	34.1	48.0
G Basin	9.1	9.6	10.7	11.9	13.0	14.5	17.6
S Pac	100.3	101.0	101.9	103.6	105.1	107.2	111.1
NORTH PACIFIC	158.1	164.2	179.7	198.1	216.7	243.7	303.8
C Pac	67.8	70.1	73.2	78.5	83.7	90.0	103.1
PNW	90.3	94.1	106.5	119.6	133.0	153.7	200.7
U.S.	1,515.4	1,589.5	1,722.4	1,910.7	2,098.9	2,338.3	2,832.2

Table E-11. COST OF STANDARD TREATMENT, BY LEVEL OF TREATMENT AND REGION: 2020 LOW

($ million)

	Treatment level *(percent)*:						
	70/50	70/60	70	80	90	95	97½
NORTHEAST	589.0	610.5	643.7	702.9	760.9	834.9	989.6
N Eng	64.4	64.7	65.9	69.8	73.7	79.7	93.3
D & H	148.5	151.5	155.4	161.8	167.9	175.2	189.2
Ches	62.3	64.7	69.0	75.2	81.5	89.4	106.2
Ohio	73.6	79.3	88.1	104.3	120.1	140.3	182.0
EGL	77.9	79.7	82.2	87.1	92.0	98.0	110.5
WGL	96.8	99.9	103.8	109.8	115.7	122.2	135.1
U Miss	54.0	58.2	64.2	76.5	88.3	103.7	136.2
L Mo	11.5	12.5	15.1	18.4	21.7	26.4	37.1
SOUTHEAST	236.5	248.3	277.8	320.9	364.4	427.0	564.0
SE	157.4	163.5	179.8	206.3	232.9	272.1	359.5
Cumb	9.3	10.3	12.3	14.6	16.9	19.7	25.0
Tenn	15.3	16.6	19.4	23.1	26.9	32.2	43.2
L Miss	38.9	41.2	46.1	52.3	58.6	67.1	84.9
L AWR	15.6	16.7	20.2	24.6	29.1	35.9	51.4
MID-CONTINENT	120.3	127.7	141.5	163.1	184.7	213.3	272.8
U Mo	32.5	34.5	39.6	47.8	56.0	67.9	94.7
U AWR	13.7	14.7	17.0	20.2	23.5	28.1	37.7
W Gulf	74.1	78.5	84.9	95.1	105.2	117.3	140.4
SOUTHWEST	135.0	137.4	143.3	153.9	164.3	179.9	215.1
RG-P	11.8	12.3	13.7	16.5	19.3	23.6	33.4
Colo	20.3	21.1	23.8	28.8	33.8	41.5	59.2
G Basin	8.1	8.6	9.7	11.0	12.2	13.9	17.6
S Pac	94.8	95.4	96.1	97.6	99.0	100.9	104.9
NORTH PACIFIC	137.7	142.6	156.2	172.5	189.0	213.3	268.2
C Pac	57.4	59.1	61.7	66.3	70.8	76.6	88.9
PNW	80.3	83.5	94.5	106.2	118.2	136.7	179.3
U.S.	1,218.5	1,266.5	1,362.5	1,513.3	1,663.3	1,868.4	2,309.7

Table E-12. COST OF STANDARD TREATMENT, BY LEVEL OF TREATMENT AND REGION: 2020 MEDIUM

($ million)

	Treatment level *(percent)*:						
	70/50	70/60	70	80	90	95	97½
NORTHEAST	788.4	822.2	875.4	957.1	1,037.9	1,137.3	1,338.8
N Eng	85.6	86.2	87.9	92.8	97.8	105.3	122.5
D & H	200.4	205.1	211.7	220.9	229.9	239.8	258.2
Ches	83.6	87.5	94.6	103.6	112.6	123.9	146.7
Ohio	100.5	109.8	124.0	146.4	168.6	195.6	249.5
EGL	102.3	105.2	109.4	116.2	122.9	131.0	147.0
WGL	129.5	134.1	140.3	148.8	157.1	166.0	182.8
U Miss	70.1	76.3	85.4	101.6	117.4	137.3	178.8
L Mo	16.4	18.0	22.1	26.8	31.6	38.4	53.3
SOUTHEAST	329.4	349.0	396.0	458.0	520.6	608.1	796.6
SE	212.5	222.5	248.0	285.1	322.4	376.3	495.0
Cumb	15.1	17.0	20.5	24.1	27.9	32.1	39.8
Tenn	22.4	24.5	29.2	34.8	40.5	48.0	63.3
L Miss	57.8	61.6	69.6	78.9	88.3	100.5	125.6
L AWR	21.6	23.4	28.7	35.1	41.5	51.2	72.9
MID-CONTINENT	171.3	183.6	206.0	237.0	268.1	307.3	387.3
U Mo	42.7	45.7	53.3	64.5	75.7	91.8	127.9
U AWR	19.2	20.9	24.5	29.2	33.9	40.2	53.4
W Gulf	109.4	117.0	128.2	143.3	158.5	175.3	206.0
SOUTHWEST	169.5	172.9	181.9	195.8	209.9	230.7	277.7
RG-P	15.1	15.7	17.9	21.5	25.2	30.8	43.8
Colo	25.8	27.0	31.0	37.6	44.2	54.5	78.0
G Basin	11.6	12.4	14.1	15.8	17.6	20.1	25.5
S Pac	117.0	117.8	118.9	120.9	122.9	125.3	130.4
NORTH PACIFIC	186.9	193.9	213.9	236.9	260.5	294.3	371.7
C Pac	74.6	77.0	80.8	86.9	93.3	100.4	116.4
PNW	112.3	116.9	133.1	150.0	167.2	193.9	255.3
U.S.	1,645.5	1,721.6	1,873.2	2,084.8	2,297.0	2,577.7	3,172.1

Table E-13. COST OF STANDARD TREATMENT, BY LEVEL OF TREATMENT AND REGION: 2020 HIGH

($ million)

	Treatment level *(percent)*:						
	70/50	70/60	70	80	90	95	97½
NORTHEAST	1,407.5	1,489.5	1,612.2	1,770.4	1,925.4	2,100.3	2,432.0
N Eng	136.6	137.8	141.0	148.4	155.8	166.9	191.9
D & H	364.7	376.3	392.2	411.1	429.6	448.2	479.9
Ches	147.5	156.8	172.6	190.5	208.1	228.6	267.3
Ohio	188.2	211.4	245.4	289.4	332.6	380.3	468.7
EGL	177.5	184.6	194.8	208.1	221.2	235.5	261.7
WGL	239.1	250.4	265.1	283.0	300.1	317.1	346.9
U Miss	124.2	139.2	160.1	190.4	220.0	253.9	321.0
L Mo	29.7	33.0	41.0	49.5	58.0	69.8	94.6
SOUTHEAST	586.1	630.7	726.7	839.1	952.1	1,101.4	1,409.8
SE	359.2	381.2	431.6	496.1	560.8	650.1	841.0
Cumb	33.9	38.9	47.4	55.5	63.6	72.1	86.2
Tenn	43.5	48.8	58.9	69.9	81.0	94.4	120.4
L Miss	112.8	121.6	138.7	156.7	174.7	196.7	238.9
L AWR	36.7	40.2	50.1	60.9	72.0	88.1	123.3
MID-CONTINENT	320.6	348.9	397.1	454.9	512.6	580.4	709.8
U Mo	69.8	76.2	90.6	109.5	128.4	154.7	212.0
U AWR	34.7	38.6	45.9	54.5	63.2	73.9	95.2
W Gulf	216.1	234.1	260.6	290.9	321.0	351.8	402.6
SOUTHWEST	258.6	265.2	281.7	304.7	327.8	360.9	434.3
RG-P	22.2	23.4	27.1	32.8	38.6	47.3	66.9
Colo	38.4	40.6	47.6	57.9	68.4	84.3	120.6
G Basin	21.7	23.3	26.7	30.2	33.6	38.0	47.3
S Pac	176.3	177.9	180.3	183.8	187.2	191.3	199.5
NORTH PACIFIC	318.9	333.1	369.0	409.0	449.1	506.7	635.4
C Pac	132.7	138.4	146.4	157.7	168.7	181.6	207.9
PNW	186.2	194.7	222.6	251.3	280.4	325.1	427.5
U.S.	2,891.7	3,067.4	3,386.7	3,778.1	4,167.0	4,649.7	5,621.3

Table E-14. RECIRCULATION RATES REQUIRED TO OFFSET THERMAL WASTE LOADS, SELECTED REGIONS

	1980	2000	2020
N Eng	3.5	10.1	29.0
D & H	8.8	8.8	8.8
Ches	4.3	4.3	4.3
Ohio	27.6	27.6	27.6
EGL	70.0	70.0	70.0
WGL	16.6	16.6	16.6
U Miss	5.1	5.2	6.3
L Mo	4.1	4.1	5.1
Tenn	3.1	3.1	3.7
L Miss	5.6	5.6	5.6
L AWR	1.3	1.5	1.9

Note: Rates are the ratio: G/I. See text.

Table E-15. THERMAL WASTE LOADS: COOLING WATER DISCHARGE, BY INDUSTRY AND REGION, 1960

(million gallons per day)

	Food	Pulp & paper	Chemicals	Petroleum	Primary metals	Textiles	Lumber	Rubber	Stone, clay, glass	Leather	Other mfg.	Steam-electric	Total
NORTHEAST	379	1,608	2,939	727	5,722	26	4	180	400	4	403	47,577	58,336
N Eng	11	199	30	2	52	14	0	36	6	1	48	584	924
D & H	55	151	309	223	407	8	0	11	73	1	85	3,920	4,588
Ches	27	93	321	0	89	2	0	11	17	1	12	3,444	3,901
Ohio	61	49	1,306	73	2,437	1	2	13	39	0	54	17,364	21,399
EGL	22	79	540	123	1,269	0	0	87	47	0	102	6,417	8,686
WGL	63	134	349	285	1,319	1	0	11	136	1	56	9,264	11,618
U Miss	129	885	80	21	141	0	2	7	75	0	44	5,725	6,313
L Mo	11	18	4	0	8	0	0	4	7	0	2	853	907
SOUTHEAST	98	446	940	209	153	43	6	23	20	0	9	14,451	16,256
SE	48	295	229	9	113	38	4	11	17	0	8	7,619	8,352
Cumb	1	0	0	0	0	0	0	0	0	0	0	33	34
Tenn	3	66	396	0	18	4	0	7	2	0	1	4,187	4,682
L Miss	43	29	254	171	0	1	0	5	0	0	0	1,247	1,675
L AWR	3	56	61	29	22	0	2	0	1	0	0	1,365	1,513
MID-CONTINENT	68	24	265	222	52	1	2	3	13	0	5	2,734	3,348
U Mo	57	0	25	48	0	0	0	2	7	0	1	1,077	1,217
U AWR	5	0	33	24	46	0	0	0	2	0	1	431	543
W Gulf	6	24	207	150	6	1	2	1	4	0	3	1,226	1,588
SOUTHWEST	23	9	9	36	28	0	0	2	19	0	7	325	387
RG-P	0	0	0	25	0	3	0	0	0	0	1	168	194
Colo	1	0	0	0	14	0	0	0	0	0	0	82	97
G Basin	7	0	0	0	0	0	0	0	0	0	0	67	75
S Pac	15	9	9	11	14	0	0	2	19	0	6	8	21
NORTH PACIFIC	66	239	48	17	85	0	179	0	19	0	6	5	431
C Pac	32	13	10	13	4	0	26	0	15	0	4	5	52
PNW	34	226	38	4	81	0	153	0	4	0	2	0	379
U.S.	634	2,326	4,201	1,211	6,040	70	191	208	471	4	430	65,092	78,758

Note: Totals in coastal regions are less than the sum of constituent items to adjust for manufacturing discharge into coastal or estuarine waters. See table B-6.

Table E–16.   THERMAL WASTE LOADS: COOLING WATER DISCHARGE AT ORIGINAL RECIRCULATION RATES, BY INDUSTRY AND REGION, 1980 MEDIUM

(million gallons per day)

	Food	Pulp & paper	Chemicals	Petroleum	Primary metals	Textiles	Lumber	Rubber	Stone, clay, glass	Leather	Other mfg.	Steam-electric	Total
NORTHEAST	508	1,100	5,523	1,069	8,261	37	6	423	670	4	687	141,306	158,318
N Eng	11	242	54	4	59	20	0	86	10	1	75	1,932	2,435
D & H	74	156	508	385	459	12	0	25	123	1	148	6,442	7,386
Ches	31	238	697	0	166	3	0	25	28	1	21	7,760	8,728
Ohio	91	50	2,388	59	3,145	1	3	29	65	0	92	55,699	61,622
EGL	26	115	1,117	117	1,946	0	0	206	77	0	175	17,959	21,739
WGL	105	138	534	480	2,321	1	0	26	229	1	97	29,863	33,795
U Miss	159	90	173	18	156	0	3	17	126	0	76	18,366	19,185
L Mo	11	41	52	6	9	0	0	9	12	0	3	3,285	3,428
SOUTHEAST	123	942	2,348	236	308	60	7	55	27	0	14	29,131	33,023
SE	63	689	476	19	194	54	5	26	23	0	13	11,785	13,271
Cumb	4	46	491	6	0	0	0	0	0	0	0	108	655
Tenn	5	90	575	6	20	5	0	16	3	0	1	10,281	11,002
L Miss	47	38	684	203	36	1	-1	13	0	0	0	3,008	3,878
L AWR	4	79	122	2	58	0	3	0	1	0	0	3,949	4,217
MID-CONTINENT	74	43	503	296	59	1	2	6	21	0	8	4,787	5,733
U Mo	57	0	52	42	1	0	0	4	13	0	2	3,452	3,622
U AWR	7	0	108	15	53	0	0	0	2	0	2	24	210
W Gulf	10	43	343	239	5	1	2	2	6	0	4	1,311	1,901
SOUTHWEST	59	14	20	35	97	0	0	4	30	0	12	78	234
RG-P	0	0	2	21	0	0	0	0	0	0	2	9	34
Colo	5	1	1	0	13	0	0	0	0	0	0	33	53
G Basin	26	1	5	1	60	0	0	0	0	0	0	18	109
S Pac	28	12	12	13	24	0	0	4	30	0	10	18	38
NORTH PACIFIC	127	1,335	93	11	148	0	274	0	31	0	10	1,932	3,299
C Pac	62	21	14	8	6	0	39	0	25	0	7	22	95
PNW	65	1,314	79	3	142	0	235	0	6	0	3	1,910	3,204
U.S.	891	3,434	8,487	1,647	8,873	98	289	488	779	4	731	177,234	200,607

Note: Totals in coastal regions are less than the sum of constituent items to adjust for manufacturing discharge into coastal or estuarine waters. See table B–6.

Table E–17. THERMAL WASTE LOADS: COOLING WATER DISCHARGE AT ORIGINAL RECIRCULATION RATES, BY INDUSTRY AND REGION, 2000 MEDIUM

(million gallons per day)

	Food	Pulp & paper	Chemicals	Petroleum	Primary metals	Textiles	Lumber	Rubber	Stone, clay, glass	Leather	Other mfg.	Steam-electric	Total
NORTHEAST	685	1,496	8,149	1,535	10,768	50	8	817	1,098	4	1,048	222,470	246,294
N Eng	12	418	63	6	60	28	0	167	16	1	99	3,358	4,097
D & H	94	170	691	553	658	16	0	47	202	1	231	10,281	11,613
Ches	44	291	1,176	0	231	4	0	47	45	1	31	12,166	13,660
Ohio	130	80	3,544	81	3,443	1	4	55	106	0	140	86,704	94,289
EGL	36	130	1,571	168	2,857	0	0	398	125	0	272	30,589	36,146
WGL	148	150	774	703	3,357	1	0	52	378	1	151	45,764	51,480
U Miss	209	116	251	15	153	0	4	34	208	0	119	28,603	29,713
L Mo	12	141	79	9	9	0	0	17	18	0	5	5,005	5,296
SOUTHEAST	163	1,646	4,324	342	458	82	8	108	33	0	21	48,707	55,458
SE	91	1,140	905	28	288	74	6	52	27	0	20	19,187	21,686
Cumb	5	79	923	9	0	0	0	0	0	0	0	445	1,461
Tenn	6	157	895	9	21	7	0	30	5	0	1	18,164	19,294
L Miss	57	134	1,433	295	61	1	-2	26	0	0	0	4,541	6,246
L AWR	4	136	168	1	88	0	4	0	1	0	0	6,370	6,771
MID-CONTINENT	88	320	889	341	77	1	2	11	31	0	10	5,624	7,294
U Mo	65	212	79	38	2	0	0	9	21	0	2	4,475	4,903
U AWR	8	34	221	5	63	0	0	0	2	0	2	23	359
W Gulf	15	74	589	298	12	1	2	2	8	0	6	1,126	2,032
SOUTHWEST	95	163	22	26	103	0	0	9	47	0	16	128	434
RG-P	1	37	4	17	1	0	0	0	0	0	2	8	71
Colo	7	57	1	0	11	0	0	0	0	0	0	60	136
G Basin	42	28	5	0	58	0	0	0	0	0	0	26	161
S Pac	45	41	12	9	33	0	0	9	47	0	14	34	66
NORTH PACIFIC	199	2,196	139	8	258	0	381	0	51	0	16	7,692	9,873
C Pac	101	72	14	5	9	0	52	0	40	0	11	48	169
PNW	98	2,124	125	3	249	0	329	0	11	0	5	7,644	9,704
U.S.	1,230	5,821	13,523	2,252	11,664	133	399	945	1,260	4	1,111	284,621	319,353

Note: Totals in coastal regions are less than the sum of constituent items to adjust for manufacturing discharge into coastal or estuarine waters. See table B–6.

Table E-18. THERMAL WASTE LOADS: COOLING WATER DISCHARGE AT ORIGINAL RECIRCULATION RATES, BY INDUSTRY AND REGION, 2020 MEDIUM

(million gallons per day)

	Food	Pulp & paper	Chemicals	Petroleum	Primary metals	Textiles	Lumber	Rubber	Stone, clay, glass	Leather	Other mfg.	Steam-electric	Total
NORTHEAST	975	2,039	11,614	2,295	13,223	69	12	957	1,778	6	1,546	399,359	431,889
N Eng	16	662	70	9	45	38	0	321	27	1	115	5,584	6,693
D & H	134	160	912	825	866	22	0	85	330	1	352	17,628	19,472
Ches	64	361	1,812	0	283	5	0	85	72	1	45	21,164	23,346
Ohio	188	137	5,020	109	3,698	2	6	102	170	1	205	152,601	162,238
EGL	51	122	2,058	253	3,804	0	0	161	197	0	411	57,189	64,847
WGL	220	114	1,283	1,073	4,386	2	0	101	616	2	230	83,341	91,367
U Miss	288	156	347	14	134	0	6	68	339	0	181	52,529	54,062
L Mo	14	327	112	12	7	0	0	34	27	0	7	9,323	9,864
SOUTHEAST	231	2,867	6,923	515	615	113	18	203	29	0	30	89,283	100,732
SE	133	1,913	1,425	43	351	102	6	101	20	0	30	34,683	38,601
Cumb	6	137	1,518	13	0	0	0	0	0	0	0	1,253	2,927
Tenn	7	272	1,304	13	37	9	0	51	9	0	0	34,292	36,632
L Miss	80	309	2,460	445	96	2	6	51	0	0	0	7,713	10,635
L AWR	5	236	216	1	131	0	6	0	0.09	0	0	11,342	11,937
MID-CONTINENT	118	836	1,278	413	99	2	0	17	45	0	16	10,097	12,785
U Mo	86	613	112	39	3	0	0	17	36	0	4	7,908	8,818
U AWR	10	98	366	5	72	0	0	0	0	0	4	43	598
W Gulf	22	125	800	369	24	2	0	0	9	0	8	2,146	3,369
SOUTHWEST	151	435	11	29	92	0	0	17	72	0	23	264	815
RG-P	1	104	6	12	2	0	0	0	0	0	4	15	144
Colo	12	159	0	0	9	0	0	0	0	0	0	132	312
G Basin	68	78	2	0	43	0	0	0	0	0	0	52	244
S Pac	70	94	3	17	38	0	0	17	72	0	19	65	115
NORTH PACIFIC	305	3,692	185	12	436	0	522	0	81	0	22	20,162	23,692
C Pac	156	165	4	10	11	0	67	0	63	0	15	100	296
PNW	149	3,527	181	2	425	0	455	0	18	0	7	20,062	23,396
U.S.	1,780	9,869	20,011	3,264	14,465	184	552	1,194	2,005	6	1,637	519,165	569,913

Note: Totals in coastal regions are less than the sum of constituent items to adjust for manufacturing discharge into coastal or estuarine waters. See table B-6.

Table E-19. COSTS OF RECIRCULATION, STEAM-ELECTRIC POWER: 1960

	(1) Intake (bgd)	(2) Recirculation rate	(3) Flow-through Col. (1) × Col. (2)	(4) Annual flow-through Col. (3) × 365 (bgy)	(5) Annual intake Col. (1) × 365 (bgy)	(6) Amount recirculated Col. (4)– Col. (5) (bgy)	(7) Cost of recirculation Col. (6) × 0.0113 ($ mil.)
NORTHEAST	48.3		50.7	18,507	17,631	876	9.8
N Eng	0.6	1.25	0.8	292	219	73	0.8
D & H	4.0	1.08	4.3	1,570	1,460	110	1.2
Ches	3.5	1.04	3.6	1,314	1,278	36	0.4
Ohio	17.6	1.05	18.5	6,753	6,424	329	3.7
EGL	6.5	1.02	6.6	2,409	2,373	36	0.4
WGL	9.4	1.02	9.6	3,504	3,431	73	0.8
U Miss	5.8	1.08	6.3	2,300	2,117	183	2.1
L Mo	0.9	1.06	1.0	365	329	36	0.4
SOUTHEAST	14.7		16.9	6,181	5,378	803	9.0
SE	7.7	1.13	8.7	3,176	2,811	365	4.1
Cumb	0.03	1.11	0.03	11	11	0	0
Tenn	4.3	1.09	4.7	1,716	1,570	146	1.6
L Miss	1.3	1.11	1.4	511	475	36	0.4
L AWR	1.4	1.47	2.1	767	511	256	2.9
MID-CONTINENT	2.9		10.3	3,760	1,060	2,700	30.5
U Mo	1.1	1.70	1.9	694	402	292	3.3
U AWR	0.5	4.49	2.2	803	183	620	7.0
W Gulf	1.3	4.77	6.2	2,263	475	1,788	20.2
SOUTHWEST	0.4		4.1	1,497	143	1,354	15.3
RG-P	0.2	4.77	1.0	365	73	292	3.3
Colo	0.1	11.89	1.2	438	37	401	4.5
G Basin	0.07	6.72	0.5	183	26	157	1.8
S Pac	0.02	70.00	1.4	511	7	504	5.7
NORTH PACIFIC	0.01	72.19	0.7	256	4	252	2.8
C Pac	0.01	70.00	0.7	256	4	252	2.8
PNW	*	2.19	*	*	*	*	*
U.S.	66.3	1.25	82.7	30,201	24,216	5,985	67.4

Source: Appendix D.
*Less than 10 mgd.

Table E-20. COST OF RECIRCULATION AT ORIGINAL RATES: 1980 MEDIUM

	(1)	(2)	(3)	(4)	(5)	(6)	(7)
						Amount recirculated Col. (4)–	Cost of recirculation
	Original intake	Original recirculation	Flow-through Col. (1) ×	Annual flow-through Col. (3) × 365	Annual intake Col. (1) × 365	Col. (5)	Col. (6) × 0.0113
	(bgd)	rate	Col. (2)	*(bgy)*	*(bgy)*	*(bgy)*	*($ mil.)*
NORTHEAST	142.6		162.6	59,351	52,052	7,299	82.4
N Eng	2.0	1.14	2.3	840	730	110	1.2
D & H	6.5	1.14	7.4	2,701	2,373	328	3.7
Ches	7.8	1.14	8.9	3,249	2,847	402	4.5
Ohio	56.3	1.14	64.2	23,433	20,550	2,883	32.6
EGL	18.1	1.14	20.6	7,519	6,607	912	10.3
WGL	30.1	1.14	34.3	12,520	10,987	1,533	17.3
U Miss	18.5	1.14	21.1	7,702	6,753	949	10.7
L Mo	3.3	1.14	3.8	1,387	1,205	182	2.1
SOUTHEAST	29.4		33.6	12,265	10,732	1,533	17.3
SE	11.9	1.14	13.6	4,964	4,344	620	7.0
Cumb	0.1	1.14	0.1	37	37	0	0
Tenn	10.4	1.14	11.9	4,344	3,796	548	6.2
L Miss	3.0	1.14	3.4	1,241	1,095	146	1.6
L AWR	4.0	1.14	4.6	1,679	1,460	219	2.5
MID-CONTINENT	5.0		30.3	11,060	1,826	9,234	104.4
U Mo	3.5	2.58	9.0	3,285	1,278	2,007	22.7
U AWR	0.1	70.00	7.0	2,555	37	2,518	28.5
W Gulf	1.4	10.21	14.3	5,220	511	4,709	53.2
SOUTHWEST	0.2		13.3	4,856	70	4,786	54.0
RG-P	0.03	70.00	2.1	767	11	756	8.5
Colo	0.07	70.00	4.9	1,789	26	1,763	19.9
G Basin	0.04	70.00	2.8	1,022	15	1,007	11.4
S Pac	0.05	70.00	3.5	1,278	18	1,260	14.2
NORTH PACIFIC	2.1		9.2	3,358	752	2,606	29.5
C Pac	0.06	70.00	4.2	1,533	22	1,511	17.1
PNW	2.0	2.51	5.0	1,825	730	1,095	12.4
U.S.	179.3	1.39	249.0	90,890	65,432	25,458	287.6

Table E-21. STEAM-ELECTRIC POWER: COSTS OF RECIRCULATION AT ORIGINAL RATES, 2000 MEDIUM

	(1)	(2)	(3)	(4)	(5)	(6)	(7)
	Original intake *(bgd)*	Original recirculation rate	Flow-through Col. (1) × Col. (2)	Annual flow-through Col. (3) × 365 *(bgy)*	Annual intake Col. (1) × 365 *(bgy)*	Amount recirculated Col. (4) – Col. (5) *(bgy)*	Cost of recirculation Col. (6) × 0.0113 *($ mil.)*
NORTHEAST	225.2		274.7	100,268	82,200	18,068	204.1
N Eng	3.4	1.22	4.1	1,497	1,241	256	2.9
D & H	10.4	1.22	12.7	4,636	3,796	840	9.5
Ches	12.3	1.22	15.0	5,475	4,490	985	11.1
Ohio	87.8	1.22	107.1	39,092	32,047	7,045	79.6
EGL	31.0	1.22	37.8	13,797	11,315	2,482	28.0
WGL	46.3	1.22	56.5	20,623	16,900	3,723	42.1
U Miss	28.9	1.22	35.3	12,885	10,549	2,336	26.4
L Mo	5.1	1.22	6.2	2,263	1,862	401	4.5
SOUTHEAST	49.4		60.3	22,010	18,069	3,941	44.5
SE	19.5	1.22	23.8	8,687	7,118	1,569	17.7
Cumb	0.5	1.22	0.6	219	183	36	0.4
Tenn	18.4	1.22	22.4	8,176	6,716	1,460	16.5
L Miss	4.6	1.22	5.6	2,044	1,679	365	4.1
L AWR	6.5	1.22	7.9	2,884	2,373	511	5.8
MID-CONTINENT	6.1		44.8	16,353	2,227	14,126	159.7
U Mo	4.6	3.46	15.9	5,804	1,679	4,125	46.6
U AWR	0.1	70.00	7.0	2,555	37	2,518	28.5
W Gulf	1.4	15.65	21.9	7,994	511	7,483	84.6
SOUTHWEST	0.5		25.9	9,455	135	9,320	105.2
RG-P	0.05	70.00	3.5	1,278	18	1,260	14.2
Colo	0.16	70.00	11.2	4,088	58	4,030	45.5
G Basin	0.07	70.00	4.9	1,789	26	1,763	19.9
S Pac	0.09	70.00	6.3	2,300	33	2,267	25.6
NORTH PACIFIC	8.0		31.5	11,498	2,930	8,568	96.8
C Pac	0.13	70.00	9.1	3,322	47	3,275	37.0
PNW	7.9	2.83	22.4	8,176	2,833	5,293	59.8
U.S.	289.2	1.51	437.2	159,584	105,561	54,023	610.3

Table E-22. STEAM-ELECTRIC POWER: COSTS OF RECIRCULATION AT ORIGINAL RATES, 2020 MEDIUM

	(1)	(2)	(3)	(4)	(5)	(6)	(7)
	Original intake *(bgd)*	Original recirculation rate	Flow-through Col. (1) × Col. (2)	Annual flow-through Col. (3) × 365 *(bgy)*	Annual intake Col. (1) × 365 *(bgy)*	Amount recirculated Col. (4) – Col. (5) *(bgy)*	Cost of recirculation Col. (6) × 0.0113 *($ mil.)*
NORTHEAST	404.7		526.1	192,027	147,717	44,310	500.7
N Eng	5.7	1.30	7.4	2,701	2,081	620	7.0
D & H	17.9	1.30	23.3	8,505	6,534	1,971	22.3
Ches	21.4	1.30	27.8	10,147	7,811	2,336	26.4
Ohio	154.8	1.30	201.2	73,438	56,502	16,936	191.4
EGL	58.0	1.30	75.4	27,521	21,170	6,351	71.8
WGL	84.3	1.30	109.6	40,004	30,770	9,234	104.3
U Miss	53.2	1.30	69.2	25,258	19,418	5,840	66.0
L Mo	9.4	1.30	12.2	4,453	3,431	1,022	11.5
SOUTHEAST	91.3		118.8	43,363	33,326	10,037	113.3
SE	35.2	1.30	45.8	16,717	12,848	3,869	43.7
Cumb	1.3	1.30	1.7	621	475	146	1.6
Tenn	35.5	1.30	46.2	16,863	12,958	3,905	44.1
L Miss	7.8	1.30	10.1	3,687	2,847	840	9.5
L AWR	11.5	1.30	15.0	5,475	4,198	1,277	14.4
MID-CONTINENT	11.2		111.8	40,807	4,089	36,718	414.9
U Mo	8.3	4.34	36.0	13,140	3,030	10,110	114.2
U AWR	0.3	70.00	21.0	7,665	110	7,555	85.4
W Gulf	2.6	21.09	54.8	20,002	949	19,053	215.3
SOUTHWEST	0.8		56.0	20,440	293	20,147	227.7
RG-P	0.1	70.00	7.0	2,555	37	2,518	28.5
Colo	0.4	70.00	28.0	10,220	146	10,074	113.8
G Basin	0.1	70.00	7.0	2,555	37	2,518	28.5
S Pac	0.2	70.00	14.0	5,110	73	5,037	56.9
NORTH PACIFIC	21.1		86.5	31,573	7,702	23,871	269.8
C Pac	0.3	70.00	21.0	7,665	110	7,555	85.4
PNW	20.8	3.15	65.5	23,908	7,592	16,316	184.4
U.S.	529.1	1.70	899.2	328,210	193,127	135,083	1,526.4

Table E-23. STEAM-ELECTRIC POWER: COSTS OF RECIRCULATION AT ORIGINAL RATES, 2020 HIGH

	(1)	(2)	(3)	(4)	(5)	(6)	(7)
	Original intake *(bgd)*	Original recirculation rate	Flow-through Col. (1) × Col. (2)	Annual flow-through Col. (3) × 365 *(bgy)*	Annual intake Col. (1) × 365 *(bgy)*	Amount recirculated Col. (4) – Col. (5) *(bgy)*	Cost of recirculation Col. (6) × 0.0113 *($ mil.)*
NORTHEAST	799.3		1,039.2	379,310	291,747	87,563	989.4
N Eng	11.2	1.30	14.6	5,329	4,088	1,247	14.0
D & H	35.3	1.30	45.9	16,754	12,885	3,869	43.7
Ches	42.4	1.30	55.1	20,112	15,476	4,636	52.4
Ohio	305.7	1.30	397.4	145,051	111,581	33,470	378.2
EGL	114.6	1.30	149.0	54,385	41,829	12,556	141.9
WGL	166.7	1.30	216.7	79,096	60,846	18,250	206.2
U Miss	104.9	1.30	136.4	49,786	38,289	11,497	129.9
L Mo	18.5	1.30	24.1	8,797	6,753	2,044	23.1
SOUTHEAST	180.4		234.6	85,631	65,848	19,783	223.5
SE	69.6	1.30	90.5	33,033	25,404	7,629	86.2
Cumb	2.5	1.30	3.3	1,205	913	292	3.3
Tenn	70.1	1.30	91.1	33,252	25,587	7,665	86.6
L Miss	15.5	1.30	20.2	7,373	5,658	1,715	19.4
L AWR	22.7	1.30	29.5	10,768	8,286	2,482	28.0
MID-CONTINENT	22.0		215.4	78,622	8,031	70,591	797.7
U Mo	16.3	4.34	70.7	25,806	5,950	19,856	224.4
U AWR	0.5	70.00	35.0	12,775	183	12,592	142.3
W Gulf	5.2	21.09	109.7	40,041	1,898	38,143	431.0
SOUTHWEST	1.5		105.0	38,325	549	37,776	426.9
RG-P	0.2	70.00	14.0	5,110	73	5,037	56.9
Colo	0.7	70.00	49.0	17,885	256	17,629	199.2
G Basin	0.3	70.00	21.0	7,665	110	7,555	85.4
S Pac	0.3	70.00	21.0	7,665	110	7,555	85.4
NORTH PACIFIC	41.5		164.2	59,933	15,148	44,785	506.1
C Pac	0.5	70.00	35.0	12,775	183	12,592	142.3
PNW	41.0	3.15	129.2	47,158	14,965	32,193	363.8
U.S.	1,044.7	1.70	1,758.4	641,821	381,323	260,498	2,943.6

Table E-24. STEAM-ELECTRIC POWER: COSTS OF RECIRCULATION AT REVISED RATES, 1980 MEDIUM

	(1)	(2)	(3)	(4)	(5)	(6)	(7)
				Annual flow-through Col. (3) × 365 = G	Annual intake Col. (1) × 365 = I	Amount recirculated Col. (4) − Col. (5) = R	Cost of recirculation Col. (6) × 0.0113
	Revised intake (bgd)	Revised recirculation rate	Flow-through Col. (1) × Col. (2)	(bgy)	(bgy)	(bgy)	($ mil.)
NORTHEAST	13.4		165.6	60,446	4,894	55,552	627.8
N Eng	0.5	3.5	1.8	657	183	474	5.4
D & H	1.1	8.8	9.7	3,541	402	3,139	35.5
Ches	2.1	4.3	9.0	3,285	767	2,518	28.5
Ohio	2.3	27.6	63.5	23,178	840	22,338	252.4
EGL	0.3	70.0	21.0	7,665	110	7,555	85.4
WGL	2.2	16.6	36.5	13,323	803	12,520	141.5
U Miss	4.0	5.1	20.4	7,446	1,460	5,986	67.6
L Mo	0.9	4.1	3.7	1,351	329	1,022	11.5
SOUTHEAST	20.1		34.3	12,521	7,339	5,182	58.5
SE	11.9	1.14	13.6	4,964	4,344	620	7.0
Cumb	0.1	1.14	0.1	37	37	0	0
Tenn	3.9	3.1	12.1	4,417	1,424	2,993	33.8
L Miss	0.7	5.6	3.9	1,424	256	1,168	13.2
L AWR	3.5	1.3	4.6	1,679	1,278	401	4.5
MID-CONTINENT	5.0		30.3	11,060	1,826	9,234	104.4
U Mo	3.5	2.58	9.0	3,285	1,278	2,007	22.7
U AWR	0.1	70.00	7.0	2,555	37	2,518	28.5
W Gulf	1.4	10.21	14.3	5,220	511	4,709	53.2
SOUTHWEST	0.2		13.3	4,856	70	4,786	54.0
RG-P	0.03	70.00	2.1	767	11	756	8.5
Colo	0.07	70.00	4.9	1,789	26	1,763	19.9
G Basin	0.04	70.00	2.8	1,022	15	1,007	11.4
S Pac	0.05	70.00	3.5	1,278	18	1,260	14.2
NORTH PACIFIC	2.1		9.2	3,358	752	2,606	29.5
C Pac	0.06	70.00	4.2	1,533	22	1,511	17.1
PNW	2.0	2.51	5.0	1,825	730	1,095	12.4
U.S.	40.8	6.2	252.7	92,241	14,881	77,360	874.2

Table E-25. STEAM-ELECTRIC POWER: COSTS OF RECIRCULATION AT REVISED RATES, 2000 MEDIUM

	(1)	(2)	(3)	(4)	(5)	(6)	(7)
	Revised intake (bgd)	Revised recirculation rate	Flow-through Col. (1) × Col. (2)	Annual flow-through Col. (3) × 365 = G (bgy)	Annual intake Col. (1) × 365 = I (bgy)	Amount recirculated Col. (4) – Col. (5) = R (bgy)	Cost of recirculation Col. (6) × 0.0113 ($ mil.)
NORTHEAST	21.2		286.7	104,647	7,740	96,907	1,095.1
N Eng	0.3	10.1	3.0	1,095	110	985	11.1
D & H	1.0	8.8	8.8	3,212	365	2,847	32.2
Ches	3.5	4.3	15.1	5,512	1,278	4,234	47.8
Ohio	4.5	27.6	124.2	45,333	1,643	43,690	493.7
EGL	0.6	70.0	42.0	15,330	219	15,111	170.8
WGL	3.2	16.6	53.1	19,382	1,168	18,214	205.8
U Miss	6.6	5.2	34.3	12,520	2,409	10,111	114.3
L Mo	1.5	4.1	6.2	2,263	548	1,715	19.4
SOUTHEAST	33.8		61.7	22,521	12,339	10,182	115.0
SE	19.5	1.22	23.8	8,687	7,118	1,569	17.7
Cumb	0.5	1.22	0.6	219	183	36	0.4
Tenn	7.3	3.1	22.6	8,249	2,665	5,584	63.1
L Miss	1.2	5.6	6.7	2,446	438	2,008	22.7
L AWR	5.3	1.5	8.0	2,920	1,935	985	11.1
MID-CONTINENT	6.1		44.8	16,353	2,227	14,126	159.7
U Mo	4.6	3.46	15.9	5,804	1,679	4,125	46.6
U AWR	0.1	70.00	7.0	2,555	37	2,518	28.5
W Gulf	1.4	15.65	21.9	7,994	511	7,483	84.6
SOUTHWEST	0.5		25.9	9,455	135	9,320	105.2
RG-P	0.05	70.00	3.5	1,278	18	1,260	14.2
Colo	0.16	70.00	11.2	4,088	58	4,030	45.5
G Basin	0.07	70.00	4.9	1,789	26	1,763	19.9
S Pac	0.09	70.00	6.3	2,300	33	2,267	25.6
NORTH PACIFIC	8.0		31.5	11,498	2,930	8,568	96.8
C Pac	0.13	70.00	9.1	3,322	47	3,275	37.0
PNW	7.9	2.83	22.4	8,176	2,883	5,293	59.8
U.S.	69.6	6.4	450.6	164,474	25,371	139,103	1,571.8

Table E-26. STEAM-ELECTRIC POWER: COSTS OF RECIRCULATION AT REVISED RATES, 2020 MEDIUM

	(1)	(2)	(3)	(4)	(5)	(6)	(7)
	Revised intake *(bgd)*	Revised recirculation rate	Flow-through Col. (1) × Col. (2)	Annual flow-through Col. (3) × 365 = G *(bgy)*	Annual intake Col. (1) × 365 = I *(bgy)*	Amount recirculated Col. (4) – Col. (5) = R *(bgy)*	Cost of recirculation Col. (6) × 0.0113 *($ mil.)*
NORTHEAST	38.7		554.1	202,247	14,127	188,120	2,125.7
N Eng	0.3	29.0	8.7	3,176	110	3,066	34.6
D & H	2.0	8.8	17.6	6,424	730	5,694	64.3
Ches	6.8	4.3	29.2	10,658	2,482	8,176	92.4
Ohio	8.6	27.6	237.4	86,651	3,139	83,512	943.7
EGL	1.1	70.0	77.0	28,105	402	27,703	313.0
WGL	6.0	16.6	99.6	36,354	2,190	34,164	386.1
U Miss	11.4	6.3	71.8	26,207	4,161	22,046	249.1
L Mo	2.5	5.1	12.8	4,672	913	3,759	42.5
SOUTHEAST	59.2		121.4	44,312	21,609	22,703	256.5
SE	35.2	1.30	45.8	16,717	12,848	3,869	43.7
Cumb	1.3	1.30	1.7	621	475	146	1.6
Tenn	12.6	3.7	46.6	17,009	4,599	12,410	140.2
L Miss	2.2	5.6	12.3	4,490	803	3,687	41.7
L AWR	7.9	1.9	15.0	5,475	2,884	2,591	29.3
MID-CONTINENT	11.2		111.8	40,807	4,089	36,718	414.9
U Mo	8.3	4.34	36.0	13,140	3,030	10,110	114.2
U AWR	0.3	70.00	21.0	7,665	110	7,555	85.4
W Gulf	2.6	21.09	54.8	20,002	949	19,053	215.3
SOUTHWEST	0.8		56.0	20,440	293	20,147	227.7
RG-P	0.1	70.00	7.0	2,555	37	2,518	28.5
Colo	0.4	70.00	28.0	10,220	146	10,074	113.8
G Basin	0.1	70.00	7.0	2,555	37	2,518	28.5
S Pac	0.2	70.00	14.0	5,110	73	5,037	56.9
NORTH PACIFIC	21.1		86.5	31,573	7,702	23,871	269.8
C Pac	0.3	70.00	21.0	7,665	110	7,555	85.4
PNW	20.8	3.15	65.5	23,908	7,592	16,316	184.4
U.S.	131.0	7.1	929.8	339,379	47,820	291,559	3,294.6

Table E–27. STEAM-ELECTRIC POWER: COSTS OF RECIRCULATION AT REVISED RATES, 2020 HIGH

	(1)	(2)	(3)	(4)	(5)	(6)	(7)
	Revised intake *(bgd)*	Revised recirculation rate	Flow-through Col. (1) × Col. (2)	Annual flow-through Col. (3) × 365 = G *(bgy)*	Annual intake Col. (1) × 365 = I *(bgy)*	Amount recirculated Col. (4) – Col. (5) = R *(bgy)*	Cost of recirculation Col. (6) × 0.0113 *($ mil.)*
NORTHEAST	76.4		1,096.8	400,333	27,888	372,445	4,208.6
N Eng	0.6	29.0	17.4	6,351	219	6,132	69.3
D & H	3.9	8.8	34.3	12,520	1,424	11,096	125.4
Ches	13.4	4.3	57.6	21,024	4,891	16,133	182.3
Ohio	17.0	27.6	469.2	171,258	6,205	165,053	1,865.1
EGL	2.2	70.0	154.0	56,210	803	55,407	626.1
WGL	11.9	16.6	197.5	72,088	4,344	67,744	765.5
U Miss	22.5	6.3	141.8	51,757	8,213	43,544	492.0
L Mo	4.9	5.1	25.0	9,125	1,789	7,336	82.9
SOUTHEAST	117.0		240.1	87,638	42,706	44,932	507.7
SE	69.6	1.30	90.5	33,033	25,404	7,629	86.2
Cumb	2.5	1.30	3.3	1,205	913	292	3.3
Tenn	24.9	3.7	92.1	33,617	9,089	24,528	277.2
L Miss	4.4	5.6	24.6	8,979	1,606	7,373	83.3
L AWR	15.6	1.9	29.6	10,804	5,694	5,110	57.7
MID-CONTINENT	22.0		215.4	78,622	8,031	70,591	797.7
U Mo	16.3	4.34	70.7	25,806	5,950	19,856	224.4
U AWR	0.5	70.00	35.0	12,775	183	12,592	142.3
W Gulf	5.2	21.09	109.7	40,041	1,898	38,143	431.0
SOUTHWEST	1.5		105.0	38,325	549	37,776	426.9
RG-P	0.2	70.00	14.0	5,110	73	5,037	56.9
Colo	0.7	70.00	49.0	17,885	256	17,629	199.2
G Basin	0.3	70.00	21.0	7,665	110	7,555	85.4
S Pac	0.3	70.00	21.0	7,665	110	7,555	85.4
NORTH PACIFIC	36.0		159.3	58,145	13,141	45,004	508.6
C Pac	0.5	70.00	35.0	12,775	183	12,592	142.3
PNW	35.5	3.5	124.3	45,370	12,958	32,412	366.3
U.S.	252.9	7.2	1,816.6	663,063	92,315	570,748	6,449.5

Appendix F

FLOW-STORAGE RELATIONSHIPS
AND THE COST OF FLOW

Definitions and Method of Analysis

For the purposes of this study the phrase "supply of water" refers to several different measurements, depending on the context. "Maximum supply" usually refers to the mean annual flow adjusted for evaporation from *additional* storage reservoirs. "Supply of water" occasionally refers to the flow-duration curve, i.e., the percentage of time that flows of a designated amount are equaled or exceeded. "Cost of flow" refers to the cost of additional reservoir capacity needed to raise present minimum flows to successively higher levels up to the mean annual flow net of additional reservoir evaporation. Costs of flow may be expressed as capital cost, annual equivalent cost, for marginal or average cost per unit of regulated flow, or as cumulative total cost for a specified level of regulated flow.

Data on regional distributions of flows, existing storage capacity, costs of existing reservoirs, and estimated costs of future reservoirs are only roughly accurate. Although the dollar costs of construction of existing reservoirs are known with reasonable accuracy, there are uncertainties regarding conversion to a constant price level and the inclusion or exclusion of certain preliminary costs during the investigation phase. Data on flows for a region are only approximate because the contributions of certain tributaries, the effects of diversions, and the effects of changes in land use are not accurately known — apart from the probabilistic character of flow data in general.

A major difference between this study and its predecessor, Committee Print No. 32, is the difference in the amount of storage required to raise existing minimum flows to fractions of mean annual flow equal to approximately 50 percent and above.[1]

Storage requirements given in Committee Print No. 32 are valid for flows up to roughly 50 percent of mean annual flow. Tables F-1, F-2, and F-3 show the corrected amounts of storage required for gross flows (i.e., without adjustment for additional reservoir evaporation) with a 2 percent, 5 percent, and 10 percent probability of deficiency, respectively. Figures for 2 percent and 5 percent probabilities of deficiency were taken directly from Löf and Hardison;[2] the figures for a 10 percent chance of deficiency were computed from diagrams for carry-over storage with a 10 percent chance of deficiency prepared by the same authors but not used in their article.

Costs of storage reflect the cost per unit of volume and the volume of storage required for successive increments of minimum flow net of reservoir evaporation. Costs per unit of storage capacity are dependent on the size of the reservoir and the physiographic zone in which the dam and reservoir are located. Construction costs per unit of capacity are lower, for example, in a broad, gently sloping valley than in a mountainous, steeply sloping canyon, since a comparatively low dam at the former site will impound the same amount of water as a high one at the latter. Capital costs per acre-foot of storage capacity for physiographic zones A-J related to size of reservoir and a map showing distribution of physiographic zones, both prepared by the Corps of Engineers, are given.[3] (See table F-4 and figure F-1.)

---

[1] A critique by Howard Cook of the Office of the Chief of Engineers, U.S. Army Corps of Engineers, of an earlier version of this study which used the flow-storage figures of Committee Print No. 32 revealed that storage required to raise the present minimum flow to the average flow had been understated by a factor of three for the United States as a whole.

[2] George O. G. Löf and Clayton H. Hardison, "Storage Requirements for Water in the United States," *Water Resources Research*, vol. 2, no. 3 (Third Quarter 1966), pp. 323–54.

[3] Costs are adjusted to a 1964 curve base. See Committee Print No. 32, chart 1, p. 60, for original cost curves.

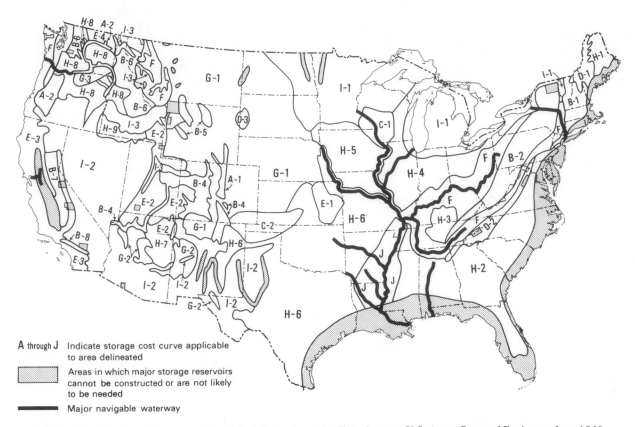

Figure F-1. Physiographic zones of the United States (see table F-4). Source: U.S. Army Corps of Engineers, June 1960.

The synthetic cost curves constructed by Löf and Hardison[4] were modified in accordance with a tabulation of completed reservoirs, those under construction, and those planned as of 1964[5] (tables F-5, F-6, and F-7). Some uncertainty attaches to the status and location of reservoirs by physiographic zone and region and to the distinction between "total" capacity and "usable" capacity. Another source of uncertainty is the likelihood that among the reservoirs still in the planning stage, some are alternatives to others. A third source of uncertainty is that in sixteen of the twenty-two regions the total number of reservoirs, including those under construction and those planned, amounted to less than 50 percent of the storage required to achieve maximum flow regulation. (In six of the eight regions of the Northeast, existing reservoirs, those under construction and those planned, accounted for less than 20 percent of the storage required for maximum regulation.)

Synthetic schedules were constructed that distributed reservoir sites among physiographic zones (table F-8) and size classes (table F-9) by an intuitive compromise between percentage distributions yielded by the inventories of existing and planned reservoirs and a rough-and-ready percentage distribution of land area within each region among physiographic zones. The results must still be regarded as tentative in spite of the effort that went into the compilation of the inventories. An average evaporation rate for each physiographic zone within a given water resource region was selected by eye from a map prepared by the Soil Conservation Service.[6]

The upward thrust of marginal cost per mgd of sustained flow resulting from diminishing marginal physical productivity of storage was augmented by the assumption that reservoirs that were both large in size and located in low-cost zones would be built first. The synthetic schedule was checked in order to discard size classes in particular physiographic zones for which no confirmation was given by the inventories. A single distribution by size class and physiographic zone was used for constructing the schedules of storage requirements with 2 percent, 5 percent and 10 percent chances of deficiency.

The meaning of "percentage chance of deficiency" or "percentage availability" as used by Löf and Hardison is limited to the percentage of *years* that a deficiency will be experienced. No information is available on the number of days in a year that flow will be deficient nor on the magnitude of the deficiency. Roughly speaking, a probability of 10 percent deficiency can be interpreted to mean that over a long period of time — e.g., a hundred years — there will be

---

[4] Löf and Hardison, "Storage Requirements for Water."

[5] Tabulated by Pum Ky Kim, Resources for the Future, under the guidance of Allen V. Kneese, from information supplied by federal agencies.

[6] See U.S. Senate, Select Committee on National Water Resources, Committee Print No. 13, *Estimated Water Requirements for Agricultural Purposes and Their Effects on Water Supplies*, 86th Cong., 2d sess. (1960), fig. 9.

120 deficient months out of 1,200 months. For the purpose of computing the combined cost of treatment and storage when short-term tertiary treatment for one month is substituted for deficient flow, we assume that a 10 percent chance of deficiency is equal to one month in twelve. This assumption may or may not be an overestimate of the frequency of deficiency on a monthly basis, depending on the intensity of the deficiency or the number of consecutive (as distinct from randomly dispersed) years of deficiency actually experienced.

Evaporation losses also contribute to the rise of marginal cost. The smaller the reservoir is, the larger the surface area for a given volume, since average depth varies directly with size class. Thus, a given aggregate of storage divided among several small reservoirs adds less to minimum flow than does the same volume in a single large reservoir. Other considerations, of course, are the merit of achieving control at several points within a region rather than at a single point and the likelihood of different evaporation rates at different locations within a region.

Costs per acre-foot of volume were based on the experience of the Corps of Engineers, verified in the West by the experience of the Bureau of Reclamation. Unit costs as originally compiled on the basis of 1954 prices were adjusted to 1964 prices by an index of construction costs.

In constructing a synthetic schedule one could, of course, adopt different assumptions. If it were assumed that the first increments of additional storage came from small reservoirs in high-cost physiographic zones where evaporation rates were also high, the effect of diminishing marginal physical productivity of storage would be attenuated by the downward trend of unit costs of storage volume. Since the inventories indicate that reservoirs of all sizes are under construction and under study, a "largest first" schedule was adopted. It should be clear, however, that the actual sequence of construction is not likely to follow this rule.

Another major difference between the flow-storage relationships given in Committee Print No. 32 and in the Löf-Hardison formulation used in this study is that in the former the volumes of storage were treated as amounts needed beyond the capacity already in place, whereas in the Löf-Hardison tables the amounts of storage measure total requirements. Thus, for any flow specified for the future the amount of flow-regulation storage already in existence (including that under construction) must be subtracted in order to show what is still needed. We have assumed that all existing storage except flood control storage can be considered available for low-flow augmentation. Existing flood control storage was assumed to be available for low-flow augmentation when full regulation is achieved. For intermediate levels of flow regulation we assumed that a pro rata share of existing flood control storage could be utilized. For example, if a minimum flow equal to 50 percent of mean annual flow were required, it was assumed that 50 percent of existing flood control storage could be included in the total of existing storage in order to compute the additional amount of regulatory capacity still needed, if any.

The procedure that we followed leaves unsettled an important question: How much of existing special purpose storage, other than flood control, should not be included in the total of existing storage counted toward low-flow augmentation? Examples are storage to maintain power head; irrigation discharges that are not coincidental with low-flow augmentation; minimum pools for fish, wildlife, and recreation; and reservoir discharges for purposes of biotic management and power production.

Unfortunately, with the data at hand it was not possible to determine the quantity of such capacity. In a period of severe stringency water reserved for power head might be devoted to other uses. But the ability of a region to make substitutions of this sort is in itself no substitute for storage capacity devoted to regularization of flow over a long precipitation and runoff cycle.

The Inventories

The "official" tabulation of reservoirs in the United States at the time of writing was that of Nathan O. Thomas and G. Earl Harbeck, Jr.[7] It includes reservoirs and lakes having a capacity of 5,000 acre-feet or more completed as of January 1, 1954, and reservoirs under construction on that date. Total usable capacity was reported as 278 million acre-feet. (Total storage minus dead storage equals usable storage.)[8]

Information received from the Corps of Engineers and the Bureau of Reclamation on additional reservoirs completed or under construction in 1960 allowed a limited updating of the Thomas-Harbeck inventory. An unofficial inventory of existing and planned reservoirs compiled by Resources for the Future (RFF) on the basis of information supplied by federal agencies and other sources brought the inventory up to 1964. Another source of information, *Western Water Development*,[9] is limited, of course, to the Western and Midwestern United States. The RFF tabulation includes all reservoirs and lakes with regulated outlets for which information could be acquired, including those with a capacity of less than 5,000 acre-feet — private and public, federal, state, and local. The compilation prepared for the Special Subcommittee on Western Water Development covered only federal water resource projects.[10]

Comparison of the various tabulations is difficult because the Thomas-Harbeck inventory contained information on usable capacity, whereas the tabulations of RFF and the Special Subcommittee on Western Water Development were primarily based on total capacity. Some conflicts in information supplied about particular reservoirs were identified. It hardly seems necessary to point out the desirability of having a current and comprehensive inventory of reservoirs containing information on size, location,

[7] *Reservoirs in the United States*, U.S. Geological Survey Water-Supply Paper 1360–A (1956). A revised edition, Water-Supply Paper 1838, by R. O. R. Martin and Ronald L. Hanson (1966), includes reservoirs completed or under construction as of January 1, 1963.

[8] Total usable capacity reported in Water-Supply Paper 1838 was 360 million acre-feet.

[9] U.S. Senate, Special Subcommittee on Western Water Development of the Committee on Public Works, Committee Print, 88th Cong., 2d sess. (October 1964).

[10] The Subcommittee report indicated the capacity assigned to different purposes or projects not yet authorized by Congress but failed to provide that information for reservoirs already authorized.

purpose, and system interrelatedness, with enough detail to support the construction of supply curves of water. The task of constructing and maintaining such an inventory does not seem unduly demanding if adequately organized. Perhaps the Water Resources Council will undertake the task.

Using the Thomas-Harbeck inventory, A. M. Piper, in *Has the United States Enough Water?*[11] reached slightly different results in his regional allocation from those in Committee Print No. 3.[12] A summary of the different regional distributions and the U.S. totals are given in table F-10. Some of the differences apparently reflect divided opinion regarding the water resource region to which a particular reservoir should be assigned. Others may grow out of uncertainty about how "usable" capacity ought to be determined in particular instances.

The results of the RFF tabulation are compared with the USGS inventory updated to 1960 (table F-10). Since the RFF inventory includes all reservoirs reported by the Corps of Engineers, Bureau of Reclamation, Tennessee Valley Administration, and Federal Power Commission, including reservoirs owned and operated by regional and state authorities, its scope is greater. The reported figures, moreover, are for *total* rather than usable capacity. Like the earlier inventory, reservoirs under construction are included.

In several regions — Delaware and Hudson, Eastern Great Lakes, Western Great Lakes, Great Basin, and South Pacific — RFF totals were below USGS figures as corrected to 1960 for Corps of Engineers and Bureau of Reclamation additions. Obviously, such an understatement could be explained either by differences of opinion regarding location or by a miscount. Since there was no way of choosing between these alternatives, it was assumed that the RFF low figure was a miscount, and the higher figures of Committee Print No. 3, as corrected, or Piper, as corrected, were used. In that way the "standardized inventory for 1964" was constructed. The results, therefore, are biased upward. Requirements for additional storage are correspondingly biased downward. Another factor contributing to probable overstatement of 1964 storage capacity is that the RFF figures are for total, rather than for usable, storage, although in many cases the two coincide.

The figures (ignoring differences in coverage and in measure of capacity) reveal that storage capacity, already built and under construction, has grown approximately as follows (million acre-feet):[13]

1947	163
1954	278
1960	320
1964	506

The figures indicate an annual rate of growth of reservoir capacity of about 6½ percent between 1947 and 1964.

[11] U.S. Geological Survey Water-Supply Paper 1797 (1965), p. 12.

[12] U.S. Geological Survey, *National Water Resources and Problems*, Senate Select Committee on National Water Resources, 86th Cong., 2d sess. (1960).

[13] Thomas and Harbeck, *Reservoirs*, p. 1. The 1960 figure represents only Corps of Engineers and Bureau of Reclamation additions since 1954.

The RFF inventory of existing reservoirs (unadjusted to the standardized inventory) yielded information on size class, physiographic zone, and function. For the United States as a whole, 10 percent of reported aggregate capacity is in reservoirs less than 200,000 acre-feet in size; 20 percent in reservoirs 200,000 to 1 million acre-feet in size; 43 percent is in reservoirs 1 million to 10 million acre-feet; and 25 percent is in reservoirs over 10 million acre-feet (table F-6).

The percentage distribution among size classes of the RFF tabulation for 1964 does not materially differ from an earlier and unverified tabulation based on Thomas and Harbeck to which new Corps of Engineers and Bureau of Reclamation reservoirs coming into being between 1954 and 1960 were added. The fact that virtually all the increase in capacity has occurred recently in fairly large reservoirs is no surprise. The apparent increase in aggregate capacity of reservoirs in the range of 100,000 to 1 million acre-feet amounts to one-third of the total increase; the remaining two-thirds is in reservoirs of over a million acre-feet.

The tabulation by function (table F-11) includes some double counting as well as an unspecified allocation for all TVA reservoirs. (For the purpose of estimating flood control storage in the Tennessee region the reported percentage in the Cumberland region was used; this figure did not differ materially from that of the Southeast division as computed with the Tennessee.) For the country as a whole, reservoir capacity in 1964 was apportioned as follows:

Flood control	22 percent
Irrigation	17 percent
Power	37 percent
Other	24 percent

The geographic distribution of total storage capacity is given in table F-12. Of the 506 million acre-feet shown for the 1964 inventory, the capacity was distributed by division as follows (percentage of the national aggregate):

Northeast	10 percent
Southeast	26 percent
Mid-Continent	32 percent
Southwest	18 percent
North Pacific	15 percent

The distribution of reservoir capacity by major geographic areas indicates that the humid Southeast and the transitional (in a pluvial sense) Mid-Continent divisions account for 58 percent of existing capacity. When capacity is related to area, it is seen that the density of storage is greatest in the Southeast and North Pacific. The most arid part of the country, the Southwest, ranks next to the Northeast (the least arid) in volume of storage per square mile of drainage area. The water resource region with the highest quantity of storage per square mile of drainage area is the Cumberland. Next come the Tennessee and the Lower Arkansas-White-Red.

The density of reservoir capacity is related, of course, to the quantity and variability of runoff per square mile. Reservoir capacity density per square mile at maximum regulation is greatest in the Southeast, followed by the North Pacific and the Northeast. It would appear that as time goes on, the absolute amount of reservoir capacity will be far greater in the East than in the West.

The classification (unverified and therefore tentative) of existing reservoirs by physiographic zone is given in table F-7. The distribution of existing and planned reservoirs was used in the construction of synthetic schedules. Without more detailed maps or a coding scheme, a satisfactory level of accuracy of classification by zone could not be achieved. Table F-7 is to be accepted, therefore, as valid in a gross sense. The synthetic schedule of additional reservoir capacity was constructed by distributing new capacity in a compromise fashion based on the distribution of existing and planned capacity and the area occupied by each zone within a region. In most regions the capacity required for full regulation is substantially above present and anticipated capacity. For this reason, some reliance was put on the relative area of each zone within a region.

Distribution by Function

The distribution of reservoir capacity according to function[14] indicates that the dominant purposes of storage planned by federal agencies are not likely to be much different in the future than they are now. (See tables F-11 and F-13.)

On the basis of planned reservoir capacity, flood control in the Northeast will be the main function of the future as it is of the present. In the Southeast, additional storage will raise somewhat the relative importance of hydroelectric power vis-à-vis flood control. In the Mid-Continent division, planned storage will add approximately equal increments of flood control and power capacity. In the Southwest, the relative importance of irrigation will decline along with power. The same change apparently will occur in the North Pacific. Taking the United States as a whole, the addition of planned capacity is marked by emphasis on flood protection and power. Roughly one-quarter of planned capacity is for "other," which means such purposes as recreation, municipal water supply, low-flow augmentation for waste dilution, and, in a few instances, nagivation. An unknown share of "other" stands for multiple purpose capacity.

Although some planned capacity consists of alternative sites, we have no information on the amount of duplication. Ignoring this qualification, we see that if all planned capacity were added to 1964 existing capacity, the Mid-Continent would have more than twice the amount needed for complete flow regulation. The Southwest, which has limited runoff, would have the smallest amount of storage but, like the Mid-Continent division, about twice as much capacity as required for complete flow regulation.

The existing and future "overcapacity" in the Mid-Continent and Southwest divisions indicates that large amounts of capacity go to the provision of hydraulic head for power purposes, reregulation, and flood protection. Without additional information it is impossible to ascertain for a given water resource region the "proper" relationship between the capacity needed to provide a specified minimum flow and the additional capacity devoted to other purposes — i.e., local flood protection, minimum pools for recreation and power, and the provision of specific seasonal flows for various purposes. In particular regions, such as the Upper Missouri and Rio Grande-Pecos, existing plus planned capacity (keeping in mind that an unknown amount of planned capacity consists of alternative sites for a particular objective) is more than four times the amount needed for raising the minimum flow to the average flow (net of evaporation losses).

Additional Storage for Flow Regulation

The amount of storage needed in any particular region depends on the criteria used to measure requirements. Schedules of flow, storage, and costs have been prepared from the following components:

1. Flow-storage relationships with 2 percent, 5 percent, and 10 percent chances of deficiency (tables F-1, F-2, and F-3)
2. Percentage distributions of additional storage among size classes (table F-9)
3. Percentage distributions of additional storage among physiographic zones (table F-8)
4. A table of capital costs per acre-foot of storage capacity, varying by size class and physiographic zone (table F-4 and map 1)
5. Average depths of reservoirs, varying by size class (see table F-14 for each region)
6. Average net loss per acre of water surface in each physiographic zone within a region (see table F-14 for each region)

By selecting the order in which increments of storage are built, the cost of each increment can be ascertained along with its contribution to flow net of additional evaporation losses. The choice of size and physiographic zone of successive increments of storage had to be established synthetically, since no systematic sequence has yet been formulated for the various water resource regions.[15] Furthermore, for most (sixteen out of twenty-two) regions, the total of existing plus planned reservoirs amounts to less than 50 percent of the capacity required for full regulation. In determining the size and physiographic distribution of regulatory capacity for the Lower Missouri, Upper Arkansas-White-Red, and Western Gulf regions, planned capacity was relied on rather substantially, since the total (planned plus existing) is well over the amount required for full regulation. In the Upper Missouri, Rio Grande-Pecos, and Colorado regions capacity now in place exceeds the amount required for full regulation. In spite of this fact, synthetic schedules were constructed, since additional capacity is under study. For all regions the synthetic schedules differ in some respects from those of Committee Print No. 32,

---

[14] The figures have not been verified. In some regions there is overcounting; in some a large fraction of multipurpose capacity is shown as "other." The percentages by division reveal what is likely to be a more accurate view.

[15] For example, the inventory prepared for the Special Subcommittee on Western Water Development includes projects that, in the words of the report, "may be mutually exclusive" (p. 3), but they are not identified.

mainly to reflect the results yielded by the inventories. Some weight was attached, however, to the area assigned to each physiographic zone in a region. In some regions a distribution of capacity among physiographic zones in proportion to area coincided reasonably well with the distribution of existing and planned reservoirs; in others there were marked divergences. As already noted, a verified distribution of existing reservoirs and of planned reservoirs, excluding incompatible combinations, would be a useful planning instrument.

In arriving at the amount of storage needed for a specified minimum flow, the amount of existing storage (including that under construction) minus a specified amount of existing flood control storage was subtracted from the quantity of storage given by the gross flow-storage schedules. It was assumed that all existing flood control storage was available for flow regulation when regulation was at the maximum attainable level. For intermediate levels of regulation the quantity of existing flood control storage available for flow regulation was given by the following:

$$\frac{a}{b} \times \text{existing flood control capacity}$$

where a is the specified level of flow and b is the maximum attainable flow.

In constructing the synthetic schedules, attention was given to the inventories of existing and planned distributions of capacity by both physiographic zone and size class in order to avoid including a size class in a physiographic zone that was not indicated in either inventory.

In order to be certain that maximum available flows were not overstated, an adjustment was made for evaporation losses attributable to new reservoir capacity completed or under construction during the period 1954–64. The nature of such adjustments is given in table F–15. Losses for all but five regions were computed on the basis of the average loss rate for each region taken from Löf and Hardison.[16] These losses amounted to less than 1 percent of mean annual flow in fifteen regions and less than 2 percent in two. In the remaining five regions the losses computed at the average rate ranged, roughly, from 4 percent to 15 percent of mean annual flow (before such losses). For these regions the losses were recomputed using maximum depth and minimum evaporation rates assigned to the regions in question. (See table F–14 for each region.) In this way the losses attributable to 1954–64 storage additions were minimized.

Although the adjustment is so crude that one might argue it should not be made,[17] its adoption reduces the likelihood of an overstatement of available flows, especially in those regions where shortages are likely to occur.

There is a further question that remains unanswered: How much existing storage capacity will be used in the

normal course of events for nonregulatory purposes? Existing dead storage presumably is not included in the 1954 inventory, hence there is no overstatement of regulatory capacity out of existing storage on that account. There is, however, capacity that is not below the point of discharge (and hence not "dead") but is likely to be reserved for nonregulatory purposes, such as the maintenance of head or as a minimum wildlife pool. There is also some capacity that will be used for purposes whose flow needs do not correspond with administration of the reservoir to augment present low flows. By counting all existing "usable" capacity as available for low-flow augmentation, we are understating the amount of capacity that will be built and used in many regions. This conclusion is obvious from what we see at present in the Upper Missouri, Rio Grande–Pecos, and Colorado regions. A more sophisticated analysis would provide measurements of special purpose capacity not "normally" available for minimum flow regulation. On the other hand, if storage is available to the level indicated by the flow-storage curve for a designated chance of deficiency, we can expect that capacity dedicated to one use — e.g., hydroelectric power — will be diverted to such "higher level" uses as municipal water supply should the "emergency" be critical enough. By giving full credit for flow regulation to existing storage (less flood control adjustment), we may be understanding the needed amount of additional storage for a year of average runoff (since special purpose uses will not give way) but not understating the needed amount for flow regulation during a period of severe emergency. However, during a period of severe emergency there probably will also be an understatement of needed capacity, since only if existing capacity is used in accordance with a long-range plan of low-flow augmentation would water be stored in adequate amounts to take care of a sequence of dry years. There is no assurance that special purpose capacity would be administered in such fashion.

Storage capacity is likely to be underestimated also, because it is assumed in the flow-storage tables that regulation is designed for the discharge point of the basin. A larger amount of capacity may be needed for regulation at points on various tributaries, rather than at the point of discharge from the basin, since the effect of naturally offsetting variability of the flows of the separate tributaries is lost. Furthermore, when storage is divided a further allowance should be made for less-than-perfect coordination of administration.

Land and Relocation Costs

Part of the cost of constructing reservoirs consists of expenditures for land and for relocation when land is preempted. Over the past fifty years, these costs, when expressed in current dollars, have probably been rising. One question was whether we should build into the model the rising costs of reservoir construction due to rising land and relocation costs. In order to determine whether to do so, regression analysis utilizing land and relocation cost data (converted into 1960 dollars) obtained from the Corps of Engineers and the Bureau of Reclamation were used. Constant dollar costs were then divided by acre-feet of storage

---

[16] Löf and Hardison, "Storage Requirements for Water."

[17] For example, the increment in capacity is based on a measure for 1964 that is a composite of total capacity and usable capacity, whereas the 1954 figure is usable capacity. Thus, the loss attributable to the new capacity is overstated.

to obtain data on land and relocation costs per acre-foot of storage. There were seventy-eight reservoirs listed in the Corps of Engineers data and the regression line obtained was

$$y = -2.74 + 0.92\,t; R^2 = 0.25$$
$$(0.58)$$

where

y = land and relocation cost per acre-foot of storage,

t = time (for 1930, $t = 0$).

The R^2 was low and the slope coefficient was not significantly different from zero at the 5 percent level of significance.

The data from the Bureau of Reclamation were divided into eastern regions and western regions. The regressions obtained were

$$\text{East: } y = 4.80 + 1.35\,t; R^2 = 0.04$$
$$(0.74)$$

$$\text{West: } y = -2.17 + 1.02\,t; R^2 = 0.04$$
$$(0.91)$$

Once again, R^2 was very low and the slope coefficients were not significantly different from zero at the 5 percent level.

In view of these results, we rejected the hypothesis that land and relocation costs — when stated in constant dollars — have risen over time. Also, no adjustment for possible future rises in reservoir costs due to this element was included. Further research with more refined data may yield different conclusions.

Schedules of Flow, Storage, and Costs

Because loss from evaporation depends on the size and location of a reservoir, and because various combinations of sizes and locations can be built, the relationship between net flow and storage is somewhat uncertain. Sensitivity to a change in the evaporation rate per unit of gross volume increases as regulation approaches closer to the theoretical limit. The maximum physical limits of regulation computed by Löf and Hardison could not be used because altering the distribution of reservoirs among size classes and physiographic zones changed the rate of evaporation per acre-foot of stored water in most cases and therefore changed marginal net flow per unit increase in storage.

The synthetic schedules are schedules of increments of reservoir capacity that would be added to existing capacity to bring total capacity to the amount required for maximum physical net flow. The schedules were constructed by scattering a percentage distribution of reservoirs classified by physiographic zone throughout a percentage distribution by size class. An evaporation rate per acre-foot of capacity was computed and its effect deducted from the increment in gross flow. The maximum physical amount of storage and the corresponding net flow were set by the rule that the last acre-foot of capacity yielded a positive contribution to net flow. Table F-16 shows maximum regulated

flows and the differences between the Löf-Hardison solutions and our own for 98 percent availability.[18] Comparatively small changes in distribution by size class can have comparatively large impact on the maximum physical limit of storage. The clearest case is the Central Pacific region, for which Löf and Hardison estimated 298 million acre-feet at maximum; our estimate was 122 million acre-feet. An explanation of the difference also illustrates how the maximum physical limit was set.

The gross flow-storage table (table F-1) gives the following for a 2 percent chance of deficiency:

Central Pacific	
Total storage	Gross flow
(mil. af)	(mgd)
4.9	5,800
9.1	11,600
13.3	17,400
19.4	23,200
28.5	29,000
42.4	34,800
68.0	40,600
122.0	46,400
280.0	52,200
299.0	52,800

When Löf and Hardison computed maximum physical storage they used an earlier distribution of capacity (taken from Committee Print No. 32) instead of the revised distribution.

	Central Pacific	
Size class	Löf and Hardison	Revised for this study
(1,000 af)	(percentage of total storage)	
0– 20	0	0
20– 40	0	1
40– 60	0	2
60– 100	5	2
100– 200	5	5
200– 400	10	5
400– 1,000	10	10
1,000– 2,000	20	20
2,000– 4,000	20	25
4,000–10,000	30	30
10,000 and up	0	0
Total	100	100

The evaporation rate assigned to the two smallest classes in the revised projection for the Central Pacific — 20,000 to 40,000 acre-feet and 40,000 to 60,000 acre-feet — was 1.5 feet per acre of surface; the assigned depths were 35 feet and 40 feet respectively. When the Löf-Hardison physical maximum of 298 million acre-feet was used as the basis of distributing reservoirs among all assigned size classes, net yield from the two smallest classes was negative — added evaporation exceeded added gross flow. This meant that either the projected percentage distribution among size classes had to be violated or the total amount of storage

---

[18] Löf-Hardison solutions were based on the synthetic schedules used in Committee Print No. 32.

had to be reduced to the point where added gross flow exceeded added evaporation. We chose to follow the second procedure, since the choice of distribution by size class preceded a determination of physical maximum flow. In the real world, the choice of size distribution will be affected by a number of factors, of which one may be the effect on net flow.[19]

One minor reason for the large difference between the Löf-Hardison maximum and our revised maximum is the use of a step-function flow-storage table rather than a relationship that varies continuously. Because of the step-function, each acre-foot of capacity within the interval makes the same contribution to gross flow. In the Central Pacific the flatness of the flow storage curve at its upper end explains the sensitivity of net flow to changes in size distribution and in the ratio of surface to volume, and therefore in the rate of evaporation per unit of storage. In adding storage beyond 122 million acre-feet, a reservoir of 20,000 to 40,000 acre-feet with a depth of 35 feet would lose more by evaporation than it would add to gross flow. The next interval, bringing total storage to 280 million acre-feet, adds 5,800 mgd to gross flow. This interval implies that it requires 27,241 acre-feet of storage to add 1 million gallons per day to sustained gross flow. An average depth of 35 feet implies that each mgd requires 778 acres of storage surface; and with an evaporation rate of 1.5 acre-feet per year per surface acre of water, evaporation per mgd of gross yield is 1,167 acre-feet, or 3 percent more than the addition to gross flow.

In a number of regions the location of the physical limit would shift with very slight changes in assumed conditions. If the average depth of the marginal-size reservoir in the Great Basin were raised by 1 foot, from 15 to 16 feet, the physical limit at a 2 percent chance of deficiency would rise from 11.3 million acre-feet, associated with a gross flow of 7,400 mgd to 17.1 million acre-feet and a gross flow of 8,400 mgd. The additional net flow, however, would be only 31,000 acre-feet or 28 mgd.

Again, note that the physical limit is based on the flow-storage step-function given in tables F-1, F-2, and F-3, which means that within each decile or semidecile of flow the yield of gross flow per unit of storage is assumed to be constant. Only by accident would a breaking point in the table coincide with a zero marginal net yield of storage. For this reason, the physical limits we have used may be above or below the real limits. It is also likely that in some regions the only explanation of a difference, usually small, between Löf and Hardison's limits and ours rests on the more precise computation carried out by the former. For the purpose of computer solution a step function was easier to use and, it is hoped, did not contribute to an unduly large error.

For the same reasons, our physical limits for 95 percent availability differed somewhat from Löf and Hardison. In comparing storage at 95 percent availability with storage at 98 percent availability, it should not be disconcerting if the former exceeds the latter, provided the associated flow is also greater. The physical maximum storage is higher in several regions when the chance of deficiency is 10 percent rather than 2 percent, a result derived from the higher physical marginal productivity of storage. In all regions the maximum sustained flow is higher for a 10 percent chance of deficiency than for 2 percent. The flows for 5 percent fall somewhere in between.

There is not, however, a consistent relationship between maximum storage at 2 percent, 5 percent, and 10 percent chances of deficiency. Because of the discontinuous gross flow-storage schedule and the abrupt changes in the size of reservoirs as blocks of new storage are added, there are a few regions in which the physical maximum of storage is highest or lowest at 95 percent availability. Because of the somewhat erratic behavior of our synthetic schedules at the upper end of the scale, marginal costs of the final increments as well as measurement of the physical limit must be considered as only approximate.

Table 65, which shows maximum storage, maximum net flows, and capital and annual costs of maximum storage, reveals that a reduction in security from a 2 percent to a 5 percent chance of deficiency raises maximum flow by about 3.5 percent, reduces maximum storage by about 16 percent, and reduces capital and annual costs by about 17 percent. In going from 95 percent to 90 percent availability, flow rises by 1.4 percent, storage declines by 9 percent, and costs decline by 9 percent. It is interesting to note that the impact of rising marginal costs per unit of storage is apparently lost when we round to millions of acre-feet of storage and millions of dollars, since both values move by the same relative amount. The other point of interest is the lesser impact on storage and costs when going from 95 percent to 90 percent security than when going from 98 percent to 95 percent.

Table 65 also reveals a wide range of response among regions to a change in the degree of security. For example, in the Ohio region the costs of full regulation are almost halved by going from 98 percent to 90 percent security, along with an 8 percent increase in maximum flow. In the Western Great Lakes region, by contrast, storage is 9 percent higher, costs are 8 percent higher, and flow is 20 percent higher at 90 percent availability than at 98 percent.

The choice of a degree of security may rest on acceptance of a modification in the projected final bill of goods when shortage strikes or on a substitution of inputs. We have done nothing about the former but have developed an example of the latter. If water security falls from 98 percent to 90 percent, this is construed as being equal to a water shortage one month out of twelve, over a large number of years. We have compared the costs of storage and treatment under two conditions: (1) by assuming that treatment is permanently at the level appropriate for flow with a 2 percent chance of deficiency, and (2) by assuming that treatment is permanently fixed at the same level of flow, but storage is reduced from 98 percent certainty to 90

---

[19] Using the Löf-Hardison maximum as a control, the 40,000–60,000 acre-foot size class raised cumulative storage from 290 million acre-feet to 295 million acre-feet, which raised gross flow from 52,511 mgd to 52,685 mgd, but lowered net flow from 50,191 mgd to 50,182 mgd. The next, and last, size class, 20,000–40,000 acre-feet, raised total storage to 298 million acre-feet (which implied 100 reservoirs averaging 30,000 acre-feet in size) and raised gross flow to 52,772 mgd, but lowered net flow further to 50,164 mgd.

percent certainty and short-term special treatment costs are incurred one month every year. The question asked is whether the savings in storage by accepting a higher chance of deficiency are more than the additional short-term treatment costs incurred during the period of deficiency. One might also compute the tradeoff between permanent treatment costs and short-term treatment costs by administering a given amount of storage so that a 10 percent chance of deficiency is accepted rather than 2 percent.

Annual storage costs for a given flow were varied by adopting three alternative annual factors: 0.0425 as the basic rate, and 0.0525 and 0.0200 as alternatives. These reflected interest rates of 4 percent, 5½ percent, and 2 percent, respectively; lives of 50, 50, and 100 years respectively; and operation and maintenance costs one-quarter of 1 percent, one-half of 1 percent (of capital costs), and zero, respectively.

Annual costs of a given amount of storage (or flow) are directly proportional to the annual factor used. What is of interest is whether a change in the annual factor used within the range of 2 percent and 5¼ percent for storage, keeping treatment costs unchanged, leads to a change in the minimum cost combination of storage and treatment.

For each region tables F–17 and F–18 show the synthetic schedules for flow, storage, cumulative capital costs, cumulative annual costs, annual average costs per mgd, and marginal costs per mgd for 90 percent and 98 percent availability with 0.0425 as the annual factor.

At 98 percent availability no costs of storage are given for the Upper Missouri, Rio Grande–Pecos, and Colorado regions; and at 90 percent availability no costs are shown for these three regions plus Upper Arkansas-White-Red because storage already in place (including that under construction) exceeds the amount specified for maximum physical development.

We followed the practice of subtracting existing storage from maximum physical capacity and distributing the remainder according to the synthetic schedule of size, physiographic zones, and evaporation rate. The schedule of "costs of storage" used for determining the minimum cost model is the schedule pertaining to storage beyond that now in existence or under construction. We selected the "minimum cost" model by minimizing the total of the cost of *additional storage* plus the cost of treatment.[20]

Since storage is added by blocks, marginal costs vary discontinuously. One might introduce an economic limit, albeit an arbitrary one, by applying a marginal cost constraint to any of the tables. If, for example, we fix an upper limit to flow by the rule that marginal cost shall not exceed 50 cents per 1,000 gallons for 98 percent availability, maximum flows are either unchanged (in eleven regions) or are reduced by 1 or 2 percent, except in the Chesapeake region, where the reduction is 3 percent. A marginal cost constraint of 10 cents per 1,000 gallons reduces flows below the maximum in every region except the Great Basin; the maximum decline is 9 percent in the Chesapeake region. In the Dela-

ware and Hudson and Eastern Great Lakes regions the decline is 8 percent; it is 6 percent in the Tennessee region and 5 percent or less elsewhere. In eight regions the reduction is only 1 or 2 percent. Since the change in maximum flow that results from minor alterations of a synthetic schedule is more than 1 or 2 percent (e.g., compare maximum flows as computed by Löf and Hardison with ours), the effective reduction in maximum flow induced by a 10-cent marginal cost limit, to say nothing of a 50-cent marginal cost, is negligible.

Marginal cost schedules reveal an occasional aberration by virtue of which marginal cost rises, then falls, then resumes its upward movement. The explanation is that blocks of storage are added by successive size classes, and when a size class changes, so may the rate of evaporation and the average depth. For this reason, a particular increment of storage may suffer a sharp increase in evaporation, inducing a more-than-expected rise in the marginal cost of net flow. Marginal cost curves could be "smoothed out" by modifying our assumptions. For example, as Löf and Hardison did, we could assume that each increment of flow is represented by a pro rata share of reservoirs of all sizes, depths, and evaporation rates. We would then use a constant rate of evaporation per unit of storage for purposes of computing net flow per unit of storage. Marginal cost curves would move continuously upward under the pressure of the diminishing marginal increment of flow per unit of storage, even if the cost per unit of storage were constant.

There is a substantial difference between mean annual gross flow and the net physical maximum, the difference diminishing with reductions in certainty. For a 2 percent chance of deficiency, maximum physical net flow is 84 percent of mean annual gross flow for the country as a whole. This percentage varies quite a bit among regions. In the Western Gulf region it is only 56 percent; in the Tennessee region it is 94 percent. The differences are attributable to several factors: "elasticity" of the gross flow-storage curve, assumed distribution of reservoirs by size, depths of reservoirs, and rates of evaporation. For higher chances of deficiency the spread between the physical maximum and the gross mean annual flow narrows. For a 5 percent chance of deficiency it is 87 percent; and for a 10 percent chance of deficiency it is 92 percent.

The amount of required storage drops by 23 percent as maximum net flow rises by 10 percent when the chance of deficiency rises from 2 percent to 10 percent. Each million acre-feet of storage at maximum regulation contributes 0.469 bgd in the country as a whole when there is a 10 percent chance of deficiency. Each million acre-feet of storage contributes 0.327 bgd when the chance of deficiency is 2 percent. In other words, it requires an average of 43 percent more storage per unit of flow at maximum regulation to reduce the chance of deficiency by 8 percent.

These relationships are reflected in costs, both marginal and average. For the United States as a whole, at full regulation with a 2 percent chance of deficiency, average annual cost per bgd is $7,469,000. For a 10 percent chance of deficiency, average annual cost is $4,783,000 — a saving per bgd of about one-third of the cost of the higher level of security.

---

[20] The cost schedules of Löf and Hardison were constructed by distributing *total* storage capacity rather than new storage capacity in accordance with the synthetic schedule.

Of equal interest is the behavior of both flows and costs when a marginal cost constraint is introduced. A maximum of 50 cents per 1,000 gallons applied to the schedule for 98 percent availability reduces aggregate flows by about 1 percent and aggregate costs by 43 percent. The rapid increase in marginal costs induced by movement up the flow-storage curve, down the size-of-reservoir schedule, and up the evaporation-per-unit-of-storage schedule, reveals possibilities for spending very large sums of money with almost negligible physical response.

What is also of interest is the possibility that "true" marginal costs will never be known because they will be lost in a succession of projects that (1) lose within themselves the marginal physical elements, and (2) confuse what is chronologically marginal — i.e. the next in time — with a "static" schedule of increments of reservoir capacity ranked by increasing costs per unit of flow.

The possibilities of overspending are made clearer by seeing what happens when we introduce a marginal cost limit of 10 cents per 1,000 gallons. With a 2 percent chance of deficiency, aggregate flows fall by 3 percent; aggregate costs fall 66 percent. With a 10 percent chance of deficiency, aggregate flows fall by 7 percent; costs fall by 36 percent. A rigid conception of "requirements" with no mechanism for acceptance and adjustment to occasional deficiencies is fairly expensive.

One can also compare the impact of a marginal cost constraint on average cost per million gallons of water. An upper limit of 50 cents per 1,000 gallons on marginal costs yields average costs that are 43 percent lower than unconstrained average costs for 98 percent availability. A limit of 10 cents per 1,000 gallons on marginal costs (at 98 percent availability) lowers average cost per million gallons from $20.46 to $7.25. Further reduction by reducing the degree of security is much less. Going to 95 percent (with a constraint of 10 cents per 1,000 gallons on marginal cost) lowers average cost per million gallons to $7.02. At 90 percent, the average cost is $6.16. Although the decline in aggregate flow at 90 percent certainty resulting from a marginal cost constraint of 10 cents per 1,000 gallons is 7 percent of the physical maximum, absolute flow of 1,033 bgd is greater than unconstrained flows with 2 percent and 5 percent chances of deficiency. Thus, the choice is not only one of paying *in money* for a higher degree of security, but also one of paying in *water*. It is hoped that in the United States there will be sufficient reduction in the rates of population growth and in the growth of water-related activity to avoid such precise calculation of tradeoffs.

The possibility of overspending is also indicated by the wide disparity between marginal and average costs of flow when regulation goes to the limit fixed by a marginal cost of 10 cents per 1,000 gallons. With a 2 percent chance of deficiency, average costs would be three-quarters of a cent per 1,000 gallons for the United States as a whole.

The *probability* of unintentional overspending will remain high until an integrated regulatory system is developed for each basin whereby increments of storage are added in such fashion that implicit, systemwide, marginal costs are not "concealed." "Concealment" would occur if high-cost storage sites were used when the basinwide "productivity" of storage was high (because the aggregate amount of regulatory storage was low) and if low-cost storage sites were used when basin productivity of storage was low. Concealment would become apparent whenever it could be shown that if the opposite sequence had been adopted the additional storage under consideration at that moment would not be justified.

We cannot, of course, rewrite history, but some reservoirs built in the past might not be built now if the decisions were to be made today. Our own history reveals that the average size of new reservoirs has increased in recent decades. This does not mean that we are now adding to capacity in such fashion as to conceal deliberately high implicit marginal costs. Unforeseen changes in technology and the geographic distribution of economic activity will justify departure from a preset maximum efficiency schedule of increments of flow.[21] However, in view of the large increments of storage that quite likely will be built in the eastern half of the United States, the possibility of achieving substantial savings by proper planning seems attractively high.

---

[21] Some departure may be justified by the desire to avoid excess capacity over an unduly prolonged interval of time. Nonmarketed benefits or costs that are not readily incorporated into an "efficiency" analysis will also warrant departure from a preset schedule.

Table F-1. STORAGE REQUIRED TO PRODUCE GROSS FLOWS EQUAL TO INDICATED PERCENTAGES OF MEAN ANNUAL FLOW (MAF), WITH 98% AVAILABILITY AND NO DEDUCTION FOR RESERVOIR LOSSES, BY REGION

(flow in billion gallons per day; storage in million acre-feet)

	10% MAF		20% MAF		30% MAF		40% MAF		50% MAF		60% MAF		70% MAF		80% MAF		90% MAF		95% MAF		Mean Annual Flow	
	Flow	Stor.	Flow	Stor.	Flow	Stor.	Flow	Stor.	Flow	Stor.	Flow	Stor.	Flow	Stor.	Flow	Stor.	Flow	Stor.	Flow	Stor.	(bgd)	(mil. af/yr)
N Eng	6.70	1.12	13.40	2.85	20.10	5.99	26.80	11.20	33.50	18.35	40.20	30.90[a]	46.90	40.50	53.60	53.20	60.30	84.30	63.60	180.0	67.0	74.90
D & H	3.20	0.72	6.40	1.43	9.60	2.68	12.80	4.94	16.0	7.70	19.20	11.20[a]	22.40	16.70	25.60	24.90	28.80	47.60	30.40	81.90	32.0	35.80
Ches	5.20	1.16	10.40	2.21	15.60	4.65	20.80	8.77[a]	26.0	16.27	31.20	24.70	36.40	37.10	41.60	53.70	46.80	97.40	49.40	174.0	52.0	58.10
SE	21.20	4.74	42.40	10.70	63.60	20.10	84.80	35.50	106.0	54.50	127.0	92.40[a]	148.0	137.0	170.0	214.0	191.0	412.0	201.0	771.0	212.0	237.0
EGL	4.0	1.34	8.0	3.13	12.0	5.14	16.0	8.49[a]	20.0	14.30	24.0	22.40	28.0	32.20	32.0	46.70	36.0	83.80	38.0	142.0	40.0	44.70
WGL			8.40	0.94	12.60	4.69[a]	16.80	11.0	21.0	19.20	25.20	29.80	29.40	44.60	33.60	70.40	37.80	137.0			42.0	46.90
Ohio	11.0	5.53	22.0	11.70	33.0	18.40	44.0	29.50[a]	55.0	44.90	66.0	63.90	77.0	90.30	88.0	128.0	99.0	223.0	105.0	495.0	110.0	123.0
Cumb	1.70	0.25	3.40	0.66	5.10	1.42	6.80	2.85[a]	8.50	5.42	10.20	8.55	11.90	12.90	13.60	19.40	15.30	37.50	16.20	60.40	17.0	19.0
Tenn					12.90	0.72	17.20	4.56[a]	21.50	11.40	25.80	20.20	30.10	31.0	34.40	47.0	38.70	87.60	40.80	192.0	43.0	48.0
U Miss			12.40	2.43	18.60	8.66[a]	24.80	18.40	31.0	27.70	37.20	42.60	43.40	58.10	49.60	81.40	55.80	165.0	58.90	274.0	62.0	69.30
L Miss	4.90	2.47	9.80	6.85[a]	14.70	13.70	19.60	21.90	24.50	31.50	29.40	43.80	34.30	58.10	39.20	82.90	44.10	158.0			49.0	54.80
U Mo	2.90	1.13	5.80	2.43	8.70	5.25[a]	11.60	9.40	14.50	14.70	17.40	20.70	20.30	27.90	23.20	39.20	26.10	75.80			29.0	32.40
L Mo	2.30	2.18	4.60	4.11	6.90	7.20[a]	9.20	11.60	11.50	18.0	13.80	26.90	16.10	38.20	18.40	63.30	20.70	130.0			23.0	25.70
U AWR	1.30	1.09[a]	2.60	2.83	3.90	5.08	5.20	8.12	6.50	12.50	7.80	18.50	9.10	27.20	10.40	43.50	11.70	80.0			13.0	14.50
L AWR	7.70	8.60	15.40	17.20[a]	23.10	29.20	30.80	45.20	38.50	61.20	46.20	83.90	53.90	113.0	61.60	157.0	69.30	280.0			77.0	86.0
W Gulf	4.60	5.14	9.20	11.80[a]	13.80	25.70	18.40	40.10	23.0	59.60	27.60	88.40	32.20	127.0	36.80	218.0					46.0	51.40
RG-P	0.36	0.10	0.71	0.28	1.06	0.46	1.42	0.70	1.78	1.08[a]	2.13	1.66	2.48	2.60	2.84	4.10	3.20	8.0			3.55	4.0
Colo	1.40	0.45	2.70	1.13	4.0	1.89	5.40	3.02	6.80	4.83[a]	8.10	6.95	9.40	9.66	10.80	14.0	12.20	25.50	12.80	55.0	13.50	15.10
G Basin	1.05	0.23	2.10	0.58	3.20	1.61[a]	4.20	3.07	5.20	4.97	6.30	7.66	7.40	11.30	8.40	17.10	9.40	36.10			10.50	11.70
PNW	14.30	4.79	28.60	11.20	42.90	18.40	57.20	28.0	71.50	41.60	85.80	68.70[a]	100.0	84.70	114.0	110.0	129.0	178.0	136.0	374.0	143.0	160.0
C Pac	5.80	4.86	11.60	9.07	17.40	13.30	23.20	19.40[a]	29.0	28.50	34.80	42.40	40.60	68.0	46.40	122.0	52.20	280.0			58.0	64.80
S Pac	0.16	0.29[a]	0.32	0.66	0.48	1.12	0.64	1.79	0.80	2.89	0.96	4.54	1.12	6.62	1.28	11.0					1.60	1.80

Source: George O. G. Löf and Clayton H. Hardison, "Storage Requirements for Water in the United States," Water Resources Research, vol. 2, no. 3 (Third Quarter 1966), table, p. 340.

[a] Approximate lowest flow for which carry-over storage is required.

Table F–2. STORAGE REQUIRED TO PRODUCE GROSS FLOWS EQUAL TO INDICATED PERCENTAGES OF MEAN ANNUAL FLOW (MAF), WITH 95% AVAILABILITY AND NO DEDUCTION FOR RESERVOIR LOSSES, BY REGION

(flow in billion gallons per day; storage in million acre-feet)

	10% MAF		20% MAF		30% MAF		40% MAF		50% MAF		60% MAF		70% MAF		80% MAF		90% MAF		95% MAF	
	Flow	Stor.	Flow	Stor.	Flow	Stor.	Flow	Stor.	Flow	Stor.	Flow	Stor.	Flow	Stor.	Flow	Stor.	Flow	Stor.	Flow	Stor.
N Eng	6.70	1.12	13.40	2.85	20.10	5.99	26.80	11.20	33.50	18.40	40.20	29.20	46.90	34.50	53.60	43.80	60.30	67.0	63.60	120.0
D & H	3.20	0.77	6.40	1.43	9.60	2.68	12.80	4.94	16.0	7.70	19.20	10.70a	22.40	14.30	25.60	21.50	28.80	36.90	30.40	57.80
Ches	5.20	1.16	10.40	2.21	15.60	4.65	20.80	8.47a	26.0	13.40	31.20	21.50	36.40	30.80	41.60	44.30	46.80	71.20	49.40	131.0
SE	21.20	4.74	42.40	10.70	63.60	20.10	84.80	35.50	106.0	54.50	127.0	78.20a	148.0	118.0	170.0	182.0	191.0	326.0	201.0	610.0
EGL	4.0	1.34	8.0	3.13	12.0	5.14	16.0	8.27a	20.0	12.10	24.0	18.80	28.0	25.50	32.0	37.10	36.0	60.30	38.0	104.0
WGL			8.40	0.94	12.60	1.64a	16.80	6.10	21.0	11.70	25.20	20.50	29.40	33.30	33.60	52.10	37.80	90.30		
Ohio	11.0	5.53	22.0	11.70	33.0	18.40	44.0	24.60a	55.0	36.90	66.0	55.30	77.0	75.20	88.0	101.0	99.0	172.0	105.0	307.0
Cumb	1.70	0.25	3.40	0.66	5.10	1.47	6.80	2.28a	8.50	4.05	10.20	6.88	11.90	10.10	13.60	15.50	15.30	26.0	16.20	47.50
Tenn					12.90	0.72	17.20	1.82a	21.50	5.38	25.80	13.70	30.10	23.80	34.40	36.70	38.70	63.60	40.80	119.0
U Miss	4.90	2.47	12.40	2.43	18.60	5.20a	24.80	11.10	31.0	19.10	37.20	32.60	43.40	47.80	49.60	67.20	55.80	118.0	58.90	218.0
L Miss	2.90	1.13	9.80	5.21a	14.70	8.88	19.60	15.30	24.50	23.30	29.40	33.20	34.30	45.90	39.20	64.40				
U Mo	2.30	2.18	5.80	2.43	8.70	4.47a	11.60	7.29	14.50	11.30	17.40	16.90	20.30	23.50	23.20	32.0	26.10	56.70		
L Mo	1.30	0.072a	4.60	4.11	6.90	6.04a	9.20	9.12	11.50	13.90	13.80	21.10	16.10	31.20	18.40	44.70	20.70	83.50		
U AWR			2.60	1.88	3.90	3.84	5.20	6.35	6.50	9.80	7.80	14.50	9.10	20.90						
L AWR	7.70	8.60	15.40	16.30a	23.10	26.20	30.80	39.10	38.50	50.70	46.20	65.50	53.90	87.30	61.60	127.0	69.30	204.0		
W Gulf	4.60	5.14	9.20	7.71a	13.80	19.50	18.40	30.30	23.0	47.30	27.60	66.80	32.20	97.70	36.80	150.0				
RG-P	0.36	0.10	0.71	0.28	1.06	0.46	1.42	0.70	1.78	1.04a	2.13	1.60	2.48	2.32	2.84	3.36	3.20	6.00		
Colo	1.40	0.45	2.70	1.13	4.0	1.89	5.40	3.02	6.80	4.53a	8.10	6.34	9.40	8.61	10.80	11.70	12.20	19.30	12.80	40.40
G Basin	1.05	0.23	2.10	0.58	3.20	1.11a	4.20	2.11	5.20	3.65	6.30	5.62	7.40	8.54	8.40	13.50	9.40	22.50	10.0	43.20
PNW	14.30	4.79	28.60	11.20	42.90	18.40	57.20	28.0	71.50	41.60	85.80	59.90a	100.0	71.90	114.0	91.90	129.0	144.0	136.0	260.0
C Pac	5.80	4.86	11.60	9.07	17.40	13.30	23.20	17.80a	29.0	25.30	34.80	36.40	40.60	55.10	46.40	87.50	52.20	196.0		
S Pac	0.16	0.18a	0.32	0.51	0.48	0.98	0.64	1.51	0.80	2.27	0.96	3.28	1.12	4.79						

Source: George O. G. Löf and Clayton H. Hardison, "Storage Requirements for Water in the United States," *Water Resources Research,* vol. 2, no. 3 (Third Quarter 1966), table, p. 340.

a Approximate lowest flow for which carry-over storage is required.

Table F-3. STORAGE REQUIRED TO PRODUCE GROSS FLOWS EQUAL TO INDICATED PERCENTAGES OF MEAN ANNUAL FLOW (MAF), WITH 90% AVAILABILITY AND NO DEDUCTION FOR RESERVOIR LOSSES, BY REGION

(flow in billion gallons per day; storage in million acre-feet)

	10% MAF		20% MAF		30% MAF		40% MAF		50% MAF		60% MAF	
	Flow	Storage	Flow	Storage	Flow	Storage	Flow	Storage	Flow	Storage	Flow	Storage
N Eng	6.7	1.12	13.40	2.85	20.10	5.99	26.80	11.20	33.50	18.40	40.20	28.2
D & H	3.2	0.77	6.40	1.43	9.60	2.68	12.80	4.94	16.00	7.7	19.20	11.6
Ches	5.2	1.16	10.40	2.21	15.60	4.65	20.80	8.20	26.00	13.0	31.20	19.0
Ohio	11.0	5.53	22.00	11.70	33.00	18.40	44.00	24.6	55.00	36.0	66.00	45.1
EGL	4.0	1.34	8.00	3.13	12.00	5.14	16.00	8.27	20.00	11.9	24.00	16.1
WGL	4.2	–	8.40	0.94	12.60	1.28	16.80	3.15	21.00	5.1	25.20	12.46[a]
U Miss	6.2	–	12.40	2.43	18.60	5.20	24.80	8.65	31.00	14.1	37.20	21.17[a]
L Mo	2.3	2.18	4.60	4.11	6.90	6.02	9.20	8.55[a]	11.50	10.89	13.80	16.06
SE	21.2	4.74	42.40	10.70	63.60	20.10	84.80	35.5	106.00	54.5	127.20	78.2
Cumb	1.7	0.25	3.40	0.66	5.10	1.47	6.80	2.28	8.50	3.67	10.20	5.2
Tenn	4.3	–	8.60	–	12.90	0.72	17.20	1.80	21.50	3.85	25.80	7.2
L Miss	4.9	2.47	9.80	5.21	14.70	8.88	19.60	12.9	24.50	17.0	29.40	24.57[a]
L AWR	7.7	8.60	15.40	15.0	23.10	21.8	30.80	28.2	38.50	33.95[a]	46.20	45.90
U Mo	2.9	1.13	5.80	2.43	8.70	4.36	11.60	6.75	14.50	9.46	17.40	12.71[a]
U AWR	1.3	0.072	2.60	1.61	3.90	2.70[a]	5.20	4.50	6.50	6.57	7.80	10.39
W Gulf	4.6	5.14	9.20	7.71	13.80	13.96[a]	18.40	21.68	23.00	32.42	27.60	48.87
RG-P	0.355	0.10	0.71	0.28	1.07	0.46	1.42	0.70	1.78	1.04	2.13	1.12[a]
Colo	1.35	0.45	2.70	1.13	4.05	1.89	5.40	3.02	6.75	4.53	8.10	6.28
G Basin	1.05	0.23	2.10	0.58	3.15	1.07	4.20	1.65	5.25	2.3	6.30	3.95[a]
S Pac	0.16	0.055	0.32	0.225[a]	0.48	0.511	0.64	0.887	0.80	1.407	0.96	2.189
C Pac	5.8	4.86	11.60	9.07	17.40	13.3	23.20	16.8	29.00	20.44[a]	34.80	29.45
PNW	14.3	4.79	28.60	11.2	42.90	18.4	57.20	28.0	71.50	41.6	85.80	57.1

	70% MAF		80% MAF		90% MAF		95% MAF		98% MAF		100% MAF	
	Flow	Storage	Flow	Storage	Flow	Storage	Flow	Storage	Flow	Storage	Flow	Storage
N Eng	46.90	34.5	53.60	43.8[a]	60.30	62.33	63.65	75.06	65.66	93.78	67.00	129.74
D & H	22.40	14.3	25.60	19.94[a]	-28.80	25.21	30.40	35.73	31.36	49.44	32.00	72.07
Ches	36.40	27.41[a]	41.60	42.23	46.80	61.11	49.40	76.92	50.96	99.57	52.00	122.40
Ohio	77.00	61.40[a]	88.00	82.31	99.00	113.06	104.50	152.42	107.80	190.55	110.00	260.66
EGL	28.00	22.38[a]	32.00	32.85	36.00	45.99	38.00	59.93	39.20	76.16	40.00	94.87
WGL	29.40	22.22	33.60	36.66	37.80	56.31	39.90	75.97	41.16	103.03[b]	42.00	121.88
U Miss	43.40	34.96	49.60	50.83	55.80	72.24	58.90	100.93	60.76	124.42	62.00	166.42
L Mo	16.10	21.99	18.40	31.27	20.70	45.69	21.85	63.16	22.54	81.59[b]	23.00	91.21
SE	148.70	102.25[a]	169.60	148.70	190.80	214.12	201.40	317.92	207.76	454.20	212.00	647.12
Cumb	11.90	7.87[a]	13.60	11.96	15.30	17.18	16.15	22.93	16.66	29.72	17.00	45.12
Tenn	30.10	15.15[a]	34.40	26.24	38.70	41.65	40.85	57.97	42.14	73.76	43.00	101.70
L Miss	34.30	33.72	39.20	46.26	44.10	65.89	46.55	85.01	48.02	113.29	49.00	144.13
L AWR	53.90	61.30	61.60	85.38	69.30	122.27	73.15	163.04	75.46	223.41[b]	77.00	261.51
U Mo	20.30	18.42	23.20	25.09	26.10	34.46	27.55	47.51	28.42	58.27	29.00	77.77
U AWR	9.10	14.79	10.40	20.78	11.70	31.41	12.35	44.71	12.74	58.63[b]	13.00	65.25
W Gulf	32.20	68.40	36.80	97.69	41.40	149.61	43.70	208.98	45.08	–	46.00	–
RG-P	2.49	1.48	2.84	2.24	3.20	3.36	3.37	5.32	3.48	7.64	3.55	10.92
Colo	9.45	8.06[a]	10.80	10.17	12.15	13.95	12.83	18.33	13.23	22.55	13.50	31.16
G Basin	7.35	6.19	8.40	9.59	9.45	14.28	9.98	19.09	10.29	26.21[b]	10.50	30.44
S Pac	1.12	3.195	1.28	4.705	1.44	7.395	1.52	–	1.57	–	1.60	–
C Pac	40.60	40.40	46.40	60.43	52.20	106.37	55.10	164.04	56.84	226.64	58.00	319.49
PNW	100.10	71.9	114.40	88.20[a]	128.70	117.00	135.85	144.20	140.14	184.20	143.00	261.00

Source: Derived from unpublished graphs prepared by George O. G. Löf and Clayton H. Hardison.

[a]Approximate lowest flow for which carry-over storage is required.
[b]Interpolated between 95% and 100%.

Table F-4. CAPITAL COSTS OF STORAGE CAPACITY PER ACRE-FOOT, BY PHYSIOGRAPHIC ZONE AND SIZE CLASS, 1964 PRICES[a]

(dollars)

Physiographic zone[b]	Size class *(1,000 acre-feet)*										
	I 0– 20	II 20– 40	III 40– 60	IV 60– 100	V 100– 200	VI 200– 400	VII 400– 1,000	VIII 1,000– 2,000	IX 2,000– 4,000	X 4,000– 10,000	XI Over 10,000
A	288	238	219	203	181	163	141	125	110	96	75
B	250	200	181	165	144	125	106	94	80	69	54
C	221	169	150	138	119	100	83	70	61	50	39
D	200	150	131	116	98	81	65	53	44	35	21
E	194	144	123	106	91	75	59	48	40	31	19
F	181	133	113	100	81	69	54	43	35	26	15
G	178	129	109	94	75	63	48	38	31	24	13
H	154	108	91	78	63	50	38	30	23	18	10
I	119	81	69	58	48	38	28	23	19	13	8
J	76	54	46	40	31	25	19	15	13	10	5

Source: U.S. Army Corps of Engineers.

[a]Equal to 1954 prices multiplied by 1.25; 1954 prices approximately the same as table 40, Committee Print No. 32, p. 58.
[b]See figure F-1.

Table F-5. CAPACITY OF RESERVOIRS IN THOUSANDS OF ACRE-FEET, EXISTING OR UNDER CONSTRUCTION: 1964

	Size class *(1,000 acre-feet)*											
	I 0– 20	II 20– 40	III 40– 60	IV 60– 100	V 100– 200	VI 200– 400	VII 400– 1,000	VIII 1,000– 2,000	IX 2,000– 4,000	X 4,000– 10,000	XI Over 10,000	Total
N Eng	2,963	517	713	1,055	1,261	1,984	1,378	1,265	0	0	0	11,136
D & H	55	116	94	68	403	299	845	0	0	0	0	1,880
Ches	154	212	89	396	378	308	0	0	0	0	0	1,537
Ohio	91	219	193	1,716	3,165	4,452	4,909	1,180	0	0	0	15,925
EGL	103	20	0	140	0	337	868	0	0	0	0	1,468
WGL	72	27	114	0	120	0	550	0	0	0	0	883
U Miss	65	0	156	144	1,814	292	5,468	1,830	0	0	0	9,769
L Mo	5	25	0	0	0	0	0	650	3,647	2,020	0	6,347
SE	194	337	214	1,197	2,504	5,960	6,904	10,042	21,284	5,815	0	54,451
Cumb	0	0	49	0	104	311	1,633	1,706	4,174	6,089	0	14,066
Tenn	86	133	129	71	1,075	1,649	2,290	4,050	2,281	4,011	0	15,775
L Miss	0	0	0	625	0	0	0	1,185	2,908	0	0	4,718
L AWR	177	31	104	228	1,149	2,679	6,422	13,362	11,842	5,408	0	41,402
U Mo	271	125	237	954	1,435	3,892	9,120	5,088	7,077	6,100	67,500	101,799
U AWR	470	502	318	240	1,298	1,181	2,038	1,332	3,848	5,530	0	16,757
W Gulf	612	698	2,915	593	2,818	3,724	7,737	6,124	7,385	9,366	0	41,972
RG-P	140	119	229	139	708	619	1,728	1,951	2,195	0	0	7,828
Colo	99	227	148	292	831	873	2,129	5,952	6,008	0	58,047	74,606
G Basin	51	53	92	136	300	489	732	0	0	0	0	1,853
S Pac	48	103	0	0	0	457	0	0	0	0	0	608
C Pac	133	219	338	376	1,571	1,295	4,197	4,847	8,100	4,500	0	25,576
PNW	236	302	328	898	2,651	4,543	12,488	13,880	3,468	9,402	0	48,196
U.S.	6,025	3,985	6,460	9,268	23,585	35,344	72,086	77,441	82,590	56,221	125,547	498,552

Table F-6. DISTRIBUTION OF EXISTING RESERVOIRS BY SIZE CLASS, U.S. SUMMARY

	Size class *(1,000 acre-feet)*										
	I 0– 20	II 20– 40	III 40– 60	IV 60– 100	V 100– 200	VI 200– 400	VII 400– 1,000	VIII 1,000– 2,000	IX 2,000– 4,000	X 4,000– 10,000	XI Over 10,000
1960[a] acre-feet	5,565	5,618	5,034	8,784	16,192	23,270	38,095	64,294	38,055	38,242	94,727
percent of total	0.016	0.017	0.015	0.026	0.048	0.069	0.113	0.190	0.113	0.113	0.280
1964 (RFF) acre-feet	6,025	3,985	6,460	9,268	23,585	35,344	72,086	77,441	82,590	56,221	125,547
percent of total	0.012	0.008	0.013	0.019	0.047	0.071	0.145	0.155	0.166	0.113	0.252

[a]Taken from Nathan O. Thomas and Earl Harbeck, Jr., *Reservoirs in the United States*, U.S. Geological Survey Water-Supply Paper 1360–A (1956), plus additional computations for 1954–60 by the U.S. Bureau of Reclamation and the U.S. Army Corps of Engineers. Tabulation made for earlier version of this manuscript; mingles total and usable capacity.

Table F-7. PERCENTAGE DISTRIBUTION OF EXISTING (1964) RESERVOIRS, BY PHYSIOGRAPHIC ZONE AND REGION

	Physiographic zone									
	A	B	C	D	E	F	G	H	I	J
N Eng	–	66	–	11	–	–	–	23	–	–
D & H	–	27	–	–	–	72	–	1	–	–
Ches	–	59	–	–	–	7	–	33	–	–
Ohio	–	21	–	–	–	40	–	38	–	–
EGL	–	8	–	–	–	23	–	4	66	–
WGL	–	–	–	–	–	–	–	62	38	–
U Miss	–	–	1	–	–	–	–	62	36	–
L Mo	–	–	–	–	–	–	–	100	–	–
SE	–	–	–	2	–	–	–	98	–	–
Cumb	–	–	–	–	–	19	–	81	–	–
Tenn	–	–	–	3	–	97	–	–	–	–
L Miss	–	–	–	–	–	–	–	13	–	87
L AWR	–	–	–	–	3	–	–	92	–	5
U Mo	–	–	–	–	4	2	85	3	4	–
U AWR	–	–	1	–	–	–	6	85	3	–
W Gulf	–	–	–	–	–	–	–	100	–	–
RG-P	–	3	–	–	–	–	14	35	48	–
Colo	–	82	–	–	5	–	4	–	9	–
G Basin	–	43	–	–	13	–	–	–	45	–
S Pac	–	9	–	–	43	–	–	–	48	–
C Pac	–	23	–	–	74	–	–	–	2	–
PNW	11	6	–	–	3	28	4	13	29	–

Note: Because of unknowns, totals do not always equal 100.

Table F-8. SYNTHETIC SCHEDULE OF RESERVOIRS: PERCENTAGE OF TOTAL NEW CAPACITY IN EACH REGION ASSIGNED TO VARIOUS PHYSIOGRAPHIC ZONES

	Physiographic zone									
	A	B	C	D	E	F	G	H	I	J
N Eng	–	45	–	10	–	–	–	45	–	–
D & H	–	60	–	–	–	40	–	–	–	–
Ches	–	55	–	–	–	5	–	40	–	–
Ohio	–	25	–	–	–	50	–	25	–	–
EGL	–	20	–	–	–	10	–	60	10	–
WGL	–	–	–	–	–	–	–	40	60	–
U Miss	–	–	10	–	–	–	–	65	25	–
L Mo	–	–	–	–	–	–	–	100	–	–
SE	–	–	–	3	–	–	–	97	–	–
Cumb	–	–	–	–	–	50	–	50	–	–
Tenn	–	–	–	20	–	80	–	–	–	–
L Miss	–	–	–	–	–	–	–	10	–	90
L AWR	–	–	–	–	10	–	–	80	–	10
U Mo	–	5	–	–	–	–	85	–	10	–
U AWR	–	–	10	–	–	–	5	85	–	–
W Gulf	–	–	–	–	–	–	–	100	–	–
RG-P	–	10	–	–	–	–	20	40	30	–
Colo	–	25	–	–	5	–	5	15	50	–
G Basin	–	–	–	–	20	–	–	–	80	–
S Pac	–	5	–	–	90	–	–	–	5	–
C Pac	–	25	–	–	75	–	–	–	–	–
PNW	10	15	–	–	10	20	5	20	20	–

Table F-9. SYNTHETIC SCHEDULE OF RESERVOIRS: PERCENTAGE OF TOTAL NEW CAPACITY IN EACH
REGION ASSIGNED TO VARIOUS SIZE CLASSES

| | Size class (1,000 acre-feet) | | | | | | | | | | |
	I 0–20	II 20–40	III 40–60	IV 60–100	V 100–200	VI 200–400	VII 400–1,000	VIII 1,000–2,000	IX 2,000–4,000	X 4,000–10,000	XI Over 10,000
N Eng	5	5	10	10	10	10	15	15	10	10	0
D & H	5	10	10	10	10	15	40	0	0	0	0
Ches	5	5	5	10	15	20	20	10	10	0	0
Ohio	2	3	5	10	10	25	25	10	10	0	0
EGL	5	5	15	20	20	20	15	0	0	0	0
WGL	5	10	10	10	15	25	25	0	0	0	0
U Miss	5	5	5	5	15	15	20	10	10	10	0
L Mo	0	40	2	3	5	10	10	10	10	10	0
SE	0	1	1	3	5	15	30	30	10	5	0
Cumb	0	0	0	5	5	10	15	15	20	30	0
Tenn	2	3	5	5	10	15	20	20	10	10	0
L Miss	0	0	0	5	5	15	15	40	20	0	0
L AWR	2	2	3	3	5	10	20	25	25	5	0
U Mo	1	4	5	5	5	10	10	10	10	20	20
U AWR	0	1	4	5	10	15	15	10	10	30	0
W Gulf	0	0	2	3	5	10	25	25	15	15	0
RG-P	0	0	0	2	3	10	15	20	50	0	0
Colo	1	1	1	2	5	10	20	20	40	0	0
G Basin	2	3	10	10	15	15	15	30	0	0	0
S Pac	5	5	5	5	20	60	0	0	0	0	0
C Pac	0	1	2	2	5	5	10	20	25	30	0
PNW	0	1	2	2	5	5	10	25	35	15	0

Table F-10. INVENTORIES OF EXISTING RESERVOIR CAPACITY, BY REGION

(million acre-feet)

	USGS[a]	Piper[b]	Additions, 1954-60[c]	USGS corrected to 1960	Piper corrected to 1960	RFF 1964[d]	Standardized inventory 1964
NORTHEAST	25.9	27.0	0.170	26.1		48.9	50.8
N Eng	9.0	8.9	0.098	9.1	9.0	11.1	11.1
D & H	3.1	3.0	0.072	3.2	3.1	1.9	3.2
Ches	0.9	0.9		0.9	0.9	1.5	1.5
Ohio	5.7	5.8		5.7	5.8	15.9	15.9
EGL	0.5	1.7		0.5	1.7	1.5	1.7
WGL	1.2	1.3		1.2	1.3	0.9	1.3
U Miss	4.3	3.5		4.3	3.5	9.8	9.8
L Mo	1.2	1.9		1.2	1.9	6.3	6.3
SOUTHEAST	69.1	64.6	3.786	70.6		130.5	130.4
SE	16.4	16.4	0.385	16.8	16.8	54.5	54.4
Cumb	6.4 ⎫	21.4		6.4 ⎫	22.1	14.1	14.1
Tenn	15.0 ⎭		0.747	15.7 ⎭		15.8	15.8
L Miss	4.5	4.5		4.5	4.5	4.7	4.7
L AWR	26.8	22.3	2.654	27.2	25.0	41.4	41.4
MID-CONTINENT	93.3		2.251	95.6		160.6	160.6
U Mo	74.8	75.9	1.078	75.9	76.9	101.8	101.8
U AWR	7.3	7.6	0.573	7.9	8.2	16.8	16.8
W Gulf	11.2 ⎫		0.600	11.8 ⎫		42.0	42.0
SOUTHWEST	44.3 ⎬	14.3	34.397	78.7 ⎬	14.9	84.9	90.1
RG-P	3.3 ⎭			3.3 ⎭		7.8	7.8
Colo	35.1	34.8	33.630	68.7	68.4	74.6	74.6
G Basin	4.1	5.1	0.277	4.4	5.4	1.9	5.4
S Pac	1.8 ⎫		0.490	2.3 ⎫		0.6	2.3
NORTH PACIFIC	45.3 ⎬	16.9	2.776	48.1 ⎬	19.9	73.8	73.8
C Pac	16.4 ⎭		2.539	18.9 ⎭		25.6	25.6
PNW	28.9	27.9	0.237	29.1	28.1	48.2	48.2
U.S.	278.0	274.0	43.380	319.1	317.2	498.6	505.7

[a]Committee Print No. 3, *National Water Resources and Problems*, prepared by the U.S. Geological Survey for the Senate Select Committee on National Water Resources, 86th Cong., 2d sess. (1960). Figures based on Nathan O. Thomas and G. Earl Harbeck, Jr., *Reservoirs in the United States*, U.S. Geological Survey Water-Supply Paper 1360-A (1956); reservoirs and regulated lakes as of 1954.

[b]A. M. Piper, *Has the United States Enough Water?*, U.S. Geological Survey Water-Supply Paper 1797 (1965).

[c]Reported additions by the U.S. Bureau of Reclamation and the U.S. Corps of Engineers.

[d]Inventory compiled by Pum Ky Kim under the direction of Allen V. Kneese, Resources for the Future.

Table F-11. EXISTING STORAGE CAPACITY, BY FUNCTION AND REGION: 1964

(thousand acre-feet)

	Flood	Irrigation	Power	Other	Total
NORTHEAST	22,848	310	12,421	11,099	46,678
N Eng	3,540	0	5,246	2,037	10,823
D & H	912	0	192	777	1,881
Ches	712	0	168	501	1,381
Ohio	11,300	1	953	3,121	15,375
EGL	415	0	747	75	1,237
WGL	0	309	466	0	775
U Miss	4,780	0	602	4,251	9,633
L Mo	1,189	0	4,047	337	5,573
SOUTHEAST	40,334	7,436	39,781	33,574	121,125
SE	11,230	4,852	19,025	10,832	45,939
Cumb	4,949	0	3,745	5,323	14,017
Tenn[a]	5,530	0	4,266	6,004	15,800
L Miss	4,412	0	0	306	4,718
L AWR	14,213	2,584	12,745	11,109	40,651
MID-CONTINENT	33,383	9,531	24,283	75,816	143,013
U Mo	15,724	5,166	17,320	51,501	89,711
U AWR	6,407	2,074	3,214	3,196	14,891
W Gulf	11,252	2,291	3,749	21,119	38,411
SOUTHWEST	8,568	40,729	32,889	3,819	86,005
RG-P	2,237	3,823	1,109	607	7,776
Colo	5,989	35,394	31,765	3,194	76,342
G Basin	0	1,272	15	0	1,287
S Pac	342	240	0	18	600
NORTH PACIFIC	19,113	33,782	91,878	11,686	156,459
C Pac	2,465	16,092	8,333	1,573	28,463
PNW	16,648	17,690	83,545	10,113	127,996
U.S.	124,246	91,788	201,252	135,994	553,280

Source: Resources for the Future.

[a]At same percentage of total as Cumberland.

Table F-12. DISTRIBUTION OF RESERVOIR CAPACITY, BY DIVISION: 1964

	Area (1,000 sq. mis.)	1964 standard capacity (mil. af)	1964 af capacity per sq. mi. of area	Maximum required storage (mil. af)	Maximum required capacity per sq. mi. (af/sq. mi.)	Maximum required capacity minus existing (mil. af)	Maximum required capacity minus existing per sq. mi. (af/sq. mi.)
NORTHEAST	664	50.8	77	1,267	1,908	1,216	1,831
N Eng	59	11.1	188				
D & H	31	3.2	100				
Ches	57	1.5	26				
Ohio	145	15.9	110				
EGL	47	1.7	36				
WGL	81	1.3	16				
U Miss	182	9.8	54				
L Mo	62	6.3	102				
SOUTHEAST	519	130.4	251	1,256	2,420	1,125	2,168
SE	279	54.4	195				
Cumb	18	14.1	700				
Tenn	41	15.8	385				
L Miss	64	4.7	73				
L AWR	117	41.4	354				
MID-CONTINENT	876	160.6	183	237	270	77	88
U Mo	518	101.8	197				
U AWR	153	16.8	110				
W Gulf	205	42.0	205				
SOUTHWEST	607	90.1	148	63	104	27	44
RG-P	136	7.8	57				
Colo	258	74.6	289				
G Basin	200	5.4	27				
S Pac	13	2.3	177				
NORTH PACIFIC	356	73.8	207	762	2,140	688	1,933
C Pac	99	25.6	259				
PNW	257	48.2	188				
U.S.	3,000	505.7	169	3,586	1,195	3,080	1,027

Table F-13. DISTRIBUTION OF RESERVOIR CAPACITY, BY FUNCTION AND REGION

(thousand acre-feet)

	Planned					Existing plus planned				
	Flood	Irrigation	Power	Other	Total	Flood	Irrigation	Power	Other	Total
NORTHEAST	71,355	38	28,203	38,205	137,801	94,203	348	40,624	49,304	184,479
N Eng	417	38	2,932	5,414	8,801	3,957	38	8,178	7,451	19,624
D & H	495	0	328	1,253	2,076	1,407	0	520	2,030	3,957
Ches	4,703	0	10,377	10,359	25,439	5,415	0	10,545	10,860	26,820
Ohio	12,289	0	2,730	3,735	18,754	23,589	1	3,683	6,856	34,129
EGL	1,139	0	1,053	326	2,518	1,554	0	1,800	401	3,755
WGL	172	0	1,106	210	1,488	172	309	1,572	210	2,263
U Miss	25,477	0	7,992	5,491	38,960	30,257	0	8,594	9,742	48,593
L Mo	26,663	0	1,685	11,417	39,765	27,852	0	5,732	11,754	45,338
SOUTHEAST	24,941	1,180	48,048	28,594	102,763	65,275	8,616	87,829	62,168	223,888
SE	6,104	777	29,601	11,379	47,861	17,334	5,629	48,626	22,211	93,800
Cumb	2,343	0	2,458	3,259	8,060	7,292	0	6,203	8,582	22,077
Tenn[a]	2,866	0	2,965	4,052	9,883	8,396	0	7,231	10,056	25,683
L Miss	180	0	0	600	780	4,592	0	0	906	5,498
L AWR	13,448	403	13,024	9,304	36,179	27,661	2,987	25,769	20,413	76,830
MID-CONTINENT	57,395	35,806	65,411	65,195	223,807	90,778	45,337	89,694	141,011	366,820
U Mo	21,195	13,454	46,585	12,187	93,421	36,919	18,620	63,905	63,688	183,132
U AWR	9,190	1,102	4,557	8,392	23,241	15,597	3,176	7,771	11,588	38,132
W Gulf	27,010	21,250	14,269	44,616	107,145	38,262	23,541	18,018	65,735	145,556
SOUTHWEST	6,717	5,574	7,583	8,831	28,705	15,285	46,303	40,472	12,650	114,710
RG-P	1,491	1,159	4,004	1,161	7,815	3,728	4,982	5,113	1,768	15,591
Colo	4,332	1,190	3,307	4,790	13,619	10,321	36,584	35,072	7,984	89,961
G Basin	621	3,225	272	2,572	6,690	621	4,497	287	2,572	7,977
S Pac	273	0	0	308	581	615	240	0	326	1,181
NORTH PACIFIC	24,039	14,444	42,922	15,693	97,098	43,152	48,226	134,800	27,379	253,557
C Pac	2,898	8,433	11,562	3,924	26,817	5,363	24,525	19,895	5,497	55,280
PNW	21,141	6,011	31,360	11,769	70,281	37,789	23,701	114,905	21,882	198,277
U.S.	184,447	57,042	192,167	156,518	590,174	308,693	148,830	393,419	292,512	1,143,454

[a]Distributed by function by using same percentage distribution as Cumberland.

Table F-14. SYNTHETIC STORAGE SCHEDULES, BY REGION

Size class	Fraction of total add. req. stor.	Physiog. zone	Evap. rate *(ft/acre)*	Depth *(ft)*	Cost per AF *($ 1964)*
Region: New England					
0 – 20,000	0.05	B	0.50	15	$250
20,000 – 40,000	.05	B	.50	20	200
40,000 – 60,000	.10	B	.50	25	181
60,000 – 100,000	.10	B	.50	30	165
100,000 – 200,000	.10	B	.50	35	144
200,000 – 400,000	.10	D	.67	40	81
400,000 – 1,000,000	.15	0.3B, 0.7H	.73	45	60
1,000,000 – 2,000,000	.15	H	.83	50	30
2,000,000 – 4,000,000	.10	H	.83	50	22
4,000,000 – 10,000,000	0.10	H	0.83	50	18
Region: Delaware & Hudson					
0 – 20,000	0.05	F	0.95	20	$181
20,000 – 40,000	.10	F	.95	25	132
40,000 – 60,000	.10	F	.95	30	112
60,000 – 100,000	.10	F	.95	35	100
100,000 – 200,000	.10	0.5B, 0.5F	.95	40	112
200,000 – 400,000	.15	B	.95	45	125
400,000 – 1,000,000	0.40	B	0.95	50	106
Region: Chesapeake Bay					
0 – 20,000	0.05	B	0.50	20	$250
20,000 – 40,000	.05	B	.50	25	200
40,000 – 60,000	.05	B	.50	30	181
60,000 – 100,000	.10	B	.50	35	165
100,000 – 200,000	.15	B	.50	35	144
200,000 – 400,000	.20	0.75B, 0.25C	.57	40	111
400,000 – 1,000,000	.20	H	.83	40	38
1,000,000 – 2,000,000	.10	H	.83	40	30
2,000,000 – 4,000,000	0.10	H	0.83	40	22
Region: Ohio					
0 – 20,000	0.02	B	–	15	$250
20,000 – 40,000	.03	B	–	20	200
40,000 – 60,000	.05	B	–	20	181
60,000 – 100,000	.10	B	–	25	165
100,000 – 200,000	.10	0.5B, 0.5H	0.25	25	102
200,000 – 400,000	.25	0.2F, 0.8H	.53	30	54
400,000 – 1,000,000	.25	F	.67	40	54
1,000,000 – 2,000,000	.10	F	.67	40	42
2,000,000 – 4,000,000	0.10	F	0.67	40	35
Region: Eastern Great Lakes					
0 – 20,000	0.05	B	0.83	10	$250
20,000 – 40,000	.05	B	.83	15	200
40,000 – 60,000	.15	0.7B, 0.3F	.73	15	158
60,000 – 100,000	.20	0.25F, 0.75H	.70	20	85
100,000 – 200,000	.20	H	.75	25	62
200,000 – 400,000	.20	H	.75	25	50
400,000 – 1,000,000	0.15	0.3H, 0.7I	0.65	25	38
Region: Western Great Lakes					
0 – 20,000	0.05	H	0.75	10	$154
20,000 – 40,000	.05	H	.75	10	108
40,000 – 60,000	.10	H	.75	15	91
60,000 – 100,000	.10	H	.75	15	78
100,000 – 200,000	.10	I	.75	15	48
200,000 – 400,000	.25	I	.75	15	38
400,000 – 1,000,000	0.25	I	0.75	15	28

Table F–14. – Continued

Size class	Fraction of total add. req. stor.	Physiog. zone	Evap. rate *(ft/acre)*	Depth *(ft)*	Cost per AF *($ 1964)*
Region: Upper Mississippi					
0 – 20,000	0.05	C	0.50	5	$221
20,000 – 40,000	.05	C	0.50	10	169
40,000 – 60,000	.05	H	1.00	15	91
60,000 – 100,000	.05	H	1.00	15	78
100,000 – 200,000	.15	H	1.00	15	62
200,000 – 400,000	.15	H	1.00	15	50
400,000 – 1,000,000	.20	H	1.00	20	38
1,000,000 – 2,000,000	.10	0.5H, 0.5I	0.83	20	26
2,000,000 – 4,000,000	.10	I	0.67	20	19
4,000,000 – 10,000,000	0.10	I	0.67	25	12
Region: Lower Missouri					
0 – 20,000	–	–	1.00	10	$154
20,000 – 40,000	0.40	H	1.00	15	108
40,000 – 60,000	.02	H	1.00	20	91
60,000 – 100,000	.03	H	1.00	20	78
100,000 – 200,000	.05	H	1.00	25	62
200,000 – 400,000	.10	H	1.00	30	50
400,000 – 1,000,000	.10	H	1.00	40	38
1,000,000 – 2,000,000	.10	H	1.00	50	30
2,000,000 – 4,000,000	.10	H	1.00	50	22
4,000,000 – 10,000,000	0.10	H	1.00	50	18
Region: Southeast					
0 – 20,000					
20,000 – 40,000	0.01	D	1.00	20	$150
40,000 – 60,000	.01	D	1.00	25	131
60,000 – 100,000	.03	D	1.00	30	116
100,000 – 200,000	.05	H	0.53	30	62
200,000 – 400,000	.15	H	0.53	35	50
400,000 – 1,000,000	.30	H	0.53	35	38
1,000,000 – 2,000,000	.30	H	0.53	40	30
2,000,000 – 4,000,000	.10	H	0.53	40	22
4,000,000 – 10,000 000	0.05	H	0.53	40	18
Region: Cumberland					
0 – 20,000	–	–	–	–	–
20,000 – 40,000	–	–	–	–	–
40,000 – 60,000	–	–	–	–	–
60,000 – 100,000	0.05	F	0.50	5	$100
100,000 – 200,000	.05	F	.50	5	81
200,000 – 400,000	.10	0.5F, 0.5H	.50	10	60
400,000 – 1,000,000	.15	0.3F, 0.7H	.50	10	41
1,000,000 – 2,000,000	.15	0.3F, 0.7H	.50	20	34
2,000,000 – 4,000,000	.20	0.5F, 0.5H	.50	50	29
4,000,000 – 10,000,000	0.30	0.5F, 0.5H	0.50	50	22
Region: Tennessee					
0 – 20,000	0.02	D	–	15	$200
20,000 – 40,000	.03	D	–	20	150
40,000 – 60,000	.05	D	–	30	131
60,000 – 100,000	.05	D	–	40	116
100,000 – 200,000	.10	0.5D, 0.5F	0.08	40	90
200,000 – 400,000	.15	F	.17	40	69
400,000 – 1,000,000	.20	F	.17	60	54
1,000,000 – 2,000,000	.20	F	.17	60	42
2,000,000 – 4,000,000	.10	F	.17	60	35
4,000,000 – 10,000,000	0.10	F	0.17	60	26

Table F-14. — Continued

Size class	Fraction of total add. req. stor.	Physiog. zone	Evap. rate *(ft/acre)*	Depth *(ft)*	Cost per AF *($ 1964)*
Region: Lower Mississippi					
0 – 20,000	–	–	–	–	–
20,000 – 40,000	–	–	–	–	–
40,000 – 60,000	–	–	–	–	–
60,000 – 100,000	0.05	H	0.67	4	$78
100,000 – 200,000	.05	H	.67	5	62
200,000 – 400,000	.15	J	.80	10	25
400,000 – 1,000,000	.15	J	.80	35	19
1,000,000 – 2,000,000	.40	J	.80	30	15
2,000,000 – 4,000,000	0.20	J	0.80	10	12
Region: Lower Arkansas–White–Red					
0 – 20,000	0.02	E	1.83	15	$194
20,000 – 40,000	.02	E	1.83	15	144
40,000 – 60,000	.03	E	1.83	20	122
60,000 – 100,000	.03	E	1.83	25	106
100,000 – 200,000	.05	J	1.00	30	31
200,000 – 400,000	.10	0.5H, 0.5J	1.25	30	38
400,000 – 1,000,000	.20	H	1.50	40	38
1,000,000 – 2,000,000	.25	H	1.50	50	30
2,000,000 – 4,000,000	.25	H	1.50	60	22
4,000,000 – 10,000,000	0.05	H	1.50	60	18
Region: Upper Missouri					
0 – 20,000	0.01	B	2.50	15	$250
20,000 – 40,000	.04	B	2.50	20	200
40,000 – 60,000	.05	G	2.00	25	109
60,000 – 100,000	.05	G	2.00	25	94
100,000 – 200,000	.05	G	2.00	30	75
200,000 – 400,000	.10	G	2.00	30	62
400,000 – 1,000,000	.10	G	2.00	40	48
1,000,000 – 2,000,000	.10	G	2.00	50	38
2,000,000 – 4,000,000	.10	G	2.00	50	31
4,000,000 – 10,000,000	.20	0.5G, 0.5I	1.34	60	18
10,000,000 and over	0.20	G	2.00	60	12
Region: Upper Arkansas–White–Red					
0 – 20,000	–	–	–	–	–
20,000 – 40,000	0.01	C	3.67	15	$169
40,000 – 60,000	.04	C	3.67	20	150
60,000 – 100,000	.05	C	3.67	25	138
100,000 – 200,000	.10	0.5G, 0.5H	3.08	25	69
200,000 – 400,000	.15	H	2.67	25	50
400,000 – 1,000,000	.15	H	2.67	30	38
1,000,000 – 2,000,000	.10	H	2.67	35	30
2,000,000 – 4,000,000	.10	H	2.67	35	22
4,000,000 – 10,000,000	0.30	H	2.67	35	18
Region: Western Gulf					
0 – 20,000	–	–	–	–	–
20,000 – 40,000	–	–	–	–	–
40,000 – 60,000	0.02	H	2.75	20	$91
60,000 – 100,000	.03	H	2.75	20	78
100,000 – 200,000	.05	H	2.75	25	62
200,000 – 400,000	.10	H	2.75	30	50
400,000 – 1,000,000	.25	H	2.75	35	38
1,000,000 – 2,000,000	.25	H	2.75	40	30
2,000,000 – 4,000,000	.15	H	2.75	45	22
4,000,000 – 10,000,000	0.15	H	2.75	45	18

Table F-14. — Continued

Size class	Fraction of total add. req. stor.	Physiog. zone	Evap. rate *(ft/acre)*	Depth *(ft)*	Cost per AF *($ 1964)*

Region: Rio Grande–Pecos

Size class	Fraction of total add. req. stor.	Physiog. zone	Evap. rate *(ft/acre)*	Depth *(ft)*	Cost per AF *($ 1964)*
0 – 20,000	–	–	–	–	–
20,000 – 40,000	–	–	–	–	–
40,000 – 60,000	–	–	–	–	–
60,000 – 100,000	0.02	B	3.00	40	$165
100,000 – 200,000	.03	B	3.00	40	144
200,000 – 400,000	.10	0.5B, 0.5G	3.00	50	94
400,000 – 1,000,000	.15	G	3.00	50	48
1,000,000 – 2,000,000	.20	I	4.67	60	22
2,000,000 – 4,000,000	0.50	0.5H, 0.5I	4.67	60	20

Region: Colorado

Size class	Fraction of total add. req. stor.	Physiog. zone	Evap. rate *(ft/acre)*	Depth *(ft)*	Cost per AF *($ 1964)*
0 – 20,000	0.01	E	3.33	30	$194
20,000 – 40,000	.01	E	3.33	35	144
40,000 – 60,000	.01	E	3.33	40	122
60,000 – 100,000	.02	E	3.33	50	106
100,000 – 200,000	.05	G	3.00	52	75
200,000 – 400,000	.10	I	5.00	57	38
400,000 – 1,000,000	.20	I	5.00	60	28
1,000,000 – 2,000,000	.20	I	5.00	62	22
2,000,000 – 4,000,000	0.40	0.62B, 0.38H	2.63	65	59

Region: Great Basin

Size class	Fraction of total add. req. stor.	Physiog. zone	Evap. rate *(ft/acre)*	Depth *(ft)*	Cost per AF *($ 1964)*
0 – 20,000	0.02	E	3.00	15	$194
20,000 – 40,000	.03	E	3.00	20	144
40,000 – 60,000	.10	E	3.00	25	122
60,000 – 100,000	.10	0.5E, 0.5I	3.00	30	82
100,000 – 200,000	.15	I	3.00	35	48
200,000 – 400,000	.15	I	3.00	40	38
400,000 – 1,000,000	.15	I	3.00	40	28
1,000,000 – 2,000,000	0.30	I	3.00	40	22

Region: South Pacific

Size class	Fraction of total add. req. stor.	Physiog. zone	Evap. rate *(ft/acre)*	Depth *(ft)*	Cost per AF *($ 1964)*
0 – 20,000	0.05	B	3.00	33	$250
20,000 – 40,000	.05	E	3.67	45	144
40,000 – 60,000	.05	E	3.67	48	122
60,000 – 100,000	.05	E	3.67	50	106
100,000 – 200,000	.20	E	3.67	53	91
200,000 – 400,000	0.60	0.92E, 0.08I	3.91	55	72

Region: Central Pacific

Size class	Fraction of total add. req. stor.	Physiog. zone	Evap. rate *(ft/acre)*	Depth *(ft)*	Cost per AF *($ 1964)*
0 – 20,000					
20,000 – 40,000	0.01	B	1.50	35	$200
40,000 – 60,000	.02	B	1.50	40	181
60,000 – 100,000	.02	B	1.50	50	165
100,000 – 200,000	.05	B	1.50	65	144
200,000 – 400,000	.05	B	1.50	90	125
400,000 – 1,000,000	.10	B	1.50	105	106
1,000,000 – 2,000,000	.20	E	1.00	120	48
2,000,000 – 4,000,000	.25	E	1.00	135	40
4,000,000 – 10,000,000	0.30	E	1.00	150	31

Region: Pacific Northwest

Size class	Fraction of total add. req. stor.	Physiog. zone	Evap. rate *(ft/acre)*	Depth *(ft)*	Cost per AF *($ 1964)*
0 – 20,000	–	–	–	–	–
20,000 – 40,000	0.01	A	–	20	$238
40,000 – 60,000	.02	A	–	30	219
60,000 – 100,000	.02	A	–	40	202
100,000 – 200,000	.05	A	–	50	181
200,000 – 400,000	.05	B	–	60	125
400,000 – 1,000,000	.10	B	–	70	106
1,000,000 – 2,000,000	.25	0.4E, 0.2G, 0.4H	0.89	80	40
2,000,000 – 4,000,000	.35	0.14F, 0.29H, 0.57I	1.66	90	21
4,000,000 – 10,000,000	0.15	F	–	100	26

Table F-15. ADJUSTED MEAN ANNUAL FLOW AFTER ACCOUNTING FOR RESERVOIRS BUILT OR UNDER CONSTRUCTION: 1954-64

	Existing capacity 1964 (mil. af)	Usable capacity 1954 (mil. af)	Increase in capacity 1954–1964 (mil. af)	Annual mean net evaporation rate (% of capacity)	Additional evaporation at average rate (bgd)	Additional evaporation at maximum depth and minimum rate (bgd)	Adjusted mean annual flow (bgd)
NORTHEAST	50.8	25.9	24.9	2.80	0.622		428.0
N Eng	11.1	9.0	2.1	2.00	0.038		67.0
D & H	3.2	3.1	0.1	2.70	0.002		32.0
Ches	1.5	0.9	0.6	1.87	0.010		52.0
Ohio	15.9	5.7	10.2	1.57	0.143		110.0
EGL	1.7	0.5	1.2	3.89	0.042		40.0
WGL	1.3	1.2	0.1	5.50	0.005		42.0
U Miss	9.8	4.3	5.5	5.52	0.271		62.0
L Mo	6.3	1.2	5.1	2.45	0.112		23.0
SOUTHEAST	130.4	69.1	61.3	2.21	1.208		398.0
SE	54.4	16.4	38.0	1.55	0.526		212.0
Cumb	14.1	6.4	7.7	3.00	0.206		17.0
Tenn	15.8	15.0	0.8	0.24	0.002		43.0
L Miss	4.7	4.5	0.2	5.12	0.009		49.0
L AWR	41.4	26.8	14.6	3.57	0.465		77.0
MID-CONTINENT	160.6	93.3	67.3	7.24	4.348		85.2
U Mo	101.8	74.8	27.0	4.44	1.070	0.5	28.5
U AWR	16.8	7.3	9.5	11.70	0.992	0.6	12.4
W Gulf	42.0	11.2	30.8	8.31	2.285	1.7	44.3
SOUTHWEST	90.1	44.3	45.8	6.27	2.562		27.51
RG-P	7.8	3.3	4.5	9.16	0.368	0.24	3.31
Colo	74.6	35.1	39.5	5.86	2.067	1.4	12.1
G Basin	5.4	4.1	1.3	8.20	0.095		10.5
S Pac	2.3	1.8	0.5	7.17	0.032		1.6
NORTH PACIFIC	73.8	45.3	28.5	1.10	0.281		201.0
C Pac	25.6	16.4	9.2	1.11	0.091		58.0
PNW	48.2	28.9	19.3	1.10	0.190		143.0
U.S.	505.7	278.0	277.7	3.64	9.021		1,139.71

Note: Adjusted mean annual flow based on mean annual flows as determined by the U.S. Geological Survey in Committee Print No. 3, *National Water Resources and Problems*, Senate Select Committee on National Water Resources, 86th Cong., 2d sess. (1960).

Table F-16. MAXIMUM PHYSICAL DEVELOPMENT, BY REGION: 98%, 95%, AND 90% AVAILABILITY

	98% availability		95 % availability		90% availability		Gross mean annual flow (bgd)	Löf & Hardison[a] 98% availability	
	Total required storage (mil. af.)	Net flow (bgd)	Total required storage (mil. af.)	Net flow (bgd)	Total required storage (mil. af.)	Net flow (bgd)		Total required storage (mil. af.)	Net flow (bgd)
NORTHEAST	1,229.0	362.0	967.9	375.8	862.2	399.3	428		
N Eng	180.0	60.9	120.0	61.9	129.7	65.1	67	172	57
D & H	81.9	28.6	57.8	29.2	49.4	30.3	32	79	28
Ches	174.0	46.7	131.0	47.3	122.4	50.1	52	174	46
Ohio	495.0	99.5	307.0	101.6	260.7	107.2	110	394	98
EGL	83.8	33.3	60.3	34.1	59.9	36.1	40	107	33
WGL	70.4	30.3	90.3	33.5	76.0	36.3	42	113	32
U Miss	81.4	46.1	118.0	50.5	100.9	54.5	62	118	48
L Mo	63.3	16.2	83.5	17.7	63.2	19.7	23	111	18
SOUTHEAST	882.0	334.0	708.0	343.1	767.0	368.4	398		
SE	412.0	186.0	326.0	187.2	454.2	202.2	212	640	189
Cumb	37.5	14.6	26.0	15.0	22.9	15.9	17	57	14
Tenn	192.0	40.4	119.0	40.6	101.7	42.8	43	158	40
L Miss	82.9	35.2	110.0	41.6	65.9	41.0	49	143	37
L AWR	157.0	57.7	127.0	58.7	122.3	66.5	77	258	61
MID-CONTINENT	175.0	58.6	171.9	60.7	149.9	66.0	88		
U Mo	68.0[b]	25.6[c]	50.8[b]	25.6	34.5[b]	25.6[c]	29	68	23
U AWR	18.5	7.1	23.4	8.4	17.7[b]	9.1	13	31	6
W Gulf	88.4	25.9	97.7	26.7	97.7	31.3	46	139	23
SOUTHWEST	50.9	22.1	44.2	23.12	40.66	24.16	29.15		
RG-P	6.4[b]	2.96[c]	4.8[b]	2.96[c]	3.36[b]	2.96[c]	3.55	6.4	2.6
Colo	28.7[b]	11.4[c]	21.1[b]	11.4[c]	18.3[b]	11.4[c]	13.5	28.7	11.0
G Basin	11.3	6.9	13.5	7.8	14.3	8.7	10.5	22.2	7.4
S Pac	4.5	0.8	4.8	0.96	4.7	1.1	1.6	5.9	0.7
NORTH PACIFIC	586.0	180.0	568.9	190.9	425.0	195.0	201		
C Pac	122.0	45.5	208.7	51.1	164.0	53.8	58	298	51
PNW	464.0	134.6	360.2	139.8	266.0	141.2	143	464	133
U.S.	2,923.0	956.2	2,460.9	993.7	2,244.8	1,052.9	1,144	3,586	959

Note: Discrepancies in totals due to rounding.

[a]George O. G. Löf and Clayton H. Hardison, "Storage Requirements for Water in the United States," *Water Resources Research*, vol. 2, no. 3 (Third Quarter 1966), pp. 323–54.

[b]Löf and Hardison, table 11, p. 348. Existing storage equals or exceeds amounts shown.

[c]Maximum attainable gross flow as given in Löf and Hardison, table 7, less evaporation from reservoirs built 1954–64.

Table F-17. SYNTHETIC SCHEDULES OF FLOW, STORAGE, AND COSTS, BY REGION: 98% AVAILABILITY, 0.0425 ANNUAL FACTOR

Size class (1,000 af)	Per-cent	Cumulative storage (1,000 af)	Existing & cumulative storage (1,000 af)	Net flow (mgd)	Unit cost ($/af)	Capital cumulative cost ($ mil.)	Annual cumulative cost ($ mil.)	Annual average cost ($/net mgd)	Marginal cost ($/net mgd)	($/1,000 gal.)
New England — Storage (mil. af): total (1964), 11.1; flood (1964), 3.5; maximum, 180; maximum minus total, 168.9; existing,[a] available for flow regulation, 7.8, which yields a 22.4 bgd net flow.										
10,000 +										
4,000 – 10,000	10	16,890	25,034	36,818	18	304	12.9	351	899	0.0025
2,000 – 4,000	10	33,780	42,253	47,324	22	676	28.7	607	1,503	0.0041
1,000 – 2,000	15	59,115	68,080	55,929	30	1,436	61.0	1,091	3,754	0.010
400 – 1,000	15	84,450	93,908	59,388	60	2,956	125.6	2,115	18,680	0.051
200 – 400	10	101,340	111,126	59,729	81	4,324	183.8	3,077	170,478	0.467
100 – 200	10	118,230	128,345	60,107	144	6,756	287.1	4,777	273,290	0.749
60 – 100	10	135,120	145,563	60,449	165	9,543	405.6	6,709	345,998	0.948
40 – 60	10	152,010	162,781	60,741	181	12,600	535.5	8,816	444,905	1.219
20 – 40	5	160,455	171,391	60,850	200	14,289	607.3	9,980	662,758	1.815
0 – 20	5	168,900	180,000	60,895	250	16,400	697.0	11,446	1,974,417	5.409
Delaware–Hudson — Storage (mil. af): total (1964), 3.2; flood (1964), 1.6; maximum, 81.9; maximum minus total, 78.7; existing,[a] available for flow regulation, 1.7, which yields a 7.5 bgd net flow.										
10,000 +										
4,000 – 10,000										
2,000 – 4,000										
1,000 – 2,000										
400 – 1,000	40	31,480	33,757	26,314	106	3,337	142	5,389	7,537	0.020
200 – 400	15	43,285	45,793	27,788	125	4,813	205	7,360	42,545	0.117
100 – 200	10	51,155	53,817	28,166	112	5,694	242	8,592	99,163	0.272
60 – 100	10	59,025	61,841	28,350	100	6,481	275	9,716	182,277	0.499
40 – 60	10	66,895	69,864	28,501	112	7,363	313	10,978	246,944	0.677
20 – 40	10	74,765	77,888	28,609	132	8,401	357	12,481	411,930	1.129
0 – 20	5	78,700	81,900	28,629	181	9,113	387	13,529	1,498,570	4.106
Chesapeake — Storage (mil. af): total (1964), 1.5; flood (1964), 0.7; maximum, 174.0; maximum minus total, 172.5; existing,[a] available for flow regulation, 0.8, which yields a 3.4 bgd net flow.										
10,000 +										
4,000 – 10,000										
2,000 – 4,000	10	17,250	18,125	26,825	22	379	16.1	601	689	0.0019
1,000 – 2,000	10	34,500	35,445	35,066	30	897	38.1	1,087	2,669	0.0073
400 – 1,000	20	69,000	70,084	42,271	38	2,208	93.8	2,220	7,734	0.021
200 – 400	20	103,500	104,722	45,331	111	6,037	256.6	5,660	53,189	0.146
100 – 200	15	129,375	130,701	45,882	144	9,763	414.9	9,044	287,055	0.786
60 – 100	10	146,625	148,021	46,250	165	12,610	535.9	11,587	328,916	0.901
40 – 60	5	155,250	156,680	46,416	181	14,171	602.3	12,975	400,797	1.098
20 – 40	5	163,875	165,340	46,556	200	15,896	675.6	14,511	524,158	1.436
0 – 20	5	172,500	174,000	46,657	250	18,052	767.2	16,444	904,255	2.477
Ohio — Storage (mil. af): total (1964), 15.9; flood (1964), 11.3; maximum, 495.0; maximum minus total, 479.1; existing,[a] available for flow regulation, 5.0, which yields a 20.0 bgd net flow.										
10,000 +										
4,000 – 10,000										
2,000 – 4,000	10	47,910	53,967	59,532	35	1,677	71.3	1,197	1,439	0.0039
1,000 – 2,000	10	95,820	102,970	79,263	42	3,689	156.8	1,978	4,334	0.012
400 – 1,000	25	215,595	225,479	95,829	54	10,157	431.6	4,505	16,593	0.045
200 – 400	25	335,369	347,988	96,642	54	16,625	706.6	7,311	338,344	0.927
100 – 200	10	383,279	396,991	97,295	102	21,512	914.2	9,397	318,024	0.871
60 – 100	10	431,189	445,995	98,376	165	29,417	1,250.2	12,709	310,794	0.851
40 – 60	5	445,144	470,497	98,916	181	33,753	1,434.5	14,502	340,971	0.934
20 – 40	3	469,517	485,198	99,241	200	36,627	1,556.7	15,686	376,706	1.032
0 – 20	2	479,099	494,999	99,457	250	39,023	1,658.5	16,675	470,926	1.290

Table F-17. — Continued

Size class (1,000 af)	Per-cent	Cumulative storage (1,000 af)	Existing & cumulative storage (1,000 af)	Net flow (mgd)	Unit cost ($/af)	Capital cumulative cost ($ mil.)	Annual cumulative cost ($ mil.)	Annual average cost ($/net mgd)	Marginal cost ($/net mgd)	($/1,000 gal.)

Eastern Great Lakes — Storage (mil. af): total (1964), 1.7; flood (1964), 0.6; maximum, 83.8; maximum minus total, 82.1; existing,[a] available for flow regulation, 1.1, which yields a 3.5 bgd net flow.

Size class (1,000 af)	Per-cent	Cumulative storage (1,000 af)	Existing & cumulative storage (1,000 af)	Net flow (mgd)	Unit cost ($/af)	Capital cumulative cost ($ mil.)	Annual cumulative cost ($ mil.)	Annual average cost ($/net mgd)	Marginal cost ($/net mgd)	($/1,000 gal.)
10,000 +										
4,000 – 10,000										
2,000 – 4,000										
1,000 – 2,000										
400 – 1,000	15	12,315	13,515	19,174	38	468	19.9	1,037	1,268	0.0035
200 – 400	20	28,735	30,053	26,398	50	1,289	54.8	2,075	4,830	.013
100 – 200	20	45,155	46,590	30,804	62	2,307	98.0	3,183	9,820	.027
60 – 100	20	61,575	63,128	32,092	85	3,703	157.4	4,904	46,049	.126
40 – 60	15	73,890	75,531	32,894	158	5,648	240.1	7,298	103,114	.283
20 – 40	5	77,995	79,666	33,137	200	6,469	275.0	8,297	143,659	.394
0 – 20	5	82,100	83,800	33,278	250	7,496	318.6	9,573	308,356	0.845

Western Great Lakes — Storage (mil. af): total (1964), 1.3; flood (1964), 0; maximum, 70.4; maximum minus total, 69.1; existing,[a] available for flow regulation, 1.3, which yields an 8.8 bgd net flow.

Size class (1,000 af)	Per-cent	Cumulative storage (1,000 af)	Existing & cumulative storage (1,000 af)	Net flow (mgd)	Unit cost ($/af)	Capital cumulative cost ($ mil.)	Annual cumulative cost ($ mil.)	Annual average cost ($/net mgd)	Marginal cost ($/net mgd)	($/1,000 gal.)
10,000 +										
4,000 – 10,000										
2,000 – 4,000										
1,000 – 2,000										
400 – 1,000	25	17,275	18,575	19,908	28	484	20.6	1,033	1,851	0.0051
200 – 400	25	34,550	35,850	25,374	38	1,140	48.5	1,910	5,105	.014
100 – 200	15	44,915	46,215	27,657	48	1,638	69.6	2,517	9,261	.025
60 – 100	10	51,825	53,125	28,473	78	2,177	92.5	3,249	28,062	.077
40 – 60	10	58,735	60,035	29,290	91	2,805	119.2	4,071	32,738	.090
20 – 40	10	65,645	66,945	29,952	108	3,552	150.9	5,040	47,910	.131
0 – 20	5	69,100	70,400	30,283	154	4,084	173.6	5,731	68,316	0.187

Upper Mississippi — Storage (mil. af): total (1964), 9.8; flood (1964), 4.8; maximum, 81.4; maximum minus total, 71.6; existing,[a] available for flow regulation, 5.6, which yields a 15.5 bgd net flow.

Size class (1,000 af)	Per-cent	Cumulative storage (1,000 af)	Existing & cumulative storage (1,000 af)	Net flow (mgd)	Unit cost ($/af)	Capital cumulative cost ($ mil.)	Annual cumulative cost ($ mil.)	Annual average cost ($/net mgd)	Marginal cost ($/net mgd)	($/1,000 gal.)
10,000 +										
4,000 – 10,000	10	7,160	13,160	21,293	12	86	3.7	171	634	0.0016
2,000 – 4,000	10	14,320	20,742	25,976	19	222	9.4	363	1,235	.0033
1,000 – 2,000	10	21,480	28,324	30,609	26	408	17.3	567	1,708	.0047
400 – 1,000	20	35,800	43,489	36,265	38	952	40.5	1,116	4,089	.0112
200 – 400	15	46,540	54,862	40,175	50	1,489	63.3	1,575	5,837	.016
100 – 200	15	57,280	66,236	42,995	62	2,155	91.6	2,130	10,034	.027
60 – 100	5	60,860	70,027	43,791	78	2,434	103.5	2,363	14,916	.041
40 – 60	5	64,440	73,818	44,587	91	2,760	117.3	2,631	17,402	.048
20 – 40	5	68,020	77,609	45,435	169	3,365	143.0	3,148	30,290	.083
0 – 20	5	71,600	81,400	46,125	221	4,156	176.6	3,830	48,800	0.134

Lower Missouri — Storage (mil. af): total (1964), 6.3; flood (1964), 1.2; maximum, 63.3; maximum minus total, 57.0; existing,[a] available for flow regulation, 5.2, which yields a 5.4 bgd net flow.

Size class (1,000 af)	Per-cent	Cumulative storage (1,000 af)	Existing & cumulative storage (1,000 af)	Net flow (mgd)	Unit cost ($/af)	Capital cumulative cost ($ mil.)	Annual cumulative cost ($ mil.)	Annual average cost ($/net mgd)	Marginal cost ($/net mgd)	($/1,000 gal.)
10,000 +										
4,000 – 10,000	10	5,700	11,027	8,799	18	103	4.4	496	1,293	0.0035
2,000 – 4,000	10	11,400	16,836	10,878	22	228	9.7	891	2,564	.0070
1,000 – 2,000	10	17,100	22,644	12,395	30	399	17.0	1,368	4,792	.013
400 – 1,000	10	22,800	28,452	13,683	38	616	26.2	1,912	7,144	.020
200 – 400	10	28,500	34,260	14,696	50	901	38.3	2,605	11,963	.033
100 – 200	5	31,350	37,164	15,185	62	1,077	45.8	3,015	15,349	.042
60 – 100	3	33,060	38,906	15,384	78	1,211	51.5	3,345	28,448	.078
40 – 60	2	34,200	40,068	15,440	91	1,314	55.9	3,618	79,390	.218
20 – 40	40	57,000	63,300	16,211	108	3,777	160.5	9,902	135,689	0.372
0 – 20										

Table F-17. — Continued

Size class (1,000 af)	Per-cent	Cumulative storage (1,000 af)	Existing & cumulative storage (1,000 af)	Net flow (mgd)	Unit cost ($/af)	Capital cumulative cost ($ mil.)	Annual cumulative cost ($ mil.)	Annual average cost ($/net mgd)	Marginal cost ($/net mgd)	Marginal cost ($/1,000 gal.)
Southeast — Storage (mil. af): total (1964), 54.4; flood (1964), 11.2; maximum, 412.0; maximum minus total, 357.6; existing,[a] available for flow regulation, 45.0, which yields a 95.0 bgd net flow.
10,000 +										
4,000 – 10,000	5	17,880	63,045	110,523	18	322	13.7	124	884	0.0024
2,000 – 4,000	10	53,640	99,777	129,839	22	1,109	47.1	363	1,731	.0047
1,000 – 2,000	30	160,920	209,973	166,945	30	4,327	183.9	1,102	3,686	.010
400 – 1,000	30	268,200	320,169	177,905	38	8,404	357.2	2,008	15,808	.043
200 – 400	15	321,840	375,268	183,023	50	11,086	471.1	2,574	22,270	.061
100 – 200	5	339,720	393,634	184,689	62	12,194	518.3	2,806	28,284	.077
60 – 100	3	350,448	404,653	185,538	116	13,439	571.1	3,078	62,268	.171
40 – 60	1	354,023	408,326	185,800	131	13,907	591.0	3,181	76,044	.208
20 – 40	1	357,599	411,999	186,030	150	14,443	613.8	3,300	99,170	0.272
0 – 20										
Cumberland — Storage (mil. af): total (1964), 14.1; flood (1964), 4.9; maximum 37.5; maximum minus total, 23.4; existing,[a] available for flow regulation, 11.0, which yields an 11.2 bgd net flow.
10,000 +										
4,000 – 10,000	30	7,020	18,980	13,427	22	154	6.6	489	2,913	0.0080
2,000 – 4,000	20	11,700	24,271	13,953	29	290	12.3	884	10,973	.030
1,000 – 2,000	15	15,210	28,240	14,247	34	409	17.4	1,222	17,230	.047
400 – 1,000	15	18,720	32,208	14,463	41	553	23.5	1,626	28,316	.078
200 – 400	10	21,060	34,854	14,607	60	694	29.5	2,019	41,439	.114
100 – 200	5	22,230	36,177	14,627	81	789	33.5	2,291	203,974	.559
60 – 100	5	23,400	37,500	14,647	100	906	38.5	2,628	251,722	0.690
40 – 60										
20 – 40										
0 – 20										
Tennessee — Storage (mil. af): total (1964), 22.0; flood (1964), 5.6; maximum, 192.0; maximum minus total, 170.6; existing,[a] available for flow regulation, 16.4, which yields a 24.0 bgd net flow.
10,000 +										
4,000 – 10,000	10	17,060	33,982	30,858	26	444	18.9	611	2,731	0.0074
2,000 – 4,000	10	34,110	51,539	34,794	35	1,041	44.2	1,271	6,447	0.018
1,000 – 2,000	20	68,240	86,654	38,427	42	2,477	105.1	2,736	16,765	0.046
400 – 1,000	20	102,360	121,770	39,128	54	4,316	183.4	4,688	111,686	0.306
200 – 400	15	127,950	148,106	39,561	69	6,082	258.5	6,534	173,462	0.475
100 – 200	10	145,010	165,664	39,884	90	7,617	323.7	8,117	202,214	0.554
60 – 100	5	153,540	174,443	40,060	116	8,607	365.8	9,131	238,149	0.652
40 – 60	5	162,070	183,221	40,237	131	9,724	413.3	10,271	268,939	0.737
20 – 40	3	167,188	188,488	40,343	150	10,492	445.9	11,053	307,951	0.844
0 – 20	2	170,600	192,000	40,413	200	11,174	474.9	11,751	410,576	1.125
Lower Mississippi — Storage (mil. af): total (1964), 4.7; flood (1964), 4.4; maximum, 82.9; maximum minus total, 78.2; existing,[a] available for flow regulation, 0.5, which yields a 1.5 bgd net flow
10,000 +										
4,000 – 10,000										
2,000 – 4,000	20	15,640	17,020	15,566	12	188	8.0	512	566	0.0016
1,000 – 2,000	40	46,920	49,960	29,648	15	657	27.9	942	1,416	.0039
400 – 1,000	15	58,650	62,312	33,030	19	880	37.3	1,132	2,801	.0077
200 – 400	15	70,380	74,665	34,633	25	1,173	49.9	1,439	7,777	.021
100 – 200	5	74,290	78,782	34,978	62	1,415	60.2	1,720	29,813	.082
60 – 100	5	78,200	82,900	35,207	78	1,720	73.1	2,077	56,702	0.155
40 – 60										
20 – 40										
0 – 20										

Table F-17. – Continued

Size class (1,000 af)	Per-cent	Cumulative storage (1,000 af)	Existing & cumulative storage (1,000 af)	Net flow (mgd)	Unit cost ($/af)	Capital cumulative cost ($ mil.)	Annual cumulative cost ($ mil.)	Annual average cost ($/net mgd)	Marginal cost	
									($/net mgd)	($/1,000 gal.)
Lower Arkansas–White–Red – Storage (mil. af): total (1964), 41.4; flood (1964), 14.2; maximum, 157.0; maximum minus total, 115.6; existing,[a] available for flow regulation, 30.9, which yields a 23.9 bgd net flow.										
10,000 +										
4,000 – 10,000	5	5,780	37,247	26,844	18	104	4.4	165	1,523	0.0042
2,000 – 4,000	25	34,680	68,761	40,290	22	740	31.4	780	2,010	.0055
1,000 – 2,000	25	63,580	100,275	48,984	30	1,607	68.3	1,394	4,238	.0116
400 – 1,000	20	86,700	125,486	53,762	38	2,485	105.6	1,965	7,815	.021
200 – 400	10	98,260	138,092	55,538	38	2,925	124.3	2,238	10,513	.029
100 – 200	5	104,040	144,394	56,467	31	3,104	131.9	2,336	8,180	.022
60 – 100	3	107,508	148,176	56,904	106	3,471	147.5	2,593	35,911	.098
40 – 60	3	110,976	151,958	57,282	122	3,895	165.5	2,890	47,523	.130
20 – 40	2	113,288	154,479	57,471	144	4,227	179.7	3,126	74,761	.205
0 – 20	2	115,600	157,000	57,661	194	4,676	198.7	3,447	100,713	0.276
Upper Arkansas–White–Red – Storage (mil. af): total (1964), 16.8; flood (1964), 6.4; maximum, 18.5; maximum minus total, 1.7; existing,[a] available for flow regulation, 16.2, which yields a 6.7 bgd net flow.										
10,000 +										
4,000 – 10,000	30	510	16,898	6,818	18	9.2	0.39	57	3,423	0.0094
2,000 – 4,000	10	680	17,127	6,856	22	12.9	0.55	80	4,184	.011
1,000 – 2,000	10	850	17,356	6,894	30	18.0	0.77	111	5,705	.016
400 – 1,000	15	1,105	17,699	6,948	38	27.7	1.18	169	7,613	.021
200 – 400	15	1,360	18,042	6,998	50	40.5	1.72	246	10,829	.030
100 – 200	10	1,530	18,271	7,029	69	52.2	2.22	316	16,151	.044
60 – 100	5	1,615	18,386	7,043	138	63.9	2.72	386	36,537	.100
40 – 60	4	1,683	18,477	7,052	150	74.1	3.15	447	49,899	.137
20 – 40	1	1,700	18,500	7,053	169	77.0	3.27	464	98,606	0.270
0 – 20										
Western Gulf – Storage (mil. af): total (1964), 42.0; flood (1964), 11.3; maximum, 88.4; maximum minus total, 46.4; existing,[a] available for flow regulation, 36.1, which yields a 15.4 bgd net flow.										
10,000 +										
4,000 – 10,000	15	6,960	43,918	17,601	18	125	5.3	303	2,944	0.0080
2,000 – 4,000	15	13,920	51,768	19,452	22	278	11.8	608	4,421	.012
1,000 – 2,000	25	25,520	64,851	22,139	30	626	26.6	1,202	7,493	.021
400 – 1,000	25	37,120	77,934	24,228	38	1,067	45.4	1,872	14,687	.040
200 – 400	10	41,760	83,167	25,064	50	1,299	55.2	2,203	21,625	.059
100 – 200	5	44,080	85,783	25,482	62	1,443	61.3	2,407	32,177	.088
60 – 100	3	45,472	87,353	25,733	78	1,552	65.9	2,563	57,825	.158
40 – 60	2	46,400	88,400	25,900	91	1,636	69.5	2,685	67,454	0.185
20 – 40										
0 – 20										
Great Basin – Storage (mil. af): total (1964), 5.4; flood (1964), 0; maximum, 11.3; maximum minus total, 5.9; existing,[a] available for flow regulation, 5.4, which yields a 5.4 bgd net flow.										
10,000 +										
4,000 – 10,000										
2,000 – 4,000										
1,000 – 2,000	30	1,770	7,170	5,981	22	39	1.7	277	2,734	0.0075
400 – 1,000	15	2,655	8,055	6,242	28	64	2.7	434	4,043	.011
200 – 400	15	3,540	8,940	6,450	38	97	4.1	641	6,866	.019
100 – 200	15	4,425	9,825	6,649	48	140	5.9	894	9,041	.025
60 – 100	10	5,015	10,415	6,775	82	188	8.0	1,181	16,370	.045
40 – 60	10	5,605	11,005	6,890	122	260	11.1	1,605	26,587	.073
20 – 40	3	5,782	11,182	6,920	144	286	12.1	1,755	36,383	.100
0 – 20	2	5,900	11,300	6,934	194	309	13.1	1,891	66,719	0.183

Table F-17. — Continued

Size class (1,000 af)	Per-cent	Cumulative storage (1,000 af)	Existing & cumulative storage (1,000 af)	Net flow (mgd)	Unit cost ($/af)	Capital cumulative cost ($ mil.)	Annual cumulative cost ($ mil.)	Annual average cost ($/net mgd)	Marginal cost	
									($/net mgd)	($/1,000 gal.)

South Pacific — Storage (mil. af): total (1964), 2.3; flood (1964), 0.3; maximum, 4.54; maximum minus total, 2.24; existing,[a] available for flow regulation, 2.2, which yields a 0.7 bgd net flow.

Size class (1,000 af)	Per-cent	Cumulative storage (1,000 af)	Existing & cumulative storage (1,000 af)	Net flow (mgd)	Unit cost ($/af)	Capital cumulative cost ($ mil.)	Annual cumulative cost ($ mil.)	Annual average cost ($/net mgd)	Marginal cost ($/net mgd)	($/1,000 gal.)
10,000 +										
4,000 – 10,000										
2,000 – 4,000										
1,000 – 2,000										
400 – 1,000										
200 – 400	60	1,344	3,585	782	72	97	4.1	5,259	46,010	0.126
100 – 200	20	1,792	4,062	801	91	138	5.8	7,301	93,124	0.255
60 – 100	5	1,904	4,182	805	106	149	6.3	7,889	119,117	0.326
40 – 60	5	2,016	4,301	809	122	163	6.9	8,569	147,778	0.405
20 – 40	5	2,128	4,421	812	144	179	7.6	9,377	200,425	0.549
0 – 20	5	2,240	4,540	815	250	207	8.8	10,809	478,946	1.312

Central Pacific — Storage (mil. af): total (1964), 25.6; flood (1964), 2.5; maximum, 122.0; maximum minus total, 96.4; existing,[a] available for flow regulation, 23.6, which yields a 25.9 bgd net flow.

Size class (1,000 af)	Per-cent	Cumulative storage (1,000 af)	Existing & cumulative storage (1,000 af)	Net flow (mgd)	Unit cost ($/af)	Capital cumulative cost ($ mil.)	Annual cumulative cost ($ mil.)	Annual average cost ($/net mgd)	Marginal cost ($/net mgd)	($/1,000 gal.)
10,000 +										
4,000 – 10,000	30	28,920	53,137	37,060	31	897	38.1	1,028	3,412	0.009
2,000 – 4,000	25	53,020	77,731	41,314	40	1,861	79.1	1,914	9,633	.026
1,000 – 2,000	20	72,300	97,406	43,283	48	2,786	118.4	2,736	19,968	.055
400 – 1,000	10	81,940	107,244	44,217	106	3,808	161.8	3,660	46,516	.127
200 – 400	5	86,760	112,162	44,673	125	4,410	187.4	4,196	56,085	.154
100 – 200	5	91,580	117,081	45,102	144	5,104	216.9	4,810	68,766	.188
60 – 100	2	93,508	119,049	45,262	165	5,422	230.5	5,092	84,677	.232
40 – 60	2	95,436	121,016	45,409	181	5,771	245.3	5,402	101,064	.277
20 – 40	1	96,400	122,000	45,478	200	5,964	253.5	5,574	119,178	0.327
0 – 20										

Pacific Northwest — Storage (mil. af): total (1964), 48.2; flood (1964), 16.6; maximum, 464.0; maximum minus total, 415.8; existing,[a] available for flow regulation, 33.3, which yields a 62.8 bgd net flow.

Size class (1,000 af)	Per-cent	Cumulative storage (1,000 af)	Existing & cumulative storage (1,000 af)	Net flow (mgd)	Unit cost ($/af)	Capital cumulative cost ($ mil.)	Annual cumulative cost ($ mil.)	Annual average cost ($/net mgd)	Marginal cost ($/net mgd)	($/1,000 gal.)
10,000 +										
4,000 – 10,000	15	62,370	97,926	107,319	26	1,622	69.0	642	1,548	0.0042
2,000 – 4,000	35	207,900	248,662	129,126	21	4,678	199.0	1,540	5,956	0.016
1,000 – 2,000	25	311,850	356,330	131,939	40	8,836	376.0	2,846	62,833	0.172
400 – 1,000	10	353,430	399,398	133,134	106	13,243	563.0	4,228	156,694	0.429
200 – 400	5	374,219	420,931	133,613	125	15,842	673.0	5,039	230,818	0.632
100 – 200	5	395,001	442,465	134,091	181	19,605	833.0	6,214	334,182	0.916
60 – 100	2	403,325	451,078	134,283	202	21,285	905.0	6,737	373,052	1.022
40 – 60	2	411,641	459,692	134,474	219	23,106	982.0	7,303	404,314	1.108
20 – 40	1	415,799	463,998	134,570	238	24,096	1,024.0	7,610	439,537	1.204
0 – 20										

Note: The Upper Missouri, Rio Grande–Pecos, and Colorado regions do not appear in the table because as of 1964 they did not require new storage for flow regulation.

[a]Existing = total 1964 storage minus prorated flood storage.

Table F-18. SYNTHETIC SCHEDULES OF FLOW, STORAGE, AND COSTS, BY REGION: 90% AVAILABILITY, 0.0425 ANNUAL FACTOR

Size class (1,000 af)	Per-cent	Cumulative storage (1,000 af)	Existing & cumulative storage (1,000 af)	Net flow (mgd)	Unit cost ($/af)	Capital cumulative cost ($ mil.)	Annual cumulative cost ($ mil.)	Annual average cost ($/net mgd)	Marginal cost ($/net mgd)	($/1,000 gal.)
New England — Storage (mil. af): total (1964), 11.1; flood (1964), 3.5; maximum, 129.7; maximum minus total, 118.6; existing,[a] available for flow regulation, 7.9, which yields a 22.6 bgd net flow.										
10,000 +										
4,000 – 10,000	10	11,864	20,083	34,475	18	214	9.1	263	761.4	0.0021
2,000 – 4,000	10	23,728	32,268	44,174	22	475	20.2	457	1,143.7	0.0031
1,000 – 2,000	15	41,524	50,544	55,423	30	1,008	42.9	773	2,017.1	0.0055
400 – 1,000	15	59,320	68,820	61,134	60	2,076	88.2	1,443	7,945.1	0.022
200 – 400	10	71,184	81,004	63,237	81	3,037	129.1	2,041	19,421.7	0.053
100 – 200	10	83,048	93,188	64,394	144	4,746	201.7	3,132	62,764.7	0.172
60 – 100	10	94,912	105,372	64,713	165	6,703	284.9	4,402	260,837.8	0.715
40 – 60	10	106,776	117,556	64,955	181	8,851	376.1	5,791	377,007.3	1.03
20 – 40	5	112,708	123,648	65,050	200	10,037	426.6	6,558	533,299.1	1.46
0 – 20	5	118,640	129,740	65,100	250	11,520	489.6	7,521	1,250,680.0	3.43
Delaware–Hudson — Storage (mil. af): total (1964), 3.2; flood (1964), 1.6; maximum, 49.4; maximum minus total, 46.2; existing,[a] available for flow regulation, 1.7, which yields a 7.1 bgd net flow.										
10,000 +										
4,000 – 10,000										
2,000 – 4,000										
1,000 – 2,000										
400 – 1,000	40	18,496	20,798	25,807	106	1,961	83.3	3,229	4,454	0.012
200 – 400	15	25,432	27,959	28,773	125	2,828	120.2	4,176	12,422	.034
100 – 200	10	30,056	32,732	29,401	112	3,345	142.2	4,836	35,051	.096
60 – 100	10	34,680	37,506	29,870	100	3,809	161.8	5,418	41,975	.115
40 – 60	10	39,304	42,279	30,073	112	4,326	183.8	6,113	108,171	.296
20 – 40	10	43,928	47,053	30,250	132	4,936	209.8	6,935	146,292	.401
0 – 20	5	46,240	49,440	30,319	181	5,355	227.6	7,506	257,591	0.706
Chesapeake — Storage (mil. af): total (1964), 1.5; flood (1964), 0.7; maximum, 122.4; maximum minus total, 120.9; existing,[a] available for flow regulation, 8.1, which yields a 34.4 bgd net flow.										
10,000 +										
4,000 – 10,000										
2,000 – 4,000	10	12,090	12,968	25,741	22	266	11.3	439	507.0	0.0014
1,000 – 2,000	10	24,180	25,127	34,540	30	627	26.7	774	1,751.8	0.0048
400 – 1,000	20	48,360	49,445	42,691	38	1,548	65.8	1,541	4,971.0	0.014
200 – 400	20	72,540	73,763	47,677	111	4,231	179.8	3,772	22,878.2	0.063
100 – 200	15	90,675	92,002	49,003	144	6,843	290.8	5,935	83,668.6	0.229
60 – 100	10	102,765	104,161	49,579	165	8,838	375.6	7,576	147,158.4	0.403
40 – 60	5	108,810	110,241	49,766	181	9,932	422.1	8,482	248,715.8	0.681
20 – 40	5	114,855	116,320	49,935	200	11,141	473.5	9,482	304,093.3	0.833
0 – 20	5	120,900	122,400	50,077	250	12,652	537.7	10,738	452,397.6	1.24
Ohio — Storage (mil. af): total (1964), 15.9; flood (1964), 11.3; maximum, 260.7; maximum minus total, 244.8; existing,[a] available for flow regulation, 5.3, which yields a 10.6 bgd net flow.										
10,000 +										
4,000 – 10,000										
2,000 – 4,000	10	24,476	30,826	49,642	35	857	36.4	733	931.9	0.0026
1,000 – 2,000	10	48,952	56,363	72,867	42	1,885	80.1	1,099	1,881.0	.0052
400 – 1,000	25	110,142	120,206	98,351	54	5,189	220.5	2,242	5,511.0	.015
200 – 400	25	171,332	184,049	104,624	54	8,493	361.0	3,450	22,385.5	.061
100 – 200	10	195,808	209,586	105,565	102	10,990	467.1	4,424	112,703.4	.309
60 – 100	10	220,284	235,123	106,367	165	15,028	638.7	6,005	214,195.8	.587
40 – 60	5	232,522	247,891	106,767	181	17,243	732.8	6,864	234,947.8	.644
20 – 40	3	239,865	255,552	107,008	200	18,712	795.3	7,432	259,651.9	.711
0 – 20	2	244,760	260,660	107,168	250	19,936	847.3	7,906	324,564.8	0.889

Table F-18. – Continued

Size class (1,000 af)	Per-cent	Cumulative storage (1,000 af)	Existing & cumulative storage (1,000 af)	Net flow (mgd)	Unit cost ($/af)	Capital cumulative cost ($ mil.)	Annual cumulative cost ($ mil.)	Annual average cost ($/net mgd)	Marginal cost ($/net mgd)	Marginal cost ($/1,000 gal.)
Eastern Great Lakes – Storage (mil. af): total (1964), 1.7, flood (1964), 0.6; maximum, 59.9; maximum minus total, 58.2; existing,[a] available for flow regulation, 1.1, which yields a 3.5 bgd net flow.										
10,000 +										
4,000 – 10,000										
2,000 – 4,000										
1,000 – 2,000										
400 – 1,000	15	8,734	9,939	17,636	38	332	14.1	800	998	0.0027
200 – 400	20	20,380	21,702	27,053	50	914	38.9	1,436	2,628	.0072
100 – 200	20	32,026	33,464	31,360	62	1,636	69.5	2,218	7,125	.020
60 – 100	20	43,672	45,227	34,577	85	2,626	111.6	3,228	13,079	.036
40 – 60	15	52,407	54,049	35,586	158	4,006	170.3	4,785	58,135	.159
20 – 40	5	55,318	56,989	35,864	200	4,589	195.0	5,438	89,018	.244
0 – 20	5	58,230	59,930	36,070	250	5,316	225.9	6,264	150,119	0.411
Western Great Lakes – Storage (mil. af): total (1964), 1.3; flood (1964), 0; maximum, 76.0; maximum minus total, 74.7; existing,[a] available for flow regulation, 1.3, which yields 12.6 bgd net flow.										
10,000 +										
4,000 – 10,000										
2,000 – 4,000										
1,000 – 2,000										
400 – 1,000	25	18,667	19,967	27,597	28	523	22.2	805	1,486	0.0041
200 – 400	25	37,335	38,635	32,355	38	1,232	52.4	1,618	6,337	.017
100 – 200	15	48,535	49,835	34,249	48	1,770	75.2	2,196	12,065	.033
60 – 100	10	56,002	57,302	35,405	78	2,352	100.0	2,823	21,405	.059
40 – 60	10	63,469	64,769	35,869	91	3,032	128.8	3,592	62,220	.170
20 – 40	10	70,936	72,236	36,167	108	3,838	163.1	4,510	115,240	.316
0 – 20	5	74,670	75,970	36,315	154	4,413	187.6	5,165	164,325	0.450
Upper Mississippi – Storage (mil. af): total (1964), 9.8; flood (1964), 4.8; maximum, 100.9; maximum minus total, 91.1; existing,[a] available for flow regulation, 5.5, which yields a 19.1 bgd net flow.										
10,000 +										
4,000 – 10,000	10	9,113	15,012	31,582	12	109	4.6	147	372	0.0010
2,000 – 4,000	10	18,226	24,559	38,233	19	283	12.0	314	1,106	0.0030
1,000 – 2,000	10	27,339	34,105	42,187	26	519	22.1	523	2,547	0.0070
400 – 1,000	20	45,565	53,198	48,643	38	1,212	51.5	1,059	4,559	0.012
200 – 400	15	59,234	67,518	51,976	50	1,896	80.6	1,550	8,716	0.024
100 – 200	15	72,904	81,837	53,567	62	2,743	116.6	2,176	22,645	0.062
60 – 100	5	77,460	86,610	53,811	78	3,098	131.7	2,447	61,793	0.169
40 – 60	5	82,017	91,384	54,056	91	3,513	149.3	2,762	72,092	0.198
20 – 40	5	86,573	96,157	54,368	169	4,283	182.0	3,348	104,805	0.287
0 – 20	5	91,130	100,930	54,477	221	5,290	224.8	4,127	393,378	1.078
Lower Missouri – Storage (mil. af): total (1964), 6.3; flood (1964), 1.2; maximum, 63.2; maximum minus total, 56.9; existing,[a] available for flow regulation, 5.2 which yields a 5.9 bgd net flow.										
10,000 +										
4,000 – 10,000	10	5,686	11,014	11,453	18	102	4.3	380	788	0.0022
2,000 – 4,000	10	11,372	16,808	13,887	22	227	9.7	696	2,185	.0060
1,000 – 2,000	10	17,058	22,602	15,947	30	398	16.9	1,061	3,519	.0096
400 – 1,000	10	22,744	28,396	17,256	38	614	26.1	1,512	7,015	.019
200 – 400	10	28,430	34,190	18,265	50	898	38.2	2,090	11,977	.033
100 – 200	5	31,273	37,087	18,625	62	1,075	45.7	2,452	20,780	.057
60 – 100	3	32,979	38,825	18,826	78	1,208	51.3	2,726	28,124	.077
40 – 60	2	34,116	39,984	18,960	91	1,311	55.7	2,939	32,810	.090
20 – 40	40	56,860	63,159	19,666	108	3,768	160.1	8,142	147,892	0.405
0 – 20										

Table F-18. — Continued

Size class (1,000 af)	Per- cent	Cumulative storage (1,000 af)	Existing & cumulative storage (1,000 af)	Net flow (mgd)	Unit cost ($/af)	Capital cumulative cost ($ mil.)	Annual cumulative cost ($ mil.)	Annual average cost ($/net mgd)	Marginal cost	
									($/net mgd)	($/1,000 gal.)

Southeast – Storage (mil. af): total (1964), 54.4; flood (1964), 11.2; maximum, 454.2; maximum minus total, 399.8; existing,[a] available for flow regulation, 44.5, which yields a 94.9 bgd net flow.

Size class (1,000 af)	Per- cent	Cumulative storage (1,000 af)	Existing & cumulative storage (1,000 af)	Net flow (mgd)	Unit cost ($/af)	Capital cumulative cost ($ mil.)	Annual cumulative cost ($ mil.)	Annual average cost ($/net mgd)	Marginal cost ($/net mgd)	Marginal cost ($/1,000 gal.)
10,000 +										
4,000 – 10,000	5	19,990	65,024	115,178	18	360	15.3	133	754	0.0021
2,000 – 4,000	10	59,970	105,990	149,673	22	1,239	52.7	352	1,084	0.0030
1,000 – 2,000	30	179,910	228,888	190,179	30	4,838	205.6	1,081	3,775	0.010
400 – 1,000	30	299,850	351,785	199,229	38	9,395	399.3	2,004	21,403	0.059
200 – 400	15	359,820	413,233	201,286	50	12,938	526.7	2,617	61,962	0.170
100 – 200	5	379,809	433,716	201,926	62	13,633	579.4	2,869	82,246	0.225
60 – 100	3	391,803	446,006	202,143	116	15,024	638.5	3,159	273,118	0.748
40 – 60	1	395,801	450,102	202,191	131	15,548	660.8	3,268	460,133	1.261
20 – 40	1	399,799	454,199	202,204	150	16,148	686.3	3,394	2,018,780	5.531
0 – 20										

Cumberland – Storage (mil. af): total (1964), 14.1; flood (1964), 4.9; maximum, 22.9; maximum minus total, 8.8; existing,[a] available for flow regulation, 12.2, which yields a 13.7 bgd net flow.

Size class (1,000 af)	Per- cent	Cumulative storage (1,000 af)	Existing & cumulative storage (1,000 af)	Net flow (mgd)	Unit cost ($/af)	Capital cumulative cost ($ mil.)	Annual cumulative cost ($ mil.)	Annual average cost ($/net mgd)	Marginal cost ($/net mgd)	Marginal cost ($/1,000 gal.)
10,000 +										
4,000 – 10,000	30	2,649	15,428	14,706	22	58.3	2.5	168	2,420	0.0066
2,000 – 4,000	20	4,415	17,572	15,318	29	109.5	4.7	304	3,553	.0097
1,000 – 2,000	15	5,739	19,179	15,527	34	154.5	6.6	423	9,199	.025
400 – 1,000	15	7,064	20,787	15,705	41	208.8	8.9	565	12,931	.035
200 – 400	10	7,947	21,858	15,824	60	261.8	11.1	703	18,923	.052
100 – 200	5	8,388	22,394	15,864	81	297.6	12.6	797	38,209	.105
60 – 100	5	8,830	22,930	15,904	100	341.7	14.5	913	47,172	0.129
40 – 60										
20 – 40										
0 – 20										

Tennessee – Storage (mil. af): total (1964), 15.8; flood (1964), 5.6; maximum, 101.7; maximum minus total, 85.9; existing,[a] available for flow regulation, 11.1, which yields a 27.9 bgd net flow.

Size class (1,000 af)	Per- cent	Cumulative storage (1,000 af)	Existing & cumulative storage (1,000 af)	Net flow (mgd)	Unit cost ($/af)	Capital cumulative cost ($ mil.)	Annual cumulative cost ($ mil.)	Annual average cost ($/net mgd)	Marginal cost ($/net mgd)	Marginal cost ($/1,000 gal.)
10,000 +										
4,000 – 10,000	10	8,590	20,133	32,010	26	223	9.5	297	2,305	0.0063
2,000 – 4,000	10	17,180	29,196	35,181	35	524	22.3	633	4,029	.011
1,000 – 2,000	20	34,360	47,322	39,360	42	1,246	52.9	1,345	7,338	.020
400 – 1,000	20	51,540	65,448	41,330	54	2,173	92.4	2,235	20,012	.055
200 – 400	15	64,425	79,042	42,123	69	3,062	130.1	3,090	47,663	.131
100 – 200	10	73,015	88,105	42,387	90	3,835	163.0	3,846	124,638	.341
60 – 100	5	77,310	92,637	42,526	116	4,334	184.2	4,331	151,808	.416
40 – 60	5	81,605	97,168	42,666	131	4,896	208.1	4,877	171,438	.470
20 – 40	3	84,182	99,887	42,750	150	5,283	224.5	5,252	196,305	.538
0 – 20	2	85,900	101,700	42,805	200	5,626	239.1	5,586	261,751	0.717

Lower Mississippi – Storage (mil. af): total (1964), 4.7; flood (1964), 4.4; maximum, 65.9; maximum minus total, 61.2; existing,[a] available for flow regulation, 0.6, which yields a 1.6 bgd net flow.

Size class (1,000 af)	Per- cent	Cumulative storage (1,000 af)	Existing & cumulative storage (1,000 af)	Net flow (mgd)	Unit cost ($/af)	Capital cumulative cost ($ mil.)	Annual cumulative cost ($ mil.)	Annual average cost ($/net mgd)	Marginal cost ($/net mgd)	Marginal cost ($/1,000 gal.)
10,000 +										
4,000 – 10,000										
2,000 – 4,000	20	12,238	13,669	19,645	12	147	6.2	318	346	0.0009
1,000 – 2,000	40	36,714	39,780	35,210	15	514	21.8	620	1,002	.0027
400 – 1,000	15	45,892	49,571	38,382	19	688	29.3	762	2,337	.0064
200 – 400	15	55,071	59,362	40,170	25	918	39.0	971	5,453	.015
100 – 200	5	58,130	62,626	40,619	62	1,108	47.1	1,159	17,974	.049
60 – 100	5	61,190	65,890	40,976	78	1,346	57.2	1,396	28,410	0.078
40 – 60										
20 – 40										
0 – 20										

Table F-18. — Continued

Size class (1,000 af)	Per-cent	Cumulative storage (1,000 af)	Existing & cumulative storage (1,000 af)	Net flow (mgd)	Unit cost ($/af)	Capital cumulative cost ($ mil.)	Annual cumulative cost ($ mil.)	Annual average cost ($/net mgd)	Marginal cost ($/net mgd)	($/1,000 gal.)
Lower Arkansas–White–Red — Storage (mil. af): total (1964), 41.4; flood (1964), 14.2; maximum, 122.3; maximum minus total, 80.9; existing,[a] available for flow regulation, 32.0, which yields a 35.9 bgd net flow.										
10,000 +										
4,000 – 10,000	5	4,043	36,521	40,066	18	73	3.1	77	742	0.0020
2,000 – 4,000	25	24,261	59,087	52,252	22	518	22.0	421	1,551	.0042
1,000 – 2,000	25	44,478	81,652	59,324	30	1,124	47.8	805	3,645	.010
400 – 1,000	20	60,652	99,704	62,965	38	1,739	73.9	1,174	7,176	.020
200 – 400	10	68,739	108,731	64,548	38	2,046	87.0	1,347	8,250	.023
100 – 200	5	72,783	113,244	65,369	31	2,171	92.3	1,412	6,484	.018
60 – 100	3	75,209	115,952	65,776	106	2,429	103.2	1,569	26,884	.074
40 – 60	3	77,635	118,659	66,143	122	2,725	115.8	1,751	34,282	.094
20 – 40	2	79,253	120,465	66,344	124	2,957	125.7	1,895	49,354	.135
0 – 20	2	80,870	122,270	66,544	194	3,271	139.0	2,089	66,490	0.182
Western Gulf — Storage (mil. af): total (1964), 42.0; flood (1964), 11.3; maximum, 97.7; maximum minus total, 55.7; existing,[a] available for flow regulation, 35.6, which yields a 22.2 bgd net flow.										
10,000 +										
4,000 – 10,000	15	8,353	44,878	24,328	18	150	6.4	263	2,972	0.0081
2,000 – 4,000	15	16,707	54,198	26,243	22	334	14.2	541	4,078	.011
1,000 – 2,000	25	30,629	69,731	28,942	30	752	32.0	1,104	6,576	.018
400 – 1,000	25	44,552	85,264	30,405	38	1,281	54.4	1,790	15,375	.042
200 – 400	10	50,121	91,477	30,924	50	1,559	66.3	2,143	22,765	.062
100 – 200	5	52,905	94,583	31,139	62	1,732	73.6	2,364	34,234	.094
60 – 100	3	54,576	96,447	31,226	78	1,862	79.1	2,535	63,256	.173
40 – 60	2	55,690	97,690	31,285	91	1,964	83.5	2,668	73,797	0.202
20 – 40										
0 – 20										
Great Basin — Storage (mil. af): total (1964), 5.4; flood (1964), 0; maximum, 14.3; maximum minus total, 8.9; existing,[a] available for flow regulation, 5.4, which yields a 7.0 bgd net flow.										
10,000 +										
4,000 – 10,000										
2,000 – 4,000										
1,000 – 2,000	30	2,664	8,064	7,750	22	59	2.5	321	3,232	0.0089
400 – 1,000	15	3,996	9,396	8,072	28	96	4.1	505	4,920	.013
200 – 400	15	5,328	10,728	8,298	38	147	6.2	750	9,541	.026
100 – 200	15	6,660	12,060	8,494	48	210	8.9	1,053	13,847	.038
60 – 100	10	7,548	12,948	8,614	82	283	12.0	1,398	25,898	.071
40 – 60	10	8,436	13,836	8,717	122	392	16.6	1,909	44,429	.122
20 – 40	3	8,702	14,102	8,741	144	430	18.3	2,091	68,075	.187
0 – 20	2	8,880	14,280	8,749	194	464	19.7	2,256	182,237	0.499
South Pacific — Storage (mil. af): total (1964), 2.3; flood (1964), 0.3; maximum, 4.7; maximum minus total, 2.4; existing,[a] available for flow regulation, 2.1, which yields a 1.0 bgd net flow.										
10,000 +										
4,000 – 10,000										
2,000 – 4,000										
1,000 – 2,000										
400 – 1,000										
200 – 400	60	1,440	3,679	1,080	72	104	4.4	4,081	34,303	0.094
100 – 200	20	1,920	4,189	1,104	91	147	6.3	5,672	76,017	.208
60 – 100	5	2,040	4,317	1,110	106	160	6.8	6,130	95,514	.262
40 – 60	5	2,160	4,445	1,115	122	175	7.4	6,658	116,691	.320
20 – 40	5	2,280	4,572	1,120	144	192	8.2	7,286	153,451	.420
0 – 20	5	2,400	4,700	1,124	250	222	9.4	8,396	337,016	0.923

Table F-18. — Continued

Size class (1,000 af)	Per-cent	Cumulative storage (1,000 af)	Existing & cumulative storage (1,000 af)	Net flow (mgd)	Unit cost ($/af)	Capital cumulative cost ($ mil.)	Annual cumulative cost ($ mil.)	Annual average cost ($/net mgd)	Marginal cost ($/net mgd)	Marginal cost ($/1,000 gal.)
Central Pacific — Storage (mil. af): total (1964), 25.6; flood (1964), 2.5; maximum, 164.0; maximum minus total, 138.4; existing,[a] available for flow regulation, 23.5, which yields a 31.0 bgd net flow.										
10,000 +										
4,000 – 10,000	30	41,532	65,655	46,812	31	1,287	54.7	1,169	3,452	0.0095
2,000 – 4,000	25	76,142	100,793	51,020	40	2,672	113.6	2,226	13,985	0.038
1,000 – 2,000	20	103,830	128,902	52,651	48	4,001	170.0	3,230	34,628	0.095
400 – 1,000	10	117,674	142,957	53,181	106	5,468	232.4	4,370	117,644	0.322
200 – 400	5	124,596	149,985	53,431	125	6,334	269.2	5,038	146,892	0.402
100 – 200	5	131,518	157,012	53,642	144	7,330	311.5	5,808	201,039	0.551
60 – 100	2	134,287	159,823	53,709	165	7,787	331.0	6,162	289,084	0.792
40 – 60	2	137,055	162,634	53,758	181	8,288	352.3	6,553	438,060	1.200
20 – 40	1	138,440	164,040	53,775	200	8,565	364.0	6,769	665,436	1.823
0 – 20										
Pacific Northwest — Storage (mil. af): total (1964), 48.2; flood (1964), 16.6; maximum, 261.0; maximum minus total, 212.8; existing,[a] available for flow regulation, 34.7, which yields a 64.2 bgd net flow.										
10,000 +										
4,000 – 10,000	15	31,920	68,616	96,926	26	830	35.2	364	1,078	0.0030
2,000 – 4,000	35	106,400	147,833	135,013	21	2,394	101.7	754	1,745	.0048
1,000 – 2,000	25	159,600	204,416	139,137	40	4,522	192.2	1,381	21,927	.060
400 – 1,000	10	180,880	227,050	139,980	106	6,778	288.1	2,058	113,737	.312
200 – 400	5	191,520	238,366	140,402	125	8,108	344.6	2,454	134,124	.367
100 – 200	5	202,160	249,683	140,823	181	10,034	426.4	3,028	194,212	.532
60 – 100	2	206,416	254,210	140,992	202	10,893	463.0	3,284	216,760	.594
40 – 60	2	210,672	258,737	141,160	219	11,825	502.6	3,560	235,001	.644
20 – 40	1	212,800	261,000	141,244	238	12,332	524.1	3,711	255,486	0.700
0 – 20										

Note: The Upper Missouri, Rio Grande–Pecos, Colorado, and Upper Arkansas–White–Red regions do not appear in the table because as of 1964 they did not require new storage for flow regulation.

[a]Existing = total 1964 storage minus prorated flood storage.

INDEX

Accelerated eutrophication model. *See* Models, stream response
Aesthetic considerations in standards of water quality, 28, 35
Agriculture
  irrigated acreage for, projected, 159–60
  water cost for, 24
  water requirements per acre for, 49
  water use by, 43–44; projected, 55, 174–75
  withdrawal uses by, 19, 49–50, 174–75
  See also Irrigation
Algae, 68, 204, 205–6
Almon, Clopper, Jr., 161, 161n
Anderson, Richard T., 221n
Annual factor in costs, 26, 27, 28, 132–33
Application efficiency of water, 174–75
Aquatic life, D.O. standards for, 27, 69, 204
Availability of flow. *See* Flow deficiency

Bacteria, pollution from, 66n, 203, 204, 208
Basic model. *See* Model, basic
Belding, D. L., 207n
Biochemical oxygen demand (BOD)
  dilution flow for, 122
  measured in population equivalents, 66, 67, 221
  production of, 66, 67
  removal of: by continuous chemical treatment, 123; by short-term treatment, 25, 122; by short-term versus permanent treatment, 74; by three levels of treatment, 66n, 67, 70
Biodegradable model. *See* Models, stream response
BOD. *See* Biochemical oxygen demand
Bonem, Gilbert W., 207, 221
Bonneville Power Administration, 44, 164
Bower, Blair T., 16n, 28n, 35n, 135n, 177n, 178, 182, 221, 221n
Brackish water, 50, 55, 177, 179, 180
Bradshaw, R. W., 206n, 213n
Brett, J. R., 207n
Bureau of Mines, U.S., 160, 176
Bureau of Reclamation, U.S., 246, 247, 249
Bureau of the Census, U.S., 155, 156, 177
Business and Defense Services Administration (U.S. Department of Commerce), 162

Central Pacific Region
  chemical treatment costs in, 123

delivery efficiency of water in, 174–75
  recirculation rate in, 180
  waste discharge in, 222
  water loss in, 58
  water requirements for, projected, 110
  water storage in, 250
Chance of deficiency. *See* Flow deficiency
Chemical and allied products industries
  recirculation of water for, 178
  value added by, projected, 161
  waste load discharged by, 221, 222
  waste treatment costs for, 178
  water use by, 50, 177
Chemical treatment, 25–26
  continuous, 123–25
  short-term, savings yields by, 121–23
  See also Biochemical oxygen demand; Waste treatment
Chesapeake Bay region
  economic activity in, projected, 163
  pollution in, 44
  storage costs in, 252
  waste discharge in, 222
Chow, C. S., 207, 207n, 208, 208n, 212n
Clawson, Marion, 183n, 184, 184n
Cobb-Douglas production function, 44
Colorado region
  cost of flow in, 100
  delivery efficiency of water in, 174–75
  recirculation rate in, 180
  urban population in, projected, 42
  water loss in, 19, 57
  water shortage in, 124, 138
Colorado Water Conservation Board, 176
Constraints
  dissolved oxygen, 68
  marginal cost, 22, 99, 252, 253
  plant nutrient, 67
Cooper, Sophia, 159n
Cootner, Paul H., 51n, 179n, 180, 224n
Corps of Engineers, U.S. Army, 246, 249, 250
Cost functions, 8, 11
Costs
  allocation of, 34–35

capital, 25, 70–71, 97, 98
concealed, 253
dilution flow, 23
effect of technology on, 11
flow, 96–100
flow versus storage, 98–99
by industry, 24
of maintaining quality, 10
marginal, 11, 22, 252, 253
minimum flow versus minimum cost programs, 135–36
problems in measuring, 4, 5, 8
recirculation, 12, 23, 72–73, 108, 223
regional variations in, 110
schedule of, 250–53
of short-term chemical treatment, 122–24
social, 5, 22, 108, 132
storage, 8, 10, 12, 13, 22, 135, 244
types of, 10
of waste collection, 12, 73, 108
of waste treatment, 11, 22, 70–74, 108–9, 136, 222–24; versus storage costs, 132–33; versus water treatment costs, 208–9
of water deficit, 24–25, 131–32
Cumberland region
    economic activity in, projected, 163, 164
    pollution in, 44
    storage of water in, 247
    storage versus chemical treatment in, 122

Dams, 34
Davidson, B., 206n, 213n
Davis, Robert K., 9n, 10n, 16n, 28n, 125, 135n
Deficiency of flow. See Flow deficiency
Delaware-Hudson region
    municipal water recirculation in, 136
    storage costs in, 252
    waste discharge in, 222
    waste treatment costs in, 28
Delivery efficiency of water, 49, 174–75
Demand for water, 9
Denitrification process, 204
Department of Agriculture, U.S., 44, 174, 183
Desalination, 15, 20, 58, 134, 210
Dilution flow, 8, 9, 12
    conditions affecting, 66
    cost of, 23
    for phosphorus, 122
    to prevent thermal pollution, 67, 72–73
    requirements for, 19–20
    "ruling," 67, 69
    for selected treatment levels, 69–70
    stream quality standards and, 68
    See also Waste treatment
Diseases, water-borne, 204
Dissolved oxygen (D.O.)
    for aquatic life, 27, 69, 204
    as a constraint, 68, 69
    dilution flow and, 6
    levels of, 14, 19, 133–34
    standards for, 27, 32, 67
Dissolved solids, 20
    treatment of, 36
D.O. See Dissolved oxygen
Downstream, defined, 9, 49

Eastern Great Lakes region, 11–13
    economic activity in, projected, 163, 164
    pollution in, 44
    recirculation rate in, 73
    storage costs in, 12, 252
    waste discharge in, 222
    water supply in, 20
East Mississippi region, water loss by irrigation in, 49
Eckenfelder, Wesley W., 66n, 67, 203, 207n, 220n, 221, 222, 223

Eckstein, Otto, 132n
Economic growth, projection of, 18, 41–44
Effluents, 67, 204
Erosion, 15, 16
Estuaries
    discharges into, 19, 66
    quality of water in, 10
    See also Potomac estuary, waste treatment costs for
Evaporation
    from heat dissipation, 178
    from reservoirs, 97, 244, 245, 250
Evapotranspiration loss, 19, 48n
    change in ground cover and, 15
    cost of, 23
    from irrigation, 174
    soil conservation and, 182–83
    from wetlands, 184

Federal Power Commission, 162
Federal Reserve Board, index of industrial production, 160, 161, 176
Fischman, Leonard L., 4n, 42n, 184, 184n
Fish, water requirements for, 42, 207
Fish and Wildlife Service, U.S., 184
Fisher, Joseph L., 4n, 42n, 184, 184n
Flood control, 247, 248, 249
Flow
    costs of, 96–100, 244
    expenditures for regulating, 107
    gross versus net, 96
    regionwide, 96–97
    schedule of, 250–53
    storage requirements for, 96–97, 248–49
Flow deficiency, 8, 35, 97, 131–32, 245–46
Flow-storage relationship, 96–100, 248–49
Flow-through, defined, 48
Flow uses of water, 8, 48n
Food and food products industries
    recirculation of water by, 178
    waste load discharged by, 221, 222
    waste treatment costs for, 70–71, 222–23, 225
    water use by, 50, 177
Fox, Irving K., 99n
Frankel, Richard J., 136n, 208n, 209n
Fruh, E. G., 207n
Fry, F. E. J., 207n

Gaufin, A. R., 207n, 208n
Geographic characteristics, water storage and, 96
Geologic characteristics, water storage and, 96
Geologic Survey, U.S., 184
Gertel, Karl, 175n
GNP. See Gross national product
Golueke, C. G., 206n
Great Basin region
    chemical treatment costs in, 123
    delivery efficiency of water in, 123
    recirculation rate in, 180
    waste discharge in, 222
    water shortage in, 124
Great Lakes, 66, 71
Great Salt Lake, 66, 71
Gross national product (GNP)
    cost of water as percent of, 108, 108n
    population change and, 42
    projection of, 159, 160,
    water requirements and, projected, 8–9, 18, 34
Ground cover, methods of restoring, 56
Groundwater
    development of, 16
    draw-down of, 19
    mining of, 97
    potential shortage of, 37
    reserve, 7

Hann, Roy W., Jr., 205n, 211
Hanson, Ronald L., 246n
Harbeck, G. Earl, Jr., 246, 247n
Hardison, Clayton H., 8n, 19, 19n, 96, 97, 98, 244, 244n, 245, 250, 251, 251n
Held, R. Burnell, 183n, 184, 184n
Herfindahl, Orris C., 99n
Horton, Harry W., 57n
Howe, Charles W., 37n, 51n, 182n
Hudson River. See Delaware-Hudson region
Hughes, William C., 15n
Hunting, 56
Hydroelectric flows, 8
Hydroelectric power, 16
Hydrologic analysis, 12, 96–97, 244–46

Industrial production index (Federal Reserve Board), 160, 161, 176
Industrial waste
    BOD of, 66
    methods of estimating, 221, 222
    reduction of, 136
    See also Waste discharge; Waste treatment
Industry
    pollution loadings for, 207
    water costs of, 24
    See also Chemicals and allied products industries; Food and food products industries; Manufacturing; Mining
Interbasin transfers of water, 3, 36, 210
Irrigation, 3, 11
    acreage under, projected, 42, 44, 159
    delivery efficiency in, 174–75
    reservoirs for, 247, 248
    water input per acre of, 49
    water loss from, 19, 49, 174–75

Johnson, Edwin L., 10n
Johnston, Denis F., 159n

Kahn, Herman, 24n
Kammerer, J. C., 175, 175n
Kaufman, Alvin, 160n, 175n
Kim, Pum Ky, 245n
Kneese, Allen V., 16n, 28n, 35n, 36, 135n, 136, 177n, 245n
Krutilla, John V., 132n

Land conservation, 56, 183
Landsberg, Hans H., 4n, 42n, 184, 184n
Lang, Karl, 180n
Larson, Gordon P., 221n
Leather manufacturing
    costs of waste treatment for, 222, 223, 224
    waste load discharged by, 221, 222
Linaweaver, F. P., Jr., 37n, 51n, 181n, 182, 182n
Livestock, water use by, 175
Löf, George O. G., 8n, 19, 19n, 51n 96, 97, 98, 136, 179n, 180, 224n, 244, 244n, 245, 250, 251, 251n
Loss of water. See Water loss
Love, Oliver T., Jr., 66n, 203
Lower Arkansas-White-Red region
    recirculation rate in, 73
    storage capacity in, 106, 247
    water loss from irrigation in, 49
    water supply in, 20, 21
    water treatment in, 105, 107, 122, 137
Lower Mississippi region
    recirculation rate in, 73
    waste discharge in, 222
    water supply in, 21
    water treatment in, 107, 124, 137
Lower Missouri region
    storage versus chemical treatment in, 122
    water loss from irrigation in, 49
    water supply in, 21
    water treatment in, 124, 137

McGauhey, P. H., 208n, 209n
MacKichan, K. A., 175, 175n
MacNamara, E. E., 207n
Malina, J. F., 207n, 212n
Manufacturing
    cost of water for, 24
    output for, projected, 42–43, 161–62
    waste load discharged by, 66, 221, 222
    waste treatment costs for, 70–72, 73
    water use by, 161, 161n
    water withdrawals by, 50–51, 177
Marginal cost
    computation of, 99n
    evaporation losses contribute to, 246
    "real," 99n
    reservoirs and, 245
    storage and, 252, 253
    water treatment and, 11, 22, 24
Marginal cost constraints, 22, 99, 252, 253
Martin, R. O. R., 246n
Michaels, Abraham, 221n
Mid-continent region, projected acreage under irrigation, 42
Minimum cost program
    compared with other programs, 21–22
    population projection and, 20
    storage requirements under, 106–7, 109, 135
    versus minimum flow program, 135–36
Minimum flow program
    compared with other programs, 21–22
    population projection and, 20
    storage requirements under, 106–7, 109, 135
    versus minimum cost program, 135–36
Minimum treatment program
    compared with other programs, 21–22
    population projection and, 20
    storage requirements under, 105–7, 109
Mining
    output for, projected, 43, 160
    water cost for, 24
    water loss from 50, 175–76
    water use by, 50, 55
Model, basic
    construction of, 6–14
    factors considered in, 4–7
    limitations of, 14–17, 33–34
    results of, 105–10
    uses of, 17
    variations of, 26–27; annual cost factor, 132–33; certainty of flow, 131–32; combined variations, 134–35; D.O., 133–34; industrial waste, 136
    waste treatment in, 25–27
Models, stream response
    accelerated eutrophication, 205–6
    biodegradable, 204–6, 210–12
    evaluation of, 209
    limitations of, 209
    multidimensional versus two-dimensional, 33–34
    nutritional, 212
    thermal, 206–7, 213
Municipalities
    cost of water in, 24
    per capita use of water in, 51–52
    pollution from, 207
    price elasticity for water use in, 37
    projected water use for, 55
    recirculation of water by, 136
    waste discharged by, 66, 222
    waste treatment costs in, 70–72, 73, 223
    water loss in, by region, 52

Nadler, Mildred, 160n, 175n
National Planning Association, 157, 158, 161, 163
National Water Commission, 4, 17
National Wetlands Inventory, 184

Navigation flows, 8
Nelson, Robert, 66n, 203, 203n
New England region
    economic activity in, projected, 163, 164
    minimum treatment program in, 107
    municipal recirculation in, 136
    pollution in, 44
    waste discharged in, 222
    water quality and treatment in, 105, 124, 137
    water supply for, 20, 21
Nitrogen, removal of, 66n, 67, 69, 212
North Atlantic region, projected urban population in, 42
North Atlantic Regional Study Group, 16, 16n
Northeast region, recirculation rate, 73
North Pacific region, projected acreage under irrigation, 42
Nutritional model. See Models, stream response
Nutritional pollution, 203, 204, 206

Office of Saline Water, U.S., 33
Office of Water Resources Research, U.S., 4, 17, 33
Ohio region
    economic activity in, projected, 163, 164
    pollution in, 44
    recirculation rate in, 73
    water supply for, 21
    water treatment in, 124
Onsite uses of water, 8
    loss from, 48–49, 56–58
    for selected population projections, 19
Orlob, G. T., 208n, 209n
Oswald, W. J., 206n
Outdoor Recreation Resources Review Commission, 159, 161
Oxygen, dissolved. See Dissolved oxygen

Pacific Northwest region
    delivery efficiency of water in, 174–75
    economic activity in, projected, 163, 164
    recirculation rate in, 180
    storage versus chemical treatment in, 122
    waste discharged in, 222
    water loss in: by irrigation, 49; from municipal use, 52
Paper and pulp industries
    production estimates for, 44
    recirculation rates in, 178
    value added by, projected, 161
    waste load discharged by, 221, 222
    waste treatment costs for, 222–23, 224
    water use by, 50, 177
Pavelis, George, 44, 44n, 159, 159n, 160, 175
Petroleum industry
    recirculation rates in, 178
    waste load discharged by, 221, 222
    waste treatment costs for, 222–23, 224
    water use by, 50, 177
Philips, Walter M., 221n
Phosphorus
    dilution flow for, 124
    removal of, 66n, 67, 69, 122, 122n, 204, 212
Physiographic zones, 244–45
Piper, A. M., 247
Plant nutrients, 67, 121, 122–23
Pollutants, types of, 203–4
Pollution
    defined, 203
    dispersed, 209
    loadings, 207–8
    from paper and pulp production, 44
    regional problems of, 33
    role of government agencies in, 32–33
    from suspended solids, 15
    treatment of, 208
    underestimation of, 16

Polyphosphates, 204
Population
    estimates of SMSAs, 41
    projected levels of: BOD measured by, 67–68, 72; comparison of, 155–56; cost of chemical treatment of water by, 123–24; economic activity and, 42–44; minimum water treatment program for, 106; GNP and, 20, 42; problems in using, 33–34; required dilution flow for, 20; sources of data for, 155; by states, 156, 157; storage and treatment costs by, 134–35; storage capacity by, 23; for urban centers, 41–42, 157–58; variations in D.O. and, 133–34; waste treatment and, 26–29, 136; water costs by, 24–25; water loss for swamps by, 57; by water resource regions, 156–57; water supply for, 20–23, 32
    rural, 41–42
    urban, 41–42
    water requirements and, 11
Population equivalent, 11, 12, 70–72
    defined, 11n
    measurement of BOD by, 66, 221
Potomac estuary, waste treatment costs for, 28
Precipitation, storage requirements and, 96
President's Materials Policy Commission, 4, 4n
President's Water Resources Policy Commission, 4, 4n
Price elasticity of water, 37
Primary metals industry
    recirculation rates in, 178
    water use by, 50, 177
Public Health Service, U.S., 175, 181

Rationing water, 19
Reaeration, 203
Recirculation
    costs of, 12, 23, 36, 72–73, 108, 110, 223
    loss rates and, 55
    for municipalities, 136
    projected, 177–78
    rate of, defined, 51
    rate of, to prevent thermal pollution, 73
    by region, 180
Recreational uses of water, 29, 42, 42n, 137
Recycling of water, 209
Reid, George W., 29n, 50, 66n, 74, 121, 122, 203, 203n, 211, 221, 222, 223
Research needs, for better water management, 35–36
Reservoir capacity
    expenditures for, 23–24
    by region, 247–48
Reservoirs
    construction costs of, 249–50
    cost of flow for, 97, 99, 244
    of groundwater, 7–8
    inventory of, 246–47
Rio Grande-Pecos region
    cost of flow for, 100
    delivery efficiency of water in, 174–75
    recirculation rate in, 180
    water loss in, 19
    water shortage in, 110, 124
Rivers
    conflict over uses of, 35
    measured flow of, 96, 97
    pollution loadings of, 207
    water supply in terms of regulated flow of, 8
Ruling dilution flow, 67, 69
Runoff loss, 19, 56
Rural areas, population projections for, 41–42
Ruttan, Vernon W., 44n, 159, 159n, 160

Salinity of water, 36, 37
Schurr, Sam H., 160n
Sediments, 15, 204
Senate Select Committee on National Water Resources, 4, 6, 9, 97

Sewage
  analysis of, 204
  collection costs, regional variations of, 110
Sewerage costs
  projected, 23
  per urban resident, 73
Sewers, separation of sanitary and storm, 107n, 108
Shortage of water, 5
  countermeasures for, 121, 209–10
  projected, by region, 110, 124
  See also Water deficits; Water requirements; Water supply
Smith, Stephen C., 177n
SMSAs. *See* Standard Metropolitan Statistical Areas
Soil conservation, 15, 56, 182–83
Soil Conservation Service (Department of Agriculture), 49, 56, 183, 245
Solids
  dissolved, 20, 36, 124n
  suspended, 15, 205
Southeast region
  projected wetlands area in, 56
  storage capacity in, 247
  storage versus chemical treatment in, 122
  waste discharge in, 222
South Pacific region
  delivery efficiency of water in, 174
  recirculation rates in, 136, 180
  waste discharge in, 222
  water loss in, 19, 52, 57
  water shortage in, 58, 110, 124
Southwest region
  cost of chemical treatment in, 123
  water supply for, 20, 29, 32
Sport fishery, flow use for, 8
Standard Metropolitan Statistical Areas (SMSAs), 41, 158–59
Steam-electric power
  projected growth of, 43, 55, 162
  recirculation costs for, 72–73
  and water cooling, 110
  water cost for, 24
  water use for, 179–81
Stein, Murray, 71n
Stephen, David G., 209n
Stoddard, Charles H., 184n
Storage of water
  artificial lakes versus dams for, 34
  cost of, 8, 10, 12, 13, 22, 23, 98, 244, 245
  cost of, versus treatment cost, 132–33, 251–52
  defined, 98
  effect of flow deficiency on, 131–32
  methods of computing, 98
  projected, 98, 106–7
  for recreation, 137
  regional studies for, 36–37
  relation between net flow and, 250–51
  requirements for, 96, 97, 244
  schedule of, 250–53
  See also Reservoir capacity; Reservoirs
Stream responses, development of, 203–7
Streebin, Leale, 66n, 203, 203n
Structural measures, for soil conservation, 182–83
Swamps, 56–57, 184

Tarzwell, M. S., 207n, 208n
Technology
  effect of, on waste treatment, 28, 207
  effect of, on water costs, 11
  maintaining quality of water through, 32–33
  water use and, 11
Tennessee region
  pollution in, 44
  recirculation rate to prevent thermal pollution in, 73

reservoir capacity in, 247
storage costs in, 252
storage versus chemical treatment in, 122
water treatment in, 124
Textile manufacturing
  waste load discharged by, 221, 222
  waste treatment costs for, 222
Thermal efficiency, 51
Thermal model. *See* Models, stream response
Thermal pollution
  costs of recirculation to prevent, 72–73
  dilution flow to counteract, 67
  effects of, 73
  waste load of, 222
Thomas, Nathan O., 246, 247n
Timber, effect of removal of, 15n
Transpiration, water loss through, 48, 52
Treatment of wastes. *See* Waste treatment
Treatment of water
  future costs for, 108, 208–9
  health considerations in, 204
  waste treatment versus, 36, 206

Underground water, 7, 97
Upper Arkansas-White-Red region
  chemical treatment costs in, 123
  delivery efficiency of water in, 174
  recirculation rate in, 180
  storage versus chemical treatment in, 122
  water loss in, 57
  water shortage in, 124
  water supply for, 20, 32
Upper Mississippi region, water treatment in, 107, 124
Upper Missouri region
  cost of flow in, 100
  delivery efficiency of water in, 174–75
  economic activity in, projected, 163, 164
  recirculation rate in, 180
  water loss in, 57
  water supply for, 30
Urban centers
  population projections for, 41–42, 157–58
  waste discharged into coastal waters by, 182
  See also Municipalities

Waste collection
  costs of, 12, 73, 108
  thermal pollution and, 36
Waste discharge
  into coastal waters, 182
  by industry, 221–22
  measurement of, 66
  reduction in, 136
  by region, 222
  See also Waste load; Waste treatment
Waste load
  as function of waste discharge, 50
  in terms of BOD, 205, 221
  See also Pollution; Waste discharge; Waste treatment
Waste treatment, 4
  for BOD removal, 10, 25, 66n, 67, 70, 74, 122, 205, 221
  chemical, 25–26, 121–24, 224
  costs of, 22, 70–71, 108–9, 132–33, 208–9, 222–23
  dilution flow and, 6, 9, 12, 68–70
  effect of technological change on, 28–29, 136
  lack of information on, 71
  levels of, 12–13, 22; projected, 107
  short-term, 25, 70, 224; alternatives to, 125; savings from, 121–23; steps in, 121; storage savings and, 122–23; versus permanent treatment, 74
  stream response to, 67
  water treatment versus, 36, 206

Water deficits, 57, 138
  alternative programs for meeting, 6–7
  cost of meeting, 24–25
  gross and net, defined, 109n
  projected, by region, 106
  projected gross, 109
  See also Shortage of water
Water loss
  by regions, 19, 52, 57
  resulting from soil conservation, 183
  upstream versus downstream, 49, 51
  See also Withdrawal uses of water
Water quality
  allocation of costs for, 33
  expenditures for, 107
  measured by D.O., 6, 27, 32, 67
  programs for, 10
  standards for, 4, 35, 134, 204
Water requirement
  agricultural, 49–50
  defined, 9
  as estimated in basic model, 6
  manufacturing, 50–51
  mining, 50
  projections of, 8–9, 18–19
  for wetland habitat, 56
Water resource regions
  cost of flow by, 97–100
  delivery efficiency of water in, 174
  economic activity in, projected, 163–64
  representative states of, 158
  reservoir capacity in, 247–48
  wastes discharged in, 222
  water losses in, 19, 57
  water shortages in, 110, 124
  See also individual regions
Water Resources Council, 4, 17, 30, 247
Water resources policy, effect of short-term chemical treatment on, 121
Water supply
  in cost-function sense, 8
  defined, 7–8, 96, 244
  as estimated in basic model, 6
  measures of, 4, 96

  methods of improving, 209–10
  need for sound projections of, 3–4
  projections of, 20
Water use
  charges for, 3
  efficiency in, 49
  "ideal" versus "actual," 174
  inter-user reuse, 48
  loss from, 48–52
  for recreation, 29, 42, 42n
  types of, 3, 8, 48–49
  See also Flow uses of water; Onsite uses of water; Withdrawal uses of water
Wells, cost of, 210
Western Great Lakes region
  chemical treatment costs in, 123
  projected wetlands area in, 56
  recirculation rate to prevent thermal pollution in, 73
  waste discharge in, 222
  water shortage in, 110, 138
  water supply in, 30
Western Gulf region
  chemical treatment costs in, 122, 123
  delivery efficiency of water in, 174
  economic activity in, projected, 163, 164
  recirculation rate in, 180
  waste discharge in, 222
  water shortage in, 124, 138
Wetlands, 56–57, 184
Wiener, Anthony J., 24n
Wildlife, water requirements of, 15, 42, 56
Withdrawal uses of water, 8, 9
  by agriculture, 19, 174–75
  coefficients of, 48–52
  downstream intake for, 179
  defined, 48
  freshwater versus brackish, 177, 179, 180
  loss from, 48–52
  by manufacturing, 50–51, 161, 177–79
  by mining, 50, 175–76
  by municipalities, 51–52, 181–82
  for steam-electric power, 51, 179–81
Wollman, Nathaniel, 6n, 207
World Power Congress, 160